D1570166

THE
JORDANIAN~ISRAELI WAR
1948–1951

A HISTORY OF THE
HASHEMITE KINGDOM OF JORDAN

THE
JORDANIAN~ISRAELI WAR

1948–1951

A HISTORY OF THE
HASHEMITE KINGDOM OF JORDAN

Maan Abu Nowar

THE JORDANIAN–ISRAELI WAR 1948–1951
A History of the Hashemite Kingdom of Jordan

Ithaca Press is an imprint of Garnet Publishing Limited

Published by
Garnet Publishing Limited
8 Southern Court
South Street
Reading
RG1 4QS
UK

Copyright © Maan Abu Nowar, 2002

All rights reserved.
No part of this book may be reproduced in any form or by
any electronic or mechanical means, including information
storage and retrieval systems, without permission in writing
from the publisher, except by a reviewer who may quote
brief passages in a review.

First Edition

ISBN 0 86372 286 5

British Library Cataloguing-in-Publication Data
A catalogue record for this book is available from the British Library

Jacket design by Garnet Publishing
Typeset by Samantha Barden

Printed in Lebanon

Contents

List of Tables   vii
Acknowledgements   ix
Preface   xi

1   Introduction: The Balance of Power   1
2   The Gathering Storm   23
3   On the Brink of War   67
4   The Battle for Jerusalem   91
5   The Battle of Bab al-Wad   131
6   The Battles on other Fronts   153
7   The First Truce   183
8   The Second Truce   223
9   Towards Arab Unity   255
10 The Armistice Agreement, 1949   293
11 The First Arab Union   335
12 The Last Days of a Great King   381
13 The Succession   411

Appendices   435
Bibliography   501
Index   507

Tables

1.1	Total strength of the Jewish force, spring 1948	11
1.2	Weapons of the Jewish force, spring 1948	11
1.3	Organisation of the Liberation Army	16
1.4	Deployment of the Jerusalem garrison	17
2.1	The National Committee in Jerusalem	52
2.2	Leadership in Jerusalem	52
2.3	Organisation of the military branch of al-Jihad	53
2.4	Jordanian troop concentration south of Kfar Etzion	60
2.5	The regiment of Abdullah al-Tel	62
3.1	Tawfiq Abu al-Huda's new government	67
3.2	Armed units of the former Jordan Arab Army	74
3.3	Areas of responsibility for each brigade	84
3.4	Disposition of units	88
4.1	Deployment of al-Tel's regiment	98
4.2	Taskforce formed from 2nd Regiment and 4th Brigade	112
4.3	The reserve force	112
5.1	Positions allocated to companies of the 4th Regiment	131
5.2	Defensive positions of the 4th Regiment	134
6.1	The Lebanese Army	154
6.2	The Syrian Army	158
6.3	1st Brigade HQ	159
6.4	The Iraqi Army	168
6.5	3rd Infantry Division	173
7.1	5th Company's reorganised defences	194
7.2	The regiment formed by Major Ali al-Hiyari	197
7.3	The Iraqi forces at the end of the truce	203
7.4	Deployment of the Egyptian Division	216
7.5	Deployment of Jewish forces	216
8.1	Czechoslovakia's arms supplies to the Jews	223
8.2	Total strength of Jewish force as at 12 August 1948	224
8.3	Reorganised Jewish fronts	224

8.4	Reorganisation of the Jordanian Arab Army	227
8.5	The deployment of the Liberation Army Brigade	233
8.6	Deployment of the Egyptian Army on 12 December	250
9.1	Appointees of the Jordanian Government to provide services, maintain law and protect property	258
9.2	Government allocation of dollars, 1947 and 1948	274
9.3	The new Congress Committee	279
10.1	The Jordanian delegation to Rhodes, 28 February 1949	294
10.2	The new Jordanian Government, May 1949	305
10.3	Cases of infection among refugees reported during 1949	308
10.4	Actual expenditure for the 16,000 officers and men of the Jordanian army	309
10.5	Administration of the West Bank, July 1949	315
10.6	Interim electoral law	331
10.7	Number of Jordanian soldiers killed in the cause of Palestine	332
11.1	Number and location of refugees in Jordan	342
11.2	Results of the April 1950 elections in Jordan	344
11.3	Chamber of Notables appointed in April 1950	345
11.4	Government of Said al-Mufti, formed on 12 April 1950	346
11.5	Officers attending the meeting at HQ of 1st Division on 5 June 1951	362
11.6	The Jordanian Arab Army, October 1950	366
11.7	Said al-Mufti's new Government of October 1950	370
11.8	Samir al-Rifai's new Cabinet of December 1950	376
12.1	Reorganisation of the 1st Division	394
13.1	Tawfiq Abu al-Huda's Government of July 1951	417
13.2	Allocation of seats for the elections to the Chamber of Deputies, August 1951	426
13.3	Results of the August 1951 elections	429
13.4	List of Senators following the August 1951 elections	430

Acknowledgements

In writing this book I was encouraged by His late Majesty King al-Hussein ibn Talal I, who urged me to publish the whole truth based on both historical facts and 'adherence to the dignity of history'. For being my King, father, brother and true friend of 47 years throughout which time he showed humanity, kindness, wisdom and courage, I will remember him for the rest of my life. May God bless his soul.

I acknowledge with much gratitude the support and attention of all at St Antony's College and its Middle East Centre at the University of Oxford; the Public Record Office in London; and the Library of the Jordanian National Assembly. I am particularly grateful to my friends in Oxford, who include Wilfrid Knapp, Dr Derek Hopwood, Dr Raghid El-Solh and Dr Ahmad Khalifah, for their help and advice. I am indebted to my friends Major General James Lunt and Colonel T. N. Bromage, both former Jordan Arab Army officers, for tolerating my many telephone calls and for reminding me of many aspects and events of the fighting during 1948–9.

In the course of writing of this book I was blessed with good neighbours in the village of Yarnton, Oxford – especially Laurence Anderson and his son John, who read the final draft.

I am blessed with 35 grandchildren, among them Hadithah and Muhammad, sons of Jamal al-Khraisha, who helped me with gathering information and documents for this volume. I am grateful to them.

To my wife Sue, I owe a special debt for her tolerance, care and kindness.

Preface

Although the four years between 1948 and 1951 may be considered a very short period of history, they were congested with many major events that deeply affected the whole of the Arab Middle East – particularly Jordan and Palestine. During these four years, the first Arab–Israeli war tested the abilities of Arab leaders and politicians, the capabilities of the Arab armies, the harmony within the League of Arab States, the loyalty to the idea and movement of Arab nationalism, and the status of the Arab countries in the international community – particularly in the United Nations. The result of the test was devastating to Arab hearts and minds. Leaders and politicians, with the exception of a small minority, were nothing more than Effendis of the Ottoman style and mind. Although they had the will to fight, the Arab armies were badly led and lacked most of the necessities of war. Moreover, there was complete disharmony in the League of Arab States; Arab nationalism was superseded by state patriotism and local jealousies; the infant democracy of Syria was destroyed by two military coups; political assassination plagued the Arab scene; and the seeds of the Egyptian and the Iraqi military coups were sown by politicised officers.

The Hashemite Kingdom of Jordan was at the heart of most of these events in their causes or consequences. That is why I have had to extend the boundaries of history to neighbouring Arab states in order to describe the general situation in which each of the events had taken place. In particular, the role of the Jordan Arab Army during the war could not be fully appreciated and discussed without reference to the roles of the other Arab armies.

Considering that Jordan was the smallest and indeed the poorest Arab country with a population not exceeding 350,000 and a national revenue of 1,593,841 Palestine pounds (P£), the significance of the role of Jordan compared with that of the rest of the Arab states was astonishing.

Maan Abu Nowar

1

Introduction:
The Balance of Power

The root cause of the conflict between the Arabs and the Jews lies deep in the history of the land that became Palestine. Around 1250 BC, the large nomadic tribe comprising about 15,000 warriors known as 'Bani Israel', or the 'Children of Israel', raided and occupied certain areas of that land. In that period, the inhabitants of Palestine consisted of tribal and settled communities such as the Canaanites, Amorites, Hittites and others. The Israelites occupied the high ground of mountains between what is now Hebron in the south and Galilee in the north of Palestine. The settled and civilized people of Canaan surrendered to the Israeli nomadic raiders after suffering countless massacres in their villages and small towns. In particular, the massacre of Jericho, during which all the inhabitants of that town were killed, broke the spirit of resistance of the people of Canaan. Thereafter, the Israeli warlords divided the occupied areas between themselves and controlled the inhabitants of Canaan as landlords rather than landowners. The Israeli nomads became the ruling class of warriors living on the tributes they imposed on the native population. They also continued to live as nomadic shepherds dwelling in tented camps and leading a primitive life without culture or civilization. Meanwhile the people of Canaan, the original people of the land, continued to live as sedentary farmers as they had done for the previous 3,000 years. In spite of all the massacres they inflicted on Canaan, the Israelites were never at any stage the sole inhabitants of that land.

The ancient Israelites, like all ancient tribes of that period, were the product of the barbaric age that existed before they came to Canaan. Even during the times of David their savagery and primitive morals regarding murder, massacres, rape, incest and tribal blood feuds continued to be the main feature of their way of life. After the death of Solomon in 927 BC, the majority of Israeli tribes rebelled against his son Rehoboam, raising the slogan 'To your tents, Israel'. At the end of the rebellion two 'kingdoms' were established: the rebels formed the Kingdom of Israel, and Judah and Benjamin established the Kingdom of Judah. The Israelites eventually settled down in the richer and more cultured agricultural areas of the land.

About 200 years later, during the year 724 BC, the Kingdom of Israel was occupied by the Assyrians, and the vast majority of Israelite tribes were removed from the land and settled in Northern Mesopotamia (Iraq). The people of Canaan remained in their country, although subject to Assyrian rule, but free from Israeli oppression. In 587 BC, the Kingdom of Judah was conquered by the Babylonians and the remaining warriors of the Israelites were removed to Mesopotamia. The original inhabitants of Canaan remained in their country. When Syrus the Persian conquered Babylon 40 years later, he allowed the Judaeans to return to Palestine. However, only a small minority returned, while the majority remained in Mesopotamia.

The dispersion of the Judaeans that followed the Babylonian conquest resulted in the spread of the religion of Judaism to North Africa, Asia Minor and Europe. Around 397 BC, Judaism assumed a new doctrine of separation adopted by the closed and fanatical Jewish community established in Jerusalem, who isolated themselves from the converts in the rest of the world. Even then the Jews of Jerusalem were not an ethnic community; they were religious fanatics who worshipped Yahweh.

After the destruction of Jerusalem by the Romans in AD 70, many Jews were killed, fled for safer areas or were forcibly exiled. The Jewish revolt of AD 135 resulted in the complete destruction of the Jewish community in Palestine, while Palestine itself remained a province of the Roman Empire. Following the conversion of the Roman Empire to Christianity, the vast majority of the people of Palestine became Christians. There were only a few hundred Jews scattered throughout the country who secretly remained devoted to the Jewish faith. Thus, until the Arab Muslim conquest of AD 633–8, the inhabitants of Palestine, who were mainly the descendants of the ancient tribes of the Canaanites, Philistines, Hittites, Amorites and Jebusites, were either pagan or Christian, with a very small community of Jews. During the following century, while enjoying the principle of the freedom of religion, a substantial majority of the people of Palestine – Arabs, Jews, Christians and pagans – adopted Islam as their religion and, gradually,

Arabic became their language. However, a large Christian community and a small Jewish minority retained their religion during the period of the Muslim Empire. Apart from the Crusader period in Palestine and during the whole era of the Ottoman Empire, there was no religious hostility whatsoever in the country. Jews, Christians and Muslims lived in peace as one civil community and as good neighbours.

Until the end of the Ottoman Empire there were no nation states in the modern political sense. The concept was not known between 1250 BC, when the Israelites invaded Palestine, until the AD 1880s, when the first wave of Jewish immigrants landed in Palestine. Thereafter, new waves of Jewish immigrants to the country began, coming mainly from Russia and Eastern Europe. These new immigrants were inspired by the Zionist Conference and the idea of a Jewish 'national home'. Towards the end of the First World War, it became evident that an attempt was being made by Britain and the United States to implant a foreign society in the land of the Palestinian Arabs who had inhabited the country without interruption for more than 3,000 Arab years and 1,300 Muslim years. When the new Jewish immigrants arrived in Palestine, there was a coherent and fully integrated Arab society in the country's ancient towns and villages: farmers, traders, craftsmen, an Arabic culture, Jewish, Christian and Muslim religious institutions, an administration that was part of the Ottoman Government, and a political élite of Arab Ottoman allegiance. However, the new Jewish settlers had no intention of becoming a part of that society. Their real objective was to create their own society with all its attributes, including the establishment of an exclusive 'religious Jewish state' in Palestine.

It is said that the motive of the Jews of the world to occupy and usurp Palestine was religious, but any religious faith or devotion can be expressed or practised anywhere in the world – especially if it is a monistic religion. The Jews of the world, particularly those in Palestine, were free to practise their devotion anywhere in the Ottoman Empire, including Jerusalem, without any constraint. As well as Palestine, they lived in Syria, Lebanon, Iraq, Yemen, Egypt, Tunisia and Morocco. Furthermore, 'the land of the Bible' to which they wanted to 'return' was never exclusively the land of the Jews. It was the land of the Canaanites and other tribes before they occupied it. It was certainly not the land of their forefathers, because they only forced their rule over it as occupiers, not as landowners, for a short period of history.

The history of Christian antagonism against the Jews of whatever country they were citizens of need not be repeated here to prove that it took more than 1,850 years for the Jews to become free from persecution as citizens in Western Europe and later in the USA, while the Jews of Russia remained isolated and persecuted. Thus, the real motive for the usurpation of Palestine was decidedly political and economic and adorned with religious symbolism. It was not strange that the Zionist Movement had started in Russia, but it was ironic that the Jews who started the movement that demanded the 'Return to Zion' were not the descendants of the Jews of Palestine. In fact, they had never set foot in the country they demanded to return to.

It is not necessary to dwell on the history of the Zionist Movement from the first Zionist Conference onwards. This movement was led by Dr Theodore Herzl and subsequently by Dr Chaim Weizmann as a political organisation that endeavoured to achieve a political aim. It was, judging by the political evidence of the time, a nationalist religious movement to save the Jews of the world from persecution and in their own countries. It is necessary, however, to mention the Balfour Declaration of 1917, initiated by Arthur Balfour, British Foreign Secretary from 1916–19, on which the Amir Abdullah ibn al-Hussein wrote:

> It is strange that the Balfour Declaration was made in favour of a people who had no previous political status in Palestine; it was similar to a birth certificate issued before the child was born. Only the Arabs were in Palestine and in the circumstances, how could it be justifiable to make a declaration in favour of a foreign people and in respect to a land in which they were not settled and, at the same time, to deprive the legitimate owners of that land of their rights. At the time of the Declaration, Palestine was considered to be an Occupied Enemy Territory, a title which could not be granted heedlessly and which in Arab eyes is inconsistent with such a queer and irregular Declaration.[1]

The Balfour Declaration was a product of British colonialist, imperialist and pro-Zionist politicians, such as Lloyd George, Winston Churchill, Balfour and others during the era of colonial and imperial power politics. It enunciated British support for the establishment of a national home, not a national state, for the Jewish people in Palestine, but on condition that it was to be established without prejudice to the rights of 'existing non-Jewish communities'; the Arab inhabitants of the country. Nothing like the political horse trading that took place between the USA and Great Britain for the support of the Jews during the First World War had occurred in the history of mankind as it had done in the Balfour Declaration. There was no legal or moral justification for that promise; the Jews were never a separate nation during the previous 1,800 years, they were national citizens of more than fifty countries. The Jews of the whole world referred to in the Balfour Declaration were not a nation, they were men and women nationals of their own countries in which they lived.

In 1922, the Council of the League of Nations granted a Mandate to the British Government, entrusting it with the task of governing Palestine as a 'trust of civilization'. According to Article 22 of the Covenant of the League of Nations, the Arabs of Palestine were classified as:

> Certain communities formerly belonging to the Turkish Empire that have reached a stage of development where their existence as independent nations can be provisionally recognised subject to the rendering of administrative advice and assistance by a mandatory until such time as they are able to stand alone. The wishes of these communities must be a principal consideration in the selection of the mandatory.

Nearly every action taken by successive British governments in Palestine has led to the denial of assistance or even advice to the Palestinian people. Instead, it was obvious that British pro-Zionist governments were determined, above all else, to implement the Balfour Declaration. Thus the wishes of the Palestinian Arabs were not the principal consideration of any British government and the status of the 'trust of civilization' was given to the Jewish usurpers rather than maintained for its Arab owners. When the Balfour Declaration was issued in 1917, the Jewish population in Palestine numbered about 56,000. By 1939, mainly through the immigration policy of the British Government, as well as through illegal immigration, the Jewish population in Palestine had increased to about 475,000. During the same period, the Arab population of Palestine increased from about 750,000 in 1917 to 1,100,000 in 1939. Between 1939 and 1947, more than 185,000 Jewish immigrants came to Palestine either with the approval of the British Government or illegally. The Jewish population in Palestine in 1948 had grown to 650,000, or more than eleven-fold since 1917.

The Jewish communities of Palestine were concentrated mainly in three strips running from north to south.

1. East Galilee, from the Lebanese–Palestinian border, with the exception of Safad, Tiberias, Baisan and their immediate environs.
2. South of Haifa, from the Jewish quarter of the city to the south of Tel Aviv, with the exception of Jaffa.
3. The Jewish quarter in Jerusalem and a few Jewish settlements.

By October 1947, the Arabs of Palestine realised the great challenge to their existence in their own country by the United Nations Partition Plan. The Palestinians, who suffered the grave injustice of having an alien people planted among them in their own small land without their consent, were completely justified in their feelings of deep and strong resentment and hostility against the Zionist Jews, as well as against the governments of Britain, the USA and the Soviet Union. To put it simply, the Palestinian Arabs have been forced to pay for the persecution of Christians against the Jews of Europe, Russia and America, and later between the two World Wars, and throughout the Second World War, the genocide of the Jews in Europe, which was committed by the Germans, not the Arabs. Thus, the Palestinians became the victims of the Jewish victims of European, Russian and American persecution.

Since the creation of the League of Arab States in 1945, the Palestine problem officially became an *Arab* problem. The League of Arab States and its Political Committee took nearly all the major decisions concerning the Palestinian people and their future. At the Sofar meeting in Lebanon of September 1947, a Military Committee was formed as follows:

1. Major General Ismael Safwat, Iraq
2. Colonel Mahmoud al Hindi, Syria
3. Lt Colonel Shawkat Shuqair, Lebanon
4. Former Major Subhi al Khadhra, Palestine.

Only General Safwat was qualified to deal with the matter at hand. The remaining three did not have any staff training, nor indeed had they even commanded units larger than one hundred men; they were either glorified police officers or officers of gendarmes. However, their first report and recommendations to the Political Committee assembled at Alai in Lebanon between 7 and 15 October 1947, which was written by General Safwat, can be summarised as follows:

1. To call for volunteers, arming and training them either by governments or People Committees.
2. To mobilise and concentrate to the maximum all regular forces near the Palestine frontiers.
3. To establish a general Arab headquarters commanding all regular and irregular headquarters.
4. To supply the Arabs of Palestine with at least 10,000 rifles and accessories.
5. To credit a sum of money not less than 1 million P£ to the Permanent Military Committee.
6. To purchase a number of weapons from foreign countries.
7. To mobilise whatever available number of aircrafts to observe the Palestinian costs.

Out of all these recommendations the P£1 million deposit from the budget of the League of Arab States was agreed to by the Political Committee and implemented. The other recommendations were the product of emotional hot air.

At the end of 1947, The United Nations Special Committee on Palestine (UNSCOP) was the final attempt to find a solution for the Palestine problem. Previous attempts such as the Royal Commission of 1937, the Anglo-American Committee of Inquiry of 1946, and the London Conference of Arabs and Jews hosted by the United Kingdom, failed to achieve a solution acceptable to both parties. Presented with the Partition Plan by UNSCOP, the Palestinians and all the Arab member states of the Arab League rejected the plan. The British Government, which anticipated great damage to its position in the Arab and Muslim worlds, was reluctant to support it. Despite Colonial Office approval of the plan as a simple and easy solution, the Foreign Office, which was more aware of the possible consequences and conscious of their effect on British relations with the whole of the Arab Middle East, resisted the idea of a Jewish State in Palestine.[2] The Foreign Office won the inter-departmental argument, and when the Plan was voted on in the United Nations, Britain abstained and declared its intention to withdraw from Palestine on 15 May 1948 rather than be party to the partition of the country in its trust.

There is no doubt whatsoever that the main architects of the Partition Plan were the Americans, who did their utmost to support the idea of a Jewish state in Palestine, and conducted intensive lobbying in the United Nations General Assembly in its favour. President Harry Truman had nothing to lose because he was not responsible for the implementation of the Plan and was therefore free from its consequences. His main motive was to win the support of the Jewish lobby and their votes in the approaching American elections (see Map 1).

On 8 December 1947, the Arab League Political Committee held a meeting in Cairo to discuss the deteriorating political and security situation in Palestine. The second report of the Permanent Military Committee was presented by its chairman, General Safwat, who explained the serious deficiencies of the Arab military strength compared with that of the Jews. He described the armaments, organisation, training and experiences of both the Arabs and the Jews, and told the Committee that defending Palestine with irregular forces was impossible, and that the Arabs must confront the Jews with regular well-armed, organised and trained Arab armies. He called for immediate action to be taken and repeated his recommendations for arming the Palestinians to defend themselves.[3]

Comparative strengths

In any military or political appreciation of a situation the aim of the planners must be clearly defined. Every military doctrine since the First World War and during the Second World War insisted on that concept. For, without a clearly defined and limited single aim, no comparative strength could be studied for the purpose of planning an operation, a campaign, or indeed a war. The Political Council of the League of Arab States, which was responsible for planning and conducting what it intended for the liberation of Palestine or even the defence of the Palestinian people, had no specific or clearly defined aim worthy of its name. Whether it related to accepting a representative of the Palestinian people in the League Council, the future of Palestine, any other policy towards the Jews or on the Arabs of Palestine, or indeed the Arab State of Palestine, they had no specific aim or plan. On the other hand, by the beginning of 1948, the Jews of Palestine, as well as Jewish Zionists all over the world, had one clearly defined aim: *the creation of the Jewish state in Palestine*. In Dr Weizmann's words, the Jewish aim was 'to make Palestine as Jewish as England is English'.

The Jews

To achieve the aim of Dr Weizmann, the Jews had a united organisation of several institutions which, although they may have had different points of view, all had one political and strategic purpose – the achievement of their aim. On an institutional level there was no comparison between the formidable Jewish civil institutions and those of the Palestinian people, if they had any. In addition to the worldwide Zionist Organisation that supported the Jews of Palestine, the Jewish Agency, the Histadrut and their local branches all over the Jewish areas of Palestine, plus the Haganah under a united command, there was a highly qualified Jewish Government already existing and effective in the day-to-day supervision of Jewish life. Most important among Jewish institutions was the Intelligence Service, which kept its leadership informed of nearly all political and military activities in Palestine and neighbouring Arab countries.

The Jews had a united leadership, while Arab leadership was divided. The Jews felt an extreme sense of urgency for they believed strongly in their hearts and minds that they had nowhere else to go if they lost the fight; the Arabs, on the other hand, with the exception of the Palestinian people, did not have this sense of urgency.

Since 1946, the Jews had carried out a cruel, ruthless and effective terrorist campaign against the British Army and the Arab inhabitants of Palestine. The British Government in Palestine, in its counter-terror strategy, was inhibited by the American attitude towards the Jews, and by the sympathy the West had shown to the Zionist cause during and after the Second World War. After all the facts of Hitler's atrocities became known, especially during the Nuremberg trials, sympathy for the Jewish cause reached its peak.

Furthermore, during the 1930s and the first half of the 1940s, while a Palestinian Arab would be hanged by his neck if he had a pistol in his possession, Jews were supplied with British weapons to protect their Kibbutz settlements. Over 30,000 Jewish men were enlisted in the British Army; they were very well trained in the arms of modern warfare and gained experience of fighting during the war. The Jewish immigrants to Palestine had gained yet more experience in the art of survival under the most dangerous and heinous conditions in the history of mankind. The Arabs had never suffered similar atrocities and had never had any experience in the art of survival. Throughout the centuries of their persecution, Jews had perfected the art of negotiation in order to survive, while the Arabs had hardly conducted negotiations during the Ottoman period and had invariably lost in any negotiations with the British Government.

By the beginning of 1947 the strength of the Haganah, the main military force of the Jews of Palestine, amounted to 43,000 men and women, of which 32,000 were Jewish settlement home guards with orders to hold out to the last man. Of the total strength of the Haganah, 27,000 had served in allied armies – mainly the British Army – where they were trained, battle inoculated and through which they gained experience of war. Within the Haganah, the Palmach units, consisting of 3,100 men and women, were the mobile élite of the Jewish forces.

In contrast, the Palestinian Arabs had no military experience whatsoever; their fighting experience was gained mainly in the Arab Revolt of 1936–9, which amounted more to partisan hit-and-run raids than military confrontation. By spring 1948, while the League of Arab States was still discussing what it was going to do and had managed to start supporting the Palestinian partisans with irregular volunteers, the Jewish Command was able to organise, arm, train and deploy its military units in Palestine. The total strength of the Jewish force at that time is shown in Table 1.1. Table 1.2 is a summary of its weapons.[4]

Furthermore, the terrorist gang Irgun Zvai Leumi (IZL), with a strength of about 4,000 members and the Stern gang, with a strength of about 1,000 men were terrorist groups employing extremely deceptive, cruel and effective guerrilla tactics. It is not known exactly what relations existed between the Haganah and these gangs. Publicly, they were opposed by the Jewish leadership, but secretly, the Jewish Agency seemed to agree to let them continue their terrorist campaign against the British Army and most certainly against the Arabs. However, the British Army estimated the strength of the Jewish forces on 14 May 1948 as follows:

TABLE 1.1
Total strength of the Jewish force, spring 1948

Name	Number	Location
Negev Palmach Brigade	2,000	Nir-Am
Yiftach Palmach Brigade	2,000	Galilee
Harel Palmach Brigade	2,000	Jerusalem
Golani Brigade	4,095	Galilee
Carmeli Brigade	2,238	Haifa
Alexandroni Brigade	3,588	Nathanya
Kiryati Brigade	2,504	Tel Aviv
Givati Brigade	3,229	Rehovot
Etzioni Brigade	3,166	Jerusalem
Training establishments	398	
Air Force	675	
Engineers	150	
Military Police	168	
Transport units	1,097	
Conscripts under training	1,719	
Total	**29,027**	
Total home guards	32,000	
Total Jewish forces	**61,027**	

TABLE 1.2
Weapons of the Jewish force, spring 1948

Type of weapon	Number held
Rifles	22,000
Light and medium machine-guns	1,550
Sub-machine-guns	11,000
3-inch mortars	195
2-inch mortars	682
Projector infantry anti-tank	86
65 mm field guns	5

Haganah (including the Palmach) fully trained and mobilised 70,000
IZL   4,000
Total   **74,000**[5]

General Safwat had estimated the Jewish strength at 50,000 men, including the Haganah, Stern and IZL (Irgun). In his report to Jamil Mardam, the Prime Minister of Syria and the chairman of the Committee for Palestine, established by the League of Arab States, estimated that the Jews had established local garrisons in all Jewish settlements with the aim of defending them against Arab attacks. He thought the strength of these garrisons was about 20,000 men and women.[6]

The Arabs of Palestine

On the Arab side within Palestine, it was only immediately after the publication of the report of the Anglo-American Committee of Inquiry that the Palestinian leadership began to think of establishing an armed movement to defend themselves against the Jews and the British forces. Two points of view represented the division within the leadership; one group recommended the doctrine of the 1936–9 Palestinian Revolt, and started supplying weapons to villagers and training them; the other group recommended the formation of regular units of local defence and other mobile striking units. It was decided that the latter should be established in Syria. However, these decisions remained on paper until the declaration of the Partition Plan by the United Nations. Thus, while the Jews expanded what forces they had at the end of the Second World War, and achieved the strength mentioned above, the Arabs began thinking about creating a new force in November 1947. The compromise that was reached in the Permanent Military Committee divided the Arab forces into what became Jaish al-Inqath (the Liberation Army) of irregular units under the command of the Permanent Military Committee, and al-Jihad al-Muqaddas (Holy Jihad) units under the command of the High Arab Committee of the former Mufti of Palestine, al-Haj Amin al-Husseini. There was no cooperation whatsoever between the two forces.

The vague and irrelevant military aim of the Permanent Military Committee was 'to prevent the establishment of a Jewish Government in Palestine; and to force the Jews to accept the Arab demands'.[7] Nothing was said regarding the destruction of the Jewish forces, or at least the defence of the Arabs of Palestine. The Jewish Government already existed and was administering Jewish life; the pretended aim did not even include what the Arab demands were. The whole strategic military debacle seemed to have been intended to shift responsibility to the people of Palestine from the Council of the Arab League to the Military Committee, which passed it to the Liberation Army, which did not exist at the time.

Soon after the decision of the Political Committee to form the Liberation Army, the Military Committee started to debate the issue of appointing a Commander. For various reasons, typical of inter-Arab divisions, rivalry and jealousies, they appointed the deserter of the 1936–9 Palestinian Revolt, Fawzi al-Qawiqji, rather than General Ttaha al-Hashimi of Iraq, who was subsequently appointed Inspector of the Volunteer Forces. Fawzi had no military experience to command even a modern military company, let alone an army, while Ttaha al-Hashimi was one of the most experienced in military affairs throughout the Arab world. The appointment of al-Qawiqji was not welcomed by Haj Amin al-Husseini, who thought him to have been 'an agent of British Intelligence since he joined the Revolt in 1938'. It was not welcomed by General Safwat either, who thought him to be 'a greedy lover of money, knave, full of exaggeration and unfit to command'. Thus al-Jihad al-Muqaddas had no confidence in him. Most certainly al-Qawiqji was out of date with, and a stranger to, the doctrines of modern warfare that existed in 1948. His appointment was the first and the worst disaster that led to the defeat of that army.

By the beginning of 1948, enlistment in the Liberation Army had begun. Several hundred highly motivated and politically minded young men from Palestine, Jordan, Syria, Lebanon and Iraq joined its units and other partisan organisations – members of the Baath Party of Syria led by Akram al-Hourani; members of the Muslim Brothers Movement from Egypt led by Kamil al-Sharif, from Syria led by Mustafa al-Sibaai, and from Jordan led by Abd al-Latif Abu Qourah; members of the Syrian Nationalist Party led by Salah al-Shishekli and Ghassan Jidid – most of whom had never fired a shot in anger in modern warfare.

The Liberation Army had its headquarters at Qudsiyah in Syria, and all volunteers were sent to the Syrian Army camps at Qattana where enlistment and training took place. At his HQ, General Safwat appointed Colonel Mahmoud al-Hindi, Colonel Shawkat Shuqair and Major Wasfi Al Tal as members of his staff for operations. Fawzi al-Qawiqji, Colonel Mohammad Safa and Colonel Adib al-Sheshekli were appointed Commanders in the field.[8] Major Wasfi Al Tal, a Jordanian who served in the British Army during the war, described the state of arms and ammunition of the Liberation Army as rudimentary and a crying shame. He thought that there was no justification for the Military Committee not to purchase effective weaponry in a short period of time. As the major stated, the weapons of the Liberation Army were antiquated: 'Some were refurbished, some were unserviceable and some were without ammunition. I remember that some of the weapons issued to the men killed more of them than the enemy was able to kill.'[9]

When enlistment started in January 1948, the officers in charge accepted whoever volunteered. According to Wasfi Al Tal,

> [M]any were able men; former soldiers, students, young civil servants, and Palestinian farmers who were loyal to their cause and very keen to fight for it. Others, were a curious mixture of mercenaries, adventurers, fugitives, former prisoners, not to mention some enemy agents.[10]

Furthermore, to any officer with the slightest knowledge of the length of time it took to build even a small military unit, not to mention an army, the idea of establishing the Liberation Army within a few weeks – even months – was not only ludicrous but also naive in the extreme.

As for the organisation of the Liberation Army, Wasfi Al Tal described it as 'chaotic' to say the least, and listed the constraints facing the planners as follows:

- The League had threatened to use force two years before, but it was only in words, because the League men did not think of providing weapons and equipment, or officers and men.
- The Arabs had no intelligence regarding the enemy, and if some information was provided, it was dismissed as unimportant.
- The League had imposed on the Political Committee to accept the Arab High Committee and the National Committees as the authorities for civil, administrative and enlistment matters.
- Palestine was divided into military areas without military considerations; it was divided for party political, local and familial considerations.
- The Military Committee was not free to select and appoint unit Commanders and local defence Commanders; the majority of them were imposed according to their political loyalties to the Arab High Committee and other political parties, not for military efficiency.
- The Military Committee thinking was dominated by the military doctrine of the 1936–9 Revolt, while the enemy, their weapons and military doctrine had changed.

- Worst of all, fighting began without discipline when the Partition Plan was declared, which was why the politicians and military Commanders lost control.[11]

Major Wasfi, who was a staff officer at General Safwat's HQ, agreed that the General had established HQ according to modern convention, with a proper order of battle and staff duties; he organised the administration and supplies and created the intelligence and communication branches. All this was undertaken on the assumption that the formations and units in the areas of Palestine would be under his direct command for operations and administration. However, according to Wasfi, these arrangements were in vain for the following reasons:

- There was no cooperation between the General Inspector and HQ regarding men, weapons and equipment.
- There was a severe lack of experienced officers in administration, supplies, training and conduct of major operations.
- It was difficult for the unit Commanders and garrisons to execute orders from the HQ, either because they did not realise their importance or because of their ignorance, or because of their political loyalties.
- There was no delimitation of jurisdiction and authorities for Commanders. For example, al-Qawiqji considered himself to be the Field Commander of the whole front, while HQ considered him to be Commander of his units and his area only.[12]

Furthermore, General Safwat had, more often than not, involved himself in various political problems and disputes between the Political Committee and the Military Committee and the Arab High Committee. Thus he travelled extensively between Arab capitals, which did not leave him enough time for the day-to-day running of his command.

Wasfi appreciated that the Syrian Army had placed all its facilities at the disposal of the HQ of the Liberation Army; it provided weapons, stores, camps and efficient officers. But all this was in vain, because there was no structure for the utilisation of these facilities. Indeed, with this chaos prevailing in Damascus, there was similar chaos in Palestine where several headquarters were established, each with its officers, regulations, formations and intelligence, none of which recognised the authority of the General HQ in Damascus and could not understand the meaning of coordination and cooperation in battle.[13]

The Liberation Army was organised as shown in Table 1.3.

TABLE 1.3
Organisation of the Liberation Army

Unit	Commander
1. Northern Area Command: commanded by	Lt Colonel Adib al-Sheshekli
2nd Yarmouk Battalion	Lt Colonel Adib al-Sheshekli
Jabal al-Arab Battalion	Major Shakib Wahab
Iraqi Company	Lt Hussein Abd al-Latif
Syrian Company – Hamah	Lt Salah al-Shishekli
Circassian Company	Lt Jalal Barqouq
Syrian Company – Idlib	Captain Abd al-Ghaffar
Jordanian Company	Captain Sari al-Funaish
Jordanian Bedouin Company	Lt Muhsin Yaaish
Syrian Regular Company	Lt Othman Hajo
Lebanese Company	Lt Mohammad Zughaib
2. Central Area Command: commanded by	Fawzi al-Qawiqji
1st Yarmouk Battalion	Lt Colonel Mohammad Safa
Qadisiyah Battalion	Lt Colonel Mahdi Salih al-Aani
Al-Hussein Battalion	Major Mahmoud al-Hindi
Hittin Battalion	Captain Madlul Aabbas
3rd Yarmouk Battalion	Major Abd al-Hamid al-Rawi
Ajnadin Battalion	Captain Michael Issa
Iraqi Battalion	Lt Colonel Aadil Najim al-Din
Lebanese Company	Captain Hikmat Ali
Furaty Company – Iraq	Captain Khalid al-Matraji[14]

3. Local Garrisons

Already in position defending their localities against Israeli attacks were the following garrisons of Palestinian armed men under command of their local National Committees.

• Western Galilee Area, including Akka and Safad in the east, commanded by Abu Mahmoud al-Saffouri (about 242 men armed with rifles).
• Southern Galilee, including Baisan, Tiberias and Nazareth, commanded by Abu Ibrahim al-Saghir (about 547 men armed with rifles).
• Haifa Area, commanded by Abd al-Haq al-Aazzawi (about 395 men armed with rifles).
• Jaffa Area, commanded by Shaikh Hasan Salameh (about 414 men armed with rifles, some hand grenades and a few machine guns).
• Jerusalem Area, commanded by Abd al Qadir al-Husseini (about 630 men armed with rifles, hand grenades, a few machine guns and explosives).
• Hebron Area, commanded by Shaikh Muhammad Ali al-Jaabari (about 250 men armed with rifles).
• Gaza Area, commanded by Tariq al-Ifriqi (about 300 men armed with rifles).

The total strength of the partisan garrisons as shown in Table 1.3 was about 2,570 men, who were static in defence of their areas and who only moved by local transport to help other villages and towns when needed. There was no general plan for these garrisons; they had extremely limited reserves of ammunition and the men were not trained for modern warfare. The best organised among them was the Jerusalem garrison, which was mainly composed of al-Jihad al-Muqaddas organised and commanded by Abd al-Qadir al-Husseini, who deployed them as shown in Table 1.4.[15]

TABLE 1.4
Deployment of the Jerusalem garrison

Number of Men	Commander
80 at the Old City	Hafith Barakat
60 at Wadi al-Jawz	Mohammad Aadil al-Najjar
60 at Bab al-Sahirah	Bahjat Abu Gharbiyah
60 at al-Musrarah	Bahjat Abu Gharbiyah
30 at Bab al-Khalil	Mohammad Abu Nab
30 at al Nabi Daoud	Ahmad Amin al-Dajani
40 at al Thuri quarter	Mohammad Said Barakat
45 at al Baqaah al-Foqa	Shafiq Auwais
100 at al-Tlibiyah	Ibrahim Abu Daiyah
40 at Bait Safafa	Abdullah al-Omari
50 at Abu Dis	Fawzi Auraiqat
40 at al-Aizariyah	Ibrahim Abu al-Rish
40 at Sur Bahir	Jadullah Mahmoud al-Khatib
30 Demolition group	Fawzi al-Qutub
35 HQ Holy Jihad	

General Safwat was in doubt about the morale and efficiency of the partisans under his command. He thought their training was below average and their efficiency low, and he reported that the reasons for this were as follows:

the lack of officers, and the appointment of Commanders of units and sub-units from retired and junior officers or non-commissioned officers. Discipline was very poor, and that is normal in units consisting of volunteers who do not feel the constraint of law and regulations, and do not fear punishment.

The partisans, whether those enlisted permanently and paid or those who participate in fighting out of a sense of national duty, have no military efficiency. But their morale, whether in volunteer units or Mujahidin is good. Their nationalist feelings make them fight stoutly, and if it was not for those feelings they would not be able to remain steadfast in front of the Jewish weapons.[16]

The Arabs of Palestine had failed to organise themselves as a united people struggling to achieve a specific aim. They were entirely dependent on the British mandatory administration in nearly all aspects of their life. They had no specific aim, no national institutions and no national leadership recognised by the majority; their leaders were divided by regional, tribal, familial and political loyalties. Apart from the Arab High Committee and the local National Committees, Palestinian society was divided by countless regional, tribal and familial loyalties, of which the following can be regarded as examples:

- In the north of Palestine: al Khayatt, al-Mahdi, al-Khalil, al-Shukri, and al-Taha of Haifa; al-Khalifah and Shuqairi of Akka; al-Tahir al-Fahoum and al-Zuabi of Nazareth; al-Khadhra of Safad; and al-Tabari of Tiberias.
- In the central areas of Palestine: al-Abd al-Hadi, al-Shakaah, al-Touqan, al-Tamimi al Masri and al-Nabulsi of Nablus; al-Aabboushi and a branch of Abd al-Hadi in Jenin; al-Taji al-Farouqi, al-Ghusain and Salamah of Ramleh; al-Dajani, al-Said, al-Haykal and al-Bittar of Jaffa.
- In the Jerusalem area: al-Husseini, al-Nusaibah, al-Khatib, al-Khalidi, al-Barakat and al-Nashashibi of Jerusalem; al-Khalaf, al-Zaru and al-Judah of Ramallah.
- In the south of Palestine: al-Jaabari, al-Tamimi and al-Umr of Hebron; a branch of al-Husseini, al-Shawa and Abd al-Shafi of Gaza.

The majority of large landowners, rich merchants, mayors, lawyers, judges and senior civil servants in the British mandatory Government – including the High Commissioner's Office, imams of mosques and Shariah courts, doctors, engineers and contractors – belonged to these families of Arab Palestine. Some of the families could trace their roots back 13 centuries, like the al-Nussaibahs of Jerusalem who had held the keys to the Holy Places ever since the Caliph Omar ibn al-Khattab.

Because of the tribal and familial attitudes of the Palestine Arab society, the influence of their leaders was local rather than national and limited to the urban areas. That may have been the reason for the psychological separation between the sedentary inhabitants of the cities and towns (*hadher*) and those of villages (*fallaheen*). But division between the two stemmed from the standard of living enjoyed by the *hadher* and the poverty suffered by the *fallaheen*.

By the beginning of 1948, nearly all the political parties were reduced, through their own docile behaviour, to a has-been status, yet competing for influence without any power over events. Only the Husseinis, who controlled the Arab High Committee, retained some influence and were active in Palestinian national affairs. In the absence of their leader al-Haj Amin al-Husseini, who was residing in Cairo, and supported by the Arab League, that influence was limited to Jerusalem, Ramallah, Lydda, Ramleh, Gaza and their environs.

Thus, when the British administrative institutions withdrew from the country during spring 1948, the Arab areas in Palestine were bereft of any kind of administration and were subsequently thrown into chaos. All the essential services collapsed; law and order, health, food supplies, public transport, post and telegraph, the police service (including fire-fighting and rescue), public administration, schools and many other services (including the judiciary) suffered immensely. Municipal and village councils attempted to control the anarchy that began to overwhelm the people, but they were short of money and failed to meet the challenge. By the beginning of 1948, therefore, when the Jews intensified their terrorist campaign and military offensive against the British Government and the Arabs of Palestine, what remained of Arab Palestinian society fell apart.

Some Arab historians and writers unjustly thought General Safwat was inefficient, but most of them, without any disrespect for their intellectual standing, were not soldiers and had very little military sense. Safwat was a graduate of a military staff college and was accurate in his appreciation of the military situation when he concluded his report as follows:

> With our forces in Palestine, whether consisting of trained volunteers or armed Palestinians, it is impossible to achieve a decisive military victory. All that they can do is to continue fighting until a certain

time determined by what reinforcements and supplies they are provided with, and whatever weapons they have.

The prevention of the establishment of a Jewish state, and to force the Jews to accept Arab demands, requires at least a force equal to their force, and that we cannot achieve within our present limitations.

We are still convinced by our previous opinion, that the armies of the Arab states must intervene and participate in fighting with all their weapons and equipment, if we want to achieve a decisive military victory.

The Arab armies are still short of sufficient transport for movement. If they do not start to overcome this deficiency, and mobilise as from now, they will not be ready for action when the mandate ends, and events will overtake us as they had done before.[17]

The history of the Hashemite Kingdom of Jordan between 1948 and 1951 is closely connected with the history of Palestine. It is also the history of the 1948 war between the Arabs and the Zionist Jews. The war was between a modern, efficient, industrial and armed society supported by the formidable Zionist Organisation and by the financial and political resources of Jews throughout the world, on the one hand, and societies consisting mainly of farming communities that had just started to develop their potential, slowly moving towards modernity, on the other. It was a war between Jewish leaders such as David Ben-Gurion, who won the support of Jews worldwide, including those of Western Europe, the Soviet Union, and the USA, and al-Haj Amin al-Husseini, who was branded a terrorist by those same nations and was a known supporter of Germany during the Second World War. The rest of the Arabs were dominated by leaders who feared each other, vying for personal influence and, with the exception of King Abdullah of Jordan, were proficient in the art of antagonising world public opinion, especially in the USA and Western European countries. It was a war between the Jews, who were able to arm themselves to the teeth, and the Arabs, who, when fighting began, were unable to buy a single round of ammunition from any country in the world. It was a war between the Jews, who were able to develop their industrial capacity to make mortar bombs and land mines, assemble armoured cars, furbish their weapons and equipment, and the Arabs, who could not make one nail, screw nor pin, and (with the exception of the Jordan Arab Army) could barely maintain what vehicles and equipment they did have.

NOTES

1 PRO. CO 733/344/11. Memorandum from Amir Abdullah to the Royal Commission, 4 March 1937.

2 M. J. Cohen, *Palestine and the Great Powers 1945–1948* (Princeton: Princeton University Press, 1982), pp. 203–28.

3 Walid al-Khalidi, *Fifty Years since the Partition of Palestine 1947–1997* (Beirut: np, 1998), pp. 99–100.

4 E. Luttwak and D. Horowitz, *The Israeli Army* (London: Allen Lane, 1975), pp. 34–6. See also Chaim Herzog, *The Arab–Israeli Wars: war and peace in the Middle East* (London: Arms and Armour, 1982), pp. 19–20.

5 PRO. WO 261/549. Extract from War Office Quarterly Historical Record, 21 March to 20 June 1948.

6 Dispatch from the Headquarters of the Palestinian Forces to the Chairman of the Arab League Committee for Palestine, no. 52/H, 23 March 1948, quoted in Walid al-Khalidi, 'Collection of Documents', *Journal of Palestine Studies* (Berkeley: University of California Press) no. 34, spring 1998.

7 Hani Al Hindi, *The Liberation Army* (Beirut: np, 1974), p. 31.

8 Wasfi Al Tal, 'The Story of the Liberation Army', *Amman al Masa* (Amman: 1–14 May 1950), p. 2. The first of a series of fourteen articles published in the newspaper. True copies of these articles in Al Tal's handwriting are among the author's private papers.

9 See Wasfi Al Tal, article no. 3 in series, p. 1.

10 *Ibid.*, article no. 2 in series, p. 2.

11 *Ibid.*, article no. 1 in series, pp. 5–6.

12 *Ibid.*, article no. 3 in series, pp. 2–3.

13 Aarif al Aarif and Hani Al Hindi, two prominent historians, agree with Wasfi Al Tal in that description.

14 Al Hindi, *The Liberation Army*, pp. 54–5.

15 Bahjat Abu Gharbiyah, *Memoirs of the Struggle of the Palestinian Arabs 1916–1949* (Beirut: published by the author, 1993), pp. 265–6.

16 General Safwat's report dated 23 March 1948, in Al Hindi's *The Liberation Army*.

17 Al-Khalidi, 'Al-Qastal', *Journal of Palestine Studies*, no. 34 (1998), p. 35.

2

The Gathering Storm

―――――

In 1945, the British Government was under pressure from the USA to allow 100,000 Jews from Europe, the United States and the Soviet Union to emigrate to Palestine. When the British Government refused to allow such a massive emigration, the Jewish leadership in Tel Aviv began to launch a terrorist campaign by the nascent Jewish army (known as the Haganah) and other terrorist organisations (such as the Irgun and Stern gangs) against British troops and British military and civilian installations in the country.

During March 1946, the Jewish terrorist gangs in Palestine planted a bomb in a British Army vehicle park killing seven British soldiers. Ungratefully, and indeed most unethically, the terrorist Jewish gangs in Palestine started their terror campaign against the British Army, whose country had awarded them the Balfour Declaration, permitted them to emigrate to Palestine in great numbers and saved millions of them from death camps in Europe. To that end, Britain had sacrificed many of her sons. As for the Arabs of Palestine, who had treated Jews as their cousins and neighbours throughout many hundreds of years, these gangs showed no mercy in the massacres of them and in the schemes by which they intended to deprive them of their homes and land.

On 18 June 1946, one Jewish terrorist killed two British officers and kidnapped three others. The British Army imposed a curfew in the area of the crime. On 27 June, the leaders of the Irgun Zvai Leumi threatened to kill the three British officers if the death sentences passed on two of their own members were carried out. On 2 July, a massive cache of illegal weapons belonging to the Haganah was discovered.

The most heinous and inhumane crime committed by the Jews against the British was carried out on 22 July 1946. The Stern gang planted a time-bomb in the King David Hotel in Jerusalem, which destroyed the wing where the HQ of the Palestine British Army Command was stationed. The official statement listed 42 officers, men and women killed; 52 others were missing, presumed dead, and 53 were seriously wounded. The crime was designed to kill all the British officers and staff at this HQ. Just after midday, a lorry, guarded by two armed terrorists, had drawn up at the hotel's basement entrance. Two other terrorists unloaded several milk churns packed with high explosives, which they placed in the kitchen of the Regency Restaurant under the office of the Secretariat. On their way out, the two terrorists fired at, and wounded, a British officer who challenged them to stop. The terrorists were able to escape in a waiting taxi, while another terrorist support group opened fire at the hotel to cover the escape. For the first time, the history of mankind recorded that the Jews had introduced the doctrine of the indiscrimnate use of time-bombs for political ends in the Arab Middle East.

Enmity against Britain was declared by the Jews in Palestine when their leaders announced a full boycott of all British goods. The announcement was followed by a new wave of terrorist bombings. On 17 November 1946, eight British Army officers and men were killed in Jerusalem and 11 other British Army personnel were seriously wounded. A few days later, four British soldiers were killed in an outrageous Jewish terrorist act, when a mine was detonated underneath their truck carrying the soldiers from a cinema to their billets. British troops near the site of the crime saw the Jewish terrorists and opened fire at them, but the criminals managed to escape. A few miles away, three British soldiers were killed when their jeep was blown up by a Jewish terrorist bomb, while another soldier was killed when he attempted to remove a mine from a railway line. On 2 December, five more British soldiers were killed in a bomb attack instigated by Jewish terrorists.

On 12 January 1947, a Jewish terrorist group blew up a Palestine police station in Haifa, killing five policemen and wounding ten others as well as an unknown number of Arabs under detention in the police station. On 31 January 1947, under the pressure of a deteriorating security situation in Palestine the High Commissioner, General Sir Alan Cunningham, commanded the evacuation of all British women and children and non-essential British civilians from Palestine. On 10 February, two members of the Irgun terrorist group were sentenced to death. Menachim Begin, leader of the Irgun, was placed at the top of the British list of wanted criminals. On 1 March, Jewish terrorists planted a bomb in the Officers' Club at Jerusalem. On 22 March, after a series of Jewish terrorist attacks throughout Palestine in which 20 British soldiers and civilians were killed, martial law was imposed on Tel Aviv as a preventive measure.

On 22 April 1947, the Jewish Stern gang blew up a British troop train near Rehovot, killing eight British soldiers and injuring another 41 soldiers and civilians – among whom six were seriously wounded. On 24 April, four British Palestine policemen who had protected the Jewish population of Tel Aviv against Arab attacks in the past, were killed and six others were seriously wounded in a massive terrorist bomb, which exploded at the police barracks at Saronà, east of Tel Aviv. Hundreds of houses suffered structural damage and broken windows, which in turn caused injuries to many civilians. The blast was heard some thirty miles away in Rehovot. The two bombs were of a new type, more powerful than any bombs previously used in Palestine. Two terrorists of the Stern gang arrived at the barracks in a Palestine post office van and claimed to have come to repair a faulty telephone line. The policeman at the gate asked them for their identity cards, became suspicious and searched the van. The bombs were well hidden under the chassis and the policeman, who saw nothing suspicious, allowed them to pass. The bombs were then planted in the barracks; a few minutes later the terrorists left – just before the bombs exploded.

On 12 July 1947, two British Army sergeants – Mervyn Paice, aged 43, and Clifford Martin, aged 20 – were kidnapped by a Jewish terrorist gang. At 0630 hours on 31 July, their bodies were discovered by a Palestine police patrol in a suburb of Nathania near Haifa. They had been brutally hung by their necks. Displayed on their uniforms were Irgun terrorists' notices saying they had been executed as spies. Such was the Zionist appreciation and gratitude for the Balfour Declaration and the protection of the Jews of Palestine during the Arab Revolt of 1936–9.

During the first half of December 1947, the Haganah carried out the following terrorist attacks against the Arab population of Palestine:

- 6 December: two Arab houses were demolished by explosives in Abu Kabir.

- 9 December: an Arab house was demolished by explosives in Kartiya.
- 11 December: an Arab house was demolished by explosives in Haifa; several buses were burnt and others destroyed by explosives at Balad al-Shaikh in the Haifa district killing or wounding many Arab men, women and children. Sir Alan Cunningham described this terrorist act as 'an offence to civilization'.[1] Also, 20 Arabs were killed at Balad al-Shaikh when a Haganah detachment opened fire at them at close range with light machine guns.
- 12 December: the Haganah attacked Ramleh; they destroyed 15 cars and vehicles, killed one Arab and wounded several others.
- 13 December: an Arab car was ambushed and destroyed on the road between Baisan and Gesher; an Arab car was ambushed on the main road between Hebron and Bethlehem opposite Kfar Etzion, where five Arabs were seriously wounded, one of whom died in hospital a few days later; an Arab house was demolished at Tal al-Reesh, killing all the members of the family living there.
- 15 December: an Arab car was ambushed on the road between Ras al-Ain and Bait Hatikfa, killing two Arabs and wounding three; two Arab lorries were ambushed and burnt on the road between Lydda and Qalqiliyah, killing one Arab and wounding four.
- 18 December: an Arab house was demolished by explosives at Salama Street in Tel Aviv. All its occupants were killed.
- 19 December: two Arab houses were demolished by explosives at Qazazah, in retaliation against the Arabs who killed a senior Haganah Commander and a Haganah intelligence officer.[2]

Also on 19 December 1947, the Irgun and Stern terrorist gangs carried out the following attacks against the Arabs:

- At al-Tirah, 14 Arabs were killed by machine gun fire.
- At Jaffa, a grenade exploded at a café killing four Arabs and wounding others.
- A bomb exploded at Damascus Gate in Jerusalem, killing three Arabs and wounding seven.
- A grenade exploded at a café in Yazur, wounding several Arabs.
- Several grenades exploded at al-Yahudiyah, wounding and killing 13 Arabs.[3]

As if Palestinian Arab life was of no value to the League of Arab States, not to mention the British Palestine Government, no action was taken to deter Jews from further terrorist acts. There was no moral, legal or political justification for the timid British and Arab policy of restraint while defenceless Palestinians were terrorised by the Jews. However, the first collision (not collusion) between the Jordan Arab Army of the Hashemite Kingdom of Jordan and the Jewish forces occurred on 14 December 1947. A Jewish convoy was passing by the British military camp at Bait Nabala, where a detachment of the Jordan Arab Army commanded by Second Lieutenant Salih al-Sharaa was posted for guard duties under the command of the British Army. A few shots were fired by the Jewish convoy at the Jordan Arab Army's sentry at the gate. The sentry fired back and his comrades joined him in opening fire at the convoy. In the skirmish that followed, 14 Jewish armed men were killed and ten were wounded. All the convoy vehicles were destroyed by fire, while the Jordan Arab Army detachment suffered no casualties. The British military policemen, who rushed to the scene, investigated the incident and the Jordan detachment were found innocent of starting the fight. The morale of the Arab inhabitants around the area rose to a high level, while the Jewish press expressed extreme anger and demanded the expulsion of the Jordanian army from Palestine.[4]

On 4 January 1948, the Jewish terrorist Stern gang exploded a car bomb in a market street at Jaffa, which caused much damage to property and caused many Arab casualties and fatalities. On 16 January, the Jewish Haganah planted a bomb in an Arab house at Haifa. When the bomb exploded, seven innocent Arab children were killed and a few of their neighbours were wounded. More than 2,000 people were killed during the period between October 1947 and January 1948. According to the officials of the United Nations the approximate number of deaths were 1,069 Arabs, 769 Jews, 123 British soldiers and 23 others.

The Arabs of Palestine became desperate and had no confidence in the British Palestine Government to defend them against the Jews or even to deter the Jews against committing terrorist acts against the British Army – not to mention the Arabs themselves. With the few weapons that they were able to smuggle from neighbouring Arab countries they started their own campaign against the Jewish forces. On 22 January, a Jewish convoy on its way from Tel Aviv to Jerusalem guarded by six armed Haganah men was ambushed near Yazour. All six guards were killed. Another convoy was also ambushed near al-Qastal; one Haganah man was killed and another wounded. A hand grenade was thrown by an Arab at a Jewish bus in Haifa; six Jews were killed and others were wounded. In retaliation, the Haganah demolished two Arab houses by explosives and opened fire on the Arab quarter of Haifa; 50 Arabs were killed and 100 others were wounded.

At that point, the Jewish terrorist policy began to succeed in frightening the unarmed Palestinian Arabs, 25,000 Arabs from Haifa and its environs began to leave the city for Lebanon in fear for their lives.

On 16 February, an Arab attack was carried out against the settlement of Tirat Tsvi in the style used during the 1936–9 Rebellion; the attack was repulsed by the Jewish home guard resulting in 38 Arabs dead and 36 wounded.[5] On 18 February, the Irgun gang also retaliated by exploding a car bomb at the market street in Ramleh.

On 20 February, units of the Liberation Army 1st Yarmouk Battalion entered Palestine through Jordan under supervision of the Jordan Arab Army Military Police, travelling on the road from Damascus, Mafraq, Amman and Damia bridge to the Nablus area in Palestine. The 2nd Yarmouk Battalion took the same route a few days later. Meanwhile, the other three battalions crossed the Syrian and Lebanese frontiers with Palestine and occupied Arab areas in the north of the country. According to intelligence reports received by Ben-Gurion, the following units of the Liberation Army entered Palestine.

- 24 December 1947: 400 men entered Palestine near al-Himmah.
- 31 December 1947: 200 men entered Palestine from Tarshiha.
- 7 January 1948: 300 men entered Palestine near Fassutta.
- 21 January 1948: 750 men crossed the Jordan to Tubas in Palestine.
- 29 January 1948: 600 men crossed the Jordan at Majamaa Bridge.
- 6 February 1948: one company of 100 men crossed the Jordan to Nablus and Tulkarm.[6]

Thereafter the British Palestine Government, particularly the High Commissioner, lost all control over events in Palestine. On 29 February 1948, 28 British soldiers were killed and 33 others injured when a mine planted on a railway line by the Stern gang exploded. If the High Commissioner and the British Army in Palestine did nothing to deter the Jews from such terrorist acts against their own officers and men, how could they have deterred the Jews against committing the same acts against the Arabs? From that point on, chaos prevailed in Palestine.

On 5 March that year, the United Nations Security Council approved a resolution appealing to all governments and peoples, particularly in and around Palestine, to take all possible action to prevent or reduce disorder in Palestine. On the same day, Fawzi al-Qawiqji arrived at Jabaa on the high ground between Nablus and Jenin. He declared that he had come to Palestine with his men, who represented all the Arab peoples, 'with one heart and for one aim; to abolish the decision of the United Nations regarding partition; to destroy Zionism; to implement the decisions of the League of Arab States and sacrifice for the Arabness of Palestine'.

The swashbuckling, inept and waffling Field Commander of the Liberation Army committed his first and major error of judgement in the field. His statement gave the Jews all the political justification they needed to attack the Arabs of Palestine, while he could not fulfil even one of his promises – neither the destruction of Zionism nor the abolition of the United Nations Partition Plan.

While in Jabaa, al-Qawiqji had a reply to his statement; on 22 March, the ugliest day of Jewish terrorism against the Arab population of Haifa took place. Two Jewish terrorist bombs were exploded in two areas of the Arab quarter killing 19 Arabs and wounding more than 150 men, women and children. The Arabs fired a few 2-inch mortar bombs at the Jewish business quarter. Four of them fell on a Palestine police station, killing one constable and wounding another. Fierce fighting between Arabs and Jews continued throughout the night. At Artoof, about 20 miles west of the city of Jerusalem, British troops opened fire with 25-pounder field guns to shell Arab positions in the hilly areas where al-Jihad al-Muqaddas armed men defended themselves and their villages against Jewish attacks. Sixty Arabs were killed and 70 others were wounded. At dawn the following morning, British troops were shocked when they heard that the bodies of two comrades were found in the environs of Artoof. Jewish terrorists had arrested the two British soldiers, beaten them to death, then stripped them of all identification, uniforms, badges, insignias and papers.

The attack on Mishmar Ha'Emeq

From Jabaa, where he had located his HQ, Fawzi al-Qawiqji directed his attention on the Jewish settlement of Mishmar Ha'Emeq, situated some 25 kilometres north-west of Jenin and 45 kilometres from Jabaa on the main road between Jenin and Haifa. Instead of planning the attack on the settlement himself, he asked his staff officer, the Commander of his artillery battery of seven guns, Lt Colonel Mamoun al-Bittar (from the Syrian Army), to plan the attack.

Although a good officer with noble nationalist intentions, al-Bittar had no previous experience in such operations. He decided that his aims were to tempt the enemy to fight a large and open battle and to capture Mishmar Ha'Emeq for its strategic location on the route to Haifa.[7] He sent a detachment to block the road to Mishmar Ha'Emeq from Affoulah; another to block the road to Haifa; and a third to block the routes to Mishmar Ha'Emeq from the north and west. He then located his assault troops to the south-east of the settlement. The Commander of the local garrison of the settlement had already noticed the movements of the Liberation Army, and asked for support. A company from the Golani Company was immediately despatched to him to strengthen the garrison defences.

On 1 April, the Security Council of the United Nations approved a resolution calling for an immediate truce in Palestine and requesting that the Secretary General convene a Special Session of the General Assembly to consider the future government of Palestine.

On 4 April, although al-Qawiqji had already lost one of the most important principles of war, the element of surprise, he mounted his attack on Mishmar Ha'Emeq. He started with five minutes of rapid fire from his artillery, followed by normal shelling and medium machine-gun support fire. The assault troops advanced and penetrated the outer perimeters of the settlement and attempted to attack its trenches and fortifications. At that point the Jewish garrison, supported by the Golani Company, opened fire forcing the attackers to withdraw to their start line. On 5 April, al-Qawiqji resumed shelling the settlement and sent a warning to its Mukhtar to surrender. The Mukhtar, accompanied by a British officer, asked al-Qawiqji to give him time to consult with the Jewish Agency. As if he was the victor, al-Qawiqji agreed and commanded his artillery to cease fire.

The Jewish garrison Commander managed to evacuate the wounded men (as well as women and children) from the settlement, reorganised his defences and was ready to fight. On 6 April, al-Qawiqji withdrew one company of the assault troops and sent it to Bab al-Wad, which was being attacked by the Palmach, while he continued to maintain his truce with the Mukhtar of the settlement. On 8 April, the Jews reinforced their forces in the area with the 1st Regiment of the Palmach Brigade, a regiment from the Carmeli Brigade and a regiment from the Alexandaroni Brigade. These fresh troops went on the offensive immediately, capturing the Arab villages and lands of Rowbiyah al-Fawqa, Khirbit al-Rass, al-Kafrain, Abu Zuraiq and Abu Shooshah. On 13 April, the Palmach continued with their attack and captured the villages of al-Naghnaghiyah and Ain al-Mansi. After all that action, while al-Qawiqji remained timid and inactive, his pretend offensive was broken and he withdrew his forces immediately after his second in command, Lt Colonel Mamoun al-Bittar, was killed among the heavy casualties that his forces suffered.

Thereafter, the forces under al-Qawiqji's command were demoralised and started to retreat; there were also many deserters. Meanwhile, the inhabitants of the Arab villages in the area lost heart and started to evacuate their homes, taking refuge in Jenin and elsewhere in the Nablus District.[8] The Arab villages in the area around Mishmar Ha'Emeq and the western end of the Jerzeel valley were in complete ruins. Not a single Arab remained in the houses and mud huts, which were all destroyed by Jewish explosives. The villages of the coastal plain were gradually evacuated one after the other as the Arabs took refuge in the eastern parts of Palestine. The Haganah and the terrorist gangs continued to mount their attacks on each village with the intention of expelling the Arabs from their homes and destroying their houses. Thus the Zionist policy of expulsion was on its merciless way.

The Jewish expulsion policy

It had become obvious that the Jews were determined to keep every inch of land they had occupied and extend their control over whatever they could usurp from Arab land. The Jewish leadership relied on high mobility and the strong defences of their outlying settlements. In spite of the few Arab attacks on the Jewish lines of communications, Haganah

HQ firmly decided that no Jewish settlement should be evacuated without a determined fight. They were extremely concerned with the future borders of the Jewish State, which would be determined by the final limits of their occupation on the ground. The Liberation Army and the Palestinian leadership, on the other hand, had no such urgency of concern for the land or the future borders of the prospective Arab State of Palestine. Instead of strengthening the local defences of Arab villages and towns, they deceived themselves by establishing a symbolic and ineffective irregular force incapable even of holding what land they had. However, from a psychological point of view, the vast majority of the Liberation Army they created did not own an inch of land in Palestine; thus defending it was not their highest priority. On the Jewish side, when the Mandate ended on 15 May, not one Jewish settlement was abandoned, except Kfar Etzion, which was captured by the Jordan Arab Army and the Palestinian partisans of Hebron, not the Liberation Army. Another psychological element played a great part in the morale of both sides: the Jews had nowhere else to go to once they abandoned their settlements, while the Arabs had the vast lands of the Arab world in which to resettle. This psychological attitude was savagely used by the Jews to justify their inhumane 'destruction and expulsion' policy against the Palestinian people and their homes.

By the beginning of April the Jewish leadership, including Ben-Gurion, approved what can be clearly defined as an expulsion policy against the Arabs of Palestine. The Haganah General Staff planned a campaign that aimed to clear out and destroy all Arab villages situated in areas dominating the main routes of movement for Haganah and their military needs. The plan was in conformity with the strategic guidelines of Plan 'D' which, among other aims, was intended to clear out and destroy all Arab communities along their main and vital lines of communications. Thus, orders from General HQ of the Haganah were issued to brigade Commanders to carry out the plan regarding the main roads between Tel Aviv and Hadera, along the road from Haifa to Jenin, and the main road from Jerusalem to Tel Aviv.

Simultaneously, another Jewish offensive, which had the same aim, was launched in accordance with operation 'Nashon' to guarantee free access to Jerusalem. The Haganah attacked and shelled al-Qastal, Qaluniyah and Khulda to rubble, forcing the inhabitants to flee their homes. Only partial success was achieved by the Haganah during the

Nashon operation for only a few Jewish convoys were able to reach Jerusalem from Tel Aviv unharmed.

The fall of al-Qastal

By the beginning of April 1948, Jewish forces had begun to attack Arab villages such as Dair Muheisin, Bait Mahsir, Suba, Qaluniyah and al-Qastal, which were adjacent to the main road between Jerusalem and Tel Aviv. Al-Qastal village, five miles west of Jerusalem, dominated the main road from its high hill. The al-Jihad al-Muqaddas fighters managed to block the road and isolate Jerusalem from the main areas occupied by Jewish forces. The village of al-Qastal was attacked several times by the Haganah without success. On 3 April the 4th Palmach Battalion attacked and captured al-Qastal unopposed – as soon as the attack started its inhabitants and the small detachment of al-Jihad al-Muqaddas swiftly evacuated fearing the huge Jewish force attacking them.

Al-Qastal was among the first Arab villages to be usurped by the Zionist expulsion and destruction policy. Soon after the occupation, the Palmach unit started to organise their defensive positions in and around the village. They also managed to hold part of the hill where it was situated.

During that operation Abd al-Qadir al-Husseini was in Damascus asking to be given weapons and ammunition for his men. Anwar Nusaibah, the chairman of the National Committee in Jerusalem and Deputy Commander al-Jihad al-Muqaddas organised volunteers for a counter-attack on al-Qastal. On 4 April, a force commanded by Ibrahim Abu Dayah, Hafiz Barakat, Kamil Auraiqat and Abdullah al-Omari, carried out this counter-attack in a battle that lasted until 5 April, when the Palmach brought in new reinforcements. On 6 April, the Palmach managed to hold the village as well as attack and capture the Arab villages of Dair Muhaisin and Khuldah near Bab al-Wad. The Liberation Army was nowhere to be seen during the battle. Fawzi al-Qawiqji seemed to have vanished into thin air.

On hearing about the fall of al-Qastal, al-Husseini returned to Jerusalem empty-handed, determined to recapture the village. On 7 April, he was able to raise about 50 armed men with whom he counter-attacked the Jewish force in al-Qastal. In the close combat that he led from the front against the Jewish force and after almost recapturing the village, he was killed at the top of the hill. It is said that, on the following day, when most of his men had returned to Jerusalem with his body to attend his funeral, Jewish forces once again captured al-Qastal. Abd al-Qadir al-Husseini was a noble freedom fighter and the most renowned leader of the people of Palestine in Jerusalem.[9] Palmach Commander Uri Ben-Ari reported the blowing up of all the houses of the village which were not needed for the defence of the Palmach positions. Immediately after the capture of the village of Qaluniyah, all the houses in that village were also destroyed.

The massacre at Dair Yasin

Two days later, on 9 April, the Irgun and Stern terrorist gangs carried out the ugliest massacre in the history of the war between the Arabs and the Jews. The unarmed village of Dair Yasin, situated near Jerusalem, which was inhabited by about 1,200 Arabs, had concluded an agreement with the Jewish population of the settlement of Givat Shaul not to use violence against each other and thus live in peace. This village was the scene of a most heinous crime against humanity. The Jewish terrorist Irgun and Stern gangs, supported by two platoons of the Palmach Brigade, along with a supply of ammunition from the Haganah, surprised the peaceful, sleeping village by an attack at dawn, just as the Shaikh was calling '*Allahu Akbar*', the morning prayer. The Jewish terrorists killed every Arab man, woman and child they could find in their homes without mercy; those who attempted to flee were also ruthlessly killed. The terrorists were most certainly bloodthirsty; they had no moral compunction in mutilating the bodies of the dead, using their knives and bayonets to stab unborn children in their mothers' womb. The ancient Israelites were not as cruel and barbaric as the Irgun and Stern gangs; 245 men, women and children were killed during that black morning of Jewish history. Without any resistance from the Arab villagers, the terrorists took 80 men, some of them wounded, as prisoners, tied them up, loaded them into trucks and paraded them in the street of the Holy City of Jerusalem in a show of Arab defeat, while singing and waving their weapons in a hysteria unknown to civilized human beings. Their audience comprised the Jewish inhabitants of the Holy City who 'insulted the prisoners with swear words and spat at them'. David Shaltiel, the regional Commander of Jerusalem, said on the following day: 'The parade of the prisoners among the people raised their morale.'[10] To display their savagery, the terrorists took the prisoners back to Dair Yasin, lined them up and shot every one of them, including the wounded, in cold blood. If barbarism in the history of mankind were given degrees, the massacre at Dair Yasin deserved a place at the top. A total of 325 innocent Arabs – men, women and children – had been killed by the end of the day.

In the House of Commons in London, the Secretary of State for the Colonies deprecated the savage attack on Dair Yasin and described it as follows:

> This barbarous aggression is a proof of savagery. It was a crime that added to a long list of atrocities committed by the Zionists to this day, and for which he could find no words strong enough to convey the feelings of repulsion and grave concern of the British Government.[11]

The representative of the Red Cross Organisation in Jerusalem, who arrived at the village the following day, searched for survivors among the dead bodies. He described an incident that had occurred during his search:

> Here they cleared the place with machine gun fire, followed by hand grenades, and finished the jobs with bayonets. When I was about to leave [the house he was in], I heard what sounded like groaning. I searched everywhere, turned over the bodies, and at last I found a small foot, which was still warm. It belonged to a girl of ten years of age, [who was] wounded but alive. All that I found was two females, that child and an old woman hiding behind some cut branches.[12]

Jewish historians have been extremely selective in their descriptions of the massacre, as can be seen in Uri Milstein's *History of the War of Independence*.[13] Avi Chlaim, in his *Collusion Across the Jordan*, was extremely brief in his description of the massacre (seven lines of text) and acquitted the Haganah from collusion with the Stern and Irgun terrorists whom he called 'fighters'.[14] However, the High Commissioner for Palestine, shed more light on the whole truth as he reported to the British Government.

> 2. A representative of the International Red Cross who visited Dair Yasin on Sunday is said to have stated that in one cave he saw the

heaped bodies of some 150 Arab men, women and children, whilst in a well a further fifty bodies were found. Arab allegations of Jewish atrocities, such as the lining up and shooting with automatic weapons of unarmed men, women and children, now seem to contain some truth. The Jewish Agency has claimed that the attack was organised and perpetrated by members of dissident groups and has issued the usual notices of condemnation which, however, deceive nobody, especially as dissidents themselves claim that Haganah let them pass through to the attack.

3. Arab reaction to this deliberate mass murder of innocent inhabitants, including women and children, of an Arab village which, by Jewish admission, has taken little part in the disturbances is naturally extremely bitter; nor have the British escaped sharp criticism for their failure immediately to intervene or to punish the criminals.[15]

With the memories of previous massacres still warm in the hearts and minds of the Palestinian people, the news of Dair Yasin overwhelmed great numbers of the Arabs of Palestine as the details of the massacre spread like a terrifying storm throughout the country. The trickles of Arab exodus caused by the previous massacres against the British Army and the Arab population of Palestine became a tidal wave in the wake of Dair Yasin, while the United Nations remained unmoved by the looming Palestinian catastrophe. To cause panic among the Arab population of villages in the area of Dair Yasin, the Haganah and other organisations distributed leaflets and used loudspeakers to threaten the Arabs to leave the area or face the same loss of life as happened in Dair Yasin. Furthermore, in a discussion between a British officer and a Jewish official, the latter said: 'Oh no, that will be fixed. A few calculated massacres will soon get rid of them [the Arabs].' There was no doubt that the massacres were intended to cause the Arab exodus, while the terrorist bombing campaign against the British Army was intended to accelerate the process of British withdrawal from Palestine.[16]

Three days after the massacre of Dair Yasin, Bahjat Abu Gharbiyah talked to one of 200 women and children who came from Dair Yasin to Jerusalem to take refuge in the city. A bereaved woman told him while sobbing her heart out and holding her child tightly as if she was frightened to lose him:

After the battle the Jews got us out from our house and killed my husband and my eldest son in front of my eyes and left my two remaining sons with me – this one whom you see and his brother who was two years older. Just before we came here a Jewish soldier took my son from my hand and said: 'This one is older, why did you keep him.' He then opened fire on him and killed him in front of me and all the others.[17]

On 13 April, a Jewish convoy passing through Jerusalem was ambushed by al-Jihad al-Muqaddas, on the main road between al-Musrarah and Wadi al-Jawz on its way to the Hadassah Medical Centre and the Hebrew University at Mount Scopus. In the battle that followed all the convoy vehicles and two armoured cars were destroyed, more than 100 Jews were killed and 20 others wounded. The British Army, which did not intervene to save Dair Yasin or any other Arab village from Jewish attacks, intervened to save the convoy. Towards the end of the battle, a British Army company intervened to save the Jews. They killed 12 Arabs and wounded others.

The fall of Tiberias
Tiberias was the first Arab urban community to be usurped by the Jews in Palestine. The town, located on the western shore of the Sea of Galilee, consisted of a mixed Arab–Jewish community of 4,000 Arabs and 6,000 Jews. Until the beginning of February 1948, traditionally peaceful Arab–Jewish relations existed. Thereafter intermittent sniping, which was started by the Haganah, continued from time to time. Being the original owners of the town, the Arabs who were concentrated in the downtown old city began sending their families to safer areas, and the Jews began to leave the old city for the adjacent Jewish area. During the first week of March, the Haganah attacked and captured the Arab village of al-Manarah (south of Tiberias) and expelled its inhabitants.

In spite of an agreement between the two sides to cease fire, sniping restarted in and around the town on 8 April. The British police inspector and the British Army Commander in the town attempted to make peace between the two sides – but without success. On 12 April, a company of the Haganah attacked and captured the Arab village of Nasir al-Din and al-Qaddumi hilltop, which overlooked the town of Tiberias. The Haganah killed unarmed men and destroyed nearly all the houses in the village, while the rest of the villagers took refuge in Lubiya and Tiberias. Thereafter the morale of the Arab inhabitants of Tiberias was undermined.

It soon became obvious that the UN was biased in favour of the Jews. The crisis in Palestine was not in the arena of the Cold War, for the Soviet Union as well as the United States supported the Jews, and they were not concerned with the looming catastrophe of the Palestinian people for whose peace and security they should have been morally responsible. Instead of taking action to save the Palestinian people they contented themselves with passing another mild and ineffective resolution. On 17 April, the Security Council of the UN approved a resolution calling upon all persons and organisations in Palestine to comply with the specific terms laid down for the maintenance of the truce called for by the resolution of 1 April. By then the Jews had little or no regard for the docile UN resolutions, and on the night of 16/17 April a battalion of the Golani Brigade and the 3rd Battalion of the Palmach Brigade mounted a massive attack on the old city of Tiberias. The attack was covered by indiscriminate fire of medium machine guns and mortars against the civil inhabitants and the very small number of armed men. When the assault started it created panic among the Arabs, and when the Palmach attackers used explosives to destroy several houses in the process, the Arab notables of the town appealed to the British Commander to save it and protect the population. However, the British Commander wriggled out of his responsibility by allowing the Arabs to be evacuated with his help. Soon after, the Arab leaders of the Tiberias community deserted their people and left the town. The British Commander scrounged what buses and trucks he could find and, under his escort, evacuated the Arabs to Jordan. In their panic the Arab population of Tiberias left their properties to be looted by the Palmach and Golani usurpers.

The fall of Safad

The Arab town of Safad, which had a population of about 12,000 people (including about 1,500 Jews in the Jewish quarter), was strategically important for both sides. The Jewish quarter had been isolated since the middle of February, but defended by a company of the Haganah and local guards. On 15 April, when the British Army was about to withdraw from the town, the Palmach sent one platoon into the town to support the Haganah. When the British Army withdrew, the Arab Liberation Army battalion, commanded by Lt Colonel Adib al-Sheshekli of the Syrian Army, sent a unit to Safad to take over the police fortress at

Mount Canaan, and other vital positions in the town including the ancient Arab citadel and Shalva House. The unit of the Liberation Army consisted of two former Arab Legion volunteer groups – one under command of Sari al-Funaish, a former cavalry police captain of the Arab Legion, and the other commanded by Lt Muhsin Yaaish, a veteran of the 1st Arab Legion Mechanised Regiment of 1941. Captain al-Funaish was assisted by Lt Imil Jumaian, a former artillery officer of the Arab Legion. The two companies were well trained with some experience in fighting during the Second World War in 1941. They took over their positions on 16 April.

Supported by the local Arab garrison, al-Funaish and Jumaian reorganised the defences of the town. During the many skirmishes that started on that day the Haganah were repulsed. On the same day the Arab defenders who inflicted heavy casualties on the attackers, repulsed an attack by the Palmach and the Haganah on the strategic village of al-Nabi Yousha overlooking the Hulah Valley. Fighting continued around the area until 28 April, when the 3rd Palmach Regiment and the Haganah attacked the police fortress of Rosh Pinna along with the British Army camp nearby. Two companies of the Palmach attacked and captured the Arab village of Biriya north of Safad; meanwhile, another Haganah force launched an attack on the village of Ain Zaitoun and captured it on 1 May. The Palmach detained all the men of Ain Zaitoun and later 70 of them were lined up and shot in cold blood. During these attacks Arabs and Jews suffered heavy casualties. While al-Funaish asked for reinforcements of men and ammunition from al-Sheshekli and got none, the Jews reinforced their forces with fresh troops and ammunition through the corridor established by the previous attacks. Thus, the final Jewish assault on Safad was planned.

The Palmach Regiment supported by the Haganah carried out a massive assault on the police fortress at dawn on 5 May and throughout 6 May 1948. Lieutenant Muhsin Yaaish and his company repulsed the attack and inflicted heavy casualties on the Palmach attackers. Yigal Allon, Commander of the Palmach, withdrew his troops for reorganisation and prepared his final assault on all the Arab positions. By 7 May, the Arab defenders of the town had nearly exhausted their ammunition during the continued skirmishes in and around it. Again, while holding their positions, al-Funaish and Yaaish appealed to Colonel al-Sheshekli for replenishment of their ammunition and reinforcements. Instead of advancing to the scene of battle with effective reinforcements, al-Sheshekli sent two platoons of around 60 men, who had never before fired a shot in anger, let alone been properly armed or trained. On 8 May, many rumours circulated that Safad had fallen to the Jews. Lieutenant Imil Jumaian sent a telegram to King Abdullah informing him that Safad was still resisting and the enemy attacks were repulsed.[18]

Although the two platoons sent by al-Sheshekli were keen Palestinian patriots who wanted to defend their country they were totally inexperienced recruits. They arrived on 9 May and took their positions in the town. Meanwhile, instead of leading his men in battle, al-Sheshekli left his command and travelled to Damascus for an unknown reason, leaving his men to face the consequences of his negligence – indeed, betrayal.

Before the end of the mandate, the fiercest battle in the north of Palestine started on 9 and 10 May, when two Palmach regiments went on the offensive. They attacked all the Arab strongholds simultaneously, fighting their way through from house to house. According to Chaim Herzog: 'The Palmach forces fought all night, attacking in waves up the hilly streets of the town, fighting from house to house and from room to room.'

As if nature had come to their aid with unexpected thunder and a heavy rain storm, they succeeded in their initial assault. At that extremely critical stage of the battle, the Arab inhabitants of Safad started a mass evacuation of unarmed men, women and children. The defenders suffered from poor visibility, the chaos caused by the evacuation and the fact that their ammunition was diminished. Captain al-Funaish decided to withdraw what was left of his troops when he clearly saw that there was no point in suffering more casualties. On the night of 11 May, Safad fell to the Jews; the Arabs lost the most vital positions in the north of Palestine. Not a single Arab was allowed to stay in Safad. Bani Israel of 3,000 years before had been a fraction more merciful to the people of Canaan. At least they allowed those whom they did not massacre to stay in their villages.

During the battle for Safad, al-Sheshekli, who was in Damascus, warned the Syrian Government that Safad was about to fall. The Syrian Foreign Minister warned the British Minister in Damascus, Philip Broadmead, that the 'situation at Safad was desperate and unless there was immediate intervention [by Britain] there would be a second Dair

Yasin. If a massacre took place, Syria would be blamed for not having intervened.'[19]

The fall of Haifa

By the end of 1947, the British Army regarded the City of Haifa and its deep sea port in the north of Palestine as the main base for their evacuation from the country. Major General Hugh Stockwell, General Officer Commanding the northern sector of the British Army in Palestine, stationed in Haifa, informed the Jewish Agency branch in the city that he intended to maintain the following positions in order of priority.

1. The security of the port.
2. The security of the railway.
3. The security of oil.
4. The security of roads.
5. The maintenance of peace between the two sides.

The population of the city of Haifa was 140,000, about 80,000 Jews and 60,000 Arabs. The Jewish population of the city occupied the high ground of Haifa and Mount Karmel, while the Arab population occupied the low ground adjacent to the coast. An Arab National Committee was established to represent the people of Haifa consisting of Victor Khayat, Farid al-Saad, Ilyas Kusa, George Muaammar and Anis Nasr.

During their service in Haifa with the 1st Garrison of the Jordan Arab Army, who were under command of the British Army, some officers did their best to help the Arabs defend themselves. Its Commander (Lt Colonel Ahmad Sudqi al-Jundi), his adjutant (Lt Mahmoud al-Rousan), Captain Abd al-Razzaq Abdullah (Commander of the 8th Infantry Company), Captain Mahmoud al-Musa Aubaidat (Commander of the 1st Security Company) and Lt Mohammad al-Hamad al-Hunaitti (an officer from the 5th Infantry Company), were all in touch with Rashid al-Haj Ibrahim and Shaikh Nimir al-Khatib of the local National Committee of Haifa. During October 1947, they encouraged the Committee to prepare for the defence of the city, and did their best to help them in the organisation and training of their partisans. For unknown reasons Mohammad al-Hamad al-Hunaitti was dismissed from the Jordan Arab

Army during November 1947. He immediately joined the local National Committee of Haifa and was appointed Commander of the local partisan garrison. In a meeting between al-Rousan and al-Hunaitti with Rashid al-Haj Ibrahim, the latter reported:

> The number of Arab defenders of Haifa did not exceed seventy-five young partisans armed with rifles and a few hand grenades. They have a small quantity of ammunition. But the number will be doubled in future days and we have seventy-five other partisans armed with pistols. All the rest of the Arabs of Haifa were unarmed.[20]

Mahmoud al-Rousan and Mohammad al-Hunaitti both thought the strength of the partisans was more than 1,000 men and were shocked that only that small number was available to defend the city against the Jewish Carmeli Brigade and Haganah garrison – about 2,500 officers and men. However, al-Hunaitti was determined to fight and started by naming his partisans, 'the National Guard'. The companies of the Jordan Arab Army were positioned in areas controlling the approaches to Haifa, Akka (Acre), Balad al-Shaikh and al-Tirah. Although they were under orders by General Hugh Stockwell not to interfere in the local fighting, they did not hesitate to support the Arabs when attacked.

On 31 December 1947, two companies of the 1st Palmach Regiment and a company of the Haganah, carried out an attack on the Arab village of Balad al-Shaikh in the environs of Haifa. Their orders were to kill as many Arab men as possible and destroy the village properties. In the close combat that followed 60 Arab men, women and children were killed, and many houses were demolished by explosives. Two Palmach officers were killed and others wounded. The Jordan Arab Army company opened fire at the attackers from their positions in support of the Arabs and the attack was repulsed. The Arab High Committee branch in Haifa lost control over their partisans and, with the approval of al-Haj Amin al-Husseini, handed over all their irregular partisans to the National Committee of Haifa to achieve a united command.[21] By the middle of January nearly 25,000 Arab men, women and children had been terrorised enough to leave the city to become refugees.[22]

During January 1948, the Jordanian Arab Army garrison company in the city managed to support the Arabs with instructors and some weapons and ammunition. They also prevented Jewish attacks against the Arabs in areas near their positions. On several occasions the Jews passing by their camps opened fire on them, which they returned effectively. On 17 January the Jordan Arab Army opened fire on a Jewish car, and in burning it killed three armed Jewish men. Under pressure from the Jews, the British Army moved the company to an area outside the city. Many skirmishes and desultory exchanges of fire continued in the city, in spite of British interventions here and there. On 3 February, the Jordan Arab Army opened fire on a Jewish convoy; five Jewish men – all armed – were killed.

During January and February, Lt Mohammad al-Hunaitti was able to raise a company of about 250 partisans and train them with the help of a few Jordanian Arab Army non-commissioned officers who, instead of going home for their annual leave, stayed in Haifa for that purpose. He organised the defences of the Arab part of Haifa in spite of the shortage of weapons and ammunition. However, on 17 February, he was on his way back to Haifa from Beirut where he had received two truck loads of weapons and ammunition guarded by himself and ten of his men. The Haganah, who were informed by their agents that al-Hunaitti was with the convoy, sent a platoon of the Palmach 1st Regiment to ambush the convoy north of the Jewish settlement of Qiryat Motskin. When the convoy reached the road block of barrels placed there by the Haganah, they opened fire and attacked the convoy. A fierce battle followed during which the two trucks exploded. Two Jewish attackers were killed and a few others wounded. Mohammad al-Hunaitti and all his men were killed. That great loss severely undermined the Arab morale in Haifa. Members of the National Committee such as Victor Khayat and Ahmad al-Khalil, who were in touch with Jewish leaders in the Rotary Club of Haifa, informed the Jews that they were trying to pacify the Arab part of the city and called for peace. But Ben-Gurion ignored their appeal.

Captain Amin Izz al-Din, a Lebanese former gendarme, was appointed Commander of the Haifa National Guard Garrison on 18 March to replace Lt al-Hunaitti. He had under his command only 240 men armed with old weapons. Additionally, his troops were short of ammunition and lacked training and experience. The Jewish strength included the Haganah Carmeli Brigade (about 2,000 officers and men) and the local garrison of Haifa (about 500 men). The men were well armed and well trained in modern warfare, and some of them had gained experience during the Second World War. By the end of March the Jordanian Arab Army 8th Infantry company was withdrawn from Haifa to be part of the prospective formation of the 6th Infantry Regiment. On 2 April the 1st Security Company was withdrawn to Jericho for the same purpose.

By the middle of April, General Stockwell was anxious to maintain the safety of his troops and to safeguard the Port of Haifa as the base for the final withdrawal of the British forces from Palestine. He was convinced that an attack by the Haganah was imminent and thought that, with the strength available to him in the city, he would not be able to hold his positions. He realised that if an attack were to be launched, he would not be able to control the situation and that his troops would suffer heavy casualties. He decided to maintain his existing deployment in eastern Galilee and to redeploy his forces in Haifa in order to safeguard his vital lines of communications with other British sectors and to maintain the security of his troops. He thus lost interest in the 'maintenance of peace between the two sides'. On 20 April, General Stockwell ordered the 1st Guards Brigade and units attached to it to redeploy in their new positions at dawn on 21 April. As soon as the sudden redeployment was completed, chaos broke out as both the Jews and the Arabs fought for the occupation of the buildings and camps evacuated by the 1st Guards Brigade.

Later that morning, General Stockwell invited the leaders of both the Arabs and the Jews to see him, and informed them of his redeployment and withdrawal from the dividing line between their forces. Captain Izz al-Din was frightened. He immediately realised the consequences of the statement, but instead of sending someone to inform the Military Committee in Damascus of General Stockwell's redeployment, he shamefully deserted his command and went himself in the afternoon of 21 April, leaving the defence of Haifa to his second in command, Younis Naffaa, a civil engineer with no military experience. Ahmad al-Khalil and the rest of the Arab leaders of the city followed him. On 22 April, Younis Naffaa also deserted his command leaving the partisans completely demoralised.

In spite of their very small numbers, and the fact that they were bereft of their Commanders and leaders compared to the Jewish forces in and around the city, the Arab partisans fought hard to defend their homes until the final attack by the Carmeli Brigade. At dawn on 22 April, the Brigade opened fire with hundreds of three-inch mortar bombs and medium machine guns, shelling the whole of the Arab quarter of

Haifa. The indiscriminate fire caused many civilian casualties among Arab men, women and children. Meanwhile, the British Army, which had withdrawn from the built-up area of the city to assemble in the Haifa port area, prevented any reinforcements from the surrounding Arab areas reaching the city. When the final assault started on the Arab quarter the young men of Haifa were incapable of showing any effective resistance. The city surrendered to the Carmeli Brigade on 23 April. At the end of the day, every one of the 240 defenders were among the 400 killed and 800 wounded – Arab men, women and children. The Arabs, who were the rightful owners of Palestine, were forced to surrender to the foreign usurpers of their city and had to evacuate it taking with them whatever they could carry from their properties, leaving the rest and their homes to be looted by the Jewish Haganah and terrorist gangs. About 50,000 Arabs of the city took refuge in the Lebanon by whatever means of transport they could find. The 10,000 Arabs who remained were subject to cruel humiliation. The Irgun organised and carried out the complete looting of the Wadi al-Nisnas quarter 'from Wednesday to 1800 hours on Sunday'; thieves and bandits joined them in the looting. The Haganah also took part in the looting; some of the looted belongings were subsequently found in the possession of their troops. Some Haganah units went on a search for Arab men, then arrested, detained, beat and tortured them. When an officer of the Haganah inspected the camp where the Arabs were detained he found a number of them still with their blindfolds on. He found that an officer had ordered the Arab detainees to stop talking and when, after a while, they resumed talking, he opened fire with his Sten gun, killing and wounding many of them. The wounded were denied medical help until the following morning. The situation report of the 1st Battalion of the Coldstream Guards of the British Army bears witness to the inhumane cruelty of the Haganah.

> During the morning they [the Carmeli Brigade] were continually shooting down on all Arabs who moved both in Wadi al-Nisnas and the old city. This included completely indiscriminate and revolting machine gun fire and sniping on women and children [who were] attempting to get out of Haifa through the gates into the docks. There was considerable congestion outside the East Gate of hysterical and terrified Arab women and children and old people on whom the Jews opened up mercilessly with fire.[23]

The whole story of the atrocities committed by the Haganah and the Irgun terrorist gang in Haifa, including the looting of all the shops, houses and stores, as well as the occupation by the Jews of all the evacuated houses, has never been fully told. Only a fraction of the truth was published.

However, the British Military Intelligence considered that 'the hasty flight of Amin Bey Azzadin was probably the greatest single factor' in the demoralisation of his partisans and the inhabitants of Haifa. On 6 May 1948, the British Military HQ in Palestine reported: 'The desertion of their leaders and the sight of so much cowardice in high places completely unnerved the inhabitants of Haifa.'[24]

Perhaps blame for the chaos inflicted upon the Arab inhabitants of Haifa should not be directed entirely at the merciless and heinous attack of the Haganah and the Jewish leaders alone, nor even at the shameful desertion of the Arab leaders. Some senior British Army officers also had a share of responsibility in the catastrophe that befell the Arab people of Haifa. When the shocking news arrived at 10 Downing Street and the Foreign Office in London, revulsion was the order of the day. Foreign Secretary Ernest Bevin was worried about the effect of the catastrophe on Britain's image and position throughout the Arab and Muslim world. On 22 April, the Chief of the Imperial General Staff, Field Marshal Bernard Montgomery of Alamein, who quelled the Palestinian Arab Revolt of 1936–9, was summoned to 10 Downing Street, where he admitted that he was not being kept informed on the situation in Haifa by his Field Commanders in Palestine. Bevin became angry and described the situation as 'catastrophic'.[25] On 7 May, another meeting was held between the Prime Minister, the Foreign Secretary and the Chief of the Imperial General Staff. During the meeting, Bevin insisted on the view that the British Army should have stopped the Haganah; he said the massacre of the Arabs had put him in an impossible position with all the Arab states. He virtually insulted Montgomery when he concluded that he was 'let down by the [British] Army'.[26] However, nothing was said about General Stockwell's collusion with the Jews in Haifa, and the whole truth may forever remain a mystery.[27]

During the fighting in Haifa on 23 April the timid and docile UN Security Council approved yet another resolution establishing a Truce Commission for Palestine to supervise the implementation of the UN resolution of 17 April. Nobody in Palestine took any notice of what was happening in the UN, and the Jewish leadership also ignored it.

[46]

The fall of Jaffa

With a population of about 70,000 Arabs, the city of Jaffa was adjacent to Tel Aviv southern areas, which had a population of about 190,000 Jews. Both cities were surrounded by Jewish settlements guarded by local Jewish garrisons, such as Herzliya, Ramat Sharon, Peta Hatiqwa, Bat Yam and Holon. Tel Aviv was the home of the Kiryati Brigade, about 2,500 officers and men; it was also defended by a Jewish garrison of about 2,000 armed men and women. The main HQ of the armed forces of the Jews was situated in Tel Aviv, and the main civil and administrative staff and military depots in and around the city. By the beginning of December 1947, the strength of the Jewish garrison of Tel Aviv exceeded 4,650 armed men, plus a few units of the Haganah.

Jaffa and its environs – the Arab villages of Tal al-Rish, Yazour, Salamah, al-Saqiyah, al-Khairiyah and Abu Kabir – were part of the proposed Palestinian state according to the UN Partition Plan. For political and propaganda reasons, and because of the presence of the British Army in Jaffa and Tel Aviv, the Jewish leadership, though determined to usurp the city and expel its Arab inhabitants, did not start its massive attack against Jaffa until April. Meanwhile it intended to gradually terrorise the civilian population into leaving the city. Using explosives, the Haganah demolished a large Arab building of two floors overlooking Herzl Street on 3 December 1947. The Haganah and the Irgun carried out several bombing attacks and sniping fire against the Arabs of Jaffa. Gradually, the border lines between the Arabs of Jaffa and the Jews of Tel Aviv were drawn by desultory exchanges of fire, when both sides evacuated what became a quasi no-man's-land between the two cities.

On 19 December, the Haganah attacked the village of Salamah with 250 men and a company of the Palmach, but the attack was repulsed by the Arabs. Soon after that attack, the Arab High Committee appointed Shaikh Hasan Commander of the Arab fighters of the local garrison in Jaffa. The Shaikh was a freedom fighter and a veteran of the 1936–9 revolt. Soon after his appointment he launched an attack on Peta Hatiqwa, but the Haganah repulsed it on 28 December. The British Army subsequently lost control over the two cities and withdrew from the built-up areas.

Early in January 1948, Captain Radhi al-Abdullah and 12 instructors from the Jordan Arab Army were sent to Jaffa to help its mayor, Dr Yousef Haikal, to organise and train the city garrison. The Jordan Arab

Army team were able to train the garrison, supply them with a certain amount of weapons and ammunition and organise the defence of the city. They also participated in many exchanges of fire alongside their trainees, and managed to hold their positions against several Jewish fighting patrols and small-scale attacks. On 4 January, the Irgun destroyed the main building of the Arab municipality of Jaffa with a powerful car bomb. The city's municipal services fell apart. The explosion terrorised the rich and middle classes of the city into fleeing from their homes, which meant that businesses closed, leaving thousands unemployed. Food became scarce and families started to abandon their city.

By the end of February 1948, Fawzi al-Qawiqji, the Commander of the central front of the Liberation Army, sent Lt Colonel Adil Najm al-Din and his Iraqi battalion to help defend Jaffa. Captain al-Abdullah handed over his task to Najm al-Din and returned to Amman. Thus, three units with three Commanders who knew nothing about each other's forces – not to mention each other – were competing for the command of the defence of the city. The forces under their various commands did not exceed 550 men. The local Arab Committees were also divided; the local branch of the High Arab Committee, the Mayor and the Liberation Army, and Shaikh Hasan of Salamah did not coordinate their efforts. There was no united Arab front in Jaffa when the skirmishes between Arabs and Jews, which had started in the middle of January 1948, developed into a series of battles towards the middle of March.

On 12 February 1948, the Haganah attacked the Arab village of Abu Kabir, killed its defenders including their Commander Abu Rahmah and, using explosives, destroyed most of its houses. Another attack was launched by the Haganah at Salamah on 28 February, but the attack was repulsed; the defenders killed six Jews and wounded others. During March 1948, the Jews attacked the Arab village of Jabaliya and destroyed many Arab houses. On 31 March another attack on Abu Kabir destroyed all the Arab houses and inflicted many casualties. Continued Jewish attacks by the Kiryati Brigade with two- and three-inch mortars, as well as by machine guns, were carried out almost daily. The Arab defenders of the city responded with less effective weapons until their ammunition was nearly exhausted. The total deaths on both sides were nearly 1,000; there were also many casualties.

On 23 April, the Kiryati Brigade, supported by elements of the Palmach as well as the Irgun and Stern gangs, launched a massive attack on the Arab city of Jaffa. The attack, which was directed at Iraq al-Manshiyah with one Regiment of the Kiryati Brigade, was held by the Arabs for 24 hours of fierce fighting until the morning of 25 April. The Jewish command committed units of the Alexandroni and Givati brigades to support the attack, which continued until 28 April without a major success. However, Iraq al-Manshiyah was isolated from Jaffa on that day. On 29 April, in a last desperate attempt to repulse the Jewish attack, two companies of the Iraqi battalion of the Liberation Army carried out a counter-attack to recapture Tal al-Rish. In the fierce fighting that followed, 33 Jews were killed and a 100 others were wounded. The Liberation Army lost 20, with 40 wounded. On the same day, al-Qawiqji decided to replace the Field Commander Adil Najm al-Din with Captain Michael Issa, a son of Jaffa, and his Ajnadin battalion of 250 officers and men.[28]

Captain Issa arrived in the city supported by a three-inch mortar platoon commanded by an Iraqi officer, Mahdi Salih al-Aani. But Adil Najm al-Din refused to hand over his command and withdrew his 290-strong Iraqi battalion back to Lebanon and Syria on 1 May 1948. With just 250 men of the Ajnadin Battalion and the remnants of the local garrison, Captain Issa was unable to control the situation; Iraq al-Manshiyah Arab quarter was captured by the Kiryati Brigade, and most of the men, women and children there were killed or wounded. The Arab villages of al-Khairiyah, al-Saqiyah, Kufr Aanah and Salamah fell one after the other. The mayor left the city on 29 April. By 4 May, over 80 per cent of the population of Jaffa had evacuated the city in fear for their lives. On the same day, Captain Issa and members of the local branch of the Arab High Committee asked the British District Governor to inform the Jews that they wished to consider Jaffa an open city. The High Commissioner for Palestine pressed the Jewish leaders to accept the offer, and on the following day the Jews agreed. Captain Issa withdrew with the 50 remaining men who had not deserted him and went back to Ramallah.

Most of the Arab population of the city, which suffered 600 deaths and over 6,000 wounded (as well as serious damage to property) were forced by continued sniper fire and other means to evacuate the city and take refuge in Jordan. Only 4,000 men, women and children remained.[29]

The fall of Akka

The Arab inhabitants of Akka continued to defend their city in spite of the fall of Haifa and Jaffa. They had formed a garrison on their own without much help from the Palestinian leadership or the Liberation Army. When Haifa fell, several thousands of its inhabitants made their way to Akka to take refuge in the city. They were able to repulse several fighting patrols sent by the Haganah to force them to evacuate the city, but they remained steadfast and continued to fight, hoping that the Liberation Army and other Arab armies would save them. By the beginning of May, the Liberation Army sent only one platoon to support them, but soon even that small force withdrew.

Immediately after they captured Haifa the Carmeli Brigade advanced to the north capturing unarmed Arab villages until they reached the high ground north of Akka. On 11 May, a battalion from the Carmeli Brigade captured Napoleon Hill to the east of Akka and advanced towards the city. On 16 May, the battalion started to shell the city and a few hours later it surrendered.

The battle of the Reutenberg hydroelectric station

The Reutenberg hydroelectric station, within Jordanian territory on the River Jordan, was the scene of violence between the Jordan Arab Army (which was responsible for the station) and the Jewish Haganah of the settlement of nearby Gesher. On 27 April, the Jewish armed settlers, who were preparing their defences east of Gesher, occupied the Palestine police station, which overlooked and controlled the road between Jordan and Palestine through the Majamaa Bridge across the River Jordan. Later that morning, they provoked an exchange of fire with the Jordan Arab Army platoon protecting the station. The HQ of the Jordan Arab Army issued orders for the reinforcement of the platoon with the 2nd company of the 4th Regiment commanded by Captain Abdullah al-Salim, as well as two platoons commanded by Lt Muhammad al-Mahasnah from the 4th Regiment. Soon after, Avraham Daskal, the Jewish station manager, nicknamed 'Abu Yousef', appealed to the Jordanian company Commander to allow him to evacuate the Jews working in the station and their families to Tiberias. The evacuation was carried out under the well-disciplined supervision of the Jordanians without a single incident.

[50]

As if timed with the end of the evacuation, the Jewish forces in Gesher and the Palestine police station across the River Jordan opened fire on the Jordanians. The exchange of fire continued all through the day, while the Jewish forces were reinforced by fresh Haganah troops from Tiberias and Samakh. Brigadier Ashton of the Welsh Guards, seconded from the British Army to command the Jordanian 3rd Brigade, sent an armoured car troop from the 2nd Regiment to support the infantry company. When the armoured cars arrived at dawn on 28 April, the Jordanians opened fire at the police station and Gesher with all guns blazing. At the same time, Lt Colonel Habis al-Majali, Commander of 4th Regiment, sent his adjutant Captain Mahmoud al-Rousan with an infantry platoon commanded by Lt Qasim al-Aayid, a section of two medium machine guns, a section of two three-inch mortars and a section of two six-pounder anti-tank guns, commanded by Lt Mohammad Naim Hashim, to reinforce the company. Later that morning, Prince Talal, the Crown Prince, arrived at the scene of the battle. General Norman Lash and Brigadier Ashton followed Prince Talal just as the Jordan Arab Army opened fire at 0730 hours. The exchange of fire continued until 1130 hours, when the Jewish forces raised white flags atop the police station. Police officer Lt Colonel Nadim al-Samman was sent to the Jewish Commander who denied the raising of white flags and, when he returned to the Jordanian line, firing was resumed. Soon after, many white flags were raised and Captain Mahmoud al-Rousan was sent to negotiate a ceasefire. While the negotiations continued, orders were issued from the Jordan Arab Army HQ to cease fire and return to base. On 29 April, an infantry platoon was left at the station, the remainder returning to Irbid and Mafraq to continue with their training programme – which had been interrupted by the incident. Four Jordanian soldiers were killed in that action and four others were wounded, including Lt Musa al-Muhasin of the 4th Regiment.[30]

Fighting for Jerusalem

In anticipation of hostilities between the Arabs and the Jews, as in every Arab city, the people of Jerusalem established their local National Committee as can be seen in Table 2.1. The National Committee worked in cooperation with the local branch of the Arab High Committee and with Abd al-Qadir al-Husseini, the Arab Commander in Jerusalem.[31] The leadership in Jerusalem appointed the Commanders shown in Table 2.2 for the various quarters and areas of the city.

TABLE 2.1
The National Committee in Jerusalem

Elected chairman	
Anwar Nussaibah	
Members	
Fawti Fraij	Salih Abduh
Asaad al-Imam	Fawzi al-Khayat
Hanna Attallah	Eid Aabdin
Tawfiq al-Dajani	Jamil Wahbah
Tahir Barakat	Yousef Abduh
Tahsin Kamal	Wadi Salah
Yousef Sabbouh	

TABLE 2.2
Leadership in Jerusalem

Commander	Area or Quarter
Mahmoud Jamil al-Husseini	Shaikh Jarrah and Wadi al-Jawz
Bahjat Abu Gharbiyah	Bab al-Sahirah
Subhi Abu Gharbiyah	Musrarah and Saad wa Said
Mohammad Aarif Barakat	The Thuri Quarter
Hafiz Barakat	The Old City
Subhi Barakat	al-Nabi Daoud Quarter
Abu Ibrahim Abu Nabb	Maman Illah Quarter
Shafiq Auwais	Qatamon Quarter

The fighting elements of the National Committee consisted of young men trained mainly by Bahjat Abu Gharbiyah, a veteran of the 1936–9 revolt. There were a few veterans like him among the defenders who gave them the benefit of their experience. The total strength of those capable of participating in the defence of Jerusalem under the National Committee was about 260 men. Their weapons consisted of rifles, a few machine guns, hand grenades and a small quantity of explosives. The main force in the Jerusalem area was al-Jihad al-Muqaddas raised by al-Haj Amin al-Husseini and the Arab High Committee, with support from the HQ of the Liberation Army. The organisation of the military branch of al-Jihad was as shown in Table 2.3.

TABLE 2.3
Organisation of the military branch of al-Jihad

Officer	Position
Abd al-Qadir al-Husseini	Commander
Kamil Auraiqat	Deputy Commander
Daoud al-Husseini	Administrative inspector
Qasim al-Rimawi	Secretary
Ibrahim Abu Diyah	Commander of companies
Malik al-Husseini	Finance and Platoon Commander
Salih al-Rimawi	Supplies and armament
Musa Abu Shaiban	Platoon Commander
Foad Auraiqat	Platoon Commander
Attallah al-Haj Ali	Platoon Commander
Fawzi al-Quttob	Commander of demolition platoon

The total strength of al-Jihad al-Muqaddas within Jerusalem was about 300 men. However, the Arabs had the advantage of the high ground of Jerusalem in an arc surrounding the city with Arab positions and villages. It was recognised by the Jews that the Arabs were better led and were determined to fight.

The Jewish part of the city of Jerusalem was defended by the Etzioni Brigade (comprising some 3,170 officers and men) and the local Jewish garrison (some 700 men, including two companies of the Palmach). The Irgun terrorist gang had about 250 terrorists in the city.

On 13 December 1947, the Jewish Irgun terrorist gang detonated two barrels of explosives in the yard adjacent to the Damascus Gate in Jerusalem. Six Arabs were killed and 20 others wounded. On 14 December, the Arabs retaliated by attacking a Jewish bus on its way to the Hadassah Hospital. Two Jews were killed and nine others wounded. The British Palestine Police came to the scene, saving the bus and the remaining Jews. On 17 December, the Jews opened fire from the Jewish quarter in the Old City against both their Arab neighbours and on al-Haram al Sharif (the Mosque of Omar), and the villages of Silwan and Ras al-Aamoud. On 25 December, an attack was carried out by the

Jewish Haganah on the village of Bait Safafa, but it was repulsed by the armed men of the village, supported by a very courageous volunteer company from Sudan, who came to the scene in time. Many other skirmishes between Arabs and Jews took place at the Arab villages of Lifta and al-Qastal, and the Jewish settlements of Gevat Shaul and Har-tuv. On 29 December another bomb was detonated by the Jewish terrorists at Damascus Gate of the Old City of Jerusalem killing 17 Arabs and wounding 30 others.

On 2 January 1948, the Arabs took positions on Bab al-Nabi Daoud and Bab al-Khalil, thus isolating the Jewish force in the Jewish quarter of the Old City from the rest of Jerusalem. On 5 January, the Haganah attacked the Arab Qatamon quarter in Jerusalem and used explosives to destroy the Samira Amis Hotel; 18 Arabs were killed and 20 others wounded. Many of the Arab inhabitants of the quarter left the area, while the company of al-Jihad al-Muqaddas, commanded by Rafiq Auwais, held its positions.[32] On 7 January 1948, the Jewish terrorist Irgun gang detonated a stolen Palestine police car containing explosives at Bab al-Khalil in the Old City of Jerusalem. Nineteen Arabs were killed – including the Commander of the area, Subhi Barakat – and 36 others were wounded. All the Jewish attackers were killed. Mahmoud Jamil al-Husseini and Shafiq Abu Gharbiyah were also killed in various incidents. On 15 January, the Arabs carried out an ambush on the main road to Jerusalem near Bait Sorik, east of the village of al-Qastal. They opened fire at a Jewish convoy, which was halted in a fierce battle. The Jews dismounted from their vehicles and took refuge in the settlement Ma'ale Ha Hamish. The Jewish forces in the area sent a Palmach company accompanied by two British armoured cars to relieve the ambushed convoy. Abd al-Qadir al-Husseini, who was among the ambushing men, would have been killed had it not been for Arab reinforcements from the villages of Biddu, al-Qubaibah, Bait Aanan and Qattanah who came to the rescue. At the end of the battle, 34 Jewish men were killed or wounded.

On 1 February, al-Jihad al-Muqaddas exploded a car bomb at the Jewish *Palestine Post* newspaper in Jerusalem causing much damage to its property; 20 Jews were killed and more than 50 others were wounded.

On 22 February, an Arab convoy of two trucks (guarded by an armoured car from the Palestine police with four British policemen who volunteered with the Arabs) set out loaded with explosives. The Arab bomber was Azmi al-Jaauni, a young man from Jerusalem, who was also dressed in police uniform. Thus, with their police identities they were able to pass through all the Jewish and British road blocks until they arrived at Ben Yahuda Street in Jerusalem where they detonated their explosives. Forty-nine Jews were killed and 132 others wounded.[33]

On 26 February, fighting broke out between the Arabs and the Jews at al-Musrarah and Wadi al-Jawz in Jerusalem. The Jews started the attack with the aim of securing the main road from al-Musrarah to the Hadassah Hospital at Mount Scopus. The attack was repulsed by the Arab local garrison commanded by Bahjat Abu Gharbiyah. Twelve Jewish Haganah were killed and 18 others wounded.

On 1 March, the Jewish settlement at Qalandiyah opened fire at an Arab bus on its way from Ramallah to Jerusalem. A few Arabs were killed and wounded. The settlement was attacked on the same day by al-Jihad al-Muqaddas men. Seventeen Jews were killed and many others wounded.

On 11 March, the offices of the Jewish Agency in Jerusalem were blown up. Twelve of its staff were killed including Leib Yaffi, Director of the Jewish National Fund. Although the Agency was heavily guarded, the Arab bomber Anton Daoud, a Christian from Bethlehem, and the driver of the American Consul in Jerusalem, used one of the cars of the American Consulate which was painted with American flags to deceive the guards.

On 13 March, Abd al-Qadir al-Husseini attempted to attack and capture the Jewish settlement of Mecore Haim, but the Jewish defenders were able to repulse the attack. On 24 March, al-Jihad al-Muqaddas ambushed a Jewish convoy at Shuafat north of Jerusalem. Two armed buses were destroyed and 14 Jews were killed. The British Army intervened and saved the rest. During the first half of April, the Haganah launched an offensive against the Arab villages in order to widen the Jewish axis through the high ground leading from Latrun to Jerusalem. In their operation code-named 'Harel', the Haganah were ordered to occupy and destroy all Arab villages adjacent to the main road including al-Nabi Samuel, Bait Surik, Bait Iksa, Shuafat, Bait Hanina and Bait Mahsir. The attack failed to capture the most important villages of al-Nabi Samuel, Bait Iksa and Bait Surik.

Qatamon was a large Arab district in the southern part of Jerusalem. It was defended by a company of al-Jihad al-Muqaddas, about 130 men, commanded by Ibrahim Abu Dayih. The district hosted the Arab consulates of Egypt, Iraq, Syria and the Lebanon, which were guarded by a few Egyptian and Jordanian soldiers. Three Jordan Arab Army armoured cars, and one platoon from the 9th Infantry Company, commanded by Captain Sulaiman Masaud, defended the Iraqi consulate. The Jews had concentrated the following forces in the Jewish part of the city, with the intention of capturing the Qatamon District:

- the 4th Battalion of the Harel Palmach Brigade
- the 5th Battalion of the Harel Palmach Brigade
- the 4th Battalion of the Jerusalem Etzioni Brigade.[34]

The Jewish Palmach and Haganah mounted their massive attack on 28 April, but in its initial phase it was checked by the defenders, who suffered a loss of 35, with 30 wounded. Abu Dayih asked for help, and the Liberation Army battalion in Jerusalem sent two platoons of 60 men, commanded by Captain Fadhil Abdullah al-Rashid to support him. On 29 April, while the Jewish attack persisted, the Liberation Army unit withdrew back to the Old City. Ignoring its sanctity, the Palmach directed their attack on the Greek Orthodox St Simon's Monastery, capturing it for its high ground and strategic importance. During the fierce fighting for control over the monastery's position and elsewhere in Qatamon, the Jordan Arab Army unit guarding the Iraqi Consulate opened fire at the attackers and forced them to halt their advance. Forty Jews were killed and 60 others were wounded. Abu Dayih left the scene of battle to go to al-Rawdhah HQ in Jerusalem to obtain ammunition and reinforcements. His men were left on their own to face the Palmach.

At that very critical stage, on 2 May, King Abdullah sent a telegram to the British Foreign Secretary Ernest Bevin in which he said:

> At this minute the Jewish organisations are attacking the Arab Qatamon Quarter at Holy Jerusalem and attacking the Royal Iraqi Consulate there which is defended by a platoon of the Jordan Arab Army. I protest against their action. The Mandate has not ended and the High Commissioner is still responsible for security. Please issue an order to His Majesty's forces to stop their attack and return them to their borders, and I will stop the Arabs from attacking. I wait for the result of my appeal, and I have commanded to prepare enough force to defend Arab lives and the holiness of the al-Aqsa Mosque and I will lead it myself.[35]

At that point and because of the very critical situation, the British Army intervened. The British District Commander arrested Ibrahim Abu Dayih for a few hours, while on his way back to his men. He commanded the Jordan Arab Army unit to leave the area and threatened to open fire on them if they did not. This, while the Jewish forces continued to advance in the Qatamon district. When the Jewish occupation of Qatamon was complete, the British Army imposed a truce on both sides.[36]

On 7 May, Kirkbride wrote to the King saying that the fighting at Qatamon 'was checked as a result of British intervention and the threat of military action by His Majesty's Forces had imposed a temporary truce on both parties'.[37] But Qatamon had already fallen.

By 13 May, the Jewish quarter in the Old City of Jerusalem was under siege within its walls, surrounded by al-Jihad al-Muqaddas. The other units of the National Committee held their positions in the Arab part of the city.

The battle of Kfar Etzion

Towards the end of 1946, Captain Abdullah al-Tel handed over his duties as adjutant of the 2nd Infantry Regiment in Maan to me, then a lieutenant, and went on a staff course with the British Army at Fayed in Egypt. For four months from August 1947, he was attached to the British Army 1st Division HQ at Sarafand to gain some experience in staff duties. While in Sarafand, al-Tel was in touch with the Mayor of Ramleh and Lydda, Mahmoud Ala al-Din, and Ismael al-Nahhas, a member of the Arab Committee of Ramleh, and helped them organise the defences of both towns. With the aid of a few Jordan Arab Army instructors, he organised the training of the town's volunteers for the defence of their homes.

On 7 April 1948, Captain al-Tel was appointed Commander of the guards for the convoys that brought weapons, ammunition and equipment from the British Army stores at Rafah, through Gaza, Beer al-Sabaa, Hebron and Jerusalem to Amman. Under his command were an armoured car squadron (commanded by Lt Hamdan al-Subaih), an infantry company (commanded by Lt Muhammad Nauman) and a three-inch mortar platoon (commanded by Sergeant Major Ali Salim). Abdullah al-Tel was 'battle inoculated' – an army expression for a soldier's first experience of battle – during a fight at al-Nabi Yaaqoub settlement, situated four kilometres north of Jerusalem on the main road to Ramallah.

On 18 April, the Haganah guarding the settlement continued with their habit of shooting at vehicles passing by from two pillboxes adjacent to the settlement main gate. When a Jordan Arab Army convoy, guarded by al-Tel, came close to the gate of the settlement, al-Tel saw a British Army officer watching a partisan Arab armoured vehicle being destroyed by the Haganah, while its wounded crew were hiding behind it to protect themselves from machine-gun fire from the settlement. Abdullah al-Tel asked the British officer to command the Haganah to cease fire while he evacuated the wounded partisans. That being done, al-Tel was able to evacuate the wounded men and take them to Ramallah for treatment. On his way back with another convoy, guarded by himself with five Marmon Herrington armoured cars, al-Tel deployed his unit and opened fire at the settlement with his two-pounder guns. Hamdan al-Subaih started by destroying the two pillboxes (also killing their occupants), and then onto other Haganah positions in the settlement knocking them out one after the other. The British Army intervened immediately and asked al-Tel to cease firing. He then withdrew after killing 16 Haganah men and wounding many others. While the battle was raging, 4th Brigade sent a platoon led by Lt Mohammad al-Auqlah to support the convoy. During the fighting al-Auqlah and two of his men were killed. Thereafter not one shot was fired by the Haganah from al-Nabi Yaaqoub, and later the Jewish force guarding the settlement withdrew to Hadassah. Abdullah al-Tel was 'battle inoculated'.

Since 9 January 1948, when al-Jihad al-Muqaddas launched an attack on Kfar Etzion and the defending Haganah repulsed it, tension between Kfar Etzion and the surrounding Arab villages had been increasing. From time to time, the Jewish force at the settlement opened fire on Arab traffic using the main road between Hebron and Jerusalem. On 14 January, the Haganah opened fire from the Jewish settlement of Kfar Etzion at Arab cars passing by on this main road. On the same day the Arab garrison at Hebron launched an attack on the settlement and managed to reach its defence perimeter. However, the settlement was well defended with barbed wire and mines and by fire from pillboxes and trenches. The defences were manned by 280 Jewish local guards, a Palmach platoon and a Haganah field company. The total strength of the settlement was about 500 fighting men and women.[38] In the fierce battle that followed, 14 Arab fighters were killed, including Naji al-Qawasmah, a veteran of the 1936–9 Palestinian Revolt. Twenty-four others were wounded.[39]

On the evening of 15 January, a Jewish convoy carrying Haganah reinforcements from Har tuv to Kfar Etzion was ambushed by al-Jihad al-Muqaddas. Thirty-five Haganah men were killed and others wounded. The settlement was completely under siege isolated for the past several weeks. It was supplied only by parachute drops and Piper Cub light aircraft.

According to Chaim Herzog, the Jordan Arab Army attack on Kfar Etzion took place on 4 May 1948. According to Abdullah al-Tel the attack took place on 7 May. Thus between 4 and 7 May 1948, Abdullah al-Tel had asked Captain Hamdan al-Subaih (a veteran of the Arab Legion during the war in 1941 and the Commander of a convoy from Rafah), to provoke the Jews at Kfar Etzion to fight. Hamdan, who was always eager for a fight, did just that, and a battle developed between his three armoured cars and the settlement. It happened that General Glubb was at al-Tel's HQ in Jericho when Hamdan asked for help. Glubb agreed that Abdullah should attempt to save the convoy, and al-Tel took two troops of armoured cars, an infantry platoon and a section of three-inch mortars to the scene of the battle and managed to save the convoy. During that night he went to Hebron to arrange for another attack on the group of settlements at Kfar Etzion. On the following morning they carried out the attack, supported by irregulars from Hebron and other villages. The Jordanian force attacked and captured Dair al-Shaar (a Russian monastery) adjacent to Kfar Etzion. Twelve of the Haganah Company were killed and many more were wounded. On the same day, General Glubb commanded al-Tel to withdraw his force. The Russian monastery positions were handed over to Hebron Palestinian partisans, and al-Tel withdrew to Jerusalem. On the following day, the Haganah counter-attacked and recaptured the monastery. On returning to his HQ, al-Tel found an order from General Glubb to move to Amman and hand over his command to Captain Hikmat Muhyar (Commander of the Infantry Company at Hebron) and Muhammad Nauman (Commander of the convoy guards).[40]

On 9 May a deputation from the city of Hebron headed by Shaikh Muhammad Ali al-Jaabari called on King Abdullah to save the Hebron

District from the harassment of the Haganah in Kfar Etzion, and King Abdullah asked General Glubb to try to put an end to the aggression. During his visit to Hebron on 10 May, General Glubb ordered Captain Muhyar to capture Kfar Etzion thus ending its harassment of the Jordanian Arab Army convoys. General Glubb was desperate to receive as much ammunition as possible before the end of the British Mandate for Palestine and the withdrawal of the British Army. On 11 May, the following force was moved to its concentration area a few miles to the south of Kfar Etzion.

TABLE 2.4
Jordanian troop concentration south of Kfar Etzion

Unit	Commander
The 12th Infantry Company	Captain Muhyar
One Platoon – 8th Infantry Coy	Lt Mohammad Muflih al-Suhaim
One Platoon of three-inch mortars	Sergeant Major Ali Salim
Two companies of irregulars from Hebron and the surrounding Arab villages	

At dawn on 12 May, the Jordanian force mounted its attack on the four Etzion settlements. They concentrated their covering fire of three-inch mortars on the Russian monastery, and in their first assault they recaptured it. Of the 32 Haganah men defending it, 24 were killed, including the Commander of the settlements area and the Jewish Commander at the Russian monastery. Eight others were wounded but they managed to withdraw to Kfar Etzion under covering fire from the settlement. The Jordanian infantry company supported by the armoured cars attacked and captured three Jewish strongholds of one platoon each with pillboxes and trenches on the high ground north of Kfar Etzion and the landing strip, and one stronghold of one platoon situated north of the Russian monastery and east of Kfar Etzion. Thus, the main settlement of Kfar Etzion was isolated from the remaining Jewish settlements in the area. By dusk on that day the Jordan Arab Army had lost about six men, with 14 others wounded. Of the Arab volunteers, 50 were either killed or wounded. The Jewish suffered 70 fatalities, plus 65 wounded, who were evacuated during the night. Captain Hikmat Muhyar realised that his men could not continue their assault and ordered them to take positions where they were. He asked the Jordan Arab Army HQ for reinforcements. On the same night, General Glubb commanded al-Tel, who was in his camp at Jericho where he was forming the 6th Regiment, to go to Kfar Etzion to deal with this critical situation.[41]

At dawn on 13 May, al-Tel arrived at the scene of battle with two platoons from the 1st Security company commanded by Lt Nawaf al-Jabr al-Humoud. He immediately planned an attack on the settlement with the forces available. When the covering fire started from the three-inch mortar platoon and the armoured cars' two-pounder guns, the Haganah raised some white flags, but as soon as the assault troops came within their range, they resumed firing at the advancing troops. Three armoured cars, and the two platoons led by Lt Nawaf al-Jabr soon managed to penetrate the defence line of the settlement protected by a mine field and barbed wire. Their war cry, reminding the attacking men of the massacres of Tiberias and Dair Yasin, was a Bedouin poem written by a veteran of the 2nd Infantry Regiment who was manning one of the armoured cars.

Tabariyah and Dair Yasin;
If we succumb who else will fight.

During the fierce fighting between the Jordan Arab Army and the Haganah, the Arab volunteers followed the Jordanian force and entered the settlement. The settlement was finally captured at noon on the same day. During the whole battle 16 Jordanian men were killed and 20 others wounded, including Lt Mohammad al-Suhaim, a veteran of the Second World War during 1941. Of the 155 men and women defending Kfar Etzion, only three (two men and a woman) managed to escape, taking refuge in a nearby settlement. Negotiations between the Red Cross and the Haganah were carried out in Jerusalem for the surrender of the remaining men in the Jewish settlements of Rivadim, Ein Zurim and Massuot Yizhak. Some 278 Jewish prisoners of war were taken by the Jordanian Arab Army to Um al-Jimal camp near Mafraq; the wounded were handed over to the Red Cross and taken to Jerusalem. The Jordan Arab Army maintained the honour of the civilised code of conduct and adherence to the Geneva conventions for the treatment of prisoners of war.[42]

On 9 May 1948, Abdullah al-Tel was rewarded for his efforts in the Battle of Kfar Etzion when he was invited by General Glubb to Amman, and was informed that he had been promoted to the rank of major and appointed Commander of the 6th Infantry Regiment. He rushed back to Jericho on the same day and started to form his regiment, which consisted of the companies shown in Table 2.5.

TABLE 2.5
The regiment of Abdullah al-Tel

Company	Officer
1st Security Company	Captain Mahmoud al-Musa Aubaidat
2nd Infantry Company	Captain Fawaz Mahir
6th Infantry Company	Captain Durgham al-Falih
8th Infantry Company	Captain Abd al-Razzaq Abdullah
12th Infantry Company	Captain Hikmat Muhyar
Support Company	Lt Ghalib Rudhaiman

One night before the end of the British Mandate, a truce was arranged in Jerusalem by the Consuls of the United States, France and Belgium. It was agreed by the Arabs and Jews, but immediately broken by the Jews who, on 14 May, advanced and captured Allenby Barracks, Alamein Barracks, al-Nabi Daoud, Dair Abu Tur, the Italian Hospital, Nôtre Dame de France, al-Mussrarah, Saad wa Said (the building adjacent to the British Consulate near Damascus Gate) and Shaikh Jarrah police fort. The Arabs of Jerusalem plus the remaining forces of the Liberation Army and al-Jihad al-Muqaddas held the remaining east, south and north-east of the city, including Bab al-Sahira, Wadi al-Jawz and the old walled city of Jerusalem (but not the Jewish quarter).

On 14 May 1948, the General Assembly of the UN approved a resolution affirming support for the efforts of the Security Council to secure a truce and appoint a mediator for Palestine. The UN resolutions remained unclear and with no effect on the ground, for by the end of the British Mandate, and the withdrawal of the British Army from Palestine on 15 May 1948, the following areas, towns and cities were usurped by Jewish forces and terrorist gangs.

• The city of Tiberias and its environs: al-Aubaidiyah, al-Majdal, al-Tabighah, Maather, Kufr Sait, Nasir al-Din, al-Dulaimiyah and al-Samikah.

- The city of Safad and its environs: al Jauniyah, al-Khait, Biriya, Aaqrah, al Tahiriyah, Ain Zaitoun and al Houlah.
- The city of Akka and its environs: al Zait, al Bassah, al-Saidiyah, Iraq al-Manshiyah and al Mazrah.
- The city of Baisan and its environs: al Aubaidiyah, al Samiriyah, Farwal, Arab al Saqr, Arab al boutti, Arab al Ghazzawiyah and Arab al Bashatwah.
- The city of Haifa and its environs: Ijzim, Jabaa, al Ttireh, Ain Ghazal, Shafa Amr and Ibillin.
- The city of Jaffa and its environs: Salamah, Yazour, Bait Dajan, al-Khairiyah, al-Saqiyah, Kufr Aanah, al Safiriyah, al Aabbasiyah, Sarafand, Shabah, Monis, Jalil, al Masaudiyah, Arab Abu Kishik, Saiydna Ali, Sarafand al Kharab and Fajjah.
- The city of Jerusalem and its environs: Qatamon, al Talibiyah, al Baqaah al Fowqa, al Baqaah al Tahta, Bab al Khalil, Dair Yasin, al-Qastal, Abu Ghosh, Muwais, Bait Mahsir, Sawbah and Bait Naqoubahm al Malihah.[43]

As a direct result of the Jewish policy of 'expulsion and destruction' by Jewish terrorist attacks, massacres against men, women and children (very similar to those committed by the nomads of Bani Israel against Canaan), the destruction of homes by explosives and other means (including a brilliant but extremely wicked psychological warfare campaign against the Arab people of Palestine), more than 300,000 Arabs became refugees. Their homes were usurped by Zionist Jews – who not only had no moral or legal right to be in Palestine, but who were also treated by the Arabs as neighbours. The injustice of it all, although not quite the same as the injustice suffered by the Jews during the Second World War, was another shameful episode in modern history.

NOTES

1 Sir Alan Cunningham's Papers, Middle East Centre Archives, St Antony's College Oxford. High Commissioner to the Secretary of State, 13 December 1947.
2 David Ben-Gurion, *War Diary: The War of Independence 1948–1949* (Hebrew), ed. Gershon Rivilin and Elhanan Orren (3 vols., Tel Aviv: Ministry of Defence, 1982), translated into Arabic by Samir Jabbour, edited by Sabri Jiriyis (Beirut: np, 1993), p. 72.

3 *Ibid.*, p. 73.

4 Abdullah al-Tal, *The Palestine Catastrophe* (Cairo: Dar al-Qalam, 1959), p. 4. Also, Ben-Gurion, *War Diary*, p. 25.

5 Ben-Gurion, *War Diary*, p. 232.

6 *Ibid.*, p. 193.

7 Wasfi Al Tal, 'The Story of the Liberation Army', article no. 4 in series, p. 1.

8 *Ibid.* Also, *The Palestine War 1947–1948*, an official Israeli account (Hebrew), translation into Arabic by Ahmad Khalifah (unpublished copy given to this author, 1998), pp. 462–4; and Abu Gharbiyah, *Memoirs*, p. 251.

9 Walid al-Khalidi, 'Al-Qastal', *Journal of Palestine Studies*, no. 34 (spring 1998), pp. 36–55. Also, Abu Gharbiyah, *Memoirs*.

10 Uri Milstein, *History of the War of Independence* (unpublished copy, Tel Aviv: 1991), translated into Arabic by Ahmad Khalifah (1999).

11 *Hansard*, records of the House of Commons, April 1948.

12 Abu Gharbiyah, 'The Dair Yasin Massacre', *Proche-Orient: Near East Monthly Review* (May 1950).

13 Milstein, *History of the War of Independence*, p. 52.

14 Avi Chlaim, *Collusion Across the Jordan* (Oxford: Clarendon Press, 1988), p. 164.

15 PRO. FO 816/117. From the High Commissioner for Palestine to the Foreign Office, secret and immediate, 13 April 1948.

16 J. B. Glubb, *A Soldier with the Arabs* (London: Hodder and Stoughton, 1948), p. 81. Also David K. Shipler, *Arab and Jew: Wounded Spirits in a Promised Land* (London: Bloomsbury, 1989), pp. 37–9; Major General Sadiq al-Sharaa, *Our Wars with Israel 1947–1973: Lost Battles and Squandered Victories* (Amman: Dar al Shurouq, 1997), p. 44; and Abdullah al-Tal, *The Palestine Catastrophe*, pp. 17–18.

17 Abu Gharbiyah, *Memoirs*, p. 222.

18 The Hashemite Documents, *The Papers of King Abdullah Ibn al Hussein* (The Royal Palace, Amman: 1995), vol. 5, part I, p. 211.

19 PRO. FO 371/68548. From Philip Broadmead, Damascus, to the Foreign Office, 6 May 1948.

20 Mahmoud Al Rousan, *The Battle for Bab al-Wad* (published by the author, Amman: 1950), p. 30.

21 PRO. CO 537/3853. Haifa District Commissioner, report for the period 16–31 January 1948, dated 3 February 1948.

22 Ben-Gurion, *War Diary*, p. 153.

23 PRO. WO 261/297. Situation report no. 10, the 1st Battalion Coldstream Guards, at 1630 hours 22 April 1948.

24 PRO. WO 275/64. Intelligence Newsletter no. 67, 6 May 1948.

25 Montgomery of Alamein, *Memoirs* (London: Allen Lane, 1958), pp. 473–4.

26 PRO. Cabinet Papers 127/341. Notes of the meeting held at 10 Downing Street on 7 May 1948.

27 Ben-Gurion, *War Diary*, p. 284. Also, Al Rousan, *The Battle for Bab al-Wad*; *Journal of Palestine Studies*, no. 34 (spring 1998); and PRO. FO 371/68505. Cyril Marriott, Report to the Foreign Office, 26 April 1948.

28 The Ajnadin Battalion consisted mainly of Palestinians who served in the former Trans-Jordan Frontier Force which was disbanded by the British Government in 1947.

29 *The Palestine War 1947–1948*, an official Israeli account. Also, Abu Gharbiyah, *Memoirs*; *Journal of Palestine Studies*, no. 34 (spring 1998); E. Luttwak and D. Horowitz, *The Israeli Army*; J. Robert and S. Hadawi, *The Palestine Diary, 1945–1948* (Beirut: np, 1970); al-Khalidi, *Fifty Years since the Partition of Palestine*; and Ben-Gurion, *War Diary*.

30 Al Rousan, *The Battle of Bab al-Wad*. Also Abdullah al-Tal, *The Palestine Catastrophe*, p. 22.

31 Abu Gharbiyah, *Memoirs*, p. 155.

32 *Ibid.*, p. 169.

33 *Ibid.*, p. 192; and Ben-Gurion, *War Diary*, pp. 204–5.

34 Herzog, *The Arab–Israeli Wars*, p. 40.

35 The Hashemite Documents, p. 207.

36 Abu Gharbiyah, *Memoirs*, p. 238–9. Also Abdullah al-Tal, *The Palestine Catastrophe*, pp. 20–1; and Herzog, *The Arab–Israeli Wars*, p. 40.

37 Abu Gharbiyah, *Memoirs*, p. 208.

38 Herzog, *The Arab–Israeli Wars*, p. 42.

39 Abu Gharbiyah, *Memoirs*, p. 175.

40 Abdullah al-Tal, *The Palestine Catastrophe*, pp. 28–9. Also Herzog, *The Arab–Israeli Wars*, pp. 42–3.

41 Abdullah al-Tal, *The Palestine Catastrophe*, p. 32.

42 *The Palestine War 1947–1948*, an official Israeli account, pp. 303–5. Also Abdullah al-Tal, *The Palestine Catastrophe*; Abu Gharbiyah, *Memoirs*; and Colonel Farouq Nawaf al Serahin, *History of the Arab Legion, 1921–1967* (Arabic) (Amman: published by the author, 1990), pp. 197–9.

43 Akram Zuaitir, *Documents of the Palestinian National Movement, 1918–1939* (Beirut: published by the author, 1980), p. 655.

3

On the Brink of War

On 27 December 1947, Prime Minister Samir al-Rifai resigned, leaving Tawfiq Abu al-Huda to form a new government (see Table 3.1).

TABLE 3.1
Tawfiq Abu al-Huda's new government

Minister	Position
Tawfiq Abu al-Huda	Prime Minister, Defence and Foreign Affairs
Muhammad al-Shanqiti	Qadhi Qudhah and Education
Hashim Khair	Internal Affairs
Said al-Mufti	Trade, Agriculture and Supplies
Falah Madadhah	Justice
Fawzi al-Mulqi	Communications
Sulaiman al-Sukkar	Finance

A few days later, on 7 January 1948, Abu al-Huda reshuffled the Government by adding the post of Minister of Foreign Affairs and appointing Fawzi al-Mulqi, a new star in the politics of Jordan, to fill the post. Abu al-Huda included al-Mulqi in his Cabinet because he knew that he 'represented the younger and more nationalist elements in Jordan'. He also wanted al-Mulqi to accompany him on a visit to London for negotiations regarding the new Anglo–Jordanian Treaty of 1948.

Soon after his arrival in London in the first week of February 1948, Abu al-Huda expressed his wish to have a private conversation with Ernest Bevin, the Foreign Secretary, in which his Minister for Foreign Affairs would not participate. His reason was that al-Mulqi 'represented the younger and more nationalist elements' in Jordan. Judging by the dispatch sent by Bevin to Sir A. S. Kirkbride, the British Minister at Amman, on 9 February, there was no serious justification for that action. It only illuminated the mentality of the pro-British Effendi, who used secrecy to hide his true identity. However, to add insult to injury Abu al-Huda took Glubb with him to visit Bevin on 7 February during which he expressed the following to Bevin as recorded in Bevin's dispatch to Kirkbride:

2. Tawfiq Pasha said that he knew that he was not entitled to speak to me officially or to enter into any negotiations about Palestine, but he would like us to know the point of view of King Abdullah without expecting us necessarily to make any comment or reply. It was expected that difficulties might arise immediately after 15 May either from Jewish action against Arabs or from the activities of unorganised gangs of Arabs. Trans-Jordan was unwilling to encourage disturbances or anarchy in Palestine because this would adversely affect the Palestine Arabs and would also react on Trans-Jordan. The Arab Legion, who were now in Palestine, had made a good impression by their discipline and behaviour. Their presence would also be beneficial in the more chaotic situation which would arise after 15 May. It was well understood that the Arab Legion would have to leave Palestine before 15 May as part of the evacuation of British forces, but after that date, when the Legion would be controlled solely by the Trans-Jordan Government and would not be in any way under British command, it would be to the public benefit if it returned to the Arab areas of Palestine to maintain law and order.

3. Tawfiq Pasha appreciated that His Majesty's Government might be held morally responsible *vis-à-vis* the United Nations and world opinion for what the Arab Legion might do, on account of our subsidy payments, and that this would cause an embarrassment if the Arab Legion attacked any part of the civil population. If, however, the United Nations saw that the Arab Legion were reducing bloodshed, they would be grateful rather than critical of its activities.

4. Trans-Jordan did not intend to act on these lines simply for its own advantage but because it was convinced that the Arabs of Palestine could not effectively set up a government of their own, whereas Trans-Jordan can ensure stability. The presence of the Arab Legion in Palestine would not prevent the execution of any United Nations decision which might ultimately be taken, but would enable such a decision to be more easily enforced. If, as His Excellency hoped, some solution was ultimately adopted involving a modification of the present arrangements in favour of the Arabs, the Arab Legion would be able to help enforce such a solution. Even if, on the other hand, the United Nations tried to enforce the present decision, the presence of the Arab Legion would limit the ensuing chaos and not increase it. Tawfiq Pasha thought it was possible that the Jews had

opened their mouths too wide and that the United Nations would come to a similar conclusion, but, however this might be, the Arab Legion could not wait for the prior permission of the United Nations to enter the Arab areas of Palestine.

5. In conclusion, Tawfiq Pasha repeated his assurance that he did not desire to create difficulties for His Majesty's Government or to involve them in responsibility. Any action that might be taken would be purely on Trans-Jordan's responsibility. He recognised that Trans-Jordan must also study the position in relation to the other Arab Governments and that it would be undesirable if her position became too isolated.

6. I asked His Excellency whether, when he spoke of the Arab Legion entering Palestine, he referred to the Arab areas as laid down in the United Nations decision or whether he thought it would also enter the Jewish areas. Tawfiq Pasha replied that the Arab Legion would not enter Jewish areas unless the Jews invaded Arab areas. He saw that the entry of the Arab Legion into Jewish areas would create such strenuous United Nations opposition as to cause great difficulty for Trans-Jordan.

7. I said that I would study the statements that His Excellency had made. Tawfiq Pasha repeated that he did not want any reply. If as a result of my study we wished to pursue the discussion he would be glad to do so, but otherwise he would not expect us to refer to the matter again.

8. Referring to the useful nature of the discussions we had had on other subjects, I said that we should be saved a lot of trouble if only other Arab countries would discuss with us in the same spirit as Trans-Jordan had done. The Prime Minster took the opportunity to say a few words on the attitude of the other Arab countries. They were at present actuated by strong feelings of nationalism. Public opinion had not thought out the fact that no government could live alone without cooperation. The problem was for us to put over to public opinion in the Arab countries that we are not trying to incorporate them in the British Empire, but that for their own sake they must join one camp or the other. Our publicity directive should be to get across the idea that everyone must have allies and that the camp we are in was the better of the two. He recognised that this would take some time but was confident that in the end the new situation would be appreciated and allegations of our imperialist ambitions would subside. I expressed general agreement with His Excellency's remarks.[1]

By the beginning of 1948, the situation in Jordan was emotionally tense and angry, with the increased flow of messages from the various Palestinian Arab communities to the Royal Palace in Amman. Until then, there had been no clear indication as to what the nature of the conflict was going to be, and therefore there was no specific aim for the Government, or indeed for the Jordan Arab Army, apart from the defence of the Kingdom. The King anticipated a special role for Jordan and its armed forces immediately after the withdrawal of the British armed forces from Palestine to protect the Palestinian people against the expected Jewish invasion. He also knew that Jordan would not be able to undertake that mission on its own. The Jordan Arab Army was still under command of the British Army in Palestine, without any effective reserve in Jordan. The Army was mainly paid for by subsidy from the British Government; in 1948 the subsidy consisted of £500,000 to secure immediate requirements of weapons and ammunition for the Jordan Arab Army and P£2,000,000 as an annual subsidy for the year 1948/9.[2] It was commanded by General Glubb, and its senior staff officers and Commanders of formations and units down to regimental level were British.[3] It was short of junior staff officers and, with only two batteries of twenty-five-pounder field guns it was also short of artillery. Just sixteen six-pounder anti-tank guns and only four guns were allocated to each regiment. There was only three weeks of reserve ammunition in the second and third lines, and with no guarantee of further supplies of ammunition it was at a risk of rationing its expenditure in the field of battle.

From the end of 1947 until the beginning of May 1948, the Jordan Arab Army carried out an intensive training programme in individual skills and advanced handling of weapons (including gun and armoured car crews, field-craft, camouflage and concealment, and zeroing of personal weapons). Collective training was carried out at section, platoon, company, squadron and regiment level. The 4th Regiment, particularly, benefitted from this type of training. Meanwhile several Test Exercises Without Troops (TEWT) were held in each brigade, and one at division level. Collective exercises with troops were held by each brigade. Only one skeleton exercise was held on the divisional level to conclude the training programme. Although the training resulted in a high degree of success, with the Jordan Arab Army considered well trained, only half of its troops had experience in modern warfare; it remained in need of battle inoculation in the field. However, two units underwent the test of battle against the Jews: the 4th Regiment in the Gesher settlement incident, and elements of the 6th and 2nd Regiments in the battles of Nabi Yaaqub and Kfar Etzion. In these latter two battles, the officers and men of the Jordan Arab Army were stout-hearted, confident and effective. Even former Jordan Arab Army men proved themselves to be good fighters in the battle for Safad, despite the loss of the city for reasons beyond their control.

The Jordan Arab Army suffered the lack of Arab senior and junior staff officers. Only Major Abdullah al-Tel and Captains Ali al-Hiyari, Yaaqoub al-Salti and Sadiq al-Sharaa had attended a junior staff college in Haifa. Other Arab officers at HQ Arab Legion, HQ I Division and brigades HQs, though well-trained by their Commanders and having some experience through training and exercises, had not attended any staff college. Captain Radhi al-Hindawi, and Lts Ali Abu Nowar, Jamil Qaawar, Maan Abu Nowar, Salih al-Sharaa, Musa Adil and Turki Hussein were appointed to staff duties.

Furthermore, King Abdullah was aware of the strength and potential strength of the British Army in Egypt and Palestine, that is more than 200,000 troops with a formidable arsenal of modern weapons and ammunition and supported by the RAF as well as Britain's ability to mobilise and commit at least three-fold more on land, sea and air in a short period of time. Thus, there was no point in antagonising that military giant. It was wise and indeed prudent to negotiate with the British Government to ensure their support and assistance for whatever the future might be – thus, the Jordanian–British Treaty of 1948 and the agreement that the Jordan Arab Army, after the withdrawal of the British Army from Palestine, may defend the Arab part of Palestine in accordance with the United Nations Partition Plan on condition that it would not attack the Jewish part unless the Jews attacked the Arabs and the Jordan Arab Army.[4] Under the circumstances existing at that time, there was nothing more that Jordan could have done.

Whatever the constraints and deficiencies might have been in the strength, organisation and training of the Jordan Arab Army, the fact remained that Jordanian soldiers were self-disciplined, stout-hearted, unafraid to fight, loyal to their King and country and, above all, full of anger at the Jews for their criminal and cowardice mass murder at Dair Yasin. They were eager to go to Palestine and fight them.

The Jordanians of 1948 were Arab nationalists in motive and behaviour. Their sympathy with the Palestinian people was stronger than any other Arab people because of their geographical closeness, along with the fact that some of their tribes and families were of Palestinian origin. After the Palestinian Revolt of 1936–9, their sympathy grew stronger than ever. King Abdullah continued to concern himself with the Palestinian problem, not only because of his strong religious faith and the fact that his father was buried at al-Aqsa Mosque in the Holy City of Jerusalem, which compelled him to do whatever he could for the cause of Palestine, but also because Palestine was the most important part of his plan for a Greater Syria, a dream that he cherished until his last day. From the day he negotiated the creation of Jordan with British Prime Minister Winston Churchill, when he said to Churchill: 'Did His Majesty's Government mean to establish a Jewish kingdom west of the Jordan and to turn out the non-Jewish population? . . . The Allies appeared to think that men could be cut down and transplanted in the same way as trees', until 1948, when he warned the British Government against chaos in Palestine, he defended the cause of Palestine on every possible occasion. Thus he could not, and did not, ignore the Palestinian appeals for help.

Although Jordan was a constitutional monarchy, it was, in a sense, ruled by autocratic ministers – most of whom could be considered effendis of the Ottoman type, who switched their loyalty to become new British-style effendis. In that sense they were quasi-benevolent autocrats controlling both the democratic institutions and political process of the country. But as a counter-weight to the effendis' executive autocracy, young Jordanian politicians had entered the political arena of the Cabinet and the National Assembly. A few of the executive and the legislative members were over fifty years of age, while the majority were in their thirties and forties. Only two members of the Cabinet were not born in Jordan – Abu al-Huda of Akka in Palestine and al-Shanqiti of Mecca in the Hijaz. The remainder of Cabinet members, all the members of the legislative, had been born in Jordan.

There was no class distinction whatsoever in Jordan. The average Jordanian considered himself (or herself) to be as good and as proud as the next Jordanian. In spite of the presence of a few rich merchants and large land owners, wealth did not contribute to the political, social, personal or public weight of those who 'have' compared to those who 'have not'; and although, in certain cases, members of large tribes had more confidence than those of smaller tribes, the inter-tribal deterrents made everyone equal, while law and order were strictly maintained by the constitution. In social and economic affairs, tribal traditions were effective and supportive to those in need.

The total population of Jordan, including those who escaped from Palestine during the first four months of 1948, did not exceed 540,000 people, 292,651 males and 247,349 females. Considering that women were not permitted to join the Jordan Arab Army by tradition, and that the age for service in the army was between eighteen and fifty years, the total number of men available for service in the army or as volunteers was about 50,000. Of that number about 7,000 men were on active service in the army and volunteers.

Needless to say, since 1921 relations between the British and the Jordanians had been conducted on the British side by the minimum number of officials (who were not in direct contact with the people) and all affairs were dealt with at the highest level. Thus the Jordanians were immune from direct foreign tutelage. They were certainly immune from economic exploitation, for they were poor enough to be aided by Britain. Indeed, immediately after independence in 1946, the Jordanians were content and more proud than ever before. When the crisis in the Middle East began to threaten, their morale was high, and their devotion to their nationalism and religion was at its zenith.[5]

When the League of Arab States decided to establish the Liberation Army, Jordan was in the lead with its contribution. The armed units of the former Jordan Arab Army as shown in Table 3.2 were organised and paid for by the Jordan Government and private contributions.

There were other former Jordan Arab Army men who joined local Palestinian garrisons. Some men of the Jordan Arab Army resigned from their units and joined the Palestinians in defending their homes. The total number of Jordanian volunteers exceeded 1,300 men. Although only three companies were under the command of the Liberation Army, the rest of the volunteers supported local garrisons and al-Jihad al-Muqaddas in Palestine. Meanwhile, with the exception of a regular infantry company at Haifa, another in Hebron and a third in Jerusalem, the rest of the Jordan Arab Army were in Jordan to carry out complete re-organisation and intensive collective training from February to May 1948.

TABLE 3.2
Armed units of the former Jordan Arab Army

Unit	Strength	Commander	Location
One Company	130	Sari al-Funaish	Safad
One Company	120	Muhsin Yaaish	Safad
One Company	130	Izz al Din al-Tel	al-Jalil
Manko Company	150	Barakat al-Khraisha	Jerusalem
Muslim Brothers	150	Abd al-Latif	
		Abu Qourah	Jerusalem
Huwaitat	100	Haroun ibn Jazi	Bab al-Wad
Bani Sakhr	100	Mohammad al-Fayiz	Bab al-Wad
One company	120	Hayil al-Surour	Bab al-Wad
One Platoon	40	Munawir al-Raja	Bab al-Wad
One Platoon	40	Suwailim Duhailan	Bab al-Wad
One Platoon	40	Falah al-Mitlaq	Bab al-Wad
One Platoon	40	Jaddoa ibn Salim	Bab al-Wad
One Platoon	40	Utaiyiq al-Aattnah	Bab al-Wad
Total	**1,200**		

By the middle of April 1948, the Jordanian Government made it clear to all concerned, and to the Council of the League of Arab States, that its intention was to attempt the temporary military occupation of the Arab areas of Palestine after the end of the British Mandate and withdrawal of the British Army on 15 May, in order to protect the Arab people of Palestine against Jewish invasion. Although this intention was specific, its method of execution was still uncertain. However, according to Kirkbride: 'There are an increasing number of indications that the presence of regular Arab troops would be welcomed by the Arabs of Palestine who are finding the various Arab partisan groups now in the country rather trying guests.'[6]

Meanwhile, after Fawzi al-Qawiqji's defeat at Mishmar Ha'Emeq, the Secretary-General of the Arab League (Abd al-Rahman Azzam) and the Chairman of the Military Committee (General Safwat) saw red lights flashing due to the inadequacy of the Liberation Army. The Political Committee, in two minds about the role of the Jordan Arab Army in the looming military crisis, agreed to the Jordanian offer to come to the rescue of Palestine. The initiative for this acceptance came from Azzam, but in the discussion that followed in the Political Committee, the Prime Minister of Syria and al-Haj Amin al-Husseini opposed the acceptance.

The Egyptian Prime Minister was able to overcome their opposition when he accused them of 'being prepared to sacrifice Palestine in their personal jealousies.'[7] When the Prime Minister of Syria criticised the conclusion of the Jordanian–British Treaty of 1948, the Prime Minister of Egypt said: 'Each state must be free to make treaties which deal with its own particular problems', and that he 'would not permit any other state to play any part in the conduct of the international relations of Egypt.' He added that he for one 'did not doubt the honesty of purpose of Arab States which had concluded treaties with Great Powers recently.'[8]

General Safwat went to Amman and had an audience with King Abdullah on 16 April. He presented the letter of acceptance of the Jordan Arab Army role in Palestine, hoping that the Army would be placed under command of the Arab League. When General Safwat mentioned that he expected the Jordan Arab Army to be under his command, the King insisted that the Liberation Army should be placed under his own command. The King also made it clear that the Jordan Arab Army would not be able to enter Palestine before 15 May. Safwat asked the King if he would consider an Iraqi brigade being posted in Jordan, and the King agreed provided it came under his command.

King Abdullah's reply to the letter of the Secretary-General of the Arab League included the following points.

1. All Arab forces now in Palestine and any reinforcements including Iraqis must come under Jordan's command.
2. The Jordanian Arab Army will not be able to act independently before 15 May.
3. The number of trained Arab partisans now in Palestine is only about 3,000 men and the Palestinian levies are untrained, disorganised and short of equipment.
4. The Jordan Arab Army cannot be dispersed in order to protect Arab villages as this action would leave the Arabs without a striking force to cope with an enemy offensive to be expected after 15 May.
5. The premature action and failure of the Arab partisans has raised the Jewish morale.
6. The advance of the Jordanian Arab Army to Palestine will be made in the belief that the Iraqi Army reinforcements will be sent to Jordan.
7. Some air support must be provided by the members of the Arab League as the Jordanian Arab Army has no aircraft.

8. The Arab League must share responsibility with Jordan for action in Palestine and must act jointly in dealing with any international reaction in the future.[9]

After the fall of Haifa the King became extremely worried about the rest of the Arab areas in Palestine, particularly Jerusalem and the holy places in it. On 23 April, he sent a message to the High Commissioner for Palestine with a copy to Foreign Secretary Bevin, calling their attention to the deteriorating situation and appealing for action.

> I feel I must express to your Excellency the Arab feeling in and outside Jordan. After what happened at Dair Yasin, Nassir Al Din, Tiberias and Haifa, public opinion here is so excited and disappointed that nothing can check it except the righting of affairs. I wish to invite the attention of His Majesty's Government and your own to the position of Jerusalem, Nazareth and Bethlehem in the eyes of Christian and Muslim Arabs, a fact which makes it necessary that these trusts be placed in our hands on the termination of the Mandate. Attention is also drawn to the desirability that the Jews should abstain from committing in the Holy City and Jaffa what they have done elsewhere. Jewish quarters should be advised that their extravagance will cause great disadvantage to their desire to settle in Palestine under the name of a national home. If the Jews will stop aggression and accept negotiations with a view to attaining the right of being citizens in the Palestinian State and to admitting that Arab sovereignty in their homeland shall not be disputed or contended by any authorities, if they do this it will be in their own interest as well as in the interest of peace in these countries. This my cable is an interpretation of what every Palestinian and Jordanian has in mind. It is moreover a true expression of the feelings of every Jordanian who possesses magnanimity and manhood.[10]

On 24 April 1948, when the battle for Jaffa was raging and there were heavy Arab casualties, and when the flood of refugees started to pour into Jordan, a meeting was held at the Royal Palace in Amman to discuss the situation in Palestine. The meeting was attended by King Abdullah and Abu al-Huda, the Prince Regent of Iraq and accompanying ministers, the Lebanese Prime Minister, Riyadh al-Solh and the President of the Military Committee, General Ismael Safwat. Fawzi al-Qawiqji was in Amman at the time, but was not invited to the meeting. Owing to the gravity of the crisis, tremendous pressure was put on the King and the Prince Regent to intervene immediately with regular troops in Palestine. By then, Amman was overcrowded with Palestinian refugees, Jaffa was about to fall and a Jewish offensive against the city of Jerusalem, particularly the Qatamon quarter, was imminent. Judging by the successes that the Jews had had in various battles against the Liberation Army and the Palestinian partisans, those at the meeting were apprehensive about launching a campaign against the unknown strength of the Jewish forces and in the presence of the British forces in Palestine until 15 May. Fawzi al-Qawiqji added to that apprehension by introducing a list of the fighting capabilities of the Jews – including artillery, armour and aircraft – in his attempt to justify his defeat to General Safwat.

At the end of meeting, the King sent a letter with Riyadh al-Solh to Abd al-Rahman Azzam, making it clear that Jordan could not handle the situation alone, and that before he took any action he must be assured by the Arab League of full financial, material and military support by the other Arab states. The Prince Regent agreed with the King and felt that Iraq should not be involved in the fighting with regular troops unless the other Arab states participated. Kirkbride, who had a talk with the Regent after the meeting, reported as follows:

> As regards the Iraqi Army he [the Regent] said that a small force would probably be sent but that anything like a division was out of the question having regard to possible events in Kurdistan. The non-arrival of new fighter aircraft made the ability of the Iraqi air force to intervene doubtful. The Regent gave me the impression that his main objective was to calm public opinion in Iraq rather than to save Arab Palestine.[11]

It was obvious by 27 April 1948 that General Safwat had lost control of the Liberation Army and operations in Palestine. On that day he sent an urgent telegram to King Abdullah saying that Samakh in the Syrian sector was in extreme danger, and added: 'We could not allocate more than 300 men to defend it. But it is being attacked by many Jewish forces and is surrounded by Jewish settlements which make its defenders unable to hold it. We appeal to Your Majesty to order the Jordanian Army to cooperate with the defenders to counter the Jewish attacks.' On the following day the King replied:

> In accordance with your request, we commanded two platoons to advance to Samakh; they went and found no one in it and returned

after an exchange of fire with Jews. Where was the Syrian detachment which you conditioned their advance with the advance by the
two Jordanian platoons? We blame you for what happened.[12]

It was obvious that General Safwat's staff did not inform the Syrians
of the intended Jordanian move and, thereafter, a general slump in
Arab morale occurred at every level – heads of states, governments and
peoples, as well as in the various committees of the Arab League. There
was an inclination to indulge in recrimination instead of planning to
deal with the situation. However, the Prime Minister of Jordan and his
colleagues were counselling prudence and resisting the demands for
armed intervention with which they were inundated. On 29 April, the
Secretary-General of the Arab League visited Amman and attended the
meeting held by the King with the Regent of Iraq and his ministers.
Tawfiq Abu al-Huda conveyed all the information about the meeting to
Kirkbride. Kirkbride reported the following to the Foreign Office.

2. The Regent and his ministers brought back from Egypt an
undertaking by the Egyptian Government to engage the Egyptian
Army in southern Palestine if the other Arab States undertook to
intervene at the same time with their troops.

3. The meeting here today decided in principle in favour of
intervention by the regular Arab armies. As regards the question of
date, King Abdullah provoked a heated discussion by saying that
he could not intervene before 15 May 1948, the others maintained
that they could not be bound by this date in view of the Jewish
offensive.

The Prime Minister of Jordan overcame the difficulty by
proposing that the actual date of intervention would be decided
when everyone was ready. (Commenting to me he remarked that he
was certain that the others would not be ready before 15 May. The
Iraqi force said to be of a brigade strength was not due to arrive at
Mafraq before the 7th and no arrangements had yet been made for
its maintenance and supply.)

4. The real argument arose over command. King Abdullah
maintained that it should be in Jordan's hands at Amman. Azzam
was in favour of continuation of the present arrangement with
headquarters at Damascus under Ismael Safwat or another Iraqi
General, Nur al-Din Muhammad. The Iraqis wanted to keep an Iraqi
general in command wherever headquarters may be situated. The
Egyptians have accepted readiness to accept Jordan's control. The

Prime Minister of Jordan said definitely that Jordan would not place the Arab Legion under the existing command in Damascus.

Eventually it was agreed by those present that as far as they were concerned each State shall retain its independent command and be allocated an operational zone in Palestine. It was assumed that Syria, Lebanon and Saudi Arabia would agree to this.

5. The Arab League has allocated a sum of one and a half million pounds to finance the opening stages of the operation. The expenditure of this amount will be in the hands of the Secretary-General of the Arab League personally. (This arrangement seems to invite future friction about funds.)

6. The next step is for representatives of the general staffs of the armies concerned to meet and work out the technical details of a plan to put this decision into force both as regard troop movements and on the questions of supply, as regards which everyone is very vague. The Jordan Government have invited the meeting to take place at Amman.[13]

On 30 April, all the military representatives arrived at Amman to discuss the details of the military intervention. The Syrian Prime Minister and the Syrian Chief of General Staff arrived at Amman on the same day on their own initiative, having made a U-turn on their previous refusal to treat Jordan as an equal. Tawfiq Abu al-Huda and General Abd al-Qadir al-Jundi represented Jordan. During the meeting on 1 May, it was suggested that because the Jordan Arab Army was ready to intervene, it should act immediately without waiting for the rest of the Arab armies to occupy their positions. Abu al-Huda made it abundantly clear that the Jordan Army would not act independently under the present decision in favour of a joint intervention. He also insisted that Egypt, Syria and the Lebanon should indicate clearly to what extent they would be able to help in military forces and equipment.

The most important question during the meeting was that of Jerusalem, on which the Arab leaders were torn between the fear of the Jews being able to usurp it on the one hand, and the shock of their realisation of the fact that they were really not ready for military intervention on the scale required, on the other. They also knew that nothing could be done before the end of the Mandate on 15 May, remembering that the British Army would still be in Egypt and Cyprus. That situation worried the Secretary-General of the Arab League, who asked Kirkbride 'whether the British troops at Rafah would intervene' if the two Egyptian Army brigades moved into Palestine. Kirkbride replied: 'The British at Rafah would be bound to react to any move before the end of the Mandate.'[14] However, Britain hardly intervened at all during the last four months when the Jews usurped seven Arab towns and cities and more than 59 villages – all in Arab areas designated by the partition plan.

On 2 May, the results of the discussions in the meeting were reported to the Foreign Office by Kirkbride as follows:

> 1. I have been given the following information in confidence [most certainly by Tawfiq Abu al-Huda] and I shall be grateful if it could be used in a manner that conceals myself as the source. I believe it to be entirely reliable.
>
> 2. The Arab leaders in Amman recently decided that while they could not go on the offensive before the end of the Mandate, they could not wait until then to move their troops into Palestine as this would give the Jews too great an initial advantage.
>
> Syrian, Iraqi and Lebanese troops in the guise of volunteers will therefore enter Palestine territory on 8 May and take up positions in Arab areas. They will be ordered to avoid all contact with British and Jewish forces before 15 May.
>
> 3. The position as regards the Egyptian troops is not so clear as it would be difficult to conceal their move forward in open country and they are nervous about the British forces in Rafah.
>
> 4. As regards the Arab Legion [Kirkbride revealing his source] the Prime Minister avoided the issue by pointing out to the other Arab leaders that the Arab Legion was already in position in Arab areas of Palestine.
>
> 5. It was agreed that British representations on the subject should continue to be met by undertakings to do nothing before the end of the Mandate and that if the presence of the so-called volunteers in Palestine was discovered, the Arab governments should deny all knowledge.[15]

On 6 May 1948, the Jordanian National Assembly held a joint meeting of the Council of Senators and the Council of Deputies, which was presided over by Senator Abdullah al-Kulaib al-Shraidah, to discuss the situation in Palestine. The Prime Minister opened the debate with the following statement:

In their request to hold this meeting, in accordance with His Majesty the King's wishes and approval, [the Jordan Government] wanted to follow the path of referring to the views of the representatives of the people, senators and deputies, in these critical circumstances, and to cooperate with them, believing that it will make it easier for both the executive and legislative authorities to do their duty in the public interest.

You remember that your High Councils had decided on 2 December 1947 to support the government in what action they may take in conjunction with the states of the Arab League to prepare and act in the defence of the Arabness of Palestine. Some months have passed during which the Arab League Council and its Political Committee has made its decisions and discussed with the United Nations and its various Committees, but all that did not lead to the preservation of right and the security of justice in Palestine. You know what atrocities and catastrophes have been inflicted upon our brothers there, which indicate the behaviour of our Zionist adversaries, and shows the extent of their resoluteness in ignoring the principles of humanity and their use of savage terrorism which makes the situation grim, and it has become obvious that defence through Arab partisans has not achieved the results we hoped for. Therefore the Arab states see no alternative but to use their regular forces to defend our brothers and prevent the dangers that threaten all the Arab countries.

The Hashemite Kingdom of Jordan in accordance with His Majesty the King's wish, who has used all his time during the last few months working for the good of Arab Palestine, and in accordance with your decision mentioned before, and according to the wishes of the Jordanian people as mentioned in the resolutions of their leaders and Shaikhs, and to the requests by individuals from all walks of life, in all events, and owing to the expression by all of their will and determination, the government decided to participate with the sister Arab States in all the actions aiming to save Palestine, and to provide all that requires in effort, blood and finance.

The government is confident that you will support their stance and will help them, and agree to the needs of that stance in legislative action to that end in accordance with the constitution.[16]

It was obvious that the Prime Minister wanted a free hand in dealing with the situation. Shafiq al-Rushaidat, a member of the opposition and the deputy for Irbid, suggested that some members might wish to discuss the issues involved and asked for the meeting to be secret. Everyone approved and the secret meeting lasted for one hour, after which Shafiq offered the following draft decision.

The National Assembly, after [its] secret meeting today, following the government statement on the participation of the Hashemite Kingdom of Jordan with the Arab States to save Palestine by military forces from the Zionist usurpation, salutes His Majesty the King of the Country, the Commander in Chief of the Jordan Arab Army, places the matter in His Majesty's hands, and supports the government in all its actions for that holy aim. May God give victory to the King.

Immediately after the approval of the decision by loud applause from all present, the speaker of the National Assembly read the Royal Command for the end of the session. The government statement and the National Assembly's decision could be regarded as a declaration of war against the Zionist Jews in Palestine.

Major General Norman Lash, Commander of the 1st Division of the Jordan Arab Army, had sent Captain Sadiq al-Sharaa, one of his staff officers, to visit Palestine to report to him about the situation regarding the Liberation Army and the volunteer partisans. On 5 April, Sadiq visited Gaza and the 6th Infantry Company of the Jordan Arab Army in the area. He talked with Rushdi al-Shawa and the leaders of the city, who explained the state of affairs regarding their partisans in the city and the villages in its environ. Their main request was for weapons and ammunition. According to Sadiq, the general situation in the area was 'discomforting'. On the following day he went to Hebron and noticed the same situation as in Gaza. He then went to Jerusalem to visit the 9th Infantry Company of the Jordanian Arab Army, and ended his day in Ramleh where he visited Mayor Mahmoud Ala al-Din. He noticed that the city was crowded with volunteers who gave the impression of chaos. On 8 April, he visited Ramallah where he saw in the mayor's building a few men asking for arms to go and fight for al-Qastal, which was captured by the Jews. Captain Sadiq felt great pain when he saw an old villager who was armed with a sword, but demanded a rifle from the mayor. Sadiq was still in Ramallah on 9 April, when news of the massacre at Dair Yasin reached the city. He saw the flood of refugees from Dair Yasin and other villages. Sadiq was despondent when he came back to the division HQ.[17]

By the end of April 1948, the King commanded that the Jordan Arab Army must be prepared to intervene in Palestine. General Glubb visited the 1st Division to inform General Lash and his brigade Commanders and supporting units that it was decided that the Arab armies would intervene in Palestine. He commanded that the division would take defensive positions in the central areas of the country from the mountains overlooking the road from Tel Aviv to Jerusalem, and along the high ground running west to Latrun and Bab al-Wad, to the north to Bait Sira and thence east to Ramallah. He said that Jerusalem was not the responsibility of the division, because it was an international United Nations Zone, in addition to the fact that, with the limited number of troops available, the strength of the Jordan Arab Army would not be enough to defend the whole area – not to mention fighting in the built-up area of Jerusalem, which could swallow the majority of the troops.

General Glubb's specific aim was to hold and defend every axis from west to east, to prevent Jewish forces from advancing through the environs of Jerusalem to Ramallah, thence on to the River Jordan. The Jordan Arab Army at Bab al-Wad would block the road from Tel Aviv to Jerusalem. Thus the city would be under siege and thereafter future deployment could be reconsidered. Lydda and Ramleh were not in the Jordan Arab Army defensive area because they were situated in the low ground away from the high ground. Two regiments would be needed to defend them, which was half of the division. The defence of these two towns would be the duty of the Palestinian partisans and the Liberation Army.

On 7 May 1948, a new directive was issued by the HQ of the Jordan Arab Army to the 1st Division to include the Nablus District in the division defensive plan. This was because the Iraqi Brigade would advance through Majamaa Bridge to Affoulah north of Nablus. Considering the divisional strength, which was inadequate to defend its previous prospective dispositions, the new plan (which covered the defence of the whole area from Nablus to Jerusalem) was nearly impossible. To ask a division consisting of two infantry brigades, each of two regiments, with a total strength of only 4,500 front-line troops to cover more than 180 kilometres, against at least six Jewish brigades was, from a military point of view, an impossible mission, considering also the mobility of the Jewish forces and the many lines of approach to the said area.

On 12 May, the division Commander held an Order Group at his HQ in which he allocated areas of responsibilities for each brigade as shown in Table 3.3.

Table 3.3
Areas of responsibility for each brigade

1st Infantry Brigade to be responsible for the defence of the District of Nablus.

1st Infantry Regiment to defend the following axis:
- Bait Qad to Jenin
- Jalamah to Jenin
- Silat al-Harithiyah to Jenin
- area west of Yabad to Jenin
- Aattil to Dair al-Ghusun to Balaah to Aanabtah
- Tulkarm Aanabtah to Nablus
- Qalqiliyah to Azzoun to Nablus

3rd Infantry Regiment in brigade reserve and the defence of the following axis:
- Kufr Qasim to Bidiyah to Nablus

3rd Infantry Brigade to defend the area of Ramallah.

2nd Infantry Regiment to defend the following axis:
- Jerusalem to Ramallah
- Biddu to Ramallah
- defend al-Nabi Samuel

4th Infantry Regiment to defend the following axis:
- Rantis to Abud to Dair Nizam
- Qibbiyah to Dair Abu Mishaal to Dair Nizam
- the Latrun Triangle to Jerusalem
- the Latrun Triangle to Imwas to Bait Sira and Bait Iiqya

4th Infantry Brigade with its HQ already at Ramallah, was a small symbolic skeleton in command of:
- the 2nd Security company in Ramallah
- the 9th Infantry company in al-Taibah north-east of Ramallah
- the 5th Company in Qalandiyah
- the 12th Infantry Company of the 6th Regiment in Hebron

The 6th Regiment, which was being organised, was at Jericho

On 11 May, General Lash went on a reconnaissance to study further the deployment of the division and to check the effect of the plan on the ground. He decided on the location of his HQ in Baittin, north-east of Ramallah. He also decided on the assembly area of the division to be west of al-Shunah al-Janubiyah near the Allenby Bridge.

On 12 May, the Iraqi 1st Brigade Group, with its supporting arms, arrived at an area two kilometres north of Mafraq. Two squadrons of the Iraqi Air Force with Sea Fury fighters landed at the former RAF base in

Mafraq, which was previously handed to the Jordan Arab Army by the RAF.

On the night of 12/13 May, the GI of the Division, Major John Downs, and the GII Captain Sadiq al-Sharaa, could not resist the temptation to accompany a demolition platoon which destroyed some small bridges near Majamaa Bridge in the north. That accomplished, they returned to HQ – enjoying every minute of their adventure. However, they left the main bridge intact for the use of the Iraqi Brigade.[18]

On 13 May, just one day before the advance of the Jordan Arab Army to their assembly area in the Jordan Valley (after all the chaos that the Arab Prime Ministers and Azzam had created in the Arab effort to use irregular forces and thence military regular forces in Palestine) Azzam arrived at Amman to discuss with King Abdullah Jordan's participation in the expected war. He had no plan to offer and it was obvious that he was extremely naive regarding military affairs. After his meeting with the King, Prime Minister Abu al-Huda summoned General Glubb for a meeting with Azzam to discuss the role of the Jordan Arab Army. Of that meeting Glubb wrote:

> [Azzam] asked me how many men the Arab Legion had. When I told him that we could send about 4,500 all ranks to Palestine, he expressed disappointment. He said he thought we had far more. He then asked me how many I thought the Jews had. I replied that intelligence reports had spoken of 65,000 as having received training. I thought they varied considerably in quality. Azzam Pasha again expressed great surprise. He said that he had no idea there were so many. 'However,' he added, 'I expect it will be all right. I have arranged to get some seven hundred men from Lybia.' 'Seven hundred is not very many,' I remarked. 'How are they armed?' 'I have sent a man to buy seven hundred rifles from Italy,' replied he. I was far more surprised, however, when he remarked casually that he would be willing to accept me as Commander-in-Chief of all the Arab Armies. I could not help laughing. 'No thank you, Sir,' I answered. 'I am unfit to command the Arab Legion – much less several different armies.'
>
> I could not understand this amazing remark. Later on Egypt offered the title of Supreme Commander to King Abdullah, but when His Majesty requested an order of battle of the Egyptian Army, his request met with no reply, nor did he ever receive or dispatch a single official letter in his capacity as Commander-in-Chief. In spite of this, however, the Egyptians on various occasions attributed the failure of the operations to the incapacity of the Royal

Commander-in-Chief. It was only a year later that it dawned upon me that Azzam Pasha's extraordinary offer to me was perhaps intended for the same purpose.

A foreign Commander could have been disregarded if the operations went well, but might have proved a useful scapegoat if the war ended in defeat.[19]

The movement from the various camps to the assembly area in the Jordan valley was carried out on the morning of 14 May 1948, in the following order of battle.

- 1st Infantry Brigade: 1st Regiment, Brigade HQ, 3rd Regiment, Support Arms.
- 1st Division Main HQ: Signal Regiment HQ, Divisional Workshops.
- 3rd Infantry Brigade: 2nd Regiment, Brigade HQ, 4th Regiment.
- Divisional Tactical HQ.

The route for the movement was from the various camps to Zarqa–Rusaifa–Amman, and thence on the back road adjacent to the Royal Palace-Suwailih – al-Salt to South Shunah. Large crowds of Jordanians gathered at every village, town and the city of Amman to say farewell to their sons who were departing for war. Emotions ran high and morale was high. I remember my father and mother standing among the crowd close to the Mahattah bridge in Amman. As I was passing by in my GMC light armoured car, my mother shouted: 'God be with you my son. Don't come back. Martyrdom my son.' I was shocked, not because my mother wished me to be killed and be a martyr, but because her head and face were bare and she was waving her black scarf. In Jordan, conservative and devout women like her did not usually appear in public without a scarf covering their heads and faces (*hijab*).

The movement was typical of the Jordan Arab Army's efficient mobility; not a single accident occurred. By the afternoon all units were in their assembly areas, dispersion was maintained, camouflage nets covered all vehicles and orders down to troop level were issued. King Abdullah, accompanied by Prince Talal, General Glubb and General Lash, visited all units, and the King made a short speech to their officers and men. At every unit he encouraged the men to save Jerusalem and added:

He who is killed will be a martyr; he who lives will be glad of fighting for Palestine, the land of peace and the Arab faithful. I place obedience in your custody my gallant soldiers, for it is the foundation of the Army. I remind you of the Jihad and martyrdom of your great-grandfathers.

At dawn on 15 May 1948, the 1st Infantry Division of the Jordan Arab Army entered Palestine through the Allenby Bridge. The 3rd Brigade was in the lead with the 4th Regiment as advanced Guard followed by Brigade HQ and the 2nd Regiment. Divisional Tactical HQ, followed by the 1st Regiment, 1st Brigade HQ, the 3rd Regiment and the main Divisional HQ, crossed the river in that order. The route of the advance was from Jericho through the Jordan valley, north to al-Jiftlic and northwest to Khirbit Hasan to the dispersal point at Nablus. Thence, the 3rd Brigade continued its advance to Ramallah followed by the Tactical and main Divisional HQs, while the 1st Brigade remained in Nablus, with the 1st Regiment advancing west to take up its position. The 3rd Regiment remained in Nablus in reserve. By nightfall, all units were in their allocated positions, digging in, concealing their vehicles and equipment and ready to fight; their dispositions were as shown in Table 3.4.

The Jordan Arab Army had no serious reserve force to reckon with east of the River Jordan; only two infantry companies were left behind to guard military installations:

- the 13th Infantry Company at Majamaa Bridge, and
- the 15th Infantry Company at Aabdulli Camp in Amman.

As the Jordan Arab Army was on the brink of war in the central area of Palestine, with the 1st Division of two brigades and a third symbolic and skeleton brigade – a total of about 4,500 front-line troops – they faced the following Jewish forces.

• The Harel Palmach Brigade	Jerusalem	2,000
• The Etzioni Brigade	Jerusalem	3,200
• The Seventh Brigade	Khulda	3,000
• The Givati Brigade	Tel Aviv	3,400
• The Kiryati Brigade	Tel Aviv	3,600
• The Alexandroni Brigade	Natanya	3,600
• The Irgun Gang	Jerusalem	1,000
• The Stern Gang	Jerusalem	500
• The Local Garrisons		15,000
Total		**35,300**

TABLE 3.4
Disposition of units

The 1st Infantry Brigade commanded by Colonel D. Goldie. Brigade HQ at the experimental farm in Aaskar four miles east of Nablus.

1st Regiment: Regiment HQ, Lt Colonel H.C. Blackden, at Dair Sharaf west of Nablus; Adjutant, Captain Khalid al-Sahin, Dair Sharaf; 1st Company, Lt Salamah Autayiq, Qalqiliyah area; 2nd Company, Lt Muhammad Muhsin al-Harbi, Tulkarm area; 3rd Company, Lt Awad Hamid, in reserve at Dair Sharaf; Armoured Cars Squadron, Lt Hamad Abdullah Abu Dukhainah, in reserve at Dair Sharaf; Support Company, Lt Sulaiman Rutaimah, Dair Sharaf; HQ Company, Lt Rushaid Marshud, Dair Sharaf.

3rd Regiment: Regiment HQ, Lt Colonel William Newman, in brigade reserve at Huwarah 15 kilometres south of Nablus; Adjutant, Captain Khalid Mujalli al-Khraisha, Huwarah; 1st Company, Lt Muhammad Nauman, Huwarah; 2nd Company, Lt Eid Adailim, Huwarah; 3rd Company, Lt Ghazi al-Harbi, Huwarah; Armoured Car Squadron, Lt Zaal Ruhayil, Huwarah; Support Company, Lt Fandi Aumaish, Huwarah; HQ Company, Lt Muharib Saad, Huwarah.

The 3rd Infantry Brigade commanded by Colonel Teel Ashton. Brigade HQ at Baituniya, 15 kilometres south-west of Ramallah.

2nd Regiment: Regiment HQ, Major R Slade, Biddu; Adjutant, Captain Akkash al-Zabin, Biddu; 1st Company, Lt Aabattah Eid, al-Qubaibah; 2nd Company, Lt Muhammad Kassab, al-Nabi Samuel; 3rd Company, Lt Refaifan Khalid Khraisha, Biddu area; Armoured Car Squadron, Lt Hamdan Subaih, Biddu; Support Company, Lt Nayif al-Hadid, Biddu; HQ Company, Lt Qasim Abu Shraitih, Biddu.

4th Regiment: Regiment HQ, Lt Colonel Habis al-Majali, Dair Nizam; Adjutant, Lt Mahmoud al-Rousan, Dair Nizam; 1st Company, Captain Kamil Abd al-Qadir, Dair Nizam; 2nd Company, Captain Abdullah al-Salim, Kharbatha; 3rd Company, Captain Salih al-Fakhuri, Bait Sira crossroads; Support Company, Captain Izzat Hasan, Dair Nizam; HQ Company, Lt Nasr al-Ahmad, Dair Nizam.

The 4th Infantry Brigade commanded by Colonel Ahmad Sudqi al-Jundi, Brigade HQ at Ramallah; Second-in-Command, Major Abd al-Halim al-Sakit, Ramallah.

6th Regiment: Regiment HQ, Major Abdullah al-Tel, Khan al-Ahmar; 1st Security Company, Captain Mahmoud al-Musa Aubaidat, Khan al-Ahmar; 6th Infantry Company, Captain Dhurgham al-Falih, Khan al-Ahmar; 8th Infantry Company, Captain Abd al-Razzaq Abdullah, Khan al-Ahmar; Support Company, Lt Ghalib Rudhaiman, Khan al-Ahmar; two 3.7 guns, Lt Abd al-Rahman al-Armouti, Khan al-Ahmar.

The Infantry Companies, also under command of the 4th Brigade, were: 2nd Infantry Company, Captain Fawaz Mahir, at the Jordan Valley; 2nd Security Company, Captain Muhammad Khalf al-Omari, Ramallah; 4th Infantry Company, Captain Radhi al-Abdullah, Ramallah; 5th Infantry Company, Captain Muhammad Ishaq, Ramallah area; 9th Infantry Company, Captain Sulaiman Masaud, al-Taybah; 12th Infantry Company, Captain Hikmat Muhyar, Hebron.

The administrative base of the Jordanian Arab Army was in Zarqa, about 150 kilometres away. The Jewish forces' administrative base was only about 10–20 kilometres away from most Brigades, except the Etzioni and Harel brigades which were about 40 kilometres away. The Jews had two ports on the coast of the Mediterranean sea from Haifa to Tel Aviv, while Jordan had the port of Aqaba, about 360 kilometres away from its administrative base and 460 kilometres away from its front line. The Jewish forces lived in the land of the expected battles; they knew and were accustomed to its geographical features. Meanwhile, the Jordanian Arab Army, though having served in Palestine, was a stranger to the geographical features of the land. With exception of the Jordanian armoured cars and field artillery, the Jewish forces had far greater advantages than the Jordanian.

On the Arab side, the League of Arab States, because of its inefficiency, lack of determination, disunited leadership, jealousy among blocks of states and, above all, because it was a new regional organisation which was only two and a half years old, had lost the most precious, indeed priceless, asset of time – time to decide on a feasible and specific aim, time to prepare its irregular and regular forces, time to train its troops, time to unite its command, time to enhance discipline and change chaos into an organised order (particularly in Palestine) and, finally, time to plan and mobilize.

For the first four months of 1948, the Arab League and the Arab states did nothing of any real consequence, except lose precious time. The united Jewish leadership had used the asset of time effectively, particularly between the end of 1947 and 15 May 1948.

NOTES

1 PRO. FO 371/62193. Conversation between Abu al-Huda and Ernest Bevin on 7 February 1948, dated 9 February 1948.
2 PRO. FO 371/68817. Telegram from the Foreign Office to Amman, 3 February 1948.
3 For details of the organisation of the Jordanian Arab Army see Maan Abu Nowar, *The Struggle for Independence 1939–1947* (Reading: Ithaca Press, 2001), Chapter 10.
4 PRO. FO 371/62193. Conversation between Tawfiq Abu al-Huda and Ernest Bevin on 7 February 1948, dated 9 February 1948.

5   PRO. FO 371/68386. Sir A. S. Kirkbride (British Minister in Amman) to Ernest Bevin (Foreign Secretary), 26 April 1948.
6   PRO. FO 371/117. Kirkbride to the Foreign Office, 13 April 1948.
7   PRO. FO 816/117. Kirkbride to the Foreign Office, 19 April 1948
8   *Ibid.*
9   PRO. FO 816/117. Kirkbride to the Foreign Office, 21 April 1948.
10 PRO. FO 816/117. King Abdullah to The High Commissioner, copied to Bevin, 23 April 1948.
11 PRO. FO 816/118. Kirkbride to the Foreign Office, 25 April 1948.
12 The Hashemite Documents, p. 191.
13 PRO. FO 816/118. Kirkbride to the Foreign Office, 29 April 1948.
14 PRO. FO 816/118. Kirkbride to the Foreign Office, 1 May 1948.
15 PRO. FO 816/118. Kirkbride to the Foreign Office, 2 May 1948.
16 HKJOG Records of the National Assembly, 6 May 1948, pp. 204–5.
17 Al-Sharaa, *Our Wars with Israel*, pp. 57–9.
18 *Ibid.*, p. 81.
19 Glubb, *A Soldier with the Arabs*.

4

The Battle for Jerusalem

To any Muslim, the Holy City of Jerusalem is sacred in his heart and mind. The veneration of 'Bait al-Maqdis' Jerusalem started with the dawn of Islam when *al-Issraa wa al-Miaraj*, the nocturnal journey of the Prophet Muhammad from al-Masjid al-Haram in Mecca to al-Masjid al-Aqsa in Jerusalem, became known and written about in the Qu'ran. It was further venerated when the Prophet built his Mosque in al-Medinah and made its *Qiblah*, direction of prayers, towards Jerusalem. He announced the *Hadith* saying: 'You shall only set out to three mosques: al-Masjid al-Haram in Mecca, my Mosque in al-Medinah, and the al-Aqsa Mosque.' Thus, 'Jerusalem is the first *Qiblah* and the third of the two Holy *Harams*.'

The Caliph Omar ibn al-Khattab entered Jerusalem in peace in AD 637. During his visit to Jerusalem, al-Khalifah Omar ibn al-Khattab indicated the place of prayer in al Haram al-Sharif and marked the site of al-Mihrab. In AD 643 the al-Masjid al-Aqsa was completed while Omar was still alive.

Since his childhood, the author, like every Jordanian and Arab pupil, was extremely impressed by the history he learnt from his religious teacher Shaikh Baha al-Din al-Aaboudi, about the entry of Caliph Omar ibn al-Khattab into Jerusalem – he was leading his camel and his servant was riding, because it was his turn to ride – and the peace pact between Omar ibn al-Khattab and Sophronius, the Bishop of Jerusalem. He was also told of the history of the liberation of Jerusalem from the Crusaders by Salah al-Din al-Ayoubi, as well as the occupation of Jerusalem by General Allenby in 1917. Deep in the hearts and minds of the generation of the author, young Arabs, Christians and Muslims felt the holiness of Jerusalem. From their homes in Amman, as they approached Jerusalem they felt they were going home, and as they left Jerusalem to go home to Amman, they felt they were leaving home behind. Such were the feelings of the officers and men of the Jordanian Arab Army on the evening of 14 May 1948.

Early in the morning of 14 May 1948, all British officials of the British Palestine Government plus the staff of the British Army HQ evacuated their rooms at the King David Hotel in Jerusalem and left the city. At 0800 hours, General Sir Alan Cunningham, the High Commissioner for Palestine, reviewed a guard of honour at Government House wearing his uniform of Lt General of the British Army. He drove to Qalandiyah air strip and, from there, flew to Haifa. As he prepared to sail to Britain at midnight that evening, the 26-year-old British Mandate for Palestine came to an end. Sir Alan, who once said that 'the city of Jerusalem, precious as an emblem of several faiths, a site of spiritual beauty lovingly preserved over the ages by many men's hands, has been in our care as a sacred trust for thirty years', left that Holy City in a political, economic and social shambles.

Immediately after Cunningham's departure from Jerusalem, units of the Jewish Harel and Etzioni Brigades and elements of the Irgun terrorist gang advanced and captured the former British Army security areas, which consisted of nearly one-fifth of the city – including the Allenby and Alamein barracks. By noon the Haganah occupied all the undefended buildings in the new city centre including the main post office, telephone exchange, the building of the Health Department and other government offices. By the evening of 15 May, the Jewish forces occupied the Shaikh Jarrah police station near Mea Shearim and part of the area of Shaikh Jarrah. Early on 16 May, they usurped the Arab areas of the Greek Colony, the German Colony, al-Talbiyah and parts of Abu Tur. By nightfall they captured Talpiot and the railway station, and advanced further into Abu Tur. The Palestinian partisans of Jerusalem counter-attacked at Shaikh Jarrah to relieve Musrarah and Saad wa Said, but as soon as they overran it the Harel Brigade recaptured it. Fierce fighting between the Palestinian Partisans of Jerusalem and a company of the Liberation Army on the one hand, and the Jews on the other, continued all night. The Jews were attempting to break through the Old City walls at Bab al-Nabi Daoud (Zion Gate), Bab al-Khalil (Jaffa Gate) and Bab al-Jadeed (New Gate), but failed to do so. The Jewish Quarter in the Old City was under siege. The Harel Brigade under the command of Yitzhak Rabin fought all night to break through into the Old City, but failed. Appeals from the Arab leaders of Jerusalem were sent to King Abdullah, who could no longer tolerate Glubb's avoidance to engage the Arab Legion in Jerusalem. He wrote to Glubb on 16 May:

> My dear Glubb Pasha,
>
> The importance of Jerusalem in the eyes of the Arabs and the Muslims and the Arab Christians is well known. Any disaster suffered by the people of the city at the hands of the Jews, whether they are killed or driven from their homes, would have the most far-reaching results for us. The situation does not yet give cause for despair. I accordingly order that everything we hold today must be preserved, the Old City and the road to Jericho. This can be done either by using the reserve forces which are in the vicinity of Ramallah or by sending there a force from the general reserve. I ask you to execute this order as quickly as possible.[1]

General Glubb had no choice but to obey his Royal Commander-in-Chief. But on 17 May, he went on a visit to 1st Brigade HQ in Nablus and HQ 1st Division in Baittin near Ramallah, 'principally in order to escape the insistence of the King and Prime Minister for immediate action' to save Jerusalem.[2] During his visit to 1st Brigade HQ, Lt Salih al-Sharaa and I told Glubb that we noticed the men were frustrated. They had been asking: 'Why are we here in Nablus while the battle is in Jerusalem?' When Glubb asked what we thought, Salih al-Sharaa and I unashamedly said that we agreed with the men. At 1st Division HQ, Glubb heard the same from Captain Sadiq al-Sharaa, and was convinced that some form of indignation that he would not be able to control was creeping into the hearts and minds of the Jordan Arab Army.

At the Royal Palace in Amman King Abdullah, who usually prayed at dawn, was informed by Hazzaa al-Majali, a member of the staff of the Royal Palace, that Ahmad Hilmi, the Chairman of the High Committee in Jerusalem, had appealed to him to send the Jordan Arab Army to save Jerusalem. King Abdullah immediately telephoned Ahmad Hilmi and heard his report about the situation. At 0430 hours, he went to Tawfiq Abu al-Huda's house, woke him up and informed him of the situation and his anticipation that Jerusalem would fall to the Jews if the Jordanian Arab Army did not save the Holy City. Abu al-Huda replied: 'Military intervention by the Jordanian Arab Army in Jerusalem will contravene the United Nations resolutions and will lead to international consequences.'

The King, who was determined to intervene come what may, commanded Abu al-Huda to assemble the Cabinet and establish a regency for the throne. He added: 'I will command the forces in Jerusalem myself to preserve her Arabness and Islam'.³

During Glubb's visit to the HQ of the 1st Division, he discussed the situation with General Lash and his staff. While reviewing the situation in Jerusalem, a message came from King Abdullah commanding him to send a force to Jerusalem to threaten the Jews into accepting a truce. A few minutes later he also received a message from the Prime Minister and Minister of Defence telling him that the situation in Jerusalem was very critical, that His Majesty was worried and expected immediate action. Glubb, who wanted to avoid Jerusalem, had nowhere to 'escape' to and was thus compelled to take action. He commanded that a company of the 6th Regiment occupy its position at Jabal al-Zaitoun (Mount of Olives) and from there enter the Old City of Jerusalem at night.⁴

The battle for the Old City

When David Shaltiel took over command of the Jewish forces in Jerusalem on 14 February 1948, Ben-Gurion gave him orders to prevent the evacuation by the Jews of the Old City in the first stage, and in the second, after the end of the Mandate, 'to liberate the Old City and the whole of Jerusalem'.⁵

The Old City of Jerusalem was inhabited by Jews, Christians and Muslims who, until the beginning of hostilities towards the end of 1947, lived in peace as good neighbours. They constituted multi-racial and multi-religious communities with a Muslim and Christian Arab majority and a small Jewish minority. The Christians belonged to different churches: Greek Orthodox, Ethiopian, Russian, Armenian, Roman Catholic, Protestant and others. The Jews, who inhabited nearly 15 per cent of the urban area of the Old City – about 1,500 men, women and children – were mainly 'old-fashioned and completely Arabicised, most of them intensely devout and with no sympathy for the German or Russian Zionists'.⁶

When the hostilities started in Palestine, the British Army surrounded the Jewish quarter to protect it against any possible attacks by the Arabs, but they never really protected any Arab village against Jewish attacks. During a period of three months the British Army, in spite of the Jewish terrorist campaign against themselves and the Arabs of Jerusalem, took care to supply the Jewish quarter with the necessities of life – mainly food and medicine. However, by way of deception the Haganah and Harel Palmach Brigade were able to infiltrate 300 of their men, including Stern and Irgun members, into the Old City. Then they smuggled in weapons and ammunition, trained the young men of the Jewish quarter, and prepared their defences in pillboxes, loopholes and other firing positions.

By the beginning of May they were ready to fight. Their defence was all round and in depth, with direct wireless communication with their HQ. Their orders from the Jerusalem Brigade HQ were to fight to the end and never surrender.

A few minutes after midnight on 17/18 May, King Abdullah ordered the Commander of the 6th Regiment, Major Abdullah al-Tel, to join the battle in Jerusalem. On receiving that order, al-Tel sent Captain Mahmoud al-Musa Aubaidat and his 1st Security Company to Jerusalem. On his arrival at the foot of the Mount of Olives two hours later, Aubaidat was informed by Othman Badran (the Commander of al-Hussein company of Palestinian Partisans), Jamal al-Soufi (the second-in-command of the Liberation Army unit in Jerusalem) and Salih al-Alami (of al-Jihad al-Muqaddas) that the Jews had penetrated through Bab al-Khalil (Jaffa Gate) and Bab al-Jadid (New Gate) and established contact with the Jewish quarter in the Old City. Additionally, the whole of Jerusalem would fall into Jewish hands if the Jordan Arab Army did not save it.

A few minutes later, Abdullah al-Tel ordered Aubaidat to send a rescue force to support the Liberation Army and defend the city. Captain Aubaidat sent two platoons of about 40 men each under command of Lts Nawaf al-Jabir al-Humoud and Mustafa Ibrahim from the Mount of Olives to the Old City. The two platoons moved at night from their positions, past Gethsemane through the valley to the tomb of the Virgin Mary, and through Bab al-Asbatt (St Stephen's Gate), and joined the Partisans in al-Rawdhah in the Old City.

Lt al-Humoud reported to Captain Fadhil Abdullah al-Rashid, the Commander of the Liberation Army unit in Jerusalem, who seemed to have belittled the two platoons by saying: 'What could two platoons do? The Jews want to take the city.'

'Please give us the weakest position to defend,' said al-Humoud.

'It's hopeless,' said al-Rashid.

Al-Humoud insisted and after a short talk between the two, al-Humoud was asked to try to defend the New Gate. With the help of a guide, he took the two platoons to the New Gate adjacent to the huge building of Nôtre Dame in the New City. On their arrival, the two platoons took their positions on the city wall in support of a unit from the Liberation Army. A few minutes later the Jews opened heavy fire from Nôtre Dame at the Jordanian platoons. Lt Mustafa Ibrahim, under covering fire from al-Humoud and his platoon and with a platoon from the Liberation Army, crossed the road from the New Gate to Nôtre Dame, assaulted its gate, attacked the Jews and cleared them out of the eastern part of the first floor. Meanwhile, under pressure from the Jewish forces at Mount Zion, the Liberation Army unit defending Bab al-Nabi Daoud withdrew, leaving it open to a breakthrough by the Jews. The man who belittled al-Humoud and his men now asked for their help. Captain Fadhil al-Rashid sent word to al-Humoud informing him of the situation at Bab al-Nabi Daoud and asked him to go to the rescue. Al-Humoud gathered the two platoons at dawn and started on his way to recapture the lost gate.

At 0430 on 18 May, Captain Aubaidat was ordered to enter the Old City with the rest of his company. He went ahead of his troops to al-Rawdhah (where the Jerusalem HQ of the unit of the Liberation Army and the Jerusalem Committee was located), and had a meeting with its Commander, Fadhil Abdullah al-Rashid. Al-Rashid explained that the Old City would fall in a few hours, that the Jews had captured Bab al-Nabi Daoud (Zion Gate) and were in touch with the Jewish quarter, and that his troops were unable to recapture the gate because his force was small and his troops were tired. When asked by Mahmoud al-Musa Aubaidat about the strength of his force, he replied: 'only 700 men.'

Captain Aubaidat said he could recapture Bab al-Nabi Daoud and split the Jewish force if al-Rashid would help him to protect his flanks with the unit of the Liberation Army during his counter-attack. At that point, al-Rashid took Aubaidat aside and whispered in his ear: 'Do not expect any help from me; be self-reliant, if you have the ability to do anything that prevents the Jewish occupation of the Old City.'[7]

At 0200 hours on 19 May, two companies of the Harel Palmach Brigade commanded by Uzi Narkis attacked and captured Mount Zion and broke through Bab al-Nabi Daoud with reinforcements, weapons and ammunitions for the Jewish quarter.[8]

Mahmoud al-Musa Aubaidat went forward on a short reconnaissance to the Armenian monastery, where he found al-Humoud and Ibrahim and their platoons. As soon as he completed his reconnaissance, he took one section of al-Humoud's platoon – about 12 men – and, with support fire from the remaining two sections, he attacked the Jewish platoon that occupied the gate. Leading the assault himself, Aubaidat completely surprised the Jewish force, attacked their positions at the gate and pushed them out of the city wall. The Jews retreated to the al-Nabi Daoud quarter. Thus, the section held the gate and isolated the Old City Jewish quarter from the al-Nabi Daoud quarter. Meanwhile, the Liberation Army platoon holding part of Nôtre Dame withdrew, leaving the building open to Jewish occupation.

Captain Aubaidat brought the rest of his company to the Armenian school and monastery opposite and near the gate. He took another section to carry out a reconnaissance of the Jewish quarter and because he did not know the Old City well enough, he asked a passerby from Jerusalem to take him to a place from where he could observe the Jewish quarter. The passerby, who was Fawzi al-Quttob, the Commander of the Demolition Platoon of al-Jihad al-Muqaddas, asked Aubaidat: 'Are you like your fellows [meaning the Liberation Army] or do you really mean to fight?' To this quasi-insult, Aubaidat responded politely: 'Please take me there and you will see.'[9]

Al-Quttob took Aubaidat to an observation point seventy yards away from the Jewish quarter, and pointed out the Jewish positions to him. After he had studied the situation and planned his next move, Aubaidat immediately deployed the section that accompanied him and opened fire at the Jewish position with rifles, a Bren light machine-gun and a PIAT rocket launcher.[10]

At 1400 hours, Aubaidat was wounded. However, before he was carried away to hospital, he ordered the section to withdraw and wait for him at al-Aqsa Mosque. After he received treatment, he returned to the section, had lunch with them, then took them back to engage the enemy, test their fire power, pinpoint their positions and, at the same time, attract their fire to let them waste their ammunition. As soon as the section took their positions, they opened desultory and selective fire at the Jewish Synagogue area, thus attracting heavy fire from the Jews. From an area not involved in the exchange of fire, Aubaidat and a rifle group – about four men – rushed to the Synagogue from where the

Jewish fire had come and lobbed a few hand grenades inside it. The Jewish Haganah continued to fire back and during the skirmish that followed, Aubaidat was wounded again. He ordered the section to withdraw to the company.

Meanwhile, at dawn on 18 May, the rest of the 6th Regiment arrived at Jerusalem from al Khan al-Ahmar. Major Abdullah al-Tel went through to al-Rawdhah and had a meeting with Ahmad Hilmi of the Arab High Committee, Captain al-Rashid of the Liberation Army and Khalid al-Husseini of al-Jihad al-Muqaddas. They gladly agreed to hand over the responsibility of defending Jerusalem to al-Tel and to unify their command under him. Thereafter, al-Tel immediately deployed his regiment as shown in Table 4.1.

TABLE 4.1
Deployment of al-Tel's regiment

Regiment HQ at Rawdhah

1st Security Company: commanded by Aubaidat and his Platoon Commanders Lts Nawaf al-Jabir, Mustafa Ibrahim, Hussein Miflih al-Gharaybah and Rustum Yahay at Bab al-Nabi Daoud.

6th Infantry Company: commanded by Captain Dhurgham al-Falih, and his Platoon Commanders Lts Farid al-Qutub, Muhammad Khair Idris and Hasan Muhammad, to join the 1st Security Company under the command of Aubaidat.

8th Infantry Company: commanded by Captain Abd al-Razzaq Abdullah and his Platoon Commanders Lts Hathlul Sayir, Jadaan Majid and Turki Abdullah to occupy Bab al-Jadid and Bab al-Khalil.

The Support Company: commanded by Lt Ghalib Rudhaiman and Muhammad al-Aarmouti, which consisted of a platoon of three-inch mortars, a platoon of six-pounder anti-tank guns and two 3.7 Howitzer guns, plus a troop of armoured cars, which were deployed at Ras al-Aamoud and Mount Tur as required.

The total strength of the Regiment was as follows:

Regiment HQ	30
1st Security Company	194
6th Infantry Company	190
8th Infantry Company	209
The Support Company	100
Total	**723**

In spite of his new wounds, Aubaidat went to see al-Tel in the Regiment HQ, and reported to him on the strength and dispositions of the Jewish force. After consultations with the Jerusalem Committee, al-Tel issued a warning to the Jews through the Truce Committee of Consuls in Jerusalem during the afternoon of the 18 May:

> In the name of His Majesty King Abdullah, I invite the Jews of Jerusalem to surrender and save bloodshed. If they do not surrender I will be compelled to shell the Jewish quarter and destroy it.[11]

On the same day as the Jews rejected the warning, al-Tel ordered his support weapons to open slow desultory fire at various targets inside and outside the Old City of Jerusalem. There was a sudden change in the morale of the Arab people of Jerusalem. They became more confident and cooperative with the Jordan Arab Army. On the same day, the King ordered the appointment of al-Tel as Commander of the Arab forces in Jerusalem. The following units came immediately under his command.

- Hussein Battalion of the Liberation Army: about 250 men, commanded by Captain Fadhil Abdullah al-Rashid and a company of Syrian partisans.
- Al-Jihad al-Muqaddas Battalion: about 400 men, commanded by Khalid al-Husseini and his officers (Bahjat Abu Gharbiyah, Hafiz Barakat, Qasim al-Rimawi, Daoud al-Husseini, Fawzi al-Quttob, Muhammad Nimir Audah, Kamil Auraiqat, Abu Khalil Janhu, Muhammad al-Najjar, Salah al-Haj Mir, Raouf Darwish, Said Barakat and Abd al-Halim al-Joulani).
- A unit of former policemen: about 100 men, commanded by Munir Abu Fadhil and various police officers (Ibrahim Jarjourah, Jamil al-Aasali, Sulaiman Aazar, Muhammad Daoud, Sadiq Nazif and Hashim Najim).

At dawn on 19 May, the Harel Palmach Battalion was able to attack and capture Bab al-Nabi Daoud. Captain Aubaidat, who had spent a sleepless night with fever and in much pain from his wounds, was on his way to his company when he was met by Lt Hussein al-Muflih, who reported to him that the Jews had recaptured Bab al-Nabi Daoud. Four of his men had been killed and four others were wounded. Captain Aubaidat, who was a polite and traditional Jordanian, did not comment, but called on the Armenian Patriarch Guregh II on his way to Bab al-Nabi Daoud. The patriarch told him: 'I am an old man who cannot fight, but I will stay with you and do light duties.'[12]

He appealed to Aubaidat to release six young Armenians who were arrested by the Liberation Army. Aubaidat responded immediately and sent one of his sergeants to the Liberation Army to release the young men. At that point, the tension that existed between the Liberation Army and the Armenian quarter ended, and cooperation and understanding was maintained with the Jordan Arab Army.

Captain Aubaidat called on his two platoons commanded by Nawaf al-Humoud and planned a counter-attack on Bab al-Nabi Daoud. He selected one section for the assault and commanded the rest to support him with all their fire power to cover his rush on the tower adjacent to Bab al-Nabi Daoud. As soon as the supporting fire started, with the greatest possible surprise Aubaidat and the selected section rushed the tower and cleared it with small arms and hand grenades. Thence al-Humoud occupied the tower with one platoon and Aubaidat advanced at the Jewish quarter only to be wounded again. Four of his men were killed and five others wounded. He ordered the last man with him, Corporal Abd al-Karim Mahmoud, to cover each other's withdrawal.

While moving away from the scene he saw two men in uniform and, suffering from his new wounds, was unable to identify them clearly. Thinking that they were his men, and acting out of character, he poured abuse on them and accused them of cowardice. The two men took cover, and as Aubaidat came closer to them, they appeared and aimed at him. Before they were able to shoot, Corporal Abd al-Karim killed one of them; the other was killed by Private Mahmoud Khalil of the same unit. Captain Aubaidat then ordered Lt Hussein al-Muflih to recapture the other tower adjacent to Bab al-Nabi Daoud. After that objective was achieved, he ordered al-Humoud and al-Muflih to defend Bab al-Nabi Daoud to the last round and the last man, and went back to hospital.

At dusk on the same day the 6th Company arrived at Aubaidat's HQ. As soon as they were deployed by him, an attack by the Jews to recapture Bab al-Nabi Daoud was launched from outside the city walls and from the Jewish quarter simultaneously. After a fierce battle that lasted several hours, the Jewish attack was repulsed suffering heavy casualties. During the fighting for the gate, the Armenian quarter suffered heavy casualties. The patriarch and his community, who were right in the middle of the exchange of fire, remained steadfast and cooperated with the 6th Regiment.

On 20 May, Aubaidat occupied new areas in the Armenian quarter, which overlooked the Jewish quarter from the west and, with the company at Bab al-Nabi Daoud, the Jewish quarter was completely under siege. No supplies could be sent from the Jews in the New City to their besieged Haganah in the Old City. The Jews attempted yet again to break through Bab al-Nabi Daoud, but failed suffering heavy casualties. At the Headquarters of the Haganah Jerusalem Brigade, the Jewish Commander, Shaltiel, and his staff had prepared a plan to break through the Old City walls at Bab al-Khalil (Jaffa Gate), while a diversion attack would be carried out by a regiment of the Harel Palmach Brigade commanded by Yitzhak Rabin. At that time, Rabin was at Latrun attempting to penetrate Jerusalem with a supply convoy, but when he was informed of the plan by his staff officer Itiel, he immediately opposed it.

Shaltiel was so confident of his plan, he prepared a flag to hoist on top of David's Tower.[13] However, when the operation was mounted as planned, the diversion attack by the Palmach succeeded in capturing an area at Mount Zion. However, the Jordan Arab Army was not deceived and although they engaged the attackers with mortar and artillery fire, they were aware of the movements taking place towards Bab al-Khalil. Thus when the main attack planned for the Jewish breakthrough at Bab al-Khalil was launched, the Jordanians and the Palestinian partisans were ready for it. When the assaulting Jewish troops approached Bab al-Khalil and were about 50 yards from it, the defenders opened fire at them with all their weapons, and as soon as their Commander was wounded the momentum of the Jewish attack petered out. Chaos prevailed among the Jews who suffered heavy casualties and soon started to withdraw. The attack failed miserably.

On 21 May, Aubaidat moved with one platoon and two sections commanded by Lt Mustafa Ibrahim to an area north of the Jewish quarter in order to narrow the siege against it. At that position he ordered Captain Barakat al-Ttrad al-Khraisha to command the sector, and gave him the task of engaging the Haganah with his Manko Jordanian Partisans Company and to capture whatever he could of the Jewish quarter. He then went back to Bab al-Nabi Daoud and led an attack on the Jewish quarter from the east. With the help of Fawzi al-Quttob's demolition platoon of al-Jihad al-Muqaddas, he was able to destroy one house and several shops, which made it possible for a small no-man's-land of open ground between him and the Haganah defending the Jewish quarter. During that attack Lt Nawaf al-Humoud, a courageous officer with great initiative, was wounded and taken to hospital. At midnight the Haganah and Palmach units at the Mount Zion area launched an attack at Bab al-Nabi Daoud to open a gap in the siege to relieve the Jewish quarter. During the fierce fighting, which developed into hand-to-hand combat, one of the defending Jordanians prayed with the religious call 'Allahu Akbar'. The whole platoon repeated the call while fighting, and their morale soared. Thereafter, the Jewish attackers suffered heavy casualties and withdrew.

On 22 May, the Security Council of the United Nations approved a resolution calling on all governments and authorities to abstain from any hostile military action in Palestine, and to order a ceasefire to become effective within 36 hours after midnight on 22 May. But like all previous resolutions, the call for a ceasefire was ignored by both sides.

By 23 May, the front-line troops of the 6th Regiment were exhausted after a complete week of almost sleepless nights and hard fighting. Captain Aubaidat redeployed his platoons and gave orders that the majority of his men should have ample rest and sleep. He also reduced unit activities to the minimum, but with alert observation. Since they were fresh when yet another Jewish attack was mounted against several areas of the walled city, the front-line troops repulsed the attackers.

The alleys and lanes in the centre of the Jewish quarter were dominated by the domes of the Synagogue and the hospital, which overlooked all the streets and houses in the adjacent areas of the Christian and Muslim quarters. From the synagogue and the hospital, Jewish marksmen and snipers of the Haganah fired continuously at anything that moved in the Arab area. Major al-Tel did his best to spare the synagogue, but the Haganah continued sniping and caused many casualties among the civilian Arab population. Finally, he warned the Jews through Pablo de Azcazarte, the Red Cross representative, that he would be compelled to open fire if the Jews continued to shoot from the synagogue. No reply came.

Captain Aubaidat led his men from the front and set them a good example himself. On 24 May, although still suffering from his wounds, he was determined to destroy a steel works building at the southern part of the Jewish quarter and adjacent to the city wall in order to uncover the main positions of the Haganah hidden from view by it. Al-Quttob prepared a large demolition bomb and carried it with his men away from the troops. While Aubaidat was holding an order group in the front line, a locally made Jewish bomb exploded near him, lightly wounding eight of his men. Under covering fire from another section, Aubaidat and al-Quttob, with a section of men and the demolition team of four from al-Jihad al-Muqaddas, advanced and demolished the steel works building, thus leaving the Jewish hospital and the synagogue exposed to direct fire from the south.

David Shaltiel ordered the two Palmach platoons who occupied Mount Zion to attack and break through Bab al-Nabi Daoud and connect with the Jewish quarter. Rabin lost his temper and said: 'Where are all the troops? Are the 80 exhausted Palmachniks I lent you the only force that the Jewish people can muster for the liberation of the capital?'

By 25 May, the 5th Infantry Company, commanded by Captain Muhammad Ishaq Hakuz, was sent from Ramallah to the 6th Regiment in the Old City. But after two days of fighting, during which its Commander was wounded, the company was withdrawn back to Ramallah and placed under command of the 3rd Brigade in reserve. Captain Adib al-Qasim al-Nwasrah was appointed as its Commander.

Captain Aubaidat had organised his troops in detachments rather than in platoons in accordance with the needs of each position and, at the same time, keeping some adequate reserve for immediate action. On the morning of 25 May, he ordered his troops to have another day of rest. At midnight on the same day, the Haganah and the Palmach attacked Bab al-Nabi Daoud yet again, but this time with covering fire from Mount Zion, as well as an attack at the same time by the Haganah in the Jewish quarter advancing towards the gate. A detachment of the Palmach was able to reach the gate and, using an incendiary bomb, they were able to set the northern tower on fire. The officer commanding the two sections in the tower left his post, went to see Aubaidat and reported that his men had been burnt. Then Aubaidat took the officer with him to visit the tower, only to find that the men were well and in high spirits. He immediately brought Lt Rustom Yahya to take his place and send the other officer (who remains nameless because he was the only officer to desert his post during the war) to the rear echelons.

On 26 May, al-Tel managed to bring a troop of Marmon-Herrington armoured cars, armed with two-pounder guns and Browning machine guns into the Old City and sent them to Aubaidat, who positioned two of them at Bab al-Nabi Daoud (covering the two towers) and the third at Bab al-Khalil (Jaffa Gate). Their orders were to engage the Haganah in desultory fire aimed at the Jewish quarter and the New City of Jerusalem. When firing commenced, Barakat al-Khraisha and his men of the Manko company of Jordanian partisans started the assault, advanced and rushed into the Jewish quarter. They captured a few houses and demolished others with the help of the demolition platoon of al-Jihad al-Muqaddas, which were supplied by high explosives from the 6th Regiment. Thereafter, the siege started to get closer to the heart of the Jewish quarter. During the same night the Palmach launched yet another attack on Bab al-Nabi Daoud, but were repulsed by a section of the 1st Security Company.

At dawn on 27 May, Captain Aubaidat launched an attack on the Jewish quarter from the north with Barakat al-Khraisha, the Commander of the Manko Jordanian partisans Company, and his men, and Lt Mustafa Ibrahim of 6th Regiment and his platoon. They managed to capture many strongholds of the Haganah defences and held them while getting ready to attack again. At that point Captain Barakat al-Khraisha was seriously wounded and evacuated to hospital. (He was later rewarded for his endeavours by rejoining the Jordan Arab Army as a regular officer with the rank of captain, which he held until he retired.) During the afternoon of that day, al-Tel went forward for the first time and visited his front line at Aubaidat's HQ. Captain Aubaidat was encouraged by his Commander's visit and in the conversation they had Aubaidat proved again how determined and courageous he was. His body covered with bandages, he pointed out his dispositions and gave al-Tel his appreciation of the situation. He concluded by promising al-Tel that he would end the battle for the Old City either with a Jewish surrender or with the destruction of the Jewish quarter. Major al-Tel disagreed with Aubaidat's assessment, and instead of giving him encouragement and moral support, he said that the Haganah would fight him for a month or more. To this Aubaidat replied: 'My assessment will be fulfilled, God willing, and tomorrow will uncover the result of our discussion.' Major al-Tel went back to his HQ at dusk.[14] During the same evening, Abdullah al-Tel reported to King Abdullah personally on the situation in the Old City. The King, who was continually informed of the progress of the battle in the Old City, said to al-Tel: 'I want you, Abdullah, to invite me to pray the Friday prayer tomorrow in Jerusalem.'[15]

Captain Aubaidat, who was later awarded a gallantry medal for his actions, which were over and above the call of duty, planned his final attack at the Jewish quarter with a diversionary attack from the south, and the main attack by three companies from the north. At dawn on 28 May, the diversionary attack started with supporting fire from the Mortar platoon and two Marmon-Herrington armoured cars. A few minutes later, a smoke screen was laid by the armoured cars giving the impression that the main attack was advancing from the south. When the Haganah thinned out from the north of the Jewish quarter, the main attack led by Aubaidat was launched at about 0600 hours. An hour of fierce hand-to-hand fighting followed from street to street, from alley to alley, from house to house, and in some areas, from room to room. By about 0730 hours, the defences of the Jewish quarter were narrowed to an area of about 200 square yards around the Nissan Bek Synagogue and Misgav Ladach Hospital. By 0830 hours, the Commander of the Haganah reported to his HQ by wireless: 'There is no possibility from a military point of view of holding out here.' Shaltiel urged them to hold out for another day, and promised to break through and save them. However, with the remaining 36 men of the Haganah and Palmach who were still able to fight, and with about 300 rounds of ammunition, permission was given by the Haganah Commander in the Jewish quarter to the rabbi to negotiate with the Jordan Arab Army and surrender.[16]

By about 0900 hours, white flags were raised by the Haganah over the Jewish Quarter in the Old City. Two Jewish rabbis with an officer in uniform appeared holding white flags. Captain Aubaidat ordered his men to cease fire. The very well disciplined Jordanian soldiers and, with some persuasion, the irregular partisans, obeyed immediately. Before he went to meet the Jewish delegation, Aubaidat made sure that no one would say a word against the Jews as he ushered them into his HQ. He then informed al-Tel of the Jewish offer to surrender. Yitzhak Rabin, who witnessed the scene from his observation point at Mount Zion, wrote in his memoirs:

> On the 28th I went up to Mount Zion, where I witnessed a shattering scene. A delegation was emerging from the Jewish quarter bearing white flags. I was horrified to learn that it consisted of rabbis and other residents on their way to hear the Legion's terms for their capitulation.[17]

On his second visit to the front since he came to Jerusalem, al-Tel, accompanied by Shaikh Mustafa al-Sibaai of the Muslim Brothers of Syria, Kamil Auraiqat, Dr Izzat Tannous, Dr Musa al-Husseini (who was hanged two years later for his role in King Abdullah's assassination) and Captain Fadhil Abdullah al-Rashid (who tried to persuade Aubaidat not to fight) went to meet the Jewish delegation. Captain Aubaidat left diplomacy to al-Tel and his accompanying delegation, and went back to his troops insisting on discipline, strict ceasefire, and an honourable and humane treatment of the prisoners of war who were about to surrender. By then, Aubaidat was his men's hero and was obeyed to the letter.

At the Armenian Monastery, al-Tel found the two rabbis responsible for the Old City; one of them was wounded in the face, so al-Tel made sure his wounds were treated before the negotiations were begun. The rabbi spoke in Arabic when he recounted how he had been sent by the inhabitants of the Jewish quarter and the armed men to discuss the surrender of the Jewish quarter. He also said that if al-Tel accepted this surrender in principle he would leave his companion with him, return to the quarter and bring the military delegation for negotiations. Major al-Tel agreed and 15 minutes later the Jewish officers arrived with the mayor of the quarter, Mordechai von Gartin. The Haganah officer, Moshe Roznik, handed over his gun to al-Tel. After a short discussion the following terms were agreed and a document to their effect was signed by both sides.

> In accordance with the request of the Jews of the Old City of Jerusalem for surrender, the first Party presented the conditions and the second Party accepted them:
>
> - to lay down arms and hand them over to the first Party
> - take all the men fighters as prisoners of war
> - allow old men, women and children and whoever's wounds are serious to go to the Jewish quarters in New Jerusalem through the Red Cross
> - the first Party will guarantee the protection of life for all the surrendering Jews
> - the Jordan Arab Army will occupy the Jewish quarter of the Old City of Jerusalem
>
> 28/5/1948.
> First Party: Abdullah al-Tel
> Second Party: Moshe Roznik

In order to complete the surrender before nightfall, al-Tel ordered a curfew in the Old City. He asked the mayor and Roznik to gather all the Jews in the Ashkenazi Yard in the middle of the quarter. He surrounded that area with troops who had strict orders to prevent any unauthorised person from coming close to the area. The 1,500 Jews of the Jewish quarter assembled; all weapons were laid down and submitted to the officers of the 6th Regiment. Then al-Tel asked his officers – comissioned and non-commissioned – who were detailed to classify the prisoner, to behave in the manner expected of them. Thus, they separated younger men from women, children and old men, and the wounded men from those who were fit to fight. The Jews, who were terrified at the beginning of the proceedings, started to relax when men of the 6th Regiment brought them water and cigarettes, and paid special attention to the children. When that was completed, al-Tel went to the Misgav Ladach Hospital, where he talked to doctors and visited the wounded, assuring them of the most humane treatment. He then ordered their transfer to the Armenian Monastery where better conditions could be provided. At that stage of the proceedings, General Glubb, who two weeks earlier had endeavoured not to fight in Jerusalem, arrived at the scene. He wrote:

> I visited the Old City shortly after the surrender. The prisoners had been moved to a large modern building, just beyond the limits of the Jewish quarter. On the first floor of this building, many large rooms were occupied by them, while others sat or lay in the wide stone corridors. Men, women and children lay side by side, most of them looking pale and tired. A few had limbs bandaged owing to minor wounds. Arab orderlies and soldiers of the Arab Legion moved here and there through the crowd of Jews, speaking a word, giving a drink of water or talking among themselves.
>
> As I came up the passage, the soldiers smilingly came to attention with a clatter of weapons. Two or three Jews came forward and shook hands. None of them had any complaints to make. A few attempted to produce documents testifying to their good characters in the days of the British Mandate.
>
> The Haganah prisoners and young Jews of military age were transferred to a prisoner of war camp east of the Jordan. The old men, women and children were sent across the lines to the Jewish side under the supervision of the Red Cross. As the sad little caravan straggled through the narrow alley-ways of Old Jerusalem, Arab Legion soldiers were seen to be helping along the sick and the old women, and carrying their little bundles of possessions.

'Well, that is what I call chivalry,' exclaimed a European Press
correspondent, as he watched the convoy hobble past.
It was our answer to Dair Yasin.[18]

Lt Salih al-Sharaa and I were sent from Brigade HQ to observe the process
of the surrender in its final stages. I remember with great pride all the
humanity, discipline and chivalry with which the officers and men of the
6th Regiment treated the prisoners of war and the Jewish civilians, men,
women and children. At that point I remembered the speech given by
Caliph Abu Bakr al-Siddiq to the Muslim Army, commanded by Usamah,
which was on its way to Syria. As a pupil I learned the speech by heart as
part of my religious education:

> Do not betray, do not deceive, do not bludgeon and maim, do not
> kill a child, nor a woman, nor an old man, do not break palm trees,
> do not burn, do not cut a fruit tree, do not slaughter a sheep or a
> cow or a camel except to eat.
>
> If you come across communities who have consecrated them-
> selves to the shrines [churches], leave them and that to which they
> consecrated themselves.

On 29 May, Pablo de Azcazrte visited the hospital in the Jewish quarter.
He was told by Dr Laufer, its Jewish director:

> You will remember my fear and mistrust that it was decided last
> night to leave the hospital under the protection of the Arab Legion.
> Well, now I want to tell you that the Arab Legion has behaved as well
> as the best disciplined force of any European army; I must say that I
> have served as a doctor first in the Austrian Army and afterwards
> in the British. Thanks to the soldiers of the Arab Legion and their
> magnificent behaviour, we have been able to save our wounded
> from the fire that was threatening the hospital.[19]

After the surrender of the Jewish quarter, the 6th Regiment started to
reorganise the forces under its command. When it took over command
from the Liberation Army and al-Jihad al-Muqaddas units in Jerusalem
on 18 May, the left flank of its command included the areas of al-Nabi
Daoud, al-Thouri, Sur Bahir, Bethlehem, Bait Safafa, al-Malihah and
Ain Karim. When the Egyptian forces reached Bethlehem, troops of the
Jordanian Arab Army, the Liberation Army and al-Jihad al-Muqaddas

were ordered to cooperate with the Egyptian command. However, al-Thouri and al-Nabi Daoud remained under command of the 6th Regiment.

The Manko Company (about 120 men) and the al-Hussein company (about 100 men), commanded by Captain Othman Badran, were pulled out of the Old City and al-Tur, and were deployed around Mount Scopus, the Hadassah Hospital and the Hebrew University to prevent the Jews from attacking from the rear of the 3rd Regiment, which had entered Jerusalem on 22 May as well as the 6th Regiment in the Old City.

At al-Nabi Daoud, the Haganah had occupied the top of the hill, where they could overlook many of the Old City and New City quarters. The Eastern slope of the hill mid-way between the top and the foot of the hill was still occupied by Palestinian partisans. The 6th Regiment sent a platoon to the Franciscan monastery at that point and occupied it with permission from the bishop. Their mission was to prevent the Jews from attacking Silwan on the left flank of the regiment.

At al-Thouri, another platoon of Jordanian Bedouin partisans, commanded by Shaikh Yousef ibn Adwan, was sent to reinforce the positions of its defenders near the foot of the hill in a line of Arab houses. Between al-Nabi Daoud and al-Thury was the deep Wadi al-Rababah, through which the Jews could infiltrate to Ras al-Aamoud or Silwan. A detachment of al-Jihad al-Muqaddas was deployed in the Wadi as an ambush.

Meanwhile, since 15 May, the 12th Infantry Company of 6th Regiment, commanded by Captain Hikmat Mihyar, had remained in the Hebron sector. Its Platoon Commanders were Captain Qaseem Muhammad and Lt Qasim al-Nassir. Under command of 12th Company were two Jordanian partisan companies, as listed below.

- The Abu Aubaidah Company of the Jordanian Muslim Brothers, commanded by Abd al-Latif Abu Qourah, with Mamdouh al-Sarayrah, a former cadet officer, and Mashhur Hasan Haymour, a former Lieutenant – both of the Jordan Arab Army.
- The Usamah ibn Zaid Company, Jordanian partisans commanded by Arabi Jamil with Abu Abduh Faris and Muhammad al-Shalati.

The total strength of the Jordanian regular and irregular troops in the south sector of Jerusalem as well as Hebron was about 150 regulars and 250 partisans.

The battle for the New City of Jerusalem

Victory in the battle of the Jewish quarter in the Old City of Jerusalem was not that of the 6th Regiment alone, for were it not for the attacks mounted by the composite force of the 2nd Regiment and two infantry companies of the 4th Brigade on 19 May as well as the attack mounted by the 3rd Regiment on 22 May, the 6th Regiment would not have been able even to hold the Old City – let alone capture the Jewish quarter. These attacks, and the successive battles that followed in the New City of Jerusalem from 19 May until 30 May, compelled the Jews to divert the majority of their units in Jerusalem to defend their positions from Nôtre Dame to Shuafat Hill – a front of about one mile in a built-up area, which was vital to the defence of Jerusalem. The officers and men of the 2nd and 3rd Regiments and the infantry companies, who gave up their lives during these battles, died for the capture of the Jewish quarter too. In his book, *Karithat Filistin*, al-Tel ignored the role of these regiments and, to a certain extent, belittled their major and very important role in diverting the main Jewish efforts and the largest part of the Jewish forces to defend the New City against the 2nd and 3rd Regiments, while Aubaidat achieved his victory in the Old City. I know well how much Aubaidat appreciated that contribution, which made his mission possible. However, the following facts speak for themselves.

Immediately after General Glubb's visit to the 1st Division on 17 May, the 5th Infantry Company mounted an attack and captured the Jewish settlement of Atarot north of Jerusalem, and the 9th Infantry Company occupied the Jewish settlement of al-Nabi Yaqoub which it found deserted. On the following day, Glubb visited the Division HQ and remained reluctant to commit the Jordan Arab Army to fighting in the built-up area of new Jerusalem for fear of high casualties. During the meeting, Munir Abu Fadhil, a partisan Commander in the north of Jerusalem, came to the Division HQ and informed Sadiq al-Sharaa that the defence situation in the city was very critical: unless the Army attacked and recaptured Shaikh Jarrah and the Damascus Gate to relieve the pressure on the Old City it would fall in a day or two, added to which the Palmach had broken through Bab al-Nabi Daoud and maintained contact with the Jewish quarter adjacent to al Haram al-Sharif. He also told him that a delegation from Jerusalem went to Amman to call upon the King to save Jerusalem.[20] At the same time, Abu al-Huda sent a telegram to General Glubb informing him that the King commanded that the Jordan Arab Army must enter Jerusalem immediately. But Glubb remained reluctant and went back to Amman. On the morning of 18 May, General Glubb was summoned for an audience with King Abdullah at the Royal Palace. He found the King extremely anxious regarding the situation in Jerusalem. The meeting between King Abdullah, who was a most devout Muslim, and General Glubb, who was a most devout Christian, was emotional and historic. Glubb wrote of the meeting:

> 'I conjure you by God to tell me the truth,' he said. 'Can we hold Jerusalem, or will the Jews take it?'
> 'If God wills, they will never take it, Sir,' I answered.
> 'I want you to promise me,' the King went on, 'that if you ever think the Jews will take Jerusalem, you will tell me. I will not live to see them in the Holy Places. I will go there myself and die on the walls of the city.'
> 'If God wills, that will not happen,' I said.[21]

Late that same afternoon, Glubb ordered the 1st Division to attack Shaikh Jarrah, and to advance and capture Damascus Gate at dawn on 19 May. Because of the urgency of the order and the lack of time to bring in the divisional reserve – the 3rd Regiment from Nablus – General Lash decided to use part of the 2nd Regiment for the attack. Major R. Slade, Commander of the 2nd Regiment, was called to the Division HQ and ordered to set aside his intention to attack Radar Hill north-west of Jerusalem, and instead to attack and capture Shaikh Jarrah and Damascus Gate at 0345 hours on 19 May. Major Slade wrote to General Lunt many years later:

> The chances of it getting off the ground at 0345 hours were minimal. I had to return to my regiment, assemble the troops, give an order to march, get to Shuafat (a considerable distance) in the dark and unknown to us. I have been told that the difficulties were understood, but King Abdullah had insisted we should do this.[22]

During the first two hours of 19 May, the units from the 2nd Regiment and 4th Brigade (see Table 4.2) regrouped to form the taskforce and moved to the assembly area around the airstrip at Qalandiyah. In order to have a reserve force for the operation, orders were given to the 1st Brigade to move units of the 1st and 3rd Infantry Regiments to Divisional HQ at the Baittin area (see Table 4.3).

TABLE 4.2
Taskforce formed from 2nd Regiment and 4th Brigade

The 2nd Regiment:
- 1st Company from the village of Qibiyah, commanded by Lt Aabattah Eid.
- 3rd Company from the village of Biddu, commanded by Lt Refaifan Khalid al-Khraisha.
- Armoured Car Squadron from Biddu, commanded by Lt Hamdan al-Subaih al-Bliwi.
- Two sections of 3-inch mortars.
- Medium machine gun platoon.
- Two sections of six-pounder anti-tank guns.

The 4th Brigade Companies (commanded by Captain Abd al-Halim al-Sakit):
- 9th Infantry Company, commanded by Captain Sulaiman Masaud.
- 2nd Security Company, commanded by Captain Muhammad Khalaf al-Omari.
- Two platoons of 4th Company, commanded by Ahmad al-Fayadh.
- 2nd Artillery Battery, commanded by Captain Muhammad al-Maaytah.

TABLE 4.3
The reserve force

- 3rd Infantry Company of the 1st Regiment, commanded by Lt Awad Hamid.
- Armoured Car Squadron of the 3rd Regiment, commanded by Lt Zaal Ruhayil.
- Two sections of 3-inch mortars.
- Two sections of six-pounder anti-tank guns.

A few minutes after 0200 hours, Major Slade held an order group of the taskforce unit Commanders at Qalandiyah which asserted the following:

Intention
1st Division will enter Jerusalem at 0345 hours on 19 May with a view to:

- defending the Old City so it remains intact
- clearing the Arab Quarter from Shaikh Jarrah to Damascus Gate.

Method

The attack will be made in two phases:

- Phase I:
1. 8th Infantry Company will enter the Old City under direct command of 6th Regiment at 0345 hours.
2. 6th Infantry Company will occupy al-Tur.
3. Composite force will capture the Shaikh Jarrah Quarter.

- Phase II:
   One company of 5th Regiment will advance to the Damascus Gate and make contact with the 6th Regiment.[23]

Major R. Young was appointed to 2nd Command for the operation, but regretted that he could not take part on the basis that he was a British Army officer and limited by his contract with the Jordanian Army. Lt Ali Abu Nowar, Staff Captain of 3rd Brigade, volunteered for the post and was attached for the operation.

At 0345 hours on 19 May, the Armoured Car Squadron crossed the start line at the village of Shuafat. At that point the artillery battery, directed by Captain al-Maaitah, with himself as Observation Point (OP), opened fire at selected targets in Shaikh Jarrah Quarter, the Police Fort, Mea Shearim and Sanhedriya. Soon after, the mortar platoon joined in the shelling, while the armoured cars advanced to Shuafat Ridge. Immediately after they crossed the ridge and were going down a deep slope towards the junction of the Police Fort at Shaikh Jarrah, they came under heavy mortar fire from the Police Fort, which was occupied by two companies of the Irgun. Major Slade wrote to General Lunt:

> On our right flank there was a conglomeration of buildings, the Police School. This was occupied by, I was told, the IZL (Irgun) who were a particularly nasty collection, and Sanhedriya suburb on their right; from Mount Scopus, Hadassah Hospital and the Hebrew University on the left; and from Mea Shearim in the front. Covering fire from the mortar platoon and the six-pounder guns who came to Shuafat ridge soon after daylight, as well as artillery support, reduced the Israeli counter fire.[24]

It soon became obvious that, under the circumstances, no regular soldier would have undertaken voluntarily to carry out that operation. The five regiments of the Jordan Army and the infantry companies were already scattered over an area of about 2,000 square kilometres. In proper military terms, to redeploy the forces needed for the operation would have meant withdrawing nearly two of the five regiments, and would have taken at least two or three days to plan, assemble the troops, carry out the reconnaissance required, issue orders and start the attack, by which time the whole of Jerusalem, including the Old City, would have been captured by the Jews. Moreover, the taskforce consisted of about 300 officers and men advancing on a city that was defended by at least 4,000 Jewish officers and men, plus a population of about 90,000 Jews.

Furthermore, for weeks the Jews had been erecting concrete defences in their part of the New City. All the streets leading to it from the Arab part had been closed by concrete walls and road blocks, dragon teeth and concrete pillboxes, and machine gun and PIAT emplacements, trenches and barbed wire covered every approach. Very little was done in the Arab part of the city, and had it not been for the 6th Regiment and its offensive in the Old City, it would have fallen to the Jews long before the operation was even ordered.

Thus, as the operation proceeded while the situation was at its most critical, and as the Armoured Car Squadron reached the beginning of the built-up area just before the 'S' bend, the leading armoured car was held up by a concrete road block of dragon teeth. That being destroyed by six-pounder and two-pounder fire, the advance continued under very heavy machine gun and mortar fire only to find a further massive concrete road block round the 'S' bend on the edge of Wadi al-Jawz. Major Slade, who was with the leading troop of armoured cars, dismounted and went forward to examine the road block when mortar fire was directed at it. At about 0800 hours he was wounded by mortar shrapnel. Just before he was evacuated to the Field Dressing Station in Ramallah, he told Lt Ali Abu Nowar (who was close by): 'Please leave me here. I would like to die in Jerusalem.'

Ali Abu Nowar, who was impressed by his courage and leadership, insisted: 'You will certainly come back soon; you will be alright.'

He then asked Major Muhammad al-Maaitah to take over command, but al-Maaitah insisted he was going to continue directing the artillery fire and would obey Ali as Commander. He also insisted that it was wrong to change command while the attack was in progress. Ali asked

Lt Haidar Mustafa to bring in one of his six-pounder guns and destroy the dragon teeth, which Haidar and his men did from a range of about 30 metres.[25]

The taskforce, whose mission was to advance down the Ramallah–Jerusalem road, fight its way through the Arab residential quarter of al-Musrarah to the Old City and establish contact with its defenders, attempted to continue with the advance. Immediately on their right, about 300 metres away, was the Jewish quarter of Mea Sherim. The advance from Shaikh Jarrah along the 'S' bend, east to the Old City, was on a lateral axis across the front of a built-up area of houses, strongly manned and defended by the Jewish forces. The Shaikh Jarrah quarter was separated from al-Musrarah by an open space about 300 metres wide, which was commanded by fire from Mea Sherim at a range of about 250 metres. The armoured cars had to cross the space under heavy fire and immediately after it would come under fire from al-Musrarah.

By about 1330 hours, two troops of armoured cars managed one after the other to cross the hell-fire through the open space to reach the Damascus Gate of the Old City, where they established contact with the 6th Regiment in the Old City. A Jewish writer, who was in Jerusalem at the time, described the attack as follows.

> The Legion launched the attack with four batteries of heavy guns, smaller artillery units, two infantry regiments, and large units of tanks and armoured cars. After the artillery barrage, they advanced in massed strength, tanks in the lead.[26]

Just two troops of armoured cars were able to create that impression for this writer. However, Ali Abu Nowar took over command of the composite force. A few minutes later, al-Maaitah was wounded. Ali dressed his wound and was about to take him to hospital, but al-Maaitah refused and continued to direct the artillery fire. After fierce fighting from house to house in Shaikh Jarrah, all the Arab houses in the area were captured from the Haganah who withdrew through al-Musrarah. At that stage of the battle, the Jewish force at the Hadassah Hospital and the Hebrew University opened fire at the rear of the attacking taskforce, inflicting many casualties on the Jordanian infantry – including Lt Sanad Nasser of the 2nd Regiment. Orders had been given not to engage these positions because of their humanitarian nature. However, after their aggression there was no justification for avoiding an engagement against them. Under very heavy fire from Hadassah, Lt Haidar Mustafa, the Commander of the anti-tank troop of the 2nd Regiment, brought one of his six-pounder guns to an open area between the Police Fort and al-Nashashibi House, and started to engage Sanhedriya and the Police Fort as well as the Hadassah and Hebrew University with direct fire. He was able to silence all the Jewish positions at the latter.[27]

General Lash, who observed the battle from Shuafat Ridge, went back to his HQ and ordered Major Buchanan, Second-in-Command of the 2nd Regiment, to take over command of the taskforce and continue with the advance to the Damascus Gate. As soon as Buchanan was able to assess the current situation, he reported to Lash. He then assembled his order group: Muhammad al-Maaitah, Sulaiman Masaud, Muhammad Khalaf al-Omari, Hamdan Subaih, Ali Abu Nowar and Adib Omar. As he started to give his orders a mortar bomb exploded a few yards away from the group. Buchanan was wounded in his chest and was immediately taken to hospital. Two hours later, Lash sent the Reserve Armoured Car Squadron, commanded by Zaal Ruhayil, to the scene with Captain Sadiq al-Sharaa. Al-Sharaa went forward to meet Buchanan, but instead found Ali Abu Nowar and Haidar Mustafa in the middle of Shaikh Jarrah Quarter. They reported to him that Buchanan was wounded and had been taken to hospital. Lash ordered al-Sharaa to take over command.

Captain al-Sharaa immediately redeployed the taskforce, leaving Awad Hamid and his company on Shuafat Ridge. With the armoured cars unable to see well at night, he withdrew them back to an area between Shuafat Ridge and the junction to the Police Fort, where he was able to conceal them and at the same time gave them a good field of fire against the Jewish forces. He sent one troop of armoured cars to the left of al-Nashashibi House to engage Mount Scopus, another to face Mea Shearim and Saad wa Said, and a third troop in depth and opposite the Police Fort. An all-round defence of the Shaikh Jarrah Quarter was established, with the 9th Infantry and 2nd Security companies of the 4th Brigade in reserve at Shuafat Ridge and Shuafat village.

Meanwhile, the Jewish forces continued to hold the Police Fort from where they directed their fire at the 2nd Regiment companies at Shaikh Jarrah. During the afternoon, al-Sharaa planned an attack on the Fort which would take place that night. At 2100 hours, the 2nd Security

Company, commanded by Muhammad Khalaf al-Omari, attacked the Police Fort. During the fierce close combat that followed, al-Omari and his men soon gained the upper hand. After many casualties suffered by both sides, the Jewish force withdrew, and the 2nd Security company organised and prepared their defensive positions in and around the Police Fort making use of the Jewish positions. Thus Phase I of the operation was completed.

By the morning of 20 May, the taskforce was well dug in and established its defensive positions in and around the Police Fort, al-Nashashibi House (which overlooked the 'S' bend leading to Musrarah and Shaikh Jarrah Mosque) and the culvert over the Wadi. The approaches to Wadi al-Jawz were covered. Mount Scopus, the Hadassah Hospital and Hebrew University were all isolated from the New City on the road to Anata, and from Wadi al-Jawz. Captains al-Sharaa and al-Maaitah inspected every position travelling in the OP armoured GMC car. While on the roof of the Police Fort, al-Maaitah shot a Haganah soldier attempting to reach the roof-top of a building in the new front line. Thereafter, al-Maaitah went back to his OP position and directed his twenty-five-pounder field guns on Mea Shearim and Sanhedriya with a slow and desultory shelling, taking into account the shortage of ammunition. During the afternoon his position was located by the enemy, and during the counter mortar fire at his OP post he was wounded again in his arm and evacuated to the Field Dressing Station at Baituniya near Ramallah.[28] Sadiq was also nearly killed that afternoon when he was travelling in his jeep around the various positions. A mortar bomb exploded directly in front of his jeep, killing one of his men and wounding his driver and two others. In spite of his wounds the driver, Awadh Yousef, insisted on taking the other two wounded to hospital.

During the night of 20/21 May, two companies from the Harel Brigade carried out a counter-attack on the Police Fort. They advanced under cover of very heavy mortar and machine gun fire until they reached the outer barbed wire. Until then, the 2nd Security Company held their fire, and as soon as the attackers attempted to penetrate the perimeter they opened fire with all their weapons. Supported by an artillery troop, they inflicted heavy casualties on the attackers. The Harel Palmach Brigade withdrew, taking their casualties with them.

On 21 May, Lt Muhammad Najib Barakat, from the artillery battery, reported to Captain al-Sharaa's HQ to take his position as gunner

OP for the taskforce. As soon as he had his orders, he left for his allocated position near al-Nashashibi House. Instead of stopping at the armoured cars' position he went through the 'S' bend to the Shaikh Jarrah culvert where his GMC armoured car was shot at and destroyed by a Jewish PIAT rocket. Muhammad Najib, his driver, and his wireless operator were killed. Zaal Ruhayil, who saw what was happening, rushed in his armoured car shooting as he went to help Muhammad Najib. When he found that Najib and his crew were dead, he attempted to tow the destroyed GMC. His armoured car, too, was hit by a PIAT rocket and was compelled to withdraw with the only surviving soldier from his crew. Sergeant Major Salim Shubaikan, who was Zaal's second-in-command, attempted to save Zaal thinking that he needed help. But as soon as he arrived at the scene his armoured car, too, was hit and caught fire. He managed to help down a wounded soldier and, with help from his driver, he managed to withdraw. On seeing this situation, al-Sharaa sent a fighting patrol to the scene of the fighting and managed to recover the bodies of the three dead soldiers. During that afternoon the 13th Infantry Company was attached to the taskforce and positioned in and around al-Nashashibi House.

Meanwhile, since 15 May, the Iraqi Brigade, which moved to their allocated sector across the Jordan, were engaged by the Jewish force at Gesher Police Fort near Majamaa Bridge. Following a series of bitter and fierce battles, which lasted five days until 20 May, they were unable to capture Kawkab al-Hawa, a high mountain across the River Jordan. They decided to withdraw to the south and cross the river from Damya Bridge south of Majamaa Bridge. On 21 May, while the battle for Jerusalem was in its critical phase, it was decided to move the 3rd Regiment to Qalandiyah in order to take over the implementation of the unfinished Phase II of the taskforce operation in Jerusalem – the thrust from Shaikh Jarrah to Damascus Gate. The Iraqi Brigade was ordered to take over the Nablus sector defended by the 1st Brigade, and to move the latter to take over the Jerusalem sector.

On the morning of 21 May, the 3rd Regiment moved from Nablus to the Jerusalem sector. At noon they halted at Jifna and had a hot meal. The men were able to rest, while their officers were given more orders. At dusk, the regiment moved to Jerusalem without lights, and deployed in the area between Bait Hanina and Shuafat villages. Their vehicles moved to Qalandiyah airstrip, where the men had a good few hours' sleep. Meanwhile, in order to give the Jews the impression that there was no change in its position, deceptive and fighting patrols were sent along the Nablus sector front line of the 1st Regiment. In certain areas, small convoys with their lights on were dispatched randomly to give the impression that the front was still occupied and carried out as part of the deception plan.

The Iraqi Command Order Group, consisting of Brigadier Rafiq Aarif, Lt Colonels Ghazi al-Daghistani and Omar Ali, arrived at 1st Brigade HQ in the morning. After a short meeting with Colonel D. Goldie, the Brigade Commander, they left for the front for reconnaissance. While on their way to their vehicles, Rafiq Aarif asked me: 'Why are you here?' Salih al-Sharaa, nearby, could not resist saying: 'Waiting for you, Sir.' Rafiq Aarif was very polite when he said: 'zain' ('good').

Meanwhile, at 1700 hours, Lash commanded al-Sharaa to hand over his command to Major Abd al-Halim al-Sakit and report to the Division HQ. Ali Abu Nowar was also ordered back to 3rd Brigade HQ.

The situation during the night of 21/22 May was as critical as it could be for the Jordanian Arab Army. The Division was holding a front from north of Nablus to the south of Jerusalem, with four regiments – 2nd, 3rd, 4th and 6th – lopsided in the Jerusalem Latrun sector, facing three Haganah and one Palmach brigades; and the 1st Regiment was holding the whole of the Nablus sector from the north of Nablus to the south of Qalqiliyah on its own without artillery or reserve, and facing three Haganah and one Palmach brigade. The staff at 1st Brigade HQ and the officers and men of the 1st Regiment spent a sleepless night while preparing to move to Jerusalem on the following day and watching enemy movements in the front. Every shot fired, every car light, every small convoy, everything that moved was reported back to Brigade HQ and marked on the situation map. The Iraqi Brigade arrived at Nablus at dawn on 22 May, and started to deploy their units taking over from the 1st Regiment. When the takeover was completed, 1st Brigade HQ and the rest of the 1st Regiment were on their way to Jerusalem, extremely keen to fight.

Meanwhile, on 21 May, Lt Zaal Ruhayil and what was left of his armoured squadron, withdrew from Shaikh Jarrah and joined their 3rd Regiment at Qalandiyah. The artillery battery attached to 1st Brigade was placed in support of 3rd Regiment at an area near Bait Hanina. Brigadier Lash commanded Lt Colonel William Newman, an Australian seconded from the British Army, who commanded the 3rd Regiment, to advance into Jerusalem and capture the huge building of Nôtre Dame de France, adjacent to the Old City wall, the Barclays Bank building and the Italian Hospital. All these buildings dominated all approaches to them from the north where the 3rd Regiment was supposed to advance through al-Musrarah and Saad wa Said to the Damascus Gate. The vast majority of the officers and men of the 3rd Regiment were Bedouins who were not experienced in fighting in built-up areas. The Second in Command of the regiment was Major Hankin-Tervin, a former Palestine police officer with no military experience. The training officer of the regiment was Captain Patrick Grey and, although he had some experience in military affairs, most of his service was in the RAF Armoured Car Regiment. No reconnaissance was carried out and orders were given by the use of maps.

At 0350 hours on 22 May, the 3rd Regiment moved from their assembly area where they had spent the night to Shuafat with the Armoured Car Squadron in the lead, followed by the 4th Company, the 3rd Company, the regiment's tactical HQ and the 2nd Company. They crossed the start line at Shuafat Ridge at 0430 hours, at the same time as the artillery battery opened fire at selected targets. The regiment advanced down the hill from Shuafat Ridge to Shaikh Jarrah, while the artillery continued with desultory fire thereafter. As soon as the regiment reached the 'S' bend, to the east and below al-Nashashibi House, all hell broke loose from Mea Shearim and Sanhedriya, as well as from Hadassah, when the Jewish forces opened fire with all their weapons, rifles, machine guns, mortars and artillery at the advancing Jordanian troops. At the east end of the 'S' bend, Jewish PIAT rocket launchers were fired at point-blank range. Lieutenant Zaal Irhayil and his armoured cars, who were in the area a few days before, took their previous positions (which they held during the attack of the taskforce during Phase I) and started to shoot at the Jewish positions. Meanwhile, the 4th Company, commanded by Lt Ghazi al-Harbi, advanced through al-Musrarah to capture the Barclays Bank building. The mortar platoon of the 3rd Regiment took their position near al-Nashashibi house and went into action. All hell broke loose again from Sanhedriya and Mea Shearim, when the Haganah opened fire with all their weapons at the advancing company. The company suffered many casualties, and was compelled to swerve to the left and advance on the main road towards the Nussaibah and YMCA buildings. The Jews started to withdraw from the Arab houses they had occupied in the area, and shortly afterwards the 4th company cleared and occupied them.

Thereafter, it seemed as if the Regiment was lost in the hail of bullets and mortar bombs directed from everywhere to anywhere; Lt Colonel Bill Newman and his tactical HQ were bogged down at al-Nashashibi House, under fire, while endeavouring to find out where his companies were in a city that was, by then, clouded with smoke and dust. It was as late as noon when he received a message from Ghazi al-Harbi which stated that his 4th Company had reached the walls of the Old City at the Damascus Gate. There was no news of the 2nd and 3rd Companies. Newman could no longer stay put and decided to move forward with his tactical HQ escorted by a troop of armoured cars. Under fire, they crossed the open space between the 'S' bend and Shaikh Jarrah culvert to the edge of Saad wa Said and thence to the Damascus Gate where they occupied a few houses opposite the British Consulate right in the front line. Soon after, the 2nd and 3rd companies were located and guides were sent to lead them to their new positions.

From their new positions, the 4th Company was able to support the 3rd Company's advance towards the Damascus Gate. The 3rd Company, commanded by Lt Eid Adailim, passed through to the Damascus Gate supported by mortar fire and a troop of three Marmon-Herrington armoured cars. They occupied the houses across the road from the Damascus Gate south of the British Consulate building, thence turned to the right in the direction of Nôtre Dame. This was a huge building in the style of an old fortress with many loopholes and windows overlooking the open road and slope to the Damascus Gate, where the attack started. The 3rd Company advanced under very heavy fire from Nôtre Dame and the buildings located to the west where the area was strongly defended by the Jewish forces. In spite of the heavy casualties suffered by the company, the men continued to fight their way through to the building. However, as they were about to enter the northern wall, Lt Adailim, who was leading from the front, was killed during the hand-to-hand fighting that followed. Sergeant Major Flaiyih Matir, his Second in Command, took over but soon realised that the company could not achieve its objective. He was commanded to withdraw to a few small buildings close to Nôtre

Dame and continue to engage the enemy with fire. During the night he withdrew further to the buildings south of the Damascus Gate opposite the British Consulate.

The 2nd Company, commanded by Lt Muhammad Nauman (who had lost his way in the city), advanced from the rear and north of Damascus Gate to an area adjacent to Bab al-Sahirah where they took defensive positions. Thus, by the end of 22 May, the 3rd Regiment was in Jerusalem holding a front from Shaikh Jarrah culvert at the end of the 'S' bend, along the road to al-Musrarah to Damascus Gate. During the night many casualties of the regiment were evacuated to the Field Dressing Station near Ramallah.

Meanwhile, 1st Brigade HQ arrived at an area three kilometres west of Anata, and the Brigade Commander took over command of the forces in Jerusalem. The 1st Regiment arrived at Biddu and took over the al-Nabi Samuel, Bait Surik and Bait Iksa area from the 2nd Regiment. As soon as the 3rd Regiment occupied their defensive positions in the New City, the companies and supporting weapons of the 2nd Regiment regrouped at an area near Yalo and reverted back to under command of the 3rd Brigade.

At dawn on 23 May, Colonel Goldie, the Commander of the 1st Brigade, went to visit the HQ of the 3rd Regiment, still at a building opposite the British Consulate near the Damascus Gate despite the British Consul General's objection to their presence close to him and his request for them to move. Colonel Goldie travelled in his GMC command car with the Brigade Staff Captain, myself, manning the Bren light machine gun in its turret. As they approached the 'S' bend from al-Nashishibi House they were shot at by a machine gun from their right. The sound of the bullets hitting the turret was peculiar to say the least. I immediately felt my heart beating faster and my mouth go dry. It was the first time I had ever been shot at in anger, although I had instructed hundreds of commissioned and non-commissioned officers on battle inoculation. Colonel Goldie, who was decorated with DSO and MC during the Second World War, was laughing when he shouted: 'Are you alright Maan?' I did not answer, fearing that my commanding officer would detect my dry mouth. By then, the GMC had crossed the 'S' bend and was approaching the culvert when a rocket whistled by above the turret. I crossed the turret to face the direction the rocket had come from and opened fire with the Bren light machine gun. I kept firing until the magazine was empty. By that time, the GMC was covered from the right by the buildings where the 4th Company of the 3rd Regiment was located. From that point, I recovered enough to answer: 'I am all right, Sir.' I learnt later that the spot where they were fired at was where Muhammad Najib Barakat was killed. That was a real battle inoculation.

The meeting with Lt Colonel Newman and Major Hankin-Tervin, his Second in Command, was mainly concerned with the second attack on Nôtre Dame, as well as replacement for the heavy casualties suffered by the regiment and the replenishment of ammunition. All the support needed was provided by Brigade HQ on the same day and the 3rd Regiment was ready to attack and capture their objectives. Glubb later wrote:

> The attack began at 12 noon, supported by two six-pounder anti-tank guns and four three-inch mortars. The noise was soon deafening once more, but a pea-shooter would have been as effective as a six-pounder against the walls of Nôtre Dame. The Holy Catholic Church seemed to have been built for eternity.
>
> The infantry made slow progress through the narrow streets and houses, towards the towering walls of the monastery. Brick walls, little back gardens and a rabbit warren of streets and buildings were surroundings to which the Bedouins were unaccustomed. Some of the houses were occupied and had to be cleared of the enemy room by room. Five men claiming to be Russian Christians were found crouching in one house; they were captured and sent back. This incident speaks highly of the self-control of the soldiers, for the Russians were found in the house from the windows of which Eid Adailim had been shot the day before.
>
> As they drew nearer to the walls of Nôtre Dame, the infantry came under enfilade fire from the Italian Hospital, another large block of buildings about three hundreds yards to the north. Fire was also being directed at them not only from Nôtre Dame, but also from the roof of the French Hospital behind it. Our own infantry was already too close beneath the walls of the monastery to allow for any shelling by mortars or artillery to support them. The action continued indecisively throughout the afternoon and night. At seven o'clock on the morning on 24 May, a report was received that 4 Company were in Nôtre Dame. They had indeed entered the grounds of the monastery, but immediately came under heavy fire from the windows of other wings of this great block of buildings. At the same time, a party of Arab irregulars, who were occupying a

house to the right rear of the regiment, saw figures moving in the garden of the monastery and opened a heavy fire on our leading infantry.

In spite of this double fire, however, the infantry clung to the garden, and at nine o'clock, ten men actually got into the buildings, found themselves cut off and nearly surrounded, and were obliged to fight their way back to their comrades in the garden. By five o'clock on the afternoon of 24 May, the casualty situation was serious. Of the two hundred infantry who had set out to attack Nôtre Dame at noon on 23 May, nearly half were either killed or were stretcher cases; the walking wounded as usual remained in the line. 4 Company had lost all its officers and NCOs, except one. At five o'clock on the afternoon of 24 May, the attack was abandoned.

Throughout three days of battle, the officers and men of the 3rd Regiment had fought with unflagging bravery and smiling cheerfulness. Always thirsty, dirty and even hungry, they fought on with unwearying energy and determination. 'No troops would have done better and most not as well,' wrote their commanding officer, Bill Newman – and he was an Australian so knew something about fighting men. The Jews referred to 24 May as a 'bloody day of slaughter'.[29]

Many controversial accounts were written about the attack of 3rd Regiment at Nôtre Dame. Although I cannot dispute any of them, after a full investigation during my service as Assistant Chief of Staff in 1969, I was able to present the following account to add to General Glubb's summary: At 1200 hours on 23 May, the second attack on Nôtre Dame commenced, with a short period of covering fire from the artillery battery, two-inch mortars, and medium machine guns. The six-pounder troop and the Armoured Car Squadron were brought to forward positions, and started to soften their targets with armoured piercing and high explosive bombs. Ghazi al-Harbi and his 4th Company attacked through al-Musrarah from the right, and Muhammad Nauman and his 2nd Company attacked through the Damascus Gate area from the left. As the two companies came close to the Jewish positions the covering fire stopped and hand-to-hand fighting commenced. Many small houses adjacent to Nôtre Dame were cleared and occupied by the 4th Company. Ghazi al-Harbi sent a detachment to open a gap in the fences of Nôtre Dame under covering fire from the rest of his company. The detachment, which came under very heavy fire from the building, was able to open the gap, but al-Harbi did not risk penetrating the fences and entering the building because of his company's heavy casualties and the continued heavy fire from Nôtre Dame.

Meanwhile, Muhammad Nauman and his 2nd Company came close to the building from the left flank adjacent to the Old City Wall. Under heavy fire from the enemy, his company suffered many casualties, and he was later wounded and evacuated to the dressing station. Lt Khalid Mujalli al-Khraisha, who became adjutant of the 3rd Regiment, went forward to replace him, taking with him a platoon from the 3rd Company. When Khalid al-Khraisha realised that it was nearly impossible to capture Nôtre Dame from his positions he withdrew his troops, some to the Old City and others to the positions they captured before. Sergeant Major Flaiyih Matir and the rest of the 3rd Company advanced and captured a few houses to the west of Nôtre Dame and took defensive positions there.

During the night of 23/24 May, Lt Colonel Newman asked for a twenty-five-pounder field gun to be brought to the Damascus Gate area to fire point-blank at Nôtre Dame with the object of opening a gap in the thick stone wall of the building. At dawn on 24 May, while al-Harbi and his 4th Company advanced and entered the court yard of Nôtre Dame, the twenty-five-pounder gun commenced, shooting point-blank at Nôtre Dame. A gap was opened in the wall, while al-Harbi and a section of his men demolished the main gate of the building and rushed through it occupying parts of its ground floor. The rest of the company were pinned down with machine-gun fire and grenades so heavy that they were unable to enter the ground floor. At that critical moment al-Harbi reported that he was on the ground floor of the building and asked Lt Colonel Newman for reinforcements. By that time, more than 80 men of the 4th Company had been killed or wounded. Newman commanded al-Harbi to withdraw. Al-Harbi refused and insisted on staying, asking again for reinforcements. Eventually al-Harbi, who did not succumb to the hell-fire directed at him and his men, yielded to his Commander's order and withdrew. Thereafter the front line of the 3rd Regiment remained unchanged. At least 300 men of that gallant regiment were killed or wounded in the operation.

On 26 May, General Glubb visited the 3rd Regiment. His description of his meeting with Lt Ghazi al-Harbi is worthy of al-Harbi. Glubb wrote:

Bill Newman, a little drawn and unshaven, was sitting on a packing case. Others came in. Mugs of tea appeared. The rattle of machine guns began again. Ghazi al-Harbi, a veteran of thirty years of war up and down Arabia, entered and shook hands. The tears ran down his wrinkled and weather-beaten face as he begged for permission for one more try to take Nôtre Dame. 'We'll do it this time, O father of Faris,' he assured me. But I vetoed any more attempts. The 3rd Regiment was now only five hundred strong, spread out over a thousand yards of streets and houses. Behind them there was not a single soldier from Jerusalem to Amman. Without a man in reserve and with ammunition which would scarcely be enough for another fortnight's fighting, we could not afford to embark on adventures, particularly in street fighting. The Old City had been relieved, the Holy Places saved, and a thin defensive line established across the city. The Jewish drive to seize the whole of Jerusalem had been stopped short. With this we must be content. Outside Jerusalem, thousands of square miles of country allotted to the Arabs under the partition scheme must also be defended, almost without troops, ammunition or money. How was it to be done? How long might the fighting last? We could not at this stage afford to lose precious trained soldiers merely to capture one block of buildings. 'We will take it later on,' I said. 'If God wills,' replied al-Harbi quietly.[30]

Meanwhile, the 1st Regiment of the 1st Brigade had taken over the Biddu–al-Nabi Samuel sector from the 2nd Regiment on 23 May. (Al-Nabi Samuel was the traditional tomb of the prophet Samuel.) The tasks given to the regiment included holding the front and, when commanded, to capture the Radar Hill – a task aborted by the 2nd Regiment when they were ordered to attack Shaikh Jarrah earlier in the week. Radar Hill, thus named because the British Army had erected a radar station at its highest point during the Second World War, was ideally situated for observing all the main roads around it – from Bab al-Wad to Abu Ghosh, from Biddu to al-Nabi Samuel and from Latrun to Bait Ur to Ramallah. From its position, the company of the Etzioni Brigade defending Radar Hill could see every movement of the 1st Regiment in the sector covering al-Qubaibah, Biddu and al-Nabi Samuel as well as Bait Surik and Bait Iksa. Radar Hill was prepared by the British Army for all-round defence and a Haganah garrison of about 90 men manned its defences and enhanced them further with mines and barbed wire. The only approach from the Jordanian side was by a narrow track, which ran along a knife-edge ridge of hill and had been blocked by a concrete road block of dragon teeth and mine craters.

On 25 May, Colonel Goldie ordered Lt Colonel H. Blackden, Commander of the 1st Regiment, to capture Radar Hill. At dawn on 26 May, a section of two twenty-five-pounder guns from the artillery battery supporting 1st Brigade opened fire to cover the attack by 4th Company of the 1st Regiment, commanded by Lt Salamah Autayiq. The artillery fire lasted for nine minutes only because of the lack of ammunition. Thereafter, a slow rate of artillery fire was shifted to the Jewish settlement of Maale Ha Hamisha north of Abu Ghosh. General Glubb described the battle that followed in these words:

> The infantry advanced with great gallantry in the face of considerable automatic and rifle fire. The first man up to the wire cut his way through, a few yards from the Jews. Just as he jumped the last strands and ran forward, he was shot dead, but another and another were behind him. The 1st Regiment broke into the enemy's position at 4.30 a.m. The enemy left thirteen dead. Others were shot as they escaped towards the Jewish colony to the west. The garrison was about equal to the attacking force. The 1st Regiment suffered three killed and sixteen wounded, most of them in a sharp hand-to-hand engagement in the enemy's position. Both the Company Commander and his Second in Command were wounded. The Company Commander reached the enemy's position on all fours, dragging a broken leg behind him. He refused to be evacuated until the position was captured and consolidated. The wire was found to have consisted of a double apron fence, with four coils of dannert wire between them. The ground outside the wire was liberally sprinkled with anti-tank and anti-personnel mines.
>
> Israeli forces in the days following made repeated attempts to retake Radar, and suffered heavy casualties, but never succeeded.[31]

By sunrise the second phase of the attack was on its way with the 1st Company supported by a troop of armoured cars. Some parts of Maale Ha Hamisha were burning as a result of the artillery fire and when the Marmon-Herrington armoured cars opened fire with their two-pounder guns, the civilian population of the settlement started to run away towards the village of Abu Ghosh. Soon after, while the armoured cars moved forward, one was destroyed by a PIAT rocket and another lost its driver who was killed. Colonel Goldie, who was observing the battle from a high point, commanded the attacking force to withdraw, and Maale Ha Hamisha survived.[32] However, the most important part of the operation was successful, because Radar Hill was 'an ideal observation post overlooking the main Jerusalem road, which it could henceforth interdict with artillery fire'.[33] It was also a formidable defensive stronghold. Under the circumstances, according to Colonel Goldie, 'the capture of the settlement of Maale Ha Hamisha was not worth the bones of any soldier of 1st Regiment'.[34]

NOTES

1 Glubb, *A Soldier with the Arabs*, p. 118.
2 PRO. FO 371/68830. Kirkbride to the Foreign Office, 19 May 1948.
3 Hazza Al Majali, *Memoirs* (Arabic) (Beirut: Dar Al Ialm Lil Malayeen, 1960). Also, Munib Madhi and Sulaiman Musa, *The History of Jordan in the Twentieth Century* (Amman: Dar al-Muhtasib, 1959), pp. 487–8.
4 Al-Sharaa, *Our Wars with Israel*, p. 91.
5 *The Palestine War 1947–1948*, an official Israeli account.
6 J. B. Glubb, *The Changing Scenes of Life: an Autobiography* (London: Quartet, 1983), p. 150.
7 Mahmoud al-Musa Aubaidat, 'Account of the battle of Jerusalem', *The New Jordan Magazine* (Amman: winter 1990), nos. 15–16, p. 64.
8 *The Palestine War 1947–1948*, an official Israeli account, p. 491.
9 *Ibid.*, p. 65.
10 PIAT is the abbreviation for Projector Infantry Anti-Tank, a deadly man-portable rocket launcher device with armour-piercing explosive charges.
11 Abdullah al-Tal, *The Palestine Catastrophe*, p. 106.
12 *The New Jordan Magazine* (winter 1990), nos. 15–16, p. 66.
13 Yitzhak Rabin, *The Rabin Memoirs* (London: Weidenfeld & Nicolson, 1979), p. 22.
14 *The New Jordan Magazine* (winter 1990), nos. 15–16, p. 68.
15 Abdullah al-Tal, *The Palestine Catastrophe*, p. 129.
16 Martin Gilbert, *Jerusalem in the Twentieth Century* (London: Pimlico, 1997), p. 223. Also, Herzog, *The Arab–Israeli Wars*, p. 62; and Aubaidat, 'Account of the battle of Jerusalem', *The New Jordan Magazine* (winter 1990), no. 15–16, p. 69.
17 Rabin, *The Rabin Memoirs*, p. 24.
18 Glubb, *A Soldier with the Arabs*, pp. 127–30.
19 Gilbert, *Jerusalem in the Twentieth Century*, p. 225.
20 Al-Sharaa, *Our Wars with Israel*, pp. 91–2.
21 Glubb, *A Soldier with the Arabs*, p. 127.
22 The letter was kindly given to the author by Major General James Lunt.
23 From the copy of the orders given by hand to Major Slade by Major Downs at Qalandiyah. Copy given to the author by Major General James Lunt.

24 *Ibid.*
25 Major General Ali Abu Nowar, *When the Arabs Faded: Memories in Arab Politics 1948–1964* (London: Dar al-Saqi, 1990), Chapter II.
26 Glubb, *A Soldier with the Arabs*, p. 115. Also Harry Levin, *Jerusalem Embattled: a diary of the city under siege, March 25th, 1948 to July 18th, 1948* (London: Cassell, 1997).
27 *Ibid.*
28 Al-Sharaa, *Our Wars with Israel*, p. 98.
29 Glubb, *A Soldier with the Arabs*, pp. 124–5.
30 *Ibid.*, p. 126.
31 *Ibid.*, p. 131.
32 Al-Sharaa, *Our Wars with Israel*, pp. 123–4.
33 Herzog, *The Arab–Israeli Wars*, p. 65.
34 Remark by Colonel Goldie at the Officer's Mess Tent when asked why he aborted the attack at Maale Ha Hamisha.

5

The Battle of Bab al-Wad

By 1300 hours on 15 May, the 4th Regiment, commanded by Lt Colonel Habis al-Majali, passed through Ramallah on their way to their positions. Habis and his adjutant, Lt Mahmoud al-Rousan, went ahead of the regiment and allocated the positions of his companies and their supporting weapons as shown in Table 5.1 below.

TABLE 5.1
Positions allocated to companies of the 4th Regiment

- 1st Company at the top of the high ground at Dair Nizam.
- 2nd Company at an area east of Kharbatha.
- 3rd Company at the top of the mountain overlooking the triangle of Bait Sira.
- Regiment HQ at an area between Dair Nizam and Kharbatha.

While on their way to their area going west, the 4th Regiment saw two companies of the Liberation Army, which were defending the area of Latrun, withdrawing back to Ramallah and going east without handing over their positions to the 4th Regiment. It was a peculiar withdrawal since orders were given to Habis al-Majali to cooperate with the Liberation Army as closely as possible. However, as soon as the companies arrived at their positions they were deployed according to plan, then started digging their trenches and preparing their defences. In a letter dated 27 May 1999 to the author, Colonel T. N. Bromage wrote about a scene he witnessed around 28 May 1948.

> During the next few days (between 25 and 28 May 1948) we patrolled regularly. In the hills immediately east of Bab al-Wad we came across the bodies of some Huwaitat tribesmen killed in the battles for the entrance to the Wadi in which the main asphalt road starts winding upwards towards Abu Ghosh and Jerusalem. The strong smell of death was heavy. I reckoned that the main battles

between the Israelis and the Huwaitat irregulars must have been fought just at the time the Jordan Arab Army had crossed into Palestine. All credit to Shaikh Haroun Ibn Jazi and his Huwaitat tribesmen who had fought so gallantly. At the same time the Syrian based 'Liberation Army' had occupied Latrun, but had promptly withdrawn without telling the other Arab forces, leaving the important position empty until it had been occupied by 4th Regiment.[1]

The situation in Jerusalem on 17 May was still obscure, but the road from Tel Aviv to Jerusalem was open to Jewish traffic after the withdrawal of the Liberation Army companies. Thus, two Jewish convoys loaded with reinforcements, weapons, ammunition and food supplies were able to reach Jerusalem from the coastal plain. The Jews also occupied the villages of Latrun and Dair Ayoub. When the King's orders reached Glubb to enter Jerusalem, Glubb realised that if the Jordan Arab Army was engaged in Jerusalem he should prevent the Jewish supply convoys from reaching the city. For if the Jews were able to occupy the Old City with fresh troops and advance on the main road to Jericho, they would cut off the whole of Palestine from Jordan and destroy the Jordan Arab Army. At that time the situation in Jerusalem was getting critical for its Jewish inhabitants. In his book, *The Arab–Israeli Wars*, Chaim Herzog wrote,

> [General Glubb] therefore had decided to concentrate on starving the Jewish city into surrender by tightening his hold on the Jerusalem road, particularly at Latrun. Electricity supplies in the city were down to a minimum of a few hours a day, and the water pumping stations had been shut off by the Arabs since 12 May. There was no news because the radio was cut off. There was widespread hunger and thirst and, at night, total darkness. Twenty-four hours a day the city was under artillery bombardment. There was no food in the shops. The entire population lived and slept in the cellars and the shelters, and there were no sanitary arrangements because of the lack of water. As supplies ran out, it became clear to all that the limit of human endurance was not far off unless the siege could be lifted.[2]

Glubb ordered the Commander of the 3rd Brigade to send the newly formed 4th Regiment to the Latrun area – nicknamed 'Bab al-Wad' (the valley gate) by men of the 4th Regiment – with the task of preventing the Jews from using the main road to Jerusalem.

At 1640 hours on 17 May, Colonel T. Ashton, Commander of the 3rd Brigade, held an order group in his HQ. He told Habis al-Majali that the enemy may attack the police fort at Latrun, which was occupied by a platoon of the 11th Infantry Company commanded by Lt Abd al-Majid al-Maaitah with a group of Jordanian Bedouin partisans under his command, and that Shaikh Haroun al-Jazi and his Huwaitat group of Jordanian partisans were still holding the village of Yalo. Ashton ordered the 3rd Company, less one platoon of the 4th Regiment, to move to Shaikh Haroun's positions with the following intentions: first, to support al-Maaitah's platoon and the Jordanian partisans against any attack by the enemy and, second, to counter-attack if necessary. He also commanded that the 3rd Company, less one platoon, should be under command of Brigade HQ, which was located at Baituniya – far behind 4th Regiment HQ.[3] The 3rd company occupied its new position before dawn on 18 May at an area overlooking the main Tel Aviv–Jerusalem road.

On 18 May, Ashton ordered the 4th Regiment to move and reinforce the area of Bab al-Wad (Yalo and the Police Fort). Habis and his adjutant went on a reconnaissance to Bait Sira, Bait Nuba, Imwas, Latrun and the Police Fort. He was delighted by the high morale of the shaikhs of the Jordanian Bedouin partisans, who met him at the police fort with Lt al-Maaitah. The shaikhs – Haroun al-Jazi, Hayil al-Surur, Autayiq al-Aatnah, Suwailim ibn Duhailan, Nahar al-Suboua, Munawir al-Raja, Falah al-Mitlaq, Miflih al-Suboua and Jrouh ibn Salim – placed themselves and their men under Habis al-Majali's command. There was a special relationship between Habis and the shaikhs. While the Liberation Army retreated for unknown reasons, these shaikhs and their men, who volunteered to defend Palestine without any demands whatsoever (without pay, buying their own food and using their own weapons and ammunition), held their positions for their honour and that of King Abdullah and Jordan. It was for their self-respect and true Arab nationalism that these noble and courageous men stood fast. The total strength of the Jordanian partisans in Bab al-Wad was about 250 men.

On completing his reconnaissance and appreciation of the situation, Habis allocated the defensive positions of the Regiment shown in Table 5.2.

TABLE 5.2
Defensive positions of the 4th Regiment

Regiment HQ, south of the village of Imwas

- 1st Company, commanded by Captain Kamil Abd al-Qadir, at the mountain near the entrance to Imwas.
- 2nd Company, commanded by Captain Abdullah al-Salim, around the Monastery of Latrun occupying three hills overlooking the open ground to the west.
- 3rd Company, commanded by Captain Salih al-Eid al-Fakhouri, occupying three mountains at Yalo.
- Jordanian partisans, located in each company area according to the need for men to cover all approaches to their positions.
- Support Company, commanded by Captain Izzat Hasan Ghandour, deployed a section of medium machine guns, a section of three-inch mortars and a section of six-pounder anti-tank guns with each infantry company (see Map 4).

The principles of all round defence, in depth and with mutual support, were strictly implemented in the plan, and by nightfall of 18 May the regiment was dug in and ready to fight. In order to enhance the defensive positions of the regiment, Colonel Ashton ordered Habis to maintain the principle of offensive defence by sending reconnaissance, standing and fighting patrols to cover all lines of approach to their positions. At 1900 hours, the patrol Commanders were briefed and moved out on their missions. Eight reconnaissance and listening patrols were sent to the areas of Dair Ayoub, Bait Jiz, Salbit, Bir al-Hilu and Latrun. The main road to Jerusalem was thus dominated by the 4th Regiment before the Jews were able to discover the vital importance of the move.

However, it did not take the Jews long to realise what had happened. Soon after, the Haganah Alexandroni and the 7th Brigades were ordered to take Latrun. While they were planning their attack they attempted to prevent the 4th Regiment from preparing their defences by active fighting patrols and desultory artillery fire. They also sent various patrols to locate and harass 4th Regiment positions in preparation for their intended attack on the Latrun Police Fort. During the night of 18/19 May, two Haganah patrols, each of one platoon, managed to infiltrate to a point between two platoons of the 3rd Company at Yalo. As soon as they were detected the company opened fire and the Haganah patrols withdrew with unknown casualties. Another Haganah reconnaissance patrol from the direction of the Artoof track to Latrun was detected by a listening patrol at 0230 hours on 19 May, but as soon as they noticed the Jordanian patrol they withdrew. While this action was taking place, another battle was raging in Jerusalem, and the whole of the Nablus sector was defended by the 1st Regiment, less one company, which was at Jerusalem during that night.

On 19 May, the 4th Regiment continued to improve their defences in the expectation of a Haganah major attack. At 1000 hours, the sounds of explosions came from Khulda. In his daily meeting with his regimental Commanders, Ashton insisted on the offensive by patrols to keep the enemy unaware of the brigade positions. He also ordered that the Jordanian partisans should be organised and deployed to the maximum. At 1600 hours, the adjutant assembled the partisans at the Police Fort and organised them in platoon strengths, naming each for identification – Lions, Tigers, Hawks, Ibn Jabal and so on. Some 250 Jordanian partisans were thus organised and given locations and duties. One platoon refused its name of 'Vultures' because the vulture eats the carcass of dead animals. They were then named Falcons. Such is the pride of the Jordanian Bedouin. On the same day, eight mortar bombs fell on the Police Fort, but no casualties were reported.[4] The Palestinian local partisans were also organised and named in accordance with their villages – thus, Imwas, Yalo and Bait Jiz. The village of Imwas was given 20 rifles by the regiment to increase the number of their partisans from 60 to 80 men.

On 23 April 1948, the Commander of the 4th Brigade, Colonel Ahmad Sudqi al-Jundi, sent an infantry platoon of about 35 men to the village of Artoof to defend it against Jewish attacks. The platoon, which was commanded by Lt Isa Mufadhi, was ordered to wear a khaki Kaffiyah to disguise the men as partisans. They took their positions in the Police Fort at the village, and were later reinforced with two sections under the command of Sergeant Iyadah Mdanat. The Police Fort was manned by a section of former Palestine policemen with a wireless set connected to Bethlehem police HQ. During the afternoon of 20 May, the Palestinian partisans at Artoof, Ishawa, Islin and Bait Susin attacked a Haganah force in their area and pushed them out. The policemen of Artoof deserted their posts and the wireless set became redundant. On that day, Mufadhi was placed under the command of 4th Regiment, which sent a patrol with food, ammunition and a PIAT rocket launcher to support them.

On 21 May, Habis was informed at the daily meeting with Ashton that a large Jewish convoy of supplies would be passing on the main road from Tel Aviv to Jerusalem. All units were warned, and by nightfall they observed complete silence and were listening to every sound from the area of the settlement of Khuldah, Wadi al-Sarar, Latrun and from there on the main road to Jerusalem. At 2330 hours, the growing sound of engines was heard by the listening patrols; soon after, they saw the Jewish convoy moving without lights. At 2400 hours the twenty-five-pounder field artillery battery attached to the 4th Regiment, which had located pre-planned defensive targets, opened fire at the appropriate targets – including the main road. As soon as the convoy reached an area within the range of the Latrun Monastery, the 2nd Company and the Jordanian partisans opened fire at them, at which point they started to withdraw. At 0100 hours on 22 May, the Haganah attacked the Latrun Monastery area with a strong detachment, but the attack was repulsed by the Jordanian partisans who chased the attackers to Wadi al-Sarar and beyond, and killed two of them at close range. No casualties were suffered by the 4th Regiment; one Jordanian partisan was killed and two others were slightly wounded.

On the same day, more listening patrols were sent to areas where the enemy was likely to advance through the area west of the Latrun Monastery (by the 2nd company), and the area east of Yalo near Dair Ayoub. Further reconnaissance patrols were sent around the perimeter of the regiment, so that each company could have as early a warning as possible of enemy attacks. At nightfall, the whole front was absolutely silent apart from the sounds of crickets and mosquitoes. At 0120 hours on the morning of 23 May, a red signal flare followed by a green one were fired by the listening patrol at Bir al-Hilo, indicating that the enemy was advancing in the direction of the Police Fort.

The Jewish plan for the attack on the 4th Regiment called for a battalion of the Alexandroni Brigade to capture the Police Fort and the village of Latrun. Another battalion from the 7th Brigade planned to cover the right flank of the attack and secure the main road to Jerusalem. At 0230 hours, a company of the Haganah Alexanderoni Brigade was on its way to capture the Police Fort. One platoon engaged the 2nd Company and two others advanced to about 200 yards from Latrun. At that point the 2nd Company and the Jordanian partisans opened fire. Under heavy attack, the Haganah continued their advance to about

100 yards of the 2nd Company perimeter. Fighting continued until 0400 hours. Chaim Herzog wrote:

> By the time the advance units reached the Latrun–Jerusalem road, they were in full view of the defending Arab Legion in the Latrun area above the road. Completely exposed, the Israelis came under withering fire that obviated any possibility of attack. Thus began a tragic withdrawal, during which most of the hundreds of casualties suffered were incurred. At the same time, the Battalion of the 7th Brigade to the right of Alexandroni Battalion came under flanking fire from Arab Legion forces and Arab irregulars [the Jordanian partisans], who had occupied the village of Bait Jiz and Bait Susin [Jordanian Arab Army and Palestinian partisans], to the rear of the attacking forces – which had previously been assumed to be empty. The heat was oppressive. There were no water supplies and the troops carried no water bottles, an especial hardship for the immigrants. The Arab Legion artillery pounded the area mercilessly as the units tried to extricate themselves. Numerous acts of heroism and self-sacrifice were recorded. Sniping from the flanks and rear intensified. It was only with the greatest difficulty that the remainder of the force was extricated. The units, broken in disarray and followed by stragglers, gradually struggled back to the area of the high ground held as a firm base by one of the Alexandroni Battalions.[5]

Lieutenant Muhammad al-Mahasnah, a Platoon Commander of the 3rd Company, went on a fighting patrol with the object of a reconnaissance of the track between Bir al-Hilo and Artoof, and to establish contact with Lt Isa Mufadhi and his platoon. The patrol consisted of an infantry platoon, a section of three-inch mortars and one Marmon Herrington armoured car. At about 2000 hours, as they neared Islin village, a platoon of the Haganah on a fighting patrol opened fire at them. The Jordanian patrol dismounted and opened fire at the Haganah forcing them to run away, chased by three-inch mortar bombs exploding among them. The Jordanian patrol did not suffer any casualties and returned to base after completing their mission.

Meanwhile, Major Geoffrey Lockett temporarily took control of the 2nd Regiment from Major Bob Slade, who was seriously wounded in the battle for Shaikh Jarrah in Jerusalem. Lockett served with Wingate's Chindits, where he won two bars to his DSO. He and his Second in Command, Captain Nigel Bromage (seconded to the Jordan Arab Army from the Grenadier Guards), handed over the 2nd Regiment positions to the 1st Regiment at al-Nabi Samuel and Biddu. On 24 May, the 2nd Regiment was commanded to take over the positions of the 3rd Company of the 4th Regiment at Yalo area. By the evening of the same day, they were in their new positions in the hills that lie between Yalo and Dair Ayoub, covering the main road between Latrun, Bab al-Wad and Jerusalem. The 2nd Regiment was supported by the artillery battery under command of 3rd Brigade near the village of Bait Nuba. The officers of the battery were Lts Mustafa al-Khasawnah, Shahir Yousef, Samih al-Bataynah, Mahmoud al-Maaitah, Abd al-Razaq al-Sharif and Abd al-Aziz Asfour.

On the same day, Shaikh Haroun ibn Jazi and the Huwaitat partisans volunteered to join Isa Mufadhi at Artoof to support him. Thus, they missed the partisans' action which, it had been decided, was to attack on the same day the Jewish settlement of Kfar Uria to the west between Bait Mahsir and Latrun. The attack was to support the village of Bait Jiz, which the Palestinian partisans were still courageously holding and defending. During that night at 1950 hours, Shaikhs Autayiq al-Aatiyah, Suwailim ibn Duhailan, Nahar al-Suboua, Abdullah Swaimrin and their men moved in three detachments: one to the school at Bait Jiz; a second at Bait Susin; and the third to assault the perimeter of Kfar Uria and open a gap in it. At 2000 hours, the artillery battery opened fire at the settlement. As soon as the artillery ceased firing, the Jordanian partisans were able to open a gap in the settlement perimeter and the rest started to advance. At that point, Jewish reinforcements started to arrive at the scene from Khulda. The partisans withdrew to their positions after inflicting many casualties on the defenders of the settlement. One Jordanian partisan was wounded.

Meanwhile, Ashton decided to move his HQ closer to the field of action and established it near Bait Nuba and the artillery battery. Thus by nightfall the 2nd and 4th Regiments were redeployed and their patrols moved out to their locations. The 3rd Brigade was ready to fight for Bab al-Wad. At 2100 hours a fighting patrol, commanded by Lt Qasim al-Ayid of the 4th Regiment, was sent to demolish two bridges between Artoof and Ishawa, as well as to make contact with Artoof and bring as much information about the Haganah as possible. The patrol consisted of one infantry platoon and a section of the demolition platoon. The patrol completed its mission without incident and at 0115 hours on 25 May, they were on their way back to base.

Despite the critical Haganah situation at the central and Jerusalem fronts, and the presence of the Iraqi Brigade in the Nablus, Jenin and Tulkarm areas, Ben-Gurion decided to give first priority to the Latrun front in order to be able to open the way to Jerusalem for Jewish convoys with supplies. On 24 May, orders were given to the 7th Brigade to attack Latrun again. The battalion from the Alexandroni Brigade was withdrawn and replaced by a battalion from the Givati Brigade. The Jewish plan was as follows:

1. The Givati battalion to capture Bait Susin and use it as a base, thence cross the Tel Aviv–Jerusalem main road to the north and capture Dair Ayoub and continue to capture Yalo, thus cutting the Latrun–Ramallah road behind the Jordanian 4th Regiment and the main line of communications of the Jordanian 3rd Brigade.
2. The 7th Brigade, commanded by Haim Laskov, to advance with an armoured battalion followed by an infantry battalion to capture the Police Fort, the village of Latrun and neutralise the monastery.
3. The attack was to be supported by a troop of 65 mm guns and a troop of 120 mm mortars.[6]

At 0200 hours on 25 May, the Haganah artillery and mortar troops opened fire at Latrun, the Police Fort, the monastery and the village of Imwas. At 0230 hours, two Haganah companies were able to advance from the settlement of Uria and take positions near Bir al-Hilo. As soon as they came close to their objective, two signal flares were fired by the 4th Regiment listening patrol nearby. Lt Mahmoud al-Maaitah, the artillery Observation Post at the 2nd Company positions, directed his guns at his defensive targets and opened fire at the advancing Haganah. Lt Abd al-Razaq al-Sharif, the other artillery OP, directed his guns at the Haganah guns and mortar positions and opened fire. It was not known afterwards whether the silence of the Haganah guns was caused by the Jordanian artillery fire was deliberate to allow the force to assault their objectives. However, it was soon confirmed that the assault was directed at the 2nd Company positions near the monastery and Latrun. The company and the Jordanian partisans held their fire until the attackers were about 100 yards from their positions. When they opened fire with their two- and three-inch mortars, and medium and light machine guns, the attackers scattered as they suffered heavy casualties.

During the close combat that followed, one Jewish platoon managed to approach the gunner OP position of Lt Mahmoud al-Maaitah and was about to capture it. Mahmoud ordered his four gunners and the detachment of three men manning a Bren light machine gun protecting his position to withdraw to their alternative OP position 100 yards to the rear. In the rush that followed, and under very heavy fire, the wireless operator left his wireless set behind, switched on and ready for use. The Jewish platoon occupied the empty Jordanian OP position, and its Commander started to use the wireless attempting in his Arabic with a Jewish accent to direct the Jordanian artillery fire. The Commander of the gun position immediately realised what had happened and ignored the messages. In his extreme anger at what he saw as an insult to his personal pride, Mahmoud al-Maaitah ordered the seven men with him to attack the Jewish platoon. Under support fire from their Bren light machine gun, Mahmoud and his men counter-attacked with their personal weapons and hand grenades. They recaptured the OP position and chased the Jews out from the area. To their surprise they found their wireless set still switched on and immediately used it to direct their artillery fire as soon as they identified themselves. The Jews, who were taken by surprise, ran away and, chased by artillery fire, withdrew back to their former positions carrying their casualties with them.[7]

To the south of Latrun was a series of arid hilltops known as the mountains of Bait Susin, nicknamed by the 4th Regiment Jabal al-Aqra (the Bald Mountain). Jordanian patrols reported a concentration of forces behind the mountain just before dawn. On his way back to his base, Lt Qasim al-Ayid and his patrol saw the Haganah force and opened fire on them. On seeing the battle between Qasim and the Haganah, Isa Mufadhi advanced with his platoon from the Police Fort at Artoof and joined Qasim al-Ayid. Meanwhile, soon after dawn the Haganah forces were more visible and the Jordanian artillery were able to direct their rapid fire on them, inflicting very heavy casualties on their units. Qasim's fighting patrol was able to advance close to Jabal al-Aqra and pushed back the attacking Haganah to the west. The three-inch mortars of the 2nd and 3rd Companies managed to inflict heavy casualties on them. Even the six-pounder guns of the 4th Regiment joined in and, firing high explosives bombs at the enemy forces, managed to add to their casualties. At 1000 hours the Haganah attempted to recover their casualties from the scene of battle, but were stopped by a three-inch mortar that was fired at them. Fighting continued until 1200 hours on 25 May.

Meanwhile, the 3rd Brigade HQ was moved by Ashton from Bait Nuba to Yalo. He sent a troop of Marmon-Herrington armoured cars, commanded by Lt Hamdan al-Subaih, to cover the rear of Qasim al-Ayid's patrol which, after engaging the Haganah at Jabal al-Aqra, had already reported back to their HQ. However, Hamdan carried out a reconnaissance from Yalo to Artoof and on his way back to base he saw a cave in which six Haganah men were hiding. The Palestinian partisans were close by, and Hamdan asked their shaikh and one of his men to arrest the Haganah men who were pleading for their lives by mentioning the names of the prophets. Typical of a Jordanian Army officer, Hamdan took them as prisoners of war. They, as well as the Regiment HQ and the Brigade HQ treated them with the utmost humanity.

Back in the 2nd Regiment positions, another battle was about to begin, as described by Colonel T. N. Bromage in his letter to me of 27 May 1999:

> In the early hours of the morning of 25 May, there was heavy firing from the top of the hills where the forward companies were entrenched. Awake and dressed I heard movement from the valley to the east of us, which led to Yalo village, and surmised that an Israeli force was moving round to encircle us and possibly to attack the village. I collected all available men from the lower echelons, cooks, drivers, mechanics and the like, and, having talked to Geoffrey, moved down to the valley. There I found the Israelis in full retreat. We fired a few shots at them and followed them down, harassing them.
>
> The valley leads to the road junction and then a deserted police post at Bab al-Wad. Here we could see a number of Israeli troop carrying vehicles picking up the stragglers. Someone produced a PIAT anti-tank rocket launcher. I took aim from behind a stone wall and fired twice. Both were misfires, not uncommon with that weapon. The vehicles drove away unscathed. I chanced my luck and led my motley band through Dair Ayoub village to return to our lines. As we left the village, we saw by chance five Israelis, not in uniform, hiding in a hedge of prickly pear cacti. They were in a state of great alarm and pleaded for their lives. With some difficulty they were extracted from the prickly pears, and I had the opportunity to question them as we walked back up the hill. It seemed that they were refugees from Europe who had only been in the country for

about two or three days when they had been rounded up and sent into battle. I was extremely sorry for them, and was glad that my PIAT had misfired; at least they would have been safe in a Jordanian Prisoner of War Camp until the war was over.

I had always been horrified at the Israeli's penchant for murder as a solution to their problems. We had experienced it in Palestine. At a later stage Colonel Marcus was killed in Jerusalem. Probably deliberately, because of jealousy that he had been favoured by Ben-Gurion, while Count Bernadotte, the United Nations Mediator, was also to be murdered in due course. Of all the unpleasant acts of the Israelis, the dispatch of these wretched immigrants to act as cannon fodder during the attack on the 3rd Jordanian Brigade defending Latrun and Yalo must have been among the worst, ranking after the massacre of women and children at Dair Yasin and Bernadotte's murder.[8]

During that second attack at Latrun, three infantry soldiers from Qasim's patrol were killed; three others were wounded. Two Jordanian partisans were killed and three others were wounded. Four civilians of the village of Imwas were killed, and two men and four women were wounded. At least 500 Haganah soldiers were killed or wounded.[9] Chaim Herzog described the attack and the reasons for its failure with a brief account in his book, *The Arab–Israeli Wars*:

Dair Ayoub fell to the Givati attack without opposition. However, as the force moved on to Yalo, it came under flanking fire that wounded a number of soldiers in the leading platoon. Panic ensued and, without permission, the 'Givati' Battalion withdrew in disarray, abandoning also Dair Ayub. Unaware of the failure of the operation's east flank Laskov's armoured force fought bravely, reached the outskirts of Latrun village and penetrated the courtyard of the police post. However, the untrained and inexperienced infantry failed to follow through the murderous fire of the Legion [Jordanian Arab Army] artillery. The armour persisted in its attack under point-blank fire from the defence positions on the roof of the police fortress. Flame-throwers were used in the attack, but the engineers whose task it was to demolish the wall of the police station were hit and immobilised by fire from nearby Emmaus [Imwas, the scene of one of the great battles of the Maccabees 2000 years earlier]. Laskov's attacking force, without its supporting infantry and without the benefit of what would have been a major diversion at Yalo, saw victory snatched from its grasp at the last minute and was obliged to withdraw. Indeed, it later transpired that the move against Yalo and the assumption that the armoured force would be followed by a major infantry assault had alerted the Arab Legion, which had even thrown its clerks and cooks into the battle. Hastily, orders had been issued to prepare for an Arab withdrawl from the area to avoid being cut off at Yalo.[10]

Three days later, on 28 May, King Abdullah visited the 3rd Brigade HQ and the HQ of 4th Regiment. An account of the last battle and the defeat of the Haganah was briefed to him. On the other hand, the Prime Minister, Tawfiq Abu al-Huda, never visited even a peaceful village in Jordan, not to mention a regiment in the field of battle. Being the Defence Minister, at least he could have accompanied the King on his visit.

On 29 May, the UN Security Council approved a resolution calling for a ceasefire for four weeks, calling on all the governments and authorities concerned to refrain from introducing fighting personnel and from importing or exporting war material into or from Palestine or the Arab States, and calling on all governments to take all possible steps in the implementation of the resolution.

On 30 May, Prince Abd al-Ilah, the Prince Regent of Iraq, accompanied by Prime Minister Nuri al-Said, visited the 3rd Brigade and went as far forward as the Police Fort, while an account of the two battles was explained to him. During the evening of the same day, the usual patrols moved forward from the 2nd and 4th Regiments. A patrol commanded by Sergeant Major Yousef Jiryis of the 4th Regiment was near Uria when they detected a Haganah patrol of about 30 men carrying supplies and moving in the direction of Bait Susin. Yousef engaged the Haganah and forced them to withdraw. He returned to base with one of his men wounded.

At 2200 hours, the third attack on Latrun started. The Jewish forces opened fire with three-inch and 122 mm mortars and field guns on all positions of the 2nd and 4th Regiments. A patrol commanded by Lt Muhammad al-Mahasnah came under heavy fire and when its Commander was seriously wounded, Lt Turki al-Hindawi immediately evacuated his comrade to the field dressing station and took over command of the patrol. Meanwhile, the Haganah were able to destroy the culvert north of the entrance to the village of Imwas, the objective the patrol was to protect. The Haganah bombardment continued until 2230 hours.

Minutes later, a Haganah company were approaching the 3rd Company of the 4th Regiment positions at Ibn Jabal Tomb. Only a small Wadi existed between the two forces. Another Haganah company managed to come close to the HQ Company 4th Regiment. Two Haganah companies were approaching the Police Fort. With another Haganah force of two companies attacking the 1st Company of the 4th Regiment, the whole area of the Regiment came under fire from every direction and in depth, and then close combat was the order of the day. At that point the Haganah armoured units went into battle and got close to the Police Fort.

By 0300 on 31 May, the attacking Haganah infantry had been repulsed; on their retreat they picked up many casualties. Thereafter, the scene of the battle went quiet. Ten minutes later all hell broke loose at the Police Fort, which was commanded by Lt Abd al-Majid al-Maaitah; the Jordanian partisans there were commanded by Shaikhs Nahar al-Suboua and al-Aatnah. A Haganah company managed to advance to the perimeter of the Fort and opened fire at close range on its defenders. At 0330 hours the Haganah armoured unit managed to assault the defences of the Police Fort and used flame-throwers to set fire to it. To start with, the adjacent Jordanian units could not precisely identify the enemy to shoot accurately, but soon two wooden huts were on fire and the flames illuminated the scene. Thereafter, a cry of *Allahu Akbar* (God is Greater) filled the air from all directions when the six-pounder anti-tank guns opened fire at the advancing Haganah armour. PIATs, hand grenades and machine guns were used at a close range against the attackers. Lt Abd al-Majid al-Maaitah, the hero of Latrun who held the Police Fort against three Haganah attacks, was killed after throwing a hand grenade into one of the Haganah armoured cars. Just before dawn, the Jordanian artillery battery directed their fire during the attack on the rear echelons of the attackers as well as on their predetermined defensive targets. They also followed the retreating Haganah with desultory fire until the end of the battle.

Meanwhile, the 2nd Regiment was under attack at 2300 hours on 30 May in the Yalo area. After an initial bombardment with artillery and mortars covering their attack, the Haganah were able to advance to the perimeter of the 2nd Regiment at Yalo. When the Haganah started their assault and the close combat war cries were as loud as the sounds of battle, with the Haganah shouting *Kadima*; and the Jordanians singing 'Tabaria and Dair Yasin; If we succumb, who will fight? *Allahu Akbar*', the defenders of Yalo repulsed their attackers and caused them many casualties. The battle lasted until 0330 on 31 May.

By sunrise, the casualties on both sides were: one soldier killed and three wounded from the 2nd Regiment, and one soldier killed and four wounded from the 4th Regiment. The Haganah casualties were 58 killed and an unknown number of wounded in the 2nd Regiment area, and 103 killed, including one Haganah woman in uniform in the 4th Regiment area. Four armoured vehicles, two flame-throwers, 200 rifles and several machine guns were captured from the Jewish force.

Unable to capture the sector of the Jordanian 3rd Brigade and the main road to Jerusalem, the Jewish command directed their efforts to open a new road to the city. After the capture by the Jewish 7th Brigade of the two Arab villages of Bait Jiz and Bait Susin, they controlled the land connecting Khulda by a short distance from the track between Artoof and Bab al-Wad. From that area a diversion track leads to Bait Mahsir and thence to Saris on the Jerusalem main road. That area of land was about five to six kilometres of rough terrain without tracks. The Jewish command intended to build a track connecting Khulda with Bait Mahsir and Saris and thence to the main Jerusalem road within the Jewish sector. More than one thousand men worked hard to open the track and make it passable. Chaim Herzog wrote:

> David Ben-Gurion gave immediate instructions to assemble the maximum available number of earth-moving vehicles in order to exploit the possibility of building a road as proposed. Isolated units and individuals made their way across the stretch separating the two brigade areas. The area, impassable to transport, was immediately east of Beit Susin, where there was a steep rocky drop of four hundred feet. Immediately, large convoys of flour, meat on the hoof and other supplies were driven to Beit Susin under cover of darkness; there they were manhandled by hundreds of porters mobilised in Jerusalem, and taken by mule to the Hartuv road . . . The result was 'the Burma Road' first traversed – with great difficulty, jeeps and lorries frequently having to be manhandled over rocks – on 10 June by a convoy that drove straight through from Tel Aviv to Jerusalem with American correspondents on board.[11]

On 2 June 1948, as a result of many appeals to King Abdullah by the people of Ramleh and Lydda in the central areas of Palestine, a composite force of the 2nd and 4th Regiments was organised with the task of reinforcing the Jordanian and Palestinian irregulars defending Lydda and Ramleh. The force, which was code-named 'Sun Rise', consisted of

the following troops – about 120 officers and men – commanded by
Captain T. N. Bromage of the 2nd Regiment.

- **From the 2nd Regiment:** one armoured cars troop, one infantry
  platoon, one section of six-pounder anti-tank guns.
- **From the 4th Regiment:** one infantry platoon.
- **From the 5th Company:** one infantry platoon, commanded by
  Captain Adib al-Qasim.

The composite force, which assembled at Bait Sira junction, moved to
Ramleh and Lydda at about 1500 hours on 2 June, and deployed at the
police fortress located between Lydda and Ramleh on the main road to
Jaffa. In his letter to me Colonel Bromage described what followed:

> We moved down to Ramleh reaching the town soon after midday,
> having left the bulk of our administrative transport in the olive
> groves facing the Old Palestine Police District Headquarters midway
> between Ramleh and Latrun.
>
> Having called on the Mayor of Ramleh and obtained his
> agreement, we moved to the open ground to the north-west of
> the town, which covered the main road approach from Jaffa and
> Sarafand Camp. I ordered the infantry to dig in and prepare a
> defensive position. They had hardly started to dig, when they were
> heavily mortared by the Israelis, and one man from 4th Regiment
> was killed. Fortunately a 37-mm mortar bomb struck the soft sandy
> ground about a yard from where I was standing, and failed to explode.
> Given the comparatively short range of that particular weapon and
> the angle of the projectile, I judged that it had been fired from the
> near side of Sarafand Camp, near where a railway bridge used to
> cross the main Jaffa road.
>
> As I knew the area from the days of the Mandate, I climbed into
> my jeep and taking with me one armoured car, drove down the
> asphalt road towards Jaffa, turned to the left, and went south for about
> three hundred yards down a rough overgrown track that followed
> the line of the railway embankment. The drive was worrying as
> we had no knowledge that the track was not mined, nor could
> we see much, as our vision was blocked to the north by the railway
> embankment, and to the south by olive and citrus groves, but coming
> round a bend we found an immense tower of sandbags built up
> against the embankment; obviously the Israeli observation post. I
> asked the armoured car Commander to shoot at the top of the tower
> with two-pounder high explosive. This he did, spraying the area

with his machine gun. The top of the sandbag tower was demolished and one member of the observation post was killed as he dived down the front of the embrasure. I suspect a second man had been in the post who was either killed or escaped through the back, but this I was unable to confirm. We returned the way we had come and were never bothered again by mortar fire from that direction.[12]

Captain Bromage spent the rest of the day and the following morning on a thorough reconnaissance of the whole area, and talked to the Commanders of the Palestinian and Jordanian partisans, as well as to the citizens' contingents defending the area of Lydda and Ramleh. He then made his appreciation of the situation. He found himself at a position nearly midway between his base, at the 2nd Regiment and 3rd Brigade Headquarters at the Bab al-Wad area, and the Jewish main base and command headquarters of the whole Jewish military forces in the Tel Aviv area. His composite force did not exceed 120 Jordanian Army officers and men, and about 300 irregular Jordanian and Palestinian partisans, while the Jewish forces in the area exceeded four mobile infantry brigades and one armoured brigade, supported by armoured cars and guns which exceeded twice the number of men under his command. Although his task was nearly impossible, he took the initiative and adopted the tactics of aggressive defence. I had served as adjutant of the 2nd Regiment in 1946 and knew Bromage well enough to describe him, from the military point of view, as an English Bedouin combining the mentality of a well-disciplined, extremely courteous, gentle and gallant Grenadier Guards officer with that of a fiery and courageous Jordanian Bedouin combatant raider. Thus, instead of adopting the stance of static defence and waiting for the enemy to attack, he was motivated to contend for a fight. In his letter to me he wrote:

> The Israeli colony of Ben Shemen straddled the road that runs north-east towards Bait Nabala and thence to Qalqiliyah and Tulkarm. If there had been any hope of defending Lydda from the Israelis, that colony would have needed to have been captured as a first step. I had enough force to have taken it by storm, and once overrun, the irregulars would have destroyed it; but a certain number of casualties among my small force would have been inevitable. I asked for permission to attack, but Brigade HQ signaled back flatly refusing to entertain my proposal. This was dispiriting, and a refusal that was to cost Jordan dearly when hostilities resumed at the end of the

first truce; but I had an alternative plan in mind if higher authority had refused to allow an attack on Ben Shemen; that was to capture and destroy the colony of 'Gezer' to the south of the main road from Ramleh to Latrun and Jerusalem. Surprise was essential, as just to the south of Gezer was Khulda, the main Israeli base from which previous Israeli attacks on Latrun had been launched. A successful operation against Gezer would have been certain to have alarmed the Israelis, and would have relieved pressure on Latrun. A small number of casualties among my force would have been inevitable, but in addition to the other factors, the morale of the irregulars needed boosting if they were not to melt away. So I forbore to mention my proposal to Brigade Headquarters.[13]

On 7 June 1948, all units of the Jordan Arab Army were informed that the truce would begin at 0600 hours on 11 June 1948. On the same day, Bromage, who was determined to take Gezer, decided to attack and capture it on the following day. He also knew that the Lydda contingent of irregulars was planning to attack Sarafand Camp and Bait Dagan Police Fort at dawn on 10 June, an attack that Bromage judged would have no chance of success and which he had opposed. On 8 June, Bromage mounted his attack on Gezer. In his letter to me he wrote:

Our two six-pounders anti-tank guns were allocated the task of knocking out the Israeli colony's generating plant. This was done quickly and effectively by the end of the morning.

The colony itself was protected by fields of anti-personnel mines attached to trip wires, and, behind these makeshift minefields, fences of danert wire. The only infantry unit which could be spared for the attack was the platoon of the 2nd Regiment. The other two platoons had to be left behind to defend our base at Ramleh. Reckoning that the Israelis would have been unlikely to have been armed with infantry anti-tank weapons, I risked allowing the armoured cars to overrun both the wire and the anti-personnel mines. This they did successfully, but one of the armoured car Commanders was killed as he threw a grenade at an Israeli position, but didn't duck back into his turret in time.

During our advance we were shelled by our own artillery battery supporting the defences at Latrun. The shelling was at extreme range. As the projectiles were falling almost vertically onto soft, newly ploughed soil, we suffered no casualties, but each wasted shell tore at my heart; we were so short of artillery ammunition. After many frantic wireless messages to Latrun and the artillery battery at Bait Nuba, the shelling eventually stopped.

Our infantry were able to advance in the tracks of the armoured cars where the anti-personnel mines had been overrun and exploded. By mid-afternoon the colony was ours.

The non-combatants were crowded into a large underground shelter on the top of the hill. These we shouted at in English to come out with their hands up. This they did after some persuasion, but not before one had a shot at me which missed and hit a soldier of 2nd Regiment standing beside me. We had no medical facilities, so had to dispatch him to the local hospital at the former Royal Air Force Regiment camp to the east of Ramleh on the Jerusalem road. He was an Auqaidi from a semi-settled tribe of Bedouins who lived north of Daraa in Syria. He had been shot in the lung and did not look as though he would last the night. He did not. I only hoped the doctors had had sufficient morphine to ease his passing.[14]

In spite of their anger at the shooting of their comrade, Bromage and the men of the 2nd Regiment behaved in the most honourable manner towards their prisoners at the Jewish settlement of Gezer. They controlled the raging urge of retaliation in their hearts for the killing of their comrade and the massacre at Dair Yasin, and were controlled by the self-discipline in their minds. Not one Jewish prisoner was abused nor even insulted. As luck would have it, there was a bus in the settlement that had remained untouched. Bromage and his men ushered the Jewish prisoners to board it and took them to the Lydda Police Headquarters on the Ramleh road. However, during the whole of the 1948 war with Jews, the only Jordanian soldier who lost control and was about to commit a shameful act was soon discovered by Bromage and was prevented from making a fool of himself. In his letter, Bromage wrote:

> I had been over to congratulate one of the armoured cars section Commanders, and climbed on top of his turret. At the bottom was one of the prettiest girls I had ever seen, about seventeen years old with black hair and blue eyes. The captor, a staff sergeant (to remain nameless), was reluctant to part with her. After being ordered to do so, she joined the rest of the prisoners in the bus. Trouble, I thought to myself . . .![15]

Thus 'trouble' was saved and the honour of the Jordan Arab Army was preserved. Thereafter, Bromage and his men withdrew from the wreckage of the settlement of Gezer, as he had no troops to oppose a counter-attack. Before leaving, he warned all the irregulars, who followed the attack on the settlement and stripped it bare after its capture, to leave the battlefield and return to Lydda as early as possible. However, many stayed and were caught in the inevitable counter-attack, which came late in the evening. The Jordan Army losses in that attack were two killed. At the Ramleh Police Fort, the exhausted force had a good night's sleep. At about 0600 hours on 10 June, Bromage was awakened by a call from the Commander of the local Lydda partisans to say that he had attacked Sarafand Camp and that his men were pinned down in an olive grove. He also asked why the Jordan Army had not been there to support him and his men. Bromage did not remind him of his opposition to the plan and his suggestion for him and his men to leave the battlefield. He immediately turned out his troop of armoured cars and rushed to the scene of the beleaguered Lydda irregulars. Bromage wrote:

> We engaged the Israelis who were entrenched along the line of the road outside the wire perimeter of the camp in a fire fight lasting long enough to give cover for the bulk of the irregulars to withdraw back to Lydda. Unfortunately one of the armoured car drivers stalled his engine and could not restart it. My jeep driver and I fixed on a tow rope from another armoured car under heavy fire from an Israeli spandau. We were most uncomfortable. Never was a tow rope fixed so quickly. Fortunately, as so often happens in an operation, the spandau was inaccurate, and the recalcitrant armoured car after being towed down hill towards the Israelis decided to start again. Breathing a sigh of relief we were able to withdraw unscathed.
>
> As the hour of the truce struck, we had started to retire to Ramleh, when we heard heavy machine gun and mortar fire coming from the direction of Yehudia village on the main road from Lydda Airport to Bait Dagan. I drove over in my jeep with one armoured car as escort. The main road forks to the west of Yehudia. The left fork goes to Jaffa via Bait Dagan police fort, the right heads towards Tel Aviv and Petah Tikveh, scene of an appalling Zionist atrocity in the latter days of the Mandate. We stopped our vehicles just past the road junction on the Tel Aviv side, and waited to take stock of the situation.
>
> The machine-gun fire continued. Large numbers of irregulars appeared running from the direction of Bait Dagan town, with in hot pursuit, an armoured scout car of the type formerly used by the Palestinian police, firing from a machine gun in the turret. I told my armoured car Commander to hold his fire until the Israeli scout car was level with us at about 200 yards range and then fire one round of two-pounder anti-tank. This he did. The crew of the

scout car obviously never saw what hit it, as they evacuated their vehicle through the north hatch and were immediately cut down by our machine gun. I was sorry for the Israelis; they had fought bravely, but should have taken more care! Lydda town irregulars subsequently recovered the scout car, but it looked to me that it would never fight again, as the anti-tank round had destroyed the gear box and transmission and damaged the engine. The truce had now taken effect; we regrouped at Ramleh.[16]

On the following morning the assistant superintendent of police at Lydda police headquarters, where the Jewish prisoners who were taken at Gezer were incarcerated, telephoned to say that two Jordan Arab Army men were demanding the keys of the prison at pistol point. Bromage was so shocked that within five minutes he was there to rocket the miscreants sky-high. One, Mansur Shair, nicknamed 'al-Jack' as he was strong enough to lift the back of a Landrover single-handed, came from the late Salim bin Tual's section of the Shummar tribe. The second was Fantoul from the Fedaan Annezah. The whole problem was that both were besotted by the beauty of 'Trouble', the black-haired, blue-eyed Israeli girl whom Bromage had seen in the armoured car at Gezer. Miss 'Trouble' was saved again. The honour and reputation of the Jordan Arab Army was also saved again. However, in order to avoid any further incident of the 'trouble' kind and to safeguard the women prisoners, as well as the honour of the Jordan Arab Army, the 27 Haganah men prisoners were sent under escort to the prisoner of war camp at Mafraq. Meanwhile, the 35 women prisoners were loaded into a captured Tel Aviv No. 5 bus and driven through Lydda to the settlement of Ben Shemen. Bromage led the bus in his jeep waving a white flag; another was flown from a window of the bus, while two armoured cars covered the humane operation from well back on each side of the road.

The Jews were momentarily taken aback by this unexpected arrival. Bromage called to them in English across their minefield and wire, and they soon opened a path for their compatriots. A Jordanian soldier helped out one woman who had been injured in the assault on Gezer, and the transfer was soon effected. Bromage and his men returned to Ramleh with the great weight of 'Trouble' off their minds. Bromage wrote:

> Waiting for me was a signal from Brigade Headquarters ordering my small force to return to the Latrun–Yalu Salient, and for me to hand over command to Captain Adib al-Qasim, while the platoon

of 5th Company was to remain in situ and be joined by the rest of 5th Garrison Company.

Calling in at Brigade Headquarters, which had moved to Bait Sirah, I had a major row with the Brigadier. Teal accused me of all sorts of sins, the worst of which was to have suffered three fatal casualties at a time when the Jordanians had no reinforcements and no chance of getting any. I reminded him that to fight a war without casualties was impossible. In my opinion, reinforced with hindsight, we could have done so much to bolster up the defence of Lydda and Ramleh. Not to have taken Ben Shemen was a missed opportunity.[17]

Thereafter, the main aim of the 3rd Brigade of the Jordan Arab Army was well established: the main road to Jerusalem from Tel Aviv remained cut. Captain Bromage wrote:

> One of Geoffrey Lockett's last acts before the truce began, had been to blow up the pumping station at al Qubab, about three kilometres to the west of Latrun, which supplied Jerusalem with water, and which for some reason had been ignored by the irregulars, and had still been operating. Most of the water for the New City of Jerusalem came from al-Qubab station.[18]

NOTES

1 Colonel T. N. Bromage, letter to the author, 27 May 1999.
2 Herzog, *The Arab–Israeli Wars*, pp. 62–3.
3 Al Rousan, *The Battle for Bab al Wad*, p. 75.
4 *Ibid.*
5 Herzog, *The Arab–Israeli Wars*, p. 65.
6 *Ibid.*
7 Abu Nowar, *When the Arabs Faded*, p. 49. Also, an account by Lt Colonel Mahmoud al-Maaittah to the author.
8 Colonel T. N. Bromage, letter to the author, 27 May 1999.
9 Al Rousan, *The Battle for Bab al Wad*, pp. 111–15.
10 Herzog, *The Arab–Israeli Wars*, pp. 65–6.
11 *Ibid.*, pp. 67–8.
12 Colonel T. N. Bromage, letter to the author, 27 May 1999.
13 *Ibid.*
14 *Ibid.*
15 *Ibid.*
16 *Ibid.*
17 *Ibid.*
18 *Ibid.*

6

The Battles on other Fronts

_____

In spite of all the political meetings of the member states of the Arab League, no strategic or general plan for the Arab armies was even mentioned. The aim of the Arab military intervention in Palestine was not clear if one existed at all; the Chiefs of Staff did not even know the battle orders of each others' armies and there was no coordination whatsoever between the military forces in the field. The weapons, ammunition and equipment varied in origin – French in Lebanon and Syria, and British in Iraq, Jordan and Egypt, not to mention those of the Liberation Army which were from different sources. The Lebanese Army was two and a half years old with its origin in the Lebanese Gendarmerie and police. The Syrian Army was only three years old, in origin similar to the Lebanese Army, but with the advantage of having fought the French in 1945. The Iraqi Army had had some war experience in the rebellion of 1941 and the continued internal security operations against the Kurds, but was limited at the start of the intervention to only one brigade. The Egyptian Army was the oldest of all the Arab armies, but it had little war experience. With the exception of the Jordanian Arab Army and the Liberation Army, no other Arab Army had operated in Palestine before 15 May 1948.

The Lebanese Army front
The Lebanese Army consisted of the 1st Infantry Battalion supported by a mortar platoon, medium machine-gun platoon, one troop of five Renault tanks, and two troops of armoured cars. The total strength of the Lebanese Army was about 700 officers and men organised as shown in Table 6.1.

TABLE 6.1
The Lebanese Army

Unit	Commander
1st Battalion	Lt Colonel Jamil al-Husami
Second in Command	Major Habib Qashua
1st Company	Major Michael Abu Taqah
Assistant	Lt Antwan Khuri al-Bani
2nd Company	Captain Said Nasrullah
Assistant	Lt Franswa Jinadi
3rd Company	Captain Kamil Zain al-Din
Assistant	Lt Ilyas Bawab
Assistant	Lt Mohammad al-Halabi
Support Company	Major Raad al-Hashim
Assistant	Lt Ilyas al-Haj
Assistant	Cadet 3rd year Abd al-Majid Shihab
Armoured Car Squadron	Lt Jamil Husni Eid
Sapper Platoon	Lt Salah Darwish

On 14 May 1948, the 1st Battalion of the Yaftach Palmach Brigade and the Lebanese 1st Battalion were racing each other on their way to capture the al-Malikiyah, Qudus and al-Nabi Yusha police posts adjacent to the international border with Palestine. The village of al-Malikiyah is situated on a high point on the main road between Lebanon and Palestine. The mission of the Jewish battalion was to prevent the Lebanese from capturing these Arab villages, while the Lebanese intended to use them as a springboard for their advance into Palestine and a base to protect the main route between the Liberation Army in North Galilee and their base in Syria and Lebanon. The Palmach Battalion advanced on foot to the Jewish settlement of Ramat Naftali a few miles to the west of al-Malikiyah and started to prepare themselves for the attack.

By dawn on 15 May, the Palmach Battalion attacked al-Malikiyah, but was repulsed by a detachment of the Lebanese Army holding the hill. Captain Muhammad Aqil Zughaib of the Lebanese Army was killed after a fierce battle of hand-to-hand and close-combat fighting. The Palmach Battalion suffered heavy casualties, and were forced to withdraw to the high ground and road west of al-Malikiyah. They manned their new positions in the area with the aim of preventing the Lebanese Army from using the road in their advance into Palestine. The Lebanese Battalion also suffered some casualties in their attack, but they continued with their attempt to capture Ramat Naftali. Their assault on the settlement reached the outer perimeter of its defences, where a very fierce battle went on for most of the day. Finally the Lebanese attack was repulsed and the Army was compelled to withdraw after suffering very heavy casualties.[1]

On the night of 15/16 May, a company of the Yaftach Brigade launched an attack on al-Nabi Yusha police post, but were unable to capture it. On the same night, another Palmach company infiltrated to al-Laittani bridge about ten kilometres from al-Muttallah inside Lebanese territory and managed to destroy it, thus depriving the Lebanese from using it for further movements. The Palmach company repeated their attack on al-Nabi Yusha on the night of 16/17 May, starting with an air raid, which dropped incendiary bombs on the post. But the target was too small for an air raid and although a few bombs hit their targets, they were of no effect on its Lebanese defenders who experienced an air raid for the first time. However, a few minutes later the Palmach company started their artillery and mortar bombardment and in the attack that followed half an hour of heavy bombardment, they managed to open a gap in the post perimeter, assaulted and captured the al-Nabi Yusha police post. Thus the main road running north–south to the west of al-Malikiyah, and all the approaches from the Lebanese territory into eastern Galilee, came under control of the Palmach Brigade. However, the Lebanese Battalion was in no way capable of advancing further into Palestine because of the casualties they suffered during their attack on the two Arab villages and the police post.

During the following two days, 16 and 17 May, the Yaftach Palmach Brigade carried out several fighting patrols north of al-Malikiyah inside Lebanese territory. They harassed a few undefended Lebanese villages, carried out a few demolitions on the Lebanese lines of communication and destroyed a large bridge on the road between Banyas and Marj Eiyoun. Thereafter, and apart from a few patrols from both sides here and there, the Lebanese front remained quiet for the next ten days.

On the night of the 18/19 May, the Yaftach Palmach Brigade, under command of Colonel Mula Cohen, sent a mixed column of armoured cars and softskin vehicles disguised as a supply convoy to al-Manarah. The column, without their lights on, passed by the road in the open ground between al-Manarah and the part of the road between Marj Eiyoun and al-Malikiyah adjacent to the Lebanese Palestinian border. One Palmach detachment blocked the road from the direction of Marj Eiyoun to prevent any reinforcements using it. When the Palmach column reached the Lebanese road, their armour turned south to capture al-Malikiyah. At the same time, a diversionary attack was carried out by another Palmach unit so that, when the Commander of the Lebanese Battalion asked for reinforcements, the Palmach column would move south with its lights on as if it was the expected reinforcement. A wicked plan, but it worked.

The Palmach column, with its lights on, advanced towards al-Malikiyah; it was received in every Lebanese village it passed safely through with cheers since the villagers thought that it was a Lebanese column on its way to support al-Malikiyah. At Aitaroun road junction, instead of turning south towards al-Malikiyah, the Palmach column went on towards Aitaroun a few miles west of al-Malikiyah, which was being air-raided by the Jews at the time. During the turn around of the column towards al-Malikiyah, a Lebanese column had just arrived at the scene with supplies and reinforcements for al-Malikiyah. It was surprised by heavy fire from the Palmach unit which destroyed two of its armoured cars and four vehicles loaded with ammunition. The Lebanese Battalion was surprised by the Palmach attack that followed and after a fierce battle it withdrew to its previous positions. Thus al-Malikiyah and Qudus fell to the Palmach on the morning of 19 May.

General Foad Shihab planned to attack al-Malikiyah at dawn on 5 June 1948 with the Lebanese Battalion, supported by one 75-mm artillery battery, one 81-mm mortar platoon, one medium machine-guns platoon and six Renault tanks. He also coordinated his plan with the Syrian Army, which planned to launch an air raid on al-Malikiyah just before dawn in support of the attack. However, that air raid was not launched and the attack was delayed by seven hours. In fact, it started at noon on 5 June, the fourth day of Ramadan, the month of fasting. Covered by a heavy barrage of artillery and mortars the assault troops of three companies advanced on al-Malikiyah and reached the defences of the Jews at 1800 hours. At the Jewish perimeter a hand-to-hand battle from trench to trench continued until 1900 hours when al-Malikiyah was recaptured by the Lebanese Army. The Jewish force withdrew, only to counter-attack during the night, but failed to regain its positions. On the following day the Lebanese Army attacked and captured Qudus near al-Malikiyah. Three Lebanese soldiers – Naim Rashid Khadaj, Foad Muhammad Ayash, and Imil Mtanyous al-Hilo[2] – were killed.

The Syrian Arab Army front

The Syrian Arab Army was established after the creation of the Syrian Ministry of Defence on 14 June 1945. Its origin was in the Arab officers and men serving with the French Mandatory Forces in Syria, when many of them left to join the Syrian nationalist movement for independence and fought the French forces in the rebellion of 1945. After independence, the Syrian units in the French forces were handed over to the Syrian Government and were formed as the Syrian Guards and Gendarmes, commanded by Brigadier Abdullah Aatfah. The organisation and training of the Syrian Army started on 29 August 1945. During 1946, the American military attaché in Damascus offered the Syrian Government a free supply of American weapons, but the Syrians declined and asked the British Army Commander in Syria to provide them with weapons, ammunition and a training mission. Soon afterwards, a British training mission, led by Colonel Fox, was drawn from the British Army in Syria and started to advise the Syrian Army. Two squadrons of 32 Marmon-Herrington armoured cars were presented as a gift to the Syrian Army. By 5 January 1947, the newly formed Syrian Arab Army was made up as shown in Table 6.2.

Towards the end of 1947, it became obvious that the Syrian Arab Army was to intervene in Palestine. Colonel Fox, who was an utter failure, was asked to leave, and the Syrian Army began its preparations for action. On 21 April 1948, the Syrian Minister of Defence informed Colonel Abd al-Wahhab al-Hakim that his 1st Brigade was to intervene in Palestine on 15 May. The Brigade Commander thought that 25 days were not enough to prepare his brigade for action and asked for more time. On 2 May, further orders from General Safwat were sent to al-Hakim to be ready to move on three days' notice. By that time the 1st Brigade was concentrated in Qattanah, and consisted of 1,811 officers and men organised as shown in Table 6.3.

Although a minority of the brigade troops had some experience in fighting the French during the rebellion of 1945, none had experience in modern warfare – particularly in large operations. However, on 12 May 1948, the brigade was ordered to move to the villages of Bint Jubail and Blida in Lebanon on 14 May. But after issuing his orders, al-Hakim was told to abort his move and change direction by entering Palestine from the south and to establish his assembly area in Fiq and Kufr Harib

TABLE 6.2
The Syrian Army

Unit	Location	Men	Officers	NCOs
HQ and administration	Damascus	1,429	71	282
1st Brigade				
1st Infantry Battlion	Hamah	501	12	81
2nd Infantry Battalion	Damascus	408	12	68
1st Cavalry Regiment	Homs	194	7	29
1st Artillery Regiment	Damascus	287	8	50
Tank Squadron	Damascus	109	3	21
Armoured Car Squadron	Damascus	89	3	18
HQ Company	Damascus	163	71	00
Total 1st Brigade		**1,751**	**116**	**267**
South Border Guards				
2nd Cavalry Regiment	Suwaida	927	20	87
3rd Cavalry Regiment	Qunaitrah	292	9	47
Total South Border Guards		**1,219**	**29**	**134**
2nd Brigade				
3rd Infantry Battalion	Lathiqiyah	494	11	91
4th Infantry Battalion	Halab	419	10	34
2nd Artillery Regiment	Halab	225	8	38
Mechanised Regiment	Halab	296	7	34
HQ Company	Halab	376	19	51
Total 2nd Brigade		**1,810**	**55**	**248**
3rd Brigade				
5th Infantry Battalion	Hasakah	350	10	41
6th Infantry Battalion	Dair al-Zur	388	11	47
6th Armoured Car Squadron	Dair al-Zur	73	2	10
HQ Company	Dair al-Zur	152	11	22
Total 3rd Brigade		**963**	**34**	**120**
North Border Guards				
4th Cavalry Regiment	Halab	603	13	53
5th Cavalry Regiment	Hasakah	430	14	35
Total North Border Guards		**1,033**	**27**	**88**
Badiyah (Desert) Force				
Dhumair Squadron	Dhumair	416	13	39
Tadmur Squadron	Tadmur	333	6	34
Dair al Zur Squadron	Dair al-Zur	390	9	36
Total Desert Force		**1,139**	**28**	**109**
Total Syrian Arab Army		**9,344**	**360**	**1,248**

Grand Total: 10,952 officers and men.[3]

TABLE 6.3
1st Brigade HQ

- 1st Infantry Battalion of three companies.
- 2nd Infantry Battalion of three companies.
- 1st Artillery Regiment of three 75-mm batteries.
- Armoured Regiment of two Marmon-Herrington squadrons and one tank squadron of six Renault tanks.
- One Signal Platoon.
- One Engineer Platoon.

area, and thereafter advance to Samakh, west of the southern part of the Golan heights. At 1800 hours on 14 May the move was completed.

The Syrian 1st Brigade had four geographical and tactical advantages over the Jewish Golani Brigade, which defended the sector.

1. The Syrian Brigade had no major geographical obstacles ahead on the line of their advance, such as the River Jordan.
2. The open and almost flat ground, where the Jewish settlements were located, was suitable for their armour.
3. They had excellent positions for their artillery observation and direction of fire.
4. Considering the dispersion of the Jewish forces in the areas of their objectives, a breakthrough would have enabled them to fight with the support of the Arab population in Nazareth and other districts.

As regards the last point, Herzog wrote: 'This would enable the Syrian forces a firm and potentially friendly jump-off ground from which to move in the direction of Haifa, a major port and one of the terminals of the oil pipeline from Iraq to the Mediterranean.'[4]

Opposite the Syrian Army in the north of Palestine, on the evening of 15 May, was the 2nd Regiment of the Golani Brigade, with one company at the Samakh–Tiberis sector, another company at the Ashdot Yaaquv–Gesher sector, and the third company in the rear at the al-Shajarah and Tabour sectors. The Golani Brigade were deployed as follows.

- One platoon at Gesher Police Fort.
- Two platoons at Ashdot Yaaquv.

- A local garrison company at Samakh and the police station there.
- Two platoons at Tiberias.
- One platoon and two sections in reserve at south Galilee.[5]

At 0100 hours on 15 May, the Syrian brigade crossed their start line from southern Golan towards Samakh with their lights on, thus losing the element of surprise. In a night attack, two Syrian companies of the 1st Battalion assaulted and captured al-Qasir Hill, Hill 98 and the village of al-Samrah on the shore of Lake Tiberias without artillery support. At 0730 hours, the Syrian artillery and mortars opened fire at Ain Ghaif, and by sunrise a Syrian air raid was carried out against the Jewish settlements of the plain. Further artillery fire was directed at Shaar Hagolan south of Lake Tiberias. The two Syrian companies went down from al-Qasir Hill and advanced across the open ground towards Samakh. On their way to the army camp and quarantine station they were joined by a squadron of armoured cars. In the fierce battle that followed, the Jewish garrison at these two positions retreated and the Syrian companies occupied them. The Syrian force advanced next towards Samakh and engaged the Jewish garrison with artillery and mortar fire.[6]

At this stage of the battle, the Golani Battalion sent two platoons from Tiberias to Samakh, stretching the defensive line from the south of Lake Tiberias to Ashdot Yaaquv. At the same time a Syrian company, supported by artillery and armoured cars' fire, advanced from al-Duwair Hill, west of al-Hemmah towards the water station east of Shaar Hagolan settlement. After a brief fight, with the exception of one of its defenders, everyone at the Jewish garrison at the station was killed, and the Syrian company advanced towards Shaar Hagolan. At that stage the Golani Brigade sent a detachment to reinforce the garrison of the settlement supported by a troop of 20-mm guns. The Syrian company attacked the settlement but failed to capture it and withdrew to its previous positions.

During the rest of 15 and 16 May, the Syrian Brigade continued with its artillery bombardment, a few air raids, night-fighting patrols and day engagements by their armoured cars, harassing Samakh and the other Jewish settlements. It also had time to reorganise and plan its future operations. The Jewish Golani Brigade was not idle either, for the troops dug their positions in Samakh, reorganised their defences and sent a few boats to the southern beaches of Lake Tiberias in a diversionary attack, opening fire at the Syrians with the aim of giving them the wrong impression of their strength.[7]

On 17 May, two Syrian companies attacked Samakh supported by artillery and mortar fire. The attack was repulsed when the Jewish 20-mm guns opened fire at the Syrian assault troops. The Syrian artillery continued with bombardment of the village, and the artillery duel continued for some time during the day. Meanwhile, it was reported to the Golani Brigade that a Syrian force was about to cross the frontier north of Lake Tiberias, but was prevented from continuing with its advance by a minefield which killed one senior officer. During the night of 17/18 May, the Golani Brigade carried out further deception and diversionary operations; its convoys moved with their lights off from Samakh to Poriya about ten miles from Samakh and returned to the village with their lights on, thus giving the impression that reinforcements had arrived. They used bulldozers and tractors to imitate the sound of tanks. All these movements were intended to cause the Syrians to delay their attack on Samakh. The success of these deceptive operations gave the Golani Brigade much-needed time to evacuate women and children from Samakh and the Jewish settlements, as well as to improve its defences and find a few men to reinforce its positions.

However, the Syrian Brigade Commander, Colonel Abd al-Wahhab al-Hakim, was not persuaded. He launched his attack at 0400 hours on 18 May. The attack started with heavy Syrian bombardment on Samakh and Shaar Hagolan, which inflicted heavy casualties on the Jewish defenders including a number of officers. One of the two Jewish 20-mm guns was destroyed and many buildings collapsed. At 0420 hours, the artillery ceased fire. Then a Syrian squadron of Marmon-Herrington armoured cars and a troop of Renault tanks followed by the 1st Infantry Battalion were deployed, crossed their start line and began their assault against Samakh from the south. The 2nd Battalion attacked from the north of Samakh. The Syrian armoured cars and tanks methodically destroyed the Haganah positions one after the other with point-blank fire.

While the Syrian armoured unit continued to clear Samakh, the Golani garrison withdrew leaving its dead and wounded behind. During its retreat to the two settlements of Degania 'A' and 'B', the Samakh Garrison lost further casualties and, ultimately, most of the defending force was wiped out.

Later that morning, the Haganah defenders of the Police Fort in Samakh continued to hold and cover the withdrawal of the Golani troops. But under pressure from the Syrian attack, particularly from the Marmon-Herrington armoured cars, they withdrew and the whole of Samakh area was taken by the Syrian 1st Brigade, which succeeded in capturing all its objectives, including the Police Fort, and occupied its positions south of Samakh at 0815 hours on 18 May.[8]

Following the fall of Samakh, and as a result of the continued artillery fire and air raids on the other settlements, the Jewish Northern Command sent two companies of the 3rd Battalion of the Golani Brigade and a company of the Palmach Yaftach Brigade to reinforce the 2nd Battalion. Many other settlements near the scene of the battle sent reinforcements to Dagania 'A' and 'B' settlements, which, by nightfall, had become the new Jewish front line. The Syrians turned their attention to the villages of Shaar Hagolan and Massada and occupied them. During the same night the Palmach Company carried out a counter-attack on the Police Fort, but only managed to reach the school building nearby when the Syrians opened fire at them and managed to beat off their attempt and hold the fort. The Palmach Company withdrew after suffering heavy casualties.[9]

President Shukri al-Quwatli, who was delighted with the success of the 1st Brigade, visited the front with some ministers and had lunch at Hill 98. When al-Quwatli heard that 400 artillery shells were fired during the attack, he ordered the brigade Commander to reduce his expenditure of shells because the war may last for six months and there was a shortage of shells. During his visit he ordered the 2nd Brigade to send their 3rd Infantry Battlion to be attached to 1st Brigade; the Battalion arrived during the afternoon and were placed at Hill 98 in reserve.

By the morning of 19 May, the new Syrian front line was from Samakh, south to Shaar Hagolan to Massada, ready to be used as a springboard for an attack on the settlements of Dagania 'A' and 'B'. During the night of 19 May, a delegation representing the Jewish settlers in the area visited David Ben-Gurion at Tel Aviv and appealed to him to send reinforcements to the area owing to the seriousness of the situation. According to Herzog, Ben-Gurion replied:

> We do not have enough guns and not enough airplanes. There is
> a shortage of men on all fronts. The situation in the Negev is very

serious and it is serious in Jerusalem and upper Galilee. The whole country is a front line. We have no possibility to send reinforcement.[10]

On 18 May, Moshe Dayan was appointed as Sector Commander of the Haganah forces defending the two Daganias, 'A' and 'B', and other settlements. He arrived at his command post on the same day and started to reorgnise his troops.[11] On 19 May, al-Hakim planned his attack on the two Dagania settlements with the following units.

- 1st Infantry Battalion.
- 2nd Infantry Battalion.
- 3rd Infantry Battalion of 2nd Brigade.
- Armoured Regiment.
- One company of Circassian Special Force.
- Two Engineer Platoons.

At 0415 hours on 20 May, the main Syrian attack on the Dagania settlements started with a heavy artillery and mortar bombardment as well as medium machine-gun fire from the police post at Samakh. Most of the artillery and mortar bombs hit their targets in the centres of the settlements causing many casualties and damage. The artillery barrage continued for 30 minutes. Then, a Syrian company from the 3rd Battalion supported by four Renault tanks and two troops of armoured cars advanced towards Dagania 'A', shooting at the pillboxes and trenches of the settlement, manned by about 70 Jewish defenders.

To avoid the tank fire and more casualties the Jews abandoned their pillboxes and moved to their communication trenches. The tanks were able to assault and penetrate the outer perimeter of the settlement and advanced to the inner perimeter. A Syrian armoured car advancing on the northern part of the settlement was hit by the remaining 20-mm gun near the bridge on the River Jordan. Another Syrian tank was hit and started to withdraw. A third tank, which was able to cross the inner perimeter and enter the settlement, was set on fire with Molotov cocktails. But the determined and courageous Syrian crew of the tank continued to fire until further Molotov cocktails destroyed their tank. The attack continued in spite of the heavy fire from the defenders.

The Syrian Infantry Company advancing behind the tanks had not kept up with the pace and were about 100 yards behind. When they continued to advance towards the outer perimeter, the Haganah opened fire at them from close range. Nevertheless, the Syrians, who were fighting with courage and high morale rather than with efficiency and experience, attempted to assault the defences of the settlement. At about 1300 hours, after fierce fighting for about nine hours with mounting casualties on both sides, it became obvious to the Syrian Commander that the attack on Dagania 'A' had failed.

Meanwhile, the attack on Dagania 'B' by the Syrian 1st Battalion was carried out at the same time as on Dagania 'A'. The battalion advanced to an area close to the outer perimeter of the settlement during the artillery barrage and attempted to assault its defences when the barrage ceased. At that point a Haganah fighting patrol detected the Syrian advance and opened fire at them from close range. The Syrian brigade Commander turned his attention on Dagania 'B'. He directed his mortar fire and the guns of eight armoured cars and tanks at the settlement. The battalion advanced to a point about 400 yards from the perimeter with two infantry companies in the lead. The tanks halted and directed their fire at the pillboxes and defences of the settlement while the two infantry companies advanced and came as close as 30 yards from their objectives. The defenders of the settlement opened fire at the Syrian infantry, who had to withdraw because of their very heavy casualties.

Another Syrian attack was mounted by 12 armoured cars and tanks. But by that time the Haganah had managed to bring into action a troop of 65-mm mountain guns close to the scene of battle and opened fire at the attacking Syrians. After suffering heavy casualties the Syrian attack was aborted and the battalion withdrew to its assembly area.[12]

Thereafter, the Haganah's 65-mm mountain guns directed their fire at the withdrawing Syrian forces, their support weapons behind their lines and any concentration of armour in the area. The Syrians, who until then had the monopoly of artillery fire in the battle field, were surprised and, under a heavy barrage of coming Jewish artillery and mortar fire, were compelled to withdraw from Samakh, Shaar Hagolan and Massada. That afternoon the Haganah reoccupied Samakh and the other settlements.

Meanwhile, during the afternoon of 20 May, at this critical situation for the Syrian Army, a meeting of the Arab leaders was held at Daraa on the Jordanian–Syrian border. It was attended by King Abdullah, the

Prince Regent of Iraq, the Syrian President Shukri al-Quwatli, the Lebanese President Camille Shamoun and Abd al-Rahman Azzam, the Secretary-General of the League of Arab States. Kirkbride reported:

> The Syrian President took the King aside and asked him if he would move his friends, the British, to give the Syrian Army equipment and ammunition, otherwise their position would become critical. The King suggested that the request should be addressed to the British Minister in Damascus and remarked that the request came oddly from one who had organised opposition to the British treaties with Iraq and Trans-Jordan. The President replied that it was clear that the Arab interests lay in coming to terms with Great Britain as soon as possible.
>
> I met Azzam at his request. He asked me to point out to you [The Foreign Office] that the American recognition of the Jewish State and your refusal to do so had caused an immense reversion of feeling in favour of Great Britain among the Arab masses. He felt that this was the psychological moment for the Arab leaders and politicians who had been hampered in the past by the suspicions of the masses to come to agreement with Great Britain. I concurred and suggested that they should get on with the work immediately. Azzam then said that he would be glad to know first that you would be favourable to such an idea. I promised to convey the message.
>
> My own view is that having committed themselves to a war the Arab leaders, in particular Azzam and the Lebanese and the Syrian Presidents, are nervous about the outcome and would like to bring Great Britain in on their side in some way or other – the bait offered being the treaties for which they assume Great Britain to be anxious.[13]

The failure of the attack on the two Dagania settlements and the recapture by the Jews of Samakh was devastating to the high command in the Syrian Army. On 22 May, the Syrian Minister of Defence resigned, and Brigadier Abdullah Aatfah and Colonel Abd al-Wahhab al-Hakim were relieved of their commands and pensioned off. All the battalion Commanders of the 1st Brigade were also relieved of their commands.

On 23 May, the following officers were ordered to take over the following units at the front.

Brigadier Husni al-Zaim	Chief of General Staff
Colonel Anwar Bannud	Commander 1st Brigade

Colonel Tawfiq Bashur   Commander 2nd Brigade
Lt Colonel Omar Khan Thamr   Commander Armoured
                                                Regiment

Mindful of the lessons he experienced in the field of battle, Brigadier Husni al-Zaim reorganised his forces and decided to coordinate his future operations with the Lebanese Army and Liberation Army units commanded by Fawzi al-Qawiqji.

On 9 June 1948, the joint offensive of Lebanese, Syrian and Liberation armies began. The Lebanese Army attacked and recaptured al-Malikiyah, and thus controlled the heights overlooking the main road running north to south-east of their positions. On the following day they also captured Qudus. Thus, the way was clear for the units of the Liberation Army, who until then were reorganising their formations, to advance further into the central areas of Galilee.

Meanwhile, the Syrian 2nd Brigade of two infantry battalions supported by an artillery regiment and an armoured squadron attempted to attack and capture the settlement of Mishmar Hayardin on the River Jordan opposite the bridge of Banat Yaaqoub. The attack started with an artillery barrage on the settlement and on the surrounding areas where the new Haganah Oded Brigade units had occupied their defensive positions. The initial Syrian attack was repulsed and the Syrians had to withdraw back to their assembly area. Both the Syrian Brigade and the Jewish Oded Brigade suffered casualties, and both sides called for reinforcements. The Syrians sent another battalion to join the brigade, while the Jewish Northern Command sent a battalion of the Carmeli Brigade to reinforce the Oded Brigade.

On 10 June, the Syrian Brigade, consisting of three battalions, repeated the attack on Mishmar Hayardin for the second time with a two-pronged assault. The first advanced towards the road junction between the settlements of Mahanayim and Razor, situated behind Mishmar Hayardin; the second, at the same time, attacked north and south of the targeted settlement. Under cover of a heavy barrage of artillery, the two parts of the attack crossed the River Jordan and advanced on their objectives. With a vanguard of eight tanks ahead, the Syrian battalion opened fire on Mishmar Hayardin at point-blank range from their tanks, supported by their mortars. The Carmeli Battalion, which had arrived at the scene of the battle, was not able to deploy. The Syrians assaulted the outer perimeter defences and penetrated the settlement. In the close combat and hand-to-hand fighting that followed, the Syrians captured Mishmar Hayardin and took the 20 surviving Haganah of its defenders as prisoners of war.

On the same day, the Syrians launched an attack on the fortress of En Gev on the eastern shore of Lake Tiberias, almost at the same time as the attack on Mishmar Hayardin. However, the attack failed and the Syrians withdrew at about 1200 hours. Another Syrian attack was launched on Mahanayim on 11 June, but that attack also failed. On the same day at the same time al-Qawiqji's Liberation Army units attempted to capture the Jewish village of Sejera near Lubya. During the fierce fighting that followed, they succeeded in cutting the road to Kfar Tabor, but casualties on both sides were very heavy. Just as the Haganah were about to withdraw, the Liberation army units withdrew.

The massacre of al-Tanturah

On the night of 22/23 May 1948, the 33rd Battalion of the Alexandroni Brigade carried out an unprovoked attack on the Arab village of al-Tanturah, near Haifa, in the north of Palestine. Fighting for the capture of the village continued all night and until the morning of 23 May. By that time, 14 Alexandroni soldiers were killed and some others wounded. However, as soon as the village was captured an organised house-to-house search for Arab men was carried out by the battalion. Any Palestinian Arab man, young or old, was killed on the spot. Thereafter, the battalion gathered all the remaining men who did not escape and took them to the Muslim cemetery, split them into groups of seven men each and ordered them to dig large trenches. As soon as each group finished digging they were shot in cold blood by the Jews and buried by others in the trench they had dug. Ninety-five Arab men were killed in that brutal manner. The total number of those Palestinian Arabs killed during that massacre reached 200 men. This information was revealed to the Israeli press by an Israeli researcher Theodore Katz, who thoroughly investigated the massacre and compiled his findings during his research for a master's degree at Haifa University. Katz interviewed witnesses from the 33rd Battalion of the Alexandroni Brigade who took part in the attack, relatives of the Arabs killed during the massacre and Jews from the settlement of Zikharon Ya'akov near al-Tanturah.

Some details of the massacre were published in the UK newspaper *The Independent* on 29 January 2000, and *al-Rai*, the Jordanian newspaper on 20 January 2000.

The Iraqi Army front

The Iraqi Army, which intervened in Palestine on 15 May, consisted of the units shown in Table 6.4, according to the order of battle by Lt General Salih Saib al-Juburi, the Chief of Staff of the Iraqi Army.

TABLE 6.4
The Iraqi Army

1st Infantry Brigade (97 officers and 2,257 men)
- 1st Battalion, 29 officers and 658 men.
- 2nd Battalion, 24 officers and 616 men.
- 1st Battalion of the 5th Brigade, 24 officers and 643 men.
- One Field Dressing Station.
- One Engineers Squadron.
- One Signal Squadron.

Mechanised Brigade (106 officers, and 1,837 men)
- Mechanised Regiment.
- Armoured Car Regiment (Khalid ibn al-Walid).
- Mechanised Desert Regiment.
- One Engineers Squadron.
- One Signal Squadron.

The two brigade groups were supported by the 3rd Artillery Regiment of 25-pounder field guns; the Mobile Artillery Regiment of 3.7 Howitzer guns; and the total strength of the Iraqi forces was about 4,700 officers and men. Among their troops they had a large number of men who had some fighting experience during the 1941 Iraqi rebellion when they fought the British Army. Their officers were well trained and some of them attended courses in the British Staff College and at other institutions during 1942–7, when relations between Iraq and the United Kingdom improved. Their weapons and ammunition were British-made, and they had a squadron of fighter/bomber aircraft (Sea Furoy) at Mafraq airfield in the east of Jordan. Their line of advance on 15 May was from Mafraq to Irbid and down through Wadi al-Arab to North Shunah in the Jordan valley.

At dawn on 15 May, two infantry companies supported by an armoured car squadron and an engineer platoon assembled in the area of North Shunah. On observing this movement the Haganah force at Gesher destroyed the two small bridges opposite the settlement to prevent the Iraqi Army from using them to cross the River Jordan. The Iraqis, who were well equipped and well trained in river crossing operations, managed with one engineer's squadron to lay two bridges adjacent to the two that had been destroyed and crossed the River Jordan. Under cover of an artillery barrage they advanced with the intention of capturing the Police Fort adjacent to the settlement of Gesher, Gesher itself and Camel Hill north of Gesher. They attacked and captured the settlement of Naharayim and the power station to the north. During the same afternoon they attacked and captured Camel Hill, one kilometre north-west of Gesher, and continued shelling the settlement and Police Fort without attempting to capture them that night.

On the afternoon of 16 May, the Iraqi Company and Armour Squadron at Camel Hill attacked Gesher from the north. As they were about to assault it from close range, the Haganah opened fire with all their weapons and managed to halt the attack. Both sides suffered heavy casualties, and the Iraqis were compelled to withdraw back to their starting line. The Haganah thence opened the flood gates of the River Jordan to prevent the Iraqis from crossing the river again.[14]

On the following day, 17 May, the Iraqis renewed their attack from Camel Hill with armoured cars and infantry against the settlement of Gesher and the Police Fort. The Infantry Company were able to close up at the Police Fort main gate and destroy it, and an armoured car went through the gate into the courtyard. The Haganah used Molotov cocktails to destroy the armoured car and thereafter the Iraqis withdrew. The Iraqi attack on Gesher was repulsed, but it was not over. Gesher was isolated by the Iraqis who continued to harass it with desultory mortar and artillery fire. During that night, the Haganah attempted to recapture Camel Hill but were repulsed by the Iraqis who inflicted very heavy casualties on them. The Haganah renewed their attack on Camel Hill during 18 May with a company from the Golani 3rd Battalion, but the attack was again repulsed by the Iraqis, who inflicted heavy casualties on the attackers.

Meanwhile, while the right flank of the Iraqis attempted to capture Gesher, on 17 May another battalion was planning to attack and capture Kawkab al-Hawa located at a height of 400 metres above the Jordan valley and overlooking the whole area of operations. In their time, the Crusaders had realised its strategic importance and built a small citadel at its peak. The Iraqis attacked the ruins of Kawkab al-Hawa with an Infantry Company from Lt Colonel Omar Ali's battalion and managed to capture the peak by dawn on 18 May. The Golani 3rd Battalion had arrived during the night at al-Bira about 1,500 yards from Kawkab al-Hawa. During the attack they carried out at the peak, 30 Iraqi soldiers were killed and the rest withdrew back to Jordan across the river. The Golani Brigade managed to send four 65-mm guns to Kawkab al-Hawa from which they engaged many Iraqi targets below their position. Thereafter, they directed their desultory fire at nearly every Iraqi position in depth. The Iraqis withdrew to the south, and then took over the sector of the 1st Brigade of the Jordan Arab Army in Nablus.[15]

On the morning of 22 May, the Iraqi 1st Brigade deployed in the Nablus sector where, for three days, they prepared to take the initiative. On 23 May, an Iraqi Mechanised Brigade commanded by Lt Abd al-Karim Qasim struck from the Nablus hills past the town of Tulkarrn in the direction of Natanya on the Mediterranean. They took the Jewish settlement of Geulim. On 28 May, another attack supported by armour reached Kfar Yona and Em Vered. A third column attacked from Kufr Qasim and reached Ras al-Ein. Thus, the Iraqi forces were only six miles from Natanya and the Mediterranean when they were forced to halt their advance by the Alexandroni Brigade. Then the Alexandroni counter-attacked and recaptured Geulim on the same day.

It became obvious to the Jewish command that the threat of cutting their occupation of Palestine into two isolated areas and blocking the line of communication to the whole sector of Galilee was imminent. They decided to mount an offensive threatening the Nablus triangle and the northern flank of the Iraqi 1st Brigade. They planned an attack by two brigades – the Golani and the Carmeli – to capture the town of Jenin. At the same time, a diversionary attack was planned by the Alexandroni Brigade on the Tulkarm area through Wadi Ara.[16] While the massive Jewish attack was being planned, the Iraqi Army had sent the 4th Infantry Brigade Group to reinforce the Nablus sector. They arrived there on 29 May, but were commanded to move to Jenin on the following day. They advanced from Nablus to the sector of Jenin on 30 May and deployed their troops in depth with forward positions from Affulah, Sandalah to Jenin; the main road from Haifa, Givat Gadish, Kufr Dan to Jenin; Um al-Fahim, Anin, Rehan, Yaabad south of Jenin; and the roads from Faqquah, Jalaboun and Arranah to Jenin.

The major attack by the Golani Brigade started that same day. At dawn they crossed their start line at the road between Affulah and Bait Shean, advanced south and captured Zirain, Nuns and al-Mazar on Jabal Jalboua. On 2 June, they attacked and captured Arabunah and then advanced by three columns to capture Dair Ghazalah, north-east of Jenin, and Arranah, north of the town.

The Carmeli Brigade advanced and occupied Jezril on 28 May. On 29 May they advanced to Sandalah, capturing it on 1 June. On 2 June, they captured al-Muqaibilah, Jalamah and connected with the Golani unit at Arranah. On 3 June, they attacked Jenin with two battalions from the north, and managed to control the hills adjacent to the city from the south-west and the south-east. They attempted to capture the police post west of the city, but the Iraqi Company defending it managed to repulse the attack inflicting heavy casualties on the attackers. A few hours after midnight on 3 June they were able to capture a small part of Jenin, excluding the city centre and the Police Fort.

By sunrise on 3 June, the Carmeli Brigade were exhausted. The Iraqi resistance against their attacks was extremely strong, which caused them heavy casualties. Chaim Herzog wrote:

> The excessive heat and the troops' inability to dig slit trenches for personal protection on the exposed sun-scorched rocky terrace impaired the effectiveness of the Israelis holding the high ground to the west of the city . . . The Iraqis now brought up reinforcements, whose weight began to tell in the battle, which could have brought success had the 'Alexandroni' Brigade diversionary attack taken place as planned . . . But no effective attack was mounted from the west by the 'Alexandroni' Brigade, and the situation of the 'Carmeli' unit became very precarious.[17]

The Iraqis were not affected by the excessive heat. For them, even in June, the Jenin weather, compared with the summer heat in Baghdad, was cool and refreshing. The weather was even better when the Iraqi 4th Infantry Brigade Group started their counter-attack during the afternoon of 3 June. An Iraqi Battalion, commanded by Lt Colonel Omar Ali, a very experienced soldier in mountain warfare, supported by artillery and mortar fire, attacked the 1st Battalion of the Carmeli Brigade defending the high ground on the south-west of Jenin. As the Iraqis approached the Carmeli positions, a mortar bomb exploded at the Carmeli Battalion HQ where the battalion second in command and the staff of the HQ were killed.

In the close combat that followed, the Jewish Battalion suffered many casualties, and started to desert their positions and withdraw to the north-west. Followed by the Iraqis with their machine gun, mortar and later artillery fire, they suffered more casualties during their withdrawal.

At that point, the Carmeli Brigade Commander committed his reserve of infantry and armour to support the unit in the outskirts of Jenin, but was not able to affect the momentum of the Iraqi counter-attack, which was forcing his units to retreat. By dusk, the Iraqi force was able to recapture the hills surrounding Jenin and pushed the Carmeli Brigade back to their positions of 2 June. In the battle that followed, the Carmeli and the Golani Brigades suffered about 860 killed and wounded. At that point, Colonel Moshe Carmel, the Commander of the Carmeli Brigade, advised his HQ that it would be possible to continue to hold Jenin and his positions in the desperate situation his troops were in only if the Alexandroni Brigade could attack and capture Tulkarm. His HQ commanded him to withdraw.

Under a very heavy Iraqi artillery barrage, the Carmeli Brigade withdrew while they suffered further heavy casualties. From then on, they took their defensive positions at Muqaiblah, Jalamah, Arranah, Dair Ghazalah and Faqquah. Jenin was recaptured by the Iraqis on 4 June. In fact, the Nablus sector was saved by the Iraqi victory.

Opposite Tulkarm to the north-west, the village of Qaqun was still being held by the Iraqi force that had captured it on 30 May. On the night of 4/5 June, the Alexandroni Brigade attacked the village with the 3rd Battalion and two companies of the 2nd Battalion. The Iraqi platoon at the village and the Palestinian partisans held their position until it was impossible to continue fighting and they had to withdraw. The Iraqi Battalion at Tulkarm carried out three counter-attacks to recapture Qaqun, which failed.

The Egyptian Army front

The Egyptian Kingdom was the largest of all the Arab countries, and its army of 1948 was the oldest and largest Arab army that intervened in Palestine. But its officers and men, who constituted the majority of its units and formations of 1948, had never fired a shot in anger – unlike the Syrians, the Lebanese, the Iraqis and (especially) the Jordanians. The best of its armed services were the artillery regiments, who were well known for their accuracy and level of training. Their participation in the 1948 war had two elements: the first element was the regular army commanded by General Ahmad Muhammad Ali al-Mawawi, which consisted of the 3rd Infantry Division containing the two infantry brigades shown in Table 6.5.

TABLE 6.5
3rd Infantry Division

1st Infantry Brigade
- 1st Infantry Battalion, 25 officers and 700 men.
- 2nd Infantry Battalion, 25 officers and 750 men.

2nd Infantry Brigade
- 6th Infantry Battalion, 25 officers and 750 men.
- 9th Infantry Battalion, 25 officers and 750 men.

Light Infantry Company, 4 officers and 124 men
Armoured Cars Regiment, 35 armoured cars and Bren carriers
Tank Squadron, 12 light tanks
Artillery Regiment, 3 batteries of twenty-five-pounder field guns (24 guns), 1 battery of eighteen-pounder guns (8 guns).

Each infantry battalion consisted of three infantry companies, a squadron of 12 Bren carriers and a support company of three-inch mortars and medium machine guns. Each company was armed with two-inch mortars and PIAT rocket launchers. The organisation of the infantry was similar to that of British infantry battalions. The total strength of the division was about 4,200 officers and men. The Egyptian Army was supported by a small air force.

The second element was the Muslim Brothers' partisans of two battalions – about 800 officers and men – maintained by private donations of the Muslim Brothers Movement and the League of Arab States.

The Jewish forces facing the Egyptian Army were the Givati Brigade, commanded by Colonel Shimon Avidan, consisting of five battalions of about 3,000 officers and men; and the Negev Palmach Brigade, consisting of about 1,200 officers and men commanded by Colonel Nahum Sarig, which had two battalions and a mobile commando desert force. The Brigade were deployed with the 2nd Battalion responsible for the area north of Beersheba to Gaza road, and the 8th Battalion responsible for the area south of that line in the Negev desert.

The first Egyptian force to enter Palestine was the 1st Muslim Brothers Battalion commanded by Lt Colonel Ahmad Abd al-Aziz of the Egyptian Army. In its training and equipment the battalion was on a level with the Liberation Army, but they enjoyed a unity of purpose, the highest possible morale and a determination to fight for a religious cause of martyrdom. On 5 May 1948, the battalion moved from al-Arish to Khan Yunis using the railway line. As soon as they entered Palestine, Colonel Ahmad Abd al-Aziz decided, in spite of all the advice to the contrary, not to heed the lessons of the attack carried out by the Muslim Brothers on the settlement of Kfar Darom on 10 April 1948. He intended to attack and capture the same settlement in the south-east between Gaza and Khan Yunis.

On 10 May, the attack was launched supported by artillery fire. But for some reason the barrage was delayed from 0200 hours to 0430 hours. Instead of postponing the attack, Ahmad Abd al-Aziz commanded that it should continue. By that time the Jewish defenders of the settlement were alerted to the attack and could observe the Muslim Brothers advancing close to the perimeter. By the time the attacking Brothers were about to assault the barbed wire, some of their own artillery shells hit them rather than the settlement. Seventy Muslim Brothers were killed and 50 others were wounded, and the attack was aborted. The well-known Captain Maarouf al-Hadhari was among the wounded who were evacuated to Cairo. The bodies of the attacking Brothers remained around the settlement until they were recovered by Kamil al-Sharif of the Muslim Brothers on 18 June – six weeks later.[18]

On 13 May, the Muslim Brothers Battalion surrounded the settlement and placed it under siege. Soon after, an infantry company of the 2nd Battalion of the Negev Brigade, supported by a squadron of armoured cars, attempted to reach the settlement of Kfar Darom with supplies. The Brothers had an ambush of infantry supported by predetermined artillery targets ready to intervene. When the Negev Brigade convoy reached the area of the ambush, the artillery opened fire at close range – this time with accuracy. The Haganah men deserted their armoured cars and vehicles and ran towards the settlement, only to be trapped by the ambush. None of them survived. When the Haganah in the settlement attempted to rescue the convoy, and as they went out in the open, other machine guns opened fire on them killing many while they withdrew back to the settlement. Fifteen armoured cars and vehicles were captured by the Muslim Brothers.[19]

On 14 May, the Egyptian regular army, commanded by General al-Mawawi, crossed the Egyptian border into Palestine and advanced as far as Gaza, where al-Mawawi established his HQ. To begin with, he wanted to place the Muslim Brothers under his direct command, but Ahmad Abd al-Aziz refused and asked that they remain free as a partisan unit. General al-Mawawi then offered that the Brothers should occupy the Beersheba sector to protect the Egyptian Army flank. Abd al-Aziz agreed, moving his troops and HQ to Beersheba on 17 May.

On 18 May, he sent a company to attack the settlement of Bait Eshel north of his position, another to occupy al-Aujah and Asluj Arab villages and held one company in reserve at his HQ.

On 19 May, a delegation from Hebron arrived at Abd al-Aziz HQ and appealed to him to send a force there to assist the Jordanian Arab Army to defend Hebron and Bethlehem. Abd al-Aziz agreed, ignoring his Commander's plan.

On 20 May, he left Beersheba with two platoons and moved his HQ to Hebron, leaving behind Captain Mahmoud Abdo to defend Beersheba. From Hebron he took the Brothers to Bethlehem and established his HQ at the Windsor Hotel in the city. He immediately thinned out his troops from al-Aujah, Asluj and Beersheba and reinforced his positions in Bethlehem.

On 21 May, orders were given to the 12th Infantry Company of the Jordanian Arab Army through Abdullah al-Tel, Commander of the 6th Regiment, to cooperate with the Egyptian force in Bethlehem. On the same day, the Muslim Brothers' artillery and the Jordan Arab Army mortars and Marmon-Herrington armoured cars' two-pounders opened fire at Ramat Rahel. A few minutes later fires were seen in many buildings of the settlement. The shelling of Ramat Rahel continued on the following day and as soon as it stopped, an attack on the southern

[175]

area of the settlement was mounted by the Jordan Arab Army platoon in Mar Ilyas and by the Jordanian company of Muslim Brothers in Sur Bahir. The Haganah holding the settlement withdrew, but a company from the Etzioni 2nd Battalion counter-attacked and recaptured the occupied areas.

On 23 May, Lt Colonel Ahmad Abd al-Aziz decided to attack and capture the Jewish settlement of Ramat Rahel, which overlooks the Arab village of Sur Bahir and the road to Jerusalem. His plan was to attack with the following forces.

- One company of the Egyptian Muslim Brothers, about 130 officers and men.
- Two platoons of the 12th Company of the Jordanian Arab Army, with three officers and 50 men.
- Three platoons from the Jordanian partisan Usamah Company, one officer and 70 men.
- The Jordanian Muslim Brothers of Abi Aubaidah Company.
- The Artillery Battery of the Egyptian Muslim Brothers.
- A troop of Marmon-Herrington attached to the 12th Jordanian Infantry Company.[20]

At dawn on 24 May, the Egyptian artillery started their bombardment of the settlement of Ramat Rahel, and the Marmon-Herringtons advanced to a closer range and opened fire with their two-pounders at the pillboxes of the settlement and other positions. By sunrise, the infantry advanced and assaulted the barbed wire of the settlement, and then started to demolish the towers and pillboxes with explosives. They cleared their objective, fighting from house to house, until (with the exception of one building) the whole settlement was captured.

However, on the following day, units from the Etzioni Brigade and the Harel Palmach Brigade carried out a counter-attack to recapture the settlement. The platoon of the 12th Company of the Jordan Arab Army and the troop of Marmon-Herringtons at Mar Ilyas were attacked by the Etzioni Brigade on 28 May and, under pressure, they were compelled to withdraw. But the Jordanian Muslim Brothers at Sur Bahir and a platoon from al-Jihad al-Muqaddas, commanded by Hussein al-Hijazi of the Muslim Brothers, carried out a counter-attack and reoccupied Mar Ilyas. After a complete day of fighting the settlement was recaptured by the units of the Etzioni and Harel Brigades.[21] On 4 June 1948, the settlement of Talbioth continued to fire at the Muslim Brothers at Sur Bahir from a large tower south of the settlement. Late that night Ahmad Abd al-Aziz ordered Hussein al-Hijazi to destroy the tower. A fighting patrol of the Muslim Brothers commanded by al-Hijazi infiltrated to the tower, placed a high explosive bomb under it and completely destroyed it. All the Haganah men in the tower were killed.[22]

Meanwhile, the first operation by the regular Egyptian Army was an attack on Nirim (Nir Yizhaq), about 20 miles east of Rafah. The Egyptian attack was carried out by four Crusader tanks, a troop of armoured cars and a squadron of Bren carriers. At 0700 hours on 15 May, the Egyptian force started their artillery bombardment, while the mobile column advanced towards their target. Instead of rushing the settlement using their mobility and armour, they dismounted about 400 yards from the settlement perimeter. They waited until the middle of the day to start their assault, which came as close as 150 yards from the perimeter. At that point the defending Haganah suddenly opened fire. The armoured unit, who had reached the barbed wire of the settlement, halted when they saw a mines warning sign and started to withdraw. The whole force then withdrew to a deserted British Army camp two kilometres from Nirim, leaving behind them the bodies of the 30 men killed. Seven Haganah men were killed and 40 others wounded. On 16 May, the Egyptian force repeated their attempt, but only managed to shell the settlement with their artillery without assaulting it. On 17 May, the Negev Palmach 8th Battalion sent a company to reinforce the settlement, so the Egyptian Army decided not to attack and withdrew to its previous positions.

If the intention of the Egyptian Army was to capture Tel Aviv, they soon realised that wasting their efforts on small settlements was of little value, and cost them heavy casualties and precious time. Thus they changed direction and concentrated their efforts on advancing north of Gaza. The main obstacle ahead of their advance was the settlement of Yad Mordechai on the main road and railway line 20 miles north of Gaza. General al-Mawawi decided to capture it. On 19 May, after a very heavy artillery barrage which nearly destroyed the settlement, the 1st Egyptian Battalion, commanded by Major Zakariya Muhyi al-Din, mounted their second attack on Yad Mordechai. After a battle that lasted about three hours they managed to destroy a large pillbox located about 400 yards south of their objective. The Haganah withdrew from the pillbox back to the settlement. The Egyptians continued with their attack and assaulted the outer perimeter, but were forced back by very heavy fire from the defenders. Captain Muhammad al-Mouji, who led the attack with his company, was among the 40 Egyptian soldiers who were killed. Sixteen Jewish soldiers were killed and 20 were wounded. The 1st Egyptian Battalion repeated their attempt at 2050 hours, but were forced to halt again. After two more attempts the defenders suffered 18 fatalities and 20 wounded, and appealed to their HQ to send reinforcements. The 2nd Battalion of the Negev Brigade sent one platoon to support the settlement, but the Egyptian artillery continued with their barrages to the extent that the morale of the defenders became very low.

During the afternoon of 23 May, a few Egyptian tanks and Bren carriers managed to penetrate the settlement, but were halted by nightfall. During that night, a commando unit from the Negev Brigade attempted to enter Yad Mordechai from the direction of the settlement of Gevar Aam, but were intercepted by a Muslim Brothers' patrol commanded by Kamil al-Sharif. In the battle that followed, the commando unit managed to enter the settlement with a few of their vehicles and evacuated the wounded from it. The defenders suffered 38 fatalities.[23]

Just before dawn on 24 May, the Haganah and the platoon of the Negev Brigade withdrew from Yad Mordechai to the nearby settlement of Gevat Aam. An Egyptian platoon, commanded by Lt Saad al-Jammal, attacked the evacuated settlement and captured it.[24]

During the night of 25/26 May, the Commando unit of the Negev Brigade surprised the Egyptian artillery battery at their gun position near Bait Hanoun while they were shelling the settlement of Nir Aam. They managed to approach the guns to within 50 yards without being detected, then opened fire at the gunners. In the chaos that followed they killed and wounded about 40 officers and men, and destroyed the guns.

Meanwhile, the Egyptian Brigade had to face the Jewish Givati Brigade. After the Givati's successful 'destroy and expel' operation of evicting the inhabitants of several Arab villages from their homes between the settlements of Negba and Bir Tuvia, they captured the British Army camp in Sarafand, which was completely empty.

The Police Forts west of the village of Iraq Suweidan and al-Faluja were two thorns in the side of the Jewish forces. From their location on the main lateral road between al-Majdal, al-Faluja and Bait Jibrin, they linked the forces of the Muslim Brothers in the Hebron–Bethlehem sector with their main Egyptian force in the Gaza sector. Thus it was vital to the Egyptians to hold them at any cost. The Givati 3rd Battalion sent a company supported by armoured cars to capture the Police Fort and the village of Iraq Suweidan on 21 May. But the attack was repulsed by the Egyptian Muslim Brothers defending both. Later that night, another attack was mounted with the same company supported by a platoon from the 4th Givati Battalion, but they failed to achieve their objective and withdrew after suffering some casualties.[25]

On 29 May, the Egyptian 2nd Brigade, commanded by Brigadier Muhammad Najib, advanced to the north. They captured Isdud, just 25 miles from Tel Aviv. However, after they had moved forward for about two miles they halted because the bridge ahead had been demolished by the Givati Brigade during the previous night. Thereafter, the Givati Brigade, commanded by Shimon Avidan and the Jewish Air Force, carried out a heavy bombing of the Egyptian Brigade, forcing them to dig in and take a defensive posture.

On 2 June, the Givati Brigade attacked the Egyptian positions with two battalions. After a very fierce battle, the Givati Brigade attack was repulsed – but only after suffering more than 100 fatalities and a large number of wounded. An unknown number of Givati men were taken prisoner by the Egyptians. Instead of advancing north to Yibne, Brigadier Najib decided to reorganise his force, reinforce it and turn his attention to isolating the Jewish forces in the Negev desert from the north of Palestine.[26]

The Jewish command planned a massive attack on the Egyptian 2nd Brigade with the following formations.

- Givati 3rd, 4th and 7th Battalions.
- 7th Battalion of the Negev Brigade.
- One company of the 1st Givati Battalion.

The plan of the attack was as follows:

- Column 'A' consisting of four companies from the 4th Givati Battalion and another company from the 1st Givati Battalion to attack from the north and north-west of Isdud, to surprise the Egyptians from the rear.

- Column 'B' consisting of commando troops and infantry from the Negev Brigade to attack from the south of Isdud.
- Column 'C' consisting of the 7th Givati Brigade to attack from the east of Isdud.

The attack started at dawn on 2 June, with very heavy bombardment by the Jewish mortars and artillery. But the Egyptians were well dug in; they had by then some experience in fighting and were determined to hold their positions. As the attackers came close to the Egyptian trenches, the latter opened fire with all their weapons. The Egyptian artillery was very accurate in directing its fire at the advancing Jews and disrupted the momentum of their attack. All the Jewish columns failed to reach their objectives on any axis and the Egyptian 2nd Brigade won the day.[27]

Meanwhile, on the night of 2 June, another Egyptian formation attacked the settlement of Negba, which was defended by a company from the 3rd Givati Battalion. The attack started with a very heavy barrage from three artillery batteries of 25-pounders and 4.7 Howitzer guns followed by a three-pronged assault. But the attack failed to achieve its objective, and caused some 100 casualties. Unable to advance north over the blown-up bridge, especially as the Givati Brigade had captured the Arab village of Yinbe, Brigadier Muhammad Najib decided to secure his long line of communication. The Jewish settlement of Nizzanim located about ten miles south of Isdud was a threat to his line of supplies from Gaza. On 6 June, he decided to capture it. At dawn on 7 June, the Egyptian 9th Battalion and one company, supported by an armoured car squadron and an artillery regiment, attacked the settlement of Nizzanim, which was defended by a company of the 3rd Givati Battalion and two platoons of Haganah and settlers (about 150 officers and men). After a barrage by Egyptian artillery, the armoured squadron led the attack, assaulted the perimeter and captured the courtyard of the settlement. After two attempts during a fierce battle of close combat, the settlement was captured. Thirty-three Jewish soldiers were killed and, with the exception of three men who escaped, the rest were taken prisoner and sent to Gaza by the Egyptians.

During the night of 7/8 June, the 2nd Battalion of the Givati Brigade and the 7th Battalion of the Negev Palmach Brigade attempted to attack and capture Isdud, but their attack failed and they were forced to withdraw – except from Hill 69 on which a company of the Givati Brigade had been positioned the previous night.

During the night of 9/10 June, the 2nd Givati Battalion attempted to recapture Nizzanim, but failed and withdrew to Hill 69, where the Egyptian artillery directed their defensive fire. The Egyptians attacked and recaptured Hill 69.[28]

On 10 June, the 1st Battalion of the Givati Brigade occupied Yasaur and the 8th Givati Battalion captured Bttani; thus the Jewish corridor between Gan, Yafnah and Tufiya became wider and more open. The 3rd Givati Battalion captured Julis and the crossroads adjacent to it; thus the road to Negba was freed. An attempt to capture the Iraq Suweidan police post by the 7th Negev Palmach Battalion failed after a battle of close combat in which the Egyptians courageously held their positions. The Negev Palmach Brigade captured Bir Asluj south of Bir al-Sabaa.

NOTES

1 Herzog, *The Arab–Israeli Wars*, pp. 54–5. Also, the Lebanese journal *The Army* (Beirut: the Lebanese Army, 1951), no. 159, p. 38.
2 *The Army*, no. 159, p. 42.
3 *The Syrian Arab Army in the Palestine War of 1948*. Document sent to the author by Field Marshal Mustafa Tlas, the Syrian Defence Minister and Chief of General Staff, through the Syrian Embassy in London, received 17 July 1999.
4 Herzog, *The Arab–Israeli Wars*, p. 49.
5 *The Palestine War 1947–1948*, an official Israeli account, p. 505.
6 *Ibid.*, p. 505. Also, Herzog, *The Arab–Israeli Wars*, p. 51.
7 *The Syrian Arab Army in the Palestine War of 1948*, official document, pp. 17–18. Also, *The Palestine War 1947–1948*, an official Israeli account, p. 506.
8 *The Syrian Arab Army in the Palestine War of 1948*, official document, p. 19. Also, Herzog, *The Arab–Israeli Wars*, p. 51.
9 *The Palestine War 1947–1948*, an official Israeli account, p. 507.
10 Herzog, *The Arab–Israeli Wars*, p. 51.
11 Shabtai Teveth, *Moshe Dayan* (London: Oxford University Press, 1972), p. 141.
12 *The Palestine War 1947–1948*, an official Israeli account, pp. 508–9. Also, *The Syrian Arab Army in the Palestine War of 1948*, official document, pp. 22–3.
13 PRO. FO 816/120. Kirkbride to the Foreign Office, 22 May 1948.
14 *The Palestine War 1947–1948*, an official Israeli account, p. 515.
15 *Ibid.*, p. 516. Also, al-Sharaa, *Our Wars with Israel*.
16 Herzog, *The Arab–Israeli Wars*, p. 56.

17 *Ibid.*, p. 58.
18 Kamil Al Sharif, *The Muslim Brothers in the Palestine War* (Arabic) (Amman: Al Manar, 1984), pp. 82–4. Also, Herzog, *The Arab–Israeli Wars*, p. 70.
19 Al Sharif, *The Muslim Brothers*, pp. 84–5.
20 Abdullah al-Tal, *The Palestine Catastrophe*, p. 168.
21 Al Sharif, *The Muslim Brothers*, p. 94. Also, *The Palestine War 1947–1948*, an official Israeli account, p. 529.
22 Al Sharif, *The Muslim Brothers*, p. 95.
23 Herzog, *The Arab–Israeli Wars*, p. 70.
24 *The Palestine War 1947–1948*, an official Israeli account, p. 549. Also, Dan Kurzman, *Genesis 1948: The First Arab–Israeli War* (London: Vallentine Mitchell, 1992), pp. 280–7.
25 *The Palestine War 1947–1948*, an official Israeli account, p. 552.
26 Herzog, *The Arab–Israeli Wars*, p. 73.
27 *The Palestine War 1947–1948*, an official Israeli account, p. 555–6.
28 *Ibid.*, pp. 558–9.

7

The First Truce

While battles were raging at every Arab front in Palestine, at 1130 hours on 24 May 1948 the British Minister in Amman, Sir A. S. Kirkbride, sent a telegram to the Foreign Secretary, Ernest Bevin, reporting on the war and the political situation.

> 1. Although the Arab forces in Palestine appear to be fairly well placed and to be making progress the weaknesses of their supply systems and their lack of reserves of ammunition and stores is beginning to make itself felt already. The incident of the seizure of Trans-Jordan supplies by Egypt is significant.
>   The Egyptians seem to have, no doubt wisely, to advance no further and yesterday declined to make a small movement forward which was suggested by Glubb on the grounds that they might meet with opposition.
>
> 2. Though not prepared to admit it, the Arab military leaders are far from happy about their position and when their doubts infect the political leaders we shall doubtless have a new slump in morale. In fact, there is a good chance that in a relatively short period, the Arab leaders may be ready for a general truce which will lead to some settlement. The danger is, of course, that by that time the Jews will be on the upgrade and not be prepared to treat.
>
> 3. On the Arab side it will be best if the acceptance of the truce could appear as an act of generosity before the internal rottenness of their apparently successful military façade becomes evident. It should doubtless help if at the right moment they were subject to intense and public pressure by the United Nations Organisation. The Trans-Jordan Minister of Foreign Affairs yesterday expressed surprise that there had been so little pressure by the United Nations Organisation. He spoke in a tone of regret.
>
> 4. This message is intended as a warning of my feeling that on the Arab side the moment to put through a truce may be near.[1]

Bevin wasted no time. Being under pressure himself from the United States of America and the Jewish lobby in the United Kingdom, he immediately replied at 1630 hours on the same day.

1. If as I anticipate you find difficulty in persuading King Abdullah to agree to a ceasefire you should make use of as much as you think fit of the following material.

2. As King Abdullah will know, I have been and am under the strongest pressure from America in the United Nations and from sections of public opinion here with regard to the continuation of assistance to the Arab Legion by means of subsidy, loan of officers and supply of war materials. I have so far been able to resist this pressure out of regard for our good relations with Trans-Jordan of which King Abdullah has in the past given us such notable proofs. I have also been greatly influenced by the statement made to me by the Trans-Jordan Prime Minister during his visit here to the effect that the intentions of Trans-Jordan were to enter the Arab parts of Palestine and that the Trans-Jordan Government realised the difficulties that would be caused for us as well as for them if they went further than this and became involved in large scale hostilities.

3. The Arab Legion has successfully carried out the greater part of its objectives of occupying Arab areas of Palestine. It has also become involved in severe fighting in Jerusalem. Presumably also they will now have achieved their major objective by cutting off Jerusalem from the coast and securing the protection of the Moslem Holy places in the Arab city. As I have said before, an attack on Jerusalem touches on a most sensitive point in public opinion throughout the world. The sooner that the fighting there is brought to an end the better it will be.

4. It therefore appears to us that the purpose according to the Prime Minister's statement to me for which King Abdullah sent his troops into Palestine has been more or less achieved and that no advantage could consequently be lost by agreement to an immediate ceasefire, which would not prevent the consolidation of the position held by the Arab Legion and in this connection deployment of forces, provided this did not involve the exchange of fire with the Jews. If King Abdullah refuses to agree it will be difficult for me not to feel he is now aiming at objectives or those of which he informed me through his Prime Minister and I should find it very hard to avoid reconsidering our whole position with regard to the Arab Legion.

5. I do not know what the attitude of the other Arab governments will be. Even if they are reluctant to agree to a ceasefire, my advice

to King Abdullah would be on this occasion that as he has borne the brunt of the fighting and as the other Arab forces, apart from the Egyptian Army, have shown themselves incapable of making any progress in Palestine, it would be perfectly reasonable for him to accept a ceasefire on his own. We believe that such action by securing a marked improvement in his international position and prestige would be the greatest consolidation of his position in Palestine and that the advantage of this course would outweigh any possible disadvantages which might arise from disagreement between him and the other Arab governments.

6. In [reaching] agreement to a ceasefire, King Abdullah would of course make it clear that he would rely on the passage in the Security Council resolution which states that the ceasefire would be without prejudice to the rights, claims or position of the parties concerned. He could use this to show the other Arab governments that he was not in any way weakening the Arab position.[2]

The Foreign Secretary was extremely keen to achieve a ceasefire in Palestine and was trying to help Kirkbride in his effort to put pressure on the Arab leaders' meeting of the Political Committee of the Arab League to accept the truce. He further wrote to Kirkbride on the following day:

1. I have been considering how we should proceed as regards mediation in Palestine and how we can make progress towards a settlement on the assumption that the present fighting is somehow brought to an end. Please show this telegram to Sir Hugh Dow when he arrives in Amman and discuss it fully with him. It suggests one or two lines of thought which will be useful for him to explore with a view to his discussions with the United Nations' mediator.

2. One possible line of approach for the mediator with Sir Hugh Dow's assistance to follow, would be to start by considering what machinery was possible or was required at the centre in order to achieve some of the objectives of economic union as proposed in the assembly resolution on 29 November. It would, of course, be impossible to suggest to the Arabs that we were pursuing even this part of the partition resolution, but it might well be possible to interest them in the creation of common services, the joint operation of utilities and so on if this was not specifically done under the aegis of the Assembly resolution. If it were possible to make some progress in this direction we would then be able to see where we stood as regards the future political settlement – that is, whether the fact of partition had become so firmly established that it is

bound to continue with few or no joint services or whether the common services would be developed in such a way as to lead to a political framework more akin to cantonisation.

3. Another line of approach is indicated if we consider it likely that the Arab governments will prefer not to set up a separate Arab State in Palestine but to appropriate the Arab areas to themselves. We have always thought it was probably King Abdullah's intention to appropriate central Arab area and possibly Gaza to Trans-Jordan. It is possible that the Egyptians may also wish to appropriate the area between the Egyptian frontier and Gaza in view of their occupation of it. It would be useful to have His Majesty's Ambassador to Cairo's appreciation of their intentions on this point. Trans-Jordan and Egypt would no doubt wish to share the Negev between them. The position in the north would be obscure since the Jews would no doubt claim western Galilee if they lost the Negev and it seems likely that it is beyond the power of the Arabs to turn them out. There is also the position of King Ibn Saud who would resent the acquisition of territory by King Abdullah without compensation for himself and through the position of Egypt might wish to support a solution on these lines, particularly if King Abdullah had an outlet to the sea at Gaza, where it would have many obvious advantages from our point of view. It would create a strong barrier against the Jews and communist expansion south and east, and it would provide us with an extended area of friendly Arab country in which we would have strategical facilities, whereas a separate Arab state in Palestine would be so small and weak that it could not maintain itself and might well succumb at some stage to Jewish pressure or infiltration. If the inter Arab rivalries threatened any such plan, a speedy solution might perhaps be found in some inter Arab control of Gaza and perhaps of a corridor between there and Aqaba.

4. The further question would then arise whether even with some such settlement as this there would be a case for some kind of economic relations or even for the operation of certain common services between the Jewish state and this enlarged Trans-Jordan or at least parts of it in Palestine. From the broad point of view of the economic future and development of the whole area some such arrangement would undoubtedly be necessary and should if possible extend beyond Palestine to Trans-Jordan and even to other neighbouring states. The matters which would most obviously need to be handled in this way would be the rail road and air communications, oil, potash, phosphate, irrigation and power.

5. Before we go any further it is clearly essential to know rather more of King Abdullah's intentions. I suggest that when you have

discussed the above ideas with Sir Hugh Dow you should take him to see King Abdullah and have a frank discussion in an attempt to discover now how we can best cooperate with him in arriving at a peaceful settlement which would at the same time promote the well being of Palestine and Trans-Jordan.[3]

Thereafter, Kirkbride was very active in Amman during the meetings of the Arab League Political Committee; gaining information, putting pressure on the participants to accept the ceasefire, and feeding back his information and advice to the Foreign Office in London. When Captain Mahmoud al-Musa Aubaidat was about to launch his attack to capture the Jewish quarter in the old city of Jerusalem, while King Abdullah was putting great pressure on the Jordanian 6th Regiment to achieve its mission, and when the 3rd Regiment was attacking Nôtre Dame, Kirkbride wrote to the Foreign Secretary on 26 May:

1. After my talk with the Regent yesterday he asked the Prime Minister of Trans-Jordan to do all he could to secure the acceptance of the ceasefire but not to do it in such a manner as to enable the other Arab states to accuse the Hashemites of having abandoned the fight first. This attitude of mind plus the suspicion of the other states that Trans-Jordan always intended to halt short of Jewish territory gave rise to the principal difficulties encountered in connection with the ceasefire proposal.

2. This morning early the King rang me up and said apologetically that he had done all he could to get the ceasefire but that the opposition of Azzam and the Egyptian delegate had resulted in a resolution of the Political Committee of the League which was neither acceptance nor refusal. I tried to contact the Prime Minister and found he was sitting with the other delegates producing the final resolution.

3. I sent word that I had received a message from you which he should know of before the other delegates left. As they are getting tired of my personal pressure I asked the First Secretary to take up a note indicating the sense of your message and I also asked him to remind the Prime Minister of our reference to the possible acceptance by Trans-Jordan alone of a ceasefire.

4. At the interview, the Prime Minister said that there was no chance of changing the resolution, the gist of which after a long preamble was as follows:

'In view of the above mentioned reasons the Arab States which welcome every step towards the establishment of peace and order, believe that the realisation of the Security Council's wish which is shared by them necessitates adherence to the original resolution of the Security Council [of 16 April] and the adoption of practical and just measures which are indispensable in order that the ceasefire should not merely act as a breathing space for a fiercer and more violent conflict later.

'Moreover, in order to ensure that the result of the ceasefire in fact brings about a just solution and a complete peace in accordance with the wishes of the Security Council, the Political Committee of the Arab League now in session is prepared to study within forty-eight hours any proposition that the Security Council may offer as a basis for the solution of the Palestine Problem.'

The Prime Minister went on to say that it was only after great effort that he had secured so conciliatory a message, as the Egyptians had wished to refuse to consider the appeal at all. The relatively mild wording of the resolution was out of courtesy to Great Britain whose efforts on behalf of the Arabs were genuinely appreciated.

5. As regards the suggestion that Trans-Jordan should alone accept a ceasefire, the Prime Minister answered that we must realise that this was impossible for the Trans-Jordan authorities however much they wished to do so and whatever might be the international penalties if they did not. He had already said much the same thing to me in anticipation of such a suggestion. He pointed out that Trans-Jordan was a small part of the Arab world and could not defy Arab opinion to that extent.

My own view is that neither King Abdullah nor the Prime Minister could carry the blame which such an action would call upon them in the Arab world. It is not necessary for me to indicate here the obvious accusations which would be made against them. The Prime Minister could never survive the action politically and it might bring down the Hashemites both in Trans-Jordan and in Iraq. I recommend, therefore, that the proposal should not be pressed. If this necessitates a revision of His Majesty's Government's policy as regards assistance to Trans-Jordan it will be most unfortunate but I feel that it would be a lesser evil.

6. It is with a feeling of personal failure that I report this position but I am convinced that the King and Prime Minister of Trans-Jordan did their best to satisfy your wishes. I am not so sure about the Regent.[4]

Kirkbride's pressures and offers achieved nothing in the Political Committee, because all the participants were aware of the weight of Arab public opinion and what accusations they would have to face. While King Abdullah was waiting anxiously for the fall of the Jewish quarter in the Old City of Jerusalem, he was not keen to accept a ceasefire; the Jordanian and Lebanese Prime Ministers called for the acceptance of the ceasefire; Iraq and Egypt as well as Azzam of the Arab League opposed it; and the Syrian Prime Minister did not commit himself and waited for the majority to decide. However, Kirkbride was also waiting for future developments. He wrote to Bevin:

> My forecast for future events is that the military situation will become less favourable to the Arabs as time goes on and that in about a fortnight from now they will be in serious difficulties about supplies. When this happens Iraq, Trans-Jordan and Egypt will probably ask for supplies from Great Britain, and if these are refused, they may well call off the war and blame Great Britain for the result.[5]

On 29 May, the Security Council of the United Nations passed a resolution calling for a four-week truce to be observed by all combatants in Palestine. Count Bernadotte, a member of the Swedish Royal family, was appointed as the United Nations mediator between the Arabs and the Jews. Bernadotte arrived at Cairo on the same day and started his negotiations. That action by the United Nations put greater pressure on the Arab States to accept the ceasefire in the form of a truce. On the same day, Kirkbride discussed with Tawfiq Abu al-Huda the question of the future of the Arab areas of Palestine which were occupied by the various Arab armies and the subject of the immediate setting up of an Arab state over the whole of Palestine. The Egyptian Government had suggested that the Arabs should set up and recognise a unitary state over the whole of Palestine, but their proposal was opposed by Jordan and Iraq who insisted on maintaining the original decision of the Arab League that whatever area of Palestine was rescued should be placed under military rule until its inhabitants were in a position to achieve their self-determination. However, only Jordan and Egypt were in a position to claim temporary political control in the areas they occupied – for Iraq and Saudi Arabia were excluded geographically, and Syria and Lebanon had no Palestinian areas under their control.

On 30 May, the British Government decided that all British officers seconded to the Jordan Arab Army from the British Army 'were immediately to leave their commands and withdraw from battle'. The reason was the Security Council resolution of 29 May which called upon all governments to refrain from sending war material to either side, in accordance with the British Foreign Enlistment Act. There was no mention in the resolution of the recall of nationals of other countries that might be fighting. The British Government had succumbed to American pressure in New York to withdraw its regular officers from the Jordan Arab Army. No pressure was put on the Jews to withdraw the Colonel of the United States Army, David Marcus, who was commanding the Haganah in the central area of Palestine. No mention was made of the Jordanian–British Treaty of 1948, which was intended to defend Jordan. However, the move was temporary and was intended to support the Foreign Secretary's statement in the House of Commons to the effect that no regular British officers were fighting in Palestine. The officers returned to their units and formation two days later.

On 30 May, while pressure was maintained by Kirkbride on the Political Committee of the Arab League to accept the truce, all seconded British officers of the Jordan Arab Army were ordered to withdraw behind the east bank of the River Jordan. Colonel T. Ashton, Commander of the 3rd Brigade (seconded from the Welsh Guards), and Captain Bromage of the 2nd Regiment (seconded from the Grenadier Guards) had no intention of obeying the order. Ashton ignored the order and Bromage asked for two weeks' leave so that he could stay with the Regiment. However, the rest of the British officers withdrew to al-Salt area in Jordan. Nearly every senior Commander, staff officer or junior officer was affected by that decision. Although they were in direct communications with their units and HQs by wireless, the Jordan Arab Army went through a short precarious period when the Jews were about to launch an attack at Bab al-Wad. However, the decision did not affect Glubb and a few other officers.

On 1 June a Jewish aircraft bombed Amman; five people were killed and two were injured. Later in the month, a strong Jewish detachment from the southern potash works near the Dead Sea attacked the Ghur al-Safi police post, injuring eight policemen. The attackers were driven off by police reinforcements. The Jews also made an attempt to demolish Shaikh Hussein Bridge in the Jordan valley, but failed.

Discussions in the Political Committee in Amman continued until 1 June. After a 12-hour debate, during which the heat of both the war and the summer heat of Amman had affected the tempers of the participants, no decision was taken regarding the ceasefire. During the meeting on 2 June, the Egyptian delegate opened discussions with a long speech promoting the acceptance of the ceasefire. Aware of British pressure he also favoured heeding the British advice. He said:

> Although Egypt has quarrelled more with Great Britain than any other Arab State in matters of this importance, Egypt and indeed the other Arab States cannot afford to continue to ignore Great Britain's advice.

The Iraqi delegate followed this with his announcement that Iraq would continue to do its duty and 'to fight to the end'. At that point, Tawfiq Abu al-Huda lost his temper and pointed out that 'the success of the Iraqi Army consisted of occupying areas of Palestine which were already in possession of the Arab Legion'. Kirkbride reported:

> 4. After this the proceedings were a battle between Jordan, Egypt and Iraq on the one hand, and Syria, Lebanon and Saudi Arabia on the other hand who wished to continue the war to the last of their allies' soldiers.
> Owing to their utter failure in the field of battle they could not, however, prevail and they ultimately signed the decision which was in fact drafted by the Jordanian and Egyptian representatives.
>
> 5. The final effort of the opposition was to table a draft resolution which would be made public, stating that notwithstanding the acceptance of the ceasefire the Arab states would never agree to the formation of a Jewish State and that anyone who did so would in fact be implementing partition which all Arabs had agreed to refuse.
> The Prime Minister confesses to having lost his temper to pointing out that the whole effort of the three opposing states had been directed to blackening King Abdullah's good name and to throwing on to the Hashemite states the odium of stopping a war to which Syria, Lebanon and Saudi Arabia had contributed nothing. As Chairman of the Committee he ruled that it had been convened to consider one question only that was the acceptance or otherwise of the ceasefire. There was no other matter on the agenda and the meeting was over.

The opposition accepted this in silence and their delegates left Amman without bidding farewell to the Prime Minister.⁶

The main principle of the truce was that neither Arabs nor Jews should achieve any military advantages during the four weeks. This principle made it vital that neither side would be allowed to bring troops or war material into Palestine during the truce. Furthermore no weapons or ammunition would be imported by the countries concerned, and the Red Cross should supervise food supplies and water to be sent from the coastal area to Jerusalem. Kirkbride saw the danger in the main condition of withholding military supplies to the Arab Legion. He reported:

> Application to Arab States, of the part of the resolution of the Security Council which relates to withholding military supplies may, in certain circumstances, produce a situation of extreme danger to the Arabs. Supply position of the Arab Legion is that they have ammunition for seven more days fighting only. I cannot be so precise about Iraqis but there is no doubt that they are also short of ammunition. Iraqi transport is in a dilapidated state; much of it consists of commandeered civil buses, and is drawing more and more on dwindling resources of the Arab Legion for spares, repairs and fuel. Lebanese and Syrian armies are virtually out of line. Egyptians are probably best of all regards supply, but suffer from extreme reluctance to fight and would undoubtedly run if faced with adverse circumstances.
>
> Strategic key to the Arab position is Latrun which is held by the Arab Legion. If, owing to shortage of supplies, the Legion had to abandon Latrun, the road to Jerusalem would be opened to Jews and Arab forces which would have to commence a series of withdrawals which might well end in their countries of origin. These withdrawals would doubtless start a panic among the remaining Arab population of Palestine and retreat would probably be hampered by crowds of refugees. In short, Arab forces are fully extended and if the Arab Legion, which is the best of them, hastily pull out the result might well be that the whole of Palestine would be occupied by the Jews.
>
> Circumstances which would turn these conditions into danger would be a failure to secure a ceasefire in the next few days or alternatively a breakdown of the Truce or failure to secure a solution during its existence.⁷

On 7 June, the mediator, Count Bernadotte, visited Amman and had a meeting with Fawzi al-Mulqi, the Jordanian Foreign Minister, Ahmad al-Rawi representing Iraq and General Glubb. The Count informed them that the truce would begin at 0600 hours Greenwich Mean Time (0800 hours Jordan time) on 11 June 1948. Glubb, who had never experienced a truce during his military service, wrote in his book, *A Soldier with the Arabs*:

> The fighting in Palestine presented an entirely new military problem, and one which, to the best of my knowledge, has no precedent in the history of war. Military operations are usually carried out on the assumption that the war will continue until one side or the other is defeated. Hence the object of the operations is not to occupy this province or that, but to destroy the enemy's army. This done, the victor can dictate such peace terms as appear good to him. But in the case of the operations in Palestine, this was not the case. There was a third party, the United Nations, constantly intervening. In the present instance, we had four days more of fighting, after which there was to be a truce. There was no question of destroying the enemy's forces in four days. The problem was how to employ the four days in such a manner as to be in the best possible military position when the truce began.[8]

General Glubb was concerned about the situation in Lydda and Ramleh, which were part of the Arab areas allotted to the Palestinian Arabs in the Partition Plan of 1947. They were still defended by Palestinian partisan troops supported by one platoon of the Jordan Arab Army. He wrote:

> From the very beginning of hostilities, I had told both the King and the government that we could not hold Lydda and Ramleh. These two towns had been given to the Arabs in the UNO partition plan. They are situated on the flat coastal plain only fifteen miles from Tel Aviv, and were almost entirely surrounded by Jewish colonies. We had proposed to capture the Jewish colony of Ben Shemen, which lay across the only road connecting Lydda to the Arab area, but the Mayor of Lydda had begged us not to do so. He alleged that he was on good terms with the Jews and proposed to defend his town by diplomacy. If the Arab Legion came round attacking Jewish colonies, the Jews, he said, would turn on Lydda.
>
> The small numbers of the Arab Legion in comparison with the Israeli forces made it essential for us to fight in defiles at the foot of the mountains. Here, a single battalion could hold up the Israeli army, as indeed it had done at Latrun. But if a single battalion were to venture out into the open plain, it would be overwhelmed. Or, if it were to repulse every attack on itself, its line of communications across the plain would be cut off.

During the first month of hostilities, we had held our own against all comers, by holding the defile at Latrun. If we had ventured farther afield to Lydda and Ramleh, the enemy would have broken at Latrun and driven up the road to Ramallah in the Arab area.

The government had appointed military governors to Hebron, Jerusalem, Ramallah and Nablus in order to continue the civil administration. I discussed the appointments with the Prime Minister. When I asked about the arrangements for Lydda and Ramleh, Tawfiq Pasha replied: 'We have decided that we cannot hold Lydda and Ramleh. If we appoint a military governor, and then the Jews take them, it will look worse.' So Lydda and Ramleh had no governor. During the month's fighting, there had been no government in these two towns and the civil police had disbanded themselves.

I accordingly suggested to the Prime Minister that we should send a token force to Ramleh twenty-four hours before the truce began. Once the truce had begun, military movements might be prohibited. If this force went to Ramleh before the truce, we could reconstitute the police and administration as soon as fighting ceased. The Prime Minister agreed, but still did not send a governor. The 5th Infantry Company, of just over a hundred men, moved across country and into Ramleh on 9 June.[9]

On 8 June, Captain Sadiq al-Sharaa visited Lydda and Ramleh on a mission to appreciate the situation and organise the defence of the two towns. Later that night he reported to Brigadier Lash that it was impossible to defend the towns with Palestinian partisans, even if the 5th Infantry was deployed in the area. Captain Adib al-Qasim, Commander of the 5th Company, moved to the area, took over from Captain Bromage and organised its defences in cooperation with al-Jihad al-Muqaddas Palestinian partisans as shown in Table 7.1.

TABLE 7.1
5th Company's reorganised defences

Company HQ, at Lydda Police Post, commanded by Lt Jamil al-Sakran.
One platoon, at Lydda railway station, commanded by Lt Ghazi al-Hindawi.
One platoon, at the crossroads, Lydda, Ramleh, Sarafand, commanded by Lt Anwar al-Tarabishi.
One platoon, at the shrine of al Nabi Salih, south of Ramleh, commanded by Lt Abd al-Ayish al-Hiyari.

On the following day, Glubb visited the Division HQ in Ramallah and Sadiq reported on the situation. According to Sadiq, Glubb thought that the truce would be renewed according to assurances from the Tawfiq Abu al-Huda. Major Idris Sultan was appointed governor to the area of the two towns and, on his arrival, he started to organise the civil administration.[10]

On 9 June, the Jews attempted to attack and capture Shaikh Jarrah area in order to establish a corridor connecting Mea Sherim and San Hydria to Mount Scopus and the Hadassa Hospital. The area of Shaikh Jarrah was defended by the Second Infantry Company, commanded by Captain Fawaz Mahir (with its positions in the Police School area), and the 9th Infantry Company, commanded by Captain Sulaiman Masaud (with its positions in the Nashashibi House area).

Early that morning Major George Corfield, the Brigade Major of 1st Brigade, informed me that the 9th Company had two three-inch mortars with a 100 rounds of ammunition, but with no one to use them. With the shortage of ammunition for the twenty-five-pounder artillery, the Brigade Commander placed the authority for using the artillery battery under his command to himself and for the use of three-inch mortars to be restricted to the approval of regimental Commanders. Thus, the whole of Shaikh Jarrah had only two redundant three-inch mortars. Sergeant Major Musayib Sulaiman from Brigade HQ and I, who had previously been three-inch mortar instructors, volunteered to assemble and establish a mortar section.

By dusk on 9 June, one three-inch mortar in the 9th Infantry was ready to fire, and when the Jewish attack started, I (as No. 1) and Musayib (as No. 2) managed to open rapid fire at Mea Sherim and San Hydria from where the attack was launched. Lucky for both of us, the Jewish mortar fire was directed at the two companies' position and not at where the mortar position was. All hell broke loose for about 30 minutes, during which a curtain of rifle, Bren machine-gun and two-inch and three-inch mortar fire repulsed the attack. The hundred rounds of mortar ammunition were not wasted.

At 0800 hours on 11 June 1948, the truce between the Arabs and the Jews began. On the northern front, with one battalion, the Lebanese Army was holding a front line from Rosh Hanikra on the coast to Bint Jubayil adjacent to al-Malikiyah to the east. From their positions they were able to support the Liberation Army in the centre of Galilee by protecting its line of communication to Lebanon.

The Syrian Army, with one brigade, was still holding the bridgehead of Mishmar Hayarden, and with another brigade was holding the high ground overlooking the River Jordan. The Iraqi Army was holding with two brigades, the longest front from the River Jordan to Bait Qad, Arrana, Harithiyah, Bartaah, Qaffin, Dair al-Ghusun, Tulkarm, and a few kilometres south of Qalqiliyah. The Jordan Arab Army was holding, with two brigades, a front extending from Rantis, Budrus, Latrun to the south and thence to Qubaibah, Biddu, al-Nabi Samuel, Shuafat, to the Shaikh Jarrah, Damascus Gate, the Old City of Jerusalem, and parts of the south of the city. The Egyptian Army was still holding, with four brigades, a front from al-Majdal near the coast to Isdud and east to al-Faluja, to Bait Jibrin in Hebron, with the Muslim Brothers in Hebron and Bethlehem (see Map 2).

As soon as the truce was firmly established on 11 June, Glubb called on the Prime Minister and explained the precarious situation of the Jordan Arab Army at the beginning of the truce. He asked him for his approval for further enlistment of troops so that the units would in a better position to defend the front if there was any more fighting. Glubb wrote:

> 'There won't be any more fighting,' he [Tawfiq Abu al-Huda] said to me, shaking his finger of his right hand to the right and left, in a gesture of prohibition. 'No more fighting! I and al-Noqrashi Pasha [the Egyptian Prime Minister] are agreed on that. If we two are agreed, we can sway the rest. No! No more fighting!'
> I tried to point out that it might not rest solely with us. What would happen if the Jews started fighting again? But Tawfiq Pasha was adamant.
> 'No more fighting,' he said, 'and no more money for soldiers.'[11]

The Jordan Arab Army, though committed to the truce in the front line, spent the next four weeks preparing for the beginning of the possible hostilities at the end of the truce. On 12 June, the 1st Brigade was commanded to form the 5th Infantry Regiment from the garrison companies under its command – that is, the 2nd Security Company, the 4th Infantry Company and the 9th Infantry Company. Major Ali Hiyari, who was appointed Commander of the Regiment, immediately started to establish his HQ at Bait Hanina near Ramallah, and began a campaign of scrounging officers and men from the staff of the 1st Brigade HQ. Ali al-Hiyari was well known for his efficiency, self-discipline and hard work. All the officers under his command were experienced company Commanders and by the end of three weeks the regiment was formed as shown in Table 7.2.

TABLE 7.2
The regiment formed by Major Ali al-Hiyari

Commander	Major Ali al-Hiyari
Second in Command	Major Karim Ohan
Adjutant	Lt Salih al-Sharaa
Commander 1st Company	Captain Sulaiman Masaud
Commander 2nd Company	Captain Muhammad Khalf Omari
Commander 3rd Company	Captain Radhi al-Abdullah
Commander Support Company	Major Karim Ohan
Commander HQ Company	Lt Abdullah al-Aayid

Furthermore, all the recruits in the training schools were transferred to units in the front to replace the casualties, and the 19th Infantry Company was attached to the 3rd Infantry Brigade and took over its new position at al Nabi Salih. A new battery of 4.2-inch mortars was formed. The Iraqis attached two heavy field guns to the 1st Artillery Regiment. The whole process was one of reorganisation of the available officers and men, as well as weapons and other resources. Not a single soldier, weapon or round of ammunition was added to the strength of the Jordan Arab Army.

While the Jordanian Prime Minister refused to sanction any money to the Jordan Arab Army, on 16 June, the Israeli Prime Minister arranged with Menachem Begin, the Irgun leader, to unload a ship with a cargo of war materials and weapons for their forces. This cargo consisted of 5,000 rifles, 250 Bren machine-guns, 5,000,000 rounds of ammunition, 50 PIAT rocket launchers and ten Bren carriers.[12] By 26 June, nine fighter bomber aircrafts joined the Jewish Air Force. On 27 June, the following arms and ammunition were purchased in Europe.

- 50 artillery 75-mm field guns, each with 1,000 rounds.
- 150,000 rounds of 20-mm anti-aircraft guns.

- 50,000 rounds for 65-mm field guns.
- 12 mortars, 120-mm with 4,000 rounds.
- 12 anti-tank 47-mm guns with 25,000 rounds.
- 12 anti-tank 50-mm German guns with 21,000 rounds.
- 35 16-ton tanks.[13]

All the Haganah and Palmach brigades were reorganised, reinforced and deployed in preparation for the new Jewish offensive at the end of the truce.

Meanwhile, on 27 June Count Bernadotte presented his draft proposals for a solution of the Palestine problem to the Arabs and the Jews. The main points in his suggested plan were as follows:

1. The Arab areas of Palestine should be united with Jordan and thence the new Jordan should form a Union with Israel.
2. The Union between Jordan and Israel should handle economic, foreign and defence affairs for the Union.
3. In accordance with the provisions of the Union, Jordan and Israel should each control their own internal affairs.
4. All of the Negev area should be included in Jordan.
5. All of the area of Galilee should be included in Israel.
6. Jerusalem should be in the Arab area.
7. Haifa should be a free port for Arabs and Jews.
8. Lydda should be a free airport for Arabs and Jews.

The plan embodied too much too soon considering the enmity that existed between both sides. The Arabs rejected it because they felt it would give Jordan more power and control over Palestine, and the Jews rejected it because they were planning an offensive to take the Negev and Galilee as well as the whole of Jerusalem. However, an agreement was reached in Jerusalem in regard to the area and buildings of Hadassah Hospital and the Hebrew University. Glubb wrote:

> ... both great mountains of stone, situated on high ground dominating the Arab side of the city and cut off from the Jewish city by the suburb of Shaikh Jarrah. As soon as the Arab Legion had intervened in Jerusalem, Mount Scopus had been isolated. The Jews, however, had left a military garrison in the Hadassah and the Hebrew University, which continued to fire into the backs of the Arab Legion who were defending Jerusalem. When we retaliated with mortars or, on one

occasion, with the twenty-five pounders, there was an outcry about Arabs shelling hospitals. The Jordan Government was informed that both the hospital and the university had been built with funds voluntarily subscribed in the United States. Any attempt by us to destroy or capture these buildings would, we were told, produce intense indignation in America.

When, therefore, Count Bernadotte suggested that the buildings be demilitarised and handed over to the United Nations, the solution seemed to be a reasonable one. The Israeli Government agreed to the proposal, but requested permission to leave some Jewish civil police in the buildings to prevent pilfering of the valuable medical equipment and the literary treasures in the university. Count Bernadotte was very explicit in his statement that Mount Scopus would henceforward be solely under the control of the United Nations. He said that it was his intention little by little to replace the Jewish by United Nations police.[14]

Meanwhile, Count Bernadotte was hoping that the Arabs and the Jews would accept a renewal of the truce because 'from the military point of view they were in a difficult position'. He continued with his efforts to convince both sides to accept the renewal. On 7 July, the Security Council of the United Nations approved a resolution addressing an urgent appeal to the parties concerned to accept the prolongation of the truce.

On 8 July, the Political Committee of the Arab League held a meeting in Cairo to discuss the issue. Tawfiq Abu al-Huda was told by the King to do his best to convince al-Noqrashi and the other Arab delegates to accept renewal. During the meeting, the Egyptian and Jordanian Prime Ministers proposed to accept renewal, while the majority, Syria, Iraq, Lebanon and Saudi Arabia insisted on fighting. All the military Chiefs of Staff were in favour of renewing the truce. They complained of lack of ammunition and supplies and stated that their armies were not in a position to continue fighting. But the politicians insisted on terminating the truce and gave instructions to their Chiefs of Staff to take a defensive posture without attacking the Jews. The decision of the Political Committee was presented to Count Bernadotte by Azzam on the same day. On his return to Amman, Tawfiq Pasha informed the King of the decision, and when Glubb asked him in the presence of King Abdullah how he could fight without ammunition he replied: 'Don't shoot until the Jews shoot first.'

Meanwhile, on 8 July, one day before the end of the truce, the 5th Regiment had completed its organisation and short period of training. On the same day it took over the defensive positions of the 1st Regiment who were placed under the command of the Division as a reserve for the whole Jordanian front and were deployed at Dair al-Qara north of Ramallah.

The second round

On Friday 9 July 1948, the first truce came to an end with the Arabs standing still in their defensive positions along the truce line. The Jews went on the offensive at dawn that morning on all the Arab fronts, as detailed in the text that follows.

The Syrian and Lebanese front

Facing the Syrian and Lebanese front along the truce line were five Jewish brigades – the Alexandroni, Golani, Carmeli, Oded and the 7th. The Syrians had two brigades – the Lebanese 1st Battalion and the Liberation Army 1st Brigade. The Jewish offensive was planned in two operations. First was Operation 'Dekel', the aim of which was to destroy the Liberation Army. The second was Operation 'Brosh', the aim of which was to defeat the Syrian Army.

The Syrian Army posed a serious threat to the Jews with the bridgehead they had established in the area of Mishmar Hayardin, about one mile from the vital north–south road in eastern Galilee. During the truce, the bridgehead was reinforced with troops and armour supported by artillery. The 1st Syrian Brigade, commanded by Colonel Anwar Bannud, was given the task of defending a front line stretching from Banat Yaaqub Bridge to Khirbit Irbid, including Mishmar Hayardin, Aatrah Castle, Khan Yardah, Tal Abu al-Rish and Tal al-Aswad – about 15 kilometres wide. Three Infantry Battalions, one Armoured Car Regiment, one Armoured Car Squadron, supported by an Artillery Regiment, were deployed to defend the area of the Syrian bridgehead.

The Jewish plan was intended to isolate the bridgehead from its line of communication. The main attack was to be carried out by the Carmeli Brigade, while a battalion from the Oded Brigade would carry out a diversionary attack on the Syrian bridgehead from the west. Then the Carmeli Brigade would cross the River Jordan to the north of the bridgehead and take the customs house position overlooking the Banat Yaaqoub Bridge.

The Jewish attack was mounted with the usual heavy artillery and mortar bombardment immediately after dusk on 9 July. The Syrian artillery returned the fire and managed to delay the crossing of the River Jordan. The Jewish Battalion, which was given this task, was unable to do so, causing the delay of the attack by the other battalion that was meant to carry out the main assault. At that critical stage, some information was received by the Jewish Commander that the Syrian Army was about to attack the Jewish settlement of Rosh Pina. Thus some confusion occurred and the Jewish attack lost its momentum. In the fierce fighting that followed the Syrians fought well and held their positions. Their actions had disrupted the timing of the Jewish attack and forced chaos in the various stages of the Jewish operation. This disruption of the attack's timing made it extremely difficult to capture the customs house before sunrise. Thus the attack failed and the Carmeli Brigade was ordered to withdraw.

At dawn on 10 July, the Syrian Brigade, aware of their victory, launched a counter-attack supported by bombing from the air. The Brigade, which was located at the eastern heights of the River Jordan, attacked the Carmeli Battalion, which was unable to withdraw to the west bank of the river. In the fierce fighting, which lasted nearly two days and nights, both sides suffered heavy casualties. On the third night, the Carmeli Battalion was defeated, but managed to withdraw. Other positions in the narrow front were attacked by the Syrian Brigade on their way to attack the Jewish settlements of Rosh Pina and Mahanayim. In the two days' fighting that followed, more than four attacks and counter-attacks were launched by both the Syrian and Jewish forces, with very heavy casualties suffered by both sides.

On 14 July, the Carmeli Battalion mounted yet another attack with the aim of capturing the bridgehead. They approached their objective from the south under heavy cover of artillery bombardment. That attack was also defeated, and the Jewish force was compelled to withdraw. When the second truce came into effect on 18 July, no change was made on the Syrian front. Although exhausted and lacking ammunition, the Syrians managed to hold their positions intact. By the end of that day the Syrian Arab Army had suffered, since 15 May 1948, the deaths of 28 officers and 300 men, with casualties totalling about 800.

The Liberation Army front

Meanwhile, the Liberation Army was still holding its strategic positions farther to the west in the centre of Galilee near Nazareth. On 9 July, Operation 'Dekel' was launched by the Golani Brigade, with the aim of dislodging the Liberation Army from its positions in the area of the village of al-Sejara, which was a vital link along the main Jewish route leading to the north, through Kfar Tabor to Tiberias. Fawzi al-Qawiqji planned an attack to capture al-Sejara. He assembled most of his troops and launched several attacks against the Golani Battalion defending the area between 10 and 14 July, but was unable to capture any of the Jewish positions.

On 14 July, the 7th Brigade and a battalion from the Carmeli Brigade advanced from western Galilee towards Nazareth. They took Shfaram on the Akka–Nazareth road. On 15 July, a battalion of the Golani Brigade advanced from their positions in Nahalal and took Shfaram on the Akka–Nazareth road, cleared the Liberation Army unit from its positions, and established themselves in Kfar Hahoresh, west of Nazareth. The 7th Brigade captured the village of Zippori a few miles north-west of Nazareth. At that point, Fawzi al-Qawiqji began to redeploy his forces to meet the imminent danger coming from the rear, and sent his reserve force to deal with it. But the Liberation Army armoured cars were unable to defend themselves and six of them were destroyed. It was compelled to withdraw and Nazareth fell to the Jewish 7th Brigade on 16 July. Thereafter, the Liberation Army was too exhausted to continue fighting, especially after suffering heavy casualties, whom it could not replace. On 18 July, it abandoned lower Galilee for good and withdrew to the north-east, occupying a central defensive line in northern Galilee, from within the Lebanese border and extending south to the valley of Bait Netofa.

The Iraqi front

The Iraqi Army used the truce to improve its defensive positions, reinforce its formations and generally increase its strength. By the end of the truce the Iraqi forces consisted of about 10,000 officers and men in the formation of one infantry division of three brigades and supporting weapons as shown in Table 7.3.

TABLE 7.3
The Iraqi forces at the end of the truce

1st Brigade Group, commanded by Colonel Najib al-Rubaie.
3rd Brigade Group, commanded by Lt Colonel Ghazi al-Daghistani.
4th Brigade Group, commanded by Colonel Salih Zaki Tawfiq.
2nd Battalion of the 5th Brigade, commanded by Lt Colonel Omar Ali.
Armour Brigade Group, commanded by Colonel Rafiq Arif.

On 9 July, an Iraqi Battalion attacked and captured Tal al-Kharoubah north of Jenin. They also forced the Haganah out of several Arab villages to the north-west of Jenin – including Faqouah, Jalamah, Sandalah, Arranah, Arabawnah, Dair Ghazalah and al-Muqaibalh. The Haganah counter-attacked in vain to recapture some of these villages. The village of al-Majdal Yaba was attacked by the Jews immediately after the fall of Lydda and Ramleh. The Iraqi Company holding the village with a local garrison of Palestinian partisans repulsed the attack. On 12 July the Haganah attacked again and recaptured the village. Before their withdrawal from al-Majdal Yaba, the Iraqi Company had demolished the water pumping station at Ras al-Ain, which pumped water to Jerusalem. Thereafter, the Iraqis mounted two counter-attacks to recapture al-Majdal Yaba and Ras al-Ain – the first on 16 July and the second on 18 July – but failed to achieve their objectives during these two fierce battles for the villages.

On 17 July, when the Jordanian 1st Infantry Regiment was withdrawn from its previous positions to occupy Saffa and Bait Sira in the Latrun Sector, it was relieved by an Iraqi Regiment which occupied the area of Dair Nizam, thus closing the dangerous gap between the Iraqi and the Jordanian Armies.

With one Infantry Division and their support weapons of artillery, mortars and armour units, the Iraqi Army was a deterrent against the Jewish intentions of attacking the Nablus Sector. It further trained and organised many local garrisons of partisans, formed them in four partisan battalions and deployed them in certain areas in support of its formations. Thereafter it remained on the defensive.[15]

The Jordanian front

The Jordanian Arab Army was the most effective military force against any Jewish offensive, as proved by the first round of fighting in the Jerusalem and Latrun sectors. Chaim Herzog wrote:

> The main military problem facing the Israelis on the conclusion of the first truce was posed by the strongest and most effective Arab army, the Arab Legion. This was besieging the city of Jerusalem; from the towns of Lod [Lydda] and Ramleh, Arab forces also posed a direct threat to Tel Aviv, the main Jewish population centre. Furthermore, the main railway junction of the country was at Lod, in addition to the only international airport. Two Arab Legion infantry battalions supported by armour and artillery were concentrated in the Latrun sector; Ramleh and Lydda were well fortified and held mainly by local Arab forces, irregular units, several hundred tribesmen from Trans-Jordan, and small detachments of the Arab Legion.[16]

The Jewish command planned their offensive for the resumption of hostilities at the end of the truce with their main attack against the Jordan Arab Army, with the dual aims of raising the siege of Jerusalem and removing the threat to Tel Aviv. The offensive was planned in two phases (see Map 3). Phase I was to attack and capture Lydda and Ramleh, and phase II was to attack and capture Latrun and Ramallah. The attacks were to be carried out by the following formations, commanded by General Yigal Allon.

• Harel Palmach Brigade.
• Yaftach Palmach Brigade.
• Kiryati Brigade.
• One battalion from the Alexandroni Brigade.
• One battalion from the Etzioni Brigade.
• 8th Armoured Brigade.
• 89th Mechanised Commando Battalion.

Phase I of the offensive – code-named operation 'Danny' – started at 0100 hours on the morning of Saturday 10 July 1948. The Yaftach Brigade attacked from the south and captured the villages of Innabah, Kharroubah, Jimzo and Danyal to the east of Ramleh. The 8th Armoured Brigade, supported by units from the Kiryati and Alexandroni Brigades, attacked Lydda airport four miles north of the town. The airport was defended by two small groups (about 70 lightly armed men) of Palestinian partisans – one under the command of Sergeant Salah Auzair, and the other under Sergeant Ali al-Autum. The partisans had three home-made armoured cars mounted with machine-guns. The two groups held their positions until their ammunition was exhausted and their armoured cars were destroyed during the heavy artillery barrage by the Jews. After about three hours of fighting and suffering heavy casualties, they were forced to withdraw to Lydda, and the airport was captured by the Jews.

The Yaftach Brigade advanced and raised the isolation of the Jewish settlement of Ben Shemen, and then continued their advance forward towards Lydda, but were faced with strong resistance from the 5th Infantry Company of the Jordan Arab Army. The 89th Mechanised Commando Battalion, commanded by Moshe Dayan, and mounted in half-tracks and jeeps, advanced towards Lydda, then attacked the town as they passed through the main street firing at anything that moved. Following the attack, they returned to their start line. That movement created panic among the civilian population, who started to flee from the town. In the chaos that followed, the Yaftach Brigade were able to attack again and capture it.

Perhaps the most daring and courageous armoured unit of the Jordan Arab Army was the Marmon-Herrington armoured car troop of the 1st Regiment. Immediately after the fall of Lydda, the 1st Regiment, who were engaged in a fight near Dair Tarif, sent a fighting patrol of one armoured car troop, commanded by Lt Hamad Abdullah Abu Dukhainah, to Lydda to ascertain the situation in the town. As if out of nowhere, Hamad and his troop passed the Jewish settlement of Ben Shemen and attacked a large concentration of the Yaftach Brigade. Glubb described the attack as follows.

> This patrol behaved in a most gallant manner, engaging and scattering several Israeli units. For a short time, friends and enemies alike thought that they were the advanced guard of a column coming to relieve Lydda. But soon it became apparent that the armoured cars were unsupported. Hamad could see the enemy attempting to cut his road back to Dair Tarif. He was obliged to withdraw. With three armoured cars he had challenged two infantry brigades.[17]

After considering the strength of the enemy in operation 'Danny', by then surrounding Lydda and Ramleh from all directions, and the imminent danger of the destruction of the 5th Infantry Company who were surrounded at the Police Station in Lydda, Glubb approved the withdrawal of the company on 11 July. Captain Adib al-Qasim led his men out of their position during the night of 11/12 July. He managed to infiltrate through enemy lines undetected and arrived at Bait Sira without losing a man or a weapon. His operation was 'a remarkable example of good order and discipline'. The 5th Company occupied their defensive positions at the Bait Sira road junction. On the morning of 12 July, Ramleh surrendered and was occupied by units of the Kiryati Brigade.

Shortly before the end of the first truce, Bob Slade, Commanding Officer of the 2nd Regiment, who had been wounded in the first attack on the New City of Jerusalem, rejoined his regiment at Bab al-Wad. Both Brigade and Divisional HQ had become somewhat worried about the likelihood of the Israelis attacking with armour from the west and with infantry from the south. Looking at the situation objectively from Latrun, Bromage surmised that the infantry would need to attack at night when their armour would be of little value, or during the day when their armour would support them, but when the Jordanian artillery would have cut them to pieces on the rocky ground.

By 13 July, the mountains and roads west of Ramallah were congested with 30,000 refugees from Lydda and Ramleh. The tragedy of their catastrophe is still engraved in my memory and my heart. Glubb wrote:

> Perhaps 30,000 people or more, almost entirely women and children, snatched up what they could and fled from their homes across open fields. The Israeli forces not only arrested men of military age, they also commandeered all means of transport. It was a blazing day in July in the coastal plains, the temperature about a hundred degrees in the shade. It was ten miles across open hilly country, much of it ploughed, part of it stony fallow covered with thorn bushes, to the nearest Arab village of Bait Sira. Nobody will ever know how many children died.[18]

Because the 3rd Brigade units were occupied with fighting the Jewish forces in the area, Division HQ instructed the Commander of the 1st

Brigade to do what he could to help the refugees and evacuate them from the roads. The Staff Captain, myself, was ordered to use any vehicle of Brigade HQ and the 1st Motor Transport Company to carry out the task. With the much-appreciated help of the Mayor of Ramallah, and also Yousef Audah and Nadim al-Zaro, I managed to evacuate about 10,000 old men, women and children from the main roads and hilly areas to Ramallah, then accommodate them in schools, churches and mosques and feed them. Many doctors, including those of the 1st Field Ambulance of the 1st Brigade, cared for the refugees. All the Brigade's administrative units gave their rations to feed the refugees, and the people of Ramallah were a perfect example of generosity and patriotism.

Those five days in July were the worst days in my memory. I will never forget the sight of one woman sitting under a tree with her mother and two children, of whom one was a baby of about a year old. After helping them to the truck, I went back to the tree to collect the few belongings they had; I was surprised to find the sleeping baby wrapped in a blanket under the tree. As I walked back to the truck carrying the baby, suddenly an agonised cry came from the truck: 'Ya waili, ya waladi, daa ibni!' (O my catastrophe, my baby, my baby is lost!) I shouted back: 'No! He is here with me.' No words can describe how she hugged her baby, crying and laughing at the same time.

On 14 July, a reconnaissance in force was ordered by the Commander of the 3rd Brigade to ascertain whether or not the Israeli forces had reached the village of Jimzu, which lies some six kilometres east of Ramleh. In a letter to me, Bromage wrote:

> Taking two troops of armoured cars, I had driven down the main track to Jimzu, which passes through the village of Barfiliya. As we arrived near Jimzu, we had seen some hastily laid mines, half concealed. I had left my Jeep, climbed into the leading armoured car, then driven across several terraced fields in order to enter the village from the north. The Israelis had been completely surprised. We killed one soldier who had been drinking at the village well, and then withdrew, the way that we had come, to report the occupation of Jimzo.
>
> The following night, movement had been detected in the direction of Salbit village about four kilometres north of Latrun. I had led out a fighting patrol, which entered Salbit from the south.

No sooner had we arrived at the first house when a grenade had exploded and an Israeli emerged. This had been followed by exchange of fire and grenades in which the Israeli had missed me with a rifle at five yards' range, and had been shot by a member of the patrol. When the fracas was over, we had discovered that Sergeant Mohsin al-Naif of the Bani Sakhr tribe had been killed. Dawn had been upon us. We had carried Mohsin's body about half-way back to Latrun, but had to abandon it owing to the danger of moving in broad daylight. I had been hit in the head by shrapnel and was bleeding profusely.[19]

On 15 July, the Security Council of the United Nations approved a resolution declaring that the situation in Palestine constituted a threat to peace, and required the governments and authorities concerned to issue ceasefire orders and to institute an immediate unconditional ceasefire in the city of Jerusalem; any failure to comply with that resolution would demonstrate the existence of a breach of the peace under Article 39 of the Charter. All governments and authorities concerned were to conform with the resolution of 25 May.

The effect of the catastrophe of Lydda and Ramleh and the plight of the refugees was felt deeply in the whole of the Jordanian sector as well as in the whole of Jordan. Britain's Acting Minister at Amman, Perie-Gordon, reported to the Foreign Office as follows:

The loss of Ramleh and Lydda occurred on 12 July and was followed by streams of refugees making their way over to Trans-Jordan as best they could. The fact that Glubb had repeatedly warned both the King and Government that these towns could not possibly be held in the event of fighting being resumed was considered in some quarters as evidence that Glubb had deliberately lost them from malice, acting in accordance with instructions from this office to ensure that Trans-Jordan accepted a truce at all costs. Demonstrations against the Arab Legion took place in Nablus and Es Salt, and Glubb was sent for to attend an unpleasant interview with the King and Council of Ministers during which it was made clear that his stories of ammunition shortages were disbelieved as being part of British propaganda. The King took the opportunity of openly telling Glubb that there was no need for him to remain in office, unless he wished. Full details of this meeting were known throughout the Amman 'Suq' the same day, presumably having been circulated by the junior members of the Cabinet with quotations of the 'official view' that Glubb and the British officers were purposely leading the

Arab Legion to destruction in the interests of the 'policy' of His Majesty's Government. Having prudently thrown the blame on those in no position to reply, the Ministers doubtless felt themselves suitably insulated against public criticism in the all too probable event of a military collapse.

Further demonstrations took place the next day against Glubb personally and the British in general on account of the news of withholding the subsidy by His Majesty's Government, and were accompanied by wild talk in the town of impending reprisal assassinations of individuals among the Arab Legion officers and British residents in Amman. Glubb informs me that on that day, while he was visiting the Front, the inhabitants of every village he passed through on the road both in Palestine and Trans-Jordan appeared to be in a state of hysteria, spitting at him and calling him a traitor.[20]

The Harel Brigade advanced and captured several Arab villages in the Jerusalem corridor in order to pave the way for its aim of raising the siege of Jerusalem, capturing Ramallah and isolating Latrun from the rear. That was why the 1st Regiment was placed in the division's reserve, with one company supporting the 3rd Brigade. The Jordanian front had no reserve whatsoever thereafter. The 1st Regiment was ordered to move north and contact the Iraqi Army at al-Majdal Yaba in order to close the gap between the two fronts. On 16 July, it attacked and pursued the Jewish force away from its front. It engaged a Jewish unit at Qula, drove it out of its positions, and then chased it in hot pursuit to the north-west.

Phase II of operation 'Danny' started on the night of 15/16 July. The Yiftach Brigade, supported by the 8th Armoured Brigade and one battalion of the Kiryati Brigade, launched the fourth major attack to capture the Latrun sector, held by the Jordan Arab Army. They managed to capture several undefended Arab villages, including Barfiliya, Shilta, al-Burj, Bir Maain and Salbit. Had they captured Bait Sira and the road junction leading to Ramallah, where the 5th Infantry Company was, Latrun would have been isolated, and the road to Ramallah would have been free and open.

The officers and men of the 2nd Regiment were extremely angry and deeply affected by the scene of the refugees from Lydda and Ramleh moving through their positions on their way to Ramallah. During a visit by Brigadier Ashton, the Commander of the 3rd Brigade to the regiment, the men surrounded him for a talk. They interrupted him and demanded that they should attack and retaliate against the Jewish crime of evicting people from their homes.

At 1300 hours on 16 July, orders were given by the Commander of the 2nd Regiment to attack and capture al-Burj. The Armoured Car Squadron, commanded by Lt Hamdan al-Subaih, would lead the attack, with the 2nd Company commanded by Lt Muhammad Kassab on the right and the 3rd Company commanded by Lt Refaifan Khalid al-Khraisha on the left. Lt Haidar Mustafa volunteered, indeed begged, to participate. The attack was supported by the artillery battery commanded by Lt Mustafa al-Khasawnah. Major Geoffrey Lockett, DSO, MC, who took part in the attack, reported:

> I have seldom seen a more cool, steady and determined advance from the start line to the objective by the troops of any nation, under fire that was as heavy and accurate as in European attack, than the advance on al-Burj.[21]

While the artillery started their bombardmant, Hamdan al-Subaih could not wait. He rushed al-Burj with his armoured cars within a few minutes. On seeing that Hamdan would soon be under his fire from his battery, the gunner OP ordered a ceasefire just in time for Hamdan to enter al-Burj. Hamdan's armoured car was hit. His driver was wounded in his left eye and could no longer see anything. Hamdan was also wounded. The following is the dialogue between Hamdan and his driver, as it was described by Glubb and confirmed by Hamdan and his driver to the author.

The driver: I am hit! I can't see! I have lost my eye.
Hamdan: You don't have to see. Keep straight ahead and put your foot hard on the throttle.

The driver pressed on and Hamdan continued to advance until his armoured car was hit again and was a complete wreck. The driver managed to get out of the armoured car despite being wounded again. He shouted to Haidar Mustafa nearby that Hamdan was seriously wounded and still in the armoured car. Under heavy fire, Haidar Mustafa rescued Hamdan and his driver and evacuated them to the Regiment Dressing Station. At the Field Dressing Station in Ramallah, more than 100 small pieces of shrapnel were removed from Hamdan's body. When he was told that by the doctor after the operation, Hamdan said to him: 'You should not have bothered!' The fiercest counter-attack launched by any unit of the Jordanian Arab Army continued at al-Burj until the village was taken. More than 50 men from the 2nd Regiment were wounded and ten were killed. More than 40 Jewish soldiers were killed and many others wounded.

Meanwhile, the Harel Brigade attacked Latrun Ridge but were repulsed by the Jordan Army company defending it. On 17 July, the Jewish offensive continued, as described by Chaim Herzog:

> As the new truce approached, the 'Yiftach' and 'Harel' Brigades widened their respective areas of control. A distance of but two miles now separated the 'Yiftach' outposts west of the Latrun road from the 'Harel' outposts poised in the Jerusalem hills to the east of the Latrun road. Yigal Allon [the Commander of the offensive] resolved therefore to mount yet a further frontal attack on Latrun. While the 'Harel' units occupied the heights above Beit Nuba, from the west, the 'Yaftach' Brigade attacked with the support of the 8th Armoured Brigade. As a result of an error in communications, however, this support – which suffered losses from an anti-tank gun on the roof of the Latrun police station – withdrew, and the infantry did not persist in the attack. This was the last Israeli effort to capture Latrun. It continued to block the main highway to Jerusalem for the next nineteen years.[22]

Such a brief description could hardly do justice to the fierce fighting that took place on 18 July. The six six-pounder anti-tank guns of the 2nd Regiment, commanded by Haidar Mustafa, were deployed as follows.

- One gun at Latrun Ridge directed at al-Qubab.
- One gun at Latrun Ridge directed at the Wadi al-Sarar road.
- One gun directed at Bab al-Wad.
- One gun on the roof of the Latrun Police Fortress.
- One gun at the forest of the Latrun Monastery.
- One gun at the outer yard of the Latrun Police Fort.

To take the six-pounder up to the roof of the Police Fort, Haidar Mustafa had dissembled the gun and reassembled it on the roof in order to gain a wide field of fire against the advancing Jews and adjacent areas.

The Jewish artillery started their bombardment while the advance commenced towards the 2nd Regiment positions from the direction of al-Qubab. The attack was carried out by two brigades with a tank regiment in the lead. More than 300 rounds of artillery directed at the Police Fort nearly destroyed it, while the Jordanians held their fire and waited for the Jewish attackers to come closer to their positions. When the assaulting force were within close range of the six-pounders atop the Police Fort and the mortar platoon behind it, the 2nd Regiment opened fire supported by the artillery battery. The six-pounder gun on the roof of the Police Fort was aimed to give a clear view of the attacking tanks and armoured cars, and knocked out as many as possible before two of the gun crew were killed, one after the other. The rest of the gun crew remained in action in spite of their wounds. Those courageous men managed to halt the attack even when every one of them was wounded and continued to fire until the end of the battle. Thereafter, the artillery battery and the mortar platoon continued to fire at the enemy troops as they withdrew.

Meanwhile, on the 4th Regiment front, the attack on its positions started on 15 July with a heavy artillery and desultory mortar bombardment from 0800 hours until 1900 hours. It seemed that the enemy's aim was to break the morale of the Jordanian troops defending Yalo where most of the bombardment was directed. No casualties were suffered. Meanwhile, the enemy artillery directed their desultory bombardment at a previous Jordanian artillery gun position thinking that the guns were still there and without knowing that Mustafa al-Khasawnah had continued to change his battery's gun position. Although the Harel Brigade was one of the best of the Jewish forces, it was no match for the standard of training and will to fight of the Jordanian 4th Regiment. Although they advanced and captured a small hill to the east of the village of Yalo and started to open fire at the 3rd Company to cover an attack by a Harel battalion, while another regiment engaged the 2nd Company at the hills which overlooked the village of Dair Ayoub, they did not affect the determination of the Jordanians to hold their positions. The Harel Regiment had managed to occupy a house on a hill overlooking Yalo, and were by then threatening the rear echelons of the 4th Regiment. The attack was repulsed when the 4th Regiment opened fire from all directions. The fourth attack on Bab al-Wad was defeated. General Glubb sent this message to all officers and men of the 1st, 2nd and 4th Regiments:

It is my pleasure and pride to send this message to express to you my appreciation and esteem for all the heroic and valiant efforts you made between the 14th and 18th of July 1948, at the time when the enemy attacked in a strength more than four times your own, and you have been able to repulse them and achieve victory over them. May God bless you, and we must thank Him for this success. God save the King and the Jordan Arab Army.

Meanwhile, the 1st Brigade of the Jordan Arab Army defending the Jerusalem sector had made use of the first truce to reorganise and reinforce its units with new recruits to replace casualties. The 5th Regiment was holding a front in the Biddu al-Nabi Samuel area, the 3rd Regiment was holding the new city sector from Shuafat to Damascus Gate and the 6th Regiment was holding the Old City and south to al-Thuri area. On 8 July the 12th Company in Hebron was brought to the Old City of Jerusalem to take over the positions of the 8th Infantry Company, while the latter was placed in reserve at Ramallah.

On 10 July, an exchange of desultory mortar fire continued nearly all day, and the regiment used the 3.7 guns in their support at the anticipated enemy mortar positions. Many Jewish mortar bombs fell on the yard of al-Aqsa Mosque and one fell on the Dome of the Rock. Further exchanges of machine gun and mortar fire covered the whole area of al-Thuri, al-Nabi Daoud, Bab al-Jadid and Bab al-Nabi Daoud.

Just after dusk on 12 July, the Haganah attacked the whole of the 3rd Regiment front from the Damascus Gate to the Shaikh Jarrah Bridge – including Musrarah Saad wa Said and the Wadi leading to Mount Scopus. One of the fiercest battles in Jerusalem followed, in which both sides suffered many casualties. However, the 3rd Regiment held all their positions and by dawn on 13 July, the attack was repulsed.

The Jewish attack nearly succeeded because of the proximity of their positions to those of the 3rd Regiment. In certain congested built-up areas only a few yards separated them from the Jews. Until 15 July the road between Shaikh Jarrah and Damascus Gate was blocked by a few houses occupied by the Jews, and the 3rd Regiment decided to clear them. On 16 July, the following units from the 3rd and the 6th Regiments attacked the buildings at Mandelbaum, Mea Shearim and all the buildings adjacent to the Shaikh Jarrah–Damascus Gate road:

• 2nd Company 3rd Regiment, commanded by Khalid al-Khraisha.

- 3rd Company 3rd Regiment, commanded by Ghazi al-Harbi.
- One platoon, commanded by Lt Saud al-Khashman.
- One platoon, commanded by Lt Ahmad Abd al-Qadir.
- One platoon, commanded by Captain Othman Badran.
- One platoon of al-Jihad al-Muqaddas.
- The demolition platoon of 6th Regiment commanded by Lt Ahmad al-Zahir.

The attack started at dawn on 16 July and continued until early afternoon. In the close combat from house to house, and with the exception of Mea Shearim, all the other objectives of the attack were achieved. However, many casualties were suffered on both sides.

In the same evening, the Jewish artillery and mortars started a heavy bombardment of the Old City of Jerusalem covering an attack by a battalion of the Etzioni Brigade and a unit from the Irgun, which started at 0100 hours on 17 July. The Jewish aim was to capture the area from Bab al-Jadid to Bab al-Khalil and to break through to Bab al-Nabi Daoud. Other attacks were mounted on the 3rd Regiment sector, as well as al-Thuri. The Irgun unit sent a demolition detachment to the wall opposite Bab al-Jadid with a load of high explosives. The Jordanians defending the wall allowed them to come as close as they could throw grenades at them and managed to explode the load. About ten Jews were killed by their own explosives. The Irgun unit then advanced and nearly broke through Bab al-Jadid, but the Jordanians guarding the gate killed most of the attackers while the rest withdrew. Meanwhile, the battalion of the Etzioni Brigade launched their attack to break into Bab al-Nabi Daoud. The 6th Regiment allowed them to come as close as they could to making a kill. They then opened fire and threw grenades at the attackers who retreated with very heavy casualties.

At the YMCA building, close to what became the Mandlebaum Gate, many casualties were suffered by the 2nd Company of the 3rd Regiment at the hands of Jewish snipers shooting across the street from a building to the south. On a visit to the area, George Corfield and myself of the 1st Brigade HQ were told of the sniper. We took a PIAT rocket launcher and went up on the roof of the building adjacent to the YMCA building. With the usual trick of moving a steel helmet along the low wall of the roof we were able to provoke a few shots from the sniper who thereby gave his location away. George Corfield fired a rocket at the loophole from where the sniper was shooting. That was the end of sniping from that area. Suddenly, all hell broke loose where we were taking cover behind the low wall. A mortar bomb exploded on the wall about two feet above George Corfield's head, and although he was not wounded he suffered severe shell shock from which he did not then recover. He was subsequently sent to England for treatment. Corfield was a gallant officer and an honourable gentleman. He was replaced by Major Monihann, whose only qualification, as it seemed to be at the time, was to be able to drink copious quantities of Irish whiskey. He was soon dismissed from the Jordan Arab Army.

During the night, a soldier from the 3rd Regiment and myself dragged two coils of Dannert wire and placed them in the garden along the south wall of the newly occupied house. While moving back out of the garden, the soldier stepped on an anti-personnel mine which exploded and wounded him. I picked up the wounded soldier and handed him to his comrades who removed him to the dressing station. About ten minutes later I discovered that the boot and gaiters of my right leg were soaked with blood from a flesh wound to my calf.

Thus, the second truce started on the Jordanian front.

The Egyptian front
A major Jewish offensive was mounted in the south of Jerusalem with the intention of expanding the Jewish front in the area of al-Maliha and Ain Karim, in order to control the railway line from Tel Aviv to Jerusalem. On the night of 9/10 July, the Haganah attacked and captured a hill overlooking Ain Karim and al-Maliha. The Jordanian Arab Army 12th Company had been sent to defend the Old City of Jerusalem, and the whole of the area came under the command of the Egyptian Army, with the Muslim Brothers Brigade holding the Bethlehem–Hebron sector.

Further south-west of Hebron, the Egyptian Division had been reinforced with another brigade. The division was deployed as shown in Table 7.4.

The Jewish forces facing the Egyptian sector consisted of two brigades deployed as shown in Table 7.5.

TABLE 7.4
Deployment of the Egyptian Division

1st Brigade, covering the coastal main road from the Egyptian–Palestinian border to the north through Gaza to al-Majdal.
2nd Brigade, covering the northern Isdud sector.
4th Brigade, covering the al-Faluja sector controlling the line from al-Majdal, Bait Jibrin and Hebron.

TABLE 7.5
Deployment of Jewish forces

Givati Brigade, covering the sector north of the main road from al-Majdal to Bait Jibrin, along with two battalions manning their front and two battalions in reserve.
Negev Brigade, covering the area south of the Gaza–Beersheba main road with a commando battalion maintaining the lines of communication to the Jewish settlements in the Negev.

During the first truce, the Egyptian and Jewish commands planned their offensives against each other with the following aims.

- The Jewish aim was to free the road to the Negev and force the Egyptian 2nd Brigade out of the Isdud area.
- The Egyptian aim was to widen their east–west corridor, and isolate the Negev.

On 8 July, the Egyptians launched their offensive, seizing the initiative and surprising the Givati Brigade, who planned their attack for the following day at the end of the truce. The Egyptians assaulted and captured Hill 113, north of the crossroads west of Iraq Suweidan, Kowkabah and al-Hulaiqat on the main road to the Negev, south of the crossroads. Taken by surprise, the Givati Brigade Commander advanced his offensive which he had planned for 9 July.

The Jewish Negev Brigade launched a night attack on the Police Fort at Iraq Suweidan, which was held by an Egyptian infantry company. The attackers managed to break through the first perimeter of the Fort, but were unable to continue with their assault and had to withdraw after fierce close combat. However, fighting continued elsewhere and the

Givati 2nd Battalion managed to clear several undefended Arab villages in the area of the crossroads.

The Egyptian 4th Brigade attacked Bait Daras, but its defenders managed to repulse the attack. A Givati company attacked and captured the village of Ibdis. The Egyptian 4th Brigade counter-attacked with an infantry battalion and recaptured Bait Affa. They also carried out a counter-attack to recapture Ibdis, but failed to achieve their objective.

General al-Mawawi then directed his attention to Negba, a vital base for the Jewish defence. He launched an attack following a heavy artillery bombardment covering the advance of two infantry battalions and one armoured regiment. With the 9th Infantry Battalion in the lead, the assaulting troops managed to reach and break through the outer perimeter, but were halted by the defenders of Negba. The second attack managed to break through the inner perimeter and in the close combat that followed, they were compelled to withdraw. The Egyptians suffered more than 200 fatalities in both attacks.

Meanwhile, the Egyptians continued with their attacks against the settlements of Gal-On in the east and Beerot Yitzhak near Gaza to the south. But the Negev Brigade managed to repulse the attacks. In both these attacks the Egyptians suffered about 200 fatalities and wounded. The Sudanese units under command of the Egyptian Army managed to attack and capture Hill 105, near Negba, but were later forced to withdraw during a counter-attack by the commando battalion of the Givati Brigade.

Thereafter, because of their lack of ammunition, and after five days of the fiercest battles they had fought, the Egyptian Division Commander decided to take a defensive posture. The Negev Brigade continued with their offensive and launched attacks on al-Huleiqat, Kowkaba and Bait Affa, but were repulsed in all these villages. They also attacked Hatta and Kharatiya, east of Iraq Suweidan, and captured both these villages. Before the evening of the second truce on 18 July, the Egyptians counter-attacked to recapture the two villages but failed in both attempts. When the truce began no major changes had occurred on the ground. The ceasefire called for in the United Nations Security Council resolution of 15 July took effect on 18 July 1948.

After a short but heated argument between the Prime Minister and General Glubb about money for the Jordan Arab Army, both had an audience with the King who suggested that General Glubb should have a month's leave in Europe in order to rest. Glubb went on leave on 12 August taking a letter from King Abdullah to Ernest Bevin. It was to be delivered to him by hand and read as follows:

Dear Mr Bevin

Glubb Pasha is the bearer of this letter, which conveys to you my compliments and respects. In it I wish to put before you certain matters which affect your interests as much as ours.

I informed you directly about the Arab League at our last interview at the Foreign Office. I followed the advice you gave me on that occasion.

The Jewish question, which has given both you and us so much trouble, will not be solved through the Arab League. All concerned must understand and appreciate the dangers inherent in this problem and seek for a remedy. I think that we have reached at least a partial understanding with you on this subject, according to the information submitted to me by my Prime Minister, who actually met Your Excellency and discussed this problem.

The abominable massacres committed by the Jews and the driving of the Arab civilian population from their homes, led however to a real and bitter enmity. Then it became apparent to us that what had at first appeared to be merely a Jewish movement was in reality a Soviet design. We are now trying to remedy this critical situation in precisely the same manner as the Greeks are using to deal with an identical threat.

This state of affairs must be brought to an end. It is essential that we be able to stamp out Soviet influence, but our power to do so is crippled by the lack of the most essential means to this end.

We do not wish to render Britain's position more difficult in the United Nations Organisation, but, on the other hand, we have to weigh the relative importance of avoiding trouble with the United Nations, on the one hand, and the absolute necessity of preventing further strengthening of Soviet propaganda in the Arab Countries, on the other.

I feel that it is our duty to obtain the means to resist this Soviet threat, and I am also persuaded that it is the duty of our friends to help us in this, whatever the consequences may be.

This seems to me to be a reasonable measure, which it is essential to carry out, if necessary without it becoming publicly known.

Glubb Pasha will also explain to you all the activities which our jealous Arab rivals have engaged in against us, with even more alacrity than our enemies the Jews.[23]

On 12 August, General Glubb, accompanied by his family, departed for London, flying through Cairo where he found a group of reporters who wanted to know if it was true that he had been dismissed by King Abdullah. He was also surrounded by reporters in London asking him about attempts on his life by Jewish terrorists, following the Jordan Arab Army victory at Latrun. On 19 August, he had a meeting with the Foreign Secretary, Ernest Bevin, in the latter's private flat in Carlton House Terrace. With the King's letter, Glubb submitted a detailed report on how the current political and military situation in the Middle East affected relations with the Hashemite Kingdom of Jordan. The report described three problems that had to be dealt with if Britain intended to regain her credibility in the Arab world.

First, political relations between Britain and Jordan were tainted by King Abdullah's doubts about British policy and motives in the United Nations. Second, the Jordan Arab Army would cease to exist as a military fighting force unless it received fresh supplies of arms and ammunition. Third, the Jordan Arab Army was on the point of bankruptcy and its subsidy would have to be renewed. He insisted that unless His Majesty's Government turned its urgent attention to these problems, the Hashemite Kingdom of Jordan would collapse, its territory would be divided among Syria, Iraq and Saudi Arabia, and Israel would seize the West Bank territories. General Glubb warned: 'Should this occur, the extremists in all Arab countries will really have a good excuse for claiming that the British and their tool, Jordan, have really let down the Arab cause.'

Glubb endeavoured to bring the attention of the Foreign Office to the fact that the British connection with Jordan was a double-edged sword. For when the Jordan Arab Army captured the Old City of Jerusalem, King Abdullah was hailed as a saviour and the Arab leaders praised his policies and treaty with Britain, but when the Jordan Arab Army was forced to withdraw from Lydda and Ramleh, the same Arab leaders suspected King Abdullah because of what seemed to them to be the Jordan Arab Army acting on instructions from Britain.

General Glubb recommended that Britain should immediately rearm and re-equip the Jordan Arab Army; Britain should publicly guarantee the independence of the Hashemite Kingdom of Jordan in accordance with the Anglo–Jordanian Treaty of 1948, and Britain should support the Hashemite Kingdom of Jordan's right to take possession of the West Bank and warn the Israelis not to make incursions into any of King Abdullah's territories. He added:

> I venture to submit that it is essential to keep Trans-Jordan alive through the next months, because:
>
> 1. Trans-Jordan, in spite of all that has happened, has not departed from her traditional policy of friendship with Britain. Only circumstances too strong for her compelled her to fight the Jews, and to acquiesce in the fatalities and follies of the Arab League.
>
> 2. Trans-Jordan is notorious in the Middle East and further afield as the staunchest friend of Britain. For her to be the first to collapse would be disastrous for British prestige. If we can hang on a little longer, Trans-Jordan may receive a substantial increase of territory, which will make her a more valuable ally. If we abandon her now and she collapses the solution of the Palestine problem itself will be rendered much more difficult.[24]

NOTES

1 PRO. FO 816/121. From Kirkbride to the Foreign Office, 24 May 1948.
2 PRO. FO 816/121. Bevin to Kirkbride, 24 May 1948.
3 PRO. FO 816/121. Bevin to Kirkbride, 25 May 1948.
4 PRO. FO 816/121. Kirkbride to Bevin, 26 May 1948.
5 PRO. FO 816/121. From Kirkbride to Bevin, 27 May 1948
6 PRO. FO 816/122. From Kirkbride to Bevin, 2 June 1948.
7 PRO. DEFE 6/6. Kirkbride to Foreign Office, 6 June 1948.
8 Glubb, *A Soldier with the Arabs*, p. 142.
9 *Ibid.*, p. 143.
10 Al-Sharaa, *Our Wars with Israel*, p. 154.
11 Glubb, *A Soldier with the Arabs*, p. 145.
12 Ben-Gurion, *War Diary*, p. 411.
13 *Ibid.*, pp. 437–8.
14 Glubb, *A Soldier with the Arabs*, p. 146.
15 Al-Sharaa, *Our Wars with Israel*, pp. 214–15. Also, Sulaiman Musa, *Unforgettable Days: Jordan in the 1948 War* (published by the author, Amman: 1983), p. 338.
16 Herzog, *The Arab–Israeli Wars*, pp. 79–80.
17 Glubb, *A Soldier with the Arabs*, pp. 161–2.
18 *Ibid.*, p. 162.
19 Colonel T. N. Bromage, letter to author, 27 May 1999.
20 PRO. FO 371/68822. From C. M. Perie-Gordon to the Foreign Office, 25 July 1948.

21 Glubb, *A Soldier with the Arabs*, p. 167.
22 Herzog, *The Arab–Israeli Wars*, p. 83.
23 PRO. FO 371/68822. From King Abdullah to Ernest Bevin, 12 August 1949.
24 PRO. FO 371/68822. General Glubb, the Trans-Jordan Situation, 12 August 1948.

8

The Second Truce

On 19 August 1948, the Security Council of the United Nations approved a resolution making each party in Palestine responsible for the actions of both regular and irregular forces operating in its territory and stating that no party was entitled to gain military or political advantage through violation of the truce. But the Jews wasted no time during the first truce and the ten days of fighting in July. They continued to reorganise their forces, reinforce their strength, and import new weapons and equipment. In spite of the United Nations calling upon all members to abstain from supplying weapons, ammunition and war material to both the Arabs and the Jews, the Jews won an agreement with Communist Czechoslovakia, approved by the Soviet Union, to supply them with aircraft and weapons as shown in Table 8.1.

TABLE 8.1
Czechoslovakia's arms supplies to the Jews

Date	Arms
21 June	19,500 rifles; 113 military 4 x 4 Jeeps.
26 June	7 C.46 Aircraft.
27 June	50 field guns, 75-mm, each with 1,000 rounds of ammunition; 50 field guns, 75-mm, each with 1,000 rounds of ammunition; 50,000 rounds of ammunition for 65-mm guns; 150,000 rounds of ammunition for 20-mm guns; 144 guns of various calibres with 52,000 rounds of ammunition; 57 tanks of various weights.

By 12 August, the total strength of the Jewish forces was as shown in Table 8.2.

By the last week of September, the Jewish forces were completely reorganised into four fronts as shown in Table 8.3.

TABLE 8.2
Total strength of Jewish force as at 12 August 1948

Type of force	Officers and other ranks
Regular brigades	30,600
Local garrisons	11,300
Women soldiers	16,200
Services	22,000
Various forces	4,000
Total	**84,100 officers and other ranks**

TABLE 8.3
Reorganised Jewish fronts

- **Northern front**, commanded by General Moshe Carmel.
- **Central front**, commanded by General Dan Even.
- **Jerusalem–Tel Aviv front**, commanded by General Zvi Ayalon.
- **Southern front**, commanded by General Yigal Allon.[1]

The following brigades were brought up to full strength with mobility and full support arms and services:

- Golani Brigade.
- Carmeli Brigade.
- Alexandroni Brigade.
- Kiryati Brigade.
- Givati Brigade.
- Etzioni Brigade.
- 7th Brigade.
- Oded Brigade.
- Harel Brigade.
- Yaftach Brigade.
- Negev Brigade.
- 8th Armoured Brigade.

The new Jewish Air Force consisted of 9 fighter aircraft, 3 bombers and 10 bomber/transport aircraft. Gradually, the Jewish forces were developing into an efficient regular army with fighting abilities and close cooperation between the various arms and services. Particularly in night operations, they started to avoid the many mistakes they had previously made in major operations.

During the same period, the Arab armies took a defensive posture without any increase or major developments in their strength. Although some reorganisation and troop reinforcements took place, no major replenishment of ammunition, weapons or equipment had been carried out. The western powers adhered to the Security Council resolution and refused to supply both sides. The Arabs had no contact or close relations with the Communist bloc, and with the exception of the good relations between Britain and Jordan, the rest of the Arabs found themselves without friends, isolated in the world and in the United Nations.

The northern front

At the northern front, the Lebanese Army had increased its strength to one brigade and one battalion very thinly deployed from Rosh Hanikra (on the Mediterranean coast) to Bint Jubaiyil (near al-Malikiyah in the east). Their main aim was to protect their southern border with Palestine and to support the Liberation Army by protecting their line of communications from Lebanon to the areas adjacent to the Lebanese border, Muttallah, an area west of the Sea of Galilee, al-Lubban, al-Majdal Karm and Tarshihah. The Lebanese Army fought by instinct rather than by training and experience – and with hearts full of loyalty to the Arab cause rather than by the rules of war.

The Liberation Army was reduced to three Yarmouk battalions – the 1st, 2nd and 3rd – supported by six 75-mm guns and eight armoured cars. It was an army defeated by its outdated leadership rather than by the efficiency of its opponents. The men's morale was low, supplies were also low, and the administration was antiquated. The army lacked discipline and tended to indulge in looting and imposing levies of money on the civilians inhabiting the areas they occupied. It became a burden rather than an asset to the Palestine cause.

The strength of the Syrian Army was increased to three brigades manning the border line from the Lebanese–Syrian border in the north to al-Hammah on the River Yarmouk in the south. Although the soldiers and non-commissioned officers were good, natural fighters who had gained some experience during the first round of fighting, their collective training was still below average, and their senior officers and Commanders had the mentality of gendarmes rather than military Field Commanders. The Syrians fought gallantly with their hearts and emotions rather than with strategy and tactics.

The Iraqi front

The Iraqi front was defended with a strong division and one battalion holding a wide front stretching from Bardala in the north to Jenin to the west and then south to Tulkarm, Qalqiliyah and al-Majdal Yaba. The Iraqi Army suffered from the lack of an efficient logistics system and supplies, particularly in transport and replenishment of ammunitions.

The Jordanian front

The main problem facing the Jordanian Arab Army was the lack of ammunition and money. Glubb had complained to Tawfiq Abu al-Huda that he could not fight a war on the peacetime budget. The £3,000,000 promised by Abd al-Rahman Azzam amounted in reality to only £250,000 – and even that amount was overspent. Azzam, who wanted the Jordanian Arab Army to continue fighting, refused to pay a penny more. The Syrians offered to supply Jordan with some Belgian ammunition which they were not using, but when an officer went to Damascus to collect the shells, he was bluntly told by the Prime Minister, Jamil Mardam, to go away. The Egyptians were more generous – they returned a fraction of the twenty-five-pounder shells confiscated by them on the ship *Ramsis*, a total of 400 shells.[2]

However, reorganisation was the order of the day during the first truce and afterwards, including the formation of the regiments shown in Table 8.4.

The expansion of the Jordan Arab Army within six months from four regiments on 15 May to ten regiments by 1 December was due to the presence of 16 infantry companies and the hard work and dedication of their commanding officers and the staff officers at the 1st Brigade HQ, under whom five new regiments were formed. The support provided by the Division HQ and the dedication of all the officers concerned in the formation of these regiments was unprecedented and remarkable. Scrounging was the order of the day for those months, and the staff of 1st Brigade became experts in that field.

TABLE 8.4
Reorganisation of the Jordanian Arab Army

- **8th Infantry Regiment**, formed under the command 1st Brigade at Maaloufiyah near the Brigade HQ on 15 August 1948. The regiment was commanded by Captain Fawaz Mahir (former Commander of the 2nd Infantry Company). It consisted of the 2nd Infantry Company and the 8th Infantry Company, commanded by Captain Abd al-Razzaq Abdullah. The regiment was deployed later as a reserve for the brigade in the area of Bir Zait near Ramallah. It was later placed under the command of 3rd Brigade in the area between Budros, al-Nabi Salih and Bait Sira.

- **7th Regiment**, formed under the command of 1st Brigade in the secondary school at Bait Hanina near Ramallah on 21 August 1948. The regiment was commanded by Major Khalid al-Sahin, the former adjutant of 1st Regiment. It consisted of officers and men of the 13th Infantry Company commanded by Captain Faris al-Abid, and the 19th Infantry Company commanded by Captain Qasim Abu Shraitih. By 20 September, the 7th Regiment relieved the 5th Regiment in the Biddu, al-Nabi Samuel sector and was deployed as follows:

  – Regiment HQ, at Biddu
  – 1st Company, at Biddu
  – 2nd Company, at al-Nabi Samuel
  – 3rd Company, at Khirab al-Lahim
  – 4th Company, at al-Qubaibah
  – Support Company, at Biddu
  – HQ Company, at Bait Ijra.

- **9th Infantry Regiment**, formed under the command of the 1st Brigade on 15 November 1948. It took over from 'G' Force in the area of Hebron Tarqumiya under the command of Captain Dhurgham al-Falih.

- **10th Infantry Regiment** (later titled 'the Hashemite Regiment'), formed at the Abdulli Barracks under the command of Jordan Arab Army HQ on 1 December 1948. The regiment was commanded by Lt Colonel Habis al-Majali, and took over the Hebron Sector from the 9th Regiment with one company deployed at Wadi Araba.

On the political front, the British Minister, Sir A. S. Kirkbride, who had been on sick leave in England, returned to Amman on 5 August. He immediately reported to the Foreign Office as follows:

1. I have just resumed duty after three weeks' sick leave during which period I was entirely out of touch with current events. You may be interested in my impressions.

2. I am struck principally by the extreme precariousness of our position in Trans-Jordan. Even at the moment we have reached a

degree of unpopularity which I would have described as impossible six months ago. The main danger now is that of a Jewish attack on the Arab Legion which that force is in no position to resist, being without artillery or mortar ammunition. The anti-British outbreaks, which followed the fall of Ramleh and Lydda for which the Arab Legion was not directly responsible, is an indication of what would happen following a major defeat of that force.

3. The line that the Arab Legion is being prevented from using its maximum strength against the Jews both through the treachery of its British officers and withholding of supplies by His Majesty's Government is being propagated actively by Syrian and Iraq authorities and Azzam. The Iraqi Army personnel operating in Trans-Jordan are particularly hostile to both British and to the Arab Legion, and they have practically ceased to have any relations with the latter.

4. One cannot help feeling that many Arab leaders would rejoice in the downfall of Trans-Jordan. Their motives vary. The Syrians regard Trans-Jordan as a potential danger to their régime; others would like to be able to point to the object lesson of the uselessness of depending on His Majesty's Government and to the fact that Trans-Jordan's long history of loyalty to Great Britain had counted for little at the end. Our argument about international obligations could do little to counter the effect of such propaganda in the rest of the Arab World. I have a growing conviction that if a disaster overtakes Trans-Jordan while we are withholding supplies and ammunition we might as well abandon the present policy of building defensive alliances in the Middle East.

5. I realise, of course, that it is impossible to judge from here the importance of other major issues involved in the withholding of supplies, but judged from a purely local point of view the policy is becoming increasingly difficult to justify. The Trans-Jordan Government has complied with our wishes to the best of its ability, both as regards general conduct of the campaign and as regards the truces. The restoration of the subsidy is an acknowledgment of this fact, but it is difficult to explain away the fact that, while paying the subsidy which enables the Arab Legion to exist, we should also reduce it to impotence, by denying it supplies of ammunition. The fact that the Jews are undoubtedly receiving ammunition, arms and equipment from overseas, renders the position all the more untenable.[3]

By the beginning of September, the Arab League Political Committee held a meeting at Cairo to discuss the military situation in Palestine. Kirkbride, who was kept informed of such developments by Abu al-Huda, reported on the meeting as follows:

> 1. The following is a precis of the instructions given to the Ministers of Defence and of Communications, who are representing Trans-Jordan at the current meeting of the Political Committee of the Arab League, as to the attitude which they are to adopt towards the various items of the agenda. You may find them interesting.
>
> (i) Resumption of hostilities if solution proposed by the mediator is not accepted by the Arab States. Trans-Jordan would only resume fighting on three conditions:
>
>   (a) that all the Arab States did so
>   (b) that the Arab League provided Trans-Jordan beforehand with all the arms and ammunition needed by the Arab Legion and with sufficient funds to meet the cost of the Arab Legion for a year
>   (c) that the Trans-Jordan Government should be entitled to satisfy themselves that the other Arab armies were pulling their weight and to withdraw from the war if this condition was not satisfied. [Commenting, Tawfiq Pasha expressed the view that he anticipated that none of these conditions could be fulfilled.]
>
> (ii) The formation of a Palestine Arab administration. Trans-Jordan would not agree to any change from the existing arrangement whereby each Arab Army was responsible for the administration of that part of Palestine which it occupied.
>
> (iii) The formation of a Palestine Army. Trans-Jordan had no objection in principle to the formation of a Palestine Arab Army but no units of that Army would be permitted to be stationed or to operate in areas of Palestine occupied by the Arab Legion.
>
> (iv) United Nations Organisation assistance to Arab refugees. Trans-Jordan did not mind whether this assistance was issued direct by United Nations Organisation or through the Arab League but would insist that the division should be made on the basis of the number of refugees for which each Arab State was responsible.
>
> 2. A final instruction, which did not relate to the agenda of the meeting, was that if any member of the Committee attacked

Trans-Jordan, as was the case at the last meeting, the Trans-Jordan representatives were to withdraw.[4]

During September, an Arab Airways passenger aircraft returning from Beirut was shot down over Jordanian territory by a Jewish fighter; all the passengers and crew were injured, three of them fatally.

In December, there was a series of incursions into Jordanian territory by Jewish forces in the Wadi Araba. One Jewish detachment kidnapped three Jordanian civilians who were subsequently released unharmed. A British warship came to Aqaba early in November, and while the individual ships were changed, there was a naval unit at that port for most of the time until the end of the year.

On 26 October, Radio Israel announced that Aqaba must be captured. Because Aqaba was within Jordanian territory, and consequently covered by the Anglo–Jordanian Treaty of 1948, the Government of Jordan asked the British Government to assume responsibility and obligation for the defence of the town and port. By the beginning of November, a British battalion landed at Aqaba and a British warship had anchored offshore.

The Egyptian front

The Egyptian Army in Palestine had taken a defensive posture on the whole of its front; it suffered severely from a lack of ammunition and modern arms compared to the Jewish forces. The Egyptian revolution of 1952 unintentionally tarnished the image of the Egyptian Army of 1948, but the fact is that the junior officers and men fought with their hearts and emotions and did their best under the circumstances in every battle they fought.

The assassination of Count Bernadotte

Count Bernadotte, the United Nations mediator, was actively pushing his new proposals for a peaceful settlement of the Palestine question. The proposals suggested that the whole of the Negev would be returned to the Arabs, and the whole of north Galilee would be given to the Jews; Lydda and Ramleh would be returned to the Arabs and Jerusalem, and the international airport at Lydda would be placed under United

Nations control. (For the detailed proposals, see Appendix C.) The Jewish command realised that, with the Negev isolated and not within their control, it would be nearly impossible to oppose Count Bernadotte's proposals. It became vital to them to break the Egyptian front line between the Jewish areas in the centre of Palestine and the whole of the Negev in the south and place it under their control.

On Friday 17 September, after completing his new proposals and submitting his report to the Security Council of the United Nations, Count Bernadotte flew from Damascus to Qalandiyah, an air strip north of Jerusalem in the Jordanian sector. He drove to 1st Division HQ for talks with General Norman Lash, during which the continuous sniping by the Jews against the Jordanian front was discussed. At the end of the meeting, Lash offered an armoured car to escort the mediator to Jerusalem. The Count declined the offer and said: 'We cannot allow ourselves to be frightened out of doing our work.'

Lash insisted and said his safety within the Jordanian sector was his responsibility. Thus the Arab Legion escort accompanied the mediator from Division HQ to the area of Mandelbaum Gate where he crossed over to the Jewish sector of the city. He had lunch at the YMCA building with a few United Nations observers. In his book,[5] Glubb summarised what happened next.

> After lunch, with a convoy of three cars, the Count drove out to Government House, the former official residence of the British High Commissioner for Palestine. After inspecting the house and garden [where it was proposed that UNO headquarters be established], and viewing the city from the roof, the party returned to Jerusalem. As they drove through the Katamon quarter, they came suddenly on a jeep, which was standing in the middle of the road. As the convoy approached, the driver appeared to be trying to turn. He fumbled with the gears, went backwards and forwards, and finally stopped in the middle of the road again. There were four men in the jeep, in the uniforms of the Israeli army. The Count's convoy consisted of three cars, containing United Nations personnel and an Israeli liaison officer. There was no Israeli escort. No one in the convoy was armed.
>
> Three of the occupants of the jeep jumped out and walked towards the UNO convoy, which had been obliged to halt because the Jewish jeep was blocking the road. Count Bernadotte was in the third or rear car. One of the Israelis walked down one side of the

cars and two walked down the other. They went straight to the third car. The driver remained seated in the jeep.

The single man went up to the window of Count Bernadotte's car. The passengers thought that he was a Jewish soldier about to ask for their passes, and began to pull them from their pockets. Suddenly the man thrust the mouth of an automatic pistol through the window and fired a burst of shots at point-blank range at the Count and at the French Colonel Serot, who was sitting beside him. At the same instant, the other two Israelis pulled out automatic pistols and fired at the wheels and radiators of the cars, presumably to prevent pursuit. The men then jumped into the jeep, which disappeared at full speed. A truck, full of Israeli soldiers, was seen to be halted some forty yards away. It subsequently transpired that the murderers in their jeep had been waiting on the road for at least an hour before the convoy arrived. Count Bernadotte had received six bullet wounds, one of which, through the heart, must have caused death instantaneously. Colonel Serot had received seventeen bullets. Next day, the murderers, who belonged to the Stern Gang – Jewish terrorists, sent the following letter to the Press:

> *'Although in our opinion all United Nations observers are members of foreign occupation forces, which have no right to be on our territory, the murder of the French Colonel Serot was due to a fatal mistake: our men thought that the officer sitting beside Count Bernadotte was the British agent and anti-Semite, General Lundstrom.'*

General Lundstrom was Count Bernadotte's chief of staff and an officer in the Swedish army.

The Count's body was taken by road to Haifa on 18 September. The convoy passed our positions at Latrun, where an Arab Legion guard of honour was drawn up to pay the last homage to the dead.

Count Bernadotte was the representative of the United Nations, the first mediator of the Security Council, a close relative of the King of Sweden, and a man who had devoted his life to charitable and humanitarian causes. The United Nations should have imposed a punishment of some kind against the Jews who had so brutally assassinated their representative. This new Jewish terrorism and the failure of the United Nations to take appropriate action sent a message to all parties that the United Nations Organisation was impotent.

The end of the Liberation Army

In the north of Palestine, the Liberation Army Brigade was deployed as shown in Table 8.5.

TABLE 8.5
The deployment of the Liberation Army Brigade

- **1st Yarmouk Battalion**, supported by a company of Lebanese volunteers, was deployed in the high ground south of the Akka to Safad road.
- **2nd Yarmouk Battalion**, deployed opposite Safad between Meron and Sasa.
- **3rd Yarmouk Battalion**, holding the western part of the sector including Tarshiha.

The Jews must have been pleasantly surprised by the political justification given to them by al-Qawiqji, who stated that he and his army were not members of the United Nations, and that the ceasefire resolution did not apply to his forces. The Jews were planning for weeks to clear Galilee of any Arab forces, destroy the Liberation Army and extend their control to a defensive front along the international boundary between Lebanon and Palestine. To achieve that aim, the Northern Command planned operation 'Hiram' and deployed the following formations:

- 7th Brigade, consisting of two infantry battalions – an armoured regiment and the Circassian Company.
- Oded Brigade, with the Druze Company.
- One battalion from the Carmeli Brigade.
- One battalion from the Golani Brigade.
- Two batteries of 75-mm guns.
- Two batteries of 65-mm guns.

On the night of 28/29 October, the first phase of operation 'Hiram' started with the advance of the 7th Brigade from Safad with a troop of armoured cars and the Circassian Company in the lead, and captured all the Arab villages north of the road from Safad to Meron and east to Safsaf. The Circassian Company were engaged in a bitter infantry action at Meron as a result of which the Arabs withdrew, leaving 80 dead on the battlefield. A composite detachment from the Carmeli and the 7th

Brigade advanced to capture Meron. When the attack on Meron was mounted, the defenders of the village fought well and repulsed the attack. The attackers had to wait until dawn when they launched another assault with two troops of armoured cars and a squadron of half-tracks and captured the village. The village of Safsaf was captured later on the morning of 29 October. Thereafter, al-Jish was attacked by the composite force at the same time as a Syrian battalion was about to launch a counter-attack. In the chaos that followed, the 2nd Yarmouk Battalion started to withdraw to the hills around al-Jish, leaving their Battalion HQ to be captured by the Jews. The Syrian Battalion and what remained of the 2nd Yarmouk Battalion suffered 200 fatalities, with the survivors being taken prisoners.

Meanwhile, the Oded Brigade advanced from the west in the direction of Tarshiha, which was well defended by the Liberation Army. The attack on Tarshiha started with a heavy bombardment of artillery and mortars all through the night of 28/29 October. Just before dawn a battalion of the Oded Brigade mounted an assault on the two hills overlooking the village. In the fierce battle that followed, the attackers were repulsed and had to withdrew back to their assembly area. The Druze Company were able to occupy the village of Yanuh after forcing a Yarmouk company to withdraw, but as soon as the attack on Tarshiha failed, the Yarmouk Battalion counter-attacked and reoccupied Yanuh.

The second phase of operation 'Hiram' started late in the evening of 29 October. The 7th Brigade attacked and captured Sasa, and took defensive positions at the road junction between Jist and Tarshiha. The Oded Brigade was about to attack Tarshiha, but at dawn white flags were seen raised on the village which was deserted by the Liberation Army.

Thereafter, the Golani Battalion advanced northwards from Eilabun and, by the evening of 29 October, reached the Tarshiha–Sasa road. By that time the Liberation Army was no more, and the situation ended in complete defeat. It was not the Arab volunteers who were defeated, it was the Political Committee of the Arab League, every one of them, along with al-Qawiqji. Thereafter, the Commander of the Jewish northern front ordered the Oded Brigade to clear the sector between Nahariya and Sasa, south of the Lebanese border. The 7th Brigade advanced from Sasa to the north-east in the direction of al-Malikiyah, while the rest of the Liberation Army withdrew into the Lebanese border. Thus the Jews controlled the whole Lebanese–Palestinian border from al-Nabi Yusha in the east to Rosh Hanikra on the Mediterranean coast. Thereafter, two battalions from the Carmeli Brigade broke through the Lebanese border into Lebanon and captured 14 Lebanese villages – including the near bank of the Litani River. The Arab deaths and casualties during the Jewish offensive were as follows.

- 200 killed from the Syrian Battalion.
- 200 killed from the Liberation Army.
- 500 prisoners taken from the Syrian Battalion and the Liberation Army.

The Jews captured 1,500 rifles, three field guns, two armoured cars, 20 vehicles and four medium machine-guns.[6]

The final battles of the southern front

By the beginning of October, neither the Jewish nor the Egyptian forces were the same as they had been at the beginning of the war in May 1948. The Egyptians had been through a severe battle inoculation and become experienced fighters at officer level, the ranks of lieutenant colonel and below and at the level of non-commissioned officers and soldiers. Although most of their senior officers had little experience in conducting large operations, they had had some experience during the previous battles and had learnt some expensive and hard lessons. The Jewish forces, on the other hand, were radically different from four or five months previously. They acquired and used with telling effect an air force of bombers and fighter-bombers, several regiments of field artillery and mortars, and four armoured car and tank regiments. Most of their senior officers had experience of fighting during the Second World War, and their junior officers had the experience of both military and guerilla tactics. An example of their tactical abilities was the intricate operation of the infiltration of the Yaftach Palmach Brigade into the Negev through the Egyptian front to relieve the Negev Brigade, which had suffered the brunt of fighting in the southern front since the beginning of the war. An example of the Egyptians' abilities was the defeat of the seven Jewish attacks on Iraq Suweidan, which was still held by its Egyptian defenders. Another example is provided by Chaim Herzog in his book:

A typical battle was the one that took place in the area of Khirbet Mahaz, a hill overlooking the main road running from north to south through the Negev, and which was within artillery range of the airfield at Ruhama, a vital supply link for the Israeli forces in the Negev. After a fresh force from the 'Yiftach' Brigade had occupied the area of Khirbet Mahaz, the Israeli positions were unsuccessfully attacked seven times by Egyptian forces, particularly by the 6th Infantry Battalion, whose operation officer at the time was a Major Jamal Abd al-Nasser.[7]

The plan for the massive Jewish offensive on the Egyptian Army was completed by the first week of October 1948, and code-named 'Yoav'. The following formations were deployed to carry out the operation.

- Givati Brigade.
- Yaftach Brigade.
- Negev Brigade.
- Oded Brigade.
- 8th Armoured Brigade.

The plan aimed to open a corridor from the centre of Palestine to the Negev so that it could first cut the Egyptian lines of communications along the coast, second isolate the Egyptian sector of Hebron-Jerusalem from the rest of the Egyptian forces and finally, isolate and defeat the Egyptian forces and remove them from Palestine.

In order to justify their offensive, the Jewish command sent a supply convoy on 15 October to the Negev settlements under the supervision of United Nations supervisors and in accordance with the terms of the ceasefire agreement. On its way through the Egyptian lines, when the convoy reached the road junction exactly as the Jews anticipated, the Egyptians opened fire at it, destroying one of its vehicles while the rest withdrew back to their lines. The Jews now had a pretext on which to launch their massive operation (see Map 5).

At 1800 hours on the same day, the Jewish air force bombed al-Arish airport, Gaza, al-Majdal and Bait Hanun. Thereafter the Jews had complete air superiority. The 9th Commando Battalion of the Yiftach Brigade advanced and mined the railway between Rafah and Khan Yunis west of Nirim, and began to harass the Egyptian installations and camps. At the same time, the 1st and 3rd Battalions of the Yaftach

Brigade advanced from Nir-Am near Gaza and occupied their positions east of Bait Hanun, about 600 yards east of the main road, and started to intercept the Egyptian traffic.

The 3rd Battalion of the Givati Brigade advanced to the road between Iraq al-Manshiyah and Bait Jibrin, occupying the village of Masarah north of the road and Khirbit al-Raai to the south. The Muslim Brothers carried out a counter-attack against the attackers of Masarah, but failed, although the road to Bait Jibrin was cut. They also moved south to the east of Iraq al-Manshiyah and cut the road from al-Faluja to Bait Jibrin. On the morning of 16 October, the 9th Tank Regiment of the 8th Armoured Brigade and the 7th Battalion of the Negev Brigade supported by an infantry battalion mounted a major attack against Iraq al-Manshiyah with the aim of opening the corridor to the rest of the Negev. The attack was repulsed by accurate Egyptian artillery fire from the area of al-Faluja. Within minutes, one Jewish company suffered the loss of one-third of its troops and retreated in panic. At that point a reserve company in half-tracks attempted to evacuate the wounded and tow away the damaged tanks knocked out by the Egyptian defenders. The Jews suffered very heavy casualties, and four tanks were completely destroyed. Herzog wrote:

> This attempt failed because of the lack of experience of the Israeli forces in co-ordinating armour and infantry; much of the armoured force was damaged when it was caught exposed in an artillery killing ground previously prepared by the Egyptians, and the Israeli force was obliged to withdraw. In the course of the action, one of the two Cromwell tanks that had been acquired from the British Army was damaged, and the second Cromwell was involved in the task of extricating it from the battlefield. Very heavy losses were incurred in this attack, which had all the indications of slovenliness, lack of co-ordination and poor overall command. Of the total attacking force, only about fifty men managed to make their way back to the Israeli trenches. In addition to the heavy casualties, four Hotchkiss tanks of the small Israeli tank force were lost and all the remaining tanks were damaged.[8]

On the same day, General Yigal Allon made a change in his plan and decided to attack and capture the road junction on the main road about three kilometres west of Iraq Suweidan, and break through in the area of the village of al-Hulaiqat. The Egyptian defensive positions in the area were designed to protect the junction and block every road out of it. It was a defensive plan in accordance with standard principles: all round, mutual support and comprehensively organised. All the defensive positions were based on the famous Police Fort at Iraq Suweidan, which had repulsed seven previous Jewish attacks. To be able to break through, the Jews had to capture Hill 113 and Hill 100 dominating the junction in the north, along with the hilltop Arab villages of Kawkabah and al-Hulaiqat, two strongly fortified positions held by two very courageous units – one company of the Saudi Arabian Army and an Egyptian company.

The 1st Battalion of the Givati Brigade were given the task of capturing Hill 113 and Hill 100. At 2230 hours on 16 October, Israeli artillery, mortars and medium machine-guns opened fire at the two hills. At the start of the assault, Hill 103, near Hill 113, was taken. Then the two assaulting Givati companies attacked and had to fight the fiercest battle in the history of the battalion. But following a battle of close hand-to-hand and bayonet assaults the two hills were captured by the Jews. Many counter-attacks were carried out by the Egyptian force in the area and some air raids by the Egyptian Air Force on Jewish positions near the junction. The counter-attacks failed. The Givati Battalion continued to advance and captured the high ground near Kawkabah.

The 1st Battalion of the Yaftach Brigade mounted an attack on the Saudi Arabian company at al-Hulaiqat supported by a heavy artillery bombardment. When the attackers came close to the perimeter, the Saudi Arabians opened fire with all their weapons and inflicted heavy casualties on the leading assault troops, and once they were able to break the momentum of the attack, they left their trenches and chased the Jews out of their area. Thus, the Saudis won the day and kept the road to the Negev blocked by their positions.

Meanwhile, on the night of 15/16 October, the Egyptian artillery near Yad Mordechai started to shell the Jewish positions near Bait Hanun, while the Egyptian forces located at Isdud and al-Majdal, which were threatened by isolation and encirclement, started to withdraw south using an alternative road track adjacent to the beach towards Gaza. On the night of 18/19 October, the Oded Brigade was brought into action and attacked the Egyptian positions at the area of Kharatiya, which comprised the new Egyptian bypass, Burma Road. The Oded Brigade had no experience in desert warfare and were fighting an open battle for the first time. Their attempt to capture Kharatiya failed and the road to the Negev remained blocked.

General Allon was under heavy pressure from Ben-Gurion to open the corridor to the Negev, for Ben-Gurion himself was under pressure from the United Nations and Britain to accept a ceasefire. On 19 October, the Security Council approved a resolution regarding the fighting in the Negev, adopting a modified form of the Acting Mediator's report, which recommended an immediate and effective ceasefire, and a withdrawal of both parties from positions that were not occupied at the time of the outbreak of fighting. The Jews completely ignored this resolution. Thus General Allon decided to attack al-Hulaiqat and gave the task to the 2nd Battalion of the Givati Brigade and a company from the 4th Battalion, supported by artillery and mortars. The Arab force defending al-Hulaiqat consisted of one Egyptian infantry company, one Saudi Arabian infantry company and a support company, including Bren Carriers, in six defensive positions. The fiercest battle in the Negev so far followed.

After very heavy bombardment by artillery and mortars, which lasted for about 30 minutes and inflicted casualties on the defenders, the Jewish forces advanced and started to assault the Saudi Arabian and Egyptian positions. As the assaulting troops came close to the perimeter, the defenders opened fire with their two-inch mortars, machine-guns and minor arms and were able to halt the attack. The battle for the perimeter lasted for nearly an hour during which the Egyptian and Saudi ammunition was almost exhausted. At that stage the Jewish force managed to break through the perimeter and approached the trenches. With their ammunition exhausted the Egyptians and Saudi Arabians came out of their trenches shouting 'Allahu Akbar', and in the close combat that followed, bayonets, hand grenades, attacks and counter-attacks were the order of the day. During the fighting for the last hill, the Saudi Arabian soldiers started biting their attackers once they had run out of ammunition. Thereafter, the fiercest hand-to-hand fighting in the 1948 Arab–Israeli war inflicted a heavy toll of casualties on both sides. All the Saudi and Egyptian soldiers were either killed or wounded and al-Hulaiqat, at last, fell to the Jews on 20 October leaving the corridor to the Negev wide open.

While the attack on al-Hulaiqat was in progress the 1st Battalion of the Givati Brigade attacked the Police Fort at Iraq Suweidan on the night of 20/21 October. With the use of a vehicle loaded with high explosives an attempt was made to destroy the wall on the fortress, but a PIAT rocket hit the vehicle before it reached its target and only the water tower was subsequently damaged. At one point the attackers reached the gate of the fortress. However, they were forced back with a determined close combat by the defenders and the whole attacking force withdrew after suffering many casualties.

Nearly 12 hours after the opening of the corridor to the Negev, Yigal Allon decided to capture Beersheba. He regrouped and formed a composite force as follows.

- One infantry battalion from the Negev Brigade.
- 9th Commando Battalion of the Negev Brigade.
- 2nd Regiment of the 8th Armoured Brigade.
- One regiment of artillery and mortar batteries.

Allon's intention was to isolate the Egyptian Hebron–Bethlehem sector and its line of communications. Thereafter, he would deal with each isolated Egyptian force one after the other. His composite force moved from Mishmar Hanegev to their assembly area in Hatzerim. At 0400 hours on 21 October, they advanced to an area near Abu Irqiq, three kilometres north of the town of Beersheba. At the same time an artillery and mortar bombardment started, while a troop of armoured cars mounted a diversionary operation from the direction of Hebron in the north. After fierce fighting, which lasted for four hours, the Egyptian battalion – about 500 officers and men – had exhausted their ammunition, and the capital of the Negev fell to the Jews.[9]

By 22 October the Egyptian Division was broken up into five isolated forces as follows.

- One brigade in the Gaza–Rafah area.
- One brigade withdrawing from the al-Majdal area to the south.
- One brigade of approximately 2,500 officers and men were under siege in the al-Faluja area.
- Two Muslim Brothers Battalions in the Hebron–Bethlehem area.
- One Muslim Brothers Battalion in the Gaza–Rafah area.

During the withdrawal of the Egyptian forces to Gaza, the Commander of the Muslim Brothers there, Kamil al-Sharif, had realised the critical situation of the Egyptian Army and suggested to General al-Mawawi that the Muslim Brothers should take new positions on any high ground facing the Jewish settlements in the area and protect approaches to the Egyptian positions while they prepared their new defences. When al-Mawawi agreed, Kamil al-Sharif sent his troops forward. They occupied their new positions, laid minefields on the roads and tracks leading to the Egyptian positions, and generally harassed the Jewish settlements with fighting patrols and random ambushes. Their bases were in the areas of, for example, Wadi al-Shallalah, Tel-Jumaah, al-Rabiyah and al-Shauth. During these operations the Muslim Brothers were supported by Palestinian Bedouin tribes including al-Tarabin, al-Hanajirah, al-Nussairat, al-Tayaha and al-Maaliqah. Thus, the withdrawal of the Egyptian forces succeeded. During one week of operations, 15 Jewish armoured cars and one tank were destroyed. Many water pipes and telephone lines between Jewish settlements were also destroyed.[10]

While operation 'Yoav' was in progress, operation 'Hahar' was launched by the Harel Brigade with the intention of expanding the area under their control in the Jerusalem corridor to the south against the Egyptian force in the Bethlehem–Hebron Sector. On the night of 18/19 October, the 4th Battalion of the Harel Brigade advanced to the south-east and captured Bait Shamish and Bait Jammal without resistance. In the east they captured Dair al-Hawa. The 6th Battalion of the Harel Brigade captured Jarash, Sufla, al-Qabo and Wadi Fawkin. On the night of 21 October, the 8th Battalion of the Etzioni Brigade captured al-Walajah. The Harel 4th Battalion of the Givati Brigade attacked and captured Bait Jibrin and Ajjour. On 22 October, the 4th Battalion of the Harel Brigade captured Bait Natif and reached the village of Hausan.

On the same day, the Mayor of Hebron, Shaikh Muhammad al-Jaabari, accompanied by a large delegation, went to Amman and appealed to King Abdullah to send a Jordanian Army force to save Hebron from the imminent Jewish attack. The United Nations Security Council passed a resolution on 22 October ordering a ceasefire and the withdrawal of all combatants to the positions they had held on 15 October. But the Jews refused to withdraw. At this very critical stage for the Egyptians and the Palestinian people, President Truman of the United States of America prevented a vote on the enforcement of sanctions against Jews and Arabs who did not obey the Security Council. The Jews had succeeded in defying the United Nations.

It soon became obvious that the Jews, whether in the international political field or on the battlefield, could occupy Hebron and Bethlehem undeterred by the United Nations or the Egyptian force in the Hebron–Bethlehem sector. Aware of the possibility that the Jordan Arab Army might be asked to help the Egyptian Army or defend the Hebron–Bethlehem sector, General Glubb commanded the 1st Division to form a composite force pending further orders. On the same day the division assembled the following units – about 350 officers and men – at Ramallah under command of the 1st Brigade.

- Two infantry companies of the 1st Regiment.
- One armoured car squadron of the 1st Regiment.
- One battery of 4.2-inch mortars from the Artillery Regiment.

Known as 'The G Force', these units were commanded by Major Geoffrey Lockett, DSO, MC, an eccentric British officer who liked his pinch of snuff and tot of whisky, and who was an unconventional and gallant man with a great love for fighting. After Shaikh al-Jaabari's appeal, King Abdullah asked General Glubb to send a force to Hebron. On the same day, Major Lockett led his force through a detour to the east of Jerusalem and along the rough track from Bethany to Bethlehem. Furthermore, Captain Sadiq al-Sharaa and myself were sent to Bethlehem and Hebron to obtain information regarding the state of the Egyptian force in the sector. We were baffled by the lack of interest and cooperation shown by the Egyptian officers – especially in Bethlehem.

On 23 October, the Political Committee of the Arab League held a meeting in Amman to discuss how to support the Egyptian front. Mahmoud Fahmi al-Noqrashi of Egypt and Jamil Mardam of Syria were the principal speakers. Mardam condemned the other Arab armies for their 'disgraceful' reluctance to help the Egyptian Army. As if goaded by him, the others agreed that they would provide assistance next time (as if what was going on in the Egyptian sector was not enough), but said that there was no need at present because the ceasefire had been accepted. Mardam promised that 'next time' the Syrian Army would break through between al-Hulah and Galilee to recapture Nazareth and Safad. He hinted at a condition that the Iraqi army would capture Affula. The Iraqi General Salih al-Saib, remarked: 'If the Syrian army did all that Mardam proposes, the Iraqi army would cooperate.' All that rhetoric while the Egyptian Army was being destroyed.

In an attempt to bring the discussion down to earth, General Glubb explained that the most urgent problem was how to rescue the Egyptian Brigade besieged at al-Faluja. He later wrote:

> The Arab Legion column had reached the Hebron area, but was too weak to undertake any offensive operations. We consequently suggested that the Iraqi army extend its front to take over Latrun from us, and that we then transfer the troops in the Latrun sector to Hebron. This would enable us to build up in Hebron a force sufficient to extricate the Egyptians from al-Faluja. The Iraqis, however, replied that they were not in a position to take over Latrun. As a result, the Arab Legion was left to do everything; to defend its original front from Beit Nabala to south-east of Jerusalem, to hold the whole Hebron district and in addition to rescue what it could from the debacle in the south. Neither the Iraqis, the Syrians, nor the Lebanese, were prepared to change their dispositions.[11]

On 24 October, Israeli Radio announced that Jewish forces would soon recapture Kfar Etzion. On that same day, two columns were moving parallel to each other from north to south. The Jewish column was advancing from Artoof to Bait Jibrin and, unknown to them, the Jordanian 'G Force' was moving down from Bethlehem to Hebron. The Jews attacked all the Arab villages on their route and conducted expulsion and destruction operations against the Arab inhabitants, who poured into Bethlehem and Hebron as refugees. As in every area of Palestine, the destruction of houses and the expulsion of Arab civilians had, by that stage, developed into a clearly recognised feature of official Jewish policy. A tragic and savage example of that policy in action occurred in the village of al-Dawaayimah. In his account of the massacre committed by the Jews against this village's inhabitants, Benny Morris wrote:

> Hundreds of refugees who made their way up the hills towards Hebron were from al-Dawaayimah, survivors of the massacre in the village on 29 October. Ben-Gurion, quoting General Avner, briefly referred in his War Diaries to the 'rumours' that the army had 'slaughtered 70–80 persons'. What happened was described a few days later by an Israeli soldier-witness to a Mapam member, who transmitted the information to Eliezer Prai, the editor of the party daily *Al Hamishmar* and a member of the party's Political Committee.

The party member, S. (possibly Shabtai) Kaplan, described the witness as 'one of our people, an intellectual, 100 per cent reliable'. The village, wrote Kaplan, had been held by 'Arab irregulars' and was captured by the 89th Battalion [8th Brigade] without a fight. 'The first [wave] of conquerors killed about eighty to a hundred Arabs, women and children. The children they killed by breaking their heads with sticks. 'There was not a house without dead,' wrote Kaplan. Kaplan's informant, who arrived immediately afterwards in the second wave, reported that the Arab men and women who remained were then closed off in the houses 'without food and water'. Sappers arrived to blow up the houses. 'One Commander ordered a sapper to put two old women in a certain house . . . and to blow up the house with them. The sapper refused . . . The Commander then ordered his men to put in the old women and the evil deed was done. One soldier boasted that he had raped a woman and then shot her. One woman, with a new-born baby in her arms, was employed to clean the courtyard where the soldiers ate. She worked a day or two. In the end they shot her and her baby.' The soldier-witness, according to Kaplan, said that 'cultured officers . . . had turned into base murderers and this not in the heat of battle . . . but out of a system of expulsion and destruction. The less Arabs remained the better. This principle is the political motor for the expulsions and the atrocities.[12]

On the evening of 26 October, 'G Force' turned east at Hebron and moved towards Tarqumiya, where it remained for the night. On 28 October, Lockett took a fighting patrol of two troops of Marmon-Herrington armoured cars to reconnoitre the area of Bait Jibrin. According to Glubb's book, *A Soldier with the Arabs*, Captain Spring, who took part in the operation, reported thus:

Just outside Bait Jibrin village the road rises slightly and runs through a small copse before it twists and turns through the white buildings of the village. It was inside this copse that the first car in the column halted while the sergeant commanding the vehicle jumped out, cocked sub-machine gun in hand, and crept forward to see what lay immediately over the rise; during this period the other armoured cars slipped up behind and stopped in line on the road, engines were switched off and the dust settled while no sound disturbed the stillness of the morning except harsh metallic scrapings as the silent crews of the armoured cars slipped belts of ammunition into their Browning guns, and the breech-blocks of two-pounder cannons were opened in readiness.

All eyes were now fixed on the sergeant, who was perhaps one hundred yards forward of the leading armoured car, his khaki-clad body, topped by scarlet headdress, the only thing moving in the landscape. He was crawling with irritating deliberation to the top of the small tree-crowned rise, where his body stiffened on the ground as his eyes rose above the level of the hill and he looked down into the valley and on to the village itself. There was no movement from him for perhaps a minute, and just for that moment there was no sound at all, everything still, and the cars stood waiting.

Suddenly he leaped to his feet and came running back to the column of vehicles, shouting excitedly, almost dancing across the ground and waving his gun in the air. As he clambered on to his vehicle, panting with exertion, his face split with an excited grin, he shouted: 'There are about thirty Jewish armoured cars coming along!' He had hardly said these words before a vague humming and sound of vehicle engines, many and moving fast, could be heard from the direction of the village, steadily increasing in volume and sounding rather ominous and strangely disturbing with each second that passed.

There was hardly any sound from the armoured cars as they fanned out left and right on either side of the road and stood there in an inverted 'V' with the point towards Bait Jibrin, the muzzles of their guns moving smoothly round in the direction of the oncoming vehicles like the snouts of a band of some queer monsters scenting their enemy.

The leading armoured car moved a little forward in order to catch first sight of the oncoming vehicles, and it was from this car that the first shot of the engagement came. It was debated with a certain amount of seriousness afterwards if the sergeant in charge of the vehicle had any knowledge of billiards and knew the meaning of 'in off', or if he had perhaps been influenced by war-time reports of 'skip bombing', but the fact remains that the first shot from his car sailed deliberately across the valley, over the village and striking the ground about thirty yards short of a Jewish half-track vehicle, ricocheted off the ground and flipped into the vehicle, which spun round in a half-circle, smoke pouring from its engine and stood still there, flaming. The Jewish crew of the vehicle jumped out, but were met with a burst of machine-gun fire which left their bodies twitching on the road beside their burning vehicle.

The first shot was the signal for all the guns to crash into life, and for the next thirty minutes the situation was almost too confused to recall. Jewish armoured cars were racing in every direction all over the landscape, vainly trying to escape the fire of the Arab guns, but spread out in the valley the cars were an easy target, and as one after the other slewed round flaming, the excited Arab Legionaries were almost screaming with delight. Scattered burning vehicles dotted the landscape, and the Arab Legion troops found themselves under very heavy machine-gun and light-automatic fire, which indicated that they were in the midst of quite a strong position. So, deliberately, the fire of the Arab armoured cars was turned on to these machine-gun nests, and one after the other they were silenced. As their green-clad soldiers fled for the shelter of houses, they dropped on to the ground under the intense fire from the armoured cars, sometimes to rise again and stagger forward a few yards only to meet a hail of tracer bullets which left them motionless on the ground while the Arab troops in their armoured cars slapped each other on the back, yelling with laughter, and now and then popped their heads out of their cars to scream out: 'Al Jeish al Arabi', 'the Arab Legion is here!' By this time, the Arab armoured cars had worked their way forward into the village of Bait Jibrin. The undamaged armoured cars had all fled from the scene and the machine-gun nests having been silenced, there was a lull in the battle while the Arab Legion armoured cars moved slowly forward with the houses of Bait Jibrin village on their left and a deep Wadi on their right.

It was about this time that Major Lockett decided that the purpose of the recce had been fulfilled and he began giving orders for the vehicles to withdraw from the village. The enemy must have been waiting for just this chance, for no sooner had the cars started turning round than a hail of large calibre mortar bombs began to fall in the narrow area of the road and Wadi. It is estimated that in ten minutes more than eighty bombs fell around the cars. The whole area was thick with the dust of the Wadi as the crashing bombs churned it into the air, and the air itself was full of flying pieces of metal, chunks of masonry and slivers of wood torn from nearby trees by the exploding bombs.

One armoured car received a direct hit when a bomb exploded inside it, killing the crew of three, and another was so damaged by a bomb bursting close to it that, despite many attempts, it was found impossible to tow it away, and so the noise was increased as these cars were destroyed by our own guns. As they burst into flames, the ammunition and shells inside them exploded, sending streams of tracer bullets into the air, and pillars of smoke from the armoured cars climbed slowly upwards.

As this work was completed and the mortar bombs were still falling, the five remaining armoured cars withdrew to Tarqumiya village, leaving behind them at least six burning Jewish armoured cars and one truck destroyed, while the ground in the whole area was doffed with the corpses of at least forty Jewish soldiers whose spread-eagled bodies paid adequate tribute to the power and accuracy of Arab Legion fire. The Israeli force had been about five times as strong as the Arab Legion party.

During the heavy mortar fire in the defile, special tribute should be paid to two sergeants of the Arab Legion. One of them, with astounding coolness, attempted to fix the tow rope to the damaged armoured car under very heavy fire directed immediately at his vehicle. The other assisted him in this work and carried on, refusing to leave, even though seriously injured by a bullet through his thigh; with a blood-soaked trouser leg he hopped on one leg to his armoured car, took command, led it out of battle and then collapsed through loss of blood.

Under an olive tree in Tarqumiya village, there are three mounds of earth that hide all that is left of three very gallant soldiers from Trans-Jordan who will never see their country again, but the manner of whose death was an inspiration to the whole Arab Legion.[13]

On 4 November, the Security Council of the United Nations approved a resolution regarding the fighting in the Negev. The resolution called upon the Jews and Egyptians to withdraw their forces, which had advanced beyond positions held on 14 October, and to establish a neutral or demilitarised zone to secure the full observance of the truce. The Jews took no notice of the United Nations. Instead of withdrawing, on 9 November, Yigal Allon directed his attention to the Iraq Suweidan Police Fort. At 1400 hours, while the sun was against the sights of the defenders, Jewish artillery and mortars bombarded the fortress in an attack that lasted for two hours. At 1600 hours, the assault began with the 9th Regiment of the 8th Armoured Brigade, a company mounting half-tracks and a troop of tanks. The barbed-wire fence was broken and the wall of the Fort was demolished by a section of sappers. At that point the Egyptian garrison surrendered. The gallant defenders of Iraq Suweidan had no other choice. The main consequence of the fall of Iraq Suweidan was that the position of the Egyptian Brigade at al-Faluja was reduced to a small, totally besieged enclave.

On 11 November, al-Mawawi, the Commander of the Egyptian Army in Palestine, was relieved from his duties and transferred to Cairo. He was succeeded by Major General Ahmad Fuad Sadiq.

No one knew the real situation in al-Faluja except those who were trapped there. The issue of the rescue of the al-Faluja Brigade became the main concern of the Political Committee of the Arab League; a plan was devised by them to provide one battalion each from Jordan, Iraq and Syria to relieve the besieged brigade. The Jordanians continued to press for their plan of handing over Latrun to the Iraqi Army and the 3rd Jordanian Brigade to relieve the al-Faluja Brigade. Meanwhile, Major Lockett and a Jordanian corporal were sent on foot through the Jewish lines to al-Faluja. The Major spent two days with the Egyptian Brigade and then walked back to 'G Force' HQ. On his return he reported that the Jews were bombarding the Egyptian positions with artillery and mortars day and night, but that the troops, who were mainly Sudanese, were in good spirits. Colonel Sayyid Taha, the Brigade Commander, refused to accept any plan of evacuation presented to him by Major Lockett.

The 4th Egyptian Brigade became the most popular formation in the Arab army because they refused to surrender and were determined to defend their positions to the last man. There was strong sympathy for them, and great pride in their courage and honour. Because of the Egyptian radio reports about them, the Arabs hoped that some action would be taken to save them by the United Nations or the Great Powers. On 16 November, the Security Council of the United Nations approved a resolution to establish an armistice in all sectors of Palestine, calling on parties directly involved to seek agreement with a view to its immediate establishment – including the delineation of permanent armistice demarcation lines beyond which the armed forces of the respective parties should not move. But instead of accepting the UN resolution, on 17 November, between 0700 hours and 1900 hours, the Jewish forces bombarded al-Faluja. On 19 November, despite another very heavy bombardment, which lasted an entire day, white flags were not produced over the Egyptian positions at al-Faluja. On 25 November, a white flag was raised by a Jewish officer who approached the Egyptian lines with a loudspeaker asking to meet the Egyptian Commander. Major Jamal Abd al-Nasser went forward to see him and was told by the Jewish officer that it was better for them to surrender, to which Jamal replied: 'Surrendering is not in our thoughts.' (See Map 6.)

The Jewish Command decided to attack al-Faluja. By the beginning of December they had relieved the Givati Brigade with the Alexandroni Brigade and transferred the Golani Brigade to the Southern Command in the Negev. On the night of 27/28 December, the Alexandroni Brigade attacked al-Faluja. But after a battle that lasted six hours, they were unable to capture a single Egyptian trench and subsequently withdrew after suffering heavy casualties.

Operation 'Horev'

Meanwhile, while the Egyptian Army was fighting in Palestine and Sinai, a storm of political friction between the Muslim Brothers and the al-Noqrashi Government was in progress. The Egyptian Government decided to disband the Muslim Brothers Movement. By the beginning of December, orders were issued from Cairo that the Muslim Brothers should withdraw from their positions in Wadi al-Shallalah, Tel Jumaah, al-Rabiyah and al-Shauth, a move that allowed the Jewish forces freedom of movement, without harrasment, in a wide area adjacent to the Egyptian front. Whoever issued that order had, whether he knew it or not, betrayed the Egyptian Army in its hour of dire need for reinforcements on the field of battle. As expected by Kamil al-Sharif, as soon as the Muslim Brothers withdrew, the Jews attacked and captured Shaikh Nuwairan Hill on 4 December. One battalion of the Egyptian Army mounted a counter-attack against the Jewish forces with the aim of recapturing the hill. However, they failed and had to withdraw with some casualties. The Jews occupied Tel Jumaah Hill on 15 December, and al-Faraah Hill on 18 December.

On 11 December 1948, the General Assembly of the United Nations approved a resolution establishing a Conciliation Commission with a mandate to bring about direct or indirect negotiations between the parties concerned for a final settlement, and to prepare a plan for a permanent international régime for the Jerusalem area. The resolution stated that Jerusalem should be placed under effective United Nations control and requested the Security Council to take further steps to ensure the demilitarisation of Jerusalem at the earliest possible date.

By 12 December, the Egyptian Army was deployed in a crescent shape facing Beersheba as outlined in Table 8.6.

On 7 December, Kamil al-Sharif was called to see General al-Bardini, the second in command of the Egyptian Army in Palestine, who told him that the Muslim Brothers would be disbanded on 8 December. Bardini had requested the disarming of the Brothers be postponed until the situation had calmed down. Kamil al-Sharif replied:

The issue of disbanding the Brothers was expected, and we are not surprised given that the English and their protégés rule the country; we believe that this mission cannot be disbanded, because it is God's mission, and our role does not exceed our loyalty and endeavours to achieve it. Disbanding the Brothers, to us, does not exceed the removal of banners and the closing of doors, but the mission's place is in the hearts of the faithful. Our hearts are strong citadels which cannot be assaulted or overcome. Even if the Government erects the gallows on the roads and hangs every member without exception, they will not achieve their aim. Because the mission of Islam will find those who will work for it even after generations.[14]

TABLE 8.6
Deployment of the Egyptian Army on 12 December

- Division HQ at Rafah, commanded by General Ahmad Fuad Sadiq.
- One brigade besieged at al-Faluja.
- Two reinforced brigades deployed in the Gaza area.
- One brigade deployed in the area of Abu Agailah and al-Arish.
- Two battalions of the Muslim Brothers in the Hebron Sector.
- One battalion of the Muslim Brothers in the Gaza area not deployed, but concentrated in their camp since they were withdrawn from their task.

On the following day, General Fuad Sadiq saw the Brothers in their camp and assured them they could keep their weapons and continue training until they were needed. The Brothers did not have to wait long before that happened. General Yigal Allon had decided to attack the Egyptian Army through its line of communications in the rear of its main force at Gaza. He planned operation 'Horev' to be carried out by the following formations.

- Negev Brigade.
- Golani Brigade.
- Harel Brigade.
- 8th Armoured Brigade.

On 22 December, while the Alexandroni Brigade continued to besiege al-Faluja and frustrate any attempts for its relief or supplies, operation 'Horev' was launched with a very heavy artillery barrage on Gaza and

Rafah. In a diversionary attack, the 3rd Battalion of the Golani Brigade attacked and captured Hill 86 near the coast between Rafah and Gaza and south of Dair al-Balah. The capture of the hill made it possible to isolate the whole of the Egyptian Army in Gaza. Late on the night of 23 December, General Mahmoud Refaat, the Commander of the Dair al-Balah Sector, rang Kamil al-Sharif and told him that the Jews had penetrated his lines and taken Hill 86 and that the Jewish forces were attempting to reach the main road. He also said that his forces had isolated Hill 86 in order to recapture it. He asked al-Sharif to be ready to fight. At dawn on 23 December, the Egyptian unit at Dair al-Balah mounted a counter-attack on Hill 86. The Golani Battalion resisted wave after wave of assaults carried out by the Egyptian force, which suffered heavy casualties. Egyptian tanks were brought to the scene, but two of them were destroyed at the foot of the hill. General Mahmoud Refaat asked the Muslim Brothers to attack.

The Brothers' plan was to attack in three groups of about a company each. Two groups were to assault the Hill from the front on the north and a third group were to attack round the Hill from the rear. The frontal assault was to be supported by a squadron of tanks. The speed with which the Brothers attacked the Hill was a surprise for the Golani Battalion. Soon they were forced to fight in hand-to-hand combat for every trench on the Hill. By dusk the Golani Battalion had had enough and began to withdraw after evacuating their wounded. Among those killed was the Commander of the battalion. The Brothers paid a very heavy price for their victory. Kamil al-Sharif wrote:

> The number of casualties was high, many died because of their wounds in hospitals; others were sent on leave and had medical treatment in Huckstep and al-Tour Detention Centres. Please, readers do not think I am joking; I do not record except the true facts; two of the wounded in that battle, Auwais Abd al-Wahab and Said Abd-Yousef were sent to the Egyptian hospital for treatment for their serious wounds. But the political police ordered their removal to al Tour Detention Centre where they were without food or treatment. One of them is still (1984) suffering from the pain of a bullet in his body.[15]

Meanwhile the Jewish Air Force carried out raids on Rafah, al-Arish and Khan Yunis, excluding the eastern areas for deception purposes.

During the night of 23/24, the 8th Armoured Brigade and the Negev Brigade advanced without lights from Beersheba, and on the morning of 24 December swung to the east, occupying Mishrafeh on 25 December. Another unit of Jewish–French commandos captured al-Thamilah on the same day.

On 27 December, the 8th Armoured Brigade captured al-Auja, while the Negev Brigade attacked and captured all the Egyptian positions between Asluj and al-Auja. On the night of 28/29 December the Negev Brigade, supported by a tank regiment, broke through the International Egyptian–Palestinian border into the Sinai Peninsula and captured Abu Agailah. On the 29th the brigade advanced and captured Bir Lahfan, then reached the airport at al-Arish. At the same time, the Harel Brigade attacked and captured an area south-east of Abu Agailah.

At that point of military development in the field, on 29 December the United Nations Security Council approved a resolution calling on the governments concerned to order an immediate ceasefire in southern Palestine and to implement without further delay the resolution of 4 November 1948. The Egyptians were desperate. They appealed to their Arab brothers to take action on their fronts to attract some of the Jewish forces in the south, but no Arab country responded. The Egyptians found themselves compelled to invoke the Egyptian–British Treaty of 1936 which they had wanted to abrogate, and to seek help from the British forces in Egypt which they had wanted to be removed. Thus, on 1 January 1949, the Ambassador of the United States in Tel Aviv delivered an ultimatum from the British Government that unless the Jewish forces withdrew from the Egyptian territory of Sinai, the British Government would be compelled to invoke the provision of the Treaty of 1936. The Jews withdrew from Sinai on 2 January.

On the night of 3/4 January, the Golani Brigade, the Harel Brigade and a battalion of the Negev Brigade attacked and captured some positions near Rafah and threatened to isolate the Egyptian Army in the Rafah–Gaza sector. At that point, the Egyptian Government declared its acceptance to negotiate for an armistice agreement.

Meanwhile, the British Royal Air Force sent a flight of fighter aircraft to reconnoiter the battlefield in Sinai and to find out if the Jewish force had been withdrawn. The Jewish Air Force intercepted the British fighters and shot down five RAF aircraft. Two British pilots were killed, two others were taken prisoner and a fifth managed to escape, making his way to the Egyptian positions. The British reaction was extremely violent, and the Jewish command thereafter agreed to the ceasefire on 7 January. Fighting finally came to end in Palestine on 11 January 1949.

NOTES

1 Herzog, *The Arab–Israeli Wars*, p. 88.
2 PRO. FO 371/68822. From the acting British Minister at Amman, C. M. Perie-Gordon to B. A. B. Barrows at the Foreign Office, 25 July 1948.
3 PRO. FO 371/68822. From Kirkbride to the Foreign Office, secret, 6 August 1948.
4 PRO. FO 371/68822. From Kirkbride to the Foreign Office, 6 September 1948.
5 Glubb, *A Soldier with the Arabs*, p. 182.
6 *The Palestine War 1947–1948*, an official Israeli account, pp. 656–60.
7 Herzog, *The Arab–Israeli Wars*, pp. 91–2.
8 *Ibid.*, p. 93.
9 *The Palestine War 1947–1948*, an official Israeli account, p. 643. Also, Herzog, *The Arab–Israeli Wars*, p. 95.
10 Al Sharif, *The Muslim Brothers*, pp. 129–30.
11 Glubb, *A Soldier with the Arabs*, p. 202.
12 Benny Morris, *The Birth of the Palestinian Refugees Problem 1947–1949* (Cambridge: Cambridge University Press, 1987), pp. 222–3.
13 Glubb, *A Soldier with the Arabs*, pp. 206–9.
14 Al Sharif, *The Muslim Brothers*, p. 147. The author has no doubt whatsoever in Kamil Al Sharif's words. He is a man of honour.
15 *Ibid.*

9

Towards Arab Unity

The dangers and difficulties that faced Jordan during 1947, which were then considered serious, were of little consequence in comparison with the dangers and difficulties that threatened the whole country during the war year of 1948. King Abdullah was under extreme pressure from the Jordanian people, as well as from every Arab country, to fight a war in Palestine before the end of the mandate. In that critical situation – as well as in many others far more serious and dangerous – the King led Jordan to do its duty towards Palestine while maintaining a moderate stance in the Arab League and in his relations with the United Nations and Great Britain. The King could have done nothing more than he did with his small army, his financial limitations, and his political and diplomatic constraints.

In spite of all his efforts and those of his people and army, King Abdullah, his Government and the people of Jordan were unjustly treated with criticism, and sometimes abuse, by the surrounding Arab countries. By the end of 1948, however, the peoples of the neighbouring Arab countries realised that Jordanians did not deserve the criticism or abuse hurled on them and that the attitude adopted by Jordan was, after all, better than their own.

The main internal problem for Jordan at the beginning of the year was how to care for the Palestinian refugees who came to the country, plus the vast administrative and economic problems resulting from their great numbers and the tragic state they were in. The flow of refugees, which started as early as January 1948, when whole families took refuge in Amman, the capital, at the start of hostilities in Palestine, continued until after the fall of Lydda and Ramleh. The early groups of refugees were able to look after themselves using their own funds, but the huge increase in the price of renting accommodation and the cost of living in general affected their political attitudes. They were also highly critical of the British policy in Palestine and blamed Britain for their catastrophe. Their criticism of Britain found receptive audiences in Jordan and had some effect on anti-British feelings in the country. The whole atmosphere of the Palestinian rebellion of 1936–9 was revived in 1948.

As the volume of hostilities increased during March and April 1948, the flow of refugees from areas occupied by the Jews increased. That second wave of refugees was in an extremely bitter frame of mind. With them came the demands, which were supported by Jordanians, for an immediate intervention by the Jordan Arab Army in Palestine. Thereafter, Jordanian petitions, strikes and demonstrations in protest against the British Zionist policies and the Jews increased. Scare bombs were planted outside the Prime Minister's house, General Glubb's house and the British Legation.

After the fall of Lydda and Ramleh into Jewish hands, the population of Amman – including refugees – doubled in three weeks. There were no houses or even tents to accommodate the unfortunate Palestinian refugees. I remember coming to Amman to deliver a message from Colonel Goldie to General Glubb. Then, going home to spend the night, I was met by my father at the door, who told me that there was no room for me because the house was full of refugees and that my own family were sleeping on the roof. All unfinished buildings, schools, mosques, yards and tented camps around the city were full of destitute Palestinians. Violent demonstrations by anti-British and anti-foreign crowds marked that very sad period.

Between February and October, the Government of Jordan provided for the Palestinian refugees in Jordan, and the tens of thousands of them who remained in the areas occupied by the Jordan Arab Army and the Iraqi Army, from its own resources, aided by a single meagre remittance of £20,000 from the Arab League and private donations from Jordanians, the extent and generosity of which will never be fully known or appreciated. Furthermore, some financial difficulties were caused by the over-expenditure of free sterling following the decoupling of the Palestinian pound from the sterling bloc in February 1948. They were, however, overcome by the release of frozen sterling later in the year.

By October 1948, the first supplies of the United Nations Disaster Relief Fund arrived in Jordan, just as the over-strained financial resources of the Government of Jordan were drained. Thereafter the whole situation started to improve and by the end of 1948 all destitute refugees were housed in organised camps in Amman, Zarqa and Irbid. Food and health care was provided by the United Nations. All through this tragedy public health suffered from the influx of refugees, the lack of adequate health care and the unhygienic conditions under which people lived for many months. The reported cases of diseases included:

- smallpox   (43 people)
- dysentery   (820 people)
- pneumonia   (610 people)
- typhoid   (363 people).

Meanwhile, by February 1948 the disbandment of the Trans-Jordan Frontier Force had commenced and was completed in April. There were individual desertions, and two parties of Palestinian and Arab troops made off to Syria with their motor vehicles and weapons to join the Liberation Army in Damascus. All Trans-Jordan Frontier Force installations were taken over by the Jordan Arab Army and a considerable number of officers and men of Jordanian and Palestinian nationality enlisted in the Jordan Arab Army immediately after their demobilisation.

During May 1948, a law was enacted making all forms of communism illegal. That was because from time to time pamphlets addressed to the refugees, obviously with communist inspiration, appeared in Trans-Jordan and steps were taken to trace and expel from the country communist agents among refugees who appeared to be extremists and anti-Jordanian.

Since the occupation of the Jordan Arab Army of its sector in the Arab area of Palestine on 15 May 1948, military governors were appointed by the Jordanian Government to provide the necessary services, maintain law and order, and protect the lives and properties of the inhabitants of those areas under their control. Table 9.1 shows those who were appointed for the task.

With the help and advice of former senior civil servants of the British Administration of Palestine, the governors were able to lay the foundation for a new Civil Service in each of the areas concerned. For the first time since the beginning of the year, the Government authority was neutral and immune from political bias and unauthorised interference by the former quasi-military partisan leaders. While most of the municipal servants remained at their posts during the initial fighting between January and May 1948, many of the Arab civil servants of the former British Administration deserted the country in fear for their lives. However, the

TABLE 9.1
Appointees of the Jordanian Government to provide services, maintain law and protect property

Name	Role	Date
• Ibrahim Hashim	Governor General	19/5/1948
• Bahjat Tabbarah	Governor of Ramallah	18/5/1948
• Mustafa al-Rifai	Governor of Hebron	19/5/1948
• Salih al-Majali	Governor of Hebron	29/6/1948
• Ahmad Hilmi	Governor of Jerusalem	12/6/1948
• Thawqan al-Hussein	Governor of Jericho	18/5/1948
• Ttahir Muhammad	Governor General	26/7/1948
• Abdullah al-Tel	Governor of Jerusalem	26/9/1948

few that remained began to reorganise their departments and managed, under the new governors, to create a reliable skeleton of a purely Palestinian staff. The police officers and policemen were enlisted in the Jordan Arab Army and started to maintain law and order. The medical, telephone and post, public works, water and civil defence services were re-established. The Sharia and Civil courts resumed their functions and an adequate degree of stability in the Arab areas controlled by the Jordan Arab Army started to affect the lives of the people.

On 22 September 1948, the Political Committee of the Arab League approved the formation of an Arab Government for the whole of Palestine with its capital at Gaza in the Egyptian sector. The Government was formed by Ahmad Hilmi and the supporters of al-Haj Amin al-Husseini. On 30 September the first Palestinian National Council consisting of 75 unelected members held a conference in Gaza during which an independent Palestinian State for the whole of Palestine was proclaimed and the Government of Ahmad Hilmi confirmed. King Abdullah sent a telegram to Abd al-Rahman Azzam:

> Ahmad Hilmi Pasha in his telegraphic reply to us said that the formation of a Palestine Government in Palestine was effected by a decision by the Arab League.
>
> The Jordanian delegation denies that, and, in any case, such an action, in our opinion, is a return to the situation as it was before 15 May. As the Jordan Arab Army is fighting today in sacred Jerusalem, continuing alone in spite of the truce, and as the central front to the plain and Ramallah is in the charge of the Jordan Arab Army

and as matters are still complicated, we cannot allow other hands to interfere in the responsibilities of our military Government, and in particular those persons who aspire to government and are exerting themselves to that end.

Secondly, and in order to maintain brotherhood and preserve the integrity of the Arab League, we declare that we shall not tolerate any adjustments in the security zones of the Jordan Government from the frontiers of the Egyptian Kingdom to the frontiers of Syria and Lebanon. Further, the formation of such a Government is an act which is forced on the Palestinians without their consent; we do not approve this and we shall contest it. In addition, if that Government is formed and is acknowledged by the United Nations Organisation as it had acknowledged the Jewish State, this would mean that the League is seeking the partition against which it had fought.[1]

On the same day King Abdullah sent the following telegram to Ahmad Hilmi in Gaza, rejecting the formation of the All Palestine Government:

What is desired to form, in the name of a government in Palestine, whether by a decision of the Arab League or by the wish of those who aspire to government, would be a return to the situation which existed before 15 May. It may entail the possibility of recognition of this instrument by the United Nations in the same way as most of them recognised the Jewish claims and thus bring about the partition against which you have fought. In any case the souls of the martyrs in the Jordan Arab Army, who have fallen during the months of fighting, refuse to play with the fate of the country.[2]

During the rest of September, Ahmad Hilmi, with support from the Egyptian Army in Gaza, sent arms to Hebron and Bethlehem as well as to Ramallah to arm some pro-Mufti Palestinian partisans to carry out guerrilla operations against United Nations observers and any Jewish targets facing the Jordanian sector. A pro-Mufti group started to levy contributions of money, enlist recruits from villages and hold courts of justice in the Mufti's name. The situation became critical with the danger of provoking the Jews in the front line to attack the Jordan Arab Army and disturb the stability of the people in the Jordanian sector. The Jordan Arab Army had no reserve to deal with internal affairs within their sector and action had to be taken to restore law and order. With Egypt, Saudi Arabia, Syria and Lebanon supporting the Mufti, Jordan was defending its sector in Palestine on its own. Even the Regent of Iraq, who forgot King Abdullah's role in restoring the Kingdom of Iraq to what it was before the rebellion of 1941, deserted his uncle, who had given him protection, and spoke against him. The British Minister at Baghdad wrote:

> I am rather perturbed by the strength of criticism of King Abdullah, which the Regent and Prime Minister constantly express to me. The Regent has always said that his uncle talks too much but he now suggests his health is failing and that he is too old for the job. I have, however, no reason to suppose that the Regent would support Mufti against his uncle.[3]

It soon became evident that the Egyptian Government and the command of its forces in Palestine were encouraging anti-Jordanian propaganda within the areas under control of the Jordan Arab Army, not only in the Hebron–Bethlehem sector, but also to the north in Jerusalem and Ramallah, as well as the Nablus sector controlled by the Iraqi Army. The Egyptians showed no signs of loosening their military and administrative control of the area immediately south of Jerusalem. The road between Bethlehem and Jerusalem was closed by the Jordan Arab Army to avoid any clash between Egypt and Jordan, and all units within the Bethlehem sector were withdrawn to the Jordanian southern Jerusalem sector.

However, whatever the attitudes of the Egyptian, Iraqi or the All Palestine Government in Gaza, the attitude of the Palestinian Arabs in these areas was the most important of all. By the beginning of October 1948, their attitude was still bellicose, and despite all the catastrophes they endured and the real hardships they had suffered, they wanted to fight. They showed no wish to be incorporated into any other Arab country and they did not take Ahmad Hilmi and his Government seriously.

The Jordan Government did not even bother to visit the area under its control. Tawfiq Abu al-Huda had never even visited his soldiers, and no contact was made between the Jordan Government and the leaders of Palestinian public opinion. The burden of such action was left to the King, who was wholly occupied with the general situation rather than the details of the administration of the areas. No political advantage was taken from the victories of the Jordan Arab Army in Bab al-Wad and in Jerusalem, when Jordan's reputation was at its zenith and the other Arab armies' reputations were at their lowest because of all the defeats they had suffered. Then came the catastrophe of the fall of Lydda and Ramleh, which caused much damage to the Jordanian image in the hearts and minds of the Palestinian people, goaded by Egyptian and Syrian anti-Jordan propaganda.

Furthermore, with no money available to build an administration and provide adequate services to satisfy the people, and the fact that the choice of Governors by Abu al-Huda was, to say the least, unwise, the administration failed to achieve its most basic objectives. The Palestinian business community and the more sophisticated élite saw little attraction in Jordanian political and economic prospects. They were aware of the non-viability of the Jordanian economy, and soon realised that Jordan and Palestine combined would be even less of a going concern than they would be individually.

King Abdullah saw no other option than unity for the survival of the Arab inhabitants in the areas under his control. He thought unity with Jordan was the only chance. That is why he continued to struggle for it despite opposition from the Arab League, the Mufti and the indifference of the inhabitants of the areas under his control. The British were half-hearted in their approach to the question. Richard Beaumont, the British Consul in Jerusalem, wrote to the Foreign Office:

> It is not, of course, a question of King Abdullah conducting an independent political campaign in defiance of the Arab League. External dangers of that course have been well pointed out in British Middle East Office. Inside Arab Palestine itself the effect would almost certainly be to alienate still further the Arabs who would resent him 'cashing in on partition' at their expense. It would lead immediately to intrigues against him with Syria and other members of the League. (On the other hand a decision of the Arab League, if it could be achieved, agreeing to Trans-Jordan's annexing of Arab Palestine would immeasurably strengthen his hand here by reducing the possibilities of intrigue.) But even now in advance of any territorial award King Abdullah could start an intelligent campaign of propaganda with their aid and proper administration using Palestinians combined with those personal attentions to leading Palestine Arabs which count for so much, on basis of turning over a new leaf. Our advice and our money will be needed for this and while we should be wary of saying anything which would show that we were intending to extend our political hold on the Middle East, we should leave the Arabs of Palestine in no doubt that the political integrity and economic future of the new Jordan Kingdom would

be assured by us. As seen from here only thus can the present rapid decline in King Abdullah's popularity be stemmed and only thus the Arabs of Palestine be given some better guidance than the bleak data at present before them by which to reconcile themselves to a unification which they may otherwise resist.[4]

Those who did not know King Abdullah well enough were not able to realise that he was not alone in being opposed by the Egyptian, Iraqi, Syrian, Saudi, Lebanese and Yemeni Governments in regard to the recognition of the All Palestine Government in Gaza. Even when he wrote to the Prince Regent of Iraq regarding the situation in Palestine, the latter did not care to answer when the letter was delivered to him while he was in Amman. Thereafter neither were able to talk politics to each other.[5]

King Abdullah had his down-to-earth political acumen and the power of conviction to support him in his attempt to save what remained of Palestine from Jewish usurpation. In his desperation, he exploded a huge political thunder flash when he threatened that he might have to withdraw the Jordan Arab Army from Palestine, if the continued friction between the Jordan Arab Army and the Mufti's men developed into fighting.[6]

Meanwhile, on 1 October 1948, a Palestinian congress was held at Amman to consider the situation in Palestine. The organising committee consisted of the following Palestinian leaders:

- Sulaiman al-Taji al-Farouqi
- Hikmat al-Taji al-Farouqi
- Aajaj Nuwaihidh
- Shaikh Saad al-Din al-Alami
- Khidhir Mansur
- Hashim al-Jauosi
- Nure al-Ghusain
- Rashad Abu Gharbiyah.

After debating the situation in Palestine, the congress passed the following decision:

1. The Conference decides that the task of the Arab armies in Palestine has not been and will not be accomplished except when the Zionists have been finally defeated.

[262]

2. The Conference decides that the Arabs of Palestine will await eagerly and impatiently the decision to be taken at the United Nations Organisation. They hope that it will be just and fair.

3. The Conference urges the Arab Governments to leave words and statements and to resort to real deeds.

4. The Conference draws the attention of the Arab Governments and peoples to the fact that the formation of a Palestine Government at Gaza at a time when the Palestine people are scattered is an action that will be harmful and detrimental, especially as it imposes on the unwilling people the leaders of a single party which is notorious for its negative policy. The action paves the way for the recognition of the new Government by certain states, just as others have recognised the Jewish pretence. Its result will be the partition which we are fighting against. For all these reasons the conference will not support the Government or have any confidence in those who do so.

5. The Conference places responsibility for any disasters or calamities which befall Palestine from now on, on the shoulders of those Arab Governments who support the Government of Gaza. Deeds of the men of the new Government will be the cause of grave miseries in the future in the same way as they were throughout the last thirty years.

6. The Conference sees that the formation of that Government in its present form is contradictory to the early decisions of the Arab League when it was agreed that no government was to be instituted until the whole of Palestine soil had been freed from the Zionist tyranny and the Palestinian people enabled to decide for themselves the form of Government they want.

7. The Conference requests the Government and press of sister Egypt to refrain from supporting the Government of Gaza which lies within their zone of occupation. If this weak and feeble Government remains in existence it will be the biggest and greatest disaster to befall the Arabs of Palestine as it will make it possible for the Jews to conquer the whole country.

8. The Conference calls upon the Arab armies to carry out a determined attack in order to restore dignity to the Arab nation and rescue the country.

9. The Conference urges the United Nations Organisation to seek justice in regard to Palestine.

10. The Conference begs the Arab Kings and Governments to redouble their efforts for the liberation of the country.

11. The Conference hails the Arab armies who have expressed their full readiness to die for Palestine.

12. In view of the existing national connections and ties between Palestine and the Hashemite Kingdom of Jordan, the Conference places on His Majesty King Abdullah the greatest hopes for the defence of Palestine and the preservation of its Arabism and sacredness. The Conference is confident that His Majesty will never agree that solutions be imposed on Palestine by people who yearn for authority, from whose bad deeds and selfishness during thirty long years the Palestine people escaped. The Conference gives His Majesty unrestricted power, to speak in the name of the Arabs of Palestine and to negotiate and do everything on their behalf for the purpose of reaching a solution to their case in the form he wishes. His Majesty is our representative in all respects of relation to the future of Palestine. The Conference supports His Majesty in every step he will take towards solving the Palestine deadlock. The Conference considers His Majesty the only authority and resort for the Arabs of Palestine who have placed in him all their confidence and loyalty.

13. The Conference decides to send a telegram to the Arab Higher Executive notifying it that the Arabs of Palestine have withdrawn their confidence from them and that the Arab Higher Executive has no longer any right to represent them or speak on their behalf, because the Arab Governments have taken up the Palestine case.

14. The Conference decides to elect a permanent executive committee to ensure that the decisions shall be put into effect.

15. The Conference decides to send copies of these decisions to the Government of the Hashemite Kingdom of Jordan and to all Arab and foreign legations at Amman for submission to their Governments.[7]

While the Palestinians were attempting to come closer to Jordan, the Iraqi Prime Minister was moving away from the Hashemite bloc for better relations with Egypt. He became a strong advocate of a firm Iraqi–Egyptian understanding. On his way from Baghdad to Cairo he stopped at Amman and had a talk with Kirkbride, who reported:

He found Egypt well disposed not only towards better relations with Iraq but also towards a friendly settlement with Great Britain. I said I hoped, in this connection, that he would not lose sight of Jordan and the continuing need for a strong Hashemite understanding. I had been somewhat disturbed of late by sundry reports tending to show that Iraq was less well disposed in that quarter than in the past. His Excellency replied that the personality of King Abdullah was the trouble. His Majesty was indiscreet to a degree, unreliable in so many ways and not of a stature demanded by the problems of the day. It would be much better if he were to 'retire'. I said I heard that His Majesty was occasionally indiscreet but I was very much astonished to hear His Excellency speak in this way.[8]

King Abdullah was not well understood by the Iraqi Prime Minister, not to mention King Farouq and al-Noqrashi, the Prime Minister of Egypt. He may have been indiscreet in certain situations, but only when it was necessary for his political purpose. In his attitude towards Palestine he kept all the Arab leaders guessing as to what was his next move, as can be seen from Kirkbride's report of 8 October:

1. It seems quite clear that none of the Arab States wants to have the Mufti in any position of authority in Palestine. But it remains to be seen whether they will dare either to haul him out or, if they let him remain in Palestine, prevent him from making a nuisance of himself. The best information is that he has about 2,000 men at his disposal in the southern area, and that these men were responsible for the blowing up of Latrun Power Station and the recent attack on a Jewish convoy. Neither of these feats of arms was, I understand, welcome to the Arab Governments but hitherto they have done nothing about it despite assurances given to Brigadier Clayton by Azzam a month ago that the Mufti's forces would be brought under control. The fact that the Mufti has now engaged an Aberaizani refugee to organise bands of 'Fidais' shows that he is still on the warpath.

2. There seems therefore some justification for Abdullah's fear that the Arab Legion and the Mufti's men may come to blows. Nevertheless, it is clear that if Abdullah were to carry out his threat and withdraw the Arab Legion, the result to the Arab cause would be disastrous and its repercussions on our own position equally so.

3. It is difficult to advise what action we should now best be advised to take. With some hesitation I would, however, suggest the following:

Do what we can to prevent Abdullah from doing anything precipitating in the way of breaking the Arab front.
Having by now made our views about the Mufti abundantly clear, give the Arab Governments a chance of working out the situation themselves. For reasons given in

paragraph 1 above we may be forced by events to exercise further pressure but there is a danger lest repeated protests against the Mufti's activities may only serve to build up his position.

Leave it now to Abdullah to fight the battle of the Arab Palestine Government. Our own representations on this subject have had no effect and are unlikely to have any. As seen from here, our outspoken insistence on giving the Arab areas to Jordan is spoiling our case generally. Plainly the Jews and the Arabs are at one in thinking, or at least saying, that our attitude is dictated by selfish imperialist motives and this will strengthen the hands of all who wish to see the whole of the Bernadotte plan rejected by the United Nations.

Bear in mind that the more we line up with Abdullah on the Palestine problem the less influence we have in other Arab States. All recent reports show that he is thoroughly distrusted in every Arab capital and thoroughly disliked by the Palestine Arabs. As has been forcibly pointed out in recent telegrams from Baghdad the key to the situation in the Arab world lies in Egypt. It may be a pretty poor key but it is the only one there is.[9]

On his way back from Cairo, the Iraqi Prime Minister, with the approval of the Regent, had an audience with King Abdullah and did his best to convince him to recognise the All Palestine Government temporarily, and on the basis that it would fail and that ultimately the Palestinian people would want to be united with Jordan. Kirkbride reported:

2. The King and the Prime Minister of Jordan countered by pointing out that recognition would merely implement partition of Palestine before it was known what the United Nations was going to decide. They declined to commit themselves in any way about the future but promised to consider with other Arab States what action was possible once the United Nations' decision was known.

While they were here a telegram arrived from the Imam of the Yemen also counselling temporary recognition. The move was obviously pre-arranged and elicited the same reply as was given to the Iraqis.

The King got a bit of his own back by declining to sign the order placing the Arab Legion under supreme command of Iraqi Commander on the grounds that it would be meaningless in the absence of active operations. He also stated that if the other Arab states insisted on recognising the Gaza Government the Jordan Government might feel compelled to withdraw the Arab Legion from Palestine. This warning was given by the King personally and was not repeated by the Prime Minister.[10]

On 28 October 1948, a Palestinian Conference was held in Nablus attended by all the notables and leaders of public opinion from Nablus, Tulkarm, Jenin, Qalqiliyah and the rest of the district. The Conference elected Sulaiman Touqan as Chairman and Ahmad Touqan as Secretary-General. It decided to proclaim King Abdullah ibn al-Hussein the Constitutional King of Jordan and Palestine in a United Hashemite Kingdom of the two countries. Thus, with the decisions of the first Palestinian Conference at Amman on 1 October, the majority of all the areas under control of the Iraqi and Jordanian armies from Nablus to Hebron had proclaimed King Abdullah and the Hashemite Kingdom of Jordan as their own. Thus while the Iraqis were working hard with Egypt to support the Mufti and the All Palestine Government, King Abdullah had won the hearts and minds of the Palestinian people in the Iraqi and Egyptian Hebron–Bethlehem Sectors.

King Abdullah was seeking a political solution to the Palestine problem through unity when he saw no other possible solution. His main aim was to save whatever land he could from Jewish usurpation. He knew that the Lebanese army was incapable of freeing its own territories recently occupied by the Jews. The Liberation Army was no more, and on its way to being disbanded. The Syrian Army could hardly hold its positions within Syria and had it not been for the strategic advantage of the high ground it was defending, it would have been destroyed. The Iraqi Army did not intend to go on the offensive, especially when the Jewish offensive against the Egyptians started. The Jordan Arab Army had no reserve, was short of ammunition and could hardly make ends meet in a peacetime budget. The Egyptian Army was in no position even to defend the isolated defensive areas it occupied. To add to its predicament, the massive Jewish offensive in the Negev started on 16 October, as mentioned earlier. The Acting General Consul in Jerusalem reported on 30 October:

The misfortunes of the Egyptian Army in Southern Palestine and the reported hasty withdrawal from Gaza of the 'All Palestine Arab

Government' which is regarded locally as being under Egyptian protection, have tended not unnaturally to diminish such slender dominion as that 'Government' had succeeded in establishing over the territories of the Arabs of Palestine. The political trimmers in Palestine – and for lack of any clear indication in the future of Arab Palestine, they are many – are coming to the conclusion that the likelihood of the establishment of an independent Arab State here is receding while union with Trans-Jordan appears more probable and, perhaps, more profitable. There has, therefore, been a perceptible movement towards King Abdullah.

The District Officer of Bethlehem who visited me yesterday and who has, hitherto, worked on amicable terms with the Egyptian Military authorities, left me in no doubt that this was his view. He also told me that Eisa al-Bandak, a former mayor of Bethlehem and a staunch supporter of the Mufti, had gone to Amman to spy out the land on his own behalf. He had previously taken the precaution of refraining from any act which might commit him to overt support of the Gaza Government and the arrival of the Arab Legion and the prospect of a Trans-Jordan military Governor in Bethlehem impelled him to take time by the forelock.

I am also informed that the Mayor of Nablus, Sulaiman Tuqan visited King Abdullah at Amman on 25 October, on behalf of one of the Palestinian notables who had been insulted by King Abdullah, but he had also taken care to place the letter from Ahmed Hilmy Pasha announcing the formation of the Gaza Government unanswered in the drawer of his desk. The present discomfiture of the Gaza Government has doubtless made him feel that despite the 'insult' he can again approach King Abdullah without loss of dignity and with the credential of non-recognition of the Gaza Government to recommend him. The remainder of the population of Samaria (Nablus) have been slower off the mark and the 'District Commissioner' of Nablus informed a member of my staff on 26 October that they still support the Gaza Government. I suspect however that they too will waiver in their allegiance when the implications of the Egyptian reversals become more widely known.

The upshot of all this is that King Abdullah has probably been presented with a new and unexpected opportunity of rehabilitating himself with the Arabs of Palestine and it is once more seen that the Arab armies hold off the Jews [the District Officer at Bethlehem stated that their reappearance in Bethlehem gave a tremendous boost to the morale of the population who were on the point of evacuating] and it is also seen, though not stated as yet, that the logic of events has spoken in favour of the King's realism as opposed to the bombastic self-deception of other Arab countries. A great amount of spade work has thus been done for the King which he could otherwise only have achieved by strenuous personal effort and diplomacy.

If I am right in assuming that His Majesty's Government desires the unification of Arab Palestine and Trans-Jordan not merely to gratify King Abdullah nor even in order to achieve the settlement of the Palestine question which offers a prospect of temporary stability locally, but also for strategic reasons of mere direct military significance, then it seems to me doubly important that the King should make the best possible use of this opportunity to further his case inside Palestine and it is most unfortunate that at the outset he has found himself impelled by the economic situation of Trans-Jordan to discourage the Arabs of Palestine by a broadcast message to them (so I am informed) stating that he is unable to offer them further economic aid. In earnest of this is the fact that for the last fortnight there have not been the customary deliveries of flour from Trans-Jordan to Ramallah for the feeding of refugees. On this same assumption and subject to the views of His Majesty's Minister at Amman, it seems to me that the time has come for His Majesty's Government to secure their base here by the offer if possible of economic aid (disguised perhaps as a loan) to King Abdullah to help pro-Arab Palestine and, certainly, by advice to the King as to the conduct of his propaganda. At the same time it might be found possible to advise the Regent of Iraq to use such personal influence as he has over chosen officers in the Iraqi areas of occupation to further the cause of his uncle in the important Nablus District. I realise that this may achieve little (particularly since the departure of General Mustafa Ragheb Pasha whose personal loyalty to the Regent was undoubted) and will require delicate handling but so suitable an opportunity may not occur again.[11]

Meanwhile, on the internal Jordanian front, democracy and political debate in the Jordanian Parliament were at their best ever since the beginning of the constitutional state of Trans-Jordan in 1930. On 1 November 1948, the King opened the second ordinary session of the First National Assembly with a speech from the throne in which he said:

The day of 15 May is an eternal date in history, for it was the day that saw the withdrawal of the soldiers of the mandatory from Palestine, and when the Arab States discharged their duty towards that brotherly country by standing up to those who claimed it and usurped part of it from its owners who were not ready. The Arab Nation was taken by surprise without being prepared, except in determination, courage and a sense of right. We must not be overwhelmed by delay or by aggression against unarmed peaceful cities, as we saw. We must persevere, endure and be ready without hesitation or weakness. We mention the jihad of the Egyptian Army and their endeavours during October and the jihad of the Jordan Arab Army in Holy Jerusalem and the central front; that successful jihad, which deserves thanks to Allah, praise upon him, and pray for more success from his blessing.

We also mention every Iraqi, Najdian, Syrian and Lebanese who threw himself and what he owned, governments and peoples in the field which the Arab Nation face in the era of independence praying for success from Allah. We are from a nation that knows the worth of countries and the value of honour, and the duty of manhood. We salute in that field their Majesties and Excellencies the Kings and Presidents and praise the Arab League on the path taken, hoping that we succeed in our efforts, and brotherhood in our ranks.[12]

In their reply to the speech from the throne, the deputies expressed disappointment and sadness at the Arab situation. They said:

Your Majesty

This stage of the Arab States today, is the most critical in its modern history. This end at which our dear Palestine has arrived, and the anxiety which has overwhelmed the Arab States in their economic and political life and this suspicion which nags them in their historic values and national pride is shaking us with severe shocks and alerting us to what we are in and what we have come to be.

As we think of our position from the day of the departure of the armies of the Mandatory State from Palestine, and the Arab States held their responsibilities towards that holy country, and as we think of the preceding incidents and the decisions and actions of the League of Arab States dealing with the Palestine problem, we are grieved by their political failure and military stillness. They did not achieve political settlement; their armies did not achieve what they entered Palestine for; their prime ministers did not fulfil their promises or implement their statements; and the League of Arab States did not achieve any victory in the field, instead they put the Arabs in the dark without guidance or known aim.

We are saddened to see our brothers, the Palestinians, at the time when the Arab armies entered their country to save it, expelled from their land, their houses destroyed, the properties looted and the Zionist brigands occupying their towns and villages one after the other without any respect for the United Nations or commitment to the truce agreements, while our armies are standing still receiving the Zionist blows one army after the other.[13]

[270]

On 11 November 1948, the Chamber of Deputies debated various issues, among them an entreaty by nine prominent lawyers. The entreaty was a comprehensive attack on the Jordanian Government and other Arab governments in the light of the Palestinian catastrophe. It criticised chaos on various issues, and the chains that crippled the freedom of the nation and its sons. They attacked the Arab governments thus: 'They are exerting great efforts for the sake of Palestine, is not true but a deception. The Arab tragedy of the sister Palestine, that catastrophe which hurts every Arab, is the consequence of the neglect of these successive Arab governments.'[14]

They criticised the constitution for its lack of respect for the people, and the absence of the principle of the separation of powers. They demanded a new constitution to be written by a founding committee which would guarantee the rights of the people and government, separate powers and respect for the rights and freedoms of the citizens. They objected to the 1948 Treaty between Britain and Jordan, the Reutenburg project and the Dead Sea project which 'helped the Zionists to fight the Arabs of Palestine'. They said:

> We demand a popular government, benevolent, clean and worthy of the responsibilities of a national government, capable of developing the country, achieving its legitimate demands and fighting the three enemies of the people: ignorance, sickness and poverty.[15]

On 16 November, the Prime Minister, Tawfiq Abu al-Huda, issued the following Defence Order:

> In accordance with Article 9 of the Defence Regulations, No. 2 of 1931, I command the following:
>
> 1. The arrest of Dhaifullah al-Humud and Nabih al-Rushaidat and intern them at Bayir police post.
>
> 2. The arrest of Abd al-Karim Maath, Ratib Darwazah and Muhammad Abd al-Rahman Khalifah and intern them under guard at the al-Quwairah police post.[16]

The lawyers' entreaty was again debated in parliament on 18 November. The arrest and internment without trial of these five lawyers had angered the members of the opposition who attacked the Government. The Prime Minister tried to appease the deputies by using some articles of the internal regulations of the Chamber of Deputies, but failed to satisfy the young élite among the members. He was angry enough to attack the Speaker of the Chamber who ignored him and allowed the entreaty to be debated. Farah Abu Jabir, who defected from the opposition lines to support the Prime Minister, suggested that the entreaty be struck off the record. Shafiq al-Rushaidat took the opportunity and launched his strongest criticism against the Government, saying:

> The young who are more educated and more patriotic and national-istic among us, presented their entreaty to our Chamber criticising the Arab situation and the Arab governments because of their attitude towards the Palestine problem, and the Jordan Government internally, accusing them of contravening laws and regulations, against the public interest. The Government abused their authority, despised public freedoms, arrested and interned the lawyers as if they were thieves and criminals only because they complained to the Government. I must say it is incredulous that this cabinet has among its members the popular member Said al-Mufti.
>
> How could this action by the Government be interpreted? What would the people say about us? Were they imprisoned because they demanded reform? Or because they alerted the Government to their mistakes? No, they will say, they are the liberals who wanted freedom for their country; they demanded their rights; they could not tolerate diversions and mistakes committed against them and their interests. Why is it that our exalted Government are disturbed because of the entreaty of the young liberals?
>
> Had not our Government, with its respected sisters, failed in dealing with the Palestine problem? Had not our seven victorious governments entered Palestine while most of it was in the hands of the Arabs and now most of it is in the hands of the Jews? Had not the Jews occupied Lydda, Ramleh, Nazareth, Galilee and hundreds of towns and villages during the historic invasion of our armies? Are not the seven Arab governments responsible for all those innocent souls, the martyred members of the Arab armies? Are not our governments the traders in words and speeches?[17]

Shafiq's attack on the Government in internal affairs was eloquent and devastating. He highlighted poverty, ignorance and illness in his constituency of Irbid where only two doctors were responsible for the health care of 200,000 people. He accused the doctors of spending most of their time treating private patients in their private clinics, while the rest of the people suffered. He accused senior civil servants of corruption by trading in wheat and paraffin. He attacked corrupt government control over the dollar allocations for external trade. He said: 'Ministers allocated dollars to themselves and later sold them to Nadim al-Tabbaa for the profit of £760 for each minister.'[18] He repeated the accusations of the young liberals and added his own.

Abd al-Halim al-Humud supported Shafiq and the young lawyers. He demanded the release of those arrested and their return to their homes from their exile in the desert. Aakif al-Fayiz supported the sacred right of the people to speak, write and think freely in accordance with Articles 17, 18 and 19 of the Constitution, and demanded the release of the detainees.

In his reply, the Prime Minister was uncertain and took refuge in the internal regulations. He said that he needed time to study Shafiq's speech. He attempted to hide behind the King's name by revealing that he informed him of his intention of arresting the young liberals and added:

> I appreciate what Abd al-Halim had said about not using His Majesty's name in debates, and that the ministers are responsible. But according to our constitution the Cabinet is responsible to the King not to the Chamber of Deputies and I have always informed His Majesty of every action I have taken. I have no objection to informing you that some of those who signed the entreaty are moved by instigators and communist principles, and two of them are members of a communist party. Two others are in Damascus working against the country and His Majesty. When His Majesty pardoned them, they came back and again repeated their ills. I could have allowed their entreaty had it been kept in the Chamber, but they printed and published it. This is my authority and no one has the right to question it.[19]

At that point Said al-Mufti, who was the leader of the independent bloc, lost his temper and said:

> Shafiq's statement could be directed against any government in the world: Britain, America, even the Soviet Union, and I will not deny the action taken yesterday because they are seekers of employment and they are the trumpets of others whom we know.[20]

When Shafiq attempted to reply, Said al-Mufti left the Chamber in anger, and the meeting ended.

During the 6th meeting of the Chamber of Deputies on 2 November 1948 the Prime Minister delivered his reply to the accusations made by Shafiq al-Rushaidat regarding dollars, paraffin, cars and wheat. He explained that the allocation of dollars was according to shares of US$2,500 each and was issued to merchants according to the level of their tax payments. The total number came to 184 merchants, plus 12 doctors and chemists. He said that the smallest share was US$2,500 and the largest was US$25,000. He then endeavoured for personal political reasons to compare his Government's allocations of dollars in 1948 with those of the previous Government of Samir al-Rifai during 1947, as shown in Table 9.2.

TABLE 9.2
Government allocations of dollars, 1947 and 1948

Name	1947	1948
Sabri al-Tabba	1,815,953	25,000
Yasin al-Talhuni	435,844	25,000
Tabakh and Samman	210,000	Nil
Shafiq al-Hayik	233,268	25,000
Ismail al-Bilbaisi	219,200	12,500
Tawfiq Qattan	147,837	25,000
Hamdi Manqu	385,033	25,000
Haddad and Shashah	194,499	25,000
Total	**3,641,634**	**162,500**

Abu al-Huda intended to criticise the previous Government of Samir al-Rifai in the process of defending himself. He said that, in the past, dollar allocations were made to people other than merchants and importers; 'They were even made to persons who had no business in Amman and no trade relations with this country, and that was what we wanted to avoid.'[21] He then accused the previous Government of corruption, without using the word, when he said:

> The allocation of cars during 1946–1947 was made to ministers, civil servants and others. A civil servant used to get two or three cars and sell them to benefit from the difference in prices. Some of them did not even touch the cars, for they were transferred to others and they were paid the difference in price.[22]

[274]

In the process of defending his ministers against Shafiq's accusations, Abu al-Huda continued to attack the previous Government and intended to insult and hurt them. He said:

> During the last year, an official letter stated that because the government was certain that a certain shop was an agent for a Jewish agent in Palestine, the owner was denied a license for imports, work or cars and all his property was to be held until a decision regarding the shop was taken. But later, this letter was cancelled by another which stated that it was certain that the shop was not a subsidiary agent, but a full agent in the Hashemite Kingdom of Jordan. What is amazing in this case is that the action was taken because of the certainty and the same action was cancelled because of the certainty. It might be true that a retreat from a mistake is a virtue, but it was said that the car was of a known type, known number and was given as a gift to an important person who sold it.[23]

Abu al-Huda admitted the chaos and lack of control over the sale of paraffin, and said that he had taken action to avoid any mistakes or mishandling of the provision of paraffin to the people. He then mentioned that the Minister of Justice would reply regarding paraffin and bread, and concluded:

> Will the Honourable Members remember that this is the first parliament of our country, and it is a strong test for our awareness. I appeal to every member to be pious to God for his country and our dignity, and not to oppose for personal aims, but to be careful to prove our political rationale and self-reliance for the reason for which we were elected.[24]

Shafiq al-Rushaidat persisted in his attack against the Government by saying that he was not convinced by the Prime Minister's reply. He repeated his defence for the young liberals and demanded their release, which the Prime Minister avoided, insisting that not one of them was a communist. He named traders of dollars on the black market: 'Farhat al-Haj, who was a hairdresser in Amman, and Haj Dairaniyah, a merchant whose shop was closed, and Issa al-Suwais.'[25] He named others who were not Jordanians but were issued with licences and sold them on the black market: 'Wajih Aqil, Baghdadi and Aqqad, Ilyas and Aajur and Abd al-Majid Omar Pasha.'[26] He said: 'If the Prime Minister wants to state the truth about dollars, will he please publish all the names of those 483 persons who were issued with licences?'[27] Shafiq intended to wound the Government and did so when he said:

> Regarding the dollars, I have stated that I have heard from the ministers themselves. They told me that they were given licences of $4,000 which they sold to Nadim al-Tabbaa for £767 at the black market price, and bought cars for the price of £1,200, thus the Ministers bought cars for less than what normal people will pay.[28]

Another devastating blow was dealt to the Prime Minister by Ismael al-Bilbaisi who said: 'I must point out that my name was mentioned by the Prime Minister in the list of those issued with dollar licences, that I have a merchant shop in the name of Ismael al-Bilbaisi and Company. I must state that I personally have no relations with dollars and have no record of them, and do not know how to deal with them.' The Prime Minister did not comment.[29]

Meanwhile, on 5 November 1948, ten Palestinian leaders from the city of Nablus wrote to the Speakers of all Arab parliaments regarding the situation in Palestine. They described the history of the British Mandate for Palestine until the departure of the British Army from the country on 15 May 1948. They mentioned the occupation of what was held by the irregular Arab units and by regiments of the regular Arab armies. They said these regiments did not advance from the Arab areas, but retreated from some areas until the establishment of the one month truce. They continued:

> The Jews became stronger during the month, while the Arab regular regiments remained as they were. Fighting was resumed; the Zionist forces expanded the areas they occupied while the Arab areas shrank. Arab losses increased, catastrophes rampaged and the second truce was enforced. The Arabs accepted.
>
> That means allowing the Jews to kill the Arabs, group by group. It means the destruction of the Arab flag of Palestine for ever as a result of the intervention by the Arab States, their inaction and their competition for what would bring shame to all. That means the desertion of the states from the sacred issue of Palestine, and throwing the Arabs of Palestine as the sacrificial price for their schemes and desires.[30]

The ten leaders visited Amman on 5 November and had an audience with King Abdullah and visited the Prime Minister. Kirkbride, who had a talk with Sulaiman Touqan, reported to the Foreign Office thus:

1. The attitude of the Palestine delegations that have visited Trans-Jordan recently was that in view of the unfortunate events in southern Palestine, they would now be graciously pleased to permit the Trans-Jordan authorities to earn their support to the scheme to unite Arab areas of Palestine with Trans-Jordan. The visitors made it clear that they expected immediate and ample supplies of foreign exchange, oil fuels and foodstuffs. They also indicated that they regarded the Trans-Jordan standard of emoluments for civil servants as being too low and that they required to be paid at Palestine Government rates if given Government appointments.

2. People here are tired of the fickleness and pretensions of the Palestinian leaders and it was made clear to recent visitors, including Sulaiman Touqan, that in the view of the Trans-Jordan authorities, it was the Palestinians who stood in need of Trans-Jordan favour and not the reverse. They were informed that their protestations of loyalty were accepted with pleasure but that their past rapid coat-turning had rather discounted the value of their present statements.

Finally they were told that Trans-Jordan was nearing the end of its economic tether and that a general tightening of belts seemed to be inevitable.

Sulaiman Touqan was very annoyed and expressed the conviction that if the King pressed hard enough His Majesty's Government would be bound to provide him with the means of satisfying the needs of Palestine.

3. The Prime Minister of Trans-Jordan feels that, after recent developments, the surviving Arab areas in Palestine, if any, will have no alternative but union with Trans-Jordan. He also appreciates the fact that the ability of Trans-Jordan to carry the additional economic burden which would be imposed by such a union is decreasing while the potential weight of the burden is increasing.

He does not see any point in trying to deceive the Palestinians regarding Trans-Jordan's economic position as evidence of the true position could not be concealed for long.[31]

The attitude of the leaders of public opinion in the Arab areas of Palestine started to be more down to earth and in favour of King Abdullah's policy for a peaceful solution. In the district of Nablus, the most belligerent of the Palestinian cities and towns, the defeat of the

Egyptian Army was felt deeply. Thus the population was in favour of a moderate policy towards peace rather than war. The Acting Consul General in Jerusalem reported to the Foreign Office as follows:

> Events in northern and southern Palestine have certainly led Palestine Arabs to abandon their recent bellicose attitude and to favour some sort of negotiated settlement of the Palestine question. The Mayor of Nablus in private conversation with a member of my staff on 2 November even expressed the view that direct negotiations with Jews might be advisable since the United Nations was obviously incapable of finding any fair settlement.
>
> Both Sulaiman Touqan and the District Commissioner of Samaria were thinking in terms of a possible Jewish occupation of Nablus, and both expressed the firm intention of staying put and encouraging the others to do likewise. It remains to be seen whether this intention will still be firm when the Jews get nearer.
>
> Touqan also said that when he visited Amman, he had broached with King Abdullah the question of uniting Arab Palestine and Trans-Jordan and had found His Majesty enthusiastic for the union. When, however, he broached the same question with the Prime Minister and other ministers he found them opposed to union or at best lukewarm. He attributed this to the fact that Trans-Jordan ministers fear that in a unified state they would quickly be superseded by the more intelligent and educated Arabs of Palestine. No doubt Sulaiman Bey was thinking primarily in terms of himself in saying this, but it is a natural corollary of objection of the Palestine Arab to being subordinated to the more backward Trans-Jordanians, though he is the first Palestinian I have met who realises it. The rest appear to think King Abdullah is wedded to his former cronies to the exclusion of the newcomers.[32]

By the end of November 1948, after consultations between the leaders of the areas of Palestine under control of the Iraqi and Jordanian armies, including the Bethlehem and Hebron sector, it was decided to hold a third Palestinian congress to discuss their future. On 1 December 1948, delegations consisting of more than 3,000 Palestinian national, municipal and village leaders and representatives of the various political parties assembled in Jericho. Among them were some of the Mufti's supporters who were dissatisfied with his policies. Musa Abdullah al-Husseini, Ali al-Dajani and Yahya Hammoudah were present. At 1030 hours, the Congress was opened and the delegates elected the participants shown in Table 9.3 as the Congress Committee.

TABLE 9.3
The new Congress Committee

Name	Post
Shaikh Muhammad al-Jaabari	President
Fuad Attallah	Vice-President
Aajaj Nuwaihidh	Secretary
Kamal Hannun	Member
Hikmat al-Taji al-Farouqi	Member

After a long debate, during which many delegates spoke in favour of unity with the Hashemite Kingdom of Jordan, the Conference approved the following decisions:

> As Palestine used to form a part of *natural Syria* and as the mandate was imposed thereon against the will of the people and remained in force up to 15 May 1948, preventing Palestine from attaining independence or joining one of the sister, independent Arab countries, and in view of the fact that the people of Palestine today consider, in the light of the present political and military situation in Palestine, that the time has come when a decisive step should be taken to safeguard their future, to exercise their right of self-determination finally and to participate with adjacent Arab countries in a settled and free life; in view of all these reasons, the Conference decides that *Palestine and the Hashemite Kingdom of Trans-Jordan* should be incorporated into one Kingdom and acknowledges His Majesty King Abdulla ibn al-Hussein as the Constitutional King of Palestine.
>
> The Conference thanks the Arab states for the military and political efforts they have made for the preservation of Palestine Arabism and Sacredness. The Conference hails the Arab armies now stationed in the various parts of Palestine and demands from the Arab governments that they accomplish the task of liberating the country which they assumed when first they entered it.
>
> The Conference requests state members of the Arab League, as well as the United Nations Organisation, to take immediate and decisive action to enable Palestinian Arab refugees to return to their homes as soon as possible and to give them adequate reparation for their losses.
>
> The Conference decides that the decision, which was taken unanimously in regard both to acknowledging His Majesty King Abdullah as King of Palestine as well as the incorporation of the two sister countries, must, on conclusion of the Conference, be

submitted immediately to His Majesty King Abdullah Ibn al Hussein, King of the Trans-Jordan Hashemite Kingdom. It also decides that the decisions as a whole should be conveyed to member states of the Arab League, United Nations Organisation and to all diplomatic representatives at Amman.

Sgd. Muhammad Ali al-Jaabari.
Sgd. Fuad Attallah.
Sgd. Aajaj Nuwaihidh.
Sgd. Kamal Hannun.
Sgd. Hikmat al-Taji al-Farouqi.[33]

Thereafter all the delegates crossed the River Jordan to the Mussalla Palace in al-Shunah and proclaimed King Abdullah King of Palestine. The King delivered the following speech to the delegates:

> I consider your decisions a blessing from Allah and a great responsibility. During last April when Palestinian delegates came to me because of the painful event of Dair Yasin, I said that I place myself at the disposal of the people of Palestine until victory or they say enough. Allah helped us to do what we promised. The situation is not that of speeches, but a situation of study and action. I will take these decisions and present them to the Government, and it is imperative that the Arab States must know them. They will save Palestine from catastrophe.

Kirkbride reported the details of the proceedings of the Congress and its decisions to the Foreign Secretary, Ernest Bevin, on 8 December. He said that the initiative for holding the Conference came from the Palestinians themselves which indicated 'a growing volume of dissatisfaction among them with (a) their old leaders in general and the Mufti in particular; (b) the political tactics of the Arab League; and (c) the conduct of military operations by the various Arab armies'. He added:

> 4. The original intention had been that the present Congress should decide to unite Arab Palestine and Trans-Jordan under King Abdullah, to remove the settlement of the Palestine problem from the hands of the Arab League and to authorise King Abdullah to effect a settlement on behalf of the Arabs of Palestine.
> It will be seen from the decisions that only the first of these objectives was secured.
> It is believed that the enclosed decisions were edited after the conclusion of the Congress and that the original version included a

decision that any settlement which did not preserve the unity of Palestine could only be temporary.

5. During the debates at Jericho there were exhibitions of the personal and party jealousies which have done so much harm to the Palestinians' case in the past. It was also evident that the younger representatives were determined to get rid of the 'old gang' and to see that control of the movement remained in the hands of new and younger men. In this they were successful.

A number of hostile persons, led by Farid Fakhr al-Din of Beisan, started heckling on the first day but dispersed when their leader was arrested.[34]

Instead of immediate action by the Prime Minister, Tawfiq Abu al-Huda, in support of the King's wishes (which he knew well), for some unknown reason he hesitated, preventing an immediate response. He further created a gratuitous ministerial crisis. Kirkbride reported:

1. I have not reported on this matter before because it caused a ministerial crisis which was only solved yesterday.

2. Communication made by King Abdullah to the United States on this subject on 4 December took the form of an oral reference to the Congress which he made to Mr Stabler in the course of a routine visit of the latter to see the King. Stabler is a member of the United States Foreign Service but his official status in Trans-Jordan is that of a representative of the Jerusalem Truce Commission. It is therefore surprising to see this informal conversation referred to as an official announcement.

3. The original idea was that the Jericho Congress should pass resolutions pressing for an urgent settlement of the Palestine problem and so strengthen the hand of the Trans-Jordan Government if the latter came to negotiations either direct with the Jews or otherwise. In the event the Congress, through Palace influence, proclaimed the union of Palestine and Trans-Jordan and acknowledged Abdullah as King of the united country. It went further astray through influence of Arabian Palestinian elements and pressed for Arab States to complete their task of liberating Palestine.

4. As it was clear that the King expected something to happen immediately as regards implementation, the Prime Minister, accompanied by the rest of the Council of Ministers, went to the Palace and said that the most they could do at present would be to welcome decisions as promoting unity of Arab world so desired by all Arabs

and promised to take the necessary constitutional and international measures to secure their implementation as soon as circumstances permitted. The Prime Minister pointed out that in view of the treaty, His Majesty's Government was directly concerned and that Trans-Jordan could not act in a matter of this kind with complete disregard of their ally, the United Nations and the Arab world. The King lost his temper and said rudely that they could go away and decide anything they liked.

5. The Council of Ministers returned to the Prime Minister's office where he, the Minister of Defence and the Minister of the Interior expressed the intention of resigning immediately. The other Ministers agreed to resign if the King persisted in his attitude, but pressed that the Council should pass a resolution, present it to the King and resign if his attitude was unsatisfactory. This was agreed eventually and the resolution was passed in the sense indicated above with the addition of a paragraph to the effect that the Trans-Jordan Government would continue to do all in its power to assist refugees from Palestine and secure their return to their homes.

6. A delegation of three of the Council, not including the Prime Minister, took the resolution to the Palace. The King had by that time decided to climb down. He apologised for his outburst remarking that he was only one of eight (the other seven being ministers) and that he would accept any decision of the majority. When he read the resolution he said it conformed exactly with his own ideas and he telephoned the Prime Minister to congratulate him on the decision. Decision of the Council of Ministers has now been placed before Parliament where it will doubtless be confirmed.

7. Throughout this episode I supported the Prime Minister's view. This morning he came to see me unexpectedly and said that he was too tired to carry on and proposed to resign for reasons of health. I said that having steered the ship of state through the worst of the storm he could not give up just as it seemed about to make port. After some argument he agreed not to resign at present.[35]

During the joint meeting of the deputies and the senate in the national assembly on 13 December 1948, the Deputy Speaker of the senate, Abdullah al-Shraidah, read Cabinet decision No. 583 of 7 December 1948:

The Cabinet have studied the resolutions adopted by the Second Palestinian Arab Conference held in Jericho on 30 Muharram 1368 AH; of 1 December 1948, and decided as follows:

1. The Government of the Hashemite Kingdom of Jordan appreciates fully the wish expressed by the Conference and the majority of the people of Palestine regarding what relates to unifying the two brotherly countries, and consider it to be agreeable to her aims, and she welcomes it and will endeavour to achieve it by constitutional and international means and to implement it at the appropriate time in accordance with the methods of self-determination.

2. The Government has been informed of the wish of the Conference for the Arab countries to complete the mission of liberation which they declared when they entered Palestine, and they consider the efforts that have been made and are being made to achieve the required aim and believe that it is in the interest to achieve an appropriate solution to this problem in the soonest possible time.

3. The Government partakes in the Conference's wish to endeavour through the United Nations Organisation to return the refugees to their country in the shortest possible time and grant them financial compensation, and she is persistent in her efforts to achieve this wish.

4. Owing to what this decision has of relations with the entity of the country and her future, the Government considers that it must be presented to the national assembly to give their opinion of it.[36]

After a short debate, during which every speaker approved the Government's decision, the absolute majority of the national assembly approved the following decision:

The Jordanian National Assembly in its joint meeting held on 13 December 1948, after being informed of the Government decision No. 583, dated 7 December 1948, which was taken due to the resolutions of the Second Palestinian Arab Conference held in Jericho on 1 December 1948, has decided unanimously to agree with the Government policy in her said decision.[37]

Kirkbride reported the decisions of the Jordanian National Assembly and asked for instruction. The Foreign Office replied:

I appreciate the need for decisions by Jordan. We have made it clear that we favour a settlement by which Jordan would get at least the greater part of Arab Palestine. Details of the settlement which might be appropriate in present conditions to carry out these principles are given in my immediately following telegram. In these circumstances we are justified in suggesting to King Abdullah and the Jordan Government to keep open the discussions which they have begun with Jewish representatives in the hope of ascertaining Jewish intentions and if possible of preparing the ground for a final settlement on the above lines. It will no doubt be best for the discussions to be pursued as part of an armistice arrangement but the lines of a desirable final settlement should always be borne in mind and nothing should be done to make this more difficult of achievement.

We do not know when the Conciliation Commission will actually be appointed or what the result of its intervention will be but King Abdullah should not rule out the possibility that participation of the Commission in any negotiations might strengthen Jordan's bargaining position. It is clear in any case that they will have to take part in bringing about a final settlement and that there are some questions (for example, Jerusalem, Haifa and Lydda) which would best be left for them to deal with from the beginning. But subject to this there would be nothing wrong if Trans-Jordan was able to lay the foundations for a settlement by private discussion if they wished to do so and felt in a strong enough position.

So far as we can judge, it would greatly strengthen Jordan's position if they could act in concert with Egypt. This would be most difficult to arrange in view of Egyptian criticisms of King Abdullah and of his message to the Sudan. But we believe the attempt should be made. If, however, the Jordan Government has felt unable to make any proposals to Egypt for acting in concert or if their proposals were refused, we should still feel that Jordan should go ahead alone.

As regards timing, the Jews are claiming that a settlement should be made before their elections because this will help the moderates to win. We are not convinced by this. It seems more likely that no final settlement involving concessions by the Jews could be made before the elections since any party making such concessions would be vulnerable to extremist attacks and criticism. The object should therefore be to keep the Jews in play pending the arrival of the Commission and the Jewish elections, after which it would be hoped that finality could be reached.

You should speak on the above lines to King Abdullah and the Jordan Prime Minister. You should tell them that we are fully conscious of our treaty obligations to Trans-Jordan and that we wish to help to the greatest possible extent in the difficult task which lies before them.[38]

The British Middle East Office in Cairo participated in the proceedings and reported their views regarding the general Arab situation to the Foreign Office:

> While I fully realise the unconstructive attitude of every Arab Government except that of Jordan I cannot help feeling that if King Abdullah now goes ahead alone with our blessing and without necessarily even trying to get the Egyptians to act in concert with him we may find ourselves in a very embarrassing position. It will be apparent from Cairo that the Egyptian Government already feels strongly about Abdullah's latest actions. The same is no doubt true of Saudi Arabia and Syria and His Majesty's Minister in Beirut has uttered a warning that, if Abdullah makes an open deal with the Jews he will inevitably cut the ground from under the feet of his sympathisers and of moderates everywhere.
>
> It seems to me that if we identify ourselves too closely with Abdullah's policy and ambitions and advise him to go ahead in disregard of all the other Arab states we may run very grave risks. In the first place our present hopes of getting on better terms with Egypt with all that that involves to our strategic position in the Middle East may receive a serious setback. Secondly, we may find ourselves involved in greater commitments in Jordan than we would wish to incur. Even lesser Trans-Jordan in times of tranquillity is a financial liability. One hesitates to suggest what the liability would be for a greater Jordan at open odds with all her Arab neighbours. I do not suggest that they would necessarily attack her with their military forces but they should not find it difficult to cause her great embarrassment in other ways and would probably not hesitate to let loose the Mufti's supporters and other disturbers of the peace for that purpose. The fact that Jews might be chief beneficiaries of such action would be unlikely to deter them from such action.
>
> I submit with all respect that before we nail our flag completely to King Abdullah's mast and encourage him to defy all other Arab opinion, a serious endeavour should be made to bring him and at least the Egyptians together. Khashaba Pasha suggested some such action in his conversation with His Majesty's Ambassador on 15 December and it appears from Beirut telegram and Baghdad telegram that the Lebanese and Iraqi Governments may be willing to lend a hand.[39]

The British Ambassador in Cairo participated in the diplomatic debate and reported to the Foreign Office:

I feel some misgiving over the situation developing in respect of Jordan. I fully understand how desirable it is to ensure cessation of hostilities in Palestine and the establishment of peace and a settlement. On the creation of a Conciliation Committee it seemed to me that this body offered the best chance of negotiations with these ends in view while at the same time offering the Arabs a medium through which they could work in common and to some extent mitigate the effects of their disadvantageous military situation. For this reason the initiative of King Abdullah seemed to me both untimely and unwise as weakening the Arab position, giving away piecemeal some of the concessions forming common stock of Arab bargaining means and playing into the hands of the Jews more than was likely to suit us. However, I see from your recent telegram to Amman that delay is probable before the Commission gets to work thus making desirable some initiative which might expedite peace and forestall resumption of hostilities.

At the same time would initiative on the lines offered by Abdullah really be the best method?

I was struck by Sassoon's proposals to Jordan's representative in London, which seemed highly disingenuous constituting a trap for Jordan, the Arabs and His Majesty's Government by which Arab disunity would be crystallised, Jordan put in the wrong *vis-à-vis* other Arab states and His Majesty's Government indirectly, if not directly, not only put in the wrong along with Trans-Jordan, but also aligned with Israel (and Jordan) in opposition to the other Arabs. Since unilateral action by Jordan would be universally condemned by the others as treachery, His Majesty's Government would be tarred with the same brush. This might not matter if his Majesty's Government were indifferent whether they were on good terms with the other Arab states. But since for strategic reasons it seems essential for us to keep in with all the Arab states and especially with Egypt, this prospect appeared most disturbing. I imagine that our aim is to have with as many as possible of the Arab states an agreement which might form part of a general Middle East strategic mosaic. If so, I venture to repeat a passage in a minute I wrote in London on last October as follows: 'Relations between Egypt (still the leader and strongest among the Arab states) and Jordan are strained. We are supporting arrangements in respect of Palestine which encourage the aims of Jordan lying at the base of this strained relationship': if we build a defence system on a regional basis there will be this flaw in its very foundations.

Jordan it is true may prove rather less unreliable as a friend than Egypt though this has yet to be put to the real proof. But would any such great reliability of Jordan counter balance the disadvantage of a serious weakness in the foundation of our regional edifice?

A Jordan augmented by Arab Palestine seems unlikely to be more viable than Jordan in its present form. We would therefore risk antagonising other Arabs in favour of Jordan and a state which could only be of use to us at the price of a continual drain on our financial and military resources and of constant support not only against Israel but also against other Arab states, thus widening the breach between the latter and ourselves.

While therefore in supporting Jordan in a separate peace with Israel we might make an immediate gain by promoting *partial* Judeo/Arab peace, would we not start a train of consequences which would at least neutralise this advantage, certainly give it a mere temporary character and prevent a *general* Judeo/Arab settlement?

Would it not be better for us to do all we can to discourage unilateral action by Jordan and work for joint peaceful action between Jordan and Egypt?

Firm agreements between Jordan and Egypt (to which Iraq might perhaps also be persuaded to adhere) would I think undoubtedly be a great step forward. I have been thinking lately of suggesting that His Majesty's Government might come forward boldly and try to bring this about; and Khashaba's remarks to King Farouk the other day deplored encouraging this line of thought. Could we not act as honest broker? I think the Egyptians (the King, Khashaba and Haidar at all events) are very likely to readily come to an agreement with Abdullah about dividing the Negab but are unwilling to approach him direct. I do not think the Egyptians are ready to accept partition publicly but they might be prepared to consolidate Egyptian administration of their part of the Negab on the basis of an armistice if Abdullah would do the same in respect of his part and without raising at this time the contentious issue of Palestine and a sovereign. It may seem doubtful whether the Jews would be prepared to accept a prolonged armistice under such conditions; but I feel pretty certain that if the Arabs are in due course to accept partition and recognise the existence of a Jewish state much patience will be required because the result can only be achieved by gradualness – that is, an armistice leading to acquiescence and finally to recognition. This would surely in the long run prove to be the most satisfactory outcome even from the Jewish point of view.

If you are in agreement with this line of thought perhaps you would consider instructing His Majesty's Minister at Amman to advise Abdullah to leave on one side the question of sovereignty for the time being and ask him to say whether he would be prepared through inter-mediation of His Majesty's Government to discuss with the Egyptian Government the territorial questions mentioned above, together with those affecting the other parts of Palestine still under Arab control. If he is agreeable in principle and would say so quickly I could return an encouraging answer to Khashaba's approach to me. A secret meeting might then be arranged between representatives of the two Governments in the presence of a British representative. Opportunity could then be taken of trying to get both sides to accept what His Majesty's Government may decide upon as the best solution.[40]

On 24 December an unidentified aircraft, suspected of being from the Egyptian Air Force, dropped heavy calibre bombs near King Abdullah's winter residence at al-Shunah in the Jordan valley. These bombs were found to have borne Arabic inscriptions consigning them 'from King Farouq'. It was not finally established whether that air raid was by an Egyptian aircraft or a Jewish aircraft dropping bombs of Egyptian origin. The former was most likely, because on 24 December the Jewish forces were nowhere near an Egyptian airfield.

It was obvious that the Middle East Office in Cairo and Kirkbride were batting for Britain and its strategic interest in the Arab world, rather than endeavouring to act as the mediator of peace between the Arabs and the Jews, not to mention justice for the Palestinians, the victims of Britain's Balfour Declaration. British diplomats who, in the past, created division rather than unity in the Arab world, were keen to bring about better understanding between Egypt and Jordan for their own ends and interests rather than the national interests of the Palestinians whom they deserted unarmed and unable to defend themselves against the Jews. Kirkbride, who saw the benefit of encouraging the idea of discussions between Jordan and Egypt for a peaceful settlement in Palestine, had a meeting with King Abdullah on which he reported the following to the Foreign Office:

1. I have omitted possibility of Trans-Jordan–Egyptian discussions regarding Palestine with King Abdullah. He was not in a receptive mood principally because of the aerial bombing which was reported in my unnumbered telegram of 25 December for which he holds the Egyptians responsible and which he assumes to have been an attempt at intimidation.

2. After argument (irritable on his side) I got him to admit that Trans-Jordan would be in a stronger position in discussions on a

settlement if there was prior agreement with the Egyptians. He next said that he would accept an exchange of views with the Egyptians if this was desired by His Majesty's Government but he added quickly that if, as he anticipated, the Egyptians tried to make abandonment of decisions at Jericho Congress a condition to a meeting or raised the subject during the meeting he would not agree to continue. He also said that he would not take the initiative in suggesting a meeting as he would certainly be rewarded by a snub. In reply I pointed out that if it was an ideal as I understood it of Egypt and Trans-Jordan presenting a united front when discussing the boundaries between them and the Jews there should be no necessity to bring up the status of Arab areas at present.[41]

It may have been by coincidence rather than by intention that the British diplomatic initiative was launched at the same time as the Jewish invasion of Egyptian territory and the occupation of the area of al-Arish, thus threatening the destruction of the Egyptian Army in Palestine. Kirkbride seemed in a hurry to see the Prime Minister of Jordan on the same day of his meeting with King Abdullah. He reported back to London:

1. I spoke to the Prime Minister and he expressed willingness to discuss the Palestine question with the Egyptian authorities at any time. He made one stipulation which was that the initiative should now come from the Egyptian side. His overtures (including an offer to go to Cairo) to the late Prime Minister of Egypt after the Sudanese telegram had been ignored and he therefore felt the next move was due from Egyptian side.

2. The King's assent mentioned by me was given grudgingly and he is quite likely to attempt evasion if and when the time comes for a meeting. The Prime Minister on the other hand seemed anxious to come to terms with the Egyptians and that being so he and I should be able to keep the King up to the mark.

3. The problem now is to arrange a meeting to which Egyptians think they have been invited by Jordan and the Jordanians think they have been invited by Egypt.[42]

King Abdullah was a leader of men rather than a constitutional monarch limited by domestic or international law. His main aim was to unite Jordan and Palestine in one Kingdom, with himself as King. He thought he did not need the consent of Egypt, Saudi Arabia, Iraq or

Syria for the achievement of his aim. Above all, he needed the support of the leaders of public opinion in Palestine, particularly former British Mandate Civil Servants, Muslim Shaikhs, Christian leaders of all denominations and anti-Mufti political parties. At his Royal Palace and his Winter Palace at al-Shunah he met large numbers of delegations and individuals, taking time to explain to them the dangers of leaving eastern and central Palestine in a vacuum bereft of government and policies for defence, economic, social and political development and the rule of law. King Abdullah was not worried about the consequences of his policy and action. It was Abu al-Huda, for his own unknown reasons, and Kirkbride for British reasons, who wanted to avoid inter-Arab jealousies and media attacks by the rest of the Arab Governments concerned. The King, however, had to face limitations on all fronts, the strongest of which was the attitude of the British Government, as can be seen from the following telegram from the Foreign Office to Kirkbride:

1. I presume from 'restrictions' mentioned in . . . your telegram that King Abdullah should negotiate for an armistice leaving the final settlement to be reached with the help of the Commission and that he should, if possible, work in concert with Egypt and that he should bear in mind the desirability of a final settlement on the lines suggested in my telegram.

2. I still believe that this advice was right, and it would seem particularly difficult and dangerous for King Abdullah to negotiate while the Jews are on Egyptian territory. Nevertheless, I appreciate the serious danger that if we advise King Abdullah to refrain from any negotiations which he wishes to undertake, we are assuming a very heavy responsibility.

I have informed you separately of measures being taken or contemplated to strengthen Trans-Jordan. I can not (repeat *not*) agree to the issue of war material to the Arab Legion at this stage.

You will also have seen from the Washington telegram a very strong message sent by the United States Government to the Jewish Government with regard to the Jewish attitude towards Tans-Jordan.

I hope these two factors will enable King Abdullah and the Trans-Jordan Government to spin things out or at least to obtain a desirable settlement. I do not suggest that you should try to restrain King Abdullah from any course of action on which he decides in full knowledge of the facts, but you will no doubt ensure that he is aware of the considerations mentioned above.

I think you should also make it clear that if King Abdullah formally accepts the union of Palestine and Trans-Jordan (that is, without some reservation showing that he is referring to Arab Palestine) we shall have to make it clear that we do not recognise and cannot support any claim by him to areas which may be incorporated in the Jewish State. Apart from this we would not wish to advise him on the best way of giving effect to the wishes of his Government and Parliament with regard to the Jericho resolutions.[43]

NOTES

1　PRO. FO 371/68642. From King Abdullah to Abd al Rahman Azzam, 25 September 1949.
2　*Ibid.*
3　*Ibid.* From Baghdad to the Foreign Office, 29 September, 1948.
4　*Ibid.* From Mr Beaumont to the Foreign Office, 30 September 1948.
5　*Ibid.* From Kirkbride to the Foreign Office, 2 October 1948.
6　*Ibid.*
7　*Ibid.* From Kirkbride to Bevin, 4 October 1948.
8　*Ibid.* From Kirkbride to the Foreign Office, 10 October 1948.
9　*Ibid.* From Kirkbride to the Foreign Office, 8 October 1948.
10　*Ibid.* From Kirkbride to the Foreign Office, 12 October 1948.
11　*Ibid.* From the Acting British Consul General to the Foreign Office, 30 October 1948.
12　*TJOG* no. 28, 9 November 1948.
13　*HKJOG* no. 31, 25 November 1948.
14　*Ibid.*
15　*Ibid.* The nine lawyers were Dhaif Allah al Humud, Mohammad Abd al Rahman Khalifah, Nabih al Rushaidat, Mahmud al Mitlaq, Hamdi Fariz, Abd al Karim Maath, Attallah al Majali, Ratib Darwazah and Abd al Razzaq Khalifah.
16　Bayir is located in the desert south of Ma'an. Al Quwairah is located between Ma'an and Aqaba.
17　*HKJOG* no. 33, 18 December 1948.
18　*Ibid.*
19　*Ibid.*
20　*Ibid.*
21　*Ibid.*
22　*Ibid.*
23　*Ibid.*
24　*Ibid.*
25　*Ibid.*
26　*Ibid.*
27　*Ibid.*

28 *Ibid.*

29 *Ibid.*

30 *HKJOG* no. 31, 25 November 1948. The ten leaders were Sulaiman Touqan, Adil Zuaitir, Farid Anibtawi, Dr Mustafa Bushnaq, Shaikh Abd al Hamid al Sayih, Hashim al Jayusi, Faiq Anibtawi, Hikmat al Masri, Hilmi al Abbushi and Fadhl al Tahir.

31 PRO. FO 371/68642. From Kirkbride to the Foreign Office, 11 November 1948.

32 PRO. FO 371/68643. From the Acting General Consul to the Foreign Office, 5 November 1948.

33 PRO. FO 371/68644. From Kirkbride to Ernest Bevin, 8 December 1948.

34 *Ibid.*

35 PRO. FO 371/68642. From Kirkbride to the Foreign Office, 9 December 1948.

36 *HKJOG* no. 35, 29 December 1948.

37 *Ibid.* The speakers were Abu Jabir, Al Bilbaisi, Al Minwir, Abd al Rahman al Rushaidat, Shafiq, Al Muasshir, Al Humud, Al Tel, Mirza, Abu al Shaar and Al Fayiz.

38 PRO. FO 371/68644. From the Foreign Office to Kirkbride, 16 December 1948.

39 *Ibid.* From the British Middle East Office (Cairo) to the Foreign Office, 20 December 1948.

40 *Ibid.* From the Middle East Office (Cairo) to the Foreign Office, 21 December 1948.

41 *Ibid.* From Kirkbride to the Foreign Office, 28 December 1948.

42 *Ibid.* From Kirkbride to the Foreign Office, 29 December 1948.

43 *Ibid.* From the Foreign Office to Kirkbride, 31 December 1948.

10

The Armistice Agreement, 1949

By January 1949, the strength of the Jordan Arab Army in Palestine had increased to 11,143 officers and men defending the Jordanian and Hebron–Bethlehem sectors. The strength of the Iraqi Army had increased to about 19,000 officers and men defending the Nablus sector. The total strength of both armies was about 30,000 defending a front of about 420 kilometres. The Egyptian, Syrian and Lebanese armies were in no position to fight, not to mention defending their own positions. Against the Iraqi and Jordanian armies in Palestine, the Jews had between 130,000 and 150,000 officers and men. While the Jordan Army was about 100 kilometres away from its base, the Iraqi Army was 1,100 kilometres away from Baghdad and both armies were short of ammunition. The Jewish forces opposing the Iraqis and the Jordanians were about 10–20 kilometres from their supply base all along the front. Under these circumstances the Jews could have attacked and destroyed both armies any time they wished.

On 25 January 1949, the Jews held their general elections for a Constituent Assembly in all the areas occupied by their forces, whether allocated to them by the Partition Plan or usurped by their forces during the fighting, including Jerusalem.

On 15 February 1949, Dr Ralf J. Bunche, who replaced Count Bernadotte as the United Nations mediator, issued an invitation to the Government of Jordan to send a delegation to Rhodes for the negotiation of an armistice between Jordan and the Jews. Mindful of the relative strengths, the invitation was accepted and the Jordanian delegation shown in Table 10.1 proceeded to Rhodes on 28 February.

March 1949 was full of great anxiety about future development of the Palestinian question and the discussions in Rhodes. The negotiations between the Jordanian and Jewish delegations were at a stalemate while the aggression of the Jewish forces in the Negev including their seizure of large areas in the Bethlehem–Hebron sector went undeterred. A Jewish

TABLE 10.1
The Jordanian delegation to Rhodes, 28 February 1949

Name	Role
• Colonel Ahmad Sudqi al-Jundi	President
• Lt Colonel Muhammad al-Maaitah	Member
• Major Radhi al-Hindawi	Member
• Captain Ali Abu Nowar	Member
• Lt Fathi Yasin	Member
• Riyadh al-Muflih	Legal advisor
• Abdullah Nusseir	Legal advisor

mobile force advanced and occupied Um Rashrash on the Palestinian side of the Gulf of Aqaba and carried out various infringements of Jordanian territory. The Jews continued with their expulsion policy against the Palestinians. They drove out the inhabitants of al-Faluja and Bait Jibrin from their homes after the Egyptian Armistice Agreement and the evacuation of the 4th Egyptian Brigade from al-Faluja. The new refugees were accommodated in the Hebron sector and Jordan. There was no action by the United Nations or the great powers to put an end to Jewish aggression. It was believed that in international affairs there was one law for the Jews and another for the Arabs.

The negotiations between the Jordanian and Jewish delegations at Rhodes continued during the month of March. In order to delay the negotiations while usurping more Palestinian land, the Jews sent a message saying: 'The Jordanian delegation was of insufficiently high standing and suggested that Samir Pasha [al-Rifai], the former Prime Minister, should be sent with full powers.'[1] The Jordan Government rejected the complaint and replied that it considered its representatives at Rhodes to be of adequate seniority for the purpose of negotiations.

The most critical issue during the negotiations was the arrangement whereby the Iraqi forces in the Nablus area were to hand over their front line to the Jordanian Arab Army. The Jews took the opportunity of using this issue for the intention of usurping by intimidation and threats further concessions in return for not regarding the handover between the Iraqi and Jordanian forces as a breach of the truce. In relation to this Glubb wrote in his book:

Dr Ralph J. Bunche was conducting the Rhodes negotiations. His plan was that both sides should immediately sign ceasefire agreements for their whole fronts in order to ease the tension. The armistice agreement could then be negotiated in a less strained atmosphere. The ceasefire draft agreement provided that: 'No elements of the ground or air forces of either party would advance beyond or pass over the line now held.' The Jordan Government expressed its readiness to sign such an agreement. It requested that the undertaking be made to cover both the Iraqi and Jordan fronts, in view of the fact that the Iraqis were about to withdraw from Palestine. The Israelis demurred, whereupon the Jordan Government offered to sign forthwith for the Arab Legion only, but with a clause automatically extending its provisions to the Iraqi front, when that army withdrew. While this argument was in progress, the departure of the Iraqi army was agreed on between the Jordan and Iraqi Governments. It was to commence on 13 March 1949. The argument on the application of the preliminary ceasefire to the Iraqi front was still in progress on 8 March. We could not but suspect that the Israelis would postpone signing the ceasefire until the Iraqis withdrew on 13 March, and then seize the opportunity to follow up the retreating Iraqis and occupy some more territory before the Arab Legion could take over. As the days passed, the tension and anxiety increased. The Israelis were intoxicated at their successes in the field, their cordial reception in the United Nations, the enthusiastic support of the USA, and the swing of opinion to their side in Britain, as evidenced in the parliamentary debate on the Middle East. The whole world was on their side.[2]

The Egyptians and the Jews had signed their Armistice Agreement at Rhodes on 24 February 1949. On the following day, the Jordan Government sent a strong protest to Dr Bunche against Israeli troop movements north of the Gulf of Aqaba in the Negev. Dr Bunche cabled General Riley of the United States Marines and a representative of the United Nations, to which the latter replied that no such movements had occurred. Further Jewish movements continued, but when Jordan complained to Dr Bunche, the Jews denied that there was any military movement.

The occupation of Um Rashrash

Since 15 May 1948, the Jordanian Police in the District of Maan in the south of Jordan had controlled the internal security of the Negev area south of Palestine. They based their police posts at Um Rashrash, north-west of Aqaba, Ain Husub, about 40 kilometres south of the Dead Sea, and Karnab, south of Beersheba. Jordanian flags were raised over these police posts and the Jordan Arab Army considered the line between Ain al-Hofairah, about 30 kilometres south of the Dead Sea in a south-westerly direction, and across to the Egyptian–Palestinian frontier west of Biyar Idaid near point 826, to be under their control. The whole area and the front were defended by one company of two platoons, commanded by Lt Sulaiman Jarad. During November 1948, Captain T. N. Bromage was appointed Commander of what became the 'South Force' consisting of the following:

- One company of two platoons commanded by Lt Sulaiman Jarad.
- One detachment of Bedouin partisans commanded by Lt Saqr Aabtan al-Jazi.
- One troop of armoured cars.

Bromage established his headquarters at Um Rashrash, and sent reconnaissance and fighting patrols to the north within the Jordanian area. Ten days before the end of the Jewish offensive against the Egyptian Army on 7 January 1949, the Jewish Command turned their attention to Jordan. The Israeli General Staff had planned to make extensive conquests and expansions on the West Bank during February 1949, and to capture the whole of the Negev and the rest of the south of Palestine down to Um Rashrash. With increased patrolling against the Jordanian 'South Force', the HQ of the Jordanian Arab Army sent another infantry company of the 10th Regiment, supported by a troop of six-pounder anti-tank guns and a troop of Orlecan anti-aircraft guns, commanded by Lt Muhammad Mitlaq al-Habhibah. A section of sappers managed to plant some minefields in forward areas in order to delay any Jewish penetration into the Jordanian line. On 28 December, Bromage was inspecting a minefield when one mine exploded, threw him on his back, wounded Lt Muhammad al-Habhibah and killed the sapper soldier Musa Sulaiman. Bromage sent the body of the dead soldier to his family in Wadi Musa and sent Muhammad al-Habhibah to the Royal Navy doctor in Aqaba, where he was treated and later sent to Fayed in Egypt for further treatment. In the middle of January 1949, the company of the 10th Regiment was relieved by a company and two troops of armoured cars from the 3rd Regiment, commanded by Lt Flaiyih Matir. Bromage deployed them in the plain of al-Saidiyah, west of Gharandal within Palestine. Lt Ghazi al-Harbi, who was by then unpopular with Glubb, was also sent to the 'South Force', but soon left to retire. With the increase of Jewish activity, a further platoon from the Badiyah District was sent to support the 'South Force'.

On 3 March 1949, the 'South Force' was facing an expected three-pronged attack by the following Jewish forces:

- The Negev Brigade, with the task of advancing through the Negev mountains and desert to Um Rashrash.
- The Golani Brigade, with the task of advancing through Wadi Araba along the Palestine–Jordanian frontier to Um Rashrash.
- The Alexandroni Brigade, with the task of capturing Ain Jadi on the Dead Sea.

Captain Bromage had to choose between fighting a battle against forces 20 times stronger than his own and armed with tanks mounting 76-mm guns in which he would have lost all his forces, or withdraw and save the men under his command. On 7 March he sent a message to the Jordan Arab Army HQ reporting on the situation and asking for instructions. The reply was:

> Withdraw your forces from the following positions: first, Jabal al-Radadi; second, Wadi al-Hayani; third, Ras al-Nagab; fourth, Um Rashrash. Withdraw what you can of weapons and ammunition and destroy heavy equipment.[3]

On the night of 9/10 March, Captain Bromage withdrew his forces including all his weapons, ammunition and heavy equipment, leaving nothing for the advancing Jewish forces, while the Jewish Brigades were advancing towards his positions. He deployed his forces in the Aqaba–Gharandal area within Jordanian territory. On 9 March, the Jews attacked his previous positions only to find them evacuated. On 10 March, the Jews occupied Um Rashrash on the Gulf of Aqaba, as well as certain areas along the front line in the Hebron–Bethlehem sector, as mentioned above. It seemed that certain elements at the United Nations were in collusion with the Jews. Most certainly General Riley was a dedicated pro-Zionist. For on 2 March, 'the United Nations observers in Jordan informed General Lash, Commander of the 1st Division, that they were aware of the Israeli troop movements in the south, and had reported them to their immediate superiors, the United Nations observers in Haifa'.[4] General Riley had concealed the Jewish movements.

While the Iraqi withdrawal from Palestine, which started on 13 March, was on its way, King Abdullah knew very well that the Jordan Arab Army on its own could not defend the Nablus front line as well as its own and the Hebron–Bethlehem sector. The Jewish forces of about 120,000 officers and men could have destroyed the Jordan Arab Army in five days, especially after the defeat of the Egyptian Army and the withdrawal of the Iraqi Army. The now formidable Jewish forces were available to implement the Jewish threat, which constituted the most dangerous situation that had faced Jordan since its creation in 1920.

Under severe pressure, and in a series of night meetings carried out at the Winter Royal Palace at al-Shunah between Jordanian and Jewish negotiators, 'the Jordanians were given to understand that failure to cede the remaining areas of the plain land to the Jews would result *in the loss of the whole of Samaria, if not all Arab Palestine'.*[5] The aim of the Jewish manoeuvres in the negotiations became obvious when they suggested that they would consent to the replacement of the Iraqi Army by the Jordanian Arab Army if the latter agreed to withdraw a certain distance all along the Iraqi front after the takeover. Such a withdrawal amounted to the cession of a belt of an average width of two to three kilometres on the Iraqi front line and with a length of about 180 kilometres (see Map 7). As soon as King Abdullah heard of the Jewish threat he passed on the information to Tawfiq Abu al-Huda, who sent a letter to Glubb asking for a written answer to two questions. According to Glubb the questions were:

1. If we refused this offer, and the Israelis renewed hostilities, could we hold their attack everywhere on the present line?

2. If we could not hold them on the present line, and hostilities were resumed, against the Arab Legion alone, was it possible that the Israeli forces might seize a greater area than that now demanded?
    I replied in writing that, if hostilities were renewed against the Arab Legion alone, we could not hold the present line after the

Iraqis had gone. Moreover, if war recommenced, the Israelis might seize more territory than they were now asking for.[6]

On the morning of 23 March, during the absence of Tawfiq Abu al-Huda, who had gone to Beirut, King Abdullah held a meeting in the Winter Palace at al-Shunah which was attended by the following:

- Said al-Mufti, Acting Prime Minister.
- Muhammad al-Shanqiti, Minister of Education.
- Falah al-Madadhah, Minister of Justice.
- Hussein Sraj, Under Secretary of the Foreign Ministry.
- General J. B. Glubb, Commander of the Jordan Arab Army.
- Abdullah al-Tel, Governor of Jerusalem.
- Dr Shawkat al-Sati, the King's doctor.

According to Abdullah al-Tel, the King opened the meeting by saying:

> You all know that the Arab states had disappointed us and we are alone in the field. The Jordan Army is small and had been planned to defend the frontier and not to occupy Palestine which is full of strong Jews who were brought in by the British. We cannot rely on the Iraqi Army who might disappoint us, and they are compelled to return to Iraq for internal reasons more important than Palestine, and we have promised them to take over from them. The Egyptian, Syrian and Lebanese armies have gone their way. The West has deserted us and we cannot rely on them. If war breaks out we might lose more than the Jews demand and we will lower our foreheads. Then you might lose me, and if I go you will not find one who is better than me or similar to me . . .![7]

Abdullah al-Tel, who was satisfied enough to obey the orders, arranged the meetings between the King and the Jews and attended many of them himself, especially with Moshe Dayan. Al-Tel said:

> My Master, the Jews demanded in yesterday's meeting frontier adjustments for their benefit. Their demands were not logical and they refused our demands. I suggest that Glubb Pasha or Lash should go with the Committee which is negotiating with the Jews because the Jewish Chief of Staff is a representative in the Jewish delegation.
> My Master, the British have commanded the Jordan Arab Army in the war with the Jews. Had you commanded it yourself we

would not be in this situation. It is unjust if you carry the burden of responsibility. The British must negotiate with Jews and carry the responsibility instead of your Majesty.[8]

The King asked Glubb whom he would send along with the Committee, and Glubb replied:

Sir,

You know that the capabilities of the Army are weak, and the British did not give us ammunition after they withdrew from Palestine, and we are alone in the field and it is unthinkable to fight the Jews after they have concentrated their forces against us. As regarding the officers, if Abdullah al-Tel refuses to take part in the Committee, I will send the Director of Operations. I apologise for not attending because I do not wish to see the faces of the Jews. Sir, the Jews are greedy, they want to increase their occupation of land by every means. More important they want to expand Israel at the narrow part because the width of their territory does not exceed ten kilometres there.[9]

In his book, Glubb wrote about the current situation as follows:

On thinking over this problem, only one course seemed to me to be still open. It was a direct appeal to the USA and Britain. It must be remembered that both Israel and Jordan were still bound by the Security Council truce of 18 July 1948. For Israel to resume hostilities with Jordan, merely on the grounds that she was greedy of more territory, would therefore be an even more flagrant defiance of the United Nations than any yet perpetrated. UNO itself, having no forces, would be unable to act, but Britain and America together could undoubtedly call Israel to order. I drove down to see the King at Shuna. The Prime Minister had gone to Beirut. The King liked my suggestion and telegrams were accordingly sent off to London and Washington. Meanwhile the pressure was too much for the Jordan Government. Further Israeli troop movements were reported. The Jordan Government agreed to initial an agreement covering the surrender of territory, in order to gain time. They inserted a clause to the effect that the agreement would not be valid unless it was counter-signed by the Jordan Prime Minister, who was away in Beirut. This would provide a way out if the British and Americans agreed to intervene. Soon afterwards, the reply came from the United States Government. It was to the effect that Washington had been informed that a preliminary agreement had already been initialed.

In view of this fact, the United States Government was unwilling to intervene.[10]

The Government of Jordan, aware of the aggressive designs of the Jews, asked the British Government that the strength of the British Battalion at Aqaba should not be reduced on the signature of the Armistice Agreement. However, the failure of the British and the United States Governments to assist Jordan to resist the Israeli aggressive demands for the land concessions in the Nablus Sector during the negotiations went far to compel King Abdullah and the Jordan Government that, ultimately, they would have to make their own terms with the Jews.

Thus the Jordanian concessions were made under duress after the Jews made some similar concessions. On 23 March 1949, the first agreement was signed to allow the Jordan Arab Army to take over the Iraqi front in the Nablus Sector (see Appendix E and Map 8). An agreement for the amendment of the March 23 agreement was also signed on 31 March 1949 (see Appendix F). The negotiations at Rhodes continued until 3 April 1949, when the Armistice Agreement was signed by both parties, thus officially ending the war between Jordan and the Jews (see Appendix G). The Jordanian Arab Army completed the takeover of the Nablus sector from the 19,000-strong Iraqi force, who completed their withdrawal to Zarqa and Mafraq in Jordan on 12 April 1949.

The incorporation of the areas of Palestine occupied by the Jordan Arab Army and the Iraqi Army was carried a step further by the announcement of the Jordan Government in the *Extraordinary Official Gazette* published on 16 March 1949 laying down the details of administration and procedure and making various heads of departments in Palestine directly responsible to the relevant ministers in the Government at Amman, instead of, as previously, being responsible to the Governor General in the areas occupied. For the Hashemite Kingdom of Jordan, the titles Palestine and Trans-Jordan, used in the past, were changed to West Jordan, or, more colloquially, West Bank of the River Jordan, while the former Jordan became known as East Jordan or East Bank of the River Jordan.

Instead of endeavouring wholeheartedly to work for Arab understanding and a united front against Jewish aggression, the Syrian Government made an attempt to assassinate King Abdullah. On 26 March 1949, a mine was discovered on the main road between Wadi al-Shuaib and al-Shunah, which would have been set off by an electric device connected to a battery, as the King's car passed by on its way between Amman and al-Shunah. Two Palestinians were arrested, one of whom was a known terrorist. In their confessions they implicated another man in whose possession two other mines of the same type were found on the al-Salt main road. They also confessed that they were sent by a man who was acting on behalf of Shukri al-Quwatli, the Syrian President, and al-Haj Amin al-Husseini.

Perhaps the worst tremor that struck the Arab world was the military coup in Damascus by Brigadier Husni al-Zaim, the defeated Commander of the Syrian front. Husni al-Zaim was nothing more than a glorified Sergeant Major with a certain flare for swashbuckling. He was politically naive with no idea of how to run a country, especially Syria, the most ungovernable country in the Arab world. On 30 March, he carried out his military coup against al-Quwatli, and Khalid al-Azm, the Prime Minister. Like a soldier, he disbanded the Syrian Government and Parliament, and claimed power for the armed forces in the interest of the freedom of the people of Syria, whom he later oppressed. Shukri al-Quwatli resigned on 6 April, and on the following day Khalid al-Azm also resigned. Furthermore he disbanded all political parties and seemed to rule Syria as if he was commanding a regiment. King Abdullah was genuinely taken by surprise, and while delighted at the elimination of Shukri al-Quwatli, he saw no immediate hope for the realisation of his dream of Greater Syria. However, on 1 April, Lt Colonel Abdullah al-Tel was sent as the King's personal representative to see Brigadier Husni al-Zaim, the new ruler of Syria, and to assure him that he should have no fear of Jordanian interference in Syrian affairs. The King's trusted messenger was given a friendly welcome and a reply to the King with vague suggestions of exchanging military liaison officers and of a closer union between the armed forces of the two countries. However, Husni al-Zaim did not mention that he and Abdullah al-Tel had agreed to stage a military coup by al-Tel in Jordan with support from Syria. Al-Zaim agreed to the following:

1. He would receive King Abdullah and exile him to the desert of Dair al-Zur, without harming him.

2. Provide financial assistance after the coup for the Jordan Arab Army, if the British stopped their subsidy.

3. Commit part of the Syrian Army on the Jordanian border to help al-Tel against Jewish or British aggression.[11]

A few days later, Sudqi al-Qasim, the Governor of Amman, was the second messenger to Damascus. By this time, Husni al-Zaim was less forthcoming, although still friendly. On his return to Amman, Sudqi al-Qasim informed King Abdullah that, 'as far as he could judge, there was no prospect of making any progress with the Greater Syria scheme'. No further reference was made to closer military contact. It soon became clear that the establishment of contact between the new Syrian régime and Saudi Arabia and Egypt, together with the news that Great Britain, France and America were to recognise the régime, put an end to the speculation about the formation of 'Greater Syria' or, alternatively, the 'Fertile Crescent'.

The friendly contacts between Jordan and the new Syrian régime did not survive beyond the end of April. On the 27th, Syrian military detachments appeared on the Jordanian frontier, and defensive works designed to meet what were said to be imminent attacks from Jordanian territory were commenced in Syrian territory. Husni al-Zaim issued a number of declarations hostile to Jordan. Not a single Jordanian Arab Army soldier was anywhere near the Syrian border at the time. In fact, all the Jordanian Arab Army was in the West Bank. However, al-Zaim's statements drew, in turn, a Jordanian statement in favour of 'Greater Syria'.

King Abdullah sent a telegram to King Abdul Aziz ibn Saud on the subject of the coup in Syria asking for his reaction, and saying that Jordan would remain neutral and would not interfere in Syria. The reply from Ibn Saud was: 'The movement was a disaster for the Arabs and menaced Syria's independence.' It added: 'Saudi Arabia would not tolerate any interference in the internal affairs of Syria.' In this connection, Kirkbride reported:

> King Abdel Aziz does not seem to have been convinced by King Abdullah's first declaration of neutrality because the Saudi Chargé d'Affaires was summoned to Riyadh a few days later. He appears to have convinced his master that Trans-Jordan did not propose to intervene in Syria at present because a second message arrived for King Abdullah thanking him for the wise policy which he was following.

In the meantime, however, reports continued to be received of Saudi troop concentrations round Hayil and some uneasiness on this score was shown by the Trans-Jordan authorities.[12]

The British efforts to mediate between the Egyptian and the Jordanian Governments advanced a step further with friendly talks between Khashabah, the Egyptian Foreign Minister, and Tawfiq Abu al-Huda, the Jordanian Prime Minister, at Beirut. Meanwhile, the Egyptian military command in Hebron was inciting the Palestinians to organise demonstrations and hostile actions against the Government of Jordan and the proposed union between Jordan and the Arabs of Palestine.

The armistice agreement was received very badly in Palestine. It was believed that the Jordanian takeover of the Iraqi positions and the withdrawal of the Iraqi Army was part of a conspiracy to allow Jordan to surrender more Palestinian land to the Jews. Some statements were made by Iraqi soldiers claiming that their withdrawal was a betrayal of the Arab cause and that 'they were all prepared to fight to the death' reinforced this belief. Soon after, a deputation of agitated notables from the district of Nablus went to Amman to protest against the terms of the armistice agreement and demanded that the Iraqi Army should remain in position. They also proposed to visit Baghdad and appeal for the same. They had a meeting with the Iraqi Minister of Defence who was at Amman, during which he told them that 'Iraq had made sufficient sacrifices for an unworthy and ungrateful Palestine and that nothing would induce him to delay the withdrawal of the Iraqi army'.[13]

The Nablus deputation had an audience with King Abdullah and expressed their concerns to him. King Abdullah explained that Jordan had been abandoned by its Arab allies and the international boycott had deprived the Jordan Arab Army of ammunition, which was usually supplied by the British Government. He assured them that he had no alternative but to accept the terms imposed by the Jews and ended by saying that he wanted less argument and more obedience from his new subjects. The Arab press attributed to King Abdullah this statement: 'Great Britain and the United States had pressed him strongly to accept the armistice.' That was not quite correct. What he actually said was: 'The attitude which [he] had observed in the case of Great Britain and America had compelled [him] to accept the armistice.'[14]

By the beginning of May 1949, the application of the armistice lines between the Hashemite Kingdom of Jordan and Israel in accordance with the Rhodes Agreement commenced under supervision of the Armistice Commission. A number of map discrepancies were found in the demarcation of the lines, which had to be sorted out by the United Nations observers. In the Bethlehem area the Israelis used force in order to push the Jordan Arab Army back from the claimed line. In the Jenin area, the Chairman of the Armistice Commission, General Riley, made a decision in favour of Israel – as usual.

During the first half of 1949, the Jordan Government was engaged in negotiations with the Jews regarding the situation in Syria, and in caring for the refugees who had doubled the population of the country. It was not active in the day-to-day administration of the occupied areas of Palestine. However, with the intention of starting the constitutional process for the unity of Jordan and Palestine, the King formed a new Government on 2 May 1949. Abu al-Huda was appointed Prime Minister for the seventh time and three Ministers were appointed from Palestine (see Table 10.2).

TABLE 10.2
The new Jordanian Government, May 1949

- Tawfiq Abu al-Huda, Prime Minister.
- Muhammad al-Shanqiti, Qadhi Qudhah (Chief Justice) and Education.
- Said al-Mufti, Internal Affairs.
- Rouhi Abd al-Hadi (WB),* Foreign Affairs.
- Falah al-Madadhah, Justice.
- Sulaiman al-Sukkar, Finance and Economics.
- Khulousi al-Khairi (WB), Trade and Agriculture.
- Musa Nassir (WB), Communications.

*WB = West Bank.

The Ministry of Foreign Affairs addressed a note to all the diplomatic representatives in Amman indicating that in future the correct title of the country, as provided for in the Jordanian constitution of 1947, should be used. He stated that when using the English language, reference should be made to 'The Hashemite Kingdom of Jordan'. Among the diplomatic representatives who still used the title Trans-Jordan were the British diplomats. All Palestinian residents in areas controlled by the Hashemite Kingdom of Jordan would be deemed Jordanians for all purposes, and a promise for elections to be held for a Parliament representing both Palestinians and Jordanians was made public.

The spread of the news that Syria had received arms, ammunition and war material from France long before the armistice was signed between Syria and Israel, and without treaty obligations to supply arms on the part of France, while the Hashemite Kingdom of Jordan was still being deprived of arms and ammunition for the Jordanian Arab Army even after the armistice agreement, caused a mounting wave of resentment in Amman. The fact that the arms supplied to Syria were of somewhat ancient vintage and not of great military value did not affect the reaction in the political and military circles in Jordan. Furthermore, the admission of the Jewish state to the United Nations, while the earlier application of the Hashemite Kingdom of Jordan for admission remained unanswered, also caused discontent and frustration. The British Government was criticised for failing to support Jordan and for not opposing Israel's admission by its veto power.

Meanwhile, during the month of May, reports were received by the British Legation in Amman from various sources that a military coup in Jordan was imminent. No evidence was found of such plans. The reports seem to have originated from a certain amount of talk by Iraqi Army and Jordan Arab Army junior officers about removing power from the political leaders who had mishandled the Palestine affair. Abdullah al-Tel later wrote that he had been contemplating a coup with a few officers, but this remained within the bounds of mere talk with the junior officers around him.[15] Thereafter, a Royal Command was issued to amalgamate the Royal Guards with the 10th Infantry Regiment and to award the new unit the title of the 'Hashemite' Regiment, commanded by Lt Colonel Habis al-Majali, the former Commander of the 10th Regiment.[16]

Meanwhile, the King spoke to Kirkbride about the application of the Anglo–Jordanian Treaty of 1948 to the defence of the West Bank of the River Jordan. Kirkbride wrote to the Foreign Office regarding the problem of how far the British Government could give Jordan the support that might be needed to resist further Israeli pressure during the forthcoming negotiations for a final peace settlement. Kirkbride suggested: 'The immediate application of the Anglo–Trans-Jordan Treaty to Eastern Palestine would be of value if no effective pressure can be exercised on

Israel while the Peace Settlement is being negotiated; but that otherwise it might tend to crystallise the present frontier to the disadvantage of the Arabs.' The Foreign Office replied as follows:

> We cannot rely on the United States exerting any effective pressure on Israel during the negotiations for a Peace Settlement, if we are to judge from past experience. There were a number of reports recently that President Truman was becoming impatient with Israel but that has not prevented the United States from being largely instrumental in securing a preliminary vote of 33 to 11 for the admission of Israel in the Ad Hoc Political Committee at Lake Success.
>
> It would, however, be unwise for Trans-Jordan to make any formal annexation of the area. And the Legal Adviser has ruled that to extend the Treaty before a settlement is reached would be contrary to the terms of the Israeli–Trans-Jordan Armistice and to our obligations as a member of the United Nations.
>
> In these circumstances I think that not only would there have to be no formal annexation of Eastern Palestine by Jordan, but also any assurance we gave to King Abdullah would have to be informal and confidential. I would therefore suggest telling King Abdullah that in the light of the Anglo–Jordanian Treaty we should give him all the support in our power in the event of any Israeli attack on his forces arising from an attempt to put further pressure on Jordan during the negotiations for a Peace Settlement. We should inform the US Government that we were giving this assurance to Jordan and point out to them that we in no way wished to crystallise the present frontier but that we regarded it as a minimum from the point of view of the Palestine Arabs. We should of course have to clear this with the Chiefs of Staff.[17]

On 11 May 1949, the General Assembly of the United Nations approved a resolution admitting the State of Israel to the United Nations, noting Israel's declaration that it unreservedly accepted the obligations of the United Nations Charter and undertook to honour them. Until that date, and since the beginning of 1946, the Jews had not honoured even one principle of the Charter of the United Nations and had never adhered to any of the United Nations resolutions.

Many political and administrative problems were heaped on Jordan during the second half of 1949. The presence of a large number of displaced and disgruntled Palestinian refugees had an extremely disturbing effect on the life and economy of the country. Later in the year, however, there was a tendency of the refugees to establish themselves and their business in Amman, Irbid and Zarqa. Some of them decided to settle down, bringing new and better methods of agriculture, handcrafts and businesses of various kinds. The main problem was education, where Jordanian schools were not able to accommodate all Palestinian children. Classrooms were congested and a severe shortage of teachers affected the standard of education for all. The Health Department was overwhelmed with an abnormally large number of cases of infection among refugees (see Table 10.3).

TABLE 10.3
Cases of infection among refugees reported during 1949

Type of infection	Number of cases
Smallpox	194
Typhus	42
Dysentery	819
Pneumonia	442
Relapsing fever	38
Enteric fever	258

A report by UNICEF on Jordan indicated that out of the total number of 518,488 refugees present in the country, no less than 270,613 were children below the age of 15 and nursing or expectant mothers in receipt of milk and supplementary alimentation. Of these beneficiaries about one-fifth were in the East Bank and four-fifths in the West Bank. The total number of refugees quoted by the officials of UNICEF was considerably higher than the estimate given by various institutions in the East Bank and the West Bank. This appears to indicate a drift of refugees back to the West Bank. The increase in the total may well have been due to refugees moving back from Syria and the Lebanon as well as to additions from Palestine itself following various readjustments of the truce line with Israel.[18]

However, the main problem facing Jordan during the year was the reorganisation and development of the Jordan Arab Army, which was thinly deployed in a defensive role along an armistice line of about 600 kilometres. The Army was still short of weapons, ammunition and equipment; the shortage of senior and junior staff officers became a major task of enlistment, training and appointment at all levels, and the promotion and appointment of qualified Arab officers was much needed. Above all, the financial burden was astronomical. Compared with other Arab countries the financial burden of Jordan due to the war and its aftermath is worthy of mention.

During the war and until the middle of 1949, Jordan had maintained an army with average strength, including expansion, of about 16,000 officers and men, whereas the budget provided for an army of only 6,507 (See Table 10.4.)

TABLE 10.4
**Actual expenditure for the 16,000 officers and men
of the Jordanian Army**

Source	Expenditure (sterling)
British Subsidy	£2,500,000
Arab League	£230,000
Debt to HMG	£2,000,000
Jordan Government	£84,000
Debts carried to next year	£380,000
Total	**£5,194,000**

Glubb drew a comparison between the financial situation of the Jordanian Army and that of the Egyptian Army:

On the day that the Egyptian Army crossed the frontier into Palestine, the Egyptian Parliament voted, I think, £45,000,000 for war expenses, in addition to the army peacetime budget. The Arab Legion spent £2,694,000 during this year over and above their peacetime budget. The average strength of the two armies was possibly about the same. The Egyptians had fewer soldiers at the beginning but more at the end. Nevertheless during the year, the Egyptian Army spent twenty times as much as the Arab Legion.

At the end of the year, in spite of this expenditure, the Egyptian Army had lost nearly all the part of Palestine for which they were responsible. The Arab Legion, for one-twentieth part of the Egyptian expenditure, were still holding all the area for which they were responsible (except Lydda and Ramleh) and had also taken over the Hebron area for which the Egyptians were responsible.[19]

While on leave in England during May 1949, General Glubb negotiated with the Foreign Office regarding the subsidy for the Jordan Arab Army. The British Government offered a subsidy of £3,000,000 for maintenance and £500,000 for capital equipment for the financial year 1949/50. This amount was enough for 11,000 men in peacetime, not for the state of no-war-no-peace in which the Jordan Arab Army found itself. On 1 April 1949, however, the strength of the Jordan Arab Army rose to 17,500 regulars – or 5,770 soldiers more than could be paid for with the British subsidy. (The Hashemite Regiment of 730 men has to be added to the 11,000 officers and men to find the authorised establishment.)

Furthermore, as from 1 April 1949, the Jordan Arab Army took over about 2,000 irregular Palestinian partisan men from the Iraqi Army. A further 750 men were taken over from al-Jihad al-Muqaddas and remnants of the Liberation Army. Thus, the strength of the Jordanian Arab Army was increased to about 17,500 regulars and 2,750 irregulars; a total of 20,250 on a budget sufficient only for 11,730 regulars for the year 1949/50.

While General Glubb was endeavouring to convince the British Government of the need to increase the subsidy for the Jordanian Army, the Chief of General Staff pointed out to the Minister of Defence that if the Jordan Government retained more than 11,730 men during the first half of the year, it should have to reduce the strength to about 6,000 during the second half of the year. The basic 11,730 of the regular army were, by then, all highly trained soldiers with good experience of war. Had they been discharged, they could not have been replaced with equally good soldiers later. With the aggressive designs of the Israelis looming and threatening, a reduction of the strength of the Jordan Arab Army would have meant its destruction in the event of renewed hostilities. The Chief of General Staff argued that it was most undesirable to allow the strength to fall below 11,730 officers and men during the second half of the year. He then requested the following:

1. That the surplus regulars and irregulars be discharged as quickly as possible.

2. That the Jordan Government pay for the surplus regulars and the irregulars until they were discharged.

3. That the British subsidy of £3,000,000 be reserved for the maintenance of the regular army of 11,000.[20]

An agreement was reached with the Minister of Finance to pay for the additional strength of 7,250 officers and men, and for the HQ of the Jordan Arab Army to carry out a gradual reduction of its strength starting in June by 6,000, during July by 5,000, in August by 3,500 and September by 2,500. However, these reductions remained ink on paper, for during June 1949 the Israelis suddenly attacked and captured Jabal al-Mukabbir and their troops opened fire with all weapons at the whole Arab part of the city of Jerusalem inflicting heavy casualties on the civilian population. Thereafter, the Jordan Government ordered that the discharge of regular and irregular troops should cease.

While in London, General Glubb made an after-dinner speech to the Anglo-Arab Association, where he made some sincere, but critical, remarks about British Government policy in the Middle East. He particularly criticised its decision not to supply Jordan with arms and ammunition during the periods of the ceasefire. He argued that it was far better for Britain to increase its support for King Abdullah and show the rest of the world that he was a valued ally. Among those listening to his speech, the Labour Minister at the Colonial Office, Lord Hall, thought that Glubb's remarks were an attack on the British Government. In the altercation that followed dinner, Lord Hall threatened to report his criticism to the Foreign Office. Glubb was not in the mood to tolerate the storm that his sincere and refreshing remarks were to engender; he wrote in his defence that he was entirely innocent of any intent to criticise the Government:

> I am, of course, no longer a British officer, and can say what I like. But my intention is quite otherwise. I still wish to work as if I were a servant of His Majesty's Government and my object was to improve, not to injure, the understanding between Britain and Trans-Jordan. I was therefore somewhat distressed by this unfortunate incident.[21]

On 15 May 1949, an Israeli force on patrol in their area of Wadi Araba crossed the armistice line into Jordan and molested some Jordanian farmers who were harvesting crops. In the skirmish that followed the Jordanian farmers inflicted some casualties on the Israeli patrol. Soon afterwards, the Israelis appeared to be attempting to move into Jordanian territory with a large force. The United Nations observers were immediately informed by the Jordanian side of the Mixed Armistice

Commission. Later in the day, representatives of both parties met at the scene of the incident and restored calm to the area.

Meanwhile, there was a general and progressive deterioration taking place in the West Bank in both the economic and political spheres. Most of the leading notables and former British civil servants of the British Mandate blamed King Abdullah and the Jordan Government for this state of affairs. Kirkbride sent this report to the Foreign Office:

> The crisis, which is now threatening both sides of the Jordan, is inevitably the result of loss of Arab wealth and property in Palestine, the dissipation of liquid assets of refugees and general disruption of trade. There is every sign of these economic conditions continuing to worsen . . .

> 3. Factors affecting the political side seem to be the growing realisation in Palestine that the Arab states other than this country (Jordan), have in fact washed their hands of the problem and that the only changes likely to be effected in the present front line are more likely to be to the benefit of Israel than the Arabs, having regard to the relative weakness in the military sense of the Kingdom of Jordan. The delay in final union of both sides of the Jordan has also enabled those elements in Palestine which are opposed to the Hashemites to regain some of their lost ground and resume political activity.

> 4. Shortcomings of the Ramallah broadcasting station and the much more objectionable tone that has been adopted recently by the Arab press which is published in Palestine are symptoms of the unhealthy state of the country. I have spoken to the King and the Prime Minister about both press and broadcasts on more than one occasion but they appear to feel that there is no point in stirring up trouble over superficial matters while the real cause remains untouched. Their view is that little can be done to remedy the matter until formal union of the two countries is completed.

> 5. I am inclined to believe that they are right. It would deprive the opposition in Palestine of the opportunity of suggesting that union is not a foregone conclusion, it would enable representatives of the Palestine Arabs to be elected to both Chambers of Parliament and to voice the opinions and complaints of their constituents and it would enable the Palestinians to share equally in the few economic benefits which are available at the moment. Finally, it would enable the authorities to deal firmly and as of right with the many mischief makers present in Palestine, a thing they are reluctant to do so long as they are technically only caretakers. It would not, however,

produce any large sums of money with which to restore prosperity in Palestine as those just do not exist.

6. In brief, therefore, things in Palestine are not right and the obvious remedies at the hand-over are:

(a) Union of the two countries (and application of the Anglo–Trans-Jordan Treaty to the whole).
(b) Issue of arms and ammunition to the Arab Legion which would do something to remove the feeling of weakness which is prejudicing all negotiations with Israel and has produced unfounded accusations of bribery and corruption.[22]

During June, while the negotiations between Jordan and Israel were suspended, the Israelis attempted to approach King Abdullah with a trap whereby they could attack and capture the whole of the West Bank, including Jerusalem. Glubb was very alert to the Israeli intentions and methods as can be seen from his letter to Kirkbride:

> You said the other day that the attitude of the Jews to King Abdullah had changed a lot, because they are afraid of Husni Zaim. You quoted their offer to return Qatamon as an indication of this.
>
> In practice, however, the offer to return Qatamon seems to me more like a trick. In return they want Shaikh Jarrah and Mount Scopus, the police fortress and the country almost to Shaafat, so as to connect them with Hadassa and the Hebrew University by a solid block of country. Shaikh Jarrah and the police training is the most important plot of ground in all Palestine. If they got these, they not only dominate all Jerusalem, but they have completely isolated Hebron from Jabal Nablus. They only have a couple of kilometres more to advance in order to occupy Bethany (a village in a tiny valley under a spur of the Mount of Olives) and drive down the Jericho road, which means taking the whole of Palestine. Thus while superficially Qatamon, Beqa'a (and so on) are much more valuable as house property than Shaikh Jarrah, and the offer thus seems tempting, it all looks to me merely a subtle trap!
>
> Apart from this question of Qatamon and Shaikh Jarrah, the Jews are being extremely arrogant and aggressive all along the front. I see no indications that they mean to modify their hostility towards us.[23]

During July 1949, the last units of the Iraqi Army finally left Jordan for Iraq. In spite of a few political chinwags here and there in Jordan and Palestine who criticised the Iraqi Army for not attacking the Jews while the Egyptian Army was being attacked, the Iraqi rank and file did their best for Palestine and made great sacrifices for its cause. To say the least, they defended the sector of Nablus and handed it over intact to the Jordan Arab Army. Their presence and comradeship with the Jordanian Arab Army until the armistice agreement was signed was remembered with gratitude then and in later years.

On 1 July 1949, the King issued a Royal command appointing the administration of the West Bank as shown in Table 10.5.[24]

On 7 July 1949, Tawfiq Abu al-Huda left Jordan, taking two months' leave during which he visited Turkey, Italy, Switzerland, France and England. Said al-Mufti was appointed Acting Prime Minister during his absence. Just before he left, the relations between al-Huda and the King, which had been deteriorating for some time past, became again more strained. The apparent inability and reluctance of other ministers to take any decisions in the absence of the Prime Minister caused the King considerable irritation, which culminated in his insistence on taking Samir al-Rifai, Abu al-Huda's most outspoken opponent, with him on his visit to Tehran. When the decision became known to the Cabinet, King Abdullah sent a message to the ministers to the effect that they should 'reflect well on his action and draw what conclusions they wished'. When, during the course of his visit to Iran, he nominated Samir al-Rifai to a specially created post of Minister of the Palace with a rank equal to that of the Prime Minister, the members of the Cabinet had doubts as to whether they retained the King's confidence. The question of the resignation of the Government was discussed at a Cabinet meeting when efforts to contact Tawfiq Abu al-Huda in Europe had proved abortive, and it was decided to wait until his return in early September. In the circumstances it was felt that a new government would not be formed until the King's return from his proposed visit to London.[25]

On 14 July 1949, the King, accompanied by the Turkish Minister, visited the Jerusalem and Ramallah areas of Palestine. The welcome he received was enthusiastic; crowds waited patiently for hours by the road side and whole villages turned out to applaud as the royal car went by.

On 11 August 1949, the Security Council of the United Nations approved two resolutions: the first expressing appreciation of the work of the Acting Mediator, and the second noting with satisfaction the Armistice Agreements, considering that they superseded the truce provided for in the resolutions of 29 May 1948 and 15 July 1948, and relieved the mediator of any further responsibility.

TABLE 10.5
Administration of the West Bank, July 1949

The Administration
- Falah al-Madadhah, Governor of the Administration and Wali of Jerusalem
- Jamal Taoqan, Assistant Governor
- Najib al-Bawarshi, Qaim Maqam Jerusalem
- Adnan al-Husaini, Qaim Maqam Jerusalem
- Muhammad Abd al-Hadi, Qaim Maqam Ramallah
- Ibrahim Taqtaq, Qaim Maqam Bethlehem
- Saad al-Din al-Majali, Qaim Maqam Ariha (Jericho)
- Ahmad al-Khalil, Mutasarrif of Nablus
- Ishaq al-Nashashibi, Qaim Maqam Nablus
- Muhib al-Khayyat, Qaim Maqam Tulkarm
- Said al-Dajani, Qaim Maqam Jenin
- Naim Abd al-Hadi, Mutasarrif of Hebron
- Kashif Murad, Qaim Maqam Hebron
- Najati al-Nashashibi, Director Passport Office

The Judiciary
- Majid Abd al-Hadi, President Court of Appeal
- Hasan al-Katib, Member of Court of Appeal
- Ali Zain al-Aabedin, Member
- Hikmat al-Taji, Member
- Ilyas Khuri, Member
- Shukri al-Muhtadi, President of Central Court
- Daoud Abu Ghazalah, President of Central Court
- Faiq Halazun, Recorder of High Court
- Bisharah Aazar, Judge
- Fayiz Saadah, Judge
- Salim Aazzuri, Judge
- Jaafar Hashim, Judge
- Musbah al-Kazimi, Judge
- Khalil al-Aabushi, Judge
- Muhammad Ali Nashashibi, Judge
- Naim Touqan, Assistant Attorney
- Hanna Khalaf, Assistant Attorney
- Kamal al-Dajani, Attorney General

Information
- Azmi al-Nashashibi, Director of Information
- Thabit al-Khalidi, Assistant Director
- Ihsan Hashim, Jerusalem Broadcasting Station
- Muhammad Adib al-Aamiri, Director of Censorship Office

The plague of military coups in Syria shocked that country again, when at 0430 hours on 14 August 1949, Husni al-Zaim and his Prime Minister, Muhsin al-Barazi, were attacked and arrested at their homes.

They were taken to al-Mazzah Prison, where they were tried by court martial, convicted and executed by firing squad within two hours. Some 176 bullets were found in al-Zaim's body when his family examined it four months and 20 days later.[26]

Sami al-Hinnawi, another glorified Sergeant Major, took over the country and appointed Hashim al-Atasi as Prime Minister. The new coup came as a complete surprise to political circles, including King Abdullah who calmly foresaw the disintegration of Syria. In spite of the critical situation in the region, the King refused to change his plans to visit England. However, both King Abdullah and the Government recognised the new regime and exchanged messages with al-Hinnawi. Thus, the Syrian people lost their will and what democratic institutions they had before al-Zaim's and al-Hinnawi's quasi-military rule of the country.

During his visit to London in August, King Abdullah met the Foreign Secretary, Ernest Bevin, to discuss the situation in Jordan and the Middle East – including the recent coup in Syria. They also discussed the situation in the Muslim world – particularly Turkey, Pakistan and Iran. Lessons of political wisdom and acumen could be learnt from their words as can be seen from the minutes of their meeting in Appendix D. The King left England for Spain by sea on 3 September after a highly successful visit. The Spanish tour hosted by General Franco was also successful. The King asked King Farouq for a meeting in Alexandria on his way back to Jordan, but typical of his immature political attitude, King Farouq did not respond and King Abdullah diverted his route to Beirut.

At Beirut, Tawfiq Abu al-Huda met the Prime Minister of the Lebanon in the presence of the President of the Republic and Hamid Franjiyah, the Minister for Foreign Affairs. They asked him whether he had any objection to sending a representative or to attending a meeting of the Arab League which they felt was now due. The *Official Gazette* recorded his reply as follows:

> He had no objection in principle but would prefer first to endeavour to come to some agreement with them, and, if possible, the Syrian ministers also, regarding two matters which seemed likely to be a cause of disagreement at such a meeting. The two points he had in mind were, firstly, the desirability of removing Abd al-Rahman Pasha Azzam from the post of Secretary-General, or at least, the necessity of curtailing his powers; secondly, the hostility of the

Egyptian Government to the formal union of Eastern Palestine and the Kingdom of Jordan, and the recent activities of al-Haj Amin al-Husseini in that connection.

The Lebanese Ministers replied that, as regards Azzam Pasha, they shared Tewfiq Pasha's views but they felt that, if that point was raised first, the Egyptian reactions might prejudice any chance of the meeting of the League producing useful results. They proposed, therefore, that Tewfiq Pasha's second point should be given priority and that the attack on Azzam Pasha reserved for a favourable but later opportunity.

As regards the future of Arab Palestine they expressed the view that any attempt to set up an independent Arab Palestine state at the present moment would be folly and an invitation to further Israeli aggression; the urgent need was to preserve and consolidate the areas left to the Arabs and to ensure their future safety by including them in existing Arab states; it was obvious that Gaza could only go to Egypt and Eastern Palestine to the Jordan, while any remnant of Galilee that could be rescued should be attached to Syria.

It was agreed that this policy should be supported at the League by the Lebanese and Jordan delegations and Tewfiq Pasha was asked to endeavour to secure Syrian support on his way through Damascus.[27]

Abu al-Huda proceeded to Damascus on his way to Amman, and met with the Syrian Prime Minister, Hashim al-Atasi, who had the same views about Abd al-Rahman Azzam as the Lebanese Prime Minister. In his presentation of his points of view, Tawfiq Abu al-Huda covered the same subjects he discussed with the Lebanese. Before giving his reply on the issue of incorporating Eastern Palestine into Jordan, Hashim al-Atasi inquired about Tawfiq's attitude towards the question of 'Greater Syria'. According to the *Official Gazette*, Tawfiq replied:

His Government still maintained its earlier stand, namely, that it was in principle, in favour of closer union but that it did not consider the time to be ripe; it was, in any case, entirely opposed to any form of compulsion from either party. He added that the attitude of King Abdullah on this matter had been modified by the present moves towards union between Syria and Iraq. The King, for selfish reasons, did not view such a union with favour and he feared that any activities in connection with the Greater Syria scheme might precipitate the Syrian–Iraqi union and so extinguish finally any chance which he might have of expanding his realm northwards.

It was for this reason that his recent utterances on the subject had been in line with Tawfiq Pasha's own views.[28]

Hashim al-Atasi promised to support the Lebanese and Jordanian delegates at the meeting of the League of Arab States with regard to the future of Eastern Palestine. He also undertook to examine the question of exchanging diplomatic representatives with Jordan.

King Abdullah and the Prime Minister returned to Amman on 25 September. Also accompanying the King was Samir al-Rifai, the Minister at the Royal Palace, the most outspoken critic of Tawfiq Abu al-Huda and his Government. Perie-Gordon, the Acting British Minister at Amman, reported:

> Samir Pasha makes no secret of his determination to do all he can to oust the Prime Minister while Tawfiq Pasha Abu al-Huda for his part, invigorated by his two-month tour in Europe, shows the greatest reluctance to relinquish office. Larger and bigger triumphal arches than ever before were erected all over Amman (to the great confusion of the traffic) to indicate the Government's joy at the Monarch's safe return to his Capital and the Prime Minister himself gave a state banquet in the King's honour on the last day of the month. If the object of this costly entertainment was to keep the Government in the King's good graces, it must have failed at least partially in its object as His Majesty expressed considerable displeasure that his Minister of the Palace had not been invited to attend.
>
> Samir Pasha al-Rifai in the meanwhile appears to be making use of his office accommodation in the Royal Diwan for 'consultations' with potential members of a future government under his direction. His general line of policy at present is 'realism' as regards refugees, the incorporation of Arab Palestine in the Jordan if necessary at the cost of a breach with the Arab League and eventually a peace with the Jews.
>
> The King in his turn has privately confessed to considerable amusement at being able to study the antics of the Prime Minister and his would-be successor at short range and is anxious to try the experiment of seeing how long they can both remain simultaneously in their respective offices. He remarked that the present set-up makes them both far more considerate to his personal wishes than either has ever found it possible to be in the past.[29]

Meanwhile, following King Abdullah's visit to London, the incorporation of Arab Palestine into Jordan was discussed by the various departments of the British Government, and information was passed to all British embassies and legations concerned – including the British representative at the United Nations. By the middle of September, the attitude of the British and United States Governments was described in a telegram from the Foreign Office to Ernest Bevin in Washington:

1. In your conversation with King Abdullah on 22 August you told him we favoured the incorporation of Arab Palestine into Jordan but felt that the time for this was not yet quite ripe. You mentioned that you had discussed the point with Mr Acheson previously and hoped to discuss it with him again in America. As I understand you may be discussing Middle East question with Mr Acheson this afternoon, I am telegraphing urgently some relevant considerations on this point.

2. When we have previously discussed this question with the United States Government they have felt that the unilateral annexation of Arab Palestine by the Jordan Government might provoke the Israelis into some rash action and would also freeze the Israeli frontiers and remove any possibility of compensation being given to the Arabs for e.g. Western Galilee.

3. The United States Government have also in the past advised the Jordan Government against separate negotiations with Israel. We have given similar advice.

4. The Conciliation Commission is about to adjourn until 20 October. It is doubtful whether even then it will make any progress with the territorial settlement, at any rate in advance of lengthy discussions resulting from the work of the Economic Survey Mission. Unless therefore some special action is taken the incorporation of Arab Palestine in Jordan may be postponed for many months.

5. Arab Palestine is at present comparatively quiet. The Jordan Government are unobtrusively extending their normal administration but it has become clear that the uncertain status of the territory is a serious obstacle to co-ordinated economic development and to the orderly resettlement of refugees. It seems most unfortunate that these obstacles should continue to exist when almost everyone concerned recognises that the incorporation of Arab Palestine in Jordan is inevitable and desirable. There seems no fundamental reason why this particular part of the Palestine settlement should not be dealt with in advance. This could be entirely without prejudice to further work by the Conciliation Commission and the Economic Survey Mission and also without prejudice to the Jerusalem settlement and

to the final fixing of frontiers outside the area now held by Jordan and to the conclusion of arrangements for outlets to the sea in the interests of both Israel and the Arabs. The work of the Economic Survey Mission would be much easier if this part of the territorial settlement could be finally decided at once.

6. As you know the difficulties of giving assistance to Jordan in the event of armed attack have been emphasised by the Chiefs of Staff. This makes it desirable not to risk provoking such attack if this can be avoided. On the other hand once the annexation took place and was recognised by us we should certainly have to regard the treaty with Jordan as extending to this new territory and the consequences of our failing to honour it in the event of attack on Jordan would be exceedingly serious throughout the Middle East.[30]

The Palestine Arab Liberal Party, which was founded by Ahmad al-Khalil, the Governor (Mutasarrif) of the Nablus District, held a meeting in Nablus on 28 October at which its executive committee decided to submit a memorandum to the Prime Minister and the Governor-General demanding the abolition of customs and visas between the East and West Banks of the River Jordan; a larger allocation of hard currency to West Bank merchants; and the abolition of taxation on imports and exports. The Party had increased its membership and decided to open more branches in the West Bank. Among the members of the Party were Walid Salah, Naim Touqan, Fuad Atallah and Jamil Abd al-Hadi. All these members and many others held Civil Service posts in the West Bank.

The old Palestine Defence Party went into action by holding several meetings in Jerusalem and Ramallah during the month of October. The party was established in 1934 and was active during the revolt of 1936–9. Since then, the party had tended to fade away; thus the attempt to revive its influence. The leader of the party was Raghib al-Nashashibi, the newly appointed Governor-General of the West Bank and the Wali of Jerusalem.

The two branches of the Arab Baath Socialist Party were secretly active in Jordan and Palestine. Two of its founding members in the West Bank – Abdullah al-Rimawi and Abdullah Niawas – were arrested on orders from Abu al-Huda and sent to a detention camp in Bayir in the southern desert of Jordan. Both were lawyers and extremely eloquent in opposing the armistice agreement. They had established several branches of the Baath Party in the Jerusalem–Ramallah area and had members all over the West Bank. Abdullah Niawas was released and returned to Jerusalem, where he practised law, but al-Rimawi remained in detention and went on a hunger strike on 18 October 1949. Raghib al-Nashashibi was using his good office with the Prime Minister to release him. Meanwhile, the moderate and down-to-earth mayors of the cities and towns in the West Bank held several meetings and decided to send telegrams to the Secretary-General of the Arab League and the delegations of the Arab States at Cairo. Reporting on the meeting, Kirkbride wrote:

> The Palestinian Arabs, both Moslem and Christian, fully supported the union of Arab Palestine with the Kingdom of the Jordan under the sovereignty of King Abdullah. They deprecated the policy of their former political leaders, which had been responsible for the Palestine disaster, and denied them the right to set up any separate government for the country. They affirmed that the Jordan delegation at the Arab League Council was the only body with the right to speak in their name. The press stated that the conference which drafted the Jerusalem telegram was attended by representatives from Jerusalem and district, the Supreme Muslim Council, representatives of the Christian Communities, the Chamber of Commerce, the Palestine Arab Workers Society, and notables. The telegram was dispatched as a result of a meeting of the village Councils of the Ramallah District, who added for good measure that they would not accept the internationalisation of Jerusalem. Although it appears that this widespread action was most likely the result of some special suggestion from Amman, the universal response was quite noteworthy and indicative of the comparative ease with which anti-Mufti sentiment could be consistently exploited in Arab Palestine if a proper degree of harmony between Jordanians and Palestinians in this and other matters could be maintained. Baha al Din Touqan, the Jordan Minister in Cairo, is reported to have produced these telegrams at a meeting of the Arab League, and to have been forced to admit that the political opinions of the Mayors of Arab Palestine were not necessarily those of the people.[31]

On 25 October, Kamal Nasser, a member of the Baath Party of Ramallah, published an article in the Jerusalem newspaper *Filistin*, in which he deprecated the action of 'the hypocritical Palestinian Mayors and other notables sending telegrams to the Arab League at the bidding', he implied, 'of [King Abdullah]'. The newspaper was suspended for a month. Sources other than the press stated that the Mayors' telegrams all contained support for King Abdullah on the specific question of internationalisation, which, in view of the Christian representation in the conferences that preceded them, scarcely seemed likely. The King was angry and asked Raghib al-Nashashibi to send Kamal Nasser to Bayir on detention, but Raghib declined and informed the King that suspension of the newspaper for one month was enough punishment.

Abdullah al-Tel, the former Governor of Jerusalem, who was instrumental in the preparations and conduct of the negotiations between King Abdullah and the Jews on the armistice agreement and other agreements in Jerusalem, decided to leave Jordan and take political asylum in Egypt. On 4 October, he managed to send all his secret papers to Damascus, and on the following day, as prearranged, he crossed the frontier to Damascus where he met Muhammad Subhi Abu Ghanimah and Mishel Aflaq, the leader of the Baath Party in Syria, who encouraged him to go to Cairo. On 10 October, al-Tel flew to Cairo with his mother, his wife and his brother.

On 9 October, King Abdullah started a tour of the West Bank, visiting every district. Accompanied by Raghib al-Nashashibi, he spent the first night in Hebron at al-Jaabari's house and was entertained by him at a dinner attended by notables and leaders of public opinion. On the following day he had lunch with the Mayor of Bethlehem and was greeted by all the notables of the city – of all religious denominations. During the lunch given in his honour by the Mayor of Bethlehem (Eisa al-Bandak) the King, in reply to the Mayor's welcome, did not forget the outspoken statement by the Mayor in favour of the internationalisation of Jerusalem. The King said:

> I have taken note of what you have said today as I took note of what you said when things were not going well for us. Right cannot be vanquished. The Arabs are a great and ancient race and they must work together if they are to reach their objectives. Our views regarding Jerusalem, Bethlehem and Bait Jala are known to all. There are some who talk about their being internationalised, but they are Arab places, containing the tombs of Christians and Moslems alike, and we shall not forsake them. We know both our past and our future, and, if God wills, we respect religion and preserve tradition. I thank the Mayor for the speech and extend my affection and protection to all the religious minded.[32]

On both occasions, speeches were made by notables recognising Arab unity between Jordan and Palestine and King Abdullah as their King.

The King spent the nights of the 11th and 12th in his house at Ramallah. He visited Jerusalem, prayed in the al-Aqsa Mosque and was entertained by Raghib al-Nashashibi at lunch. He visited Nablus on the 12th and 13th, and resided in the house of Haj Maazuz al-Masri. During his tours, he stopped at many villages, visited schools, units of the Jordan Arab Army, units of the newly formed al-Haras al-Watani (National Guard) and other institutions. Each mayor made a speech of welcome, and to each the King made a speech in reply. During his visit to a Nablus school he saw a demonstration of the students' military training, which became part of the curriculum of all secondary schools in Jordan. The King was pleased with the outstanding welcome he had received all over the West Bank. Glubb wrote about an example of the reception given to the King in the rural area of Qalqiliyah:

> Qalqiliyah had suffered particularly from the Rhodes armistice demarcation line. It was a little town in the coastal plain, immediately at the base of the last foothill. Three hundred yards west of the little town began the orange groves, which seemed to stretch as far as one could see across the plains to the sea. These orange groves had all been planted by the people of Qalqiliyah, or their fathers before them, and had provided their only means of subsistence. Then had come the Rhodes armistice which had drawn the Demarcation Line between the houses of the little town and their orange groves. All the oranges had been taken over by the Jews, and the people of Qalqiliyah were left sitting in their houses destitute. In the autumn, they could see the Jews, only three hundred yards away, picking their oranges. All round the country north, south and west of Qalqiliyah, on the coastal plain, and in gaps in the orange groves, new Jewish colonies were springing up like mushrooms, groups of little white houses like the pre-fabs used in England after the Second World War or like huge chicken farms with rows of little white hen-houses. The greater part of the Israeli Army was only a few miles away across that plain; an Israeli aerodrome was only three or four miles distant; the aircraft could be seen taking off and landing all day long. East of Qalqiliyah lay the long range of the Palestine mountains, crossed only by occasional winding narrow roads, along which any Arab Legion reinforcements would have to come if the little town were attacked.
>
> But the people of Qalqiliyah were more virile than most. After a first period of despair, they had set to work. Behind the little town on the east lay the barren rocky hills; all their fertile land had gone to Israel. But they had already started to dig and level and terrace,

to remake a living when all their old livelihood was lost. But there still remained the threat of those ever-increasing Jewish colonies so near to them.

If the people of Azzun had been enthusiastic, the people of Qalqiliyah went mad. As soon as we drove into the edge of the little town, we were surrounded by a seething crowd. The Boy Scouts and schoolboys had tried to line the streets, and were to cheer the King, but they also were swept away. We advanced into the main street at less than a walking pace. The escort cars in front and behind were cut off from the royal car by a surging sea of faces. Some crowded round, some climbed on the car, some stood on the running boards on either side and took advantage of the extra four inches of height to bellow to the others: 'Long live the King! Long live His Majesty the King!'

The noise was deafening. I forced my way out of the car, pushing the door by main force to get rid of several men packed against it. I tried to struggle forward to clear some people who were dancing and shouting in front of the car and had thereby reduced it to a standstill. 'Open a road!' I roared. 'Iftah Tariq.' Nobody took any notice. I thumped them on the back to make them listen, but they looked round at me with excited faces and bellowed, 'Long live the King!' One or two of them grinned, and shouted: 'Long live the father of Faris!' [meaning Glubb, whose son's name was Faris]. But they made no attempt to move. Suddenly I also felt a thump on the back. I looked round and saw the sergeant of my escort. 'Get back into the car,' he yelled in my ear. 'You don't know who is in this crowd.'

In a sudden lull, a voice called out: 'O father of Talal, protect us!' In an instant, the whole crowd took up the words in a thunderous chorus, 'O father of Talal [meaning King Abdullah], protect us!'[33]

During September and October 1949, there was a movement for unity between Iraq and Syria, mainly encouraged by Nuri al-Said, who never let the idea go, and kept proposing it whenever he could in inter-Arab politics. As soon as King Abdullah heard of the scheme, he sent Muhammad al-Shuraiqi, Jordan's Minister to Afghanistan, Pakistan and India – and one of the keenest advocates of the 'Greater Syria Scheme' in Jordan – to Damascus to examine the attitude of the Syrian leaders of public opinion as well as Government ministers towards the scheme. Meanwhile, a new statement regarding the scheme, its plan and the manner with which it could be achieved was circulating in the Syrian capital. Kirkbride sent a translation to Ernest Bevin as an enclosure to his report about its revival.

1. Northern and Southern Syria will unite under the name of 'The United Hashemite Kingdom'.

2. In Syria, a national Hashemite Cabinet will be formed, while the Hashemite Jordanian Cabinet will remain in Office until a Constituent Assembly shall have been convened to draw up a constitution providing for the unification of the United Kingdom.

3. The two Cabinets will consider jointly the amendment of the law for the purpose of its unification and for the creation of a firm internal policy to secure to the people their rights and to punish trouble makers severely. The two Cabinets will also consider the amendment of the Press Law in order not to prevent the sons of the nation from expressing their views and fears without sedition, disrespect or agitation against the country's Government or Governments.

4. The Constituent Assembly, which will be convened, shall have the full right to lay foundations within the framework of these articles.

5. The State shall be given a period of five years to be followed by another five years during which the nation shall maintain support its Government or Governments in executing decisions wisely and consistently.

6. Necessary measures will be taken to remove intriguers and self-seekers. The State shall not admit to the public service anyone of those whose policy was rejected by the nation and against whom the army carried out its well known *coup d'état*. The Syrian Army and its honourable officers are to be thanked for their wise point of view and for the gallantry with which they ended a worn-out policy. They are asked to devote their entire efforts to ensuring that the united army shall have the qualifications for which it was created and to be faithful to the nation and to the King and to the law in general.

7. Any treaties or alliances between the United Hashemite Kingdom and an Arab or foreign state will be given due consideration until such time when it is possible to adjust and amend these in a manner suitable to the new form of the United Kingdom.

8. The decision of the General Syrian Conference on 8 March 1920, is to be the basis of discussions.

9. Union with the Hashemite Iraqi Kingdom is the objective of the United Kingdom and discussions shall start at once to this end on the basis of the decisions of 8 March 1920.[34]

Soon after his return to Amman, al-Shuraiqi reported to the King that there was not much support for the idea in Damascus. On 20 October, a

Royal speech was read in the presence of King Abdullah from the balcony of the Municipality of Amman to a large crowd that had assembled in the city centre. A translation of the speech was sent by Kirkbride to Ernest Bevin on 22 October. It read:

My dear people

During our last visit to the municipal building on the occasion of our return from the visit to Britain and Spain, we did not have the chance of talking to our people as we usually do. But now after we visited West Jordan, we say this word in clarification of our plans for our dear country. We thank the Gracious God and pray on His Prophet and say: 'This people has done on both sides of Jordan, West and East, what every individual is supposed to do in sacrifice, wisdom and patience.'

Today we are facing the problem of the internationalisation of Jerusalem, the problem of refugees and lastly, the final peace settlement.

As to the internationalisation of Jerusalem, there is no hope for this since this important position is the key to peace to East Jordan and of security for the West. About the refugee problem, we are ready to cooperate fully with the Conciliation Commission provided it acts quickly. We draw attention to the necessity of finding a just settlement for the property of refugees who do not wish to return to their homes, this would guarantee a settlement in the future and be a service for the peace. But, as to the final settlement, we have to work hard to create the necessary peaceful conditions and so avoid the repetition of complaints and disputes.

We shall, with God's will, order the execution of irrigation and building schemes that will lead to prosperity and peace to those who temporarily lost these blessings. We shall follow plans that will lead to respect for this Kingdom, the lover of peace and its defender, which wishes to live a life of non-aggression with its neighbours. I am to say from this place with regard to predictions about the existing situation in dear Syria that we shall not use force against any country. We have fought for her sake, we laid her foundations, and for her we shed our blood and sacrificed our money. We say that we shall not force Syria to something she does not want. Syria is a country the natural boundaries of which from north, east, south and west are well known. Syria's security lies in her unity. We ask God to witness that we say, and announce that we are always careful not to harm Syria or do her any mischief. We also realise that separation is harmful. Therefore, we shall work to reach the unity, which will lead to the protection of Syria, through understanding and agreement. We are sure that the future leads to unity because of the present international and political situation, especially now that Arabs are not the only race living within the natural boundaries of Syria. God is our witness when I say this word which will be recorded in history. I ask the Almighty God to lead this people to every prosperity. I pray God to lead us all to our common good, for He alone could unite our word and nation. We are also striving to see that the Arab League directs its attention to the purposes for which it was established, that of securing the tranquillity of the Arab world, the removal of disputes between its nations and the union of its natural parts which were separated by the political situation which arose from the First World War. The present situation is the inheritance of those ambitions which are known to every one who heard and understood and finally found the right path. On God we depend and God's peace be with you.[35]

On 25 October 1949, the Egyptian Delegate at the United Nations raised in the Security Council the question of securing the demilitarisation of Jerusalem in accordance with the resolution of 11 December 1948. The President suggested that in view of the forthcoming Assembly discussion it would be preferable to postpone the Security Council discussion indefinitely and to leave the item on the Council's Agenda. This suggestion was accepted without a vote.

During the first week of November 1949, the Prime Minister, Tawfiq Abu al-Huda, and the Foreign Minister, Rouhi Abd al-Hadi, a Palestinian member of the Cabinet, attended the meeting of the League of Arab States at Cairo. They were faced with the request by Ahmad Hilmi of the All Palestine Government, through the Egyptian Prime Minister, to be present at the meeting. The request was refused without debate. The Egyptian Prime Minister then requested that, instead, a Palestinian representative be elected by the Political Committee in the same way as Musa al-Alami had been elected previously. The Jordanian delegation disagreed and claimed that the whole situation in Palestine had changed since the arrangement was made in 1945, on the establishment of the League. They also pointed out that two members of the Jordanian delegation were Palestinians and could therefore represent the people of Palestine. The Egyptian Prime Minister suggested the compromise of King Abdullah nominating one Palestinian and Egypt nominating another. Tawfiq Abu al-Huda said that if that was done the Jordanian delegation would withdraw from the meeting. Nuri al-Said, in turn, said that if the Jordanian delegation withdrew, the Iraqi delegation would also. The compromise failed to gain support from the remaining delegates. In return for Nuri al-Said's support, Abu al-Huda defeated a request by the Egyptian and Saudi Arabian delegates to discuss the question of the proposed unity between Iraq and Syria, and the issue was not debated.

Tawfiq Abu al-Huda won the support of the Political Committee for the rejection of the internationalisation of Jerusalem when, after explaining the dangers of that proposal, all the delegates decided to oppose the proposal at Lake Success. The question of the Arab League Security Pact was raised by the Egyptian Prime Minister, who explained: 'The Arab World was faced with two dangers: Israel, the most imminent, and Russia, the greatest. In view of a new world conflict, no one in the Middle East should be neutral.'[36] He then asked the Arab states members of the League to decide on which side they would stand. The decision was unanimous that all Arab states would stand on the side of Western democracies. Finally, it was decided that the execution of the League Council decisions would not rest with the Secretary-General but with the chairman of the previous meeting, who would remain in charge of the executive until the following session. Thus, Abd al-Rahman Azzam's authority was limited, as agreed between the three Prime Ministers of Syria, Lebanon and Jordan, and the standing of al-Haj Amin al-Husseini was reduced in the political affairs of Palestine.

Tawfiq Abu al-Huda had a meeting with the Egyptian Prime Minister, Hussein Sirri, after the League meeting and discussed with him the future of the Gaza Strip (as it came to be known), Eastern Palestine and the Negev, including any other part of Palestine that might be recovered. Abu al-Huda conveyed the discussion to Kirkbride, who in turn reported it to the Foreign Office as follows:

> Sirri Pasha said that, for reasons of internal politics, Egypt would have to retain Gaza but that, if Jordan ever obtained access to the port, Egypt would give all possible trade facilities. He went on to say that there was no alternative to the union of Jordan and Eastern Arab Palestine. He expressed the belief that it would be possible to recover part of the Negev from Israel and his readiness to divide any such area between Jordan and Egypt.
>
> The two of them thereupon agreed in principle that it would be desirable to provide for these matters in a secret treaty which would bind subsequent cabinets in both countries. They proposed that this treaty should lay down the following principles in regard

to the future of any areas of Palestine which now remain in Arab possession or which may be restored to the Arabs.

1. Such areas of which the frontier ran with Israel and one Arab State should be annexed by that Arab State.

2. Such areas whose frontiers ran with Israel and more than one Arab State should be divided between those Arab states, the division being made in the light of strategic and economic considerations with due regard being paid to the wishes of the Arab inhabitants.

3. Any such areas that constituted enclaves in Israel would be administered by the nearest Arab State. (Areas of the third category do not exist at present but their future appearance was not ruled out entirely.)

The two Premiers agreed to obtain the assent of their respective Monarchs to the proposed treaty and then to meet again in order to discuss its terms further.

I anticipate that Tewfiq may meet with some difficulty in getting King Abdullah to accept the proposed treaty, but it does appear that he managed to get on better terms with Sirri Pasha than has been possible in the past between the Egyptian and Jordan delegations. If this *rapprochement* can be maintained, or improved, it will benefit both countries.[37]

On 9 December 1949, the General Assembly of the United Nations approved a resolution restating the intention that Jerusalem should be established as a *corpus separatum* under United Nations administration, and requesting the Trusteeship Council to complete its preparation of a statute for the Jerusalem area and to proceed immediately with its implementation. On 14 December 1949, the Israeli Government announced that it had decided to transfer a number of Ministries, including the office of the Prime Minister, and the Israeli Parliament to Jerusalem. On 20 December 1949, the Trusteeship Council of the United Nations approved a resolution expressing the opinion that the Israeli action was likely to render the implementation of the statute more difficult, calling upon Israel to revoke it.

On 19 December 1949, a group of Jordanian intellectuals, including members of the Young Liberals, applied to the Minister of the Interior to permit them to hold a conference in Irbid with representatives of all organisations, popular associations and leaders of public opinion in the Kingdom and the unoccupied Arab part of Palestine for the purpose of discussion of the following issues:

1. The internal affairs of the country.
2. The general situation in Palestine.
3. The formation of a new political party on a reform basis.

Permission was denied and the formation of the political party was disallowed.[38]

King Abdullah, the most eloquent speaker of Arabic, led the prayers in al-Aqsa Mosque in Jerusalem on Friday 10 December. He delivered the usual speech from the *minbar* (pulpit), but sounded very emotional when he appealed to the true believers to trust in God and resist the internationalisation of the Holy City of Jerusalem.

Following that visit, it was announced that, in future, the King would spend every Thursday night and Friday morning in Jerusalem, in order to keep himself in closer contact with its affairs. The emotions the King raised by his speech, especially his resistance against internationalisation of Jerusalem, were very strong indeed and the response of '*Allahu Akbar*' by the thousands attending the prayer was thunderous and sincere; most of those present, including myself, wept with emotion.

On 18 December, at the request of its inhabitants the King made a special visit to the village of Tubas in the Nablus district. During the course of his speech he again emphasised his determination to resist the internationalisation of Jerusalem. Meanwhile, on 7 December, Wadia Diamis, the Christian Mayor of Bait Jala, sent the following telegram to Fawzi al-Mulqi, the Jordanian representative at Lake Success:

> The Christians of this area fully support you in rejecting any form of internationalisation, since their inclusion in the Hashemite Kingdom of the Jordan is a sufficient solution to the Jerusalem problem. As loyal subjects of King Abdullah they are confident of his protection and no other solution will have their support.

A copy of the telegram was sent to the Secretary-General of the United Nations, and on 9 December, two telegrams were sent from Jerusalem to Fawzi al-Mulqi and the Secretary-General of the United Nations protesting against the Ad Hoc Committee's decision on internationalisation. They were signed by the following Muslim notables: Anwar al-Khatib, the Mayor of Arab Jerusalem; Amin Abd al-Hadi, the President of the Supreme Muslim Council; and Shaikh Abd al-Hamid al-Sayih, the President of the Sharia Courts. The following Christian notables also signed: Wadia

Diamis, Mayor of Bait Jala; Butrus Abu Khalil, Deputy Mayor of Bethlehem; Jirjis Qamissa, President of Bait Sahur Municipal Council; and eight Arabs from the Greek Orthodox Church.

On 11 December, the religious heads of the Christian communities in Jerusalem, Bethlehem, Bait Jala and Bait Sahur sent a telegram to the Pope asking him to intervene with a view to putting the Holy Places under Hashemite protection.

During December 1949, in order to pave the way for a constitutional unity between the two Banks of the Jordan – Palestine and the Hashemite Kingdom of Jordan – the King dissolved both Chambers of the Jordanian National Assembly with effect from 1 January 1950. Meanwhile, the Government amended the electoral law with a temporary law on 12 December 1949, adding ten Senators from the West Bank to the existing ten from the East Bank, with 20 members to be elected from the West Bank and added to the 20 members from the East Bank as shown in Table 10.6.

TABLE 10.6
Interim electoral law

Constituency	Members	
	Muslim	Christian
Jerusalem and Jericho	2	1
Bethlehem	1	1
Hebron	4	
Nablus	4	
Jenin	2	
Tulkarm	2	
Ramallah	2	1
Total	**17**	**3**

The proposed elections, which were due to be held on 11 April 1950, were the first of their kind in Arab Palestine since the Ottomans left the country in 1917 during the First World War. The Government amended the Nationality Law making all persons normally resident in Jordan, and in that part of Palestine under Jordanian administration, provided they held Palestine passports, Jordanian subjects with effect from the date of publication. By the end of December, special instructions affecting the preparation of the electoral lists in the constituencies of the West Bank were already in the hands of District Administrations. The period for registration by the electorate, publication of the lists and their final adjustments was set for between 2 January 1950 and 27 March 1950. Nominations of candidates were set to take place between 27 March and 6 April.

However, the main democratic system of elections remained unchanged. The Electoral Law provided that any male of 18 years of age and of Jordanian nationality had the right to vote, provided he was not subject to the usual disqualifications such as insanity or being in prison. Bedouin representation was subject to a special method of nomination of candidates. All Jordanians could present themselves for election to the Chamber of Deputies, provided they were not disqualified by the requirements of the Constitution or by occupation of public office (including Municipal office) from which they must otherwise resign within 14 days of the announcement of the election date.

By the end of 1949, the number of Jordanian soldiers who gave up their lives for the Palestinian cause totalled 408 martyrs as listed in Table 10.7.

TABLE 10.7
Number of Jordanian soldiers killed in the cause of Palestine

Post	Totals
Captain	2
First Lieutenant	8
Second Lieutenant	2
Staff Sergeant	3
Sergeant	18
Corporal	17
Lance Corporal	34
Private	324
Total	**408**

The total number of wounded who were retired from the Army as a result of their wounds amounted to around 900 men. Considering that the strength of the Jordan Arab Army in 1948–9 did not exceed 6,000 officers and men, the number of casualties, killed and wounded, was 22 per cent – a very high percentage indeed. The total number of Jordanian partisan martyrs was about 210, which included mainly Bedouins and Muslim Brothers.[39]

NOTES

1 PRO. FO 371/75273. Monthly situation report for March 1949, 4 April 1949.
2 Glubb, *A Soldier with the Arabs*, pp. 227–9.
3 Colonel T. N. Bromage, message to Jordan Arab Army HQ, 7 March 1949.
4 An interview with Colonel T. N. Bromage, 6 June 1999. Also, Glubb, *A Soldier with the Arabs*, p. 229; Sulaiman Musa, *Unforgettable Days: Jordan in the 1948 War* (Amman: published by the author, 1983), pp. 504–6; and PRO. FO 371/75381. From Kirkbride to the Foreign Office, 11 March 1949.
5 PRO. FO 371/75273. Monthly situation report for March 1949, 4 April 1949.
6 Glubb, *A Soldier with the Arabs*, p. 237.
7 Abdullah al-Tal, *The Palestine Catastrophe*, pp. 508–9.
8 *Ibid.*
9 *Ibid.*
10 Glubb, *A Soldier with the Arabs*, p. 237.
11 Abdullah al-Tal, *The Palestine Catastrophe*, p. 589.
12 PRO. FO 371/75273. Monthly situation report for April 1949, 2 May 1949.
13 *Ibid.*
14 *Ibid.*
15 Abdullah al-Tal, *The Palestine Catastrophe*, pp. 588–91.
16 *HKJOG* no. 980, 1 May 1949.
17 PRO. FO 371/75333. Minutes by J. Bieth on the future of Arab Palestine, 2 May 1949.
18 PRO. FO 371/75436. From Kirkbride to Bevin, 4 May 1949.
19 PRO. FO 371/827151. Note on the financial situation of the Arab Legion, 29 April 1949.
20 *Ibid.*
21 PRO. FO 371/75295. Glubb to the Foreign Office, 9 May 1949.
22 PRO. FO 371/75376. From Kirkbride to the Foreign Office, 23 May 1949.
23 Letter from Glubb to Kirkbride, 7 June 1947, held at St Antony's College, Oxford.
24 *HKJOG* no. 986, 16 June 1949. Also, *HKJOG* no. 987, 1 July 1949.
25 PRO. FO 371/57273. Monthly situation report for July 1949, 15 August 1949.
26 Nasuh Babil, *Journalism and Politics in Syria in the Twentieth Century* (London: Riad el-Rayyes Books, 1987), p. 381.
27 PRO. FO 371/75333. From Kirkbride to Bevin, 4 October 1949.
28 *Ibid.*
29 PRO. FO 371/75273. Monthly situation report for September 1949, 8 October 1949.
30 PRO. FO 371/75287. From the Foreign Office to Washington, 13 September 1949.

31 PRO. FO 371/75273. Monthly situation report for October 1949, 5 November 1949.

32 *Ibid.*

33 Glubb, *A Soldier with the Arabs*, pp. 272–3.

34 PRO. FO 371/75077. Enclosure from Kirkbride to Ernest Bevin, 22 October 1949.

35 *Ibid.*

36 PRO. FO 371/75076. From Kirkbride to the Foreign Office, 7 November 1949.

37 *Ibid.*

38 *Al Mithaq* newspaper, no. 10, December 1949. The signatories were Dhaif Allah al Humud, Shafiq al Rushaidat, Sulaiman al Soudi, Najib al Shraidah, Mahmoud Khalid, Turki al Kayid, Salim al Hindawi, Mohammad al Amin, Mohammad al Ittan, Ali al Malkawi, Muflih al Saad al Battaynah, Abd al Karim al Khass, Khalf al-Tel, Musa al Awad Hijazi, Ratib Darwazah, Yousef al Hasan, Ghazi Abu al Shaar, Ibrahim Samawi, Attallah al Majali, Hani al Aakashah, Mahmoud al Mitlaq, Mohammad al Dalqamouni, Ahmad Ramzi al Shara, Fayiz al Rousan, Ahmad Hijazi, Bashir al Hattab, Abd al Rahim al Wakid, Sulaiman al Hadidi, Abd al Razzaq Khalifah, Hamzah al Shraidah and others.

39 Musa, *Unforgettable Days*, list of casualties of the Jordan Arab Army and Jordanian partisans. Also Aref al Aref, *The Disaster*, list of casualties of the Jordan Arab Army and Jordanian partisans.

11

The First Arab Union

Much has been written about the 'annexation' rather than 'unity' between the Jordanian and the Palestinian peoples at the height of the Arab nationalist movement. The unity of the two countries was one of the major consequences of the 1948 war with the Jews and the creation of the State of Israel in the heart of the Arab world. The unity was the product of free election of a joint Palestinian–Jordanian parliament representing constituencies from all parts of the country on both the East and the West Bank of the Jordan River. Subsequent developments in the new Kingdom consisted mainly of drastic changes and political stresses which occurred as a result of formulating and implementing that unity. King Abdullah, the Government of Jordan and people from every part of the country spent 1950 in the throes of a peaceful revolution. The political, social and economic influence of the Palestinian presence overwhelmed the East Bank Jordanians, as can be seen from the events that took place during the year. There were a number of unprecedented ministerial crises and changes; a large number of senior civil servants from the West Bank were appointed in East Bank posts, while only a few from the East Bank were appointed in West Bank posts; the economic strength of the Palestinian business community overwhelmed the east Jordanians; and the pressure of inter-Arab and international relations were very serious indeed both in content and consequences.

By the beginning of 1950, the main concerns of King Abdullah and the Jordan Government were the process of unity between the West and East Bank and the defence of the new Kingdom against Jewish aggression. The process for achieving unity started with preparations for the elections on both Banks. On 2 January 1950, the registration of the electorate started on both Banks and continued without incident until the 17th of the month. On 10 January, Tawfiq Abu al-Huda, the Prime Minister, gave a press conference at Amman during which he endeavoured to clear up certain misunderstandings that had occupied public minds on the East Bank. He emphasised that the elections would be free and that there would be no interference by the Government. He explained why Government and Municipal civil servants could not combine their duties and responsibilities with those of the membership of the Chamber of Deputies. He also explained that the refugees should not withhold their votes on the assumption that voting would in any way prejudice their right to return to their homes at some later date. He assured the inhabitants of the West Bank that the Jordan Government would not abolish British Mandate laws and that the unification of Jordan and Palestine laws would be dealt with by the new Parliament of both Chambers, the Notables and the Deputies in accordance with the recommendations of a Joint Committee of Jordanian and Palestinian jurists. He admitted that the Jordanian constitution would require some amendment, but such an amendment was the right of the Parliament of both Chambers.

For the defence of Jordan, King Abdullah, the Government and General Glubb knew that alone it was unable to defend the West Bank. Thus, during December 1949, the need for the application of the terms of the 1948 Anglo–Jordanian Treaty was raised with the British Government. In his letter of 10 December 1949 to Kirkbride, the Jordanian Minister for Foreign Affairs stated that the Jordan Government claimed that the British Government was bound under the terms of the Anglo–Jordanian Treaty to come to the assistance of Jordan in the event of an attack on the West Bank, which they regarded as 'territory controlled by Jordan', in accordance with Article 1(b) of the Annex to that Treaty. On 21 December, the British Foreign Secretary approved the text of a telegram sent to the Jordan Government: 'Whatever the legal position at present it is our firm intention that the Anglo–Jordanian Treaty should be made applicable to those areas of Arab Palestine which are eventually incorporated into Jordan.' On re-examination of the question by Sir E. Beckett of the Foreign Office, he came to the following conclusion:

> His Majesty's Government could not escape the obligation under Article 3 of the Anglo–Jordan Treaty to come to Jordan's assistance in the event of an Israeli attack on Jordan forces wherever they may be, including Arab Palestine, unless there are obligations under the Charter conflicting with this. Article 4 subordinates Article 3 to the Charter. The only obligation under the Charter which could so

conflict would be those arising from Security Council Resolutions, mandatory under Article 25 of the Charter. The department does not consider that there are any Security Council Resolutions now in force which would have this effect.[1]

On 28 December 1949, during his visit to Baghdad, King Abdullah was criticised by Jamil al-Madfaai and Tawfiq al-Suwaidi for his opposition to the internationalisation of Jerusalem, arguing that it was in the interest of the Arabs. The King said: 'Iraqi ideas in the past as to what was best for the Arabs of Palestine have produced sorry results. If they had followed my advice in the first place the Arabs would have been left with two thirds of Palestine instead of one third.' He added that he was 'amazed that after the Arabs had lost so much it should now be suggested that I should surrender one of the most holy places of Islam to an authority [the United Nations] that was proving itself irresponsible'.[2] Some aspects of the King's foreign policy were reiterated in the following terms.

1. Jordan would not be bound by the Arab League. It would be present at its sittings and that was all.

2. He would not interfere in Syria, but he insisted that no other state should interfere and he was so informing the Iraqi Government.

3. His friendship with Great Britain would continue.

4. He wished to be on non-aggressive terms with Israel, but was in no hurry for a settlement, because any that might be made at present would be unfavourable to him.[3]

On 2 March 1950, Tawfiq Abu al-Huda submitted his resignation on the grounds of ill health. However, the real reason, according to Kirkbride, was his 'reluctance, for personal reasons, to be party to a settlement with Israel', despite the fact that he had conducted the affairs of the country during the war, the first and the second truces and the negotiations for the armistice agreement. Since the end of 1949, his plans had been to stay until the end of the elections of the new Parliament in April 1950, then resign and take over as speaker for the Chamber of Notables (Senate). He wanted to hand over his post as Prime Minister to Said al-Mufti, his close friend and a member of his Cabinet, hoping that he would be able to exercise considerable influence over him (and events) from outside the Council of Ministers. Thus any blame for any concessions on the question of Palestine would be directed at his friend, and Tawfiq would keep what reputation he had with the Arab states intact. This was the reason he kept his distance from the informal talks with the Israeli authorities for as long as possible. His timing was perfect, for after the elections in April, he would have to resign on constitutional grounds. Kirkbride wrote this report to Bevin:

> It was action by the three 'Palestinian' members – Rouhi Abdul Hadi, Musa Nasser and Khulousi al-Khairi – that precipitated the resignation. These three had agreed to the decision of the council unwillingly, and appear to have decided, later on, to stage a revolt. They were given an opening by an ill-advised attempt of King Abdullah to force the issue of reopening trade with Israel, which he made on Thursday 2 March. The general reaction of the council to the King's intervention was so hostile that the Prime Minister decided to resign, on the somewhat unconvincing grounds of ill-health, before his position became more difficult.
>
> King Abdullah accepted the resignation, with ill grace, but asked the ministers to continue to function until he had formed a new council.
>
> 4. The King first asked Said Pasha al-Mufti [outgoing Minister of Interior] to form a council, but the latter declined. The offer was then made to Samir Pasha al-Rifai, who accepted notwithstanding his previous assertions that he would not do so.
>
> At the outset, Samir Pasha obtained half promises from five members of the old council to join him, but in the meanwhile, the inevitable rumours appeared, not without assistance from some of the outgoing ministers, to the effect that the resignation had really been provoked by the King's desire to give way to Israeli demands, and that the ministers had been motivated by the purest patriotism in resisting these plans. The attacks on Jordan and the King, which then appeared in the Syrian and Egyptian presses, resulted in the five members of the outgoing council hastily withdrawing from Samir Pasha and emphasising their solidarity with their other colleagues.
>
> Further efforts by Samir Pasha to find candidates made it evident, by Saturday morning, that he would only be able to produce a somewhat second-rate team if the King agreed that he need not undertake to resume trade with Israel, the one point on which the outgoing council had disagreed with the King.
>
> The King actually offered to let Samir Pasha off on this question, but with the fairly obvious intention of going back on his

word as soon as a new council was formed, as Samir Pasha himself admitted.

5. Up to the Saturday morning I had managed to keep clear of the various manoeuvres, but by that time, both the King and the Prime Minister were becoming frightened by the public uproar they had created and Samir Pasha was beginning to look for a way out of his dilemma. I was then brought into the picture and consulted by the Amir Talal, Tewfiq Pasha, Samir Pasha and, finally, King Abdullah, late in the afternoon. In brief, the Amir Talal was worried about the public attacks on his father; Tewfiq Pasha expressed his readiness to withdraw his resignation or to assist Said al-Mufti to form a council, on condition that no further negotiations took place until after the elections; Samir Pasha more or less admitted failure and wanted to extricate himself; the King wanted to express his violent disapproval of all Ministers, actual or designate, and to get some outside advice as to what he should do.

6. I also was worried by the violent reactions, both in and outside and, in particular, by the immediate increase of propaganda, among the Palestinians to boycott the coming elections, which, if allowed to continue, might cause serious future difficulties in connection with the proposed formal union, after these elections of the two halves of the Jordan.[4]

Kirkbride saw no point in changing Abu al-Huda at such a very high price for a council under Samir al-Rifai, who would not be able to go further in a settlement with Israel. It was also obvious that the best course of action to stem the flood of rumours and abuse to which Tawfiq Abu al-Huda's resignation had given rise, was for Tawfiq to withdraw his resignation. At Kirkbride's suggestion, Samir al-Rifai himself recommended that course of action to the King; Abu al-Huda withdrew his resignation on the condition that no further progress was to be attempted in the negotiations with Israel until after the elections in April. The flagrant attacks against King Abdullah in the Egyptian press following the publication of some material provided by Abdullah al-Tel against his King and country caused more concern. Abdullah al-Tel told *al-Masri* magazine on 19 March that he suggested the following courses of action by the Arab League:

1. That King Abdullah should be asked to abdicate in favour of his son or else rule as a constitutional King.

2. That Jordan should be asked to denounce the Anglo–Jordanian Treaty and remove British officers from the Arab Legion so that the Arabs could be sure of the participation of the Arab Legion in Arab collective security.

3. That the Arab League should demand a modification of the Jordan Constitution so that power might be entrusted to the exiled liberals led by Dr Subhi Abu Ghanimah.

4. That Arab States should undertake to give the financial assistance to the Arab Legion at present given by the British. The Arab Legion should then be attached to the Syrian or Egyptian army under the trusteeship of the Arab League, or of Egypt, as the leader of the Arab League.[5]

All these activities against Jordan, combined with the refusal of the Egyptian Government to recognise the unity between Eastern Palestine and the Hashemite Kingdom of Jordan, and the aggressive acts by the Israeli forces in the Hebron Sector, did a great deal to heal the rift between the King and Tawfiq Abu al-Huda. At that point Abu al-Huda withdrew his resignation.

Meanwhile, the Egyptian Government continued to take a strong and uncompromising anti-Jordan line at the meeting of the Arab League and in the Egyptian press. In response, King Abdullah declined to send a delegation to Cairo. He considered the League's decision to recognise al-Haj Amin al-Husseini as the representative of Palestine, and its unwillingness to recognise the union of Palestine and Jordan as an insult to Jordan. He made clear that if the League showed signs of expelling or censuring Jordan, he might walk out of the League. In this regard G. W. Furlonge of the Foreign Office made the following comment:

> The Egyptians are being incredibly silly and doing the Arab cause much harm. Top secret reports indicate that the Egyptian Government, while professing support for the League, are opposing all the measures which might make the League useful – for example, a customs union, abolition of visas and so on. If they succeed in driving Jordan out, Iraq may well follow, in which case even they must surely realise that they will have accomplished nothing but to demonstrate to the world – and to Israel – that the Arab States are split in two.[6]

On 28 March, the Jordan Minister at Cairo attended the first meeting of the Political Committee of the Arab League and asked to be informed of the attitude of the Committee regarding two points: first, whether the so-called Palestine Arab Government would be represented in the meeting; and second, the attitude of the Committee regarding the union of Eastern Palestine with Jordan. He was informed that the Egyptian Prime Minister had already committed himself to a representative of the Palestinian Arabs being present and that non-recognition of the union with Palestine was the considered policy of the present Egyptian Government. The Jordanian Minister announced that in that case Jordan would not send a delegation to the meeting and then withdrew himself.[7]

The decision not to send a delegation to Cairo was taken by the Jordanian Cabinet with the approval of King Abdullah. Had it only been a question of agreeing to the presence of a representative of the Palestinian Arabs, the Cabinet might have been able to overcome the King's objections to Jordan's attendance, but the Ministers could not all swallow the decision of not recognising the union that had already been established. This action of the Egyptian Government helped to rally public opinion in Jordan and Palestine in favour of the King and his policy for unity.

When the future elections were announced, the policy of the followers of al-Haj Amin al-Husseini appeared to be designed to secure as great a number of Palestinian representatives in the new Parliament as possible. Towards the end of March 1950, this attitude seemed to have reversed as a result of the rumours spread by Abu al-Huda and his Ministers about a settlement with the Jews. Then the Mufti's followers joined the Arab Communists in denouncing the forthcoming elections as an Anglo–Hashemite scheme. Thus, the agitation against the elections, which started in the West Bank of the Jordan, compelled the King to issue a statement that after the new Parliament was elected, the Constitution of the country would be amended to make the Council of Ministers responsible and accountable to the Parliament and not to the King personally.

The followers of al-Haj Amin al-Husseini relied on the Palestinian refugees for support in the elections as shown in Table 11.1.

The political storm in the Council of the Arab League regarding the elections and the prospect of the new Parliament proclaiming unity of both Banks had little or no effect in the country. Baathist and Communist agitation against the elections during March were equally ineffective. Plans were made for the election of deputies on 11 April and the new Parliament to be opened by the King on 1 May 1950. It was

TABLE 11.1
Number and location of refugees in Jordan

Location	Number of refugees
Amman	26,085
Amman District	10,216
Al-Shunah	10,389
Irbid	26,716
Zarqa	6,915
al-Salt	7,693
Jerusalem	39,063
Jericho	48,534
Ramallah	69,037
Nablus	117,200
Bethlehem	43,000
Hebron	76,858
Total	**481,706**[8]

also planned that shortly after the opening of Parliament, a group of deputies from the West Bank would move a resolution proclaiming the formal union of the two parts of the Kingdom. It was expected that the resolution would be carried by acclamation of the rest of the deputies who, by the very fact of their having nominated themselves for election, had accepted the principle of unity. In anticipation of the success of these plans, Kirkbride reported to the Eastern Department in the Foreign Office suggesting the recognition of unity. He wrote:

> The purpose of this letter is to ask that there should be as little delay as possible in the recognition of this union by His Majesty's Government. How this should be done is not a matter on which I could presume to offer an opinion but it would help locally if the procedure could include some formal *démarche* here.
>
> I sincerely hope that it will not be suggested that our recognition should have to wait until the future of Jerusalem is settled. It may be years before that happens and it is most important in connection with a settlement between Jordan and Israel, and the attitude of the Arab League on that subject, that the union should have our blessing and that no further doubt should exist as to the future of eastern Arab Palestine.[9]

The Egyptian Foreign Minister approached Sir Ronald Campbell, the British Ambassador in Cairo, and said that the elections in the areas controlled by Jordan may no doubt lead to 'annexation of the area by King Abdullah'. He also said that the other Arab governments did not agree and a resolution was under consideration at the meeting of the Council of the Arab League, 'where feeling was very strong on the subject'. Sir Ronald Campbell reported:

> If Abdullah proceeded with his intention this might lead to something which neither of us would like [meaning no doubt a break between Jordan and the League].
>
> The Minister for Foreign Affairs asked whether we could give counsel in Amman either in the sense that the election should be put off or that the Jordan Government should announce that they would not lead to annexation but only to the entitlement of the area in question to the welfare services of the Jordan Government or some such formula.
>
> The Minister said that he felt able to make this request to us because of the suggestions recently made to him by Mr Chapman-Andrews on the subject of Jordan, after which he had used his influence in the press and other quarters with a view to restraint.[10]

On 11 April, in accordance with a protest made by the All Palestine Government of Ahmad Hilmi, the Political Committee of the Arab League discussed the Jordan elections and the intention of the Jordanian Government to implement their proposed union of Arab Palestine with Jordan. Although no formal resolution was taken, reports from Cairo said that all the delegations, except the Jordanian, agreed that the union would be illegal and a violation of the charter of the League. However, the debate ended with the suggestion that those parts of Palestine now occupied by the Arab States should be considered held in trust until such time as the future of Palestine would be finally decided.[11]

The general elections in Jordan took place on 11 April and passed off on both Banks of the Jordan 'in an atmosphere of complete calm and without so much as a hint of a disturbance', as Glubb put it in a dispatch to the Foreign Office. He added: 'What was more remarkable is that polling was absolutely free. It was a remarkable achievement in the Arab world, where the rigging of elections is normally accepted absolutely as a matter of course.'[12] The results of the elections are shown in Table 11.2.

TABLE 11.2
Results of the April 1950 elections in Jordan

The East Bank

1. The District of Amman
   Said al-Mufti, Circassian; Wasfi Mirza, Circassian; Sulaiman al-Sukkar, Christian; Rashad Touqan, Muslim; Muhammad Minwir al-Hadid, Muslim

2. The District of al-Salt
   Salih al-Muaashir, Christian; Abd al-Halim al-Nimir, Muslim

3. The District of Madaba
   Muhammad Salim Abu al-Ghanam, Muslim

4. The District of Irbid
   Shafiq al-Rushaidat, Muslim; Dr Muhammad Hijazi, Muslim; Sulaiman al-Khalil

5. The District of Ajlun
   Salman al-Qudhah, Muslim

6. The District of Jarash
   Muflih al-Birmawi, Muslim

7. The District of Karak
   Ahmad al-Tarawnah, Muslim; Atallah al-Majali, Muslim; Hani al-Aakashah, Christian

8. The District of Tafilah
   Salih al-Auran, Muslim

9. The District of Maan
   Omar Mattar, Muslim

10. The Northern Bedouins
    Aakif al-Fayiz, Muslim

11. The Southern Bedouins
    Shaikh Hamd ibn al-Jazi, Muslim

The West Bank

1. The District of Jerusalem
   Abdullah Niawas, Christian; Kamil Auraiqat, Muslim; Anwar Nusaibah, Muslim

2. The District of Bethlehem
   Tawfiq Qattan, Christian; Abd al-Fattah Darwish, Muslim

3. The Hebron District; Abdullah Bashir Umr, Muslim; Rashad al-Khatib, Muslim; Rashad Maswadah, Muslim; Said al-Aazzah, Muslim

4. The District of Nablus
   Qadri Touqan, Muslim; Hikmat al-Masri, Muslim; Dr Mustafa Bushnaq, Muslim; Dr Abd al-Majid Abu Hijlah, Muslim

5. The District of Jenin
   Abd al-Rahim Jarrar, Muslim; Tahsin Abd al-Hadi, Muslim

6. The District of Tulkarm
   Dr Kamal Hannoun, Muslim; Hafiz al-Hamdullah, Muslim

7. The District of Ramallah
   Musa Nasser, Christian; Khulousi al-Khairi, Muslim; Abdullah al-Rimawi, Muslim

On 14 April 1950, the Chamber of Notables (Senate) was appointed by the King as shown in Table 11.3.

TABLE 11.3
Chamber of Notables appointed in April 1950

Chairman
Tawfiq Abu al-Huda, Former Prime Minister

Members
Samir al-Rifai, Former Prime Minister
Falah al-Madadhah, Minister of the Interior
Al-Sharif Sharaf, Member of the Hashemite family
Sabri al-Tabba, Merchant of Amman
Ismail al-Bilbaisi, Merchant of Amman
Muaarik al-Majali, Landowner from Karak
Muhammad Kraishan, Landowner from Maan
Muhammad Abu Tayih, Tribal Shaikh of al-Huwaitat
Hussein Khawaja, Circassian from Wadi al-Sir
Nawfan al-Saud, Landowner from Shunet Nimreen
Salim al-Bakhit, Landowner from al-Salt (Christian)
Raghib al-Nashashibi, Minister of Agriculture
Muhamed Ali al-Jaabari, Mayor of Hebron
Suleiman al-Taji Farouki, Imam from Ramleh
Sulaiman Touqan, Mayor of Nablus
Abd al-Latif Salih, Lawyer from Nablus
Farid Irshaid, Landowner from Jenin
Wadia Diamis, Mayor of Bait Jala

Although only seven West Bank notables were appointed, it was considered then that Tawfiq Abu al-Huda and Samir al-Rifai were of Palestinian origin. Thus the numbers were nine from each Bank of the Jordan.

Said al-Mufti, the former Minister of Internal Affairs in Abu al-Huda's Government and leader of the Circassian community in Jordan, was appointed Prime Minister on 12 April 1950. His Government is shown in Table 11.4.

The Ministers for Defence, Public Works, Agriculture, Post and Telegraph and Trade and Industry were from the West Bank. On 5 August 1950, a reshuffle in the Government was made. Ahmad Touqan was appointed Minister of Communications, and Anistas Hananiya was appointed Minister of Refugees, Construction and Development.

TABLE 11.4
Government of Said al-Mufti, formed on 12 April 1950

- Said al-Mufti, Prime Minister
- Muhammad al-Shanqiti, Qadhi Qudhah and Education
- Falah al-Madadhah, Internal Affairs
- Muhammad al-Shuraiqi, Foreign Affairs
- Rouhi Abd al-Hadi, Justice
- Fawzi al-Mulqi, Defence
- Sulaiman al-Sukkar, Finance and Economics
- Ahmad Touqan, Public Works, Construction and Development
- Raghib al-Nashashibi, Agriculture
- Anstas Hananiya, Post and Telegraph
- Said Ala al-Din, Trade and Industry

Before the opening of Parliament, King Abdullah went on a tour of the West Bank visiting Hebron, Bethlehem, Jerusalem, Ramallah, Nablus, Jenin, Tulkarm and Qalqiliyah, including the villages between these main towns and cities. General Glubb accompanied the King on his tour and reported the following to the Foreign Office:

We had all heard so much of the alleged resentment felt by the public at His Majesty's approaches to the Jews, that some were inclined to look forward to those visits with a certain apprehension. Their fears were utterly unjustified. The King's reception was delirious – more enthusiastic than ever before.

In Jerusalem, the crowds were shouting: 'We are sheep without a shepherd'. 'We want you as our leader.'

His reception everywhere was the same and deeply impressive. In every village, the crowds pressed round the royal car, clapping, shouting and cheering. Everybody was laughing. Anyone who has spent many years in the East is familiar with 'spontaneous joy' arranged by the police. But there was nothing artificial about the enthusiasm of these demonstrations. I was beside the King and was immensely impressed.

The Palestine Arabs have suffered for thirty years for lack of a leader. The only man they chose, al-Haj Amin al-Husseini, proved a broken reed. All the others were merely lining their own pockets and those who are still left today are little better. It would seem that the common people of Arab Palestine have decided that King Abdullah can play the role of the leader so long awaited. When we returned to Nablus, I remarked to the Governor on the enthusiasm we had witnessed. 'The politicians had told us he was hated,' I said.

'Don't believe them,' the Governor answered. 'The common people of Palestine have decided that King Abdullah is their man.'

These paradoxes in Palestine are perhaps due to the educational results of the Mandatory Regime, which produced a relatively small number of highly educated people who form a class distinct from the simple villagers. The clever ones cannot resist the temptation to show off their cleverness by destructive criticism of all and sundry from President Truman to Mr Bevin to the private soldier of the Arab Legion. To them everything about everybody but themselves is wrong. But ninety per cent of the people have entirely different mental and psychological reactions. It is those latter – not the high brows – who have taken King Abdullah to their hearts.

Not for the first time in history, a King seems to be nearer to the common people than are the intervening job-hunters and axe-grinders.[13]

On 24 April 1950, the King opened the extraordinary session of Parliament with a speech from the throne. He said:

It is my pleasure to open, for the first time in the constitutional life of Jordan, the National Assembly which combined the two Banks of the Jordan, emanating from the will of one people, one country, and one hope. It is a blessed step for unity which the two Banks took and the people moved to achieve, motivated by the Arab national unity, patriotic pride and mutual interests. Jordan is like a bird, its wings east and west, it is its natural right to be united, its people to meet. As notables and deputies you know that the unity of the two Banks is a national and practical fact. It is a national fact proven by the unity of origin, interests and pain and hope. It is a practical fact proven by the strong ties of unity between the two Banks since 1922, ties of currency, of mutual defence, of ports, of frontier security, of the ease of customs and travel, cultural legislative exchanges, which made each Bank important to the other.

After the King's departure from Parliament, the Speaker of the National Assembly of both chambers, Tawfiq Abu al-Huda, stood up and swore the usual oath: 'I swear by The All Mighty Allah, to be loyal to His Majesty King Abdullah ibn al-Hussein the Exalted, to adhere to the Constitution, to serve the Nation and to carry out my duties truthfully.' Thereafter, every member swore the same oath. Muhammad al-Shuraiqi, the Foreign Minister, read the proposed draft resolution for the unity of both Banks:

Resolution for the decision of unity

In expression of the people's faith in, and in recognition of efforts spent by, His Majesty King Abdullah ibn al-Hussein, King of the Hashemite Kingdom of the Jordan, towards attainment of national aspirations, and basing itself on the right of self-determination and on existing *de facto* position between Jordan and Palestine, their national, natural and geographic unity and their common interests and living space, Parliament which represents both sides of Jordan resolved this day 7th Rajab 1369 coinciding with 24 April 1950, and declares:

One: Its support of complete unity between both sides of Jordan, Eastern and Western, and their Union into one State which is the Hashemite Kingdom of the Jordan at whose head reigns His Majesty King Abdullah ibn al-Hussein on the basis of constitutional representative government and equality of rights and duties of all citizens.

Two: Its reaffirmation to preserve full Arab rights in Palestine, to defend those rights by all lawful means in exercise of its natural rights but without prejudicing final settlement of Palestine's just case within the sphere of national aspirations, inter-Arab cooperation and international justice.

Three: That this resolution, adopted by the two Houses of Parliament representing both sides of Jordan, be laid before His Exalted Majesty and be considered effective as soon as it gains Royal approval.

Four: That the Government proclaim and execute this resolution as soon as it has obtained Royal Sanction, and notifies its contents to the sister Arab States and foreign friendly states in the usual diplomatic manner.[14]

Before opening the debate, the Speaker, Tawfiq Abu al-Huda, explained all the stages through which the process of unity had developed:

> The idea of establishing a Government for Palestine came from the deceased al-Noqrashi, who justified it by the fact that the Jews had a state recognised by many states with the intention of joining the United Nations. This makes it essential in order to hinder this endeavour, to have a recognised Palestinian Government which will face the Jews, and speak in the name of Palestine. I opposed the idea and told him that it would not be of any benefit, and the Arab States had committed themselves to the defence of Palestine in both political and military affairs and they have negotiated and are now negotiating with the representatives of the United Nations, and that

the establishment of a Government in Palestine needs to be reverted to the inhabitants, and that under the circumstances they cannot assemble and give their opinion and agree on persons. He accepted my reply. During my talks with some Arab leaders I found that the object of forming the Palestine Government was to burden it with the responsibilities which the Arab Governments had not succeeded in achieving. That, al-Noqrashi told me, would save the Arab States from accepting partition and negotiating with the Jews, for it would be carried out by the Palestinians themselves. That remained the object of some Arab Governments which ended in the assembly of the Gaza congress, the appearance of the weak Government which had nothing and which had dispersed except for two.

Abu al-Huda continued to describe all the events mentioned in this and the previous chapter with accuracy and details in his long speech. He concluded:

Gentlemen, you see that the Jordanian Government had honourably executed its decision which was approved by the National Assembly, and was careful to maintain understanding with its sisters the Arab States and relations with the Arab League, and that it did not take the constitutional steps to complete the unity between the two Banks except after achieving an understanding with the majority of these states. The first step was the participation of our brothers of the West Bank in the elections for the Chamber of Deputies, and it is the right of their deputies to determine their future after taking part in the elections, which indicates their wishes in unity on condition that it will not prejudice the final solution as specified in the resolution presented by the Government today.

Abu al-Huda was much applauded by the members and opened the debate, which was commenced by Anwar Nusaibah, the Member for Jerusalem, as follows:

To begin with I thank Your Excellency for your candid statement, and I have no doubt that it will help us in the debate; and secondly, we the sons of the West Bank are proud and happy in this day in which we are assembled with our brothers the notables and deputies, to establish one Assembly and to endeavour to achieve one aim for which we came to this Assembly.

Please do not interpret our talk contrary to our wish in this unity, but there are some procedures and formalities that I wish to raise. We have sworn to abide by the constitution and it is our duty

[349]

to do so. There are only two situations where both Chambers can hold a joint meeting in one place.

The first: when a speech from the throne is delivered and in that meeting we only listen to the speech.

The second: when a conflict occurs on a draft law approved by the Chamber of Deputies and not approved by the Chamber of Notables, and vice versa.

I cannot find anything in the constitution that allows us to approve a draft law before presenting it to the Chamber of Deputies, and although I am glad and honoured to be sitting in this case, I think the constitution provides for a decision by the Chamber of Deputies and thence referred to the Chamber of Notables. Again from the procedure point of view, in His Majesty's Speech it was mentioned that this is an extraordinary session, but the provision in Article 41 of the constitution shows how the extraordinary session should be conducted, that it is the right of the King to invite the National Assembly for an extraordinary session with the object of approving certain issues which must be announced with the invitation.

I do not know how my brothers received the invitation, but for me the invitation was issued by the District Commissioner of Jerusalem, and I had no idea of the proposed resolution.

Tawfiq Abu al-Huda attempted to explain the justification of the invitation by recalling precedents. He went on to refer to three cases, but failed to realise that even procedure was part of the constitution and could not be prejudiced by precedence or tradition. He concluded by saying: 'It is the wish of His Majesty and the Government to speed up the process and if unity is not approved, and it has been approved by your presence here officially, how could a member from the West Bank debate an issue of the East Bank and vice versa? The question of procedure is not important if the members approve.' Abu al-Huda, with his autocratic attitude, was debating against a graduate with an LLB degree from Cambridge University and who was a prominent lawyer; he was not convincing in his argument.

Sulaiman Touqan, the notable from Nablus said:

Please let me say that we all came here while knowing that the meeting was for opening the session and that the sons of the West Bank had approved the desired unity, and while I agree with what Anwar Nusaibah had said, we are in an extraordinary session, and came for unity. We must give the decision of amalgamation and

[350]

constitutional issues and the chance for debating the constitutional issues will come in future meetings. [Applause by the members.]

Khulousi al-Khairi, the Member for Ramallah, said:

This proposed resolution stirs in the being of every one of us a beloved tune, and touches the heart in its depth, and for these reasons it must be accomplished in accordance with constitutional procedures so that no gaps may be left open through which people of self-indulgence can penetrate to the contrary.

I imagine, from the Speaker's statement, there are some possibilities that must be examined carefully, especially that the Arab National unity movement had ceased by the actions of some elements who do not seek except their personal interests. I hope that the approval of the resolution will be the starting point in the destruction of separatism, and I say we must study and examine so that no gaps can be opened for the seekers of personal interests.

Many constitutional points have been raised and while there might be some more points, which time does not allow us to point out, we must not hurry in deciding this serious subject without giving the notables and deputies enough time to study them, not with the aim of delay and postponement, but with the aim that our work should be comprehensive and complete.

Hikmat al-Masri, the Member for Nablus, said:

The decision for Arab unity does not need examination or study, for it is the constitution of every Arab who is loyal to his country and it is taken for granted. This is why I ask his excellency to begin the process of voting on the proposed resolution of the Government.

Muhammad al-Minwir al-Hadid, the Member for Amman, said:

I wish to welcome our brothers, the Members for the West Bank, who are meeting with us and participate with our responsibilities for the first time, and I salute them with loyalty and faith in unity, because in this our meeting is the accomplishment of unity hoped for by the loyal sons of our Nation.

Wadia Diamis, the notable from Bait Jala, said:

We have listened with interest to the long statement by the Speaker and, of course, it explained what the Jordanian Government had carried out in talks and research with the Arab Governments regarding the destiny of the Arab part of Palestine and other matters. But we are meeting here as representatives of the people of Palestine. We are its owners and we came here to unite our country with this side of the Jordan and I do not think that anybody has a right upon us to consult with him for our self-determination. We have decided our self-determination in many conferences, and we came to this Parliament to take legal action for unity. We have decided for unity for our own benefit and to protect what is left of our country and not for negotiations or international interests.

Abdullah Niawas, the Member for Jerusalem and a member of the Baath Party, said:

> I do not think that there is among us anyone who does not wish for the unity of one country and one people. Our attitude until now was to support unity between two parts of one country, but, Your Excellency, I was also invited verbally. It is proven from the Speech from the throne that this is an extraordinary session and therefore its subjects must be limited. With my thanks for your explanation of the legal aspect, please give enough time to study the subject. Although I think your justifications were clever, in the study of a constitutional matter, I do not think, whatever the numbers of precedence were, they could be equal to the text.
>
> The second point: I think many of my brothers have not been able to study the constitution and the internal regulations. We have read it in general terms and we need two days to know whether we can achieve unity from our constitutional position as Palestinian deputies. We have accepted unity as we participated in the elections and became ministers, but we hoped to be given time to see whether we have the constitutional right to commit the people to this unity and how to transfer sovereignty to the Jordanian Government. The matter is a serious one, and it is related to the interests of a people and hundreds of thousands of refugees. We have in front of us the sister Arab States, and the Conciliation Commission is still studying this issue and we do not wish to block her way to study our case, and therefore we hope you will give us time to study these matters.
>
> The Palestine people are of you, and Palestine is part of your country, and therefore, Your Excellency, I suggest you give us enough time to study the matter with the Government and the notables and deputies.

Sulaiman Touqan, the notable from Nablus, said:

We see ourselves in procedural matters raised by our brothers the lawyers who are accustomed to talk in courts. We came here for unity and the Palestinian people have elected their Deputies for that aim; please put this opinion to the vote.

Shaikh Muhammad al-Jaabari, the notable from Hebron, said:

You all know the situation in Palestine; aggression was committed against our honour and our sacred places, and we are still talking of this and that. We came to you appealing to accept us and defend us. [Applause by the members.] Your Excellency, Arab Palestine had endured what it had endured, the Congress of Jericho and all the Palestinian people have said the word: Palestine and Jordan are one. Anybody who does not wish that, wants to see the Israeli flag hoisted on the al-Aqsa Mosque and the Tomb of Ibrahim.

Abdullah al-Rimawi, the Member for Ramallah, said:

It appears that there is misunderstanding in the matter for which we came here. Raising the emotions, sentimental speeches and the playing on the strings of hearts, we suffered. We are here for the judgement of our minds on the light of truth. Your Excellency and brothers, we are facing a serious situation . . .

Sulaiman Touqan interrupted, saying:

We are facing a discussion that can never end. I suggest we end the discussion.

The Speaker said:

The Assembly has the right of debate.

Abdullah al-Rimawi continued:

I say we are facing a serious situation which compels us to slow down and study matters. From the unity point of view the principle stands as in the Speech from the throne, in the past as in the present, if we slow down in time we do that for study.

Your Excellency, the length of your statement is the strongest evidence to the need of time to support this decision and study it in the light of its consequences in the Arab camp, and, as Khulousi al-Khairi said, we want to close that gap. Unity means that we the Palestinians declare our wish, and that cannot be achieved in this procedure. Please follow the constitutional procedure.

Sulaiman Touqan interrupted:

Enough. [*Khalasna.*]

The Speaker asked the members to vote on ending the debate, which the majority did. Musa Nasser and Abdullah al-Rimawi objected and left the Chamber. The Speaker announced a ten-minute rest and later called the Assembly to order. Shaikh Hamd ibn al-Jazi, Member for the Southern Bedouins, said:

> Your Excellency, God said in His Noble Quraan: 'Obey God, His Prophet and those in authority among you.' We will not advance in our work except in accordance with our Master's [the King's] wish, and we would like to unite the two countries whether we talk more or less.

In his second statement, the Speaker explained the constitutional procedure in accordance with Article 41 and attempted to convince the members of his argument. Thereafter, more comments were made by Nusaibah, Hannoun, Maswadah, al-Farouqi, al-Rimawi, al-Rifai, Salah, al-Khairi and Auraiqat – all of whom were from the West Bank.

Then the Speaker put the motion of postponement to the vote, which was defeated by the majority. Following that, the Speaker put the motion for the resolution of the Government for unity, and was approved by the overwhelming majority of the Members.[15]

The resolution was ratified by His Majesty King Abdullah and became effective in both Banks of the Hashemite Kingdom of Jordan with effect from 24 April 1950. The first Arab union between two Arab countries was achieved by the Palestinian and Jordanian peoples. A few days later the union was recognised by the British Government, with certain reservations regarding Jerusalem; and the 1948 Anglo-Jordanian Treaty of Alliance was made applicable to the whole of the Hashemite Kingdom of Jordan.

Jordan had had a stormy passage in the Council of the League of Arab States over the union. Instead of encouraging members for more unity, they opposed the union between the two countries. The Egyptian Government's move to expel Jordan, one of the founding members, from the League was only defeated by the Iraqi decision to support Jordan. In spite of strong pressure from the other members of the League, including Iraq, Jordan steadfastly refused to agree to a formula that it held the West Bank as a trust. That formula was inserted in the King's Speech from the throne: 'The act of union was without prejudice to any future settlement of Palestine.'

The new kingdom

It soon became obvious that King Abdullah would have to deal with a new kind of politician in Parliament. In spite of the catastrophe that struck Palestine at the heart of its people, there were still a few people in existence who would never learn from the lessons of the past. While the majority of the Palestinian people wanted unity and voted for it, there were some who were more interested in laying conditions for that unity. Others, like Anwar Nusaibah, wanted unity on firm foundations in accordance with the constitution. Kirkbride reported:

2. As my earlier letters had indicated, the original idea was to proceed with the act of union some time after the new parliament was opened on 1 May.

It was evident, however, that as soon as the elections were over, strenuous efforts were being made by the Saudi and Egyptian legations here and by hostile Palestinian organisations in Lebanon and Syria (working under the covert encouragement of the Syrian Government and probably that of the Lebanese Premier also) to influence the Palestinian deputies and senators and ministers against the proposed union. The means used were persuasion, money and threats.

In the circumstances, it was decided to put forward the opening of Parliament to 24 April and to put the act of union through as soon as was possible so as to reduce the period during which these attempts could produce effect.

3. There was also another factor to dispose of. The Palestinians love to deal in a form of political bargaining closely akin to blackmail and, although the indulging in this pastime has brought them nothing but trouble in the past, they must make another attempt at the opening of Parliament.

A group led by Khulousi al-Khairi and Musa Nasser (both of whom should have known better) decided to try and make the declaration of the union conditional on a revision of the constitution so as to make the Council of Ministers responsible to Parliament.

It was they who raised the point of order as an opening gambit, whether the houses should meet together or separately. The plot was weakened by the outburst of temper which the move induced among another party of Palestinians and, when Tewfiq Pasha Abul Huda eventually turned his heavy guns upon them, they collapsed and voted with the rest.

It should be noted, in connection with this incident, that the promoters were not opposed to union as such but merely wanted to use it to acquire something which they will obtain in any case.[16]

After union the main problem facing Jordan was the defence of the country against continued and expected further Israeli aggression. Since the formation of the National Guard in the West Bank, their training was limited to drilling with sticks and education in discipline. There was little training with weapons because of the shortage of weapons in the Jordanian Arab Army. In April, the first consignment of rifles bought for them began to arrive. Many villagers volunteered and were full of enthusiasm for training. The first National Guard training camp was established in Nablus on 1 May 1950. The National Guard was under training for one month every year without pay, but they were fed and clothed with fatigue uniforms. In the villages near the Armistice Line, the men of the National Guard were armed and carried out patrols to defend their villages.

A significant incident took place on 22 April 1950 when an Israeli patrol, consisting of a sergeant and nine men, lost their way and crossed into Jordanian territory in the Hebron Sector. The patrol was located by ten men of the National Guard, and in the engagement that followed two Jewish soldiers were killed, three were taken prisoner and the rest escaped back to their line. The National Guard patrol suffered no casualties.

Although the skirmish was a small incident, it must be compared with others. For example, six months earlier Arab villagers would flee at the mere approach of a Jewish patrol. Unlike the Israeli forces who took no prisoners and lined up unarmed villagers and shot them in cold blood, the National Guard, consisting mainly of Palestinians who suffered untold savagery by the Israeli Army, had the dignity to take prisoners and treat them with honour and humanity. Since this incident, large numbers of men were anxious to undergo military training to defend what was left of their country. They were impressed by the Jordanian Arab Army and wanted to be associated with the men who defended them. No Arab propaganda or Jewish aggression was able to change their hearts and minds after what they had been through during the previous two years. I, who was deeply involved in the organisation and training of the National Guard during my service in the West Bank, witnessed their genuine and wholehearted keenness to serve with discipline and honour. This came at a time when it was envisaged that the National Guard could assume an effective military role in the defence of frontier villages and persuade their inhabitants to stand fast and remain in their homes. The problem was no longer that of manpower, for it was estimated in 1950 that 100,000 men of military age could be raised. The problem was entirely one of finance, weapons and equipment, so that after scrounging here and there, about 3,000 men were raised from frontier villages.

The National Guard plan continued to be successful on the West Bank, but was followed with less enthusiasm on the East Bank, for most Jordanians wanted to join the Jordan Arab Army. To encourage enlistment in the National Guard, recruits for the Jordanian Arab Army and the police force were only accepted if they had completed their National Guard training.

Instead of supporting Jordan to defend what was left of Palestine, and help in caring for the Palestinian refugees, who constituted one-third of the people of Jordan, the Egyptian Government and al-Haj Amin al-Husseini planned to carry out terrorist acts in Jordan. Kirkbride reported:

> Detailed reports continue to be received of the activities of the ex-Mufti and the Egyptian Government. Egyptian deeds are fortunately apt to fall short of Egyptian plans, but there seems to be no doubt that the Egyptian Government is giving active support to the ex-Mufti in his plans to cause disorders in Palestine by means of political murders and acts of terrorism. The Egyptians are perhaps deceived by their own propaganda into believing that Arab Palestine is prepared to revolt.
>
> It is not, however, possible to guarantee that the Egypto-Mufti party will not succeed in bringing off a few isolated murders.[17]

Towards the middle of May 1950, British intelligence picked up information about a plot to assassinate General Glubb in Damascus airport while on his way to London for his annual leave and his usual talks with the Foreign Office. At that time there was no direct international link from Amman Airport. In order to fly to London, passengers had to travel to Damascus and then take an onward flight to Cyprus or to Cairo, which had direct links to London through Rome or Paris. When Glubb was warned about the attempt on his life, he changed his route to Cairo and immediately suggested to the Foreign Office that they should put pressure on the British airline, BOAC, to establish a direct flight from Amman to Cyprus. Such a service would also provide secure transportation for the growing number of British officers seconded to the Arab Legion and Arab officers attending courses in British Army schools and colleges. Glubb was shocked to hear that former Lt Colonel Abdullah al-Tel was the one who was planning that attempt on his life.

Until May 1950, the Jordan Government and people, particularly charitable organisations, maintained their assistance and support to the Palestinian refugees. By the beginning of May, the United Nations Relief and Works Agency (UNRWA) took over the responsibility for their care and resettlement. Works of reforestation and road building began, but no progress was made in any of the schemes to enable the refugees to be reintegrated. Not only had none of the refugees been resettled in Jordan as a result of the Agency's activities, but also the number of destitute refugees was increasing because of the following causes:

- Persons of means reaching the end of their resources.
- Refugees were moving to Jordan from other parts of the Arab world.
- Arab residents from the Jewish-occupied Palestinian areas were moving to join their families in Jordan.
- There was a natural increase in the population among the refugees.

By the beginning of June 1950, two years had passed since the Mandate for Palestine. Although the Arabs had committed all the mistakes typical of the behaviour of Third World countries, the situation at the end of the Mandate was a chapter without justice in British colonial history and was not a chapter of honour and humanity in the life of the United Nations Organisation. Indeed, it was a chapter of a policy of inhuman massacres, expulsion and destruction that had been premeditated and executed by the Israeli Government and its armed forces. After two years of bloody struggle by the Palestinian and Jordanian peoples, what was left of Palestine under Arab control was in Eastern Palestine (West Bank) and the Gaza Strip. The West Bank became part of the Hashemite Kingdom of Jordan and the Gaza Strip was hypothetically under the All Palestine Government of Ahmad Hilmi, but in reality was under the military control of the Egyptian Government. The difference in the two situations was immense, to say the least. For example, King Farouq never visited the Gaza Strip. Nor did he come anywhere near contact with its people, not to mention his own Egyptian people and his soldiers in the field. Meanwhile, King Abdullah visited nearly every village, town and city under his control, as well as every unit of the Jordan Arab Army, even before the union of the two Banks. In the Gaza Strip, the Palestinians were objects of military control, while in the West Bank they were free citizens with equal rights with their Jordanian brothers.

After the elections and union of the two Banks of Jordan, Basil Judd of the British Consulate-General in Jerusalem reported:

> The recent elections were conducted in an unexceptionable manner in the best British tradition and the union with Jordan is accepted with considerable satisfaction if not with enthusiasm. The general administrative and judicial system remains largely as it was under the Mandate with the superimposition of a Director General of Administration over the three Mutassarifs [District Governors] of Jerusalem, Hebron and Nablus. The administrative machine, fortunate of course in that it is not burdened with the problem of the refugees, works with a smoothness not to be found even in certain European states. In particular it has been possible to maintain public accounting at a high level, departmental budgets being regularly scrutinised and accounts verified while corruption is being kept to the minimum compatible with the oriental temperament. Emergency taxes, which were imposed in the early days of the Jordanian military government, have been suppressed and a return made to the more modern fiscal methods of mandatory period. Public health services are functioning normally and it has been possible to obtain Israeli cooperation in such matters as combating mosquito breeding areas in no-man's land. The schools even in Jerusalem have been open again for some time. The Holy Places are the administration's particular care; also the tourists who are now reappearing to visit them.
>
> The general level of security is high, but non-political murders are more common than under the mandate, probably as the result of the propinquity of so many refugees of the *fallah* class — that is,

the section of the community most prone, with the exception of the Bedouin, to self-redress and to blood feuds. The authorities are, however, active in negotiating 'tribal peace' between hostile families. The courts are now functioning normally under experienced judges of the mandatory régime, and an energetic young Attorney General is visiting all prisons and other places of confinement with a view to a goal delivery of persons left confined without trial as a perhaps inevitable result of disturbed conditions. It has been found possible to maintain the special institutions for juvenile delinquents set up under the mandate in spite of financial stringency. Police measures, particularly as regards political suspects, have been somewhat Ottoman, but the Attorney General is bringing the police to heel and, although it is perhaps outside his normal functions, is endeavouring by argument to convince suspected Communists of the erroneous nature of their political views. In this, of course, he is assisted by the fact that Communism in this area shows unmistakable signs of its origin in Israel.[18]

The old Trans-Jordan law making communism illegal was applied to the West Bank and successful measures were taken there against such Communist organisations as existed. There were two types of communists in existence – those who understood something about the dogma they professed to follow, and those who called themselves communists because they were dissatisfied or out of work. There also existed in the Orthodox Christian quarters in Jerusalem some support for Russia (as distinct from communism) on the grounds that the Western powers had failed in their moral duty as protectors of the Christian minority. A number of scare bombs were exploded on the West Bank and there was some sabotage of the telegraph routes on both Banks. At first, all these incidents were attributed to Communist agencies, but it was proved later that some had been carried out by Arabs in Israeli pay.[19]

Five months of war and 19 months of anticipating attack or aggression by the Jewish force along a long armistice line of about 650 kilometres from Bardala in the north to Aqaba in the south would have been enough to bankrupt even some European countries, let alone poor Jordan, which, without British subsidy, could have imploded. Thus, the economic conditions in the West Bank, which were grave during the war and after, needed all the help that could be provided and all the energy that the people could muster for a better life. By June 1950, normal commerce was flourishing. Agriculture workers revived the land that had been neglected for some time, and the partial restoration by the Jerusalem Electric Corporation of the supply of electricity to the Jordanian part of the city of Jerusalem was greatly welcomed by the population and had done much, in so far as power is concerned, to reanimate small local industries. In Jerusalem, water was reconnected from Ain Farah, but water supplies did not meet the needs of the people. Anwar al-Khatib, Mayor of Jerusalem, did a magnificent job of creating a spirit of revival in the city.

Meanwhile, there was some deterioration of the situation along the armistice line between the middle of May and the middle of June 1950. During that period 28 frontier incidents were reported. The most important of these took place on 3 June 1950, when the Israeli Army expelled 120 Palestinian Arabs without food or water over the frontier into the desolate part of south Jordan in Wadi Araba. Only 87 of the expelled Arabs were found, in the most miserable condition. The remainder had perished from thirst and starvation in the extremely hot summer of June. In this connection, Kirkbride reported:

> These people appear to have been the occupants of a concentration camp in Israel run on Nazi lines and many of them bore marks of torture and ill-treatment.
>
> Many of the incidents were due to Arab trespassers, both innocent and otherwise, over the frontier and to the savage retaliation by Israel troops [not police] on the first Arabs they saw. Various measures to remedy the position were considered in the Mixed Armistice Commission, but the execution of the one measure decided upon, mixed patrols on the frontier, was postponed by an Israeli refusal to cooperate until three Israeli soldiers captured [by the National Guard] in Jordan territory had been released. There is no doubt that the situation would have been improved greatly if cooperation on frontier control could have been kept at a police level and the Israeli army excluded.[20]

On 5 June 1951, a meeting was held at the HQ of the 1st Division, attended by the officers shown in Table 11.5. The object of the meeting was to decide on what alterations should be made to the existing dispositions of the units of the Jordan Army in the West Bank in order to counter further Israeli aggression and what additional measures could be taken to prevent further acts of aggression from occurring along the Jordan–Israeli frontier. After some discussion, it was concluded that

TABLE 11.5
Officers attending the meeting at HQ of
1st Division on 5 June 1951

- Lt General J. B. Glubb, CGS
- Lt Colonel W. A. Salmon, GSOI
- Brigadier S. A. Cooke, Commander 1st Brigade, Acting Commander of 1st Division
- Lt Colonel C. I. F. Coaker, GSOI 1st Division
- Lt Colonel W. D. Edwyn-Jones, AA and QMG 1st Division
- Major Sadiq al-Sharaa, GSOII 1st Division
- Brigadier J. O. H. Ashton, Commander 3rd Brigade
- Colonel Radhi Ennab, Chief of Police Jerusalem District
- Lt Colonel Muhammad Maaitah, Chief of Police Nablus District
- Colonel Benet de Reeder, Mixed Armistice Commission

there were two reasons for most of the incidents that had taken place during the previous few months.

1. Arab farmers and villagers wandering over the border

It is known that the Arab villagers do cross the border frequently in certain places along the frontier. This is due largely to the fact that the frontier is not marked, and therefore not easy to determine. In all these cases the Arabs have been in the habit of grazing their flocks and sowing crops on land, which the Mixed Armistice Commission have decided is to be part of the new country of Israel. As they have in most cases considered this land as theirs for countless generations it is understandable that they should continue to use it, particularly as there is no physical barrier to prevent them from entering it.

In any case such acts of 'Trespassing' cannot be considered as malicious acts of aggression; and the offence committed never warrants the outrageous reprisals that are being inflicted on these people by the Jews.

2. A general state of indiscipline in the Jewish Armed Forces

In every case, these incidents occurred in places where there are Jewish armed forces on the opposite side of the frontier. All acts of aggression are caused by members of the Jewish Army and Air Force. Some days ago, the Head of the Mixed Armistice Commission in Jerusalem stated that the CGS of the Jewish Army and certain prominent Jewish officials had stated that the acts of aggression, which were occuring along the Jordan frontier, were greatly deplored by them and they would give anything to be able to stop them. It was therefore assumed by all present at the meeting that the Jewish armed forces must be completely out of control. This was confirmed as being the case, by the representative of the Mixed Armistice Commission present at the meeting.[21]

During the discussions regarding the action that should be taken to counter Jewish aggression, it was suggested that Jordan should retaliate by shelling Jewish positions including Tel Aviv, but it was pointed out that the aim was to prevent future incidents, and that retaliation would only lead to further aggression and may indeed cause a renewal of active hostilities. Thus, the meeting decided that the incidents could be prevented by peaceful means if the Jewish authorities cooperated, and the whole problem should be dealt with by the police forces on both sides, not by military forces. The representative of the Mixed Armistice Commission, Colonel de Reeder, agreed. At the end of the meeting certain actions were recommended to the Jordan Government including the following:

- That the Government propose to the Mixed Armistice Commission, that both countries withdraw their forces five kilometres inside their own frontiers. No entry by military forces will be permitted into the demilitarised zone thus created. The police of both countries alone will be responsible for maintaining law and order within this zone. The police will be armed only with personal weapons.
- That all refugee camps to be moved back to a distance of at least twenty kilometres from the frontier.
- That village Mukhtars [leaders] assume responsibility for all refugees who are living in their respective villages, and all Mukhtars be made to give written undertakings to prevent their villagers from infiltrating into Jewish territory, stealing or smuggling.
- That in every case where an incident takes place, the police will immediately carry out an investigation and open a separate case file for each incident.
- That as soon as any incident takes place, the police are to contact immediately the Jewish police officer in the area, and arrange mutually for an emergency meeting to be held on the spot.[22]

On the following day, Kirkbride reported Glubb's conclusion to the Foreign Office:

> The conclusion he [Glubb] has reached is that the central authorities of Israel do not approve of the attitude of their army but that the latter is out of hand and refuses to follow directives from headquarters.

This conclusion is supported in official remarks of United Nations observers and by Israel police officers who are usually cooperative and reasonable and who frequently complain of the conduct of their military colleagues.[23]

Since the signing of the Israeli–Jordanian Armistice Agreement in April 1949, King Abdullah wanted to negotiate and achieve a peaceful settlement with the Jews. His main aim was to deter any aggressive plans by the Jews to occupy what was left of Palestine and prevent any further deterioration along the armistice line. He had been approached by many leaders of the West Bank who were also anxious for a settlement. He endeavoured to convince the Prime Minister and the Cabinet that everyone he spoke to was in favour of peace. According to Kirkbride, 'the Ministers retorted, as respectfully as was possible, that anyone they spoke to seemed to be against any settlement with the Jews.' After many discussions on the matter, the Prime Minister and the Minister for Foreign Affairs were delegated by the King to make a tour of the West Bank to ascertain the facts regarding public opinion on the subject of a peaceful settlement. The tour lasted four days, between 22 and 26 July 1950. The result was two resolutions of condemnation of a separate peace and a grudging mandate to the Jordan Government to contact the Palestine Conciliation Commission (see Appendix I). Kirkbride reported on the result of the tour as follows:

> Although the Ministers were on a fact-finding mission, they appear to have let it be known in advance what facts they wished to find.
> Some of the signatories of these resolutions are persons who have, in the past, encouraged King Abdullah to press for a separate peace. It is typical of the lack of moral courage prevailing in Middle Eastern countries that they should have said one thing to the King and expressed an opposite opinion in a public meeting.
> However, even after making allowance for weak-mindedness and double dealing, there seems to be no doubt that there is a consensus of opinion on the West Bank against direct peace negotiations between Jordan and Israel.[24]

As hopes of an agreement between Jordan and the Jews faded, the Jewish military forces adopted a much more aggressive stance on the frontier and the armistice line. This was not coincidental; indeed, it was certainly deliberate. Aggression accelerated with a long series of shootings, cattle thefts and incursions across the frontier. Many Arabs lost their lives, and there were Jewish casualties when the National Guard managed to defend themselves and properties, or when Arab citizens retaliated against the Jews. Irritation and anger rose on both sides, and the task of the Jordanian Arab Army to control their side of the frontier became extremely difficult because of the refusal of the Jews to cooperate in the measures suggested for the improvement of that control, which they themselves had proposed shortly before. The Mixed Armistice Commission did not deal with these incidents effectively, and the belief arose on the Jordanian side that the American chairman, General Riley, was biased in favour of the Jews.[25]

During August, the Jewish forces occupied an area of land east of the River Jordan, at Majamaa Bridge, which had been recognised as Jordanian territory since 1920. They attempted to justify their aggression by producing a map showing that the area occupied was west of the armistice line in accordance with the 1949 Rhodes Treaty. The Government of Jordan reacted immediately by challenging the authenticity of the map, invoking the Anglo–Jordanian Treaty of 1948, asking for British support, appealing to the authors of the Tripartite Declaration – Britain, France and the United States – and submitting a strong protest to the Security Council.

Early in September, the Jordanian Cabinet took a decision to use force to eject the Jewish intruders. Kirkbride did his best to prevent the use of force and was successful in convincing the Government not to take action. Anger and resentment against the Jewish aggression made any progress towards a settlement, or working arrangement between Jordan and the Jews, almost impossible. Even King Abdullah, who wanted a settlement, informed Kirkbride that 'it was hopeless to come to an agreement with such people'. The Jordan Government appealed to Iraq by invoking the Iraqi–Jordanian Treaty of Brotherhood and Alliance. In response, a senior Iraqi staff officer came to Jordan and visited the area where aggression had taken place.[26]

Advice to refer the question of Majamaa Bridge to the Mixed Armistice Commission was disregarded – which was not wholly surprising in view of local opinion about the efficacy of that timid body – and an appeal was made direct to the Security Council of the United Nations. The appeal was issued on the ground that the map of the Rhodes Agreement was a forgery, but the assertion was rejected. The rejection was received badly in Jordan, and there was a feeling of intense irritation and annoyance directed at the British Government for having failed to come to the rescue of Jordan against the Jewish aggression.

Inevitably, perhaps, the task of building up the Arab Legion and the strain of being responsible for the defence of the Israeli–Jordanian border took its toll on General Glubb. Not only was he responsible for the reorganisation of the Legion into three brigades – consisting of ten infantry battalions, three artillery regiments, one armoured car regiment and an engineer regiment – but he also had to negotiate the subsidy with the Foreign Office and Treasury, and deal with the day-to-day administration of all aspects of the Jordan Army and police work. He was forced to act as Chief of Staff, Commander-in-Chief, Director of Police and Minister for War. By the beginning of October 1950, the strength and organisation of the Jordanian Arab Army was as shown in Table 11.6.[27]

TABLE 11.6
The Jordanian Arab Army, October 1950

Unit	Commander	Strength
HQ 1st Division	Major General N. O. Lash	186
Field Ambulance	Lt Colonel Muhammad Talhuq	102
Div Workshops	Major W. Brace	286
Field Engineers	Major A. W. K. Condon, RE	263
Div S and T	Major Jubran Hawwa	235
Signal Regiment	Captain J. C. Pearsehouse	516
Div APM	Captain Nasr al-Ahmad	100
AOD	Tuamah Atallah	20
1st Brigade	Brigadier J. J. McCully	123
6th Regiment	Anwar al-Daoud	541
9th Regiment	Salamah Etayiq	538
2nd Brigade	Brigadier S. A. Cooke, OBE	112
Hashemite Regiment	Colonel Habis al-Majali	706
1st Regiment	Lt Colonel H. C. Blackden	532
3rd Regiment	Lt Colonel T. H. S. Galletly	560
5th Regiment	Lt Colonel Ali al-Hiyari	545
7th Regiment	Major Khalid al-Sahin	657
3rd Brigade	Brigadier J. O. M. Ashton	156
2nd Regiment	Lt Colonel H. F. Slade	605
4th Regiment	Lt Colonel Abd al-Rahman al-Sahin	527
8th Regiment	Major Fawaz Mahir	566
Artillery Regiment	Lt Colonel G. H. F. Chaldecott, RA	967
Armed Car Regiment	Lt Colonel C. J. Smith	474
Total strength		**9,317**

By the beginning of October the population of Amman, the capital city of Jordan, had increased to 120,000 persons, against a population of 50,000 in 1947 before the first Palestinian refugee came to the country. The vast majority of the 70,000 Palestinian refugees were living in refugee camps, but more than 10,000 of them had deliberately taken root in Amman, transferring their business and what activities they had in the West Bank to the East Bank. All through the 1930s and 1940s, trade and business in Amman was mainly controlled by Jordanians of Syrian origin, with a very small minority of Jordanians of Trans-Jordanian origin. However, by October 1950, these were nearly all superseded by Jordanians of Palestinian origin through active competition. It soon became clear that the Palestinian artisans were more skilled and industrious than their Jordanian compatriots, and Palestinian farmers and workers were more efficient than their fellow Jordanians. The Government's policy of forestalling any inclination towards patriotic regionalism of East and West Bank nature, by transferring West Bank civil servants to the East Bank and vice versa, had encouraged Palestinian competition in the East Bank, while no Jordanian business was established in the West Bank. Kirkbride reported on the political consequences of the movement of people and business within the country:

> In the old days, the Trans-Jordanians were mostly ready to accept without question decisions taken by King Abdullah; the Council of ministers taking the necessary executive action and the Legislative Council enacting the legislation required. It was almost unheard of for ministers to be attacked in the Legislative Council, and any differences which arose between the executive and legislature were composed in private.
>
> King Abdullah is now unable to enforce his wishes, and the Palestinian members of the Council of Ministers and of both houses of Parliament have demonstrated their readiness to resist Palace pressure and to express disapproval of the King's actions publicly.
>
> Now, Ministers are frequently subjected to hostile interpolations in Parliament and draft legislation is examined and debated in detail.
>
> Pressure continues to be exerted for the amendment of the Constitution so as to make the Council of Ministers responsible to Parliament and it is improbable that the Palestinians will remain content for much longer with the number of seats given to them in practice in the Council of Ministers, or allotted to them by law in Parliament.

5. The result of these political changes is a feeling of frustration on the part of King Abdullah, which has given rise to a tendency to go back on the promises he made at the opening of Parliament on the subject of the amendment of the Constitution regarding the transfer of the responsibility of the Council of Ministers to that institution.

Fear of attacks in Parliament is driving Ministers to adopt the pose of extreme nationalism, which has been a familiar feature in neighbouring Arab states for long past and which has had such regrettable results in the administration of the affairs of these countries.

6. The Palestinians are more Anglicised than the old Trans-Jordanians, and many of the Ministers and officials from the West Bank are graduates of British universities. They are, however, less ready to seek or accept advice and it is clear that, in spite of their outer veneer of English language and culture (one of them went as far as speaking Arabic in a high-faluting English accent), they are potentially more hostile to Great Britain and the West than are the less educated and more simple-minded Trans-Jordanians.

Their unwillingness to accept advice is doubtless due partly to an unwillingness to admit, by implication, that they are inferior.

They still believe that Great Britain and the United States of America were largely responsible for the disasters that overtook Arab Palestine. This belief shows every sign of becoming an established fact in Arab histories and it must continue for long to affect our relations with Palestinians in particular.

7. Given the circumstances, it was inevitable that these changes should come about and there was no chance of extending to Arab Palestine the feudal (or if you like reactionary) but happy system of government which was obtained in the old Trans-Jordan.

It is inevitable that the new Hashemite Kingdom of Jordan will gradually assume the pattern of its neighbouring Arab states and the process will be expedited by the disappearance of King Abdullah, whose influence is still a powerful brake. Much that is admirable will be lost and much that is undesirable will be acquired but, again, the geographical position makes it inevitable that Jordan should follow, for good or ill, the lead of the more advanced parts of the Arab World.[28]

It soon became obvious that the King was not pleased with the performance of the Government. The King, who considered Shaikh Muhammad Amin al-Shanqiti, Falah al-Madhah and Muhammad al-Shuraiqi as his own candidates when he formed Said al-Mufti's

Government, lost confidence in them because 'they failed to keep him properly informed with the views of their colleagues and the public at large'.[29] He thought that al-Shuraiqi, the Foreign Minister, was largely responsible for the unfavourable result of the fact-finding mission in the West Bank that he undertook with the Prime Minister in July. Muhammad Amin al-Shanqiti was responsible for the debacle in connection with Munir al-Aajlani and Lt Colonel Bahij al-Kallas of the Syrian Army in regard to the Greater Syria scheme. He was also responsible for the shortage of funds for education and the restrictions of the facilities available for the secondary schools in the West Bank. That step was extremely unpopular among the people who were accustomed to the lavish facilities offered by the British Palestine Government. Falah al-Madhah was very heavy-handed in his treatment of the people of the West Bank when he was Governor and became even more unpopular as Minister of Internal Affairs. All three were close friends of Said al-Mufti, but were disfavoured by the King, who wanted them out of the Government. Furthermore, the fact that Samir al-Rifai was in constant touch with the King, criticising the Government every step of the way, made it difficult for the King and his Government to reach mutual understanding.

Said al-Mufti tendered his resignation to the King on 11 October 1950, and the King started his consultations on the same day, but until the 13th he could find no one to form a new government. The spread of various rumours and the fact that the public became aware that a crisis was looming between the King and his Prime Minister – which was probably leaked by some ministers, or more likely, by some in the Royal Palace – and the notion that the King wanted to force the pace in the matter of negotiations with Israel, caused much concern. In Kirkbride's words, the fact that 'the King was unable to find anyone who would accept the task of forming a new government was a clear indication of where the sympathy of the people lay and of the state of public opinion on the subject of negotiations with Israel. The King offered the task to all the suitable candidates and also to many who were unsuitable, to be faced in every instance with completely negative replies.'[30]

However, on 15 October 1950, after conceding that al-Shuraiqi should remain in the Cabinet as Minister of Justice, and with al-Shanqiti and al-Madhah removed, Said al-Mufti formed his new Government (see Table 11.7).

TABLE 11.7
Said al-Mufti's new Government of October 1950

- Said al-Mufti, Prime Minister
- Shaikh Ahdullah Ghoshah, Qadhi al-Qudhah
- Muhammad al-Shuraiqi, Justice
- Rouhi Abd al-Hadi, Foreign Affairs
- Fawzi al-Mulqi, Defence
- Sulaiman al-Sukkar, Finance
- Ahmad Touqan, Education
- Anistas Hananiya, Development and Reconstruction
- Abd al-Rahman Khalifah, Interior
- Hashim al-Jayousi, Communications
- Ahmad Tarawnah, Agriculture and Trade

Ministers Ghoshah, Abd al-Hadi, Touqan, Hananiya and Jayousi were from the West Bank, while the rest of the ministers were from the East Bank. In spite of the fact that the King had acquiesced in the appointment of Muhammad al-Shuraiqi as Minister of Justice, this did not mean that he had forgotten al-Shuraiqi's role in the fact-finding delegation in the West Bank. Thus, he made it clear that al-Shuraiqi's appointment was not his wish. He started to show his irritation to some members of the opposition in parliament; he criticised the Ministers on minor matters, and, in general, he hinted at his displeasure with the Government's performance.

On 1 November, al-Shuraiqi called at the Royal Palace without an appointment asking to have an audience with the King. The King declined to receive him. On the following day, Said al-Mufti with the members of the Cabinet, except al-Shuraiqi, called on the King. Said al-Mufti spoke on behalf of his colleagues, saying they could not understand the King's attitude towards them and expressed their readiness to resign if they did not enjoy the King's confidence. The King was extremely candid. He replied that they had his confidence and that he felt he could not ask for a better Government, but with one exception. He did not name al-Shuraiqi, but said that they were aware of the identity of the exception, and that his departure would end the problem. To add to the Government's problems, on 2 November, Israeli soldiers killed two Arab children and seriously wounded another while they were gathering firewood in an area close to no-man's land in the West Bank. This cowardly and sadistic crime inflamed Jordanian and Palestinian public opinion. It certainly hardened the feelings of all the people against having anything to do with the Jews.[31]

No secrets could be kept in Amman, and the King's displeasure with the Government and al-Shuraiqi became known – particularly at the National Assembly, where the deputies were debating the reply to the speech from the throne. The opposition took the advantage of the absence of the Cabinet from the Chamber while they were at the Royal Palace, and demanded the insertion in their reply of several controversial passages against the wish of the Government. When the ministers returned to the Chamber, they endeavoured to revise the new insertions but failed to achieve a satisfactory text. The ministers had taken the deputies for granted as usual in replies to speeches from the throne, but this was before the presence of Palestinian deputies in Parliament. The Government felt almost demoralised, and Said al-Mufti had no choice but to convince al-Shuraiqi to resign. On 4 November, Muhammad al-Shuraiqi tendered his resignation and Abd al-Rahman Khalifah was appointed Minister of Justice.

While the political joust between King and Cabinet was won by the King, the other jousts between Parliament and Cabinet were, on several occasions, won by the opposition. Constant barrages of criticism were directed at various ministers who could not defend themselves except with weak and inept replies. The morale and discipline of the refugees deteriorated everywhere in the country and in their camps because of the continued uncertainty about their future and the failure of the promised capital works and other forms of aid to materialise. As Kirkbride reported, 'There were minor riots and demonstrations at various points and a lot of wild talk, inspired apparently by the refugee organisations at Beirut and Damascus, of a mass peaceful march of the refugees into Israel.'[32] Public criticism of the United Nations Relief and Works Agency on the grounds of inefficiency and the corruption of its employees was common. Such reports also appeared in the press.

On 20 November, and for the first time since the demonstrations of 1948, a demonstration of refugees in the East Bank of Jordan was staged by about 1,000 men who gathered outside the Ministry of Reconstruction and Development at Amman. They protested against the reduction of the number of ration cards and the general lack of progress to settle the fate of the refugees. Although the demonstration ended peacefully, it was regarded as 'a symptom of the feelings of unrest, which seems to have been growing among the refugees on account of the continued uncertainty about their future and because of the failure of the capital development works promised but as yet unforthcoming'.[33]

On 21 November, the opposition mounted a vicious attack on the Government for its failure to free the area occupied by the Jews at Majamaa Bridge in August, and complaining it was subservient to the British Government. An attack on General Glubb for the loss of the area was combined with attacks on the British Government for failing to support Jordan in accordance with the Anglo-Jordanian Treaty of 1948, and for preventing the Jordan Government from using force to free the Majamaa Bridge area.

By November 1950, the political atmosphere in Jordan had changed significantly, with the presence of Palestinian notables and deputies in Parliament, who had little regard for the tradition of obedience to the King's wishes or the down-to-earth attitude of the Kingdom for the desperate need of British support – including the British subsidy, without which the whole Kingdom would have collapsed economically. Kirkbride reported thus on the new situation:

> You will realise that we are in the throes of a revolution here. What has happened hitherto are just the first skirmishes in a major battle for power between a Legislature stuffed with politically minded Palestinians, and the Executive, which consists of King Abdullah and his ministers. The Executive has lost the preliminary encounters for two reasons: one, the impatience of the King which leads him to take up stands in untenable positions; two, the unfortunate fact that the Prime Minister of the moment got at cross purposes with the King and has, by now, virtually given up the struggle.
>
> As regards myself, my famous influence was exercised over a number of Jordanians, including the King himself, but when those whom I can influence lose their power to guide events, I also lose potency. The tendency of the Palestinians is to react in the negative to all British suggestions and, with one exception, they are people with whom I have not worked before.
>
> The second round between the Legislature and the Executive will be staged before long but, if the position of the latter is to be restored, it will be necessary for a new team of ministers to be formed; the present Council is a spent force. It is to this last aspect that I am now devoting my attention.
>
> I note your reference to the Arab Legion subsidy. My experience is that the withdrawal, or the threat of withdrawal, of a grant in aid

or a subsidy, is a double-edged weapon which is as likely to wound the wielder as his opponent unless it is handled with care.

If, for any reason, the Arab Legion subsidy is withheld, Jordan will crash economically and political chaos will follow economic chaos inevitably. The alternative will then be to abandon the place to ultimate division between the neighbouring states, or to commence, at great expense and trouble, to try and reconstruct the edifice which we built during the twenty-six years of British mandate.

I suggest, therefore, that great patience should be exercised before resorting to extreme measures to secure our way.[34]

Towards the end of November 1950 it became obvious that the Government was completely demoralised by pressure from the King, the National Assembly and the general public. The Prime Minister became indifferent in his dealings with internal affairs. The day-to-day running of the country suffered. The Jews became more aggressive than ever, and negotiations with them in the conciliation commission were at a standstill. The Mixed Armistice Commission did nothing to stem Jewish aggressions. Through no fault of the Prime Minister's, the economy was in decline and poverty prevailed in many areas of the country. Relations with the British Government were not as warm as usual and criticism was directed at Kirkbride in private and public. Kirkbride reported:

1. I am becoming increasingly uneasy about the effect of current events on the Jordan–Israel frontier on our own relations with the Jordanians.

2. No one can question the truth of the statement that the Israelis have been aggressive and often provocative on the common frontier ever since the chances of some sort of agreement with Jordan faded early this year.

3. The Israeli policy was, doubtless, based on their belief that the best way to treat the Arabs was to terrorise them. (They often urged this theory on me when I was District Commissioner of Galilee in 1937–39). The result has been to inflame public opinion in Jordan to a dangerous degree, to make armed clashes (such as the recent event in the Wadi Araba) probabilities instead of possibilities and to make any agreement or working arrangement between the two countries virtually impossible.

4. It is the role played by His Majesty's Government and by myself as their representative that worries me. It is natural that, whenever

the irritation of the Jordanians leads them to consider the use of force, I should do my utmost to restrain them from doing so; and my efforts are usually followed up by advice from His Majesty's Government to resort to the Mixed Armistice Commission.

Advice to refer to the Mixed Armistice Commission and to the United Nations observers is regarded here as, at best, a bad joke because, in practically every case submitted by Jordan, the matter has either been hushed up and allowed to die or the Israelis have got away with whatever they were after at that moment. How or why this should happen is not important for the purposes of this letter. What matters is that it is a fact.

The unfortunate reference to the Security Council did further damage and the Jordanian delegation to Lake Success has given the impression in its reports that the British member of the Council was not as sympathetic towards them as he might have been.

The effect on the Jordanians has been to produce a feeling of annoyance and frustration directed as much against ourselves as against the Israelis. People get up in Parliament and say that Jordan will never get justice until resort is made to force and articles appear in the newspapers to the same effect. If anyone asks why force was not used, the reply is always that I and/or Glubb prevented it. Members of the Council of Ministers have blamed us on more than one occasion for decisions with which they, in their hearts, agreed.

The belief that either I or Glubb are pro-Israel has not yet arisen but it is believed that we carry out the instructions of His Majesty's Government who are, and always have been, biased in favour of the Jews. A short time ago, demands were made in Parliament in connection with the Jerusalem affair that Glubb should be court-martialled and that my recall should be asked for.

There is no point in going into the question as to whether or not this feeling is justified; again what really matters is its existence and its increasing strength. It has not reached very dangerous proportions yet, but it will do so if it is not checked.

The only means of checking the rot is a demonstration that Israel cannot disregard and defy everybody and always get away with it. How or by whom this should be done is beyond my province but I suffer from a growing conviction that, unless it is done, our position here will be affected most seriously and that I shall be discredited personally to a degree that will reduce my value to His Majesty's Government to vanishing point.

Please do not let this letter be dismissed as a personal outburst of pessimism. Both Glubb and I are seriously worried about the present trend here.[35]

Kirkbride's report was written in the wake of a major crisis that erupted between Jordan and Israel, causing an armed clash between the Jordan Arab Army and the Israeli forces. The Jews had constructed a diversion to the main track from Um Rashrash (named Eilat by the Jews) to the Dead Sea. The diversion was built in Wadi Araba within Jordanian territory for approximately five kilometres in length between Kilometre 73 and Kilometre 78. The diversion had presumably been constructed to provide a better track than that previously in use, one that ran along the bed of the Wadi, thereby being unserviceable in rainy weather. On 20 November the Jordan Government decided that the part of the diversion that lay within Jordanian territory must be closed to Jewish traffic. On 22 November, General Glubb ordered Brigadier Sam Cooke, Commander of the 2nd Brigade, to send a force to close the diversion. Cooke chose Captain T. N. Bromage to command a composite force, code-named 'IBEX', to carry out the mission. It consisted of the following:

- Two Infantry Companies of the 1st Regiment.
- Two Armoured Car Sections of the 1st Regiment.
- Four Carriers of the 1st Regiment.
- Two MMG Vickers Teams of the 1st Regiment.
- Nineteen Wireless Set Rear Link.

(For the operation order, see Appendix J).

By 0500 hours on 29 November 1950, Captain Bromage deployed his force in the area of the diversion, closed it to Jewish traffic at both ends and was ready to fight. On the same morning a Jewish lorry was driven to the diversion, where the driver saw the road block and returned to where he had come from. On 1 December, General Yigael Yadin reported the incident to the Israeli Cabinet and obtained its approval to send a force to evict the Jordanian road blocks by force.

On 1 December, an Israeli force commanded by Major General Moshe Dayan was sent to Wadi Araba with the mission of removing the 'IBEX Force' from the diversion. On 3 December, the Jewish force was deployed on the slopes facing the diversion at both ends, and started a bombardment of artillery and mortars as well as anti-tank guns at the Jordanians. The Jordanian 'IBEX Force' opened fire at the Jewish force and, during the exchange of fire, which lasted nearly all day, one Israeli officer was killed. On the Jordanian side one soldier was killed and one armoured car was destroyed. General Dayan and his Israeli force, which was sent to open the diversion for traffic, failed to dislodge a small unit of the Jordanian Arab Army, in spite of their superior numbers and armaments. However, the Jordan Army had to obey an order of the United Nations observers to fall back. The case was reported to the Mixed Armistice Commission. That action was taken without the King being consulted, or even informed beforehand. This decided the fate of the Council of Ministers, which was already about to fall.

On 4 December 1950, Said al-Mufti tendered his resignation to the King, and Samir al-Rifai was ready with his new Cabinet to take over on the same day (see Table 11.8).

TABLE 11.8
Samir al-Rifai's new Cabinet of December 1950

- Samir al-Rifai, Prime Minister and Foreign Affairs
- Shaikh Abdullah Ghoshah, Qadhi al-Qudhah and Justice
- Abbas Mirza, Interior
- Omar Matar, Defence
- Dr Jamil al-Tutinji, Health and Social Services
- Hazza al-Majali, Agriculture
- Raghib al-Nashashibi, Public Works
- Ahmed Touqan, Education
- Anistas Hananiya, Development and Reconstruction
- Sulaiman al-Nabulsi, Finance
- Anwar al-Khatib, Trade

Ghoshah, al-Nashashibi, Touqan, Hananiya and al-Khatib were from the West Bank, and Ghoshah, Touqan and Hananiya had been Ministers in the previous Cabinet. Mattar was the Speaker of the House of Deputies, al-Majali was the Mayor of Amman and al-Khatib was the Mayor of Jerusalem. Sulaiman al-Nabulsi and al-Nashashibi were in al-Rifai's previous Cabinet. Dr al-Tutinji joined the Cabinet for the first time.

Kirkbride reported the change of Government to the Foreign Office on 5 December as follows:

Samir al-Rifai, originally a Palestinian, was Prime Minister in 1945 for eight months and again for ten months in 1947. Recently he has been Minister of the Palace, a post created by King Abdullah in order that he might always have a spare Prime Minister on tap. He failed to form a Ministry earlier this year, when Said Pasha resigned in protest against Abdullah's insistence on negotiations with Israel.

He is intelligent, but is inclined to apply the principle that the end justifies the means in public business, with results that are not always happy.

He is likely to be more amenable than his predecessor with regard to Abdullah's policy towards Israel. He acted as Chief Representative of Jordan (or more accurately the King's representative) in the negotiations at the beginning of the year. It will be interesting to see how long he lasts.[36]

On assuming office, Samir al-Rifai took certain measures to reduce the political temperature of the Chamber of Deputies to a more subdued frame of mind. He stated in Parliament and in public that he was not prepared to conclude a peace with the Israelis independently of the other Arab States. But in private he added that he would, nevertheless, be prepared to do all he could, within the scope of the Rhodes Agreement, to remove causes of friction. However, there was no progress towards a peaceful settlement with Israel. On the contrary, relations between the two sides continued to deteriorate progressively and culminated in the middle of December 1950 in an armed clash between the two sides. By the end of December there were signs of an understanding between the two Governments, and the situation had been largely restored to calm. However, both the members of the Chamber of Notables and Deputies remained 'firm in their opposition to any contacts with Israeli authorities and the personal intervention of King Abdullah failed to shake them on this point'.[37]

King Abdullah, who was determined to oppose any move for the internationalisation of Jerusalem, insisted on the Government maintaining their complete opposition to any proposal connected with it. The Government declined to accept an invitation to send a delegation to Athens to discuss the so-called 'Garreau' plan for the future of the Holy City. As regards the Swedish–Dutch draft resolution about Jerusalem, which was prepared for submission to the meeting of the General Assembly of the United Nations in the autumn, the Jordan Government refused, in spite of strong pressure, either to accept or reject the resolution. The failure of the United Nations to produce a new decision about the future of the city was regarded locally as a victory for Jordan.

In the economic field Jordan remained a poor country, relying mainly on the British subsidy and assistance. Owing to the loss of the former market in Palestine for its surplus produce, the local consumption of a great part of that produce by the unproductive refugee population, and the enhanced cost of transportation of imports and exports through Beirut, Jordan continued to draw heavily on its sterling balances in order to fill the gap between income and expenditure. In October, it became apparent that the releases from the balances agreed on earlier in the year were inadequate, and a supplementary release was requested and secured. The original provision for revenue from exports made in the estimated balance of payments on the basis of which the original release had been approved, was too optimistic. Furthermore, the redemption of the Palestine currency had been virtually completed during the year and the new currency of the Jordanian dinar was issued in its place. At the end of the year, just less than ten million dinars of the new currency were in circulation – a figure demonstrating the severe shrinkage of the amount of ready money in Jordanian hands. By the end of 1950, there was no doubt that there had been a progressive deterioration of the country's economic position.[38]

Tension along the Jordan–Israeli demarcation line did not just remain static, it even increased. Throughout that period, Israeli statesmen continued to claim on the international stage – whether in Lake Success or elsewhere – that Israel was holding out the hand of friendship to the Arabs. The actual situation on the demarcation line, however, presented a different picture: the Israelis were constantly aggressive.

In the ten months from December 1949 to October 1950, 117 incidents of crossing the demarcation line (or of firing across it) were carried out by Israeli uniformed forces. During the same period, not one incident of crossing the line by men of the Jordan Arab Army or the National Guard was reported. During the same ten months, 76 cases of Israeli aircraft flying across Jordan territory were recorded. As Jordan had no aircraft, the Israeli Air Force ran no risk flying over Jordan. From the signing of the Rhodes Armistice Agreement to October 1950, 5,648 Arabs were expelled from their homes in Israeli-occupied territory to find refuge in Jordan. (Infiltrators captured by the Israelis and returned to Jordan are not included.) The planting of a foreign state in the heart of the Arab world was on its way to creating yet more tension and conflicts.

NOTES

1 PRO. FO 371/82714. Memorandum by Wright, 22 January 1950.
2 PRO. FO 371/82707. From Kirkbride to the Foreign Office, 4 January 1950.
3 *Ibid.* From Sir H. Mack, Baghdad, to Mr H. McNeil, the Foreign Office, 7 January 1950.
4 PRO. FO 371/82705. From Kirkbride to Ernest Bevin, 6 March 1950.
5 PRO. FO 371/82755. From the Cairo Chancery to the African Department at the Foreign Office, 23 March 1950.
6 PRO. FO 371/81930. Minutes by G. W. Furlonge, 28 March 1950.
7 *Ibid.* From Kirkbride to the Foreign Office, 28 March 1950.
8 PRO. FO 371/82703. Monthly report for March 1950.
9 PRO. FO 371/82718. From Kirkbride to G. W. Furlonge, 4 April 1950.
10 *Ibid.* From Cairo to the Foreign Office, 11 April 1950.
11 PRO. FO 371/82710. From the British Middle East Office in Cairo to the Foreign Office, 13 April 1950.
12 PRO. FO 816/162. From General Glubb to the Foreign Office, 25 April 1950.
13 *Ibid.*
14 *HKJOG*, special edition, Records of the Jordanian Parliament, April 1950. Also, PRO. FO 371/82718. Resolution presented to the Foreign Office on 25 April 1950.
15 *HKJOG*, special edition, Records of the National Assembly, April 1950.
16 PRO. FO 371/82719. From Kirkbride to the Foreign Office, 28 April 1950.
17 *Ibid.*
18 PRO. FO 371/82705. From Basil Judd to the Foreign Office, 17 June 1950.
19 PRO. FO 371/91788. From Kirkbride to Ernest Bevin, 3 January 1951.
20 PRO. FO 371/82703. Monthly situation report for June, 1950, 1 July 1950.
21 PRO. FO 371/827151. Minutes of meeting on 5 June 1950, Kirkbride to the Foreign Office, 6 June 1950.
22 *Ibid.*
23 *Ibid.* From Kirkbride to the Foreign Office, 6 June 1950.
24 PRO. FO 371/82179. From Kirkbride to the Foreign Office, 29 July 1950.
25 PRO. FO 371/91788. From Kirkbride to Ernest Bevin, 3 January 1951.
26 PRO. FO 371/82703. Monthly situation report for September 1950, 1 October 1950.
27 Documents of the Arab Legion, HQ 1st Division No. G/1/2/269, 12 October 1950. Divisional diary for the period ending September 1950, author's private papers.
28 PRO. FO 371/82705. From Kirkbride to Clement Attlee, 5 October 1950.
29 *Ibid.*
30 *Ibid.* From Kirkbride to Ernest Bevin, 16 October 1950.
31 PRO. FO 371/82703. Situation report for November 1950, 1 December 1950.
32 PRO. FO 371/91788. From Kirkbride to Ernest Bevin, 3 January 1951.
33 *Ibid.*
34 PRO. FO 371/82716. From Kirkbride to Furlonge, 30 November 1950.
35 *Ibid.*, 5 December 1950.

36 PRO. FO 371/82705. Minutes by J. Brinson, 5 December 1950.
37 PRO. FO 371/91788. Kirkbride to Ernest Bevin, annual report on the Hashemite Kingdom of Jordan, 3 January 1951.
38 *Ibid.*

12

The Last Days of a Great King

On 15 January 1951, Reuven Shiloah, a senior official at the Israeli Foreign Ministry, visited Amman to deliver a reply to a letter dated 3 January from the King to Dr Chaim Weizmann, Israel's first President, demanding the evacuation of Jewish forces from the Jordanian territory at Majamaa Bridge and Wadi Araba. Samir al-Rifai, the Prime Minister, had a meeting with Shiloah in the presence of King Abdullah. The reply was from David Ben-Gurion, the Israeli Prime Minister, who said Shiloah had been delegated to discuss the matter and trusted 'that the new Government of Jordan headed by Samir Pasha would enable some progress to be made'. Shiloah stated that the road in Wadi Araba was in Jordanian territory and it would cease to be used. Regarding the question of the occupied land in the Majamaa Bridge area, Shiloah said that it was more difficult and the Israeli Government had been advised that they had a strong case legally. In spite of this, though, it was prepared to drop the legal aspect and deal with the matter politically if Samir al-Rifai would undertake to implement the provisions of Article 8 of the Armistice Agreement. Samir al-Rifai replied that, while admitting the liability of the Jordanian Government to implement Article 8, he was not prepared to link the two territorial questions with it. As soon as the two areas in question were restored to Jordan, he would be ready to go through the whole Armistice Agreement and discuss the implementation of all its terms; if there remained something for Jordan to do under Article 8, there was a great deal under the Article for Israel to do. Samir Pasha kept his promise to Parliament when he added that: 'he wished it to be understood that he would not be able to conclude peace with Israel independently of the other Arab states, but he was ready to do everything possible to remove the causes of friction and to develop the Armistice Agreement in the interests of both parties.'[1]

Much has been written about the Jordanian Government preventing the Jews having access to the Wailing Wall and the cemetery on the Mount of Olives. During that meeting, Samir al-Rifai asked Shiloah if he really thought that the time was ripe for Israelis to gain access to these holy places. Shiloah admitted that there were difficulties from a security aspect and said that 'if agreement was reached in principle, the actual application could be postponed until circumstances were more favourable.'[2] After the meeting, Samir told Kirkbride that he was not going to attend any more of these secret meetings and that future contacts must be made through the Mixed Armistice Commission or the Special Committee.

However, a further meeting was held between Samir and Shiloah on 26 February in which it was agreed that both parties should produce plans in writing for the full implementation of the provisions of the Armistice Agreement. During the following meeting on 15 March 1951, Samir al-Rifai was the only one to do so, and gave Shiloah the following English copy of the Jordanian plan.

Proposed Jordan Plan (copy)
(Communicated to Mr Shiloah by Samir Pasha on 15 March 1951.)

The following is the proposed Jordan Plan for agreement on certain questions aiming at the implementation of Article VI and VIII of the GAA between HJK and Israel.

General Principles
This Plan will be carried out as follows:

1. (a) Evacuation of the land within Jordan territory at Naharayim and rectification of the Armistice Line in that area to follow the international boundary between Trans-Jordan and Palestine.

    (b) Special arrangements will be agreed upon to facilitate the harvesting of any crops sown there by the Israeli cultivators.

2. An interval of two months to take place between the date of evacuation as in para 1 above, and the date on which the Special Committee provided for in Article VIII of the Armistice Agreement should begin to deal with the following subjects which aim at the implementation of Article VI and VIII of the Armistice Agreement.

3. The Special Committee shall be instructed to deal with the following questions in the order as set out hereunder.

(A) Article VI
(i) Borderline villages (in ex-Iraqi sector). Villages on the border line which have been affected by the demarcation of the Armistice Line in its present form and the lands of which have thus fallen

either wholly or in part in the territory of either party shall be considered to be covered by the provisions of Article VI of the GAA. Their rights under the said article shall be fully recognised and secured.

(ii) Special arrangement, to be agreed upon, shall be made to accord to the inhabitants of such villages facilities for free movement and crossing of the Armistice Line to enable them to cultivate their lands subject to normal frontier controls. (Special frontier passes or some other similar form of control may be arranged.)

(iii) Subject to the provisions of Article VI of the GAA, such lands shall be treated as being under the administration of the Government concerned.

(B) Article VIII

(i) Free movement of traffic on Latrun–Jerusalem road. This shall be put into effect. In connection with this point it is desired that the division of no-man's land in that area should be discussed and agreement thereon reached.

(ii) Resumption of the normal function of the cultural and humanitarian institutions on Mount Scopus and free access thereto.

For the implementation of this clause the following steps should be taken forthwith:

(a) UN will surrender control of the area and the military agreement dated 7 July 1948 will be terminated.

(b) The Jordan Government will undertake its full responsibility for the protection and security of the area, as is the case for other similar buildings in Jordan.

(c) The Hadassah Hospital and Hebrew University will retain legal ownership of the properties registered in their names and will be regarded as foreign property owners in Jordan.

(d) Free access to these institutions will be awarded to persons proceeding from Israel, subject to the normal frontier controls on entering Jordan territory. (Detailed arrangements for this purpose will be agreed upon. Such arrangements may include the issue of special frontier passes for staff and students who come and go regularly.)

(e) The Hadassah Hospital being a humanitarian institution and the Hebrew University a cultural institution, both will continue to be used for such purposes only.

(iii) Free access to the Holy Places and cultural institutions, and use of the cemetery on the Mount of Olives. In view of the present situation it is proposed that this point will continue to be agreed upon in principle as provided for in Article VIII of the GAA, and that its implementation must remain subject to security conditions permitting this.

(iv) Resumption of operation of the Latrun Pumping Station. This will be implemented in conjunction with the Latrun–Jerusalem road (see B(i) above).

(v) Resumption of operation of the railroad to Jerusalem. This has already been accomplished by the demarcation of the Armistice Line.

(vi) Bethlehem road and electricity for the Old City. Jordan will agree to renounce the two advantages awarded to her under the provisions of Article VIII, viz. (a) free movement of traffic on the Bethlehem road, and (b) provision of electricity for the Old City. It is evident that this should be taken as an integral part of the present plan.

(C) Division of no-man's land in Jerusalem

(i) It is proposed that the no-man's land in Jerusalem be divided in accordance with ownership – that is, Arab property to fall within the Jordan section of the City and Israeli property to fall within the Israel section of the City.

(ii) If as a result of the above mentioned division, absurdities in the line are found to exist, adjustments will be made by the exchange of property with a view to making the frontier line as appropriate and practical as possible.

(D) Financial compensation for Arab property in Israeli section of Jerusalem

It is proposed that financial compensation should be paid for Arab property situated in the Israeli section of the City. The same action will apply to Israeli property in the Arab section of the City.

(E) Frozen balances in Israel

It is proposed that the frozen balances of money belonging to Jordanians (ex-Palestine Arabs) in Israel should be released. (Particulars of agreement on this subject will be discussed.)

15 March 1951.

NB:

GP(2) The intention is that agreement would be reached on the details of execution before any part of this agreement is implemented. Thus the discussions in the Special Committee would be only for the public but in fact they would just serve to announce the previous agreement.

(B) (i.) The proposed division would include the road and pumping station within the Israeli area. Jordan would be compensated by the inclusion in its territory of Shilta, al-Burj and Bir Mayin, as well as Khirbet Hitan es Sunaubar – that is Hill 538.

(B) (vi.) This would not prejudice the Hashemite Kingdom of Jordan claiming these rights at a later date.[3]

During another meeting between Samir and Shiloah on 19 March, Shiloah agreed to the evacuation of Naharayim. Samir Pasha maintained that the term 'village' in the agreement was not restricted to houses only but included the village land. Shiloah disagreed. They agreed that the movement of traffic on the Latrun–Jerusalem road would be provided by the division of no-man's land. Shiloah insisted on Israeli sovereignty over the Hadassah Hospital and Hebrew University, but Samir disagreed. It was agreed that the Latrun pumping station should be left in Israel by the proposed division of no-man's land.

The Israeli reply to the Jordanian Plan was, in general, negative. The question of the territorial status of the Hadassah Hospital and the Hebrew University was the main problem retarding agreement. According to a strong recommendation by General Glubb, 'The existence of an Israeli enclave on Scopus will prejudice to a most serious extent the possibility of defending Arab Jerusalem against an attack from Israel, or in other words, it makes the strategic position of the Arab Legion forces in Jerusalem untenable.'[4]

Samir al-Rifai refused to agree to the Israeli demand. He also consulted the legal adviser J. Foster, PC, who advised him that 'the Jordan Government have a good case for claiming, on legal grounds, that the whole of the enclave is basically Jordan territory.'[5]

On 14 April, Ernest Bevin, a trusted friend and supporter of King Abdullah and Jordan, died at the age of 70. The friendship between Britain and Jordan had lost its most devoted supporter.

On 16 April, Shiloah transmitted to Samir al-Rifai the following reply to the Jordanian Plan of 15 March:

His Excellency
Samir Pasha al-Rifai

I have the honour to transmit to you my Government's comments and views on the 'Proposed Jordan Plan' which you were kind enough to give me on the occasion of our last meeting. I regret that owing to unforeseeable and unavoidable difficulties this communication has been delayed so long.

My Government has considered carefully the text of your proposals, as well as a detailed report on our last conversation, and I am instructed to convey to you the following.

1. The Government of Israel agrees that under existing circumstances the best procedure to be adopted in our efforts to settle some of the outstanding problems between Jordan and Israel would be that suggested in writing and orally by His Majesty and Your Excellency – namely, that we address ourselves in the first instance to the full implementation of the General Armistice Agreement. Only after the implementation of all Articles of that Agreement, which neither party claims have been properly put into effect so far, will it be possible to proceed with a wider and more far-reaching discussion. It is therefore proposed that all items mentioned in the 'Proposed Jordan Plan' that do not fall within the scope of the General Armistice Agreement should for the present be excluded from our talks. Such questions could be properly taken up in the Special Committee referred to in Article 8 of the General Armistice Agreement, after the specific injunctions of the General Armistice Agreement are implemented.

2. **Naharayim**. As I have stated on previous occasions, the Government of Israel in response to His Majesty's special appeal, agrees to hand over to Jordan the area near Naharayim referred to in para 1 of the 'Proposed Jordan Plan' and rectify the Armistice Line in that area so that it should follow the former international boundary between Trans–Jordan and Palestine.

It is understood that all details regarding the methods and dates of implementation of those parts of the General Armistice Agreement which are still outstanding will be agreed upon before this area is handed over.

3. **Article 6**. The Government of Israel has considered carefully your suggestion that villages east of the Armistice Demarcation Line in the ex-Iraqi sector be covered by the provisions of Article 6 of the General Armistice Agreement. It cannot accept this reading of the Article, the language of which is perfectly clear, and which refers only to villages on the Israel side of the Armistice Line. As I have stated on previous occasions, we recognise the right of any landowner on the Israel side of the Armistice Line in the ex-Iraqi sector who has chosen to move to Jordan, to receive compensation for lands left behind, and I am authorised again to inform you that my Government will favourably consider any such claims. I am also

authorised to reiterate our readiness to pay the Jordan Government for the stretch of road specifically alluded to in Article 6 (5) of the General Armistice Agreement.

As to landowners on the Jordan side of the Armistice Line, we cannot recognise their right to any claim from the Government of Israel. The Jordan Government was fully compensated for the ex-Iraqi sector by substantive deviations of the armistice line in the Hebron area in favour of Jordan (Article 6 (4) of the General Armistice Agreement). I am, however, authorised to agree that the case of these landowners may be placed on the agenda of the Special Committee provided for under Article 8 of the General Armistice Agreement, after the specific injunctions of Article 8 have been carried out.

4. **Free movement of traffic on the Latrun–Jerusalem road and resumption of operation of the Latrun pumping station**. My Government accepts in principle your suggestion that these purposes be achieved by the division of no-man's land in this area. It is suggested that details of such a division be worked out and agreed upon by military representatives of the two Governments.

5. **Mount Scopus**. Your suggestion that Mount Scopus be treated as Jordanian territory caused my Government considerable amazement. There can be no doubt whatever regarding the sovereignty over this area. The entire Mount Scopus area, which was held by Israeli forces prior to the Military Agreement of 7 July 1948, is and must remain Israeli territory. It is only on this clear understanding that we can approach this problem and discuss practical arrangements for free access to and the resumption of the normal functions of the cultural and humanitarian institutions on Mount Scopus.

6. **Free access to the Holy Places and so on**. The Government of Israel desires to achieve agreement in the course of the present negotiations on the detailed implementation of this provision of Article 8, on the understanding that the exact date of the implementation of such agreement should be the subject of a special agreement.

7. **Bethlehem road and electricity for the Old City of Jerusalem**. My Government will be ready to work out detailed plans for the implementation of the provisions of Article 8 on these two points.

Allow me, Excellency, to reiterate my sincere regret for the delay in replying to your latest plans, which was caused by unforeseeable difficulties.

Please accept my sincere compliments and good wishes, and please convey our highest esteem to His Hashemite Majesty, King Abdullah.

R. Shiloah[6]

Samir al-Rifai had insisted from the beginning of the talks with Shiloah that he wanted a comprehensive agreement on the implementation of the Armistice Agreement. Thus far the Israeli Government did not take any steps to make that aim possible. In his reply and comments on the Israeli proposals of 16 April, Samir Pasha stated the following:

Jordan comments on the Israeli Note of 16 April 1951

1. Regret that a little delay has taken place in this reply to the Note dated 16 April 1951, from Mr (R. Sh.), due to certain pre-occupations.

2. In reference to Para 1 of the above Note, it is fully agreed that under existing circumstances the best procedure to be adopted in the joint efforts to settle some of the outstanding problems between Jordan and Israel would be that the two parties should confine themselves, in the first instance, to the full implementation of the provisions of the General Armistice Agreement. It is also agreed that after the implementation of any Articles of that Agreement, which neither party claims have been properly put into effect, or which have not been implemented so far, it may then be possible to proceed with a wider discussion.

3. In adoption of the above principle, agreed to by both sides, it is the view of the Jordan Government that the scope of the present discussions should now be reduced to the application of Articles VI and VIII of the General Armistice Agreement.

4. In connection with these two articles, the Jordan Government observes that the Israeli contention expressed in Paras. 3 & 5 of the Note under reference, constitutes a fundamental difference to the Jordanian contention in the manner of understanding as well as in the *meaning* of the provisions of the said two Articles. This basic dispute appears to a far greater extent in the Israeli interpretation of the specific provisions relating to the Mount Scopus Institutions in Article VIII.

It is, therefore, considered that any attempt to reach agreement on these questions, by the continuance of the present discussions before the legal dispute (which appears to exist in the understanding of the two parties as to the correct meaning of the reference to these matters in Article VIII and Article VI) is decided one way or another, would serve no useful purpose, nor would it bring about any conclusive results.

In order to realise the mutual earnest desire of both sides to settle those questions in the right manner, and because the points at issue, particularly with regard to the reference to the institutions on

Mount Scopus in Article VIII, are entirely *legal* ones, it becomes obviously essential that these points should be decided by a competent judicial tribunal. In the opinion of the Jordan Government the International Court of Justice seems the proper Tribunal for such a decision. Consequently, it is proposed that if early agreement on such legal procedure were reached by the two parties, their true desire to settle the points at issue would thus be more progressively achieved.

The Israeli Government is cordially invited to agree to this proposal, or to suggest, for consideration by the Jordan Government, any alternative proposals they may wish to make for the settlement of the disputed legal points by a competent judicial authority.

PM 30 April 1951.[7]

Meanwhile, Prime Minister Samir al-Rifai and his Government were the targets of aggressive criticism by the members of the Chamber of Deputies. After their approval of the unity in April 1950, the Deputies did not pass a single act of legislation during the extraordinary session. Instead, they concentrated their efforts on making relations between the legislature and the executive as awkward and difficult as possible, and in each debate making it clear that their intention was to introduce constitutional reforms. When Samir al-Rifai assumed office, he was able to calm the tension between the Legislature and the Executive for a short period, but soon the majority of the Deputies reverted back to their previous attitude of flagrant criticism. The National Assembly was called for another extraordinary session between 24 April and 7 May 1951 for the purpose of considering the draft budget for the year 1951/2, as well as a number of Acts for unifying the Palestinian and Jordanian laws on both Banks, which the Deputies had failed to complete during the previous ordinary session.

It became obvious from the beginning of the session that the majority of the Deputies were attempting to hinder the legislative process until their demands for constitutional reforms giving the National Assembly greater powers and making the Executive responsible to the Legislature were accepted or promised. Some Deputies went as far as threatening to boycott the session until these demands were met. However, good sense prevailed and the Deputies approved a few laws unifying legislation on both Banks of the Jordan.

When the debate on the budget started, an intended delay in approving it in the Financial Committee was imposed by some members.

Comments and criticisms in the report of the Financial Committee and outspoken speeches by many members made it obvious that the budget would not be approved within the limited period of the extraordinary session. There were some subtle and indirect hints against the Royal Palace and the Royal Guard (the Hashemite Regiment), direct attacks against the Prime Minister and individual Ministers, the establishment of the Council of Ulama (religious shaikhs and imams), excessive appointments of Ministers and Consuls in the Diplomatic Service, the control of the Jordanian Arab Army by foreigners (British officers), the high salaries allocated for foreign advisers and experts and here and there anti-British inferences. There was also some legitimate criticism of the budget. The revenue was overestimated, new appointments were excessive considering the prevailing economic conditions, and the cost of running the Diplomatic Service was excessive. On 5 May, Samir al-Rifai saw no hope of having his budget approved and recommended to the King that the National Assembly be dissolved. The King approved the *Iradah* (Royal Command) on the same day.

During the first half of 1951, major developments took place in the Jordan Arab Army and on the front along the armistice line. The tense and sometimes violent atmosphere between the small Jordanian Army, which was stretched very thinly along 480 miles of the line, and the twenty-times larger and more aggressive Jewish forces, who crossed the line during 1950, developed into a sub-war. While the Jews were stretching the hand of peace to the Jordan Government during January 1951, they maintained and later increased their violence along the demarcation line. The Jordan Army did its best to protect this line against infiltration by Palestinian refugees, who could see their homes across it being occupied by the Jews who had expelled them from the source of their livelihood. From time to time they could not resist crossing the line to reap the fruits of their land or recover some livestock. They were all civilians and in nearly every case they were extremely poor. Only a few of them crossed the line to attack those responsible for their catastrophe. While the Jordan Army and the National Guard did their best to prevent infiltration, never crossing the demarcation line themselves, the Israeli forces carried out an offensive operation within Jordanian territory against civilians.

Within the Mixed Armistice Commission, as well as in negotiations between Samir al-Rifai and Shiloah, the Jordan Government suggested that instead of military operations across the line by the Israeli Army, Jordan would cooperate fully in establishing joint police patrols to help prevent infiltration, direct telephone communication across the demarcation line between police officers and set up meetings between them. The Israelis ignored all these proposals and continued with their aggressive policy of using their military forces in raids similar to those carried out by the Israelite tribes against the Canaanites during the barbaric age. Two of these Jewish crimes were described by the magazine *Truth*:

Murder of Jordan Arabs

When people perish in a Swiss or Austrian avalanche, or when they are killed by an earthquake in distant New Guinea, or when they meet death in any violent form, that fact is usually given bold headlines in British newspapers. There is one kind of violence which seems to be immune from press publicity. It is the murdering of Jordan Arabs by Jews. News has reached *Truth* that, on 29 January, about sixteen Jewish soldiers approached Yalu village, near the Latrun salient, and fired at and threw hand grenades at the villagers before being beaten off by the National Guard, but not before they had inflicted casualties. On 3 February, a party of armed Jews attacked Saffa village, near Ramallah, killing two civilians and wounding another. The Jordan authorities are convinced that these 'frontier incidents' are part of a campaign of aggression designed to provoke retaliation and so justify the rape of more Arab lands. Why does the British press, which seeks out violence in the ends of the earth, draw the line at the Israeli–Jordan border?[8]

After all the terrorism committed by the Jewish military forces between 1946 and 1951 and the untold suffering of the Palestinian Arabs, and indeed that of the British Army in Palestine until mid-May 1948, the Jewish media and newspapers started calling the Palestinian refugee infiltrators 'terrorists'. It was Jewish terrorism that prevailed all along the demarcation line. Typical of such terrorism was that described by Glubb, who wrote:

On 7 February 1951, at 3 a.m., three trucks emerged from Jewish Jerusalem. At a point two miles south-west of the city, they stopped and switched off their headlights. Some thirty Israelis dismounted, crossed the demarcation line and climbed the hill on the Jordan side of the line, to the little Arab hamlet of Sharafat. This tiny village was inhabited by only four or five Arab families. The Jews quietly surrounded the house of the headman, placed explosive charges beneath it and blew it up, with all the occupants still asleep. They then blew up the house next door, after firing indiscriminately on the inhabitants of the village or anyone attempting to escape. Two men, three women and five children were blown up in the headman's house. Three women and five other children in the village were wounded. The ages of the five children killed were thirteen years, ten, six, one and one. The wounded children were twelve, ten, eight, four and four years old respectively. As a pressman wrote at the time: 'These were doubtless formidable enemies of the State of Israel.' The reason for this outrage was never known. The hamlet of Sharafat contained no police, troops or armed Arabs of any kind.

Two nights later, a party of four or five Israelis knocked down the door of a house in Falama, a similar hamlet two kilometres inside Jordan. They threw in a hand grenade, killing a man, his son and daughter, who were asleep within.

Thus day by day the tale of murder and bloodshed continued.[9]

While manning the front line, the Jordan Arab Army was facing the main problem of developing from a division of two infantry brigades of ten regiments, supported by two artillery batteries and some miscellaneous services in their rudimentary stage, into a well-balanced army capable of large operations. The aim was to form a mobile infantry division of the three brigades with three regiments each, and supporting units of artillery, armour, engineers and signals, as well as base and field sevices of transport and supplies, hospitals, field ambulances and workshops. More development was much needed in the administration and organisation of the HQ of the Army and for police to be able to cope with the needs of the security and defence of the country and update its requirements. Above all, more money was desperately needed, which the Jordan Government could not afford. It was up to the British Government to provide Jordan with the subsidy, without which nothing could have been done.

Furthermore, the number of Arab and British officers had doubled. It was necessary to enlist new cadet officers with matriculation qualifications, and to train and promote non-commissioned officers and educate them to a standard suitable for officer training. Officers with instructor qualifications were much needed; thus more than 100 were sent to the British Army schools in England, and Jordanian officers attended British Army training exercises at Fayed and the Sinai desert in Egypt. Since 1948, when the strength of the Jordan Army was about 6,000, the majority of units lived in tents or trenches on the front line. In 1951, when the strength was increased to about 12,000 officers and men, there were only five military camps with barracks – Mahatta in Amman, and Zarqa, Khaw, Mafraq and Irbid in the East Bank. There were none on the West Bank. More camps and barracks were needed.

By the beginning of 1951, it was estimated that the national revenue of Jordan was £5,255,122. The Jordan Arab Army alone needed £6,500,000 to make ends meet and develop to the needed strength, armament and organisation mentioned above. However, while some deputies were heckling the Jordan Government about the budget, and criticising the British Government and British officers during the extra-ordinary session in April–May, the British Government approved the subsidy of £6,755,122 for the Jordan Government – £1,244,878 more than the national revenue of Jordan.

On 1 April 1951, Major General Norman Lash, Commander of the 1st Division, retired and was replaced by the Commander of the 2nd Brigade, Brigadier Sam Sidney Arthur Cooke of the Lincolnshire Regiment. It did not take long for the Arab officers of the Division to realise the difference between Lash and Cooke. Lash was a police officer in Palestine who became a soldier through 'on-the-job training' with the old Arab Legion, while Sam Cooke was a regular British soldier with fighting and staff experience. He was, according to Glubb, 'a magnificent organiser and trainer'.[10] He immediately speeded up the process of reorganising the 1st Division, and at the end of April the order of battle was as shown in Table 12.1.

The majority of soldiers in the Jordan Arab Army were illiterate; those who were educated did not exceed the sixth elementary standard and were not technically minded. The need of the Jordan Arab Army to train and qualify soldiers capable of meeting the needs of a mobile Infantry Division and its technological requirements were compelling. Thus, courses for the training of signallers, drivers, mechanical engineers, gunners, armoured car crews, medical orderlies, store keepers, clerks and many others were established in the various schools and training centres. Thereafter, the Jordan Arab Army was on its way to modernity.

During his three-month attachment to the Divisional HQ at Khaw, I, now a captain, suggested to General Cooke that in order to enhance the *esprit de corps* of the various units and raise the standard of their physical fitness, an annual sports and shooting competition should be established. I was asked to produce instructions for that purpose, and one

TABLE 12.1
Reorganisation of the 1st Division

Unit	Commander	Location
HQ 1st Division	Major General S. A. Cooke	Khaw
Medium Workshops	Major W. Brace	Zarqa
Field Engineers	Lt Colonel Constant	Khaw
Div Supply and Transport	Major Jubran Hawa	Zarqa
Signal Regiment	Major Eliot	Khaw
DAPM	Lt Riziq al-Salih	Khaw
AOD	Captain Tuaamah Atallah	Khaw
HQ 1st Brigade	Brigadier T. H. S. Galletly	Mafraq
3rd Regiment	Major P. Grey	Irbid
5th Regiment	Lt Colonel Ali Hiyari	Mafraq
7th Regiment	Major Khalid al-Sahin	Mafraq
HQ 2nd Brigade	Brigadier J. J. McCully	Khaw
1st Regiment	Lt Colonel Pilford	Khaw
Hashemite Regiment	Colonel Habis al-Majali	Amman
HQ 3rd Brigade	Brigadier J. O. M. Ashton	Ramallah
2nd Regiment	Major Nigel Bromage	Bethlehem
4th Regiment	Major Mahmoud al-Musa Aubaidat	Jenin
6th Regiment	Major Izzat Hasan Qhandour	Jerusalem
8th Regiment	Major Fawaz Mahir	Kharbatha
9th Regiment	Major Peter Young	Tulkarm
1st Artillery Regiment	Lt Colonel G. H. F. Chaldicott	Ramallah
2nd Artillery Regiment	Lt Colonel Tarr	Khaw
1st Armoured Regiment	Lt Colonel Wormald	Zarqa

week after my presentation, General Cooke wrote a more comprehensive standing order for the division adding much to the proposals and making a masterly piece of a comprehensive programme to take effect from the summer of 1952. A small arms shooting competition, track and field events, football, basketball, a marathon, platoon endurance and swimming were some of its main features.

On the morning of 16 July 1951, Riyadh al-Solh, the former Prime Minister of Lebanon, visited Amman and called on King Abdullah. When driving back to Amman Airport preceded by an escort of a police car, and as he reached the middle of the slope a few hundred yards from the main gate of the airport, another car started to overtake him.

When that car was in a parallel position with al-Solh's car, four men armed with sub-machine guns opened fire at al-Solh from the windows. Riyadh al-Solh, the Arab nationalist and one of the most honourable men in the Arab world, was killed by Arabs. The police car stopped immediately and the escort opened fire at the murderers' car. All the murderers, except one who escaped, were either arrested or killed. Because al-Solh was the King's guest, and because it was the first major political assassination in the history of Jordan, Amman was deep in consternation at the murder, and when it became known that the murderers were Lebanese, anger was added to the tense atmosphere in the city.

On the following day, having returned to the Jordan Army Training Centre as Commander of the Administration and Infantry Training Wing at Abdulli Barracks in Amman, I was ordered to run a course of training for the special guards and escort detachment protecting General Glubb. The course lasted four days, after which I was seconded to the special guard and to act as ADC to General Glubb, while at the same time continuing to train the guards.

On Thursday 19 July 1951, King Abdullah was due to present the first eight Jordanian Air Force pilots – Amir Basim Khammash, Minthir Ennab, Ihsan Qaqish, Ibrahim Othman, Ziad Hamzah, Ali Shuqum, Muhammad Nur Eisa and Fuad Aarif Salim – with their wings. On that morning General Glubb called on the King to accompany him to the ceremonial parade at Amman Airport. The King had received an anonymous letter, telling him that both he and General Glubb were to be assassinated. Before leaving for the airport, the King handed the letter to Glubb. After the parade, the King was due to leave Amman for Jerusalem to pray in al-Aqsa Mosque on the following day, Friday. Just before he left he was urged by the American Minister in Amman not to go to Jerusalem because of the threat to his life. Prime Minister al-Rifai begged him to be cautious. The King replied: 'I believe in God. My life is in His hands.' The King left for Jerusalem on Thursday afternoon. After spending the night in his residence, he travelled to Nablus on Friday morning and visited its Mayor, Sulaiman Touqan, who suggested to him to pray in the Nablus Mosque. The King replied. 'What is written, must come to pass.' Glubb wrote in his book:

> Ever since the murder of Riyadh al-Solh, I had felt tense and anxious. I had sent Colonel Habis al-Majali with the King, and had

told him to be on the alert, especially at prayers in the Great Mosque. I thought of telephoning to the Commandant of Police in Jerusalem to urge him also to be particularly careful at prayers in the Mosque, but I restrained myself. 'They all know their jobs,' I thought. 'I must not be fussy.'

The King entered the vast courtyard of the Great Mosque of Jerusalem a little before twelve. It was packed with untold thousands of people, as was usual for the noon prayer on Friday. The people opened a narrow lane down which the King walked, with the dense crowd hedging him in on every side. He loved talking to his subjects, and stopped several times to speak to people he recognised. Colonel Habis and the escort surrounded him had tried to hold back the crowd, but the King turned half irritably: '*La tihbisni, ya Habis!*' he said 'Don't imprison me, O Habis!' As the party drew near to the door of the Great Mosque, Habis and the escort again tried to surround the King, who repeated with increased vehemence: 'Don't imprison me, O Habis.'

The King accordingly stepped across the threshold first, with all the escort behind him. The old shaikh of the Mosque, a venerable ecclesiastic with a long white beard, stepped forward to kiss his hand. At that instant, a man stepped out from behind the massive door of the Mosque and found himself beside the King and only a yard from him. He presented a pistol and fired at King Abdullah's head at a few inches' range. The bullet entered behind his ear and emerged from his eye. The King fell forward dead on the floor of the Mosque. His white turban rolled away across the marble pavement.

The murderer fired wildly right and left, as the escort dashed forward and shot him dead in his turn.[11]

Thus, the Hashemite King Abdullah ibn al-Hussein, who saved Jerusalem from Jewish usurpation, was killed by one of those Arabs of Jerusalem who had failed to defend it and who had appealed to him to save it. The assassin was an instrument; the real killers were those who planned the assassination. It was alleged that the plan to assassinate King Abdullah had been suggested during a meeting in the early part of 1950 between Abdullah al-Tel, the former Governor of Jerusalem, and Musa al-Husseini, a former head of the Jordanian Ministry for Foreign Affairs Branch Office in Jerusalem, who was then the owner of a travel agency in Jerusalem and the correspondent of the *al-Sharq al-Adna* (Near East) broadcasting station in the city. At that meeting it was decided that the assassination of King Abdullah would be the beginning of a series of other political assassinations of Arab leaders. Musa al-Husseini returned to Jerusalem to wait for further instruction. Thereafter, Abdullah al-Tel discussed the assassination plan with Musa Ahmad al-Ayoubi, a Jordanian from al-Salt who lived in Cairo as one of al-Haj Amin al-Husseini's entourage and who was a former member of the assassination squad. He was given an amount of money and was sent to Jerusalem to meet Musa al-Husseini.

On his arrival at Jerusalem Musa al-Husseini got in touch with his fellow member of the assassination squad, Abed Mahmoud Aukkah, a cattle merchant who was employed by the Higher Arab Committee. A series of meetings were held between the two, and it was decided to recruit the assassins from Syria and pay them £2,000 for the murder. Musa al-Ayoubi went to Damascus and returned to Jericho with four men. He accommodated them in the orange grove owned by his brother on the outskirts of the town, and Musa al-Husseini gave them £200 for their keep. Musa al-Husseini did not give them any more money and, after waiting for several weeks, the men returned to Damascus.

During October 1950, Musa al-Husseini went to Cairo to collect money from al-Tel, and to work out the details of the plan for the assassination of the King at Friday prayers at al-Aqsa Mosque in Jerusalem. The assassin would be assured of his escape and safety, and he would be covered by others who would use grenades. In fact, it was planned that if the assassin was not killed by the King's guards, he would be killed by one of the group of assassins. Musa al-Husseini returned to Jerusalem with an unknown amount of money, and then met Abed Mahmoud Aukkah and informed him that the money for the assassination was available. Aukkah asked where it came from and al-Husseini replied: 'From a high source in Cairo' ('min masdar aali fi al-Qahirah'). Aukkah asked al-Ayoubi the same question and Ayoubi replied: 'From the group' ('min al-jamaah'). Aukkah understood that it was from the Arab Higher Committee.

Abed Mahmoud Aukkah and his brother Zakariya enlisted Mustafa Shukri Ishu, a tailor from Jerusalem and a former member of al-Jihad al-Muqaddas, to carry out the murder for a large sum of money. He was given an advance and a written order in the handwriting of Musa al-Ayoubi, which said: 'Kill and do not be afraid, you are assured of your safety.' The written order included a fatwa that he would be exempt from punishment in the *akhirah* (the Hereafter). The Aukkah brothers enlisted Abd al-Qadir Farhat, alias Muhammad al-Sidmir, a blacksmith and coffee shop owner in Jerusalem, and Mahmoud Ishaq al-Antabli, a butcher, and offered them £1,000 each to join Zakariya in throwing grenades to cover the assassin. The assassination was planned for Friday 12 May 1951. The date was set so that al-Ayoubi would have time to fly to Cairo on the morning before the assassination. However, al-Ayoubi missed the flight to Cairo from Qalandiyah and he aborted the attempt to avoid arrest, being a close friend of al-Tel. King Abdullah did not pray in Jerusalem during June, and by the middle of the month al-Ayoubi returned to Cairo leaving the supervision of the assassination plot to Musa al-Husseini.

During July, the assassins kept a close watch on the Old City of Jerusalem to see if there were any signs of an imminent visit by King Abdullah to pray in al-Aqsa Mosque. They found that there would be a visit on Friday 20 July and decided to carry out the assassination on that day. At about 1130 hours, Mustafa Shukri Ishu, armed with a Webley 0.38 pistol given to him by Abd al-Qadir Farhat, went to the Mosque and hid behind the large main door, ready for the murder of the very King who had saved him from Jewish occupation and oppression.

Inside the Mosque a shaikh was reading a verse from the Qur'an when the King approached the main door of al-Aqsa Mosque. It is part of the Muslim devotion to keep complete silence during the reading of the Qur'an. It was in that kind of silence that the King walked about four steps inside the Mosque to be received by the Imam, who stepped forward to kiss the King's hand. At that moment Ishu came out from behind the massive door of the Mosque, fired his pistol at the King's head at a few inches' range – the bullet entering behind the King's ear and emerging from his forehead – then he turned his pistol on the guards, wounding five of them. No bombs were thrown by the rest of the assassins as they kept far away from the scene. Ishu was killed by one of the guards and with his death the rest of the group thought they were immune from detection.

It was Mustafa Shukri Ishu's mother who gave the Jerusalem police and the investigator, the Attorney General Walid Salah, the names of all her son's friends and associates. The pistol with which Ishu killed the King was identified by Abd al-Qadir Farhat's son. All the conspirators were arrested and interrogated by the Attorney General Walid Salah. Musa al-Husseini revealed the names of all the conspirators and their roles in the assassination, including his, but he claimed that he did not want to kill the King; he only wanted to frighten him. Abed Mahmoud Aukkah made a full confession of his role and that of the others. Muhammad Ishaq al-Antabli also made a full confession.[12]

Meanwhile, Glubb, who was shopping at the Amman market, was sent for by Samir al-Rifai when the assassination took place. On arriving at the al-Rifai residence Glubb saw several Ministers sobbing openly, and as al-Rifai stepped forward he began by saying 'Our Lord' ('*Sayidna*'), then broke down sobbing. 'Call out the Army and move troops into the town. There may be a revolution!' he said. Glubb gave orders to General Cooke to send a regiment to Amman and be responsible for law and order in the city. Two hours later the whole situation was under control and the Government proclaimed a curfew.[13]

On the following day – Saturday 21 July – black flags were raised on every house in Amman, all the shops were shut and the whole atmosphere was one shrouded in grief. Rumours started to circulate that the British Government had prevented the Amir Talal from returning to Jordan from Geneva where he was under treatment. On the same day, the Prince Regent of Iraq, Prince Abd al-Ilah, who was in London, asked to see the Minister of State at the Foreign Office and spoke to him about King Abdullah's plans for the unification of Iraq and Jordan on his death. He recalled the suggestion, which he had rejected, that he himself should become King of Jordan, and said that the only possibility would be a union under King Faisal II of Iraq. In a telegram from the Foreign Office to all British Embassies and Legations in the Arab Middle East the Minister recounted what the Prince Regent had told him:

> In the spring of this year Abdullah had given him [the Prince Regent] a draft of a declaration announcing his intention of making Faisal his heir, and the Regent had submitted this to the Iraqi Government. The latter had put forward a counter draft, which apparently proposed that Faisal should ultimately succeed Abdullah and that for the next five years steps should be taken to align the two countries in such a way that they could be united on Abdullah's death. Since then the Regent did not know what had happened. Nuri Pasha [al-Said] had telephoned him yesterday to ask

what had become of the proposal, and the Regent had replied that he did not know but would doubtless find out on reaching Amman.

The Regent said that he did not wish to take any action without our advice and approval. He would let us know what emerged at Amman but in the meantime would be grateful if we could pass to him any preliminary observations we might have.

Our preliminary view is that union of the two countries would have serious repercussions in the Middle East as a whole. Furthermore there is a danger that our position in Jordan might be weakened if and when she came under the domination of Baghdad. For these reasons you should not favour the proposal.

We do not, however, wish to influence a decision one way or the other; and we are therefore instructing Sir A. Kirkbride to speak to the Regent on the following lines.

1. We greatly appreciate his action in coming to us for advice.

2. The future of the two kingdoms must be determined by the wishes of their Governments and peoples. We would not wish to advise a step that might not be endorsed by the great majority, nor would we wish to advise against it if union were in accordance with the general desire.

3. We would, however, earnestly hope that in considering their next step the two Governments would carefully examine and take full account of all possible results not only in their own countries but in the Middle East as a whole effecting a change of such importance in the structure of the Arab States as the result of the assassination of one of the Arab Rulers.[14]

On Sunday 22 July, Kirkbride called on Samir al-Rifai to discuss with him the question of succession to the throne. The Prime Minister told him that it was confirmed by the investigation that the assassination had been planned and carried out by supporters of al-Haj Amin al-Husseini. He also told him that the proclamation of the Amir Nayif as Regent had been decided unanimously by the Cabinet and by the three former Prime Ministers Tawfiq Abu al-Huda, Ibrahim Hashim, and Said al-Mufti. Kirkbride reported: 'Finally, the Prime Minister asked me if I could work in a word in support of the present Council of Ministers when I saw Nayif as he suspected (with justification) that intrigues to bring about a change of Government were already under way.'[15]

On the same day, Kirkbride called on the Prince Regent and was impressed by his sensible reactions to the extremely difficult situation and the courage with which he dealt with the various problems that arose. Queen Musbah, Prince Talal's mother, had announced that she would not permit the funeral of the King to take place until her son Talal had returned to Amman; Talal's sister, Princess Maqboulah, said in public that Samir al-Rifai was responsible for the King's death and should be killed next. The Regent asked Kirkbride if he agreed to an immediate change of Government on the grounds that Samir Pasha was unlucky (with the drought and the murders of Riyadh al-Solh and the King); that the people were tired of Samir Pasha's associates; and that from a constitutional point of view, the Government should resign on the death of the Monarch. Much had been said in Amman about Prince Nayif wanting the throne of Jordan for himself, but no one was sure in spite of the apprehension that overwhelmed the city regarding their much beloved and admired Prince Talal. However, Kirkbride wrote:

> As regards the succession, Nayif said that he had no designs on anything which was not his as of right and had been reluctant to accept the appointment of Regent. He realised, however, that he was the only candidate available. At the outset his attitude with regard to the succession was correct but you will see that latterly he has shown signs of wanting the throne for himself.[16]

On Monday morning, 23 July 1951, the ceremonies for the King's funeral started at the Raghadan Royal Palace, where special envoys and delegations assembled and were ushered to the throne Room. In the presence of the Regent of Jordan, Prince Hussein ibn Talal, the Regent of Iraq and the Jordan Government they paid their last respects to the flag-covered coffin. It was carried by non-commissioned officers of the Iraqi and Jordanian Armies to a waiting gun-carriage. The late King's charger and officers bearing his decorations led the funeral procession followed by the two Regents and Prince Hussein. They were followed by the Jordan Cabinet Ministers, the Prime Minister of Iraq and leading Court officials. Kirkbride (representing the British Monarch) and General Sir Brian Robertson, Air Marshal Sir John Baker and Rear Admiral Campbell (representing the three British Services) led the special envoys and delegates. Prince Fahd ibn Abdul Aziz represented Saudi Arabia. The Foreign Minister of Lebanon, Charles Helou, represented Lebanon. Dr Khalid Shatilla represented Syria, and General Aughily represented the Republic of Turkey. The Indian

Ambassador in Cairo, who was accredited to Jordan as Minister, with members of his staff, was also present, together with the Afghan Minister in Cairo and representatives of Indonesia and Argentina. Delegations from Syria were led by Dr Sami Kabara, Minister of the Interior. From Lebanon they were led by Rashid Beydoun, Minister of Defence, and from Egypt by Mahmoud Sulaiman Ghannam, Minister of Commerce. At the graveside, the Prime Minister made a short speech in which he said:

> Gratitude to Allah of the Universe, and pray and peace be upon His Noble Messenger, and His Family the pure and good.
>   I did not anticipate that I would be destined to stand in this catastrophic and devout situation to say the word of last farewell [al-Rifai started crying and could hardly control himself] to my Lord and Master the Exalted Hashemite the founder of this Kingdom and the builder of its pride, the Scion of the Noble Prophet's Family, the Grandson of the most Gracious of Mankind and the Heir of the Great Arab Revolt, His Majesty King Abdullah ibn al-Hussein.[17]

After the funeral the two Regents and Prince Hussein ibn Talal received the condolences of all present at the Royal Diwan. Thus ended the last day of the Great King.

Under a photograph of the late King Abdullah the Jewish newspaper *Herut* published a statement by the Jewish terrorist Menachem Begin, the leader of the Jewish terrorist organisation Irgun Zvai Leumi, which he made in a public meeting in the Armon Cinema at Haifa on Saturday 21 July:

> THE DAY WILL NOT BE FAR OFF, IF YOU WANT IT, WHEN
> OUR TROOPS WILL MARCH JOYFULLY INTO JERUSALEM
> AND AMMAN, LIBERATED FROM THE ARABS

At the Cairo Conference, attended by Herbert Samuel, Winston Churchill, and the British agent adventurer Lawrence, it was decided to tear out from the 'national home of the Jewish people' the East of Jordan, which is the inheritance of Reuben, Gad and half of the Menasse, and to hand this area to the son of the Hashemite dynasty, Abdullah.

I have to point out that the Israeli people never recognised, and I believe shall never recognise, this tearing out of our historic heritage, which was the granary of the Mediterranean.

> On Friday last the rule of Abdullah came to an end by means of a few grams of gunpowder . . . the people of Israel have no reason to mourn. Abdullah was the symbol of the dismembering of our country, and the robbery of our heritage. No doubt Abdullah was a pillar of the 'British Order' in the Middle East, and this pillar was crushed yesterday. This is the political value of yesterday's incident in the Old City, but it has also another meaning: this land, holy to our people from ancient times to years to come, will not bear foreign rulers.[18]

That kind of statement was to be expected from a man who used murder for political ends, as Begin was very experienced in that field. However, the moderate and more responsible Jewish newspapers, including the leading independent *Ha'aretz* and the *Histadrut Davar*, deplored the murder. *Histadrut Davar* called it 'a blow to the stability of the Middle East and to the prospects of peace' and *Ha'aretz* made the same point and added that 'King Abdullah was a person of culture, wisdom and ability with no equal in the Arab Middle East'. The other extremist, but less influential newspapers, reacted as expected of them. The Mapam paper *Al Hamishmar*, in a vulgar and tasteless article headed 'Death of a salesman', described King Abdullah as 'a British puppet who was . . . even more hypocritical than other Arab rulers'. It admitted, however, that its view of King Abdullah was 'not shared elsewhere in Israel'. The Communist paper *Kol Ha'am* said bluntly that 'King Abdullah was killed by American agents'.[19]

General Glubb sent a telegram to the editor of the British newspaper *News of the World* on 23 July in which he said:

> King Abdullah of Jordan was great in many fields in an age which has produced few great men. Perhaps his most outstanding characteristic was his political moral courage. He never hesitated to speak out what he thought was true and right, with absolute disregard for his personal safety or popularity. His constancy to his pledged word and his faithfulness to his friends were no less than his courage. To meet him was at once to receive the impression that here was a man that one could trust, a man who would never buy his own advantage by abandoning his friends.
>
> In 1940, at the time of the fall of France, even the greatest nations in the world held back in hesitation when they saw Britain, alone, at bay. Not so King Abdullah. He was the only ruler in the world who openly proclaimed that he and his little country would

stand and fall with Britain come what may. 'We Arabs,' he said 'do not abandon our friends when times are bad.' But in addition to these rugged virtues he possessed many other qualities which served to win for him the affection of his people and the friendship of a great number of foreigners.

He was extremely democratic and accessible and a true father of all his people, possessed of a knowledge of every class of society and mixing as much with Bedouins as with cabinet ministers, with villagers as with ambassadors. No man in the world could be more charming in his conversation or more delightful in his sense of humour. He has been taken from his people at a moment when they were most in need of him, standing as he did like a rock amid the storms and troubles of the Middle East.

He was fully aware that his life was threatened by fanatics but he refused to give up his lifelong custom of praying in public in the mosque amid a crowd of thousands of worshippers. Only a few days ago when he was asked to be careful he replied: 'I believe in God, my life is in His hands.' With the passing of King Abdullah the people of Jordan and the world at large have lost a very brave, kindly, wise and honourable ruler and a very great gentleman.[20]

In the House of Commons, Winston Churchill expressed his sorrow for the passing of King Abdullah and remembered his association with him adding that he was: 'A skilled and consistent worker for peace and prosperity of that part of the world, and for the interest and honour of the Arab peoples wherever they may be.'[21]

Clement Attlee, the British Prime Minister, described the loss of the King in these words: 'Great Britain has lost a trusted ally. His was no fair weather loyalty. He stood by us in all circumstances and came unhesitatingly to our aid when it seemed that we had little to rely upon except our own faith in our survival.'[22]

In Damascus, news of the assassination was received with moderate emotions and sorrow, as well as with much speculation regarding the consequences. While most people condemned the assassination (especially so soon after the passing of Riyadh al-Solh) and expressed regret, the attitude of those inveterately opposed to the Greater Syria Plan was one of ill-concealed relief that King Abdullah, the symbol of the Plan, was out of the arena. There was also some satisfaction in certain circles that Britain had lost one of the main supporters of her policy in the Middle East. Amongst others there was a certain uneasiness that as a result of King Abdullah's absence Jordan might unite with Iraq, and

Syria's integrity would consequently be imperilled. However, on 21 July, the Prime Minister and President of the Chamber of Deputies paid tribute to King Abdullah at the session of the Syrian Chamber of Deputies. While the Prime Minister's attitude was correct, Maarouf al-Dawalibi saw fit to blame the assassination of King Abdullah on the policies of foreign powers who had misled the King. The Chamber of Deputies observed one minute's silence in honour of the King but Akram al-Hourani, one of the leaders of the Baath Party, deliberately walked out beforehand as he did in the case of a similar tribute to Riyadh al-Solh. This was strange behaviour, alien to Arab custom and tradition.[23] There were also some rumours that Britain supported Prince Nayif against Crown Prince Talal, 'who is considered to be opposed to British policy'.[24]

There was sadness in Baghdad, particularly in the Royal Palace, because the Hashemite family had lost its doyen. 'The religious susceptibilities of almost all Iraqis have been offended by the fact that the murder was committed on a Friday and in a holy place which King Abdullah was about to enter in order to pray.'[25] Most Iraqis deplored the use of violence for political purposes and have had misgivings about the effect of two assassinations of major political figures in the space of a few days on the international prestige of the Arabs. There was much speculation in political circles about the succession and about the possibility of an Iraqi–Jordanian union. Reported statements in support of Crown Prince Talal by the Egyptians, the Syrians and Azzam Pasha were treated in Baghdad as interference in the internal affairs of Jordan and were privately regarded as a rather clumsy attempt to forestall any move towards Hashemite union. The British Ambassador in Baghdad reported:

> There are signs that King Abdullah's death is going to throw into sharper relief the differences between the pro- and anti-Palace parties here. The organs of the Istiqlal and National Democratic Parties were the only newspapers which did not publish appreciations of the King on the day following his death. These two parties and the United Popular Front were also misguided enough to decline an invitation to appoint representatives to participate in the Iraqi delegation which flew to Amman to attend the funeral. This is the sort of thing which the Regent does not readily forget. What is perhaps more significant is Salih Jabr's reaction when told by one of

his supporters that Sadiq al-Bassam (who is a leading member of the United Popular Front), while drunk in a cabaret, had been rejoicing in a loud voice at the death of King Abdullah and inveighing against the Hashemite house in general and had been claiming that his colleagues in the United Popular Front shared his views. Salih Jabr commented that in order to preserve the stability of Iraq it would be necessary for those parties which support the monarchy to cooperate closely.[26]

In Saudi Arabia, the general view was that King Abdullah was an old man who should have been allowed to live out his remaining years in peace. The British Ambassador reported the opinions expressed by Princes Abdullah, Faisal, Talal and Mishaal and other Saudis who unanimously 'deplored the death of a great Arab King, and have expressed particular abhorrence at the place and circumstances of the outrage and it is understandable that Ibn Saud, upon whose life at least two attempts have been made, should condemn regicide'.[27]

The Cairo of 1951 was soaked in the extreme Arab nationalism based on xenophobia rather than on the harsh realities of Arab life; it deeply resented the utter failure of the League of Arab States whose headquarters resided in Cairo; it was saturated with corruption, bribery and political intrigue; it was ruled by a King who spent more of his time in seedy nightclubs than in the service of his people; Cairo was in a mess. Cairo was influenced by al-Haj Amin al-Husseini, who had failed in his attempt to do anything good for the Palestinian people, a man who caused disasters for them, an absentee leader who could not constructively bring practical solutions to the Palestine problem.

The Government of Egypt continued to accuse Jordan of betraying the Arab cause by endeavouring to make peace with the Jews, in spite of many assurances to the contrary; it was extremely jealous of the Egyptian primacy in the Arab League, which it controlled, and strenuously opposed King Abdullah's plans for real Arab unity in fear of the emergence of a strong Hashemite state that would rival Egypt in size and wealth; it supported certain Palestinian factions who opposed unity between Jordan and East Palestine, and instead supported the Government of All Palestine, which had neither popular sanction, authority nor institutions; and it was extremely sensitive to its neglect of its army which had led to its defeat, despite the courage of its men and untold sacrifices, during the 1948 war with the Jews. All these factors had to be explained.

Hence, the violent and abusive propaganda campaign launched in 1950 against Jordan and King Abdullah and was still raging when the King was assassinated in July 1951. The day after the death of the King, one Cairo newspaper accused him of treason. He was nicknamed by the much lesser man, King Farouq of Egypt, 'the Bedouin King'. While King Abdullah made Jordan a Kingdom of Arab virtues of simplicity, austerity, discipline, plain living and loyalty to moderate Arab nationalism and Islam, King Farouq allowed Egypt to decline into demagoguery, ostentation, extravagance and xenophobia against moderate, logical and practical politics. 'King Abdullah', the *Times* correspondent from Cairo reported,

> spent less on his yearly household expenses than many a Pasha spends in a week in Paris. Jordanian standards of honesty and efficiency were a standing reproach to some other states. Many politicians were stung by King Abdullah's criticisms, gleaming with barbed wit but rarely rancorous.[28]

It would be discourteous to the late King's memory to repeat what the Egyptian press of 1951 said about his death, but the words of General Glubb describes its reaction well:

> When the Mufti's men brought off the murder, there was an unconcealed outburst of joy in the Egyptian press. The Egyptian Government alone sent no representative to the funeral. Columns of abuse appeared in the Egyptian papers in lieu of an obituary. The general set-up was made plain by a cartoon in the Egyptian magazine *Rose al-Yousef*. Their front full page cartoon showed a man being murdered by a gangster, with the label 'Cooperation with the English'. The caption read: 'There is no law which forbids political murder of this kind.'
>
> There seems to be no doubt that the plan put into execution was the original Mufti's idea to kill the King and raise rebellion and civil war between 'Trans-Jordan' and 'Arab Palestine'. The Egyptians and perhaps the Mufti secretly fully realised that they could do nothing about the Jews. Thus they concentrated their efforts against Arabs. It was arranged (or at least anticipated) that rioting in Amman, Jerusalem, Irbid and Nablus would follow the King's death. Nothing happened but the Egyptian and Syrian press had it all laid on, and described hundreds of killed, fire and sword and particularly battles between natives of East and West Jordan. This

was what they were trying to organise; civil war between Trans-Jordan and 'Arab Palestine'.

In actual practice, the King's murder caused a remarkable demonstration of solidarity. The West Jordanians seemed to be very nearly, if not quite, as distressed as the Easterners.

There now remains the next part of the programme, to carry out rebellion in West Jordan. Reports indicate that gangs are being organised in Syria and Gaza to infiltrate into West Jordan and start disturbances. It is possible that some might try pin-prick raids on the Jews to provoke counter-attacks against the Arab Legion and pin them to forward positions, while the gangs take possession of the interior of the country.[29]

NOTES

1 PRO. FO 371/91364. From Kirkbride to the Foreign Office, 15 January 1951.
2 *Ibid.*
3 *Ibid.*, proposed Jordanian Plan, 15 March 1951.
4 *Ibid.* From Kirkbride to Furlonge, 31 March 1951.
5 *Ibid.*
6 PRO. FO 371/92364. From R. Shiloah to Samir al Rifai, 16 April 1951.
7 *Ibid.* Comment by the Jordanian Government on the Israeli Note of 16 April 1951, 30 April 1951.
8 *Truth* (2 March 1951).
9 Glubb, *A Soldier with the Arabs*, pp. 286–7.
10 *Ibid.*, p. 260.
11 *Ibid.*, pp. 276–7.
12 PRO. FO 371/91839. Kirkbride to K. Younger, events leading up to the murder of King Abdullah, 17 September 1951. Also, the author, who reported back to the Jordan Arab Army Training Centre at Abdulli Barracks at the end of August, attended every session of the Trial at Abdulli while commanding the guards protecting the Court Hall.
13 Glubb, *A Soldier with the Arabs*, p. 278.
14 PRO. FO 371/91797. From the Foreign Office to the British Embassy at Baghdad, repeated to all embassies and legations in the Arab countries, 22 July 1951.
15 PRO. FO 371/91789. From Kirkbride to Furlonge, secret, 25 July 1951.
16 *Ibid.*
17 The author's private papers. The author attended the funeral as General Glubb's aide-de-camp.
18 *Herut* newspaper, 22 July 1951.
19 PRO. FO 371/91839. From J. K. Chadwick at Tel Aviv to Furlonge at the Foreign Office, 24 July 1951.
20 Jordan Arab Army HQ document no. All/18/1446. From Glubb to the editor of the *News of the World*, London, 23 July 1951, copy in the author's private papers.

21 *Hansard*, 23 July 1951.
22 *Ibid.*
23 Akram al-Hourani had taken refuge in Jordan towards the end of his life. He was treated with honour and great generosity by King Hussein ibn Talal, King Abdullah's grandson.
24 PRO. FO 371/91838. From Damascus to the Foreign Office, 23 July 1951.
25 *Ibid.*
26 PRO. FO 371/91839. Letter from Sir H. Beeley to Furlonge, 25 July 1951.
27 *Ibid.* From the British Embassy in Jedda to Herbert Morrison, 2 August 1951.
28 PRO. FO 371/91203. An article from the *Times*, 26 July 1951.
29 PRO. FO 371/91839. From Glubb to Lt Colonel R. Melville, 6 August 1951.

13

The Succession

Since the autumn of 1947, Jordan had borne, and was still bearing in August 1951, nearly all the strain of the Palestinian catastrophe, of which King Abdullah's death was the climax. Yet, in spite of losing its father, founder and wise leader, the little country and its poor but gallant people remained almost the only stable place in the Middle East. This was due, no doubt, to the character and sound leadership of King Abdullah which had kept the former Trans-Jordan quiet, stable and content through the 25 years of its life – between 1921, when he founded the Emirate, and 1946 when he built it into the Hashemite Kingdom of Jordan. It was due to his political acumen and courageous initiatives that Jordan managed to fight a war and win freedom for the Palestinian people of the West Bank and unite them in a free and democratic way with their brothers, the Jordanians of the East Bank. Even after Abdullah, and in spite of some summer clouds of uncertainty, the Palestinian and Jordanian people remained steadfast and determined to hold on to Abdullah's and their own achievements. Three forces played the main role in the continuity of the country and its monarchy: first, the devotion, confidence and loyalty to the Crown Prince Talal by the Jordanian people of both Banks; second, the loyalty, discipline and professionalism of the officers and men of the Jordanian Arab Army; and third, whatever motives they had, it was due to two men – Tawfiq Abu al-Huda, the Prime Minister, and Sir Alec S. Kirkbride, the British Minister in Amman – that the security, stability and the smooth constitutional succession to the throne took place between July and September of 1951.

Abu al-Huda had developed his capabilities from being an autocratic clerk into a politician and Prime Minister. A politician without self-interest could be regarded as a prophet, and the history of mankind has never mentioned political prophets. It was a combination of personal interest and the interest of the country that motivated Abu al-Huda to do his best to become Prime Minister at that critical stage of development in Jordan. He came to Trans-Jordan in 1924 and by 1951 he had been

Prime Minister seven times. Being Prime Minister was his whole life and his main aim, if only to spite Samir al-Rifai; to take the office from him was enough incentive for Abu al-Huda to make the effort. Although he was of Palestinian origin his devotion to Jordan was not questioned and although he was, in his political behaviour and policies, subservient to Britain – and particularly to Kirkbride – no objective historian could accuse him of betraying his King and country at that critical time.

Kirkbride served in Palestine and Jordan between 1917 and 1938 when he became British Resident in Trans-Jordan. Thereafter, he continued to serve in Jordan until the middle of 1952. Thus Kirkbride lived in Jordan for 34 years of his life. He saw Jordan as a territory in the middle of nowhere; a no-man's land on the fringe of nothing and inhabited by people who lived in poverty and deprivation. He witnessed every important event and development throughout Abdullah's struggle to create his Kingdom. Although he was British to the bone and Scottish to the marrow, he must have had some loyalty to what he had helped to build in Jordan. Thus he did his best for the country, its King and people at that critical stage.

Immediately after the King's funeral on Monday 23 July, Kirkbride called on the Prince Regent of Iraq. He gained the impression from that visit that the Prince was being led by Nuri al-Said and Salih Jabr, and that the Prince himself was not the prime mover of the idea of unity between Iraq and Jordan. During the afternoon of the same day, Tawfiq Abu al-Huda called on Prince Nayif and discussed the change of government with him. Later that afternoon, he asked to see Kirkbride. During their meeting it became evident to Kirkbride that Abu al-Huda was trying to induce him to withdraw his opposition to an early change of government. Kirkbride reported:

> His case was that a change of government was desirable because Nayif, who was superstitious, was convinced that Samir's [al-Rifai's] continuation in office would bring further bad luck. (This sounds silly on paper but is of some importance locally.) He was anxious that Samir and his associates should not be in charge of elections because they were going to interfere too drastically and some of the Council of Ministers would take bribes. Tewfiq was convinced that Samir could not last much longer and, as the most probable successor, he did not want to have to deal with a Parliament that Samir had elected. He would prefer, therefore, to take over immediately and to

manage his own elections. Finally, he said that all the Iraqi visitors were opposed to Samir and were doing their best to undermine Samir's position.

I stopped Tewfiq here and asked whether he was in favour of the union for which the Iraqis were working and whether the idea would attract much support locally. His reply was in the negative on both points. But he added, however, that he did not propose to quarrel with the Iraqis as Samir had done and he intended to find out as much as possible about their plans.

I then asked him whether he did not consider that the question of the succession was the most urgent matter before us and whether a change of government would not come more naturally after the new king had been proclaimed.

He answered that internally few people were really interested in the question of the succession, although there were a lot of wild rumours in neighbouring countries: there were no signs of parties being formed favouring one solution or the other and he considered that no action should be taken until the doctor's report at the end of the five weeks' treatment was available. He did not doubt that this report would say that Talal was unfit mentally, in which case the constitution automatically debarred him from succeeding to his father's throne. Hussein [al-Hussein ibn Talal] could then be proclaimed King and Nayif confirmed in his regency. He was opposed to the idea of sending someone to Geneva to attempt to induce Talal to waive his rights in favour of Hussein; Talal might refuse to do so, but, even if he did agree, everyone would say that he had submitted to pressure or, alternatively, that the action was of no value as Talal had not been in the proper possession of his senses at the time.[1]

During the evening of 23 July, General Sir Brian Robertson, accompanied by General Glubb, called on Kirkbride at his residence near the Royal Palace. While waiting for them to return to Glubb's house, I, the ADC to General Glubb, was told by Captain Muhammad al-Suhaimat, an intelligence officer, that there was a demonstration in Amman city centre calling for the return of King Talal, and that Glubb and his guest should avoid the road leading to the centre and use instead the road leading to Jabal al-Hussein. I had heard the rumour alleging that the British Government was delaying the return of Crown Prince Talal to Amman in order to unite Jordan and Iraq under King Faisal. To show General Glubb and his guest the true feeling of the people of Amman towards Talal, I decided to take them back through the city centre where the demonstration in support of Talal was taking place. Travelling in the same car with Glubb and his guest, and as we exited the main gate of the Palace, instead of following Muhammad al-Suhaimat to Jabal al-Hussein, I told the driver to continue on the main road through the city centre. General Glubb was talking to his guest as the car and escort arrived at the scene of the demonstration. The city centre was packed with more than 1,000 demonstrators and as the car was passing through the dense crowd hedging it on both sides, the demonstrators were shouting and singing '*Ya Talal Allah yihmik, hai Amman bitnadik*' ('O Talal may God protect you, Amman is calling you') and other slogans. There was not one incident of any kind directed at the car or its occupants, while it moved at walking pace, with Glubb translating the slogans to his guest. The message was loud and clear.

Kirkbride's next visitor on the following day (24 July) was Salih Jabr of Iraq, who requested to see him to discuss the Iraqi–Jordanian proposed union. Salih gave Kirkbride a 'lecture' on the advantages of a union of Iraq and Jordan under a single Crown. He criticised Nuri al-Said for not having crystallised the scheme during King Abdullah's lifetime. Kirkbride reported:

> The gist of his argument was that both Talal and Nayif were hopeless and that Jordan could not stand alone. Union with Iraq would give Jordan protection against Israeli aggression, secure the country from the hostile intrigues of other members of the Arab League and enable Great Britain to secure her ends in Jordan without being held responsible as at present for everything that happened here. He then produced what he regarded as an important inducement to His Majesty's Government – namely that the Arab Legion would be preserved as an independent army under British control and with its senior posts filled by British officers. (He did not add that His Majesty's Government would have to continue to pay for the Legion, but I assume that was implied.)
>
> He went on to say that the great majority of the Palestinians were in favour of the scheme and would come out openly in its support at his word. He proposed, however, to work underground at present and was in favour of the formation of a strong government here committed to work in favour of union.[2]

Kirkbride called on Prince Nayif again on the morning of Tuesday 24 July, and found that he was inclined to change the Government, although he was not as determined as he had been on Sunday. Kirkbride again advised him against haste. Nayif told him that both Salih Jabr and Nuri al-Said had spoken to him about union between Jordan and Iraq, and that he had put them off by being utterly unresponsive. He told Kirkbride that the issue would have to be decided eventually by the people of Jordan, but that in the meanwhile, he saw no reason why he should favour a scheme which seemed calculated to deprive the late King's descendents of all their rights.

Soon after he left the Palace, Kirkbride called on Glubb who confirmed Abu al-Huda's view that no great interest existed internally on the subject of the succession and that there were no signs of the country splitting into opposing parties on that issue.

On the same day, Samir al-Rifai returned Kirkbride's call and told him that he had been approached by Salih Jabr about the question of the union with Iraq. He said that his reaction had been that, 'in the absence of a King and a Parliament, no progress whatsoever was possible on the Jordan side and, indeed, with so many other distractions, it was unlikely that the responsible leaders here could give the matter serious consideration'. He also told Kirkbride that he had decided to tender his resignation on constitutional grounds, and because he felt that Prince Nayif wanted a change and he did not want to stay in office against the Prince Regent's will. Samir Pasha was particularly anxious that Kirkbride should not interfere as he would be most embarrassed if it became known that British influence had maintained him in power. He said that he was ready to serve with Abu al-Huda or Hashim, provided he remained Prime Minister, but he was not willing to accept a subordinate Ministry under some other Prime Minister.

Kirkbride was extremely active in Amman on that day. Samir al-Rifai's call was followed by another from Nuri al-Said, who discussed the union with Iraq. When Nuri left him he returned the call of Tawfiq Abu al-Huda and told him that he was not going to interfere in the question of the acceptance of al-Rifai's resignation. Abu al-Huda told him that he had discussed the issue of the union with both Salih Jabr and Nuri al-Said and, while he had not rejected the idea, he had been at pains not to commit himself. Kirkbride reported:

> He [Tawfiq] said that King Abdullah had sent certain written proposals to the Amir Abd al-Ilah about two months ago, which were designed to give the joint crown to King Abdullah during his lifetime and make King Faisal II the heir to the joint throne. The

Iraqis had sent counter proposals which could not be traced among the late King's papers and he had asked Nuri al-Said to send him a copy of the counter proposals for further consideration. He remarked that as he understood them at present, these counter proposals offered no benefits to Jordan and were framed entirely in the interests of Iraq; they would not, therefore, be acceptable to himself or any other Jordanian leaders.

He also warned me that Nayif had shown signs earlier in the day of now entertaining ideas of succeeding himself to his father's throne. Nayif was being egged on by Sheikh Muhammad Amin al-Shanqiti and Muhammad Pasha al-Shuraiqi. He expressed the view that Nayif's tendency should be checked firmly by all concerned.[3]

Kirkbride called next on former Prime Minister Ibrahim Hashim and found that Muhammad al-Shuraiqi had been trying to enlist his support for Prince Nayif's candidature. Hashim agreed readily enough with Kirkbride's suggestion that the present was no time to embark on an amendment of the constitution – the only means by which Nayif could succeed legally to the throne. Hashim did not like the idea of a change of Government but, being loyal, he volunteered his readiness to cooperate either with Samir Pasha or with Tawfiq Pasha. He was also strongly in favour of Tawfiq Pasha taking over if Samir Pasha did drop out.

On Wednesday morning, 25 July, Samir al-Rifai tendered his resignation to Prince Regent Nayif, but was asked to carry on the administration of the country for the time being. Samir Pasha called on Kirkbride to tell him about his resignation and to inform him that Prince Nayif had been open regarding the succession, and asked him whether there was any reason why his father's desire that he should succeed could not be met. He added that this desire had been expressed by the late King before the British Chargé d'Affaires. Al-Rifai had pointed out the constitutional position, and Nayif was surprised and pained that the Council of Ministers should be able to make him King if they wanted to. However, it seemed that Prince Nayif was in a hurry, and Abu al-Huda was forcing the pace of change; for although Nayif asked al-Rifai to continue with the administration for the time being, he wrote a letter accepting his resignation as well as an hour later a letter asking Abu al-Huda to form the new government.

Later in the day, Prince Nayif sent the Chief of the Royal Diwan to ask Kirkbride if there were any comments he wanted to make before sending the letters to Samir Pasha and Tawfiq Pasha, but in view of his decision not to interfere, Kirkbride confined himself to thanking the Prince for being consulted.

On the same day, Nuri al-Said called on Kirkbride again to give him copies of King Abdullah's original proposals for the union and the Iraqi counter proposals. Nuri Pasha said that he had given copies to Tawfiq Pasha and that he was postponing his departure by 24 hours in the hope that he might be able to discuss the suggestions with Tawfiq Abu al-Huda as soon as the latter had formed his Government.

On the same day, 25 July, Tawfiq Abu al-Huda did form his Government, as shown in Table 13.1, indicating that he had previously prepared for the occasion.

TABLE 13.1
Tawfiq Abu al-Huda's Government of July 1951

- Tawfiq Abu al-Huda, Prime Minister and Foreign Affairs
- Said al-Mufti, Deputy PM and Interior
- Muhammad al-Shanqiti, Chief Judge
- Falah al-Madadhah, Justice
- Rouhi Abd al-Hadi, Education
- Sulaiman al-Sukkar, Trade and Economics
- Anstas Hananiya, Agriculture and Construction
- Dr Jamil Tutinji, Health and Social Welfare
- Abd al-Rahman Khalifah, Finance
- Hashim al-Jayousi, Communications
- Sulaiman Touqan, Defence

On the first day of the new Government, internal matters appeared to have returned to normal. The few and isolated brawls between some Communist Palestinian refugees and Jordanians had ceased completely. There were no demonstrations and the whole country was still grieving the loss of the King. Investigations into his murder were progressing and the owner of the pistol used in the assassination had been arrested, together with the persons who handed the pistol to the murderer. They were persons known to have been associated with the Mufti's assassination squad, and the evidence secured up to 26 July pointed to the Mufti and his associates as being the instigators. There was no sign that Jordanian politicians and leaders of public opinion were responsive to any form of union with Iraq, and soon the Iraqi visitors in Amman realised that no decision was possible in the near future.

Kirkbride continued with his activities in Amman, gaining information, raising issues and doing his best to help the interest of Britain to maintain its influence in Jordan. He called formally on Abu al-Huda on 26 July, in order to congratulate him on assuming power and to discuss with him the various important issues facing the country. He found Abu al-Huda optimistic about overcoming any political troubles but was worried about the economic situation of the country which was most unsatisfactory. He intended to suggest to the American and British Governments that material assistance would be needed. As to the succession to the throne, Kirkbride reported:

> It was agreed that the present was no time in which to embark upon the amendment of the constitution, even if we considered Nayif the best successor to his father (which we did not). We agreed, therefore, to wait for the doctor's report on Talal at the end of the five weeks' treatment prescribed by the local board of doctors which sent Talal to Switzerland; if that report indicated that Talal's mental incapacity was permanent, Hussein would be proclaimed King and the matter settled. If the report recommended a further period of treatment, it would be awkward and we would have to think again as to whether we could afford to wait any more or whether to act at once.
>
> In the meanwhile, we should both discourage Nayif's pretensions.[4]

On 1 August, Abu al-Huda made it clear to the British, American and French Envoys that Jordan was unable to make a separate peace settlement with Israel and would act in unison with the majority of the Arab states. He also hinted that perhaps Egypt would soon take the lead towards a peace settlement. He assured them that Jordan would strictly observe the terms of the Armistice Agreement and would guard carefully against any action on the boundary or elsewhere that could give the Jews an excuse for armed aggression against Jordan. He reminded them that Jordan depended on the Anglo-Jordanian Treaty of 1948 and the Tripartite Statement for protection against aggression by Israel. He also asked the American Envoy to convey this statement of policy to the Israeli authorities and so perhaps allay the anxiety that had been evident of late in the Israeli press. He also assured the three envoys that the basic policy of his Government was to preserve the Hashemite Kingdom of Jordan in its present form and that the Government would not be party to any change in its status which was not approved by the rest of the

Arab world. He said that: 'Greater Syria as conceived by King Abdullah was dead.'[5]

The vacuum created by King Abdullah's absence from the benevolent control he exercised over events in Jordan and the absence of his influence in Arab affairs, along with the absence of an equally strong successor affected the future trend of events in Jordan and its immediate neighbouring countries. A great many people, Arab and others, anticipated that the King's death would cause immediate and drastic repercussions internally but, in spite of a most awkward situation over the succession to the throne, conditions remained normal and the country showed a satisfactory degree of internal stability. One of the main reasons for this stability was the continued steadfastness of the well-disciplined officers and men of the Jordan Arab Army and police who showed themselves to be a formidable deterrent against internal disorder and external aggression. The principal concern at the time was the campaign of murder directed against important persons and notables of Jordan who supported the Jordanian–Palestinian union or who opposed al-Haj Amin al-Husseini. On 26 July, a Cairo newspaper published a list of eminent Arabs who had been assassinated during the life of the League of Arab States, or during six years of extreme Arab nationalism:

- King Abdullah of Jordan.
- The Imam Yahya of the Yemen.
- Husni al-Zaim of Syria.
- Ahmad Mahir of Egypt.
- Mahmoud Fahmi al-Noqrashi of Egypt.
- Muhsin al-Barazi of Syria.
- Riyadh al-Solh of the Lebanon.
- Sami al-Hinnawi of Syria.
- Shaikh Hasan al-Banna, the leader of the Muslim Brothers.
- Amin Othman of Egypt.
- Salim Zaki of Egypt.
- Al-Khazindar of Egypt.[6]

According to Kirkbride, the appointment of Tawfiq Abu al-Huda, whose reputation for patriotism was higher than that of Samir al-Rifai, seems to have had a reassuring effect. However, he reported as follows:

The political leaders have overcome their original dismay at the King's disappearance and the feeling that the country could not survive without him. Although they talk of presenting a united front so as to preserve the edifice erected by King Abdullah, they are as disunited as ever and working for their personal ends as usual.

Greater Syria as conceived by King Abdullah is dead, but Greater Syria in reverse [Syria absorbing Jordan] is alive and is being supported by Egyptian and Saudi influence. It does not seem to have been met with the degree of favour here which I anticipated.

It seems likely that the Iraqis will now pull one way and the Saudis and Egyptians the other, but the fact that Tewfiq Abul Huda is in favour of avoiding any change in the present set up, may well neutralise all these intrigues.

The one question to which no one among the Jordanians is giving serious thought is what the Israelis will do. Tawfiq's only remark in this connection was to the effect that the hostile reactions in the Israeli press to his appointment had done him a great deal of good both in Jordan and elsewhere in the Arab world.

A source of great anxiety to myself is the economic condition of the country, which is most serious. Apart from the refugees, the non-displaced population has been reduced to near-famine conditions by the drought and trade is worse than ever before in the history of the country. The existence of such conditions provides many opportunities for making trouble, and there is no lack of people who want to do so here. The Jordan Government will probably put forward a request for special economic assistance soon and the satisfying of that request is, in my view, one of the best contributions towards stability in Jordan which we can make at present.[7]

On 8 August, Abu al-Huda received a reply from King Abd al-Aziz to his telegram in which he had said that he did not contemplate any early change in the status of Jordan and had asked if the King could check current intrigues for or against the union of Iraq with another state. The King's reply included the statement to the effect that he had 'informed Egypt, Syria and Iraq that he was not in favour of union of Jordan with either Iraq or Syria but wanted the rights of King Abdullah's sons preserved'.[8]

By 11 August 1951, the investigation into the murder of King Abdullah was completed, and Tawfiq Abu al-Huda announced that the following eight persons were to be brought to trial for their alleged connection with the murder:

- Dr Musa Abdullah al-Husseini.
- Abed Mahmoud Aukkah.
- Abd al-Qadir Farhat, alias Muhammad al-Sidmir.
- Zakariya Mahmoud Aukkah.
- Tawfiq Salih al-Husseini.
- The Reverend Ibrahim Aayad.
- Dr Daoud al-Husseini.
- Kamil Abdullah al-Kalouti.

In addition, the indictment mentioned the following:

- Abdullah al-Tel.
- Musa Ahmad al-Ayoubi.
- Mahmoud Ishaq al-Antabli.

The Special Court, which was held at the Officers' Mess of the Abdulli Barracks at Amman, consisted of the following:

- Lt General Abd al-Qadir al-Jundi, Deputy Chief of Staff as President.
- Colonel Habis al-Majali, member.
- Colonel Ali al-Hiyari, member.

The dual role of Attorney General and Legal Advisor to the Court was assumed by Walid Salah. The accused were represented by nine Palestinian advocates, and the proceedings were open to the public. The press, local and international, were allowed to witness and report freely on the trial.

The trial commenced on 18 August 1951, with the usual procedure, and after an initial eloquent attempt by the defence lawyers to question the legality of the Special Court, the President announced that the Court was legal and in accordance with Jordanian law. The trial continued for ten days with morning and afternoon sessions, and ended without a single incident. While the President and members of the Court behaved with commendable tolerance and patience, the lawyers were generally aggressive and outspoken in their cross-examination of witnesses and their resounding interventions in procedural issues. However, the members of the Court remained calm and replied adequately with reassuring dignity that did not fail to create a good impression on observers. Everyone was allowed to speak at length, and even the Palestinian left-wing elements and Egyptian observers admitted that the accused had a fair trial.

It would not have been difficult for the followers of Amin al-Husseini or the anti-Hashemite elements in the West Bank of Jordan to have made a political or an emotional issue before or during the trial. But as the details of the sordid story of the events leading to, and the machinery of, the assassination gradually unfolded, it became clear that the men involved were not misguided patriots, or nationalists, or religious zealots, but simply conspirators, contract killers and hired hit-men, planning a killing for cash. Thus no reaction, political or emotional, manifested itself in the West Bank.

At the conclusion of the trial, and before the verdicts and sentences were announced, both prosecution and defence representatives made speeches to the press praising each other and the Court. The Arab News Agency in particular received warm commendation from the defence.

Of the six men found guilty and condemned to death, Musa al-Husseini, Abed Mahmoud Aukkah, Zakariya Mahmoud Aukkah and Abd al-Qadir Farhat were present in the Court. Abdullah al-Tel and Musa Ahmad al-Ayoubi, who were also condemned to death, were in Cairo, and the Egyptian Government refused to extradite them to Jordan. Some sympathy was aroused by the other two Husseinis accused, but the evidence against them was so thin that they were acquitted. The remaining accused were found not guilty. It was a point in favour of the Court that although Daoud al-Husseini was known to have been a bitter opponent of King Abdullah, no attempt was made by the Court to force the evidence against him. Kirkbride reported:

> I consider that the preparation and conduct of this trial is a credit to the Jordan Government. Justice had been done, without any of the political or emotional consequences which usually follow such affairs in the Arab East.[9]

While the trial was in progress Prince Nayif had a meeting with Kirkbride in which he discussed the question of succession to the throne. Three reasons compelled Nayif to raise the issue: first, Crown Prince Talal had not sent a message to him with Said al-Mufti who had just returned from Geneva after visiting Talal; second, al-Mufti expressed his opinion that Talal was not ill; and third, Said al-Mufti added that Talal suspected that his brother Nayif had designs on the throne. Prince Nayif started the discussion with questions as to the relative claims of Prince al-Hussein and himself to the throne. Kirkbride replied that it was premature as Talal was still the rightful successor, as no one had yet certified him to be ill. Nayif then asked whether Talal was fit enough to bear the strain, to which Kirkbride replied that only time would tell. Nayif also asked who Kirkbride thought should succeed. Kirkbride replied that he recommended adherence to the constitution. He reported that he thought Nayif was rather cross, 'that he felt his position to be false and that he would not take the responsibility of confirming anyone sentenced to death in connection with his father's assassination'. Kirkbride expressed surprise and left. The rest of his report to the Foreign Office read as follows:

> Nayif then sent for two of the Ministers, expressed regret that Talal had not been brought back, and repeated to them his statement about refusing to confirm the death sentences. He added that he did not wish to retain the position of Regent and would discuss the question with the Prime Minister on Wednesday.
>
> I met the Prime Minister later in the day and dissuaded him from resigning without further ado. He will see Nayif tomorrow and if the latter opens the question of the succession explain the constitutional position to him in detail. If Nayif presses to be relieved of his duties the Prime Minister will agree and a Council of Regency will be formed.
>
> If Nayif remains as Regent and continues to make difficulties, the Council of Ministers will consider bringing Talal here if only for a few days, to settle the matter of succession finally. Talal could return to continue his treatment in Switzerland after becoming King in fact, and appoint another Regent or Regency Council.
>
> In the course of our talk the Prime Minister asked if I was aware of your views [the British Government] regarding the succession. I replied that you would be informed of this last development and I added my anticipation that you would counsel strict adherence to the constitution.[10]

In fact, Abu al-Huda had already decided to support Crown Prince Talal. Said al-Mufti, on his return from Geneva, handed a personal letter from Talal to Abu al-Huda. He told Abu al-Huda that Talal was in good health and could see no reason why he should not be proclaimed King. Prince Talal's letter read as follows:

**His Excellency Tawfiq Pasha,
The Prime Minister**

It is with pleasure that I extend to you my best wishes and heartfelt gratitude for your letter which was handed to me by the loyal friend of the family His Excellency Said al-Mufti. I cannot find a sentence to express to you my deep feelings when he came to see me here. I hope your Excellency and your council will accept my thanks and appreciation for your acceptance of my request and for sending Said Pasha al-Mufti to visit me.

I am proud of your friendship and loyalty to His late Majesty, my Father, His noble House, during his life and martyrdom. May God bless His soul, and reward goodness on His and Our behalf, and may He help you and give you success in the honour of serving the nation and the country in its noble aim, praise be God, the Responsible and the Responder.

I am still under treatment here, but my heart is with you. I must express my gratitude to my hosts for their care and gentleness, and I mention with praise my ADC, an officer of the Jordan Arab Army, for his loyalty and chivalry, and for his help in the hardest days of my life which I have endured here. Please look after his family in Amman with care and attention.

I am confident of your friendship and loyalty to the Princess [Zain al-Sharaf, his wife] and the children. They are your neighbours in the trust of God and your care, and I believe that they will not need anything, God willing.

Please your Excellency accept my salutations, support and respect.

Peace be upon you, His mercy and blessings.

8 August 1951
Talal[11]

For the kind and gentle Prince Talal, who took care to mention the family of his aide-de-camp before his own, this letter was typical of the caring man he was. Talal was most courteous and genuinely devoted to his people and family.

When Samir al-Rifai dissolved Parliament in May 1951, he intended and planned for the new elections to be conducted in a manner which would produce a more amenable Council of Deputies and 'preparations for rigging the elections were made on a large scale'. After the King's death, 'Samir Pasha showed every intention of proceeding with the original plans to control the elections, but he was replaced by Abu al-Huda'.[12]

In spite of the dogmatic and autocratic style of Abu al-Huda in conducting the affairs of the administration, from time to time he displayed a political vision worthy of his experience. When he assumed office he realised that it was impossible to resist the pressure for constitutional reform because of the absence of the personal and formidable influence of King Abdullah. Instead of attempting to control the elections, as Samir al-Rifai intended to do, he considered it preferable to yield gracefully rather than to be forced by political agitation to make concessions later on. Thus, when he announced the date of the registration of candidates for the forthcoming elections to the Chamber of Deputies as 21 August 1951, he stated that the elections would be free from interference and let it be known that, if he remained in office after the opening of the new National Assembly, he would amend the constitution. However, Abu al-Huda was determined to make one exception to his statement: that Shafiq al-Rushaidat of Irbid should not succeed.[13]

The registration of candidates was completed on 21 August. The allocation of the 40 seats, which was divided equally between the two Banks of Jordan, was as shown in Table 13.2.

During the election campaign, every attempt was made by interested parties to whip up public interest in the elections, but the political crisis that followed the assassination of King Abdullah, the uncertainty about the return of Crown Prince Talal to whom the people were devoted and the seriousness of the general economic situation had led to public apathy. Except for Nablus, where there was a bitter wrangle between leading candidates, vote catching and intrigue followed their normal course; the turnout was anticipated to be less than at the last election (50 per cent). The number of candidates was 90, of which 50 were for the East Bank seats and 40 for the West Bank. The number of voters (men only) was: 181,628 from the East Bank, and 161,086 from the West Bank, a total of 342,714. Some 50 manifestos in the form of handbills and announcements in the press appeared, of which the most extreme example came from the Communist and quasi-Communist elements of the so-called Jordan Popular Bloc. The latter demanded the cancellation of the Anglo-Jordan Treaty of 1948 and settlement of the Palestine problem on the basis of the Partition Plan of 1947, which they had opposed in the past. Two other manifestos demanded the revision of the Jordan constitution. The rest followed the usual slogans promising

TABLE 13.2
Allocation of seats for the elections to the Chamber
of Deputies, August 1951

	Muslims	Christians	Total
East Bank			
Amman	4	1	5
Irbid	2	1	3
Karak	2	1	3
Maan	1		1
Tafilah	1		1
Jarash	1		1
Ajlun	1		1
al-Salt	1	1	2
Madaba	1		1
North Bedouin	1		1
South Bedouin	1		1
Total	**16**	**4**	**20**
West Bank			
Jerusalem	2	1	3
Bethlehem	1	1	2
Hebron	4		4
Nablus	4		4
Jenin	2		2
Tulkarm	2		2
Ramallah	2	1	3
Total	**17**	**3**	**20**

relief from economic hardship, improvements in the refugees' condition and an increase in the salaries for the Civil Service, and so on. Abdullah al-Rimawi and Abdullah Niawas, who were arrested during the state of emergency following the King's assassination and subsequently released, issued a joint manifesto with the slogan, 'From Prison to Parliament'. There was no manifesto advocating the union of Jordan with any other Arab country, although several made references to Arab unity as a whole.

It was expected that the former opposition bloc in the previous Parliament would be returned and the political complexion of the new assembly was likely to be determined to a large extent by the number of seats regained by them. The members who formed the spearhead of that opposition in the former Parliament were as follows:

- Abdullah al-Rimawi of Ramallah.
- Abdullah Niawas of Jerusalem.
- Shafiq Rushaidat of Irbid.
- Abd al-Halim al-Nimir al-Humoud of al-Salt.
- Muhammad Hijazi of Irbid.

Of the five, Muhammad Hijazi had been excluded following his appointment as Consul General in Turkey, and it seemed that Abdullah Niawas was unlikely to succeed in Jerusalem against the candidature of the popular Anistas Hananiya, who was the Minister of Reconstruction and Agriculture. The general consensus of opinion was that the other members would be returned, and that they were likely to be strengthened by the addition of Dr Abd al-Majid Abu Hijlah, a member of the Popular Bloc from Nablus.

Voting started on 29 August 1951: only 37 per cent of the electorate voted in the East Bank and 30 per cent in the West Bank, and there was complete lack of interest in the elections by the citizens of Amman, the capital. There were no recognised political parties in Jordan at the time of the elections. The Jordanian branch of the Baath Arab Socialist Party, the Communist Party, the Muslim Liberation Party, the National Socialist Party and the Muslim Brothers Movement were on their way to being established. However, the elected Deputies were grouped as for or against the Government. Until then, the Governments of Jordan were of one colour and a quasi-permanent institution, changing its membership only within a narrow circle of four Prime Ministers, three of Palestinian origin and one Circassian, and about 15 ministers, the majority of whom were of Palestinian and Syrian origin. Governments were appointed by the Crown, as were the 20 members of the Chamber of Notables, many of whom were former Prime Ministers, Ministers, former Ministers and shaikhs who were leaders of the largest Bedouin and quasi-Bedouin tribes. This vested interest in Government was resented and opposed by the majority of young Jordanians and the new political élite.

The unity between the Jordanians and the Palestinians had gradually brought about a compromise in their political attitudes. The majority of Jordanians were monarchists and the majority of the Palestinians were quasi-republicans unaccustomed to monarchy. Some of the Palestinian politicians were socialists and progressive; the vast majority of Jordanian politicians were conservatives and traditionalists. In the absence of heavy or large industries, there was no effective labour movement to support the socialists in the elections on both Banks, and the call for agrarian reform or working conditions played an insignificant part in the election campaign of the so-called Left. The political competition was not about Government policies but about who should be in the Government. The opposition candidates concentrated their efforts, therefore, on 'anti-imperialism' and 'amendment of the constitution'. Without any consideration to the worst economic recession the country had ever experienced (due to the refugee problem), the 'anti-imperialists' conducted their campaign on the removal of British influence in general, the removal of the British officers from the Jordan Arab Army and even the removal of UNRWA, the agency that provided food, shelter and medical care to the refugees. Of course, they said nothing about the way they proposed to replace the British Grant-in-Aid of £6,500,000 to the Jordan Arab Army and the £3,000,000 annual budget that UNRWA spent in the country, without which it would collapse.

The argument for amending the constitution was more reasonable and had already been generally accepted by the Government of Abu al-Huda. Even at the time of the election, the Chamber of Deputies was not as powerless as it was thought to be. No government would have been able to ignore the determined will of the Deputies to force it to resign.

The results of the elections were announced by the Minister of the Interior as shown in Table 13.3.

Because of the return of the nationalists, one Jordanian and six Palestinian members, particularly al-Rimawi and Niawas, the elections were considered to be free by the majority of the people, the press and observers. The new opposition was considered to be effective in the country, where the art of criticising the Government was comparatively new and the voice of the critic had the bright ring of novelty. However, the fact remained that the Prime Minister, for his own personal reasons, did his best to prevent the return of Shafiq al-Rushaidat – and succeeded. How he was able to defeat Shafiq was never known, but his interference, though well known by Kirkbride, was only suspected by the majority.

The nominations to the Chamber of Notables were not surprising. Five were Ministers in Abu al-Huda's Government, four were leading merchants, three were lawyers, three were former Ministers, and the rest

TABLE 13.3
Results of the August 1951 elections

The East Bank

Amman
Said al-Mufti, Wasfi Mirza, Muhammad Ali Budair, Salim al-Bakhit

al-Salt
Abd al-Halim al-Nimir al-Humoud, Salih al-Muaashir

Irbid
Abdullah al-Kulaib al-Shraidah, Muhammad al-Saad al-Bataynah, Sulaiman Khalil

Karak
Hazzaa al-Majali, Ahmad al-Tarawnah, Jiries al-Halasah

Tafilah
Wahid al-Auran

Maan
Mahmoud Kraishan

Madaba
Shaikh Muhammad Salim Abu al-Ghanam

Ajlun
Fahmi al-Ali

Jarash
Shaikh Muhammad al-Aitan

Bedouins

Northern
Shaikh Sharari al-Bakhit

Southern
Shaikh Hamd ibn-Jazi

West Bank

Jerusalem
Kamil Auraiqat, Anwar al-Khatib, Abdullah Niawas

Hebron
Rashad al-Khatib, Rashad Maswadah, Said al-Aazzah, Yousef Amr

Nablus
Hikmat al-Masri, Walid al-Shakaah, Qadri Touqan, Abd al-Qadir al-Salih

Jenin
Abd al-Rahim Jarrar, Najib Mustafa al-Ahmad

Tulkarm
Hashim al-Jayousi, Hafiz al-Hamdallah

Ramallah
Abdullah al-Rimawi, Khulousi al-Khairi, Musa Nasir

Bethlehem
Abd al-Fattah Darwish, Tawfiq Qattan

were friends of the Amir Nayif and Abu al-Huda. On the day following the elections the names of the Senators were published as shown in Table 13.4.

TABLE 13.4
List of Senators following the August 1951 elections

• Tawfiq Abu al-Huda	• Muhammad Ali al-Ajluni
• Ibrahim Hashim	• Abd al-Latif Salah
• Shaikh Muhammad al-Shanqiti	• Shaikh Sulaiman al-Taji al Farouqi
• Sharif Sharaf	• Salih Bisaiso
• Falah al-Madadha	• Sabri al-Tubbaa
• Sulaiman Touqan	• Hussein Khawaja
• Anistas Hananiya	• Farid Irshaid
• Shukri Shashaah	• Adil Jaber
• Muhammad al-Shuraiqi	• Farid al-Saad
• Omar Mattar	• Najib Abu al-Shaar

The Special Correspondent of *The Manchester Guardian* in Amman, reported:

> The elections in Jordan were free. There was no interference with the nominations of candidates, and every adult man had a vote. At the time of King Abdullah's death some hundreds of suspects had been detained in prison. All but about one hundred were released before the elections; in no case were the Government's opponents prevented from contesting for seats. Two former deputies, leading Palestinian agitators who had been detained, released, and detained again on further suspicion, were finally released just forty-eight hours before nomination day. Both rushed back to their constituencies and brought election pamphlets robustly headed 'From Prison to Parliament'. Both got in, one (Abdullah Niawas) with a big majority over the former Minister for Reconstruction and Refugees, Anistas Hananiya. This Minister, a sensitive and able Palestinian, had done his best to care for the half-million refugees in Jordan. But everybody knows that with the small means at its disposal the Jordan Government can make little mark on so vast a problem. The vote for Abdullah Niawas was an anguished cry from the destitute Palestinians. He had promised them a kind of pie in the sky. He is one of the loudest of the Government's critics and it is around him that the Parliamentary Opposition tends to form.[14]

On 3 September 1951, the Regent, Prince Nayif, opened the first extraordinary session of the new National Assembly with a speech from the throne in which he did not even mention the name of his brother Crown Prince Talal. He said:

> Honourable notables and deputies
>
> At this hour when the National Assembly of both houses of notables and deputies convenes for the first time after the loss of the great monarch of the realm, our martyr Father and wise leader, we gather with heavy hearts praying to God that He may shower mercy upon his soul, always remembering how his life was full of profitable service to his nation and country and how he constantly inspired us with strength and hope. The catastrophe was therefore all the greater as people at home and abroad were struck by the news of his death. His loss was a severe test to the emotions of the people and to their loyalty to the throne as well as to their great appreciation of the man who had devoted his life for the sake of their freedom and glory and had sealed with his own blood the fulfillment of the pledge to serve them and struggle to the end for securing their rights.
>
> Honourable notables and deputies
>
> The early leaders of Islam fell as martyrs at the Battle of Mutah, a site in this realm. Their loss did not shake the Arabs' belief, subdue their ideals or dishearten them. On the contrary, it urged them to increased sacrifice and inflamed their souls, so that there never fell a leader from among them without that another picked up the standard. Our glorious past and the deeds of our forebears should thus be our guide and indisputable incentive.
>
> On the occasion of our assumption of the Regency to the throne in response to the call of duty and for the welfare of the state, the past Council of Ministers tendered its resignation in accordance with constitutional tradition. Grateful and appreciative of its services, we granted it the permission to withdraw. We entrusted the present Council of Ministers to assume the powers of Government so that it should participate with us in protecting the throne, and in upholding the good name of the homeland, and so that it should proceed to sustain constitutional life and national aspirations it should achieve the necessary improvements and maintain the good relations that exist with sister and friendly states.
>
> It is our greatest hope, nay, we are fully confident, that the nation's notables and deputies will renew their efforts to reinforce the foundation of cooperation between the legislative and executive powers of Government, and support one another in all that assures the best interests of the homeland, and promote the advancement of our people and country.

In the name of the Almighty God, I declare this extraordinary session of the National Assembly open. I call on you, Honourable notables and deputies, to start business with the devotion and zeal for which you have been renowned, praying to the Almighty that He may direct your footsteps and lead you, and us, in His bounty and generosity.[15]

On the following day, 4 September, Crown Prince Talal returned to Amman. As soon as the people of Amman heard the news of his return, almost the entire population came out in demonstrations of joy and happiness. Prince Talal enjoyed considerable devotion and confidence from the young Jordanians and Palestinians who constituted the majority of the people of both Banks. There had never been, within Jordanian memory, such rejoicing as attended his return to Amman. The welcome and the expression of confidence from both sides of the River Jordan was overwhelming. *The Manchester Guardian* wrote:

By birth and character, he was for the Trans-Jordanians the only possible ruler, while Palestinians, however much opposed to monarchy, were prepared to pay their tribute to an upright man. As Crown Prince living his own quiet life, he had never been associated with any abuse of privilege. He was thought to be fair and known to be honest. Honesty and fairness may not make a monarch, but they are valuable attributes in a country that is now beginning to grow critical of any misuse of power.[16]

Prince Talal was very popular among the Jordanian Arab Army, particularly with the Artillery Regiment. During the first round of fighting, and until the beginning of the first truce, he accompanied the Jerusalem battery in every action. He visited the front lines in Bab al-Wad and Jerusalem almost every day and spent most of his time at al-Nabi Samuel, where a gunner observation post was located. On several occasions he came under counter-artillery fire, and was almost killed during an artillery duel.

On Tuesday 4 September 1951, the Jordanian Cabinet held a special meeting and announced the following decision:

After reading the detailed memorandum presented by the Prime Minister dated 30 August 1951, and examining the state of His Royal Highness Prince Talal, the Crown Prince, the Exalted, from the constitutional and the health points of views, the Council of Ministers read the decision of the previous Council of Ministers of 20 July, no. 723, and the medical reports of various dates regarding the health of His Highness, especially the medical report issued at Geneva by the Director of the Hospital, and four doctors, of 22 August 1951. After full study, examination and detailed thought, the Council of Ministers decided that the right of accession to the throne is for the Crown Prince, and there is no objection that prevents him from assuming his mission as King. The Council of Ministers therefore decided unanimously to proclaim him King of the Hashemite Kingdom of Jordan on condition that he accepts, before he assumes his duties, to swear the Oath in the National Assembly, in accordance with Article 23 of the constitution, and to inform the said Assembly of this decision, and announce it to the people.

4 September 1951.[17]

On 5 September 1951, the National Assembly held an extraordinary meeting in which the Prime Minister presented the Council of Ministers' decision and informed the National Assembly that His Highness would arrive at Mafraq Airport, then fly to Amman Airport and arrive at 1030 hours on Thursday 6 September. Thereafter he would attend the National Assembly and swear the oath. The National Assembly approved the Council of Ministers' decision as follows:

> After reading the decision of the Council of Ministers, dated 4 September 1951, which declares that there is no objection on the ground of health that prevents His Highness Prince Talal, the Exalted, from accession to the throne in accordance with the medical reports mentioned in the Council of Ministers' decision, the National Assembly decided unanimously to proclaim His Majesty, in the name of His Majesty King Talal the First Ibn Abdullah Ibn al-Hussein, constitutional King of the Hashemite Kingdom of Jordan.[18]

On 6 September, the King arrived at the National Assembly and took the Oath: 'I swear by the Almighty God, to adhere to the constitution and serve the Nation.'

After the proclamation ceremony the King went to his father's grave and read a verse of the Qur'an with tears in his eyes.

The King was dead; God save the King.

NOTES

1 PRO. FO 371/91789. Report from Kirkbride to Furlonge, 25 July 1951.
2 PRO. FO 371/91797. From Kirkbride to the Foreign Office, 24 July 1951.
3 PRO. FO 371/91789. Report from Kirkbride to Furlonge, 25 July 1951.
4 *Ibid.* From Kirkbride to Furlonge, 27 July 1951.
5 *Ibid.* From Kirkbride to the Foreign Office, 1 August 1951.
6 The *Times*, London, 26 July 1951.
7 PRO. FO 371/91839. From Kirkbride to Sir Thomas Rapp, 2 August 1951.
8 *Ibid.* From Kirkbride to the Foreign Office, 8 August 1951.
9 *Ibid.* From M. Walker to Herbert Morrison, 3 September 1951.
10 PRO. FO 816/172. From Kirkbride to the Foreign Office, 15 August 1951.
11 Letter, *Al Sharia Magazine* (July 1972), pp. 34–5.
12 PRO. FO 371/98859. Kirkbride to the Foreign Office, note on constitutional changes in Jordan. Undated. Six weeks before the elections.
13 PRO. FO 371/91789. From Kirkbride to Herbert Morrison, 5 September 1951.
14 *The Manchester Guardian*, 16 October 1951.
15 Translation by the British Legation. PRO. FO 371/91789. Kirkbride to the Foreign Office, 5 September 1951.
16 *The Manchester Guardian*, 16 October 1951.
17 *HKJOG*, special edition, 6 September 1951.
18 *Ibid.*

Appendix A

Treaty of Alliance between His Majesty in respect of the United Kingdom of Great Britain and Northern Ireland and His Majesty the King of the Hashemite Kingdom of Jordan.

Amman, 15 March 1948

His Majesty The King of Great Britain, Ireland and the British Dominions beyond the Seas and His Majesty The King of the Hashemite Kingdom of Trans-Jordan.

Animated by the most sincere desire to consolidate the friendship and good relations which exist between them and to establish these relations on the foundations best calculated to ensure the development of this friendship.

Desiring to conclude a new Treaty of Alliance with these objects and in order to strengthen by cooperation and mutual assistance the contribution which each of them will be able to make to the maintenance of international peace and security in accordance with the provisions and principles of the Charter of the United Nations: Have accordingly appointed as their Plenipotentiaries:

His Majesty The King of Great Britain, Northern Ireland and the British Dominions beyond the Seas (hereafter referred to as His Britannic Majesty).

For the United Kingdom of Great Britain and Northern Ireland:

Sir Alec Seath Kirkbride, CMG, OBE, MC, His Envoy Extraordinary and Minister Plenipotentiary.

His Majesty The King of the Hashemite Kingdom of Trans-Jordan:

His Excellency Tawfiq Pasha Abu Al-Huda, First Class Order of the Istiqlal, Prime Minister.

His Excellency Fawzi Pasha Al-Mulqi, Second Class Order of the Istiqlal, Minister for Foreign Affairs.

Who having exhibited their full powers found in good and due form have agreed as follows.

ARTICLE 1

There shall be perpetual peace and friendship between His Britannic Majesty and His Majesty The King of the Hashemite Kingdom of Trans-Jordan.

A close alliance shall continue between the High Contracting Parties in consecration of their friendship, their cordial understanding and their good relations.

Each of the High Contracting Parties undertakes not to adopt in regard to foreign countries an attitude which is inconsistent with the Alliance or might create difficulties for the other party thereto.

ARTICLE 2

Should any dispute between either High Contracting Party and a third state produce a situation which would involve the risk of rupture with that state, the High Contracting Parties will concert together with a view to the settlement of the said dispute by peaceful means in accordance with the provisions of the Charter of the United Nations and of any other international obligations which may be applicable to the case.

ARTICLE 3

Should either Contracting Party notwithstanding the provision of Article 2 become engaged in a war, the other High Contracting Party will, subject always to the provision of Article 4, immediately come to his aid as a measure of collective defence.

In the event of an imminent menace of hostilities the High Contracting Parties will immediately concert together the necessary measure of defence.

ARTICLE 4

Nothing in the present treaty is intended to, or shall in any way prejudice, the rights and obligations which devolve, or may devolve, upon either of the High Contracting Parties under the Charter of the United Nations or under any other existing international agreements, conventions or treaties.

ARTICLE 5

The present treaty of which the Annex is an integral part shall replace the Treaty of Alliance signed in London on 22 March 1946 of the Christian Era, together with its Annex and all letters and notes, interpreting or otherwise exchanged in 1946 in connection therewith, provided, however, that Article 9 of the said treaty shall remain in force in accordance with and modified by the notes exchanged on this day on this subject.

ARTICLE 6
Should any differences arise relative to the application or interpretation of the present treaty and should the High Contracting Parties fail to settle such differences by direct negotiations, it shall be referred to the International Court of Justice unless the parties agree to another mode of settlement.

ARTICLE 7
The present treaty shall be ratified and shall come into force upon the exchange of instruments of ratification which shall take place in London as soon as possible. It shall remain in force for a period of twenty years from the date of its coming into force. At any time after fifteen years from the date of coming into force of the present treaty, the High Contracting Parties will, at the request of either of them, negotiate a revised treaty, which shall provide for the continued cooperation of the High Contracting Parties in the defence of their common interests. The period of fifteen years shall be reduced if a complete system of security agreements under Article 43 of the Charter of the United Nations is concluded before the expiry of this period. At the end of the twenty years, if the present treaty has not been revised, it shall remain in force until the expiry of one year after notice of termination has been given by either High Contracting Parties to the other through the diplomatic channel.

In witness whereof the above mentioned plenipotentiaries have signed the present treaty and affixed thereto their seals.

Done in duplicate at Amman, this 15th day of March 1948, in the English and Arabic Languages, both text being equally authentic.

(LS) A. S. Kirkbride
(LS) Tawfiq Abu Al-Huda
(LS) Fawzi Al-Mulqi
1. Treaty Series No. 67 (1948) Cmd. 7015
2. Treaty Series No. 32 (1946) Cmd. 6916

Annex to the Anglo-Jordanian Treaty of Alliance, 1948

ARTICLE 1

(a) The High Contracting Parties recognise that, in the common interest of both, each of them must be in a position to discharge his obligations under Article 3 of the treaty.

(b) In the event of either High Contracting Party becoming engaged in a war, or of a menace of hostilities, each High Contracting Party will invite the other to bring to his territory or territory controlled by him the necessary forces of all arms. Each will furnish to the other all the facilities and assistance in his power, including the use of all means and lines of communication, and on financial terms to be agreed upon.

(c) His Majesty The King of Trans-Jordan will safeguard, maintain and develop as necessary the airfields, ports, roads and other means and lines of communication in and across the Hashemite Kingdom of Trans-Jordan as may be required for the purposes of this present treaty and its annex and will call upon His Majesty's assistance as may be required for this purpose.

(d) Until such time as the High Contracting Parties agree that the state of the world security renders such measures unnecessary, His Majesty The King of the Hashemite Kingdom of Trans-Jordan invites His Britannic Majesty to maintain units of the Royal Air Force at Amman and Mafraq airfields. His Majesty The King of the Hashemite Kingdom of Trans-Jordan will provide the necessary facilities for the accommodation and maintenance of the units mentioned in this paragraph, including facilities for the storage of their ammunition and supplies and the lease of any land required.

ARTICLE 2

In the common defence of the High Contracting Parties, a permanent joint advisory body will be set up immediately on the coming into force of the present treaty to co-ordinate defence matters between the Governments of the High Contracting Parties within the scope of the present treaty.

This body, which will be known as the Anglo-Trans-Jordan Joint Defence Board, will be composed of competent military representatives of the Governments of the High Contracting Parties in equal numbers, and its function will include the following.

(a) The formulation of agreed plans in the strategic interests common to both countries.

(b) Immediate consultation in the event of a threat of war.

(c) The co-ordination of measures to enable the forces of either High Contracting Party to fulfil their obligations under Article 3 of the present treaty and in particular measure for the safeguarding, maintenance and development of the airfields, ports and lines of communication referred to in Article 1 (c) of this annex.

(d) Consultation regarding training and provision of equipment. The Joint Defence Board shall submit annual reports thereon and recommendations to the governments of the two High Contracting Parties.

(e) Arrangements regarding the joint training operations referred to in Article 6 of this annex.

(f) The consideration of and if necessary recommendation for location of His Britannic Majesty's forces at places in Trans-Jordan other than those provided for in Article 1 (d) of this annex.

ARTICLE 3

His Britannic Majesty will reimburse to His Majesty The King of the Hashemite Kingdom of Trans-Jordan all expenditure which the Government of the Hashemite Kingdom of Trans-Jordan may incur in connexion with the provision of facilities under Article (c) and (d) of the present annex and will repair or pay compensation for any damage due to the actions of members of His Britannic Majesty's armed forces, other than damage caused in military operations undertaken in accordance with Article 3 of the present treaty.

ARTICLE 4

His Majesty The King of the Hashemite Kingdom of Trans-Jordan agrees to afford on request all necessary facilities for the movement of units of His Britannic Majesty's forces in transit across the Hashemite Kingdom of Trans-Jordan, with their supplies and equipment, on the same financial terms as those applicable to the forces of His Majesty The King of the Hashemite Kingdom of Trans-Jordan.

ARTICLE 5

Pending the conclusion of an agreement between the High Contracting Parties defining in details the jurisdictional and fiscal immunities of members of the forces of His Britannic Majesty in the Hashemite Kingdom of Trans-Jordan, they will continue to enjoy the immunities that are accorded to them at present, including the provision that, in accordance with the principles of international law governing the immunities of Sovereign and Sovereign states, no demand will be made for the payment of His Britannic Majesty of any Trans-Jordan taxation in respect of immovable property leased or owned by His Britannic Majesty or in respect of his movable property, including custom duty on goods imported or exported by, or on behalf of, His Britannic Majesty. The privileges and immunities to be extended to the units and personnel of the armed forces of His Majesty The King of the Hashemite Kingdom of Trans-Jordan visiting or present in British territory shall be defined in similar agreements on reciprocal bases.

ARTICLE 6

In order that the armed forces of the High Contracting Parties should attain the necessary efficiency in cooperation with each other and in view of the desirability of establishing identity between the training and methods employed by the Trans-Jordan and British respectively:

1. His Britannic Majesty offers appropriate facilities in the United Kingdom and in any British colony or protectorate administered by the Government of the United Kingdom for the training of the armed forces of His Majesty The King of the Hashemite Kingdom of Trans-Jordan.
2. His Britannic Majesty will make available operational units of his armed forces to engage in joint training operations with armed forces of His Majesty The King of the Hashemite Kingdom of Trans-Jordan for a sufficient period of each year.
3. His Majesty The King of the Hashemite Kingdom of Trans-Jordan agrees to make available facilities in the Hashemite Kingdom of Trans-Jordan for the purposes of this joint training.
4. His Britannic Majesty will provide on request any British service personnel whose services are required to ensure the efficiency of the military units of the forces of The King of the Hashemite Kingdom of Trans-Jordan.

5. His Britannic Majesty will (a) afford all possible facilities to His Majesty The King of the Hashemite Kingdom of Trans-Jordan for the military instruction of Trans-Jordan officers at schools of instruction maintained for His Britannic Majesty's forces and (b) provide arms, ammunition, equipment and aircraft and other war material for the forces of His Majesty The King of the Hashemite Kingdom of Trans-Jordan.

6. His Majesty The King of the Hashemite Kingdom of Trans-Jordan will (a) meet the cost of instruction and equipment referred to in paragraph 5 (a) and (b) above, (b) ensure that the armament and essential equipment of his forces shall not differ in type from those of the forces of His Britannic Majesty, and (c) send any personnel of his forces that might be sent abroad for training, to military schools, colleges and training centres maintained for His Britannic Majesty's forces.

ARTICLE 7

His Majesty The King of the Hashemite Kingdom of Trans-Jordan gives permission for the ships of His Britannic Majesty's Navy to visit the ports of the Hashemite Kingdom of Trans-Jordan at any time upon giving notification to the Government of the Hashemite Kingdom of Trans-Jordan.

(Initialled)
A. S. Kirkbride
Tawfiq Abu Al-Huda
Fawzi Al-Mulqi

Appendix B

_____

Budget for the year 1948/9

On 1 April 1948, during the meeting of the extraordinary session of the Chamber Deputies, the budget for the year 1948/9, which covered the months between 1 April 1948 until 31 March 1949, was approved by the National Assembly as follows.

A Ordinary expenditure

Head	Palestine Pound
1. The Royal Hashemite Court	48,400
2. The National Assembly	12,481
3. Pensions	31,300
4. The Cabinet	19,742
5. Ministry of Internal Affairs	18,403
5A. Passports Department	3,178
6. Ministry of Justice	26,763
7. Sharia Courts	6,839
8. Ministry of Finance and Economics	23,117
9. Trade, Customs and Industry Department	28,871
10. Public Health	32,469
11. Foreign Ministry	43,605
12. Ministry of Education	52,828
13. Agriculture	31,469
14. Department of Antiquities	3,968
15. Department of Public Works	8,986
16. Department of Post, Telephone and Telegraph	44,922
17. Department of Land and Survey	74,332
18. Police, Gendarme and Prisons (Arab Legion)	326,374
19. General expenditure	427,656
20. Audit department	5,931
21. Tribal court of Appeal	424
22. Car advances	1,600
Total ordinary expenditure	**1,273,658**

B   Extraordinary expenditure

Head	Palestine Pound
23. Public Works	155,200
25. Land and Survey	21,075
26. Customs and Trade	1,350
27. Finance	3,500
29. Post and Telegraph	32,000
Total extraordinary expenditure	**213,125**
Total expenditure	**1,486,783**

C   Revenue

Head	Palestine Pound
1. Customs and Excise	810,450
2. Licences and Taxes	349,920
3. Departments and courts fees	127,850
4. Post and Telegraph	66,950
5. Revenue from Government properties	7,000
6. Interests	150
7. Miscellaneous revenue	228,361
8. Sale of Government land	2,200
9. Returned advances	960
Total national revenue	**1,593,841**

Budget for the year 1949/50

The budget for the year 1949/50 was approved by the National Assembly on 4 May 1949, and published in the *Hashemite Kingdom of Jordan Official Gazette* on 9 May 1949 as follows.

A   Ordinary expenditure

Head	Palestine Pound
1. The Royal Hashemite Court	52,646
2. The National Assembly	12,864
3. Pensions	37,363
4. The Cabinet	20,704
5. Ministry of Internal Affairs	19,861

6.	Ministry of Justice	27,889
7.	Sharia Courts	8,031
8.	Ministry of Finance and Economics	23,801
9.	Department of Customs, Trade and Industry	34,336
10.	Ministry of Health	52,854
11.	Ministry of Foreign Affairs	70,442
12.	Ministry of Education	60,071
13.	Ministry of Agriculture	34,940
14.	Department of Archaeology	4,068
15.	Department of Public Works	9,756
15A.	Recurrent Public Works	119,950
16.	Post and Telegraph	55,083
17.	Department of Land and Survey	75,044
18.	Ministry of Defence	3,546
18A.	Police, Gendarme and Prisons	506,312
18B.	The Hashemite Regiment (Royal Guards)	196,631
19.	General expenditure	369,506
20.	Department of Audit	6,378
21.	Tribal Court of Appeal	430
22.	Department of Statistics	3,905
23.	Advances	1,600
	Total ordinary expenditure	**1,808,011**

B Extraordinary expenditure

	Head	Palestine Pound
24.	Public Works	209,100
25.	The Hashemite Regiment	30,000
26.	Police and Prisons	15,000
27.	Land and Survey	151,922
28.	Customs, Trade and Industry	1,500
29.	Finance and Economics	4,078
30.	Post and Telegraph	11,850
31.	Public Health	8,000
32.	Agriculture	30,342
33.	The Royal Hashemite Court	20,000
	Total extraordinary expenditure	**481,792**
	Total expenditure	**2,288,803**

C National Revenue

Head	Palestine Pound
1. Custom and Excise	1,202,317
2. Licences and Taxes	594,795
3. Departments and Courts Fees	173,600
4. Post and Telegraph	101;030
5. Revenue from Government Properties	11,000
6. Interests	2,600
7. Miscellaneous revenue	256,200
8. Sale of State Domain	2,000
9. Returned advances	960
Total national revenue	**2,344,502**

Budget for the year 1950/1

The budget for the year 1950/1 was approved by the National Assembly on the 8–15 June 1950, and published as Law No. 20 for the year 1950 as follows.

A Ordinary expenditure

Head	Palestine Pound
1. The Royal Hashemite Court	55,809
2. The National Assembly	25,144
3. Pensions	36,700
4. The Cabinet	27,407
5. Ministry of Internal Affairs	21,567
5A. Passports Department	5,097
6. Ministry of Justice	31,639
7. Sharia Courts	8,507
8. Ministry of Finance and Economics	25,865
9. Ministry of Customs and Trade	35,110
10. Public Health	61,421
11. Ministry of Foreign Affairs	103,941
12. Ministry of Education	80,938
13. Ministry of Agriculture	36,801
13A. Veterinary Department	17,700

14.	Archaeology Department	5,334
15.	Ministry of Public Works	17,356
15A.	Public Works Recurrent	158,600
16.	Ministry of Post and Telegraph	73,662
17.	Land and Survey Department	90,455
18.	Ministry of Defence, Police, Gendarme and Prisons	566,807
18A.	The Hashemite Regiment	198,193
19.	General Expenditure	355,087
20.	Department of Audit	7,521
21.	Tribal Court of Appeal	399
22.	Department of Statistics	5,747
23.	Imports and Currency Department	6,542
24.	Advances	1,600
	Total ordinary expenditure	**2,060,949**

B Extraordinary expenditure

Head		Palestine Pound
25.	Ministry of Finance	23,615
26.	Public Health	9,390
27.	Agriculture	23,910
28.	Archaeology	2,800
29.	Public Works	222,197
30.	Post and Telegraph	39,875
31.	Land and Survey	50,045
32.	The Hashemite Regiment	25,000
33.	Police, Gendarme and Prisons	10,000
34.	West Bank Civil Service	500,000
35.	Palestine Refugees Relief	60,000
36.	Committee for Unifying the Laws	5,010
37.	Civil Service Allowance	58,239
38.	The National Guard	100,000
42.	Projects of the One Million Loan	1,000,000
	Total extraordinary expenditure	**2,130,081**
	Total expenditure	**4,191,030**

C National revenue

Head	Palestine Pound
1. Customs and Excise	1,779,500
2. Licences and Taxes	640,680
3. Fees from Courts and Departments	274,350
4. Post and Telegraph	94,200
5. Revenue from Government properties	17,000
6. Interests	3,000
7. Miscellaneous revenue	279,300
8. Sale of State Domain	2,000
9. Returned from advances	1,000
10. The One Million Loan	1,000,000
Total national revenue	**4,091,030**

Budget for the year 1951/2

On 12 May 1951, King Abdullah approved the budget for the year 1951/2 as follows.

A Ordinary expenditure

Head	Jordan Dinar
1. The Royal Hashemite Court	58,299
2. The National Assembly	32,521
3. Pensions	55,100
4. The Cabinet	36,408
4A. Publication Department	4,612
5. Ministry of Internal Affairs	46,963
5A. Passport Department	8,300
5B. Custody of Enemy Properties	1,946
6. Ministry of Justice	79,740
7. Sharia Courts	22,258
8. The Islamic Institute	5,838
9. Ministry of Finance and Economics	58,334
10. Ministry of Trade and Customs	48,802
11. Ministry of Health	216,774
11A. Department of Social Welfare	20,375

12.	Ministry of Foreign Affairs	132,136
12A.	Office of Foreign Relations	1,601
13.	The Hashemite Broadcasting Station	41,093
14.	Ministry of Education	308,194
14A.	Department of Archaeology	7,273
15.	Ministry of Agriculture	56,754
15A.	Department of Veterinary	26,728
16.	Ministry of Communications (Public Works)	65,207
16A.	Public Works Recurrent	384,250
16B.	Department of Civil Aviation	9,224
17.	Department of Post and Telegraph	99,068
18.	Department of Land and Survey	83,924
19.	Forestry Department	35,533
20.	Ministry of Defence (Police, Gendarme, Prisons)	1,224,020
20A.	The Royal Hashemite Regiment	244,692
20B.	The Arab Legion Air Force	244,692
21.	The Military Units	6,500,000
22.	Department of Audit	15,436
23.	Tribal Court of Appeal	458
24.	The Department of Statistics	8,433
25.	The Department of Imports and Exports	3,839
26.	Currency Control Department	4,342
27.	Ministry of Construction and Development	7,745
28.	General expenditure	930,815
	Total ordinary expenditure	**11,131,727**

B Extraordinary expenditure

	Head	Jordan Dinar
29.	Ministry of Finance	401,615
30.	Ministry of Trade and Customs	1,200
31.	Ministry of Health	24,000
32.	Department of Archaeology	2,650
33.	Ministry of Agriculture	16,700
34.	Public Works	321,021
35.	Civil Aviation	3,700
36.	Post and Telegraph	36,475

37.	Land and Survey	98,475
38.	Forests	1,200
39.	The Jordanian Arab Army	93,000
40.	The National Guards	279,689
41.	Committee for Unifying the Laws	900
42.	Government projects	800,000
43.	Projects of the One Million Loan	511,792
44.	The Royal Hashemite Court	20,000
	Total extraordinary expenditure	**2,612,417**
	Total expenditure	**13,744,144**

C   National Revenue

Head	**Jordan Dinar**
1. Customs and Excise	2,181,500
2. Licences and Taxes	1,029,520
3. Fees from Courts and Departments	471,890
4. Post and Telegraph	195,050
5. Revenue from Government properties	34,900
6. Interests	6,000
7. Miscellaneous revenue	954,262
8. Returned advances	1,500
9. Revenue of Civil Aviation	36,000
10. Returned from loans	20,500
11. Allocation of Military Units	6,500,000
Total revenue	**11,431,122**

Appendix C

1. Since I presented my written suggestions to the Arab and Jewish authorities on 27 June, I have made no formal submission to either party of further suggestions or proposals for a definitive settlement. Since that date, however, I have held many oral discussions in the Arab capitals and Tel Aviv in the course of which various ideas on settlement have been freely exchanged. As regards my original suggestions, I hold to the opinion that they offered a general framework within which a reasonable and workable settlement might have been reached, had the two parties concerned been willing to discuss them. They were flatly rejected, however, by both parties, since they were put forth on the explicit condition that they were purely tentative, were designed primarily to elicit views and counter-suggestions from each party, and, in any event, could be implemented only if agreed upon by both parties. I have never since pressed them. With respect to one basic concept in my suggestions, it has become increasingly clear to me that however desirable a political and economic union might be in Palestine, the time is certainly not now propitious for the effectuation of any such scheme.

2. I do not consider it to be within my province to recommend to the Members of the United Nations a proposed course of action on the Palestine question. That is a responsibility of the members acting through the appropriate organ. In my role as United Nations mediator, however, it was inevitable that I should accumulate information and draw conclusions from my experience which might well be of assistance to members of the United Nations in charting the future course of United Nations action on Palestine. I consider it my duty, therefore, to acquaint the members of the United Nations through the medium of this report, with certain of the conclusions on means of peaceful adjustment which have evolved from my frequent consultations with Arab and Jewish authorities over the past three and one-half months and from my personal

appraisal of the present Palestinian scene. I do not suggest that the conclusions would provide the basis for a proposal which would readily win the willing approval of both parties. I have not, in the course of my intensive effort to achieve agreement between Arabs and Jews, been able to devise any such formula. I am convinced, however, that it is possible at this stage to formulate a proposal which, if firmly approved and strongly backed by the General Assembly, would not be forcibly resisted by either side, confident as I am, of course, that the Security Council stands firm in its resolution of 15 July that military action shall not be employed by either party in the Palestine dispute. It cannot be ignored that the vast difference between now and last November is that a war has been started and stopped and that in the intervening months decisive events have occurred.

Six basic premises

3.   The following six basic premises form the basis for my conclusions.

One. A Jewish State called Israel exists in Palestine and there are no sound reasons for assuming that it will not continue to do so.

Two. The boundaries of this new state must finally be fixed either by formal agreement between the parties concerned or failing that, by the United Nations.

Three. Adherence to the principle of geographic homogeneity and integration, which should be the major objective of the boundary arrangement, should apply equally to Arab and Jewish territories, whose frontiers should not, therefore, be rigidly controlled by the territorial arrangements envisaged in the 29 November resolution.

Four. The right of innocent people, uprooted from their homes by the present terror and ravage of war, to return to their homes, should be affirmed and made effective, with assurance of adequate compensation for the property of those who may choose not to return.

Five. The city of Jerusalem, because of its religious and international significance and the complexity of interests involved, should be accorded special and separate treatment.

Six. International responsibility should be expressed where desirable and necessary in the form of international guarantees as a means of allaying existing fears, and particularly with regard to boundaries and human rights.

Specific conclusions

4. The following conclusions, broadly outlined, would, in my view, considering all the circumstances, provide a reasonable, equitable and workable basis for settlement.

(a) Since the Security Council, under threat of Chapter 7 Sanctions, has forbidden further employment of military action in Palestine as a means of settling the dispute, hostilities should be pronounced formally ended either by mutual agreement of the parties or, failing that, by the United Nations. The existing indefinite truce should be superseded by a formal peace or at the minimum an armistice which would either mean complete withdrawal and demobilisation of armed forces or their wide separation by creation of broad demilitarised zones under United Nations supervision.

(b) The frontier between the Arab and Jewish territories, in the absence of agreement between Arabs and Jews, should be established by the United Nations and delimited by a technical boundaries commission appointed by and responsible to the United Nations with the following revisions in the boundaries broadly defined in the resolution of the General Assembly of 29 November in order to make them more equitable, workable and consistent with existing realities in Palestine.

(i) The area known as the Negev, south of a line running from the sea near al-Majdal east south-east to al-Faluja (both of which places would be in Arab territory).

(ii) The frontier should run from al-Faluja, north north-east to Ramleh and Lydda, both of which places should be in Arab territory, the frontier at Lydda then following the line established in the 29 November resolution of the General Assembly.

(iii) Galilee should be defined as Jewish territory.

One. The dispositions of the territory of Palestine not included within the boundaries of the Jewish state should be left to the governments of the Arab states in full consultation with the Arab inhabitants of Palestine, with the recommendation, however, that in view of the historical connection and common interests of Trans-Jordan and Palestine, there would be compelling reasons for merging the Arab territory of Palestine with the territory of Trans-Jordan, subject to such frontier rectifications regarding other Arab states as may be found practicable and desirable.

Two. The United Nations, by declaration of other appropriate means, should undertake to provide special assurance that the boundaries between the Arab and Jewish territories shall be respected and maintained, subject only to such modifications as may be mutually agreed upon by the parties concerned.

Three. The port of Haifa including the oil refineries and terminals, and without prejudice to their inclusion in the sovereign territory of the Jewish state or the administration of the city of Haifa, should be declared a free port, with assurances of free access for interested Arab countries and an undertaking on their part to place no obstacle in the way of oil by pipelines to the Haifa refineries, whose distribution would continue on the basis of the historical pattern.

Four. The airport at Lydda should be declared a free airport with assurance of access to it and employment of its facilities for Jerusalem and interested Arab countries.

Five. The city of Jerusalem, which should be understood as covering the area defined in the resolution of the General Assembly of 29 November, should be treated separately and placed under effective United Nations control with maximum feasible local autonomy for its Arab and Jewish communities, with full safeguards for the protection of the Holy Places and sites and free access to them, and for religious freedom.

Six. The right of unimpeded access to Jerusalem by road, rail or air, should be fully respected by all parties.

Seven. The right of the Arab refugees to return to their homes in Jewish controlled territory at the earliest possible date should be affirmed by the United Nations and their repatriation, resettlement and economic and social rehabilitation, and payment of adequate compensation for the property of those choosing not to return, should be supervised and assisted by the United Nations conciliation commission described in paragraph Nine below.

Eight. The political economic, social and religious rights of all Arabs in the Jewish territory of Palestine and of all Jews in the Arab territory of Palestine should be fully guaranteed and respected by the authorities. The conciliation commission provided for in the following paragraph should supervise the observance of this guarantee. It should also lend its good offices, on the invitation of the parties, to any efforts toward exchanges of populations with a view to eliminating troublesome minority problems, and on the basis of adequate compensation for property owned.

Nine. In view of the special nature of the Palestine problem and the dangerous complexities of Arab–Jewish relationships, the United Nations should establish a Palestine conciliation commission. This commission, which should be appointed for a limited period, should be responsible to the United Nations and act under its authority. The commission, assisted by such United Nations personnel as may prove necessary, should undertake:

(a) to employ its good offices to make such recommendations to the parties or to the United Nations, and to take such other measures as may be appropriate, with a view to ensuring the continuation of the peaceful adjustment of the situation in Palestine

(b) such measures as it might consider appropriate in fostering the cultivation of friendly relations between Arabs and Jews

(c) to supervise the observance of such boundary, road, railroad, free port, free airport, minority rights and other arrangements approved as may be decided upon by the United Nations

(d) to report promptly to the United Nations any development in Palestine likely to alter the arrangements approved by the United Nations in the Palestine settlement or to threaten the peace of the area.

Source: PRO. FO 816/129. From a letter from Kirkbride to the Prime Minister of Jordan, Said al-Mufti, 23 September 1948.

Appendix D

RECORD OF MEETING BETWEEN SECRETARY OF STATE
ERNEST BEVIN AND KING ABDULLAH

Sir,

1. I called on King Abdullah at his hotel today. His Majesty appeared to be in good health and to be enjoying his visit. The Jordan Prime Minister, the Minister of Defence, the Jordan Minister in London and Sir A. Kirkbride were also present.

2. King Abdullah began by giving me his views upon the situation in Palestine. He said that the Arab States had not made a proper appreciation of their resources and those of the Jews before entering on the Palestine campaign. The Arab misfortunes had, moreover, largely been due to the rivalries of Arab politicians. As regards the future settlement, the Negeb and the Beersheba areas were essential to Jordan. Gaza was also very important but provided this went to Egypt, Jordan would be content. It was dangerous for Israel to hold a part of the Red Sea Coast. This interrupted the pilgrimage route between Africa and Asia. His Majesty also referred to all the other Arab areas now held by Israel and said that in Jerusalem his forces could have obtained control of Hadassah and the Hebrew University but that he had been dissuaded from this by others. The people in Jordan-occupied areas of Palestine had accepted the idea of incorporation in the Jordan State. It was impossible for them to set up a state of their own and there were no common frontiers with any other state. He had, however, not yet claimed the annexation of this area. The Arab Legion had not gone into Palestine to secure the annexation of territory but simply to restore order. It was now in full command of all the areas previously held by Iraq and (apart from Gaza) by Egypt.

3. Reverting to the past, his Majesty emphasised that he had never wanted an armed conflict, of which the result must always have been doubtful. Nevertheless, when the fighting had started he would not have made the first truce but for the confiscation by the Egyptians of supplies of war material which were being delivered to

him. Without these supplies, however, he had been forced to make the truce because otherwise the Israelis would have advanced to the Jordan.

4. His Majesty said he did not believe in a successful outcome to the Lausanne conversations.

5. His Majesty then expressed his thanks to his Majesty's Government for the recent release of war material and hoped that we would be able to expedite the provision of other equipment. He pointed out that the Israelis could mobilise 130,000 troops whereas the strength of the Arab Legion was 13,000. What he wanted was a local defence force something like the home guard or like the Israelis had in their settlements. For this force he required 15,000 rifles. Glubb Pasha was discussing this with the War Office. I said that I had not previously heard of this proposal but would consider it in consultation with the Chiefs of Staff.

6. Turning to Syria, King Abdullah said that the new Prime Minister was a reasonable man and an old friend of his. Jordan had nothing to fear from him, but His Majesty was not sure whether the situation would remain as it was.

7. His Majesty said he had received a good impression of Persia. The Shah was loyally serving his people and Islam. The Shah had mentioned to His Majesty that Turkey received more assistance from His Majesty's Government and the United States Government than Persia. The Shah had asked King Abdullah to mention this to us in London in the hope that his claims on our assistance ought to be sympathetically considered.

8. King Abdullah said he was also much interested in the idea of close cooperation between the Islamic countries and the countries of the East. There should be a Muslim League – which need not affect the position of the Arab League – and then a still larger Eastern League extending through Pakistan to India.

9. His Majesty then mentioned that he had received a message from the Imam of the Yemen. This was a primitive and isolated country which could not be expected to behave in an enlightened manner. The Imam had asked him to intervene with us with regard to attacks on him in the Aden press. King Abdullah had replied to the Imam that there was always bound to be an opposition party who would criticise him and that the press in Aden was free. But

he wished to pass on the message to us in case he could improve relations.

10. King Abdullah concluded his remarks by saying that His Majesty's Government had, for two hundred years, been a friend of the Eastern peoples, who had admired the stand taken by the United Kingdom in two wars. Responsible opinion in the East did not wish to have a third party between them and the United Kingdom. (This appears to be an oblique reference to the United States.) No one was more friendly to His Majesty's Government than King Abdullah himself. His Majesty finally referred to the prospective meeting of the Arab League Political Committee. He said that all parties saw that reform was necessary but that they all equally agreed that the general structure of the League should be maintained.

11. I replied that I had always foreseen the danger that the Arab Governments might underestimate Jewish strength. I had given them a warning on these lines at the Palestine Conference in 1940. During the fighting in Palestine one of our main difficulties had been in regard to the United States. If the truce had not been agreed, the arms embargo would probably have been withdrawn and the Jews would have received many more arms than they actually did. We had always hoped to guide United States policy into recognising and supporting the incorporation of Arab Palestine into it. His Majesty's Government and the United States Government had many other problems in common. In the framework of these general relations Palestine was an unfortunate incident that cut across every other sphere. Now, however, there was much common ground between us even on Palestine and any further difficulty on that question would, we hoped, no longer be a matter of dispute between ourselves and the United States Government. It was unfortunate that the United States Government had not adhered to their support for the Bernadotte plan, but Jewish influence was very strong there. Now, however, the United States Administration were following a sensible policy which should help towards a final settlement. I recalled that at the time of the Jewish invasion of Egypt our action and in particular the dispatch of British troops to Aqaba had checked further Jewish aggression.

12. Looking to the future I said that His Majesty's Government were stronger than ever in their determination to maintain their influence

and to support the cause of justice in the Middle East. It was unfortunate that we could not get agreement among the Arab states. Relations were better now but still very difficult and in these difficulties the Arabs, though not Jordan, seemed more concerned in attacking the United Kingdom than in settling their own problems.

13. I mentioned that we had recently reviewed with His Majesty's Representative our economic, social, financial and defence policy in the Middle East. We had a sincere interest in economic development which was necessary to give the economic strength which alone could support an effective defence system.

14. I said that we were in favour of the incorporation of Arab Palestine into Jordan but we hoped His Majesty would be careful as regards the timing of this measure. We felt that the time was not yet quite ripe. I had discussed this point with the United States Secretary of State and I hoped to discuss it with him again in America. In general I would study what His Majesty had said and would use my influence to expedite a final settlement for Palestine.

15. I told King Abdullah that we were anxious to learn of further progress in the economic development schemes in Jordan. We had loaned the Jordan Government £1 million and we hoped that further sums might somehow be obtained, particularly for the settlement of refugees. It was our view that as many as possible of the refugees should return to Israel, but we saw some advantage in an increase in the population of Jordan on a reasonable economic basis so as to provide a better balance of population. We were glad to know that His Majesty looked forward to the further development of the Jordan Valley and we wished to see Jordan get its fair share of the use of that river.

16. I hoped that the situation in Syria would soon settle down. The change of governments by assassination was not a healthy process.

17. As regards the Yemen, I said that we had arranged for the Governor of Aden to be appointed also as his Majesty's Minister to Imam. The Yemen had at first agreed but had later refused to accept this proposal. We believed that a great deal of the difficulty with the Imam arose from our lack of normal contact with him. If we had a representative there these questions of the press could be discussed and explained much more easily. King Abdullah said he hoped the Imam might now accept this proposal.

18. As regards Jerusalem, we had always adhered to the principle that there should be an international area covering the whole city, including Bethlehem. We understood that the Jordan Government was in favour of a partition of the city by which the old city would remain in Jordan control. The Israelis wanted the new city to be part of their State while the old city was internationalised. Our attitude was that either the whole should be internationalised or none. We would have to wait to see what happened on this at Lausanne.

19. We then had some discussion about the supply of war material. I said that, while we realised the difficulty that had been caused to Jordan by our refusal during the embargo to release twenty-five-pounder ammunition, I believed our decision had, on the whole, been right in relation to United States opinion and that it had contributed to the removal of the embargo which the Arab states had for so long demanded. The Jordan Prime Minister said that there was now a question of obtaining further heavy equipment for the Arab Legion. The cost of this was about £1.5 million. The War Office were proposing that the supply should be spread over three years, but this would have a very bad effect on the training programme of the Legion. Could we not arrange inter-departmentally that the equipment should all be delivered at once and that the payment should be spread over three years? I said this was a new question to me and I would look into it. We had some difficulty about the supply of war materials owing to the demands of the Western Union powers.

20. I then referred to King Abdullah's ideas about the wider Islamic or eastern area. I recalled that at the time of signing the Atlantic Pact the United States had made a declaration concerning Turkey, Greece and Persia while the United Kingdom had made a declaration concerning the area from Greece to Persia. This was enough to show that neither the United States Government nor we were inclined to neglect this region. I said that I had had opportunities to discuss with both Pakistan and Turkey the solidarity of the Moslem world. In my view this whole area from Turkey along the Russian frontier to Afghanistan with the Arab countries and Pakistan behind it was potentially one of the wealthiest areas in the world if it was properly organised and developed. At present this was

not the case. Throughout the area there was the great strengthening factor of a uniform religion and uniform principles. Building on this there was a great opportunity for economic cooperation to strengthen the whole area, to give the common people a better life and to weld the different countries into a great defensive unit. This would ensure them their proper place in the world. King Abdullah asked whether we favoured economic cooperation between these countries in order to achieve their common aims. I replied that we certainly did. If there were effective plans for economic cooperation and economic development throughout this area there would be a better chance of obtaining international bank loans. The present difficulty was in dealing with such small units. King Abdullah mentioned that the Kashmir dispute was one of the difficulties in realising this conception. Another was that Turkey was a lay state. I said that I hoped we might fairly soon see a settlement in Kashmir. Both sides were getting tired. On the other point, whatever might be Turkey's official religion, we believed the Turkish Government based themselves on the same fundamental principles as other countries in the Middle East. King Abdullah then mentioned that he had advised the Pakistan Government they should be very patient with Afghanistan. I said that I had given similar advice. Many of these difficulties were caused by the inexperience of countries that had recently acquired independence. His Majesty said he called this tendency 'Independence fever'. I mentioned as a favourable new factor the forthcoming conference in Holland between Dutch and Indonesian representatives.

I am
ERNEST BEVIN

Source: PRO. FO 371/75316. From Ernest Bevin to Perie-Gordon, 22 August 1949.

Appendix E

AGREEMENT BETWEEN THE HASHEMITE JORDAN KINGDOM
AND THE STATE OF ISRAEL, 23 MARCH 1949

The undersigned duly authorised by their respective governments have reached the following agreement.

1. Israel agrees to the taking over by the Arab Legion of the Iraqi front.
2. The demarcation line between the armed forces of the parties to this agreement shall be as marked on the map annexed hereto.
3. Establishment of the line described in Article 2 shall be effected in accordance with the following timetable.

    (a) In the area west of the road from Baqa to Jaljulia and from there to the east of Kafr Qasim within five weeks of the signature of the General Armistice Agreement now being negotiated at Rhodes between Israel and the Hashemite Jordan Kingdom.

    (b) In the area of Wadi Ara north of the line from Baqa to Zububa within seven weeks of the signature of the General Armistice Agreement now being negotiated at Rhodes between Israel and the Hashemite Jordan Kingdom.

    (c) In all other areas within fifteen weeks of the signature of the General Armistice Agreement now being negotiated at Rhodes between Israel and the Hashemite Jordan Kingdom.

4. Israel, for its part, has made similar changes for the benefit of the Hashemite Jordan Kingdom in other areas.
5. The Hashemite Jordan Kingdom agrees that the substitution of Iraqi troops by the Arab Legion in the sectors at present held by the former shall not take place until after the signing of the General Armistice Agreement now under negotiation at Rhodes. The Hashemite Jordan Kingdom guarantees for all Iraqi forces in Palestine and agrees that their numbers shall be included in any formula governing the reduction of forces provided for in the General Armistice Agreement now being negotiated at Rhodes as if they were forces of the Arab Legion.

6. It is agreed between the parties that the armistice demarcation line to be inserted in the General Armistice Agreement now under negotiation at Rhodes shall be based on the positions held on the date of the ceasefire agreement concluded at Rhodes as certified by the observers of the United Nations Truce Supervision Organisation. The General Armistice Agreement concluded at Rhodes shall provide that the armistice demarcation line shall be subject to local rectifications which have been or may be agreed upon by the parties hereto, such rectifications having the same force and effect as if they had been incorporated in full in the General Armistice Agreement.

7. The parties hereby agree that the General Armistice Agreement now under negotiation at Rhodes shall contain provisions for its revision by mutual consent at any time, and therefore that immediately after the signature of the General Armistice Agreement the present Agreement shall take effect as if it were a revision to the General Armistice Agreement.

8. In the case of villages affected by the terms of this agreement, their inhabitants shall be entitled to their full rights of residence, property and freedom. If such villagers decide to leave, they shall be entitled to take with them their livestock and other movable property, and to receive without delay full compensation for their land which they leave behind.

9. Israel will pay to the Hashemite Jordan Kingdom the cost of building twenty kilometres of first-class road in compensation for the road between Tulkarm and Qalqiliyah.

10. The Parties to this agreement shall establish a mixed commission which shall peg out the demarcation line provided for in Article 2 above. This commission shall consist of not less than two representatives of each party and of a chairman appointed by the United Nations Chief of Staff.

11. This Agreement shall not be published except with the consent of both parties, nor shall it in any way prejudice an ultimate political settlement between the Parties.

12. This Agreement is subject to ratification by the Prime Minister of the Hashemite Jordan Kingdom, such ratification to be communicated to the Government of Israel in writing not later than 30

March 1949. Failing such notification, this Agreement shall be null and void, and of no force or effect.

In faith whereof the undersigned representatives of the High Contracting Parties have signed hereunder.

Done at Shuneh, on the twenty-third day of March one thousand nine hundred and forty-nine.

For the Hashemite Jordan Kingdom
Falah el-Madadha
Hussein Siraj

For the State of Israel
Walter Eytan
Yigael Yadin
Moshe Dayan

Appendix F

---

1. It is agreed between the undersigned, duly authorised by their respective governments, that the Agreement between the Hashemite Jordan Kingdom and the State of Israel of 23 March 1949 shall be amended as follows.

    (a) Article 4 is hereby amended to read as follows:
    'Israel, for its part, has made similar changes for the benefit of the Hashemite Jordan Kingdom in the Hebron area, as delineated in blue ink on the map annexed hereto.'

    (i) Article 7 is hereby deleted.

    (ii) Article 8 is hereby amended by the inclusion of the following provisions after the first sentence:

    'Neither Israeli nor Trans-Jordan forces shall enter or be stationed in such villages, in which local Arab police shall be organised for internal security purposes.'

    (b) Article (ii) is hereby amended to read as follows:
    'This Agreement shall not in any way prejudice an ultimate political settlement between the Parties.'

    (c) Article 12 is hereby deleted.

2. The present Agreement and the Agreement of 23 March 1949 as amended by the present Agreement are to be interpreted and executed as instructions binding upon the Delegations of the State of Israel and the Hashemite Jordan Kingdom now negotiating a General Armistice Agreement at Rhodes, and their provisions are to be incorporated into the General Armistice Agreement as a condition of its signature by the representatives of the Parties.

3. The present Agreement and the Agreement of 23 March 1949 shall be considered void upon the signature of the General Armistice Agreement referred to in paragraph 2 above, and their existence as documents will not be made public by either Party.

In faith whereof the undersigned representatives of the High Contracting Parties have signed hereunder on the thirtieth day of March one thousand nine hundred and forty-nine.

For the Hashemite Jordan Kingdom
Fawzi Mulki
A. Sudki el-Jundi

For the State of Israel
Walter Eytan
Yigael Yadin
Reuven Shiloah

Appendix G

Preamble

The Parties to the present Agreement,

Responding to the Security Council resolution of 16 November 1948, calling upon them, as a further provisional measure under Article 40 of the Charter of the United Nations and in order to facilitate the transition from the present truce to permanent peace in Palestine, to negotiate an armistice.

Having decided to enter into negotiations under United Nations Chairmanship concerning the implementation of the Security Council resolution of 16 November 1948, and having appointed representatives empowered to negotiate and conclude an Armistice Agreement.

The undersigned representatives of their respective governments, having exchanged their full powers found to be in good and proper form, have agreed upon the following provisions.

ARTICLE I

With a view to promoting the return of permanent peace in Palestine and in recognition of the importance in this regard of mutual assurances concerning the future military operations of the parties, the following principles which shall be fully observed by both parties during the armistice, are hereby affirmed.

1. The injunction of the Security Council against resort to military force in the settlement of the Palestine question shall henceforth be scrupulously respected by both parties.
2. No aggressive action by the armed forces – land, sea or air – of either party shall be undertaken, planned or threatened against the people or the armed forces of the other; it being understood that the use of the term 'planned' in this context has no bearing on normal staff planning as generally practised in military organisations.

3. The right of each party to its security and freedom from fear of attack by the armed forces of the other shall be fully respected.
4. The establishment of an armistice between the armed forces of the two parties is accepted as an indispensable step towards the liquidation of armed conflict and the restoration of peace in Palestine.

ARTICLE II

With a specific view to the implementation of the resolution of the Security Council of 16 November 1948, the following principles and purposes are affirmed.

1. The principle that no military or political advantage should be gained under the truce ordered by the Security Council is recognised.
2. It is also recognised that no provision of this Agreement shall in any way prejudice the rights, claims and positions of either party hereto in the ultimate peaceful settlement of the Palestine question, the provisions of this Agreement being dictated exclusively by military considerations.

ARTICLE III

1. In pursuance of the foregoing principles and of the resolution of the Security Council of 16 November 1948, a general armistice between the armed forces of the two Parties – land, sea and air – is hereby established.
2. No element of the land, sea or air, military or para-military forces of either Party, including non-regular forces, shall commit any war-like or hostile act against the military or para-military forces of the other party, or against civilians in territory under the control of that party; or shall advance beyond or pass over for any purpose whatsoever the Armistice Demarcation Lines set forth in Articles V and VI of this Agreement; or enter into or pass through the air space of the other party.
3. No war-like act or act of hostility shall be conducted from territory controlled by one of the parties to this Agreement against the other party.

ARTICLE IV

1. The lines described in Articles V and VI of this Agreement shall be designated as the Armistice Demarcation Lines and are delineated

in pursuance of the purpose and intent of the resolution of the Security Council of 16 November 1948.

2. The basic purpose of the Armistice Demarcation Lines is to delineate the lines beyond which the armed forces of the respective parties shall not move.

3. Rules and regulations of the armed forces of the parties, which prohibit civilians from crossing the fighting lines or entering the area between the lines, shall remain in effect after the signing of this Agreement with application to the Armistice Demarcation Lines defined in Articles V and VI.

ARTICLE V

1. The Armistice Demarcation Lines for all sectors other than the sector now held by Iraqi forces, shall be as delineated on the maps in Annex I to this Agreement, and shall be defined as follows.

   (a) In the sector Kh Deir Arab (MR 1510–1574) to the northern terminus of the lines defined in the 30 November 1948 Cease-Fire Agreement for the Jerusalem area, the Armistice Demarcation Lines shall follow the Truce Lines as certified by the United Nations Truce Supervision Organisation.

   (b) In the Jerusalem Sector, the Armistice Demarcation Lines shall correspond to the lines defined in the 30 November 1948 Cease-Fire Agreement for the Jerusalem area.

   (c) In the Hebron–Dead Sea sector, the Armistice Demarcation Line shall be as delineated on Map 1 and marked (B) in Annex I to this Agreement.

   (d) In the sector from a point on the Dead Sea (MR 1925–0958) to the southernmost tip of Palestine, the Armistice Demarcation Line shall be determined by existing military positions as surveyed in March 1949 by United Nations observers, and shall run from north to south as delineated on Map 1 in Annex I to this Agreement.

ARTICLE VI

1. It is agreed that the forces of the Hashemite Jordan Kingdom shall replace the forces of Iraq in the sector now held by the latter forces, the intention of the Government of Iraq in this regard having been communicated to the Acting Mediator in the message of 20 March

from the Foreign Minister of Iraq authorising the Delegation of the Hashemite Jordan Kingdom to negotiate for the Iraqi forces and stating that those forces would be withdrawn.

2. The Armistice Demarcation Line for the sector now held by Iraqi forces shall be as delineated on Map 1 in Annex I to this Agreement and marked (A).

3. The Armistice Demarcation Line provided for paragraph 2 of this Article shall be established in stages as follows, pending which the existing military lines may be maintained.

(a) In the area west of the road from Baqa to Jaljulia and thence to the east of Kafr Qasim: within five weeks of the date on which this Armistice Agreement is signed.

(b) In the area of Wadi Ara north of the line from Baqa to Zubeiba: within seven weeks of the date on which this Armistice Agreement is signed.

(c) In all other areas of the Iraqi sector: within fifteen weeks of the date on which this Armistice Agreement is signed.

4. The Armistice Demarcation Line in the Hebron–Dead Sea sector, referred to in paragraph c of Article V of this Agreement and marked (B) on Map 1 in Annex 1, which involves substantial deviation from the existing military lines in favour of the forces of the Hashemite Jordan Kingdom, is designed to offset the modifications of the existing military lines in the Iraqi sector set forth in paragraph 3 of this Article.

5. In compensation for the road acquired between Tulkarm and Qalqiliyah, the Government of Israel agrees to pay to the Government of the Hashemite Jordan Kingdom the cost of constructing twenty kilometres of first-class new road.

6. Wherever villages may be affected by the establishment of the Armistice Demarcation Line provided for in paragraph 2 of this Article, the inhabitants of such villages shall be entitled to maintain, and shall be protected in their full rights of residence, property and freedom. In the event any of the inhabitants should decide to leave their villages, they shall be entitled to take with them their livestock and other movable property, and to receive without delay full compensation for the land which they have left. It shall be

prohibited for Israeli forces to enter or to be stationed in such villages, in which locally recruited Arab police shall be organised and stationed for internal security purposes.

7. The Hashemite Jordan Kingdom accepts responsibility for all Iraqi forces in Palestine.

8. The provisions of this Article shall not be interpreted as prejudicing, in any sense, an ultimate political settlement between the Parties to this Agreement.

9. The Armistice Demarcation Lines defined in Articles V and VI of this Agreement are agreed upon by the parties without prejudice to future territorial settlements or boundary lines or to claims of either party relating thereto.

10. Except where otherwise provided, the Armistice Demarcation Lines shall be established, including such withdrawal of forces as may be necessary for this purpose, within ten days from the date on which this Agreement is signed.

11. The Armistice Demarcation Lines defined in this Article and in Article V shall be subject to such rectifications as may be agreed upon by the parties to this Agreement, and all such rectifications shall have the same force and effect as if they had been incorporated in full in this General Armistice Agreement.

ARTICLE VII

1. The military forces of the parties to this Agreement shall be limited to defensive forces only in the areas extending ten kilometres from each side of the Armistice Demarcation Lines, except where geographical considerations make this impractical, as at the southernmost tip of Palestine and the coastal strip. Defensive forces permissible in each sector shall be as defined in Annex II to this Agreement. In the sector now held by Iraqi forces, calculations in the reduction of forces shall include the number of Iraqi forces in this sector.

2. Reduction of forces to defensive strength in accordance with the preceding paragraph shall be completed within ten days of the establishment of the Armistice Demarcation Lines defined in this Agreement. In the same way the removal of mines from mined roads and areas evacuated by either party, and the transmission of plans

[473]

showing the location of such minefields to the other party, shall be completed within the same period.

3. The strength of the forces which may be maintained by the Parties on each side of the Armistice Demarcation Lines shall be subject to periodical review with a view toward further reduction of such forces by mutual agreement of the parties.

ARTICLE VIII

1. A Special Committee, composed of two representatives of each party designated by the respective Governments, shall be established for the purpose of formulating agreed plans and arrangements designed to enlarge the scope of this Agreement and to effect improvements in its application.

2. The Special Committee shall be organised immediately following the coming into effect of this Agreement and shall direct its attention to the formulation of agreed plans and arrangements for such matters as either party may submit to it, which, in any case, shall include the following, on which agreement in principle already exists: free movement of traffic on vital roads, including the Bethlehem and Latrun–Jerusalem roads; resumption of the normal functioning of the cultural and humanitarian institutions on Mount Scopus and free access thereto; free access to the Holy Places and cultural institutions and use of the cemetery on the Mount of Olives; resumption of operation of the Latrun pumping station; provision of electricity for the Old City; and resumption of operation of the railroad to Jerusalem.

3. The Special Committee shall have exclusive competence over such matters as may be referred to it. Agreed plans and arrangements formulated by it may provide for the exercise of supervisory functions by the Mixed Armistice Commission established in Article XI.

ARTICLE IX

Agreements reached between the parties subsequent to the signing of this Armistice Agreement relating to such matters as further reduction of forces as contemplated in paragraph 3 of Article VII, future adjustments of the Armistice Demarcation Lines, and plans and arrangements formulated by the Special Committee established in Article VIII, shall have the same force and effect as the provisions of this Agreement and shall be equally binding upon the parties.

ARTICLE X

An exchange of prisoners of war having been effected by special arrangement between the parties prior to the signing of this Agreement, no further arrangements on this matter are required except that the Mixed Armistice Commission shall undertake to re-examine whether there may be any prisoners of war belonging to either party which were not included in the previous exchange. In the event that prisoners of war shall be found to exist the Mixed Armistice Commission shall arrange for an early exchange of such prisoners. The parties to this Agreement undertake to afford full cooperation to the Mixed Armistice Commission in its discharge of this responsibility.

ARTICLE XI

1. The executions of the provisions of this Agreement, with the exception of such matters as fall within the exclusive competence of the Special Committee established in Article VIII, shall be supervised by a Mixed Armistice Commission composed of five members, of whom each party to this Agreement shall designate two, and whose chairman shall be the United Nations Chief of Staff of the Truce Supervision Organisation or a senior officer from the observer personnel of that organisation designated by him following consultation with both parties to this Agreement.

2. The Mixed Armistice Commission shall maintain its headquarters at Jerusalem and shall hold its meetings at such places and at such times as it may deem necessary for the effective conduct of its work.

3. The Mixed Armistice Commission shall be convened in its first meeting by the United Nations Chief of Staff of the Truce Supervision Organisation not later than one week following the signing of this Agreement.

4. Decisions of the Mixed Armistice Commission, to the extent possible, shall be based on the principle of unanimity. In the absence of unanimity, decisions shall be taken by majority vote of the members of the Commission present and voting.

5. The Mixed Armistice Commission shall formulate its own rules of procedure. Meetings shall be held only after due notice to the members by the chairman. The quorum for its meetings shall be a majority of its members.

6. The Commission shall be empowered to employ observers, who may be from among the military organisations of the parties or from the military personnel of the United Nations Truce Supervision Organisation, or from both, in such numbers as may be considered essential to the performance of its functions. In the event United Nations observers should be so employed, they shall remain under the command of the United Nations Chief of Staff of the Truce Supervision Organisation. Assignments of a general or special nature given to United Nations observers attached to the Mixed Armistice Commission shall be subject to approval by the United Nations Chief of Staff or his designated representative on the Commission, whichever is serving as chairman.

7. Claims or complaints presented by either party relating to the application of this Agreement shall be referred immediately to the Mixed Armistice Commission through its chairman. The Commission shall take such action on all such claims or complaints by means of its observation and investigation machinery as it may deem appropriate, with a view to equitable and mutually satisfactory settlement.

8. Where interpretation of the meaning of a particular provision of this Agreement, other than the Preamble and Articles I and II, is at issue, the Commission's interpretation shall prevail. The Commission, in its discretion and as the need arises, may from time to time recommend to the parties modifications in the provisions of this Agreement.

9. The Mixed Armistice Commission shall submit to both parties reports on its activities as frequently as it may consider necessary. A copy of each such report shall be presented to the Secretary-General of the United Nations for transmission to the appropriate organ or agency of the United Nations.

10. Members of the Commission and its observers shall be accorded such freedom of movement and access in the area covered by this Agreement as the Commission may determine to be necessary,

provided that when such decisions of the Commission are reached by a majority vote, United Nations observers only shall be employed.

11. The expenses of the Commission, other than those relating to United Nations observers, shall be apportioned in equal shares between the two parties to this Agreement.

ARTICLE XII

1. The present Agreement is not subject to ratification and shall come into force immediately upon being signed.

2. This Agreement, having been negotiated and concluded in pursuance of the resolution of the Security Council of 16 November 1948 calling for the establishment of an armistice in order to eliminate the threat to the peace in Palestine and to facilitate the transition from the present truce to permanent peace in Palestine, shall remain in force until a peaceful settlement between the parties is achieved, except as provided in paragraph 3 of this Article.

3. The parties to this Agreement may, by mutual consent, revise this Agreement or any of its provisions, or may suspend its application, other than Articles I and III, at any time. In the absence of mutual agreement and after this Agreement has been in effect for one year from the date of its signing, either of the parties may call upon the Secretary-General of the United Nations to convoke a conference of representatives of the two parties for the purpose of reviewing, revising, or suspending any of the provisions of this Agreement other than Articles I and III. Participation in such a conference shall be obligatory upon the parties.

4. If the conference provided for in paragraph 3 of this Article does not result in an agreed solution of a point in dispute, either party may bring the matter before the Security Council of the United Nations for the relief sought on the grounds that this Agreement has been concluded in pursuance of Security Council action towards the end of achieving peace in Palestine.

5. This Agreement is signed in quintuplicate, of which one copy shall be retained by each party, two copies communicated to the Secretary-General of the United Nations for transmission to the Security Council and to the Conciliation Commission on Palestine, and one copy to the United Nations Acting mediator on Palestine.

Done at Rhodes, Island of Rhodes, Greece, on the third of April nineteen forty-nine in the presence of the United Nations Acting Mediator on Palestine and the United Nations Chief of Staff of the Truce Supervision Organisation.

For and on behalf the Government of the Hashemite Jordan Kingdom
A. Sudki el-Jundi
Mohammed Mowaita

For and on behalf of the Government of Israel
Reuven Shiloah
Moshe Dayan
Sgan Alouf

Appendix H

AGREEMENT OF AMITY AND NON-AGGRESSION BETWEEN
THE STATE OF ISRAEL AND THE HASHEMITE
JORDAN KINGDOM, MARCH 1950

Whereas on the third day of April 1949, the contracting parties signed at Rhodes a General Armistice Agreement to remain in force until a peaceful settlement between the Parties is achieved, and whereas the parties now desire, in order to promote normal relations and as a further step toward a peaceful settlement, to reinforce the said General Armistice Agreement and extend the scope of mutual accord between them, have therefore agreed to conclude the following Agreement of Amity and Non-Aggression and have accordingly appointed as their Plenipotentiaries

The State of Israel ....

The Hashemite Jordan Kingdom ....

who, after presentation of their full powers, found in good and due form, have agreed on the following provisions.

ARTICLE I

1. Each of the contracting parties undertakes not to resort to war or acts of armed violence or other acts of aggression or hostility against the other, or to invade territories under the control of the other, or to permit any territory under its control to serve as a base or to be used for passage for armed attack by a third party on the other.

2. If, on any occasion, there should arise between the contracting parties differences of opinion which they are unable to settle between themselves, they undertake to have recourse to the conciliatory and arbitral procedures offered under international law for the settlement thereof, or such other means of pacific settlement as shall be agreed upon by the parties.

ARTICLE II

For the duration of this Agreement the Armistice Demarcation Line described in the said General Armistice Agreement shall remain in force subject to any modifications agreed to by both parties in accordance with the terms of the said General Armistice Agreement. In order to reduce possible friction, the contracting parties agree to eliminate the various areas of 'no-man's land', the continued existence of which they consider undesirable.

ARTICLE III

The contracting parties are agreed upon the necessity for taking joint steps in order to protect the Holy Places of all faiths in Jerusalem and to ensure freedom of access thereto and freedom of worship without threat to the adherents of all faiths. A joint declaration by the contracting parties in this regard is contained in Annex I to the present Agreement. The contracting parties further agree to offer requisite assurances to the United Nations regarding the inviolability of the Holy Places and the observance of the said declaration.

ARTICLE IV

1. The contracting parties are agreed upon the desirability of establishing economic and commercial relations between them.
2. For the implementation of this Article economic and commercial accords shall be concluded between the parties. Trade delegates shall be exchanged between them not later than three months from the coming into force of this Agreement. They shall negotiate these economic and commercial accords and be responsible for their effective observance.

ARTICLE V

The contracting parties are agreed that all necessary steps shall be taken to ensure the resumption of the normal functioning of the cultural and humanitarian institutions on Mount Scopus and the use of the cemetery on the Mount of Olives and free access thereto, as well as the free movement of traffic on the Bethlehem–Jerusalem road, in accordance with Article VIII of the said General Armistice Agreement.

ARTICLE VI

1. Having regard to the purposes of this Agreement and in order to implement its provisions and to formulate the basis for a final peaceful settlement, the contracting parties hereby establish a mixed commission to be known as the Israel–Jordan Commission.
2. The Israel–Jordan Commission shall *inter alia:*

(a) Examine all territorial problems outstanding between the Contracting Parties.

(b) Consider and elaborate plans for the determination of rights to financial recompense and the assessment and payment thereof in respect of immovable property in Jerusalem which was abandoned by its owners as a consequence of the armed conflict.

(c) Examine ways and means for the settlement of the just claims for compensation of persons permanently resident in the territory of either of the contracting parties for property abandoned by them in the territory of the other contracting party. The commission may consider the feasibility, in suitable cases, of the owners of such property in person, or by their duly authorised agents, being admitted to the territory of the other party for the purpose of settling such claims. Should this not be found practicable, the Commission itself shall prepare plans for the final settlement of these claims.

(d) Devote its attention to the question of the establishment of a free zone in the port of Haifa for the Hashemite Jordan Kingdom for commercial purposes.

(e) Examine measures for the full resumption of operations by the Palestine Electric Corporation and by the Palestine Potash Company Limited.

(f) Generally supervise the proper execution of the Present Agreement.

ARTICLE VII

1. The Commission established pursuant to Article VI hereof shall be composed of representatives of each party designated by the respective Governments.

2. This Commission has the power to appoint such sub-commissions as it deems necessary in order to make possible the expeditious completion of its task.

3. The contracting parties shall immediately nominate their representatives to the Commission, which shall hold its first meeting not later than seven days from the coming into force of this Agreement. Subsequent meetings shall take place upon the first and fifteenth days of each month thereafter, unless such dates fall on a Friday or

on a Saturday, in which event the meeting will be postponed for not more than two days.

4. The Commission's headquarters shall be at Jerusalem.

5. The Commission and its sub-commissions shall establish their own rules of procedure.

6. Members of the Commission and of sub-commissions shall, while on the territory of the other contracting party, be granted the appropriate privileges and immunities.

ARTICLE VIII

The contracting parties agree that the Mixed Armistice Commission set up in accordance with the said General Armistice Agreement shall have no powers or functions in relation to the execution of this Agreement.

ARTICLE IX

This agreement shall enter into force immediately upon signature, and shall remain in force for a period of five years or for so long as the General Armistice Agreement signed at Rhodes on 3 April 1949 is in force, whichever period shall be the shorter.

ARTICLE X

A copy of this Agreement shall be communicated to the Secretary General of the United Nations for transmission to the appropriate organs of the United Nations.

ARTICLE XI

Nothing in the present agreement is intended to, or shall in any way, prejudice the rights and obligations which devolve, or may devolve, upon either of the contracting parties under the Charter of the United Nations.

In faith whereof the plenipotentiaries of the contracting parties have signed the present Agreement and have hereunto affixed their seals.

Done in duplicate in the Hebrew, Arabic and English languages all authentic, this . . . day of March 1950, corresponding to the . . . day of Adar in the year 5710 since the creation of the world, and the day of Jumada-l-ula in the year 1369 of the Hijra.

For the State of Israel
For the Hashemite Jordan Kingdom

Joint declaration concerning the Holy Places, religious buildings and sites in Jerusalem

The Government of Israel and of the Hashemite Jordan Kingdom, conscious of their responsibilities concerning the protection and preservation of the sanctuaries in Jerusalem of the three great religions; solemnly undertake by the provisions of the present Declaration to guarantee the protection and preservation of and free access to the Holy Places, religious buildings and sites of, Jerusalem.

ARTICLE I

The free exercise of all forms of worship shall be guaranteed and ensured in accordance with the Declaration of Human Rights of 10 December 1948, the Declaration of Independence of Israel and the Constitution of the Hashemite Jordan Kingdom.

ARTICLE II

The Holy Places, religious buildings and sites which were regarded as Holy Places, religious buildings and sites on 14 May 1948, shall be preserved and their sacred character protected. No act of a nature to profane that sacred character shall be permitted.

ARTICLE III

The rights in force on 14 May 1948 with regard to the Holy Places, religious buildings and sites shall remain in force.

The Governments of the Hashemite Jordan Kingdom and Israel undertake in particular to assure the safety of ministers of religion, those officiating in religious services and the members of religious orders and institutions, to allow them to exercise their ministries without hindrance; and to facilitate their communications both inside and outside the country in connection with the performance of their religious duties and functions.

ARTICLE IV

The Governments of the Hashemite Jordan Kingdom and Israel undertake to guarantee freedom of access to the Holy Places, religious buildings and sites situated in the territory placed under their authority by the final peaceful settlement between them, or, pending that settlement, in the territory at present occupied by them under armistice agreements; and, pursuant to this undertaking, will guarantee right of entry and of transit to ministers of religion, pilgrims and visitors without distinction as to nationality or faith, subject only to considerations of national security, all the above iii conform with the *status quo* prior to 14 May 1948.

ARTICLE V

No form of taxation shall be levied in respect of any Holy Place, religious building or site which was exempt from such taxation on 14 May 1948.

No change in the incidence of any form of taxation shall be made which would either discriminate between the owners and occupiers of Holy Places, religious buildings and sites, or would place such owners and occupiers in a position less favourable in relation to the general incidence of that form of taxation than existed on 14 May 1948.

Appendix I

We, representatives of the Nablus, Tulkarm and Jenin districts, having listened to explanations by their excellencies Said Pasha Al Mufti, Prime Minister and Mohammad Pasha Al-Shuraiqi Foreign Minister, who sought our opinion in relation to the Palestine case as to whether it was advisable to seek through direct talks with the Jews, the conclusion of peace or settlement, whether general or partial in order to reach stability and to settle outstanding problems, the most important of which are the refugees, compensation, immovable property and so forth.

We hereby declare, of our own free will and in the exercise of our natural rights, that we do not believe – and are not ready to believe – that there is a single person in the western part of the Kingdom who is ready to make peace with the Jews. Such a person will never exist and we will never part with any of the rights of the homeland so long as we live, so long as the homeland itself is exposed to danger, to hell with private property, buildings and lands.

We do not ask His Majesty the King and his Government to enter into direct talks with the Jews for the purpose of reaching a final settlement or an agreement on the case of our country. We refuse this categorically saying:-

> May God not reconcile any one of us who will make peace with them as long as the sun continues to shine in the high skies.

We only demand one thing and that is the realisation of the trivial rights reserved to us by the ill-fated Rhodes ceasefire agreement. We demand that that agreement be discussed in the spirit of justice and impartiality and we ask the Government to carry out that task but we refuse any direct peace settlement with the Jews. We insist on this for the following reasons.

(a) It would be futile to relinquish rights acquired internationally as described in various notes, official international resolutions and the

Lausanne protocol signed by both Arabs and Jews. It is inconceivable that the Arabs should abandon their land, which is still theirs in accordance with international custom as well as the terms of the Rhodes Agreement, without receiving anything in return. What advantage could be derived from that?

(b) The return of the refugees to the areas admitted to be Arab in accordance with United Nations resolutions is most essential in the interest of the Hashemite Kingdom of Jordan itself. This applies in particular to the coastal towns, recognised internationally to be ours, which our country cannot dispense with, even if the Jews have occupied them by force.

(c) The Jews made use of the ceasefire agreement in the worst manner. They built settlements and fortifications where they should not, they rendered homeless peaceful people, they killed innocent people and every day gave a thousand proofs of their non-respect of the ceasefire agreement, in spite of it being guaranteed internationally. The Government can ascertain their good intentions by changing the present situation so that it accords with the ceasefire agreement in so far as it concerns usurped Arab interests and rights.

(d) The compensation that the Jews offer is deceitful. Arab property in Israel has been estimated to be worth two thousand million dinars and it cannot be believed by anyone that the Jews will be able to pay this amount. The intention lying behind these offers is to secure from us the liquidation of our property at low prices and our abandonment of our country to the Jews. This we refuse categorically.

Finally these present here propose that a legal, efficient and trustworthy committee be appointed by the Government to study these subjects and submit a report for transmission to the Conciliation Committee. In proof of our unanimity of opinion on the foregoing, we hereby place our signatures.

Resolution adopted by the people of Hebron and Bethlehem districts, 24 July 1950

We, representatives of the Arab people in the Hebron and Bethlehem districts including Jericho, Bethlehem, Bait Jala, Bait Sahour, Ramalla,

Al Birih and all other villages, having met in Jerusalem this day the 24th of July 1950, and having listened to explanations by their excellencies Said Pasha Al Mufti, Prime Minister and Mohammad Pasha Al Shuraiqi, Foreign Minister, about developments in the Palestine case and their wish to know our opinion, in our capacity as representatives of the public opinion, regarding securing a solution of the Palestine case on the occasion of the arrival of the International Conciliation Committee, whether that solution be through a positive settlement (general or partial) or by other means, for the purpose of settling outstanding matters, reaching a lasting peace, securing stability and restoring plundered property to its owners.

We hereby declare of our own free will and in the exercise of our natural, national, legal and international rights, that we refuse unanimously and categorically any attempt to conclude a direct peace or settlement with the Jews which will not guarantee the recognition of the Arab rights acquired internationally and in accordance with the international resolutions and protocols that are still in force. Arabs will never abandon their homeland, country and coastal towns since if they are deprived therefrom the Hashemite Kingdom of Jordan will sustain great harm and its economical life will be paralysed. Land and property owners, those who have real interests, and the representatives of the people in all their classes – refugees and non-refugees – prefer to remain homeless, rather than to part with the country's rights or their own rights which the Jews wish to liquidate so as to send the Arabs out of their country for good, contrary to all rights, custom and law and notwithstanding the existence of legal means, international and political, to secure Arab rights.

All of those present consider that the direct contact of the Jews and the conclusion of peace with them means recognition of the Jewish state which no Arab government has yet recognised. The Jews have proved that they do not carry out or give weight to any undertakings and, since they have not proved until this date their good intentions by applying the Lausanne protocol, the ceasefire agreement and the United Nations resolutions, how could reliance be placed on any direct agreement with them, particularly in view of the fact that we held in our hand, international guarantee and in our heart national faith, all of which help us to claim all our rights with all means and guarantees of their attainment.

In view of the above, we declare once again that we refuse categorically every invitation to conclude a peace settlement with the Jews and demand from the Government of our great King that they contact the Conciliation Committee, which will arrive shortly in Jerusalem. This contact should be through a reliable and strong legal committee so as to present our case soundly and to expose the aggressive acts and intentions of the Jews and their failure to carry out pacts and decisions which define our provisional frontiers, so that the country may realise its national aspirations, please God.

In proof of the above hereby witness our signatures.

Appendix J

SECRET
2 Brigade Operation Instructions No. 3.
copy N0. 1
Ref: GI/2.
24 Nov 50.
Ref Map: 1/250,000. Palestine South Sheet.

Information

1. Israel has constructed a diversion to the main track from Um Rashrash to the Dead Sea. The diversion lies between eastings 164 and 137, and northings 953 and 953 and is approximately 5.1/2 km in length. Approximately 4.1/2 km of the diversion lie within Jordan territory.
2. The diversion has been constructed presumably to provide a better track than which was previously in use and which runs along the bed of the Wadi, and is therefore unserviceable in rainy weather.
3. It has been decided that the part of the diversion which lies within Jordan shall be closed to Israeli traffic.

Intention

4. A force from 2 Bde will close the diversion on 29 Nov to Israel traffic and will prevent any further violation of the Jordan frontier in that area.

Method

5. Force Command.   Captain T. N. Bromage
6. Troops.   Two Infantry Companies of 1st Regiment.
                        Two Armoured Car Sections 1st Regiment.
                        Four Carriers 1st Regiment.

Two MMG Vickers Teams. 1st Regiment.
Nineteen Wireless Set Rear Link.

7. Designation.   Force will be known as IBEX Force.

Task

8. Concentration. IBEX Force will concentrate at Ma'an on 27 November. Concentration will be completed as follows:

(**One**) One Infantry Company, strength 50 All Ranks, will move by rail from Amman to Ma'an on 25 November. Time of departure from Amman Railway Station, 0630 hours 25 November.

(**Two**) Road Party. Armoured cars, carriers and unit vehicles will move by road on 25 November and arrive at concentration area by PM 26 November.

(**Three**) Relief of Company of 1st Regiment at Aqaba. Company of 1st Regiment carrying out duties at Aqaba will be relieved by fifty-five Arab Legion Police who will take over duties of the garrison company on 26 November. Police Party is moving to Ma'an with the rail party on 25 November and on arrival at Ma'an will move by motor transport to Aqaba. On completion of handover, company will move by motor transport to concentration area.

9. Move from concentration area to Gharandal Police Post. IBEX Force will move from concentration area to Gharandal on 28 November. Transport to lift marching troops is being provided by Supply and Transport and will report to force Commander at Ma'an at PM 27 November.

10. Action on arrival at Gharandal.

(**One**) Road blocks will be established at both ends of the diversion where the new track enters Jordan territory, and will be manned by first light 29 Nov. Road blocks will be covered by dug-in defences.

(**Two**) No Israeli traffic will be allowed to use the diversion through Jordan territory from first light 29 November.

(**Three**) Israel troops and civilians will be warned on approaching road blocks that they are forbidden to use the diversion which is through Jordan.

(Four) In the event of Israelis using armed force to open the diversion, they will be met by fire. Commander IBEX Force will retain a mobile reserve to support Road blocks if necessary.

(Five) Extreme care will be taken to ensure that NO troops' or vehicles' veils cross the frontier between Jordan and Israeli territory.

Administration
11. Supplies.

(Ten) Rail party. One day's tinned rations will be placed in the train by S & T and handed over to officer in charge rail party at 0600 hours 25 November.

(Eleven) Road party. Two days' tinned rations will be drawn from FSP [Forward Supply Point]. Zarqa 25 November. Time to be drawn will be notified to 1st Regiment by phone.

(Twelve) Concentration area and Gharandal Area. Normal daily maintenance from Ma'an.

(Thirteen) Reserve rations. Four days' tinned reserve will be drawn in the concentration area.

12. Petrol, oil and lubricate. Road party will draw eight hundred gallons petrol from 2 Brigade operation reserve for move to concentration area. Replenishment from Ma'an.

Ammunition
13. First line scale will be taken for all weapons and arms.

Medical
14. **(One)** Strict anti-malarial precautions will be observed with effect from arrival in the Wadi Araba area.

(Two) One CWT AL 63 [anti-lice powder] will be drawn by officer in charge road party from Forward Supply Point. Zarqa on 25 November.

(Three) First field dressings to be carried.

(Four) Arrangements for evacuation of casualties will be notified later.

Clothing

15. Khaki Drill clothing will be taken, and will be worn in the Wadi Araba at the discretion of the Commander of IBEX Force.

Intercommunication

16. Communications will be by 19 set with HQ 2 Brigade, with effect from 1600 hours 26 November. Sets will be open every three hours.
17. Netting, issue of code signs and frequencies will be completed on the arrival of the road party at HQ 2 Brigade a.m. 25 November.

Acknowledge
Brigadier
Sam Cooke
Commander 2 Brigade

Time of Signature: 1625 hours.
Time issued to Signals: 1650 hours.
Method of Issue: SDR to 1st Regiment.

Source: True copy sent to the author by Colonel T. N. Bromage on 4 June 1999.

Appendix K

MAPS

Areas allotted to Jews

Areas allotted to Arabs

International Zone of Jerusalem

0   10   20   30 miles

N

LEBANON

Tyre

GALILEE

Akka

Haifa

Nazareth

MEDITERRANEAN

SEA

Tulkarm

SAMARIA

Jenin

Qalqiliyah

Nablus

Wadi Bedran

Tel Aviv(Jew)
Jaffa (Arab)

Sarafand

Lydda

Ramleh

Aqir

Latrun

Ramallah

Nabi Yaaqub

Shuafat

Al-Qastal

Dair Yasin

Jerusalem

Bethlehem

Kfar
Etzion

JUDAEA

al-Majdal

Bait Jibrin

Hebron

Gaza

Rafah

Beersheba

THE NEGEV

Al Auja

Wadi Araba

Damascus

SYRIA

Sea of
Galilee

Majamaa
Bridge

Shaikh Husain
Bridge

Ajlun

TRANS-JORDAN

River Jordan

Zarqa

Amman

Jericho

Allenby
Bridge

Madeba

Dead
Sea

Karak

MAP 1
United Nations' Partition Plan, 1947

[493]

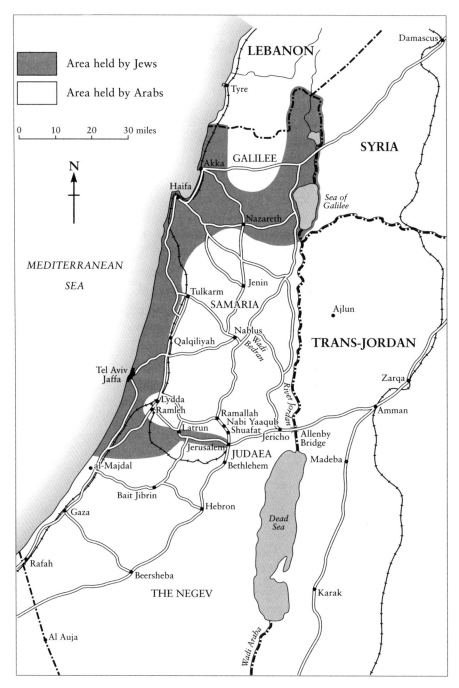

MAP 2
Situation at the beginning of the first truce, 11 June 1948

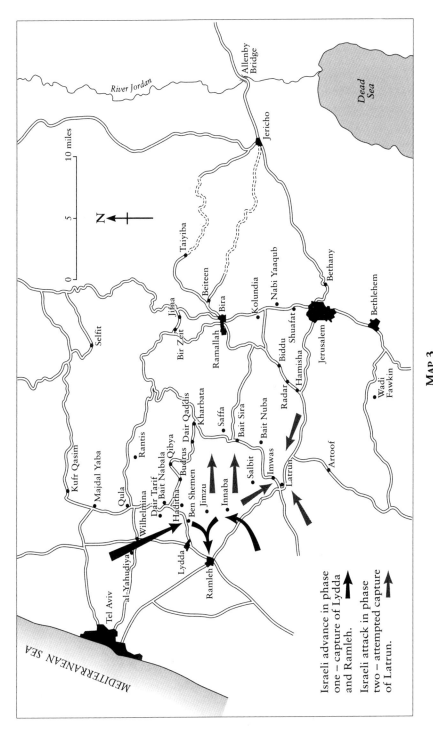

MAP 3
Israeli offensive, 9–18 July 1948

Israeli advance in phase
one – capture of Lydda
and Ramleh.

Israeli attack in phase
two – attempted capture
of Latrun.

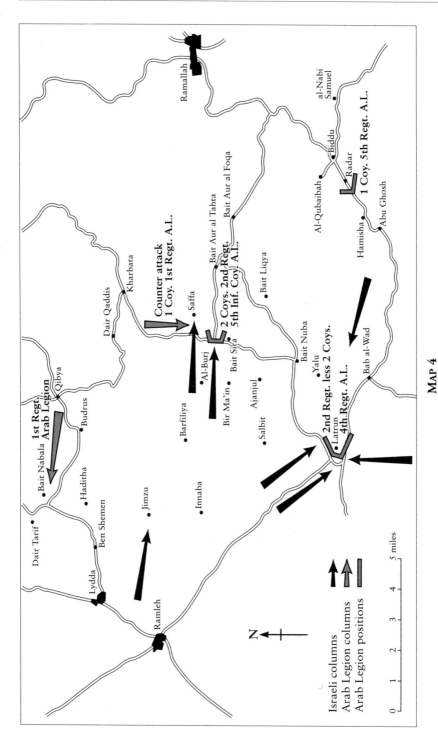

MAP 4

Abortive Israeli offensive against Latrun, July 1948

Ramallah

al-Nabi Samuel

Biddu

Radar

1 Coy. 5th Regt. A.L.

Al-Qubaibah

Bait Aur al Foqa

Abu Ghosh

Hamisha

Bait Aur al Tahta

Kharbata

Counter attack
1 Coy. 1st Regt. A.L.

Dair Qaddis

Saffa

Bait Liqya

Al-Burj

Bait Sira

2 Coys. 2nd Regt.
5th Inf. Coy. A.L.

Qibya

Bir Ma'in

Bait Nuba

Bab al-Wad

1st Regt.
Arab Legion

Budrus

Barfiliya

Ajanjul

Yalu

2nd Regt. less 2 Coys.
4th Regt. A.L.

Bait Nabala

Haditha

Salbit

Latrun

Ben Shemen

Jimzu

Innaba

Dair Tarif

Lydda

Ramleh

Israeli columns

Arab Legion columns

Arab Legion positions

N

0   1   2   3   4   5 miles

[496]

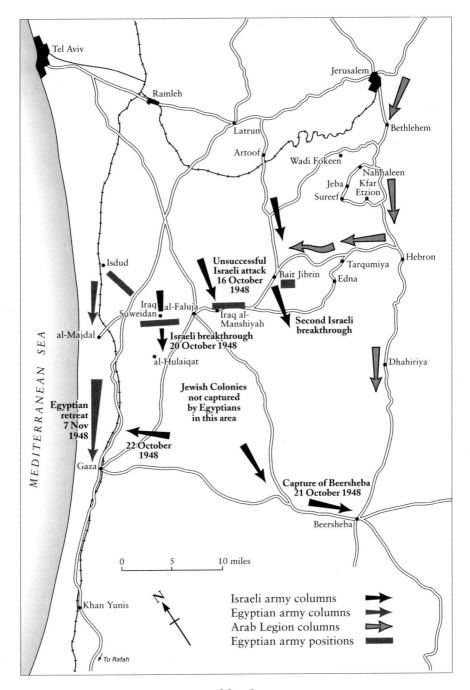

MAP 5
Israeli offensive against the Egyptian army, 15 October 1948

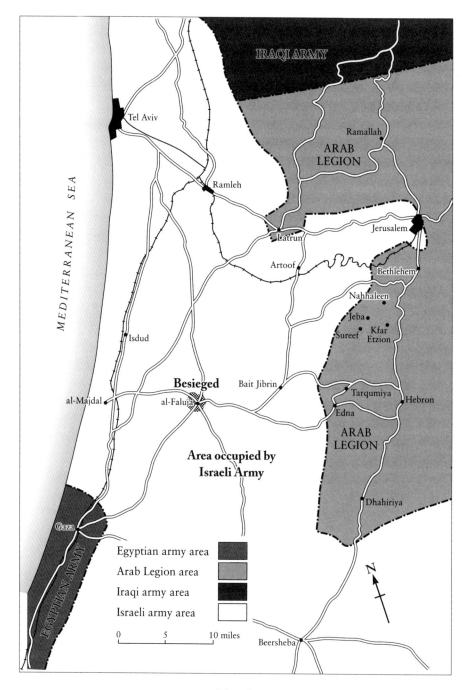

MAP 6
Situation during Israeli siege of al-Faluja, October 1948

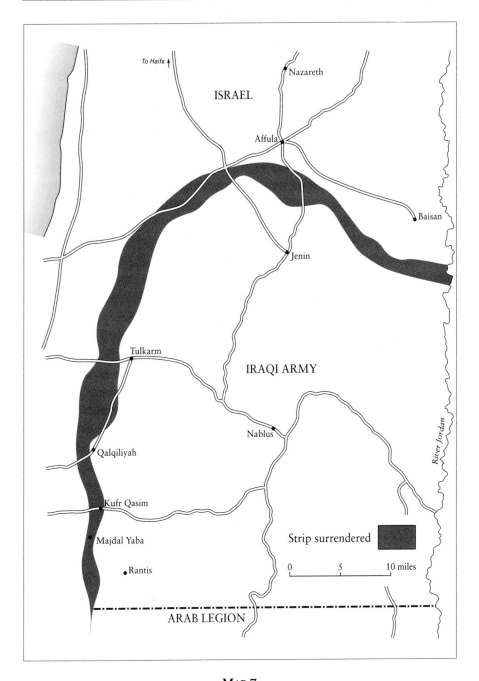

MAP 7
The strip of territory surrendered to Israel at Rhodes, March 1949, to secure Israeli agreement to an armistice on the Iraqi front

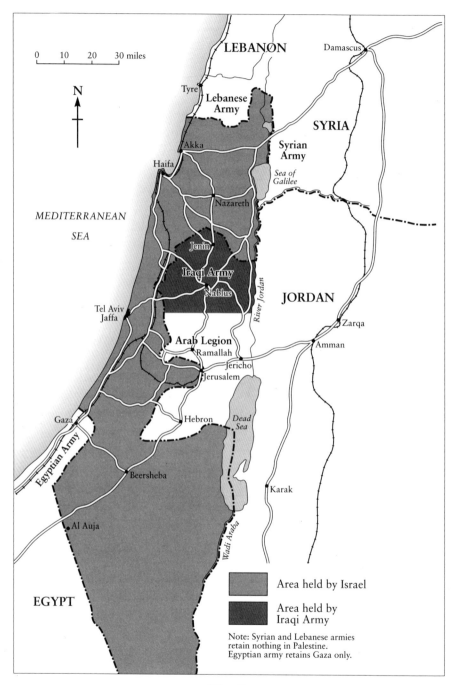

MAP 8
Situation at the time of signing the Rhodes Armistice, 3 April 1949

Bibliography

Archives

Public Record Office, London

Cabinet Papers 127/341	FO 371/75287	FO 371/91364
CO 537/3853	FO 371/75295	FO 371/91788
CO 733/344/11	FO 371/75333	FO 371/91789
DEFE 6/6	FO 371/75376	FO 371/91797
FO 371/117	FO 371/75381	FO 371/91838
FO 371/57273	FO 371/75436	FO 371/91839
FO 371/62193	FO 371/81930	FO 371/92364
FO 371/68386	FO 371/82179	FO 371/98859
FO 371/68505	FO 371/82703	FO 816/117
FO 371/68548	FO 371/82705	FO 816/118
FO 371/68642	FO 371/82707	FO 816/120
FO 371/68643	FO 371/82710	FO 816/121
FO 371/68644	FO 371/82714	FO 816/122
FO 371/68817	FO 371/82716	FO 816/162
FO 371/68822	FO 371/82718	FO 816/172
FO 371/68830	FO 371/82719	WO 261/297
FO 371/75076	FO 371/82755	WO 261/549
FO 371/75077	FO 371/827151	WO 275/64
FO 371/75273	FO 371/91203	

The Hashemite Kingdom of Jordan

Official Gazette

Hashemite Kingdom of Jordan Official Gazette (*HKJOG*), Records of the National Assembly, 6 May 1948

HKJOG, special edition, Records of the Jordanian Parliament, April 1950

HKJOG, special edition, Records of the National Assembly, April 1950

HKJOG, special edition, 6 September 1951

HKJOG, no. 31

HKJOG, no. 33
HKJOG, no. 35
HKJOG, no. 980
HKJOG, no. 986
HKJOG, no. 987
Trans-Jordan Official Gazette (TJOG), no. 28

Private papers
The author
Bromage, Colonel T. N.
Cunningham, Sir Alan, Middle East Centre, St Antony's College, Oxford
Glubb, J. B., Middle East Centre, St Antony's College, Oxford
ibn al-Hussein, King Abdullah, the Hashemite Documents, the Royal
    Palace, Amman
Al Tal, Wasfi

Newspapers and periodicals
Amman al Masa
The Army, Lebanese journal, no. 159
Filistin, Jerusalem newspaper
Ha'aretz
Al Hamishmar
Hansard, 23 July 1951
Herut (22 July 1951)
Histadrut Davar
The Independent (29 January 2000)
Al Jaish (The Army), a Lebanese journal, no. 159
Kol Ha'am
The Manchester Guardian, 16 October 1951
Majallat al-Disarat al-Filistiniyyah (Journal of Palestine Studies) (Berkeley:
    University of California Press), no. 34, spring 1998
Al-Masri magazine
Al Mithaq Newspaper
The New Jordan Magazine (winter 1990), nos. 15–16
News of the World

Palestine Post
Proche-Orient: Near East Monthly Review (May 1950)
al-Rai, Jordanian newspaper (20 January 2000)
Rose al-Yousef, Egyptian magazine
Al Shariah Magazine (July 1972)
The Times (26 July 1951)
Truth (2 March 1951)

Selected published books

Abu Nowar, Major General Ali, *Heen talashat al-Arab* (When the Arabs Faded: Memories in Arab Politics 1948–1964) (London: Dar al-Saqi, 1990).

Abu Nowar, Maan, *The Struggle for Independence 1939–1947* (Reading: Ithaca Press, 2001).

al Aref, Aref, *Al Nakbah* (The Disaster) (Beirut and Sidon: al Maktabah al Aasriyah, 1956).

Babil, Nasuh, *Sihafah wa-siyasah: Suriyah fi 'al-qarn 'al-'ishrin* (Journalism and Politics in Syria in the Twentieth Century) (London: Riad el-Rayyes Books, 1987).

Ben-Gurion, David, *War Diary: The War of Independence 1948–1949* (Hebrew), ed. Gershon Rivilin and Elhanan Orren (3 vols., Tel Aviv: Ministry of Defence, 1982), translated into Arabic by Samir Jabbour, edited by Sabri Jiriyis (Beirut: np, 1993).

Chlaim, Avi, *Collusion Across the Jordan* (Oxford: Clarendon Press, 1988).

Cohen, M. J., *Palestine and the Great Powers 1945–1948* (Princeton: Princeton University Press, 1982).

Gilbert, Martin, *Atlas of the Arab–Israeli Conflict* (New York: 1974).

—*Jerusalem in the Twentieth Century* (London: Pimlico, 1997).

Glubb, J. B., *The Changing Scenes of Life: an Autobiography* (London: Quartet, 1983).

—*A Soldier with the Arabs* (London: Hodder and Stoughton, 1948).

Herzog, Chaim, *The Arab–Israeli Wars: war and peace in the Middle East* (London: Arms and Armour, 1982).

Al-Khalidi, Walid, ed. *From Haven to Conquest: readings in Zionism and the Palestine problem until 1948* (Washington, D.C: Institute for Palestine Studies, 1987).

—Collection of Documents including the article 'Al-Qastal', *Journal of Palestine Studies* (Berkeley: University of California Press), no. 34, spring 1998.

Kurzman, Dan, *Genesis 1948: The First Arab–Israeli War* (London: Vallentine Mitchell, 1992).

Levin, Harry, *Jerusalem Embattled: a diary of the city under siege, March 25th, 1948 to July 18th, 1948* (London: Cassell, 1997).

Luttwak, E. and D. Horowitz, *The Israeli Army* (London: Allen Lane, 1975).

Madhi, Munib and Sulaiman Musa, *Tarikh al Urdon Fi al Qarn al Ishrin* (The History of Jordan in the Twentieth Century) (Amman: Dar al-Muhtasib, 1959).

Al Majali, Hazza, *Memoirs* (Arabic) (Beirut: Dar Al Ialm Lil Malayeen, 1960).

Milstein, Uri, *Out of Crisis came Decision* (Tel Aviv: 1991), translated into Arabic by Ahmad Khalifah.

Montgomery of Alamein, *Memoirs* (London: Allen Lane, 1958).

Morris, Benny, *The Birth of the Palestinian Refugees Problem 1947–1949* (Cambridge: Cambridge University Press, 1987).

Muhsin, Isa Khalil, *Abd al Qadir al Husseini* (Amman: 1986).

Munayer, Isbir, *Lydda during the Mandate and Occupation Periods* (Beirut: 1997).

al-Musa Aubaidat, Mahmoud, 'Account of the battle of Jerusalem', *The New Jordan Magazine* (Amman: winter 1990), nos. 15–16.

Rabin, Yitzhak, *The Rabin Memoirs* (London: Weidenfeld & Nicolson, 1979).

al-Sharaa, Major General Sadiq, *Our Wars with Israel 1947–1973: Lost Battles and Squandered Victories* (Amman: Dar al Shurouq, 1997).

Al Sharif, Kamil, *The Muslim Brothers in the Palestine War* (Arabic) (Amman: Al Manar, 1984).

Shipler, David K., *Arab and Jew: Wounded Spirits in a Promised Land* (London: Bloomsbury, 1989).

al-Tal, Abdullah, *Karithat Filastine* (The Palestine Catastrophe) (Cairo: Dar al-Qalam, 1959).

Al Tal, Wasfi, 'The Story of the Liberation Army', *Amman al Masa* (Amman: 1–14 May 1950).

Teveth, Shabtai, *Moshe Dayan* (London: Oxford University Press, 1972).

Unpublished sources

Abu Gharbiyah, Bahjat, *Muthakkarah fi al-nidhal al-Arabi al-Filistini 1916–1949* (Memoirs of the Struggle of the Palestinian Arabs 1916–1949) (Beirut: published by the author, 1993).

Al Hindi, Hani, *The Liberation Army* (Beirut: np, 1974).

Al-Khalidi, Walid, *Fifty Years since the Partition of Palestine 1947–1997* (Beirut: np, 1998).

Milstein, Uri, *Toldot Melhemet Ha-Kumemeyet* (History of the War of Independence) (unpublished copy, Tel Aviv: 1991), translated into Arabic by Ahmad Khalifah (1999).

Musa, Sulaiman, *Ayam La Tunsa* (Unforgettable Days: Jordan in the 1948 War) (Amman: published by the author, 1983).

The Palestine War 1947–1948, an official Israeli account (Hebrew), translation into Arabic by Ahmad Khalifah (unpublished copy given to this author, 1998).

Robert, J. and S. Hadawi, *The Palestine Diary, 1945–1948* (Beirut: np, 1970).

Al Rousan, Mahmoud, *The Battle for Bab al-Wad* (published by the author, Amman: 1950).

al Serahin, Colonel Farouq Nawaf, *History of the Arab Legion, 1921–1967* (Arabic) (Amman: published by the author, 1990).

Zuaitir, Akram, *Documents of the Palestinian National Movement, 1918–1939* (Beirut: published by the author, 1980).

Index

A

al-Aaboudi, Baha al-Din   91
al-Aani, Mahdi Salih   49
Aarif, Rafiq   119
Aatfah, Abdullah   157, 165
al-Aatnah, Shaikh   144
al-Aayid, Qasim   51
Abd al-Aziz, Ahmad   174–7
Abd al-Hadi, Rouhi   327
Abd al-Halim al-Humud   273
Abd al-Halim al-Sakit   119
Abd al-Ilah, Prince Regent of Iraq   76,
    78, 143, 164–5, 259–60, 262, 269,
    399–401
Abd al-Karim Maath   271
Abd al-Karim Mahmoud   100
Abd al-Karim Qasim   170
Abd al-Latif Abu Qourah   13
Abd al-Majid Abu Hijlah   427
Abd al-Nasser, Jamal   236, 238
Abd al-Qadir Farhat   398
Abd al-Qadir al-Husseini   17, 33–4, 52,
    54–5
Abd al-Rahman Khalifah, Muhammad
    271, 371
Abd al-Razaq al-Sharif   139
Abd al-Razzaq Abdullah   41
Abd al-Wahab, Auwais   251
Abd-Yousef, Said   251
Abdo, Mahmoud   175
Abdullah, King of Jordan   20, 40, 56–60,
    68, 71–2, 75–8, 85–6, 92–5, 104,
    111, 133, 143, 145, 164, 184–93,
    199, 208, 217–20, 241–2, 255,
    258–69, 273, 277–91, 298–307,
    311–30, 335–47, 354–5, 359,
    364–73, 377, 381, 390, 394–406,
    409, 411

al-Abdullah, Radhi   47–8
Abu Bakr al-Siddiq, Caliph   108
Abu Dayih, Ibrahim   55–7
Abu Dukhainah, Hamad Abdullah   205
Abu Fadhil, Munir   98–9, 110
Abu Ghanimah, Muhammad Subhi   322,
    340
Abu Gharbiyah, Bahjat   36, 52, 55
Abu Gharbiyah, Shafiq   54
Abu al-Huda, Tawfiq   67–9, 72, 76–80,
    85, 93–4, 111, 143, 189, 191,
    194–6, 199, 226, 229, 260–1, 271,
    274–5, 281, 290, 298, 304–5,
    314–20, 327–9, 335–41, 345,
    347–50, 356, 400, 411–25
Abu Jabir, Farah   272
Abu Kabir   25, 48
Abu Nowar, Ali   71, 113–16, 119
Abu Nowar, Maan   71, 122, 207, 393–5
Abu Rahmah   48
Adailim, Eid   121
Adil, Musa   71
Aflaq, Mishel   322
Ain Zaitoun   39
Ajnadin Battalion   49
Akka   50, 63
Ala al-Din, Mahmoud   57, 82
al-Alami, Salih   95
Alexandroni Brigade   49, 136–7, 139, 167,
    170–2, 200, 204, 248, 250, 297
Ali, Omar   119, 170, 172
Allenby, General   91
Allon, Yigal   39, 204, 211, 237–40, 247,
    250
Amman   367
Anglo-American Committee of Inquiry
    12
Anglo-Arab Association of London   311

al-Antabli, Mahmoud Ishaq   398–9
Aqaba   230
Arab High Committee   12, 14, 42, 47–53
Arab League   10, 73–9, 89, 173, 218,
    220, 256, 261, 263, 279–80,
    316–18, 321, 327, 337, 340–3, 349,
    354–5, 406
  Committee for Palestine   11–12
  Political Committee   6–8, 14, 74, 81,
    185, 187–91, 199, 229, 234, 242,
    247–8, 257, 327–8, 340–1, 343
Arab Legion   68–9, 79–80, 85, 92–3,
    107–8, 115, 137, 143, 184, 191–3,
    198, 204, 208–9, 228–9, 243, 246–7,
    265–7, 290, 295, 309, 313, 340,
    358, 366, 372–3, 385, 408, 414
Armistice Commission   305, 361–3,
    373–6, 382, 390
Artoof   29, 135, 138
Ashton, Brigadier Teal   51, 133–8, 141,
    152, 190, 209–10
Assyria   2
al-Atasi, Hashim   316–18
Attlee, Clement   404
Aubaidat, Mahmoud al-Musa   41,
    95–106, 110, 187
Aughily, General   401
Aukkah, Abed Mahmoud   397–9, 421–2
Aukkah, Zakariya   397–8, 421–2
al-Auqlah, Mohammad   58
Auraiqat, Kamil   106
Autayiq, Salamah   127
al-Autum, Ali   205
Auwais, Rafiq   54
Auzair, Salah   205
Avidan, Shimon   174, 179
al-Ayid, Qasim   138, 140–2
al-Ayoubi, Musa Ahmad   397–8, 421–2
al-Ayoubi, Salah al-Din   91
de Azcazarte, Pablo   102, 108
al-Azm, Khalid   302
Azzadin, Amin Bey   46
Azzam, Abd al-Rahman   74, 77, 85–6,
    165, 187, 189, 199, 226, 228, 258,
    265, 316–17, 328, 405

B
Baath Party   320, 341, 427

Bab al-Wad, battle of   31, 132–3, 138, 141,
    145, 147, 190, 206, 212, 260, 432
Babylon   2
Badran, Othman   95, 109
Bait Jibrin   244–7
Bait Nabala   27
Bait Safafa   53–4
Baker, Sir John   401
Balad al-Shaikh   26, 42
Balfour Declaration   4–5, 23, 25, 288
al-Bandak, Eisa   268, 322
Bannud, Anwar   200
Barakat, Muhammad Najib   117
Barakat, Subhi   54
al-Barazi, Muhsin   315–16
al-Bardini, General   249
al-Bassam, Sadiq   406
Beaumont, Richard   261
Beckett, Sir E.   336
Beersheba   175
Begin, Menachem   24, 197, 402–3
Ben-Ari, Uri   34
Ben-Gurion, David   20, 28, 32, 43, 94,
    139, 142, 145, 162–3, 239, 243, 381
Bernadotte, Count   142, 189, 192–3,
    198–9, 230–2
Bethlehem   175
Bevin, Ernest   46, 56, 67–8, 76, 183–5,
    189, 218–19, 280, 316, 319, 324,
    326, 338, 385
Beydoun, Rashid   402
al-Bilbaisi, Ismael   276
Biriya   39
al-Bittar, Mamoun   30–1
Blackden, H.   127
British presence in Palestine   3–10, 19,
    23–9, 36–41, 43–9, 53–62, 67–73,
    94–5, 255–6, 300–1
Broadmead, Philip   40
Bromage, T. N.   131, 137, 141, 146–52,
    190, 194, 206–7, 296–7, 375
Buchanan, Major   116
Bunche, Ralf J.   293, 295
al-Burj   210–11

C
Camel Hill   169
Campbell, Sir Ronald   342–3

Canaan 1–3
Carmel, Moshe 172
Carmeli Brigade 33–5, 44–5, 50, 166, 170–2, 200–2
Chlaim, Avi 35
Christianity 2–4
Churchill, Winston 4, 72, 404
Circassian Company 233
Clayton, Brigadier 265
Cohen, Mula 144
communism 360
Conciliation Commission 284–5, 319, 326, 352, 364, 373
Cooke, Sam 375, 393–4, 399
Corfield, George 195, 214–15
corruption 272–6, 313, 371, 406
Cunningham, Sir Alan 24, 26, 92
Czechoslovakia 223

D
Dagania 'A' and 'B' 162–5
al-Daghistani, Ghazi 119
Dair al-Shaar 59
Dair Yasin 34–7, 82
Dairaniyah, Haj 275
Daoud, Anton 55
Darwazah, Ratib 271
Daskal, Avraham 50
Davar 403
al-Dawaayimah 243–4
al-Dawalibi, Maarouf 405
Dayan, Moshe 163, 205, 299, 375–6
Diamis, Wadia 330, 351–2
Dow, Sir Hugh 185, 187
Downs, John 85
Druze Company 234

E
Economic Survey Mission 319–20
effendis 72
Egyptian Army 173–81, 183, 192, 196, 215–17, 230, 235–43, 247–52, 259, 267, 270, 293, 299, 309
Egyptian–British Treaty (1936) 252
elections 331–2, 335, 341–4, 349, 359, 424–30
Etzioni Brigade 53, 56, 92, 176–7, 214, 241

F
Faisal, King 413
Fakhr al-Din, Farid 281
al-Faluja 247–50
Farouq, King 265, 288, 316, 359, 407
al-Fayiz, Aakif 273
Filistin 321
Foster, J. 385
Fox, Colonel 157
France 306
Franco, Francisco 316
Franjiyah, Hamid 316
frontier incidents 361–5, 373, 378, 390–1
al-Funaish, Sari 39–40
Furlonge, G. W. 340

G
G Force 242–4
Garreau plan 377
von Gartin, Mordechai 106–7
Gaza Strip 328, 359
Germany 6
Gesher 50–1, 169
Gezer 148–9
Ghannam, Mahmoud Sulaiman 402
Givati Brigade 49, 139, 174, 178–81, 216–17, 237–41, 248
Glubb, General 59–61, 68, 70, 82–6, 92–4, 107, 111, 123, 125, 127, 132, 183, 190–9, 206–13, 217–19, 226, 231, 242–4, 256, 294–300, 309–13, 323–4, 336, 343, 346, 357–8, 363, 366, 372–5, 385, 391, 393, 395, 399, 403–4, 407, 413–15
Golani Brigade 38, 159–62, 170–2, 200, 202, 234, 248, 251–2, 297
Goldie, Colonel D. 119, 122, 127–8
Grey, Patrick 120
Guregh II 99–101

H
Ha'aretz 403
al-Habhibah, Muhammad Mitlaq 296
al-Hadhari, Maarouf 174
Hadi, Rouhi Abdul 338
Haganah, the 9–10, 23–8, 31–9, 42–61, 95–109, 115, 117, 119, 126,

134–45, 151, 162–9, 175–80, 190, 198, 203, 215
Haifa   24–9, 41–6, 63, 159
Haikal, Yousef   47
Haim, Mecore   55
al-Haj Amin al-Husseini   12–13, 20, 42, 53, 74, 302, 317, 328, 340–1, 346, 357, 397, 400, 406, 419
al-Haj, Farhat   275
al-Haj Ibrahim, Rashid   41–2
al-Hakim, Abd al-Wahhab   157, 161, 163, 165
Hakuz, Muhammad Ishaq   103
Hall, Lord   311
Hamid, Awad   116
Hamish, Ma'ale Ha   54
Al Hamishmar   403
Hananiya, Anistas   345, 427, 430
Hankin-Tervin, Major   120, 123
al-Haram al Sharif   53
al-Harbi, Ghazi   120–1, 124–6, 297
Harel Palmach Brigade   92, 95–6, 99, 101, 209–12, 241, 252
Hasan, Shaikh   47–8
Hashim, Ibrahim   400, 415–16
Hashim, Mohammad Naim   51
al-Hashimi, Ttaha   13
Hatiqwa, Peta   47
Hayardin, Mishmar   166–7
Hebron   58–60
Helou, Charles   401
Herut   402
Herzl, Theodore   4
Herzog, Chaim   40, 59, 132, 137, 142–5, 159, 162–3, 171, 204, 211, 235–7
al-Hijazi, Hussein   176–7
Hijazi, Muhammad   427
Hilmi, Ahmad   93, 98, 258–60, 268, 327, 343, 359
al-Hindawi, Radhi   71
al-Hindawi, Turki   143
al Hindi, Mahmoud   6–7, 13
al-Hinnawi, Sami   316
al-Hiyari, Ali   71, 196–7
al-Hourani, Akram   13, 405
al-Hulaiqat   239
al-Humoud, Nawaf al-Jabir   61, 95–7, 100, 102

al-Humud, Dhaifullah   271
al-Hunaitti, Mohammad al-Hamad   41–3
Hussein, Turki   71
al-Husseini, Daoud   422
al-Husseini, Khalid   98–9
al-Husseini, Mahmoud Jamil   54
al-Husseini, Musa   106, 396–9, 421–2

I
ibn Abdul Aziz, Prince Fahd   401
ibn Adwan, Shaikh Yousef   109
ibn al-Hussein, Abdullah   4
ibn al-Jazi, Shaikh Hamd   354
ibn al-Jazi, Shaikh Haroun   132–3, 138
ibn al-Khattab, Caliph Omar   91
Ibn Saud   186, 303, 406
ibn Talal, Prince Hussein   401–2, 413, 418, 423
Ibrahim, Mustafa   95–6, 101, 104
The Independent   168
Iraq
    army of   131–41, 168–72, 191–2, 196, 202–3, 226, 228, 242–3, 256, 267, 293, 295, 299, 304
    proposals for unity with Jordan   399, 412–17, 420
    proposals for unity with Syria   324–8
Iraq al-Manshiyah   49
Irgun Zvai Leumi   10, 23–8, 34–5, 45–8, 53, 92, 95, 113, 214, 402
Irhayil, Zaal   120
Ishu, Mustafa Shukri   397–8
Islam   2–3
Israel, ancient tribes of   1–2, 40, 63, 391
Issa, Michael   49
Izz al-Din, Amin   43–4

J
al-Jaabari, Shaikh Muhammad Ali   59, 241, 353
al-Jaauni, Azmi   55
Jabaliya   48
Jabr, Salih   405–6, 412, 414–15
Jaffa   26–7, 47–9, 63, 76–7
al-Jammal, Saad   178
Jarad, Sulaiman   296
Jenin   170–2
Jericho congress (1948)   278–83, 289, 291

Jericho massacre   1
Jerusalem   2, 23–6, 32, 34, 37, 53–5, 57,
    62–3, 76–7, 91–4, 249
    battle for the New City   110–28
    battle for the Old City   94–110
    status of   327–30, 337, 377
Jewish Agency   9–10, 36, 41, 55
Jidid, Ghassan   13
al-Jihad al-Muqaddas   12–13, 17, 29, 33,
    37, 52–9, 73, 99–104, 108–9, 194,
    310
Jiryis, Yousef   143
Jordanian Arab Army   27–8, 32, 41–3,
    47–51, 56–61, 70–5, 79, 82–9,
    92–5, 100–1, 108–11, 119, 132,
    142, 149–52, 175–6, 190–7, 204,
    209–15, 219, 226–7, 256–62, 270,
    293–311, 332–3, 356–7, 365–6,
    390–3, 411, 419, 428, 432
Jordanian–British Treaty (1948)   67, 71,
    75, 190, 219, 230, 271, 306–7, 313,
    336, 340, 354, 365, 372, 418, 425
Jordanian Council of Ministers   367–8,
    372, 374, 376, 423, 431, 433
Jordanian National Assembly   271–4,
    283, 331, 347–50, 389, 430–3
Jordanian National Guard   356–7, 390–1
al-Juburi, Salih Saib   168
Judah, Kingdom of   2
Judaism   2–3
Judd, Basil   359
Jumaian, Imil   39–40
al-Jundi, Abd al-Qadir   79
al-Jundi, Ahmad Sudqi   41, 135

K
Kabara, Sami   402
al-Kallas, Bahij   369
Kaplan, S.   244
Kartiya   26
Kassab, Muhammad   210
Katz, Theodore   167
Kawkab al-Hawa   170
Kfar Etzion   32, 58–61, 71, 243
al Khadhra, Subhi   6–7
al-Khairi, Khulousi   338, 351, 353–4,
    356ᵢ
al-Khalil, Ahmad   43–4, 320

Khalil, Mahmoud   100
al-Khasawnah, Mustafa   210, 212
Khashaba Pasha   285, 304
al-Khatib, Anwar   361
al-Khatib, Nimir   41
Khayat, Victor   41, 43
al-Khraisha, Barakat al-Ttrad   101, 104
al-Khraisha, Khalid Mujalli   125, 213
al-Khraisha, Refaifan Khalid   210
Kibbutz settlements   9–10
King David Hotel   23–4, 92
Kirkbride, Sir Alec   57, 67, 74, 77–80,
    165, 183–92, 227–9, 264–7,
    277–83, 288–90, 303, 306,
    312–13, 321, 324, 326, 328,
    336–9, 342, 355, 357, 361–77,
    382, 400–1, 411–23, 428
Kiryati Brigade   47–9, 204, 206, 209
Kol Ha'am   403
Kusa, Ilyas   41

L
Lash, Norman   51, 82, 84, 86, 94, 111,
    116, 119–20, 194, 231, 298–9, 393
Laskov, Haim   139
Latrun   131–43, 148, 192–4
Laufer, Dr   108
League of Nations   5
Lebanese Army   153–6, 166, 195–6, 225,
    267, 293, 299
Lloyd George, David   4
Lockett, Geoffrey   137, 141, 152, 210,
    242, 244, 246, 248
Lundstrom, General   232
Lunt, General   111, 113
Lydda   83, 147–51, 193–4, 205–8, 261

M
al-Maaitah, Abd al-Majid   133, 144
al-Maaitah, Mahmoud   139–40
al-Maaitah, Muhammad   113–15, 117
al-Madfaai, Jamil   337
al-Madhah, Falah   368–9
al-Mahasnah, Muhammad   50, 137, 143
Mahir, Fawaz   195
al-Majali, Habis   51, 131–6, 306, 395–6
al-Majali, Hazzaa   93
al-Malikiyah   155–6, 166

al-Manarah   37
The Manchester Guardian   430, 432
Manko Company   104, 109
Maqboulah, Princess   401
Mar Ilyas   176–7
Marcus, David   142, 190
Mardam, Jamil   11–12, 226, 242–3
Martin, Clifford   25
Masaud, Sulaiman   56, 195
al-Masri   339
al-Masri, Haj Maazuz   323
al-Masri, Hikmat   351
Matir, Flaiyih   121–2, 125, 297
al-Mawawi, Ahmad Muhammad Ali   173,
    175, 177, 217, 240–1, 247
Mdanat, Iyadah   135
Mesopotamia   2
Mihyar, Hikmat   109
Milstein, Uri   35
al-Minwir al-Hadid, Muhammad   351
Mishmar Ha'Emeq   30–1
Monihann, Major   215
Montgomery, Bernard   46
Morris, Benny   243–4
al-Mouji, Muhammad   178
Muaammar, George   41
Mufadhi, Isa   135–40
al-Muflih, Hussein   99–100
al-Mufti, Said   272–3, 314, 337–9,
    345–6, 368–71, 376–7, 400, 422–4
Muhammad the Prophet   91
Muhammad, Qaseem   109
Muhyar, Hikmat   59, 60–1
Muhyi al-Din, Zakariya   177
al-Mulqi, Fawzi   67, 192, 330
Musbah, Queen   401
Muslim Brothers   173–9, 196, 215, 237,
    240–1, 249–51, 333, 427
Mustafa, Haidar   97, 114–16, 210–11

N
Nabi Yaaqub, battle of   71
al-Nabi Yousha   39
Nablus   83, 87, 93, 118–19, 170–2, 268,
    277–8, 356, 395, 425
Nablus conference (1948)   267
Naffaa, Younis   44
al-Nahhas, Ismael   57

al-Naif, Mohsin   208
Najib, Muhammad   118, 179–80
Najm al-Din, Adil   48–9
Narkis, Uzi   96
al-Nashashibi, Raghib   320–3
Nasir al-Din   37
Nasr, Anis   41
Nasser, Kamal   321–2
Nasser, Musa   338, 354, 356
Nasser, Sanad   115
al-Nassir, Qasim   109
Nauman, Muhammad   57, 59, 122,
    124–5
Nayif, Prince   400–1, 405, 412–18,
    422–3, 430–2
Nazareth   202
Negba   217
Negev Brigade   174–5, 178–81, 216–17,
    237, 252, 297
Newman, William   119–26
News of the World   403
Niawas, Abdullah   320–1, 352, 426–7,
    430
Nirim   177
Nizzanim   180–1
al-Noqrashi, Mahmoud Fahmi   196,
    199, 242, 249, 265, 348
Nusaibah, Anwar   33, 349, 355
al-Nwasrah, Adib al-Qasim   103

O
Oded Brigade   166, 200, 234, 238–9
Officers' Club, Jerusalem   24–5
Ottoman Empire   3

P
Paice, Mervyn   25
Palestine
    Arab population of   3–9, 12, 19, 23,
        27–9, 278
    Arab Revolt in (1936–9)   10, 12, 25,
        46, 72, 256
    establishment of Jewish state in   7–9,
        12, 20, 165
    expulsion of Arabs from   31–3, 36
    Jewish immigration to   3–6, 10, 23
    Partition Plan for   7–8, 12, 15, 47, 71,
        185–6, 193, 266, 425

regional, tribal and familial loyalties in 18

see also West Bank of the River Jordan

Palestine Post 54

Palestinian Liberation Army 12–16, 28–32, 38–9, 48–50, 53, 56, 73–7, 83, 92, 95–7, 100, 108–9, 131–3, 167, 195–6, 202, 225, 233–4, 257, 267, 310

Palmach Brigade 31–4, 38–40, 42–3, 37–8, 53–8, 95–6, 99–105, 111, 117, 119, 154–6, 162, 174–7, 180–2, 198, 235

partisans 13, 17–19, 32, 42–6, 83, 104, 133–44, 193, 203–5, 259, 333

see also al-Jihad al-Muqaddas

Permanent Military Committee 7–8, 12–14

Prai, Eliezer 243

Q

Qaawar, Jamil 71

al-Qaddumi 37

Qalandiyah 55, 112, 118–19

Qalqiliyah 323–4

Qaluniyah 34

al-Qasim, Adib 151, 194, 206

al-Qasim, Sudqi 303

al-Qastal 33–4

al-Qawasmah, Naji 59

al-Qawiqji, Fawzi 13, 15, 29–33, 48–9, 76–7, 166–7, 202, 233–4

Qazazah 26

al-Qubab 152

al-Quttob, Fawzi 97, 101, 103

al-Quwatli, Shukri 162, 165, 302

R

Rabin, Yitzhak 92, 101, 103, 105

Radar Hill 126–8

Ragheb, Mustafa 269

al-Rai 168

Ramallah 18, 19, 82, 83, 84, 87, 88, 103, 115, 126, 131, 139, 194, 204, 206, 207, 209, 210, 213, 227, 242, 258–9, 260, 269, 314, 315, 320, 321, 331, 342, 344, 346, 394, 426–7, 429

Ramat Rahel 176

Ramleh 26, 28, 73, 145–7, 151, 193–4, 206, 208, 261

al-Rashid, Fadhil Abdullah 56, 95–6, 99, 106

al-Rawi, Ahmad 192

Red Cross 35–6, 61, 102, 192

de Reeder, Colonel 363

Refaat, Mahmoud 251

refugees 63, 255–9, 279, 282–3, 294, 305–8, 326, 342, 358, 371, 378

Reutenberg hydroelectric station 50

Rhodes negotiations (1949) 293–5, 301, 305, 365, 377

al-Rifai, Samir 67, 274, 294, 314, 318, 338–9, 345, 369, 376–7, 381–90, 395, 399–402, 412–13, 416, 419, 424–5

Riley, General 295, 298, 305, 365

al-Rimawi, Abdullah 320–1, 353–4, 426

Robertson, Sir Brian 401, 413

Roman Empire 2

Rose al-Yousef 407

Rosh Pinna 39

al-Rousan, Mahmoud 41, 51, 131

Roznik, Moshe 106–7

Ruhayil, Zaal 116, 118–19

al-Rushaidat, Nabih 271

al-Rushaidat, Shafiq 81–2, 272–6, 425, 428

S

al-Saad, Farid 41

Sadiq, Ahmad Fuad 247, 250

Safa, Mohammad 13

Safad 38–40, 63, 71

Safwat, Ismael 6–8, 11–20, 74–8

al-Saib, Salih 242

al-Said, Nuri 143, 324, 327–8, 399–400, 412, 414–17

Salah, Walid 398–9, 421

al-Salim, Abdullah 50

Salim, Ali 57

al-Salti, Yaaqoub 71

Samakh 77–8, 159–65

al-Samman, Nadim 51

Sarig, Nahum 174

Sarona   25
Serot, Colonel   232
Shair, Mansur   151
Shaltiel, David   34, 94, 101, 103, 105
Shamoun, Camille   165
al-Shanqiti, Shaikh Muhammad Amin
    72, 368–9, 416
al-Sharaa, Sadiq   71, 82, 85, 93, 110,
    116–17, 194–5, 242
al-Sharaa, Salih   27, 71, 93, 108, 119
al-Sharif, Kamil   13, 174, 178, 240–1,
    249–51
Shatilla, Khalid   401
al-Shawa, Rushdi   82
al-Sheshekli, Adib   13, 38–40
Shihab, Foad   156
Shiloah, Reuven   381–2, 385, 388, 390
al-Shishekli, Salah   13
al-Shraidah, Abdullah al-Kulaib   80,
    282
Shuafat   55
Shubaikan, Salim   118
Shuqair, Shawkat   6–7, 13
al-Shuraiqi, Muhammad   324–5, 347,
    368–71, 416
al-Sibaai, Mustafa   13, 106
al-Sidmir, Muhammad   398
Sirri, Hussein   328–9
Slade, Bob   111–14, 137, 206
al-Solh, Riyadh   76, 394–5, 405
Sophronius, Bishop of Jerusalem   91
al-Soufi, Jamal   95
South Force   296–7
Soviet Union   6, 218, 223
Spring, Captain   244
Stabler, Mr   281
Stern gang   10, 23–8, 34–5, 48, 95, 232
Stockwell, Hugh   41–2, 44, 46
al-Subaih, Hamdan   57–9, 141, 210–11
al-Suboua, Shaikh Nahar   144
al-Suhaim, Mohammad   61
al-Suhaimat, Muhammad   413
Sulaiman, Musa   296
Sulaiman, Musayib   195
Sultan, Idris   195
Sun Rise force   145–6
al-Suwaidi, Tawfiq   337
al-Suwais, Issa   275

Syria
    army of   157–67, 196, 200–2, 225–6,
        242–3, 267, 293, 299, 303
    Jordanian relations with   301–5, 317,
        326–7
    proposals for unity with Iraq   324–8

T
al-Tabbaa, Nadim   273
Taha, Sayyid   248
Tal al-Reesh   26
Talal, Prince   51, 86, 339, 399, 401, 405,
    411–14, 418, 422–5, 432
Tannous, Izzat   106
al-Tanturah   167–8
Tel Aviv   25–6, 47
al-Tel, Abdullah   57–62, 71, 95, 98–9,
    102–7, 110, 175, 299–303, 306,
    322, 339, 358, 396–8, 421–2
terrorism   10, 23–9, 34–6, 45–6, 357,
    391–2
Tiberias   37–8, 62
The Times   407
al-Tirah   26
Tirat Tsvi   28
Touqan, Ahmad   267, 345
Touqan, Baha al Din   321
Touqan, Sulaiman   267–8, 277–8, 350–4,
    395
Truman, Harry   8, 241, 307
Truth   391

U
Um Rashrash   296–7, 375
United Nations   12, 27, 36, 68–9, 81,
    83, 93, 183–4, 193, 199, 218–19,
    229, 232–3, 236, 242, 263, 266,
    278–80, 283, 295, 298, 348–9,
    376
    Children's Fund (UNICEF)   308
    Disaster Relief Fund   256
    General Assembly   30, 62, 249, 307,
        329, 377
    Israel's admission to   306–7
    Relief and Works Agency   358, 371,
        428
    Security Council   29–30, 38, 46, 62,
        102, 143, 185–92, 199, 208, 217,

223, 225, 239, 241, 247–9, 252,
  300, 314, 327, 336–7, 365, 374
Special Committee on Palestine   7
Trusteeship Council   329
United States   3–8, 20, 23, 165, 281,
  295, 300–1, 307, 319, 418

W
Wadi Araba   375–6, 381
Wasfi Al Tal   13–15
Weizmann, Chaim   4, 9, 381
West Bank of the River Jordan   301, 306,
  308, 312–15, 320–3, 336, 359, 360,
  364, 367

Y
Yaaish, Muhsin   39
Yad Mordechai   177–8
Yadin, Yigael   375

Yaffi, Leib   55
Yaftach Brigade   155, 205, 235, 238
al-Yahudiyah   26
Yahya, Rustom   103
Yalo   133–4, 139–44, 212
Yarmouk Battalion   234
Yazur   26
Yiftach Brigade   209, 211, 236–7
Young, R.   113
Yousef, Awadh   117

Z
al-Zaim, Husni   165–6, 302–3, 315–16
Zarqa   89
Zionism   3–6
Zughaib, Muhammad Aqil   154

Also available

The Struggle for Independence 1939–1947: A History of the Hashemite Kingdom of Jordan
2001 • 376pp • 235 x 155 mm • Cased £35.00 • ISBN 0 86372 283 0

The Rebirth of Uzbekistan: Politics, Economy and Society in the Post-Soviet Era
2002 • 360pp • 235 x 155 mm • Cased £35.00 • ISBN 0 86372 281 4

Iran's Rivalry with Saudi Arabia between the Gulf Wars
2002 • 308pp • 235 x 155 mm • Cased £35.00 • ISBN 0 86372 287 3

In the Wake of the Dhow: The Arabian Gulf and Oman
2002 • 276pp • 235 x 155 mm • Cased £35.00 • ISBN 0 86372 259 8

Morocco under King Hassan
2001 • 396pp • 235 x 155 mm • Cased £25.00 • ISBN 0 86372 285 7

Unfolding the Orient: Travellers in Egypt and the Near East
2001 • 324pp • 235 x 155 mm • Cased £35.00 • ISBN 0 86372 257 1

Interpreting the Orient: Travellers in Egypt and the Near East
2001 • 284pp • 235 x 155 mm • Cased £35.00 • ISBN 0 86372 258 X

Nationals and Expatriates: Population and Labour Dilemmas of the Gulf Cooperation Council States
2001 • 300pp • 235 x 155 mm • Cased £35.00 • ISBN 0 86372 275 X

Water in the Arabian Peninsula: Problems and Policies
2001 • 412pp • 235 x 155 mm • Cased £35.00 • ISBN 0 86372 246 6

Lebanon's Renaissance: The Political Economy of Reconstruction
2001 • 276pp • 235 x 155 mm • Cased £35.00 • ISBN 0 86372 252 0

Iran and Eurasia
2001 • 228pp • 235 x 155 mm • Cased £35.00 • ISBN 0 86372 271 7

Available from your local bookshop; alternatively, contact our Sales Department on +44 (0)118 959 7847 or e-mail **orders@garnet-ithaca.demon.co.uk** to order copies of these books.